STELIAN TĂNASE
AUNTIE VARVARA'S CLIENTS
Translated by
Alistair Ian Blyth

Featured Artist
Cristian Tarba

University of Plymouth Press

20 ROMANIAN WRITERS SERIES

Stelian Tănase's *Auntie Varvara's Clients* is the fifth title to be published in the series *20 Romanian Writers* by the University of Plymouth Press. The series is one aspect of the University of Plymouth's ongoing commitment to introduce Romania's vibrant artistic culture to other nations. In addition to the literature, the University of Plymouth will be hosting a series of exhibitions and performances of Romania's visual and musical arts over the next five years. The following supplement features one of Romania's leading contemporary artists.

Featured Artist

CRISTIAN TARBA

Tarba (born 1961) sees the artistic act as a means of purging tumultuous psychological states through transposing them onto paper. He does not plan his drawings or work from an initial sketch, but rather allows himself to be directed by his fluctuating thoughts and emotions. It is the transformation of the initial idea that fascinates Tarba; he may finish a piece in an entirely different state to that in which he started and so, as with Tănase's characters, the direction of his work will twist and turn in directions that he could never have predicted. Using the human face and body as a mirror to reality, Tarba explores the fears, concerns and existential frustrations of contemporary being.

Liz Wells

EA

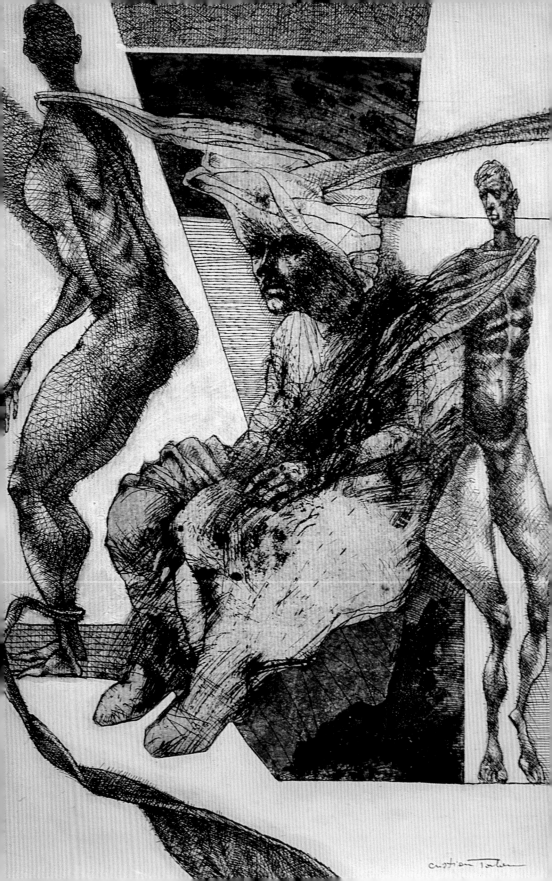

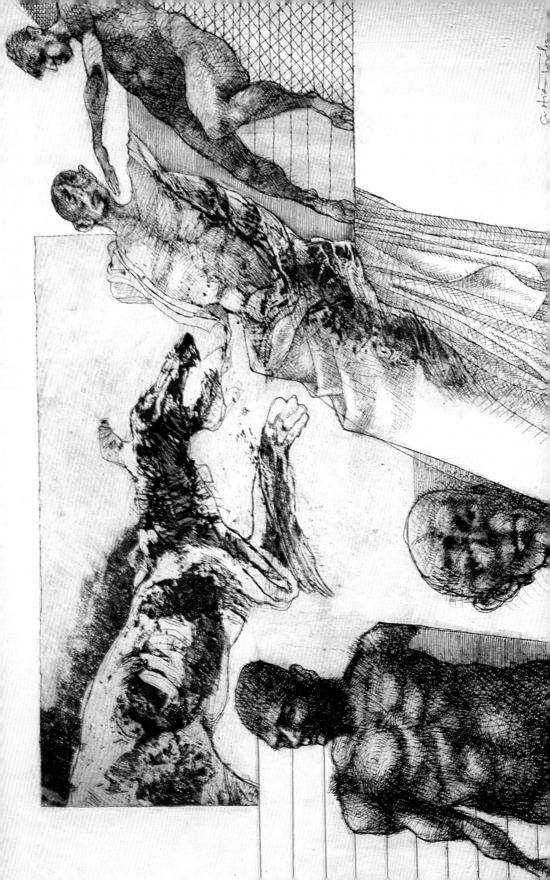

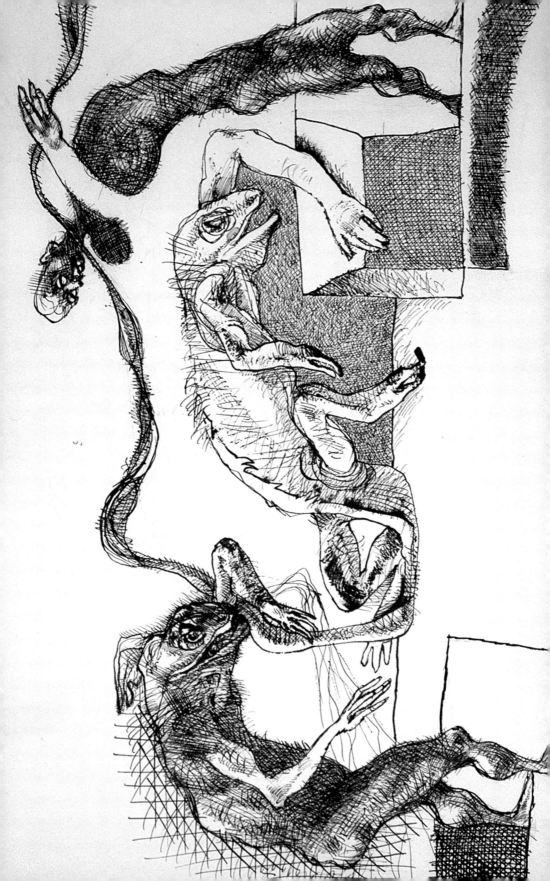

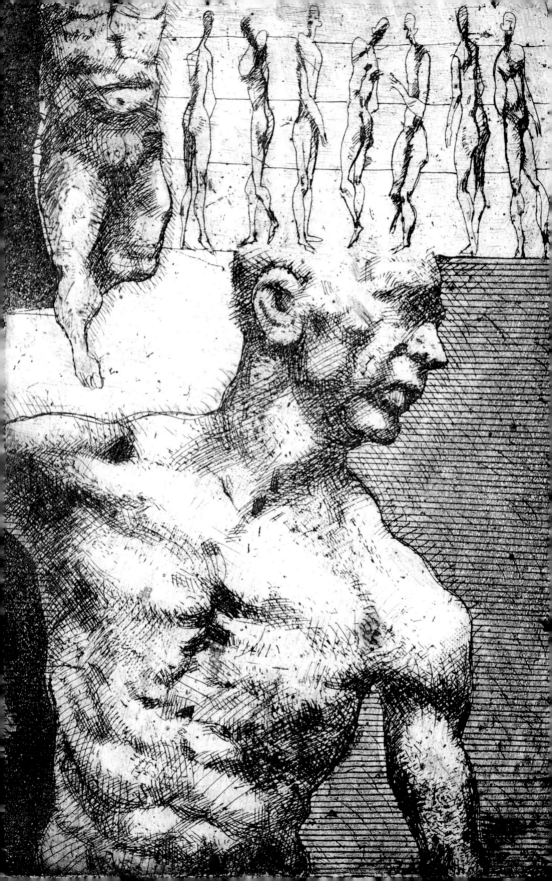

STELIAN TĂNASE

AUNTIE VARVARA'S CLIENTS

Translated by
Alistair Ian Blyth

Contents

Alistair Ian Blyth

Introducing Stelian Tănase

Stelian Tănase (born 17 February 1952) is among Romania's most prominent public intellectuals. He is a writer, historian, political analyst, journalist, scriptwriter, documentary filmmaker, and television personality. Since the Revolution of December 1989, he has been a leading figure in Romanian civil society, campaigning to declassify the archives of the Securitate (the communist secret police) and the totalitarian regime it served. In the last decade of the Ceauşescu regime, Tănase was able to publish his first novel, *The Luxury of Melancholy* (1982), but the censors banned his next two books, including the novel *Light Fittings*, which, since 1990, is in its fourth edition. Since the fall of the totalitarian state, Tănase has also published, besides his previously banned books, the 'desk-drawer' diaries he kept during the crepuscular years of the communist regime. *At Home the Talk is in a Whisper* (2002), a collection of his diaries, also includes excerpts from the files the Securitate compiled on him using secret reports written by informants, some of whom were subsequently revealed to have been close friends.

Immediately after December 1989, Tănase was active in protests against the hijacking of the Revolution by elements of the former Securitate and communist apparatus. Among the principal (and still unmet) demands made by the opposition during this period was that all those who had been members of the apparatus of the totalitarian regime should be excluded from holding public office. The protests mounted in Bucharest included a continuous demonstration, a democracy camp in University Square, which lasted from April until 13 June 1990, when, for three days, hordes of miners from the Jiu Valley, supporters of president Iliescu, rampaged through the capital to crush anti-government dissent. The toll of the so-called 'Mineriad' was a number of deaths (the official figure is seven, but non-governmental bodies have claimed that more than a hundred fatalities were covered up), numerous cases of grievous bodily harm and rapes, and widespread destruction of the offices and property of opposition parties and organisations.

In 1991, Tănase was elected vice-president of the Civic Alliance Party, one of the main opposition groups during the Iliescu period. The following year, he was elected to Parliament, serving as a Deputy for Bucharest until 1996, during which time he sat as vice-president of the Parliamentary Committee for Foreign Affairs. In 2006, he was appointed to the presidential Commission for the Study of the Communist Dictatorship in Romania, whose findings, in a 660-page report, led to president Traian Băsescu officially condemning the former regime as 'illegitimate and criminal' in a speech before a joint assembly of the two chambers of Romania's Parliament, on 18 December 2006.

As an historian, Tănase has written extensively on the communist period. His books exploring the politics of the Romanian totalitarian state and the mechanisms of repression it employed include *The Anatomy of Mystification: The Noica-Pillat Trial* (1997), about the political show trial brought against philosopher Constantin Noica, poet Dinu Pillat and other intellectuals in the 1950s, and *Elite și societate: Guvernarea Gheorghiu-Dej (1948–1965) (Elites and Society: The Gheorghiu-Dej Regime (1948-1965))* (1998). *Auntie Varvara's Clients: Clandestine Histories* (2005) is a history of the revolutionary underground in Romania during the years before the communists seized absolute power. Drawing upon Tănase's exhaustive research in the labyrinthine archives of the Securitate and the institutions of a regime pathologically obsessed with secrecy and the rewriting of history, as well as upon the archives of the pre-communist secret police, the Siguranță[1] (nicknamed 'Auntie Varvara' by the clandestine revolutionaries), *Auntie Varvara's Clients* is a vivid forensic reconstruction of a period which, for almost five decades, was mythologised by the 'illegals' once in power. At the same time, the narrative is fast-paced and often switches between past tense and historic present, thus giving the feel of a documentary film.

The history of the Romanian communist underground begins at the close of the First World War, when Russia descended into the chaos of revolution and civil war, losing the province of Bessarabia[2] to the newly formed Greater Romania. It lasted until the end of the Second World War, when the USSR re-annexed Bessarabia, which became the Soviet Socialist Republic of Moldavia, and the Red Army occupied Romania itself. In Romania, the same as in the other countries of Central and Eastern Europe, Red Army occupation brought with it a Stalinist political regime, mass repression, and economic and political vassal status as a satellite state of the Soviet Union. However, as Tănase argues, in Romania, unlike other, more industrialised countries of the communist bloc, there had never been any mass socialist movement to provide even a veneer of popular consent to the new 'people's democracy'. The Romanian communists who, thanks to Soviet military occupation, were able finally to seize complete control of the government in the fraudulent elections of 1947 had never been more than a handful of isolated activists, 'professional revolutionaries' from the margins of society, operating clandestinely, in the 'underground', with no real support even among the small urban proletariat of what was, at that time, still a mainly agricultural country.

One of the main theses of *Auntie Varvara's Clients* is that the organisational structure of the underground – a closed, rigidly hierarchical secret society, comprising 'cells', of whose members was demanded blind obedience and unthinking submission to the arbitrary will of the absolute leader, and in which dissent or apostasy was punishable by death – was extended to the whole of Romanian society once the communists seized power. Romania becomes a vast prison camp, what Tănase calls 'a carceral society'. The inmates of this prison are housed in barrack-like conditions (communal flats and shoddily built prefabricated concrete blocks[3]). They are subjected to strict rationing (food queues, shortages, central economic planning as a means of mass repression through enforced poverty; citizens are too exhausted by the time-consuming effort to obtain enough to eat for them to put up any resistance against the regime).[4] The barbed wire fence of the prison camp runs for the entire length of the national borders (travel abroad is restricted to all but a privileged few, and those attempting to escape are summarily shot). The camp guards administer hard labour (the vast Danube-Black Sea Canal construction site became a mass grave for the inter-war elites and for those peasants who opposed collectivisation) and fatigues (for example, in Romania, students and even school children were forced during their holidays to carry out unpaid agricultural labour and work in factories – so-called 'patriotic labour'). As in any prison, individual privacy is abolished: surveillance is omnipresent; the prison warders – the authorities – spy on the inmates and encourage them to spy on each other.

This vision of society as a vast prison, a carceral society, is also known as *kazarmnyy komunizm* (barracks communism) or *Nechaevshchina* (Nechayevism). Sergey Gennadiyevich Nechayev (1847-1882) was the Russian revolutionary who inspired the character of amoral fanatic Pyotr Stepanovich Verkhovensky in Dostoevsky's *Besy* (1871-72) (variously translated as *Demons, The Devils, The Possessed*). Nechayev's *Katekhizis Revolyutsionera (The Catechism of the Revolutionary)* (1869), the source of the famous revolutionary slogan 'the ends justify the means', subsequently became precisely that: the articles of faith shared by all those engaged in the clandestine struggle to destroy society. As the clandestine histories of each of Auntie Varvara's individual clients show, the revolutionaries of the

Romanian underground were no different from Nechayev's *Narodnaya Rasprava* (People's Vengeance) group or Lenin's Bolsheviks or the myriad clandestine organisations controlled by the Comintern, in that they all followed this creed to the letter. The 'demonic' nature of this creed is evident in the first of Nechayev's 26 articles of faith:

"1. The revolutionary is a doomed man. He has no personal interests, affairs, feelings, attachments, property, or even a name. Everything in him is consumed by a unique, exclusive interest, a single idea, a single passion: revolution.

2. In the depths of his being, not only in his words, but also in his deeds, he has severed every link with the civil order, with the whole of the civilised world, with all the laws, propriety, conventions and morals of this world. He is its implacable enemy, and if he continues to live in it, it is only in order that he might destroy it."[5]

In Dostoevesky's *Demons*, Nechayevism is darkly parodied as 'Shigalyovism', after the fanatical, goblin-eared theorist of the same name. It is significant that the motto Tănase chooses for *Auntie Varvara's Clients* is taken from Verkhovensky's ecstatic description of Shigalyovism to Stavrogin.[6] At a gathering of the novel's revolutionary underground, Shigalyov himself says of his system: "I have become entangled in my own data, and my conclusion stands in direct contradiction to the initial idea from which I started. Proceeding from unlimited freedom, I end with unlimited despotism. I will add, however, that there can be no solution of the social formula except mine."[7] Tănase also makes occasional reference to *Demons* during the course of narrating the clandestine histories of the Romanian underground. For example, the assassination of ousted communist leader Ștefan Foriș, bludgeoned to death with a crowbar, is compared with the brutal murder of Shatov by Verkhovensky's clandestine cell in *Demons*, which in turn was based on the killing of Ivanov, an apostate from Nechayev's revolutionary group, on 21 November 1869.

Another parallel is that the fictional Verhkovensky, like the real Nechayev, falsely claimed to be the representative of a vast underground network, ready to rise up and seize power. Likewise, in August 1944, Emil Bodnăraș, claimed to be able to muster 12,000 armed communists in Bucharest, 90,000 in Galatzi, 120,000 in Ploieşti and 70,000 in Braşov. Bodnăraş, one of the few Romanian communists not in prison or in the Soviet Union at the time, had been invited to take part in the plot to overthrow dictator and Nazi ally Marshal Ion Antonescu. The coup was being prepared by King Mihai and pro-Allied democratic politicians, who prudently decided to involve the Romanian communists, in spite of their insignificant numbers and lack of popular support, given that the advancing Red Army would soon arrive on Romanian soil. The figures put forward by Bodnăraş are fantastical, flowing from a cynical desire to deceive others in order to gain strategic advantage, but also from delusions of grandeur and an insatiable desire to falsify reality, to luxuriate in the lie even while knowing it is a lie, which will be a feature of regime propaganda and the rewriting of history once the underground comes to power. The underground's chronic psychopathological delusions of grandeur were to reach paroxysmal levels during the reign of Nicolae Ceauşescu.

In the final chapter of *Auntie Varvara's Clients*, Tănase describes the structure of Romanian carceral society as being made up of concentric circles. At the centre was the hard core of those who wielded absolute power (Dej, Ceauşescu and their closest henchmen). The second circle consisted of the former denizens of the underground, the 'illegals' of the inter-war period. The third circle was populated by those who, for reasons of opportunism and self-advantage, joined the communists once they had seized power. The fourth circle was made up of the 'fellow travellers' and sympathisers, public figures corrupted by the communists, who used them to lend the new regime a veneer of respectability and normality. At the circumference lay the society that was to be enslaved and destroyed, reduced to the lowest common denominator, the raw material for the 'utopia' of the 'classless society'. The image of the underground as a series of circles, the innermost being the most malevolent, the locus of the all-consuming will to enslave and wield power over others, is certainly meant to invite a comparison with hell.[8]

That the underground is infernal is hinted at throughout the book, although Tănase, concentrating on the historical, archival evidence, does not belabour such speculative, metaphysical interpretations. Given this evidence, the readers are left to form their own psychological, sociological, political, historical etc. interpretation of the *mysterium iniquitatis* that was the underground. However, one conclusion readers of *Auntie Varvara's*

Clients are clearly left to draw is that the creed of the underground, the revolutionaries' catechism, is ultimately one of pure, wanton destruction. The end could never justify the means, because there never was an end, except as an unrealisable utopian phantasm. The means were an end in themselves: the destruction of society for its own sake, and its replacement with an inverted hierarchy in which the lowest – the underground, the dregs – became the highest, the masters. Ultimately, the communists were incapable of building anything other than an all-encompassing replica of the underground itself, a Shigalyov state, where the solution to the formula of society is that "one-tenth [of mankind] is to receive personal freedom and unlimited rights over the remaining nine-tenths. The latter are to lose their individuality and turn into something like cattle, and with this unlimited obedience attain, through a series of regenerations, a primordial innocence, something like the primordial paradise, although they will have to work."[9]

Bibliography

Luxul melancoliei (*The Luxury of Melancholy*, novel), Bucharest: Cartea Românească, 1982, 2nd edition 1993.

Corpuri de iluminat (*Light Fittings*, novel, originally written between 1984 and 1987), Bucharest: Cartea Românească, 1990; 2nd edition, Bucharest: Allfa, 1998; 3rd edition, Jassy: Polirom, 2004; 4th edition Bucharest: Humanitas, 2008.

Șocuri și crize (*Shocks and Crises*), Bucharest: Staff, 1993.

Ora oficială de iarnă. Jurnal, 1986–1990 (*Official Winter Time. Diary, 1986-1990*), Jassy: Institutul European, 1995.

Playback (novel), Bucharest: Editura Fundației Culturale Române, 1995; 2nd edition, Pitești: Paralela 45, 2004; 3rd edition, Bucharest: Humanitas, 2008.

Sfidarea memoriei (*Memory's Defiance*; dialogues with Alexandru Paleologu), Bucharest: Editura Du Style, 1996.

Revoluția ca eșec. Elite și societate (*Revolution as Failure. Elites and Society*), Jassy: Polirom, 1996.

Anatomia mistificării. Procesul Noica-Pillat (*The Anatomy of Mystification*), Bucharest: Humanitas, 1997, 2nd edition 2003.

L.A. vs. N.Y. Jurnal American (*L.A. vs. N.Y. American Diary*), Jassy: Polirom, 1998.

Elite şi societate. Guvernarea Gheorghiu-Dej, 1948–1965 (*Elites and Society. The Gheorghiu-Dej Regime, 1948-1965*), Bucharest: Humanitas, 1998.

Miracolul revoluţiei. O istorie politică a căderii regimurilor comuniste (*The Miracle of the Revolution: A History of the Fall of the Communist Regimes*), Bucharest: Humanitas, 1999.

Acasă se vorbeşte în şoaptă. Dosar & jurnal din anii târzii ai dictaturii (*At Home the Talk is in a Whisper. Dossier and Diary of the Final Years of the Dictatorship*), Bucharest: Compania, 2002.

Zei şi semizei. La început de secol (*Gods and Demigods. At the Beginning of the Century*), Bucharest: Curtea Veche, 2004.

Clienţii lu' tanti Varvara, Bucharest: Humanitas, 2005.

Maestro (novel), Jassy: Polirom, 2008.

Racovski. Dosar secret (*Racovski: Secret Dossier*), Jassy: Polirom, 2008.

Avangarda românească în arhivele Siguranţei (*The Romanian Avant-garde in the Archives of the Siguranţa*), Jassy: Polirom, 2008.

---

[1] In Romanian, both *siguranţă* and *securitate* mean security. The latter is a neologism, employed by the communists as the name for the new secret police.

[2] In 1812, following the Russo-Turkish War, the Ottoman Turks ceded Bessarabia, the eastern half of the principality of Moldavia, to the Russian Empire.

[3] Known in the Soviet Union as *Khrushchevki* (in an ironic tribute to Khrushchev), in East Germany as *Plattenbauen*, in Czechoslovakia as *Paneláki*, and in Romanian simply as *blocuri*. In Romania, under Ceauşescu, during the drive to create a mass industrial proletariat, in conformity with the Marxist vision of the required economic stages preceding the attainment of communism, countless numbers of peasants were uprooted from the countryside and re-housed in urban blocks of flats. Indicative of the dehumanising ideological motives and prison-camp mentality behind such social engineering is the fact that some of these blocks did not even have plumbing – the toilets were situated outside, in the yard, with the inevitable result that those on the upper floors made use of the window rather than descending and ascending numerous flights of stairs.

[4] In 1989, the communists were preparing to take the prison-camp alimentary regime to its logical conclusion: in each sector of Bucharest,

gigantic communal canteens were under construction, nicknamed by the populace *cercurile foamei* (hunger clubs). All food shops and markets were to be closed down and all the citizens of Bucharest were to be forced to eat all their meals at the new 'hunger clubs', once completed. In addition, inspired by North Korea and the Chinese Cultural Revolution, it was planned that all citizens would be obligated to wear uniforms. Since the 1989 Revolution, most of the 'hunger clubs' have been turned into shopping malls.

[5] "§ 1. Революционер – человек обреченный. У него нет ни своих интересов, ни дел, ни чувств, ни привязанностей, ни собственности, ни даже имени. Все в нем поглощено единственным исключительным интересом, единою мыслью, единою страстью – революцией. § 2. Он в глубине своего существа, не на словах только, а на деле, разорвал всякую связь с гражданским порядком и со всем образованным миром, и со всеми законами, приличиями, общепринятыми условиями, нравственностью этого мира. Он для него – враг беспощадный, и если он продолжает жить в нем, то для того только, чтоб его вернее разрушить." Quoted in *Революционный радикализм в России: век девятнадцатый* (*Revolutionary Radicalism in Russia: The Nineteenth Century*), edited by E. L. Rudnitskaya, Arkheograficheskiy Tsentr, 1997, p. 244.

[6] In Part II, Chapter 8, 'Ivan the Tsarevich'.

[7] Fyodor Dostoyevsky, *Demons*, translated by Robert A. Maguire, Harmondsworth: Penguin, 2008, p. 446.

[8] Similarly, in Book V of *De Inferno et statu daemonum ante mundi exitium, libri quinque, in quibus Tartarea cavitas, parata ibi cruciamentorum genera, Ethnicorum etiam de his opiniones, Daemonumque conditio, usque ad magnum Iudicii diem, varia eruditione, describuntur* (1621), probably the most exhaustive theological treatise ever written on the subject, Antonius Rusca describes the infernal order (*ordo Tartareus*), in which the chief of all the lesser demons (*Princeps daemoniorum*) has arranged his satellites in determined divisions (*suos satellites in certas classes ordinavit*).

[9] Fyodor Dostoyevsky, *Demons*, translated by Robert A. Maguire, Harmondsworth: Penguin, 2008, p. 447.

The Clandestine Communists

FOAIA PERSONALĂ

Dimitrăr Ganev

'Auntie Varvara' was the nickname the conspirators of the communist underground gave to the 'Siguranţă' ('Siguranţă Statului' – 'State Security', the pre-communist Romanian secret police) during the decades before they seized power. 'Securitate' (short for *Departamentul Securităţii Statului* 'The Department of State Security') was a neologism chosen by the communists after 1948 to avoid any associations with the pre-communist secret services.

Ana Toma

Richard Wurmbrand

Ofelia Manole

Alexandru Iliescu

Carol Horvitz

Matei Socor

Teohari Georgescu

Nicolae Ceauşescu

Teodor Gandig

Mihail Novicov

Marin Ceauşescu

Béla Breiner

Constantin Doncea

Victor Tordai

Gustav Arnold

Imre Aladár

Petre Iobu

Ita Lerner

Moscu Cohn

Victor Nathason

Alfons Nachtigal

Miron Constantinescu

Bella Rabinsohn

Nicu Tudor

Pavel Tkachenko

Gheorghe Vasilichi

Lotti Foriș

Constantin Pîrvulescu

Ana Pauker

Golda Bancic

Boris Ștefanov

Emil Brafman

Ștefan Foriș   Ilie David   Josef Hoppe   Ghizela Goldstein

Riva Fischman   Saul Ozias   Paraschiva Breiner   Marin Păsărica

Alexandru Nathason   Iție Ozias   Mihail Povstanschi   Mihail Demetrescu

Mișu Dulberger   Alexandru Elias   David Finkelstein   Ida Felix

Ainer Goldstein   Mauriţiu Goldstein   Moriţ Goldstein   Lazăr Grümberg

Alexandru Ionescu   Gheorghe Ivaşcu   Alexandru Iacob   Mozes Kahane

Şmil Marcovici   Sender Margulis   Iancu Moscovici   Jack Blumer

Mariana Rosen   Zita Teodoru   Iţic David   Alexandru Nicholschi

The Official Face of the Underground

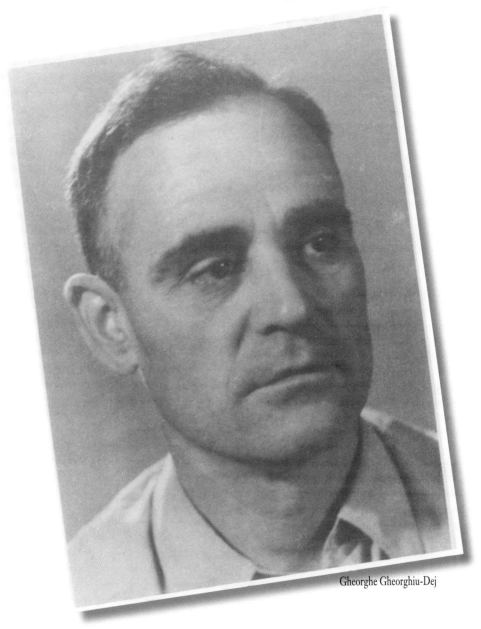

Gheorghe Gheorghiu-Dej

Cristian Racovski

Alexandru Moghioroș

Petre Constantinescu-Iași

Constantin Titel Petrescu

Dumitru Coliu

Vasile Luca

Iosif Chișinevschi

Chivu Stoica

Petre Borilă

Iosif Rangheț

Gheorghe Vasilichi

Gheorghe Pintilie
(Pantyusha Bodnarenko)

Gh. Gheorghiu-Dej, P. Groza, C.I. Parhon, Chivu Stoica, Ana Pauker, S.I. Kavtaradze, Th. Georgescu et al. on the podium at the solemn gathering held in the House of Romanian-Soviet Friendship on the occasion of the 28th anniversary of the death of V.I. Lenin (21 January 1952)

Archive no. IA006

Gh. Gheorghiu-Dej, P. Groza, Th. Georgescu, Ana Pauker, I. Chişinevschi, V. Luca et al. on the ministerial bench at the 11th session of the Grand National Assembly (26 March 1952)

Archive no. IA013

Gh. Gheorghiu-Dej, P. Groza, C.I. Parhon, V. Luca, C. Pîrvulescu, Al. Moghioroș, P. Borilă, S.I. Kavtaradze, Th. Georgescu, I. Chișinevschi, Chivu Stoica, D-tru Petrescu et al. on the viewing stand in Aviatorilor Square at the 1 May Parade (1952)

Archive no. IA046

Photographic sources: The Online Communism Photograph Collection of the National Archives of Romania and the Institute for the Investigation of Communist Crimes in Romania (http://www.arhivelenationale.ro/fototeca/fototeca/) and copies of photographs made by Mr Stelian Tănase during his archival research.

Stelian Tănase

AUNTIE VARVARA'S CLIENTS

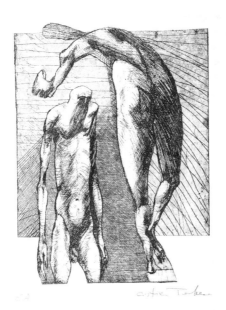

Auntie Varvara's Clients. Clandestine Histories

'It's well put in his notebook', Verkhovensky continued. 'He's got spying down. He has each member of society watching the others and obliged to inform. Each belongs to all, and all to each. All are slaves, and are equal in their slavery. In extreme cases there's slander and murder, but the main thing is equality. [...] No sooner do we have the family or love than the desire for private property arises. We will kill desire; we will foster drunkenness, gossip, denunciation; we will foster unheard-of depravity'.

Dostoevsky, *Demons* (1871)[1]

---

[1] Part II, Chapter 8 *Ivan the Tsarevich*. Translated by Robert A. Maguire, Harmondsworth: Penguin, 2008, p. 463.

I

The Diplomatically Sealed Train Carriage

> Only a revolution can save the world.
> *Lenin*

Our story commences somewhere in Switzerland, on the platform of a railway station, with an informant's report:

"Today, I learned of the departure of a number of persons and at 3.20 p.m. proceeded to the railway station, where the express train was about to depart [...] a carriage full of Russian revolutionaries [...] I also saw the Russian named Lenin, who was obviously travelling as the leader of the group. It seems that the departure should have taken place in secret, but present were another approximately one hundred Russians of both sexes, who saw off those who were leaving with mixed feelings [...] Those in favour of waging war against Germany to the very end were cursing like cabmen, shouting that those travelling were all German spies and provocateurs, or that 'you will all be hanged, Jewish instigators that you are' [...] 'Provocateurs, scoundrels, pigs' etc. [...] When the train started to move off, the travellers and many of their friends who had remained began to sing the International, while the others began once again to hurl at them 'Provocateurs, spies'."[1]

Lenin and his entourage were leaving Zurich bound for Petrograd. On German territory, they were to transfer to a diplomatically sealed carriage, with covered windows, and – via Sweden – arrive in Russia a few days later. The arrangements had been made by the German Foreign Minister, Dr Alexander Helphant, also known as Parvus: a rich Russian with revolutionary leanings, a long-standing financier of the Bolsheviks, and close to Lenin and Trotsky. Lenin was going to Petrograd with one thought on his mind: to take power. He was relying on his small party and on the Russian proletariat, also

---

[1] Martin C. Stănescu and Costin Feneșan, *Lenin și Troțki versus Ludendorff și Hoffman*. Bucharest: Editura Enciclopedică, 1999, p. 77.

a minority, circa three per cent of the population. He knew very well that a revolution could not be accomplished with such forces. Marx, his inspiration, had written that the Revolution would be unleashed and supported only by a majority. The dictatorship of the proletariat of which Marx spoke was the dictatorship of a majority over a minority, the bourgeoisie. Lenin was thus preparing not a revolution but a putsch. And his government was to be a dictatorship. In order to hold on to power, terror was to be his main political weapon. His calculations anticipated that in a short while the example of Russia would be followed by the West. The international dimension of the Petrograd coup was decisive for the adventure into which Lenin was about to plunge Russia. Immediately after seizing power, his main preoccupation would be to plot rebellions, insurrections, and uprisings in neighbouring countries, with the aim of consigning the bourgeoisie to the dustbin of history, thereby hauling Russia out of isolation. Upon this depended the very fate of the Bolshevik regime, so he believed, along with Trotsky and a number of others.

It all begins here, on the platform of Zurich railway station, at the end of March, according to the old calendar. The German authorities were pinning much hope on this deployment. The aim was to cause chaos in Russia, weaken the regime installed after the abdication of the Tsar, and secure a separate peace with Germany. The following is an excerpt from a report by the German ambassador to Copenhagen, Count von Brockdorff-Rantzau, to the Foreign Minister in Berlin. The ambassador was negotiating the entire affair with Parvus.

"[W]e are capable of continuing the war successfully until autumn [the report dates from 2 April 1917], both militarily and economically. In this case, it will be imperative to produce as much chaos in Russia as possible [...] in our interests, it is preferable to favour the extremist element, because thereby a more thorough job will be done and a conclusion will be reached more rapidly. According to the predictions, in three months it will be possible to count on the decomposition being sufficiently advanced for a military intervention on our part in order to guarantee the collapse of the Russian forces..."[2]

---

[2] *Op. cit.*, p. 64.

The Bolshevik group had been financed by German banks for many years. This support would consist of huge sums in the period to follow. After arriving in Petrograd, Lenin receives money for propaganda, the printing of newspapers, and the payment of thousands of commissars and militants. Revolution was his obsession. The Russian phase, the 'revolutionary' putsch, was merely the spark destined to light the fuse of the bomb. Capitalism was to be blown up and replaced by a paradisal world, the dictatorship of the proletariat. A utopia. No price was too high, however, if it brought him closer to this aim – neither betrayal, nor the collapse of Russia, nor millions of victims.

As a youth, Lenin had enmeshed in a vast operation of subversion. As early as 1903, in the pamphlet *What is to be done?* he had formulated the rules for a new type of party, capable of taking power by force. It would have to be limited in size, possess iron discipline, be strictly hierarchical, and lead a double life: one visible, the other underground. It would be at the latter level that decisions were taken. It would be here that secrets were shared, here that the conspiracy and the plot were woven. After gaining power, Lenin practised the same methods, drawing a dividing line between the initiates, his entourage, and the rest of the organisation. He had a pronounced aversion to democracy. He had an overriding obsession with secrecy, with conspiracy, which would not abandon him even after he had taken power. "The Great Socialist October Revolution," according to the enshrined expression, was in fact a plot with international ramifications, supported by a group of powerful interests, financed by foreign banks.[3] The plan worked perfectly. The *coup de grâce* was a putsch carried out at the beginning of November. It was then that the Red Guard, led by Trotsky, the author of the scenario, occupied the railway stations, the bridges across the Neva, the telephone exchanges, the printing presses, the Post Office…

The event served to launch an entire mythology about the brigades of soldiers and workers who that night opened up 'the horizons of a new world'. For a long time, the mystique of revolution and the liberation of man camouflaged the true meaning of things. It was a classic putsch, not a revolution. Its most approximate genus is not the English or French Revolutions but rather the 1922 'March on Rome', or Hitler's attempted coup of 1923. The Revolution sparked by the abdication of the Tsar

---

[3] Dmitri Volkogonov, *Lenin. O nouă biografie*, Bucharest: Editura Orizonturi-Lider, 1999, pp. 82-95.

in February 1917 culminates with the Petrograd and Moscow putsch of November. The storming of the Winter Palace marked the finale of this attempt. On gaining power, Lenin pursued his idea of globalising the Petrograd putsch. To this end, he unleashed a vast operation of subversion beyond the borders of Russia. He was obsessed with the idea that, were Russia to remain isolated, the 'Revolution' would succumb. This is why it was imperative that the Bolshevik example be followed. The 'avant-garde of the proletariat' was thus obliged to stage putsches in other countries. After 1918, Moscow orchestrates repeated attempts by Bolshevik groups to seize power. Hungary 1919, Germany 1919, 1920, 1923, and China 1927 are just a few examples. Many countries become the object of subversion, provocations, the fomenting of conflict, and incitement to civil war. Often, behind the protests of left-wing, pacifist movements and of trades unions, there were clandestine groups financed and politically controlled by the Bolsheviks. Subversion constantly changed its form. However, the aim remained the same until much later, until 1991: the instigation of crises, the undermining and destabilisation of democratic regimes, chaos, and seizure of power. The effects were devastating: the historical blockage of many generations within an experiment that led nowhere. It took decades for this complicated and malefic tangle to be unravelled, something that did not happen until the end of the twentieth century.

The pages that follow are nothing more than the narration of a particular case – the Romanian case – as one part of this vast history.

II

Rako, the Old Guard

> Let us leave the Russians in peace
> to continue their tragic experiment alone,
> embarked upon most unhappy adventure known to history.
> *Constantin Graur, Adevărul, 8 June 1922*

Two weeks after the report by the police agent in Zurich, another agent, this time Romanian, made the following report from Jassy: "On 18 April (1 May) 1917, at 12.00, a number of groups of Russian soldiers and officers began to make their way to the Socola Field, situated between Aviation Park and the new marshalling yard, carrying in front of them flags and red placards inscribed with 'Long Live the International', 'Long Live Free and Republican Russia, 'Long Live the Freedom of Nations', 'Land and Freedom', 'War, unto the Final Victory', 'We want Peace without annexations and reparations!' ... By 13.30, more than 5,000 men had already gathered on the Socola Field, assembled around a makeshift rostrum. Nearby, there was a military band, which played a fanfare after each of the speeches. Next to the rostrum, there were a number of motor cars and in one of them were a number of Russian superior officers, including General Belyasny. Former Member of Parliament Vadayev, the delegate of the Petrograd workers, who arrived on the 18th of this year, addressed the crowd. He explained how the Russian Revolution had taken place, adding that the Soviet of Workers' Representatives had opposed Tsar Nicholas being taken to London ... The orator Gilert (Giller) of the Russian General Staff, an engineer, delivered a violent speech against Romania. He spoke about the freedom that had been won by the Russian people, who would be neither satisfied nor content until Russia had freed all nations from slavery. The Romanian people were suffering under the same oligarchic yoke as the Russian people had suffered until now. Romanian soldiers were dying on the streets of the town and the unfortunate, starving, naked Romanian people were crawling along the roads while the Romanian oligarchy, which monopolised everything in its own hands, was pampering itself with delicacies and motor cars, without a care for the poverty-stricken people with nothing to eat. 'We', said the orator, 'must fight until the Romanian people, our ally, is freed from slavery, and we must show the King of Romania the same road as Tsar Nicholas has now taken'. … There was a visible lack of Romanians at the meeting. At 15.00 hours, the chairman of the gathering urged the soldiers to fall into rank and set off into the town to demonstrate. The demonstrators went through the streets of the town until they reached the domicile of Dr Racovski at No. 30 Aqueduct Street, where the latter was being held under police guard. They forcibly took him away by motor car and headed to Unification Square. Here, the engineer Giller, secretary of the Committee of the Soldiers' and Officers' Soviet, spoke again, in a manner more violent than at Socola … Thence, the demonstrators, together with Dr Racovski and the Russian officers, went to the house of Sub-lieutenant Gheorghiu Bujor, next to the railway station. They took him with them in the motor car and, shouting 'hooray', the Russian officers conducted Dr Racovski and Sub-Lieutenant Bujor to the hamlet of Vlădiceni, dependent on the parish of Buciumi, Jassy County. The demonstrators, in separate groups, carrying banners, demonstrated on the streets of the town, singing until evening, when it started to rain."[1]

Cristian Racovski (born 1873, near Kotel, in Bulgaria), the main character of this ludicrous escapade, had been the dominant figure of Romanian social democracy for more than 10 years, since 1905. He came from a well-known family, and was educated in the West, after having been expelled from all the lycées in Bulgaria. Racovski was a physician, with a Degree in Medicine taken in Montpellier, France, and another taken in Paris. In Switzerland, during his adolescence, he had met Friedrich Engels, Karl Marx's collaborator, with whom he had exchanged letters. Racovski was connected to a number of the leaders of the international socialist movement: Vera Zasulich, Nikolay Plekhanov, Wilhelm Liebknicht, Jean Jaurès, Jules Guesde, Karl Kautsky. He had been a friend of Rosa Luxemburg, Karl Liebknecht and others since his youth. He himself was a living history. He was closest to Leon Trotsky, whom he had met in 1903. They subsequently met each other at various congresses and in newspaper offices. Racovski also financed the gazette Trotsky published in Paris, *Nashe Slovo* (*Our Word*). In 1913, when Trotsky travelled to the region as a Balkan War correspondent,

---

[1] "Report by the Security Service of the Main Military Headquarters on 2 May 1917," in *Ideologie și structuri comuniste în România, 1917-1918* [*Communist Ideology and Structures in Romania*], National Institute for the Study of Totalitarianism, Documents, 1995, pp. 221-224.

he stayed at Racovski's estate near Mangalia.[2] Trotsky paints a flattering portrait of Racovski in the articles he writes on that occasion.[3] It is Racovski who, in 1905, when the battleship *Potemkin* – whose crew had mutinied – arrives in the port of Constanța, boards the ship, in spite of an interdiction by the Romanian authorities, in order to reconcile the conflicting groups of sailors, but also to assist in negotiations for asylum. In 1907, after the peasant uprising, Racovski, seen as one of the instigators, is expelled. This was "the most despicable act of the oligarchy," writes Trotsky, taking up the reasons as they had been related to him by Racovski: namely, that the latter was not a Romanian citizen and was an agent of the Russian General Staff. At that date, in 1907, Racovski was the head of the Social Democratic Party (Partidul Social Democrat – PSD) and its main sponsor, together with Constantin Dobrogeanu-Gherea. From 1905, he was a PSD delegate in the Bureau of the Socialist International. His expulsion occurs in August 1907, while he is at the Socialist International conference in Stuttgart, together with Nicholas D. Cocea and Alecu Constantinescu among others.[4] Reporting this occurrence, the left-wing press cause Racovski to become a familiar name throughout Europe. In any case, he remains in Europe, as a frequenter of international congresses and Socialist Party meetings. He becomes one of the most famous socialist militants. He publishes a number of books and pamphlets; he writes for various newspapers all over Europe. His articles also continue to be published in Bucharest, however. His case is a constant focus of attention. In 1909, he attempts to return to Romania clandestinely, via Sibiu,[5] but he is caught and expelled. After a stormy meeting in the Sotir Auditorium in Amzei Square,[6] a socialist meeting place, there is a trial implicating Gheorghe Cristescu and Panait Istrati among others. Cristian Racovski returns to Romania in February

---

[2] Black Sea port in the Dobrogea region of South-East Romania; the ancient Greek colony of Kallatis – *Translator's note.*

[3] Leon Trotsky, *România și răboiul balcanic* [*Romania and the Balkan War*], Jassy: Polirom, 1998, pp. 83-90.

[4] Details in Constantin Titel Petrescu, *Socialismul în România*, Bucharest: Biblioteca Socialistă, 1940, pp. 202-203.

[5] Sibiu, or Hermannstadt, a city in Transylvania, was part of the Austro-Hungarian Empire at that time, and became part of Romania after the Union of 1 December 1918 – *Translator's note.*

[6] In Bucharest – *Translator's note.*

1912,[7] after the fall of the Brătianu government, with the approval of the ruling conservatives. "The return of this extraordinary inspirer of crowds gives a new impulse to the socialist movement."[8]

The SPD congress of June 1912 enshrines the dominant position of Racovski among Romanian Social Democrats. It is the year the Balkan Wars break out. At their close, in August-September 1913, Trotsky makes the above-mentioned journey to Romania. According to the latter, Racovski stayed at Mangalia for three days to take care of domestic matters, and three days in Bucharest, where he took part in meetings, organised protests and wrote for the newspapers. Is Racovski a split personality? Is he a magnanimous man who, under given historical circumstances, would donate his estate to the peasants? It is hard to say. At Mangalia, he is viewed as a master, which is what he indeed is. He belongs to a family with traditions and a fortune. He had contacts with every ethnic group: Turks, Jews, Lipovians,[9] Russians, Ukrainians, Bulgarians. To Trotsky's amazement, they all address him in their native tongues. Racovski is a polyglot and a communicator. He feels at home in any setting: at the sophisticated, smoky conferences of the International, with their behind the scenes intrigues and tensions, but also among his barefoot, illiterate and superstitious peasants. At Mangalia, he resides in an "old house, with low windows, and also a low ceiling. The family of the master hails from Kotel, in the heart of the Balkan Mountains, the father and grandfather were sheep breeders ... The old woman who keeps watch over the house, order and traditions is 75 years old, having spent more than half her years under the Turkish yoke. Her husband, who died a few years before, had been a *çorbaci*, i.e. a wealthy man, a representative of the community before the Turkish authorities. This family, renowned in Bulgardom, is historic. Savva Racovski, the celebrated activist of the national rebirth ... served a prison sentence in Constantinople together with his father, constantly expecting death; this patriarch of the Bulgarian Revolution, who died in Bucharest in 1867, was the uncle of our host, the old woman. In the house, there is an archive, unique in its way, of the history of the Bulgarian struggle for national independence.

---

[7] Details in C. Bacalbașa, *Bucureștii de altădată* [*Bucharest of Former Times*], Bucharest: Ziarul Universul, Bucharest, 1938, vol. 4, pp. 45-49.

[8] Constantin Titel Petrescu, *op. cit.*, p. 206.

[9] Russian Old Believers, who fled Russia following the reforms under Peter the Great and settled in the Danube Delta – *Translator's note*.

Cupboards of books, old naïve chromographs, stoves of complicated shape, numerous house carpets, draperies, wherever possible, wadded blankets, and at the windows, the scent of the sea, which is 50 paces away."[10] Such is Trotsky's description of the house in which Racovski resided at Mangalia. 'Revolutionary fervour', political opposition, was in the family tradition, but also the idea that it was a leader, a natural ruler of others. Racovski's destiny is an extension of the past, albeit in a different direction. In any case, his real name is Khristo Stanchev, 'Racovski' being a borrowing from the family, ascribed to his glorious grandfather and uncle. We are in close proximity to the Orient here, and in this setting, the two, Trotsky and Racovski, are adventurers who are preparing to blow the world to smithereens. The wars of 1912-1913 also induce another idea in the two: that a solution to the Balkan problem can only be furnished by the creation of a confederacy of states between Serbia, Bulgaria, Greece, Romania and Albania. A congress in Bucharest popularises the idea. It becomes the declared aim of the socialists in these countries. The project falls into oblivion once the First World War breaks out, after Franz Ferdinand, the next in line to the throne of the Austro-Hungarian Empire, is assassinated in Sarajevo.

The Socialist International splits. Racovski takes a pacifist stance. He opposes Romania's entry into the war. On 23 September 1916, he is detained in Bucharest on suspicion of being a German agent. These accusations were not new, and there are a number of facts to bear out police suspicions toward him. In 1915, Racovski had made a trip to Italy accompanied by two German officials. His aim was to convince the Italian socialist leaders and press to fight to preserve Italy's neutrality. Racovski is also one of the initiators of the Zimmerwald Conference, where a handful of radical socialists gather in order to protest against the war. He is singled out in reports by the French secret service as a German agent. Also in 1915, he received, in Bucharest, a visit from Alexander Helphant (Parvus), who did business in Germany, Turkey, Scandinavia and Russia. He also had business interests in Romania, a neutral country at the time, from where he purchased agricultural products, bringing back medicines and surgical instruments from Germany. However, this was only one facet of Parvus' personality. There was also another facet, that of the 'professional revolutionary'. He dreamed of and plotted the overthrow of the tsarist regime. In 1905, together with Trotsky, he had been a member of the Petrograd Soviet. Arrested, sent to Siberia, he escaped

---

[10] Leon Trotsky, *op. cit.*, pp. 137-38.

and returned to the West.[11] Parvus set himself up in Constantinople, where he rapidly became rich, importing and exporting between Germany and Turkey. He supported German interests, presenting himself as a 'pacifist', a formula under which German propaganda was trying to hinder the creation of a *bloc* against the Central Powers and likewise provoke disturbances in the Entente camp. Parvus is suspected even by the socialists of working for the German government as an agent of influence and spy. Which is true. His visit to Bucharest and the meetings with Cristian Racovski attract the attention of the Romanian police. Even up to then, Racovski had played the part of a 'pacifist', an opponent of Romania's entry into the war. Police and press suspicions hovered above him. Rumours that he was a German agent were also circulating in European socialist circles. In August 1916, Romania enters the war. Suspected of being in the pay of the Berlin secret services, Cristian Racovski is placed under surveillance five weeks after Romania's entry into the war; he is forbidden to leave his domicile. He is sent to the prison in Vaslui, then, when the government retreats to Jassy, he is placed under house arrest there.

After his release from Jassy, on 1 May 1917, Racovski takes refuge in Odessa. Here, he meets Henri Stahl, the Parliament stenographer, now a refugee: "After about half an hour, Racovski came. He greeted the ladies elegantly, he shook the hand of Mr Moruzi ... Racovski is a handsome man, tall, slim, with a black beard, glittering but furtive eyes, and nervous, anguished gestures."[12] His appearances of being a civilised man are deceptive. Racovski orders requisitions, terrorises the Romanian refugees, and confiscates property, money and jewels, "for the use of the Revolution." For a time, he is regarded as the leader of the Romanian socialists, in whose name he speaks. He frequently mentions a confederation of Balkan states. The Romanian State was to be wiped from the map. In order to achieve this scenario, there would be a revolution to overthrow King Ferdinand. On the Moldavian front, the Russian Army is falling apart. Thousands of Russian soldiers abandon the trenches, and give themselves up to looting and armed attacks. Propaganda in favour of the soldiers' soviets, aimed against the government and King Ferdinand, becomes widespread. The Romanian

---

[11] Dmitri Volkogonov, *Lenin. O nouă biografie* [*A New Biography*], Editura Orizonturi-Lider, 1999, pp. 144-45.

[12] H. Stahl, *Cu Parlamentul prin URSS* [*With Parliament through the USSR*], Bucharest: Domino, 2003, p. 185.

State is in grave danger. In Odessa, Racovski gathers around him a group of extremists with whom he conspires to organise an insurrection in Romania. In proclamations, he urges the populace to rise up against the 'oligarchy', following the Russian example. He organises a Romanian revolutionary battalion of deserters, refugees and prisoners. His stance towards the Bolsheviks is nevertheless ambiguous. His relations with Lenin prior to 1917 were not good. In August 1915, Lenin wrote to Karl Radek, with reference to Racovski: "We do not share the same path as such people."[13] At the Zimmerwald Conference, Racovski had an altercation with Lenin, who stormed out of the auditorium. The two are reconciled thanks to the mediation of Trotsky in the autumn of 1917.

After the Bolshevik *putsch* of 25 October, Racovski's influence becomes very great within a short time. The question is what was such a character looking for in the company of the Bolsheviks? Racovski had, up to then, made a show of being a traditional social democrat, even if sometimes he took radical positions. From the autumn of 1917, he emerges as a Bolshevik terrorist, an adept of dictatorship, and a perpetrator of violence. There are a number of answers to this question. First of all, there is Trotsky's influence – the old friendship between the two and the dominant position of Trotsky in the Bolshevik staff. To this can be added the 'mystique of revolution'. Racovski had long-standing ties with Russia. He had been married to a Russian woman, he had lived in Petrograd for a few years at the beginning of the century, and he spoke Russian. In his family, there was a strong philo-Russian tradition. Then, he believed, like Lenin, that Russia was only the beginning of a process that would set the world aflame. In the footsteps of his ancestors, he had a heightened sense of history. He wanted "to go down in history," to be one of history's protagonists. Another reason was, of course, career.

In Petrograd, he had been offered a position he could not have hoped for anywhere else. In 1917, he was 44 years old. He was no longer young. In Romania, he was doomed to lead a modest opposition party, just a thousand strong – the number of PSD members between 1910 and 1916. Bucharest was a stage that was too narrow for him. Russia was the grand stage he craved. Racovski is a man without a homeland. He is a European, an "internationalist," like Lenin and Trotsky. He is part of that radical

---

[13] *Lenin despre România* [*Lenin on Romania*], Bucharest: Editura politică, 1960, p. 28.

intelligentsia from the beginning of the century, who felt at home in the cafés of Paris, in trains between Berlin and Vienna, in newspaper offices in London, and in the hotels of Brussels, Prague and Copenhagen. It was a world that these intellectuals detested and loved in equal measure. They dreamed of destroying it, but also of being acknowledged by it. In setting Russia aflame, they were in fact getting ready to conquer Europe. Racovski was not thinking of a Russian destiny: Russia was merely a staging post. He shared with Lenin and Trotsky the dream of a world revolution. The putsch of 25 October was merely to be the detonator. He also believed that if Russia remained isolated, its attempt to destroy capitalism would be abortive. On the other hand, Racovski was a rich, educated man. The image we have of the Bolsheviks recalls the lumpen, soot-begrimed proletariat, handing out manifestos at the gates of the industrial revolution's first factories… This image is inexact. Lenin, Trotsky, Molotov, Kollonatai, Dzerzhinsky, Manuilsky, Lunacharsky, Chicherin, Litvinov, Rykov, Kamenev and Zinoviev were not like this. Lenin had a noble title. He could have had a good career as a lawyer and made a fortune in Petersburg, had he so wished. Trotsky was the son of a rich Jewish farmer from the Ukraine. Felix Dzerzhinsky, the head of the much-feared Cheka, was a Polish noble. And so on. The Bolsheviks were part of the Russian intelligentsia and were often descended from the richer echelons of the bourgeoisie, from the families of merchants and high dignitaries. In the old guard, the déclassés, such as Stalin or Sverdlov, were the exceptions, the tools Lenin used for dirty work and dangerous operations. Having arrived in the same camp as Lenin, Racovski thus begins a career in the foremost ranks of the Russian Revolution. His international amplitude, his old contacts, and Lenin's need to utilise such well-known figures in the socialist movement assured him of a place in the Bolshevik hierarchy.

In the years that followed, Racovski was a declared enemy of Romania. He believed that a revolution was unavoidable. He was convinced that a Red Army offensive would be enthusiastically welcomed by the Romanian populace, discontent as they were with the government and the war. He is mixed up in all the actions organised by Moscow against Romania. His actions aim at unleashing a military invasion, combined with a local insurrection. Exporting the Revolution was in any case part of the vision of Lenin and Trotsky. The two send Racovski to southern Russia to lead the operation to install the Bolshevik regime there. In Ukraine, the theatre of the most violent clashes, Racovski is the president of the People's Commissars, the head of government. He also heads Rumcherod,[14] an improvised but powerful organisation, the soviet of delegates to the Romanian front in Ukraine. He is thus also a military chief. The end of 1917 is regarded as an appropriate moment to deliver the *coup de grâce* to Romania. The Bolshevik government sends a commando of around 500 men to Jassy, the location of the Royal Court and the government, with the mission of assassinating the king and arresting the government. Racovski asks for Lenin's support in the operation. The aim of the incursion was to take power in the name of a 'soviet of workers and soldiers'. Romania was to be declared a 'red republic'. The operation did not seem difficult, because the Russian Army, in falling to pieces, had provoked chaos. "The Bolshevisation and disintegration of the Russian front in our country began to accelerate with alarming rapidity. In fact, we were facing a veritable Bolshevik Revolution on our own territory."[15] Gangs of soldiers declared themselves Bolsheviks, shot their officers, set up soldiers' soviets, annihilated the local authorities. It was on these things that the Bolshevik commando led by Simion Grigorievich Roshal, one of the agitators of the Petrograd putsch, president of the Kronstadt Soviet, was relying. If the coup succeeded, a government was to be installed, made up of Cristian Racovski, Mihai Gheorghiu Bujor, Alecu Constantinescu, Ion Dic. Dissescu, and Al. Nicolau. Racovski is spotted at the beginning of December near the border. The plot is uncovered. When Roshal attempts to capture General Dmitri Shcherbachev, the commander of the Russian Army in Moldavia, he is arrested along with the other leaders of the commando.[16] Subsequently, the Bolsheviks threatening Jassy are disarmed. "Within a few

---

[14] Acronym for Румыния, Черное Море, Одесса (Romania, Black Sea, Odessa). The full title was Central Executive Committee of the Soviets of the Romanian Front, Black Sea Fleet and Odessa Military District – *Translator's note.*

[15] I. Gheorghe Duca, *Memorii*, Bucharest: Editura Machiavelli, 1994, vol. 4, p.38.

[16] See N. Iorga, *Memorii*, vol. 1, "Însemnări zilnice, maiu 1917 – martie 1920" [Daily Notes, May 1917 – March 1920], Editura Naționala S. Ciornei, pp. 166-67, 188-89, 196-200; I. Gh. Duca, *op. cit.*, vol. 4, pp. 38-45, 50, 53-54; *Ideologie și structuri comuniste în România, 1917-1918* [*Communist ideology and structures in Romania*], published by INST, 1997, pp. 280-297.

weeks, we have liquidated the Bolshevik Army in Moldavia once and for all," notes I. Gh. Duca.[17]

Consulting with Racovski, Trotsky, who is now Foreign Minister, sends a threatening note of protest, declaring that "in such circumstances the government would also take measures to support in Romania the actions of Romanian revolutionaries currently refugees in Russia. An obvious allusion to Racovski, who inspired the entire position of the Bolsheviks against us and whose hostile inclinations and machinations we detected in all things."[18] On 31 December, the Romanian Minister to Petrograd, C. Diamandy, and the entire staff of the diplomatic mission are arrested. A few days later, Racovski, now in Odessa, orders the arrest of the members of the Romanian consulate. In Odessa, there were thousands of Romanian civilians fleeing the war. Terror is unleashed among the refugees.

Racovski saw himself as a dictator, playing the role of Lenin in Romania. I. Gh. Duca was not deceiving himself as regards Racovski when he spoke of his enmity towards Romania. He was especially rancorous towards the Romanian "oligarchy." The affair of his expulsion had scarred him. He had a strong resentment towards the royal dynasty, towards the Liberals, towards I.I.C. Brătianu. Essential to Racovski's attitude was, however, the ideological schema, the vision of the 'dictatorship of the proletariat' established by the Bolshevik Revolution. The attempted putsch in Jassy in December 1917 was but one episode in a series. In 1918-1919, all over Europe governments were confronted with major problems caused by radicals, anarchists, deserters and extremists. Paramilitary groups were conspiring or else quite simply taking to the streets in arms to overthrow them. In all these cases, we can discover the involvement of local Bolshevik agitators or emissaries from Russia. Then there is the question of the vast funds they transport the length and breadth of Europe: to Germany, Finland, Hungary, France, Italy, Bulgaria, anywhere the crisis might be exploited according to the script of proletarian revolution. The Bolshevik general staff followed the situation closely, obsessed with unleashing coups wherever the occasion arose. Romania, due to its location on the corridor towards the Balkans and Central Europe, constituted a 'priority'. With Racovski in the Bolshevik staff, matters are exacerbated.

In 1917, Russia and the Central Powers signed an armistice, which

---

[17] I. Gh. Duca, *op. cit.*, vol. 4, p. 54.
[18] *Idem*, p. 55.

"sealed the fate of Romania."[19] "Chased out of our country, the Bolshevik agents moved their headquarters to Kishinev and then commenced the Bolshevisation of Bassarabia. In fact, in December, the province was in the midst of an agrarian revolution: the peasants were burning down the landowners' manor houses, emptying the granaries, dividing up the land and devastating the forests. The government of autonomous Bassarabia, which now proclaimed itself a separate republic, could barely contain this wave of anarchy. ... Lenin's men understood that it was here that the seeds of disintegration had to be sown first of all and so it was here they set to work. ... The Bolsheviks continued their work and the anarchy grew. The situation of the government and the entire fate of the new republic of Bassarabia were growing tragic. ... The government of Bassarabia asked us for the military aid necessary to defend the railways and supply depots. ... We decided to sends the troops needed to protect Bassarabia and eradicate all Bolshevik peril between the Prut and the Dniester."[20] Lenin declares the Russian government to be in a state of war and breaks all diplomatic relations with Romania. Trotsky orders the confiscation of the Romanian State treasure deposited in Moscow. Many of the plots, 'insurrections' and assassination attempts mounted outside Russia in the period that followed were funded from the Romanian State treasure. The Ionel Brătianu and Take Ionescu government is replaced with another led by General Alexandru Averescu. Russia and the Central Powers negotiate the Peace of Brest-Litovsk. Romania is in a situation with no exit. Averescu demands an extension of the armistice, trying to buy time. Rumcherod launches a massive offensive towards the Dniester. Caught between two fronts, General Averescu signs an accord with Racovski on 23 February, in Odessa. Our chronicler, I. Gh. Duca, records:

"Aversecu, with inadmissible ease, has signed a treaty with Rumcherod, which is to say with Racovski in fact, a treaty on the basis of which, in exchange for the repatriation of our compatriots, he is obliged to evacuate Bassarabia within three months."[21]

---

[19] Kieth Hitchens, *România. 1866-1947*, Bucharest: Humanitas, 1996, p. 295.
[20] I. Gh. Duca, *op. cit.*, vol 4, pp. 60-61.
[21] *Idem*, p. 92.

Thanks to this success, Racovski passes as a respected military leader among the Bolsheviks. Two weeks later, a government is formed, led by Alexandru Marghiloman. Bolshevik troops under the command of Rumerchod, led by Racovski, launch an offensive in the direction of Bassarabia. At Brest-Litovsk, the Russian delegation led by Trotsky refuses to sign the peace with the Central Powers, proposing the formula "neither peace nor war," and abandons the negotiations. The Central Powers renewed their offensive and at the end of the month occupied Odessa. The Bolsheviks abandon the city; the Romanian refugees are freed. Racovski does not look back until he reaches Moscow. After the retreats they have had to make, the Bolsheviks return to the negotiating table and sign the peace with Germany and Austria-Hungary. As an effect of this, the Marghiloman government signs the peace treaty with the Central Powers on 7 May. The situation, although dramatic for Romania – obliged to make heavy concessions – nevertheless stabilises. Russia for the time being lacks the necessary forces to threaten the existence of the Romanian State in a direct or armed fashion. It is an apparent respite. The Bolshevik regime needs time to consolidate internally. Racovski makes a short diplomatic sojourn in Berlin, whence he is expelled in November, together with the entire Russian embassy staff. The motive: his involvement in subversion. He is even arrested. He arrives in Moscow in December 1918, and in Ukraine a month later.

In 1918, a number of groups of Romanian communists are formed in Russia. Their members are, above all, former prisoners, converted to Bolshevism. Not all the recruits are former prisoners, however. Other Bolshevik groups appear clandestinely in Romania. The 'prestige of revolution', the mystique of 'fundamentally changing the world', the temptation of the 'year zero', compounded by the crisis created by the war, nourished plenty of extreme left-wing sympathies in Romania, as well as in the rest of Europe, especially among the 'trenches generation', from whom were recruited the first generation of Bolshevik agitators, conspirators and insurgents. Simultaneous with the defeat of the Central Powers and the disappearance of the pre-war system of states, a 'revolutionary situation' arises, which the Bolsheviks hasten to exploit.

In Germany, there are a number of insurrections. In Kiel, the sailors revolt. In Berlin, detachments of extreme left-wingers mount an insurrection. In Berlin and in Munich, experienced Bolshevik agitators are an active presence, utilising funds sent from Russia. Lenin is obsessed with Russia's emergence from isolation. He is convinced – a conviction he maintains until his dying day – that his regime will not resist for long unless the 'dictatorship of the proletariat' is extended across the whole continent. The situation was extremely difficult all over Europe. Convoys of soldiers, former prisoners of war and refugees were traversing the continent, provoking disorder. Countries that had just come out of a war possessed a greatly reduced capacity to maintain law and order. Many collapsed. The background of the chaos in Russia, combined with intense propaganda directed against the 'bourgeois' democracies, held guilty of the carnage, made the danger of insurrections very real. The 'wave of revolution' was at its height. Strikes, protests, street violence and attempted *putsches* erupt frequently. Soldiers heading homewards, millions of starving city-dwellers and the unemployed seeking work were easily mobilised by extremist leaders, regardless of their ideological makeup. The years 1918-1919 were those in which political violence continued unabated. Similarly relentless were the Bolshevik attempts to set Europe aflame. After the Allied victories on the Western front in particular, and simultaneous with the retreat of the Central Powers, the danger to the countries of Central and Eastern Europe was mortal. The map of Europe was redrawn in but a few weeks.

Romania gained a respite for only a short while, for as long as the Bolsheviks were tied up with domestic problems. Just two weeks after the return of the King and Queen to Bucharest, from their refuge in Jassy, there was an attempt at insurgency. On 13 December, printing press workers organised a demonstration. At the intersection of Calea Victoriei with Cîmpineanu Street and Ionică Street, in the immediate vicinity of the Social Democratic Party headquarters, in the square in front of the National Theatre, there were even serious clashes with the army, resulting in dead and wounded. Investigations showed that the organisers of the demonstration belonged to clandestine communist groups. Manifestos printed in Russia were discovered. Here is an example:

"The Revolution can no longer be stopped ... only with weapon in hand, like the Russian workers and peasants, will we become masters of our fate ... The great day approaches... Prepare your souls and arm yourselves! ... We shall lay our hands on weapons. We shall take control of the arsenals. We shall destroy all trace of yesterday's men... We shall cast out all those who are not with us... We shall occupy ... the ministries, train stations, post offices and barracks. We shall cast out the police, gendarmes, prefects, tax collectors, Members of Parliament and kings!"[22]

The aim, in the first phase, is to provoke disorder, and, in the second phase, to take power. To this end, a Committee of Action was established, with the mission of "taking action for revolution, through violent means."[23] There is a plan to occupy the railway stations and the Central Post Office, to cut off electricity and water supplies. The final ruling of the subsequent trial states, "This is what the socialists of our restless country understand by sowing the seeds of revolution … led by the great Racovski, the guide and counsellor of the socialists in our country."[24] Emissaries and agitators from Russia are behind these preparations. The investigation discovered substantial funds of the same provenance. Racovski is sent reports; he is asked for advice, emissaries and money. He cuts the figure of uncontested leader of the socialist movement in Romania. Thanks to his position at the Kremlin, his authority is even greater than it was before 1 May 1917. The instigators of the 13 December coup are the same as those who gathered in Odessa a year previously. At their head was Racovski. His lieutenants in Russia were lawyers Mihai Gheorghiu Bujor and Al. Nicolau, members of the leadership of the Social Democratic Party, and journalist Ion. Dic. Dissescu, editor of *Workingman's Romania*. The Bucharest strategist of the rebellion is Alecu Constantinescu. To these can be added leaders from the legally operating wing of the socialist movement. During the trial that takes place (15-26 March 1919), we find in the dock members of the PSD Executive Committee, including Ilie Moscovici, Ion Sion, Gaston Boeuve (a.ka. Şerban Voinea), Gh. Vasilescu-Vasia, David Fabian Finkelstein, I. C. Frimu, and Constantin Popovici. We also find militants Hugo Steinberg, Gh. Ungvari, Constantin Mănescu, Dumitru Gănescu, Moscu Cohn (who, under the name Gh. Stoica, was to have a long career – we find him present as late as 1967-1968, when he takes part in the commission of inquiry into the cases of Foriş and Pătrăşcanu), and Leon Lichtblau (who, together with Max Goldstein, in December 1920, two years later, was to plant a bomb in the Senate). Some of the accused flee abroad and are tried *in absentia*.

---

[22] *Ideologie şi structuri comuniste în România*, 1917-1918 [*Communist ideology and structures in Romania*], published by INST, 1997, p. 140.

[23] *Idem*, p. 165.

[24] *Idem*, p. 140.

Alecu Constantinescu, found guilty of plotting the violent overthrow of the government and having maintained illegal ties with Moscow, is sentenced to death. The others are sentenced to hard labour, with prison terms of varying lengths. Most of them are acquitted for political reasons. From Odessa, Racovski and the others send formal protests, make declarations, and print incendiary manifestos against the 'Romanian oligarchy'.

Although the attempted coup of 13 December is thwarted, the social and political climate remains tense. There is one strike after another. The recently unified Romanian State[25] has great difficulty in imposing its authority and maintaining order. It is a turbulent situation, which Racovski and the Bolsheviks are willing to manipulate to their own ends. Otherwise, Romania is not the only target for attempted 'revolutions'. Finland, Estonia, Latvia, Austria, and Germany (a number of times) find themselves under assailed by attempted putsches, massive street demonstration and strikes with the potential rapidly to become insurrections. It is a 'knife-edge', explosive period, which might degenerate into civil war at any time. 2-6 March, in a hall of the Kremlin, the Communist International, or Comintern, comes into being. The organisation will play a decisive role in the lives of the Romanian communists until its dissolution in 1943 and even afterwards. All the acts of subversion, attempted assassinations and clandestine operations against the governments in Bucharest, as well as their financial backing, are tied to the Comintern for a quarter of a century. The letter of invitation to the congress is published in *Pravda* on 24 January. It was signed by Lenin, Trotsky, Racovski et al. Moreover, the three dominate the congress. None of the delegates have a mandate from the socialist movements in their own countries: at that date, there were no communist parties in the proper sense. The hall was full of people who had very little idea of what they were taking part in or what ultimate effect the meeting presided over by Lenin was to have. Racovski arrives on the second day, accompanied by Angelica Balabanova, a long-time socialist militant who served him as Foreign Minister in Kharkov. She was to write in her memoirs,

"There was something artificial about this assembly, which destroyed the spirit that had presided over its convocation … The majority of

---

[25] On 1 December 1918, the provinces of Transylvania, Maramureş, Crişan and Banat declared Union with the Romanian Kingdom, comprising Walachia and Moldavia – *Translator's note*.

the 35 delegates and 15 guests had been chosen by the Russian Central Committee from the so-called 'communist parties' of the smaller 'nations' of the former Russian Empire, as well as Estonia, Lithuania, Latvia, Ukraine and Finland. Otherwise, they were prisoners or foreigners with radical views who chanced to be in Russia at the time."[26]

Everything seemed like a farce, a *quid pro quo*: none of them were what they pretended to be. The delegates were not in fact delegates, they voted in the names of 'parties' to which they did not have the slightest connection. Some also voted on the behalf of third party groups which were not present. The communists existed as extremist, secret groups, in the interior or at the margins of a left-wing political formation. The Comintern was at that date more of a political statement, a news item for the press, rather than an institutional reality. This did not make the organisation any less dangerous. The Comintern was conceived as a front. Behind it, however, lay the Bolshevik structures. Its real purpose was to export revolution. To achieve this, the Kremlin allocated vast funds, conducted repeated propaganda campaigns, and practised subversion on a grand scale. Lenin regarded the conference of 1919 as the beginning of the internationalisation of the 'Revolution'. The Comintern was to be the general staff of the world-wide proletarian revolution. It was conceived as an international movement, kept under tight control and run from a unique centre. Cristian Racovski played one of the key roles. The delegates in the hall were not prepared to vote on the proposal for the establishment of the Comintern, but Racovski's motion prevailed, while the matter of the non-representativeness of the delegates remained secondary. The Communist International was thereby established. Until 1943, it was a super-party, and the brains behind this ramified organisation were housed in the Kremlin. The parties were nothing but sections of the Comintern, and the Comintern a section of the CC of the CP(b). The leadership that emerged at the close of the congress was made up of Lenin, Trotsky, Racovski, Bukharin, Zinoviev, and Platen (who left Russia, was arrested in Romania in 1919, and released a few weeks later), while the Executive president was Grigori Zinoviev. The Comintern's first decision was to establish a Southern Bureau, based in the Ukraine, under the leadership of Racovski, who also presided over the Ukrainian

---

[26] Angelica Balabanoff, *My Life as a Rebel*, Bloomington and London: Indiana University Press, 1973, p. 213.

government. It was here that the fiercest fighting of the civil war took place. For Lenin, the Ukraine was communism's western bastion, the gateway to the West and the Balkans. This fact is indicative of Racovski's important position in the Bolshevik general staff during 1918-1919.

On 21 March 1919, a dictatorship of the proletariat is declared in Budapest. The communists and the socialists form a coalition to replace the government of Count Károlyi. Although he was not Prime Minister, Béla Kuhn, as head of the communists, was the most powerful leader. He was the son of a notary public from Transylvania, where he still had relatives. He had been a Russian prisoner of war, on which occasion he converted to Bolshevism. He took part in the 7 November coup. In Petrograd, he was trained in subversive operations and in tactics for seizing power. Before being sent to Hungary, he met with Lenin. The establishment of a Bolshevik regime on its western border doubled the dangers to which the Romanian State was exposed. Racovski had not given up on the idea of 'revolutionary penetration' through Romania and on into the Balkans, combined with the installation of a Bolshevik regime in Bucharest with him at its head. The danger of a Bolshevik invasion was very real. With the installation of the Béla Kuhn regime in Budapest, things took a dramatic turn.

"The new regime was nothing but an annex of the Moscow Soviets, with which close ties of collaboration were straight away established. Caught between the hostility of the communists to the east and to the west, Romania's situation became ever more critical."[27]

Lenin found the new combination of circumstances extremely favourable for the export of his revolution. Hungary meant an opening on to the West and the Balkans, via Central Europe. Of course, Romania would have had to be sacrificed. If the Bolshevik regime in Central Europe had been consolidated, the entire West would have been in danger. However, the greatest risk would have arisen if Russia and Hungary had achieved military and political juncture. Romanian territory lay between the two 'dictatorships of the proletariat', exposed to an attack from both directions. Which is what indeed happened. Racovski, the dictator of the Ukraine, launched a

---

[27] Gheorghe I. Brătianu, *Acțiunea politică și militară a României în 1919* [*The Political and Military Action of Romania in 1919*], Bucharest: Corint, 2001, p. 48.

military offensive. In the manifesto issued in those days by the Romanian Communist Group at Odessa, the aim of the action is formulated as follows:

"By means of the advance of the army of Russian peasants and workers towards the borders of Bassarabia and, on the other hand, by means of the disagreement that has arisen between the Workers' Government of Hungary and the Romanian ruling class, the outbreak of a revolution of workers and peasants in Romania is just a matter of days … The Army of the Soviets (Councils) of Russian workers and peasants, who now hold power in all Russia, expects the support of the Romanian workers and soldiers now taking part in the war this army has begun against the clique of boyars, the rich and all those in their pay which now rules Romania. It impatiently expects their natural support in the liberation of the Romanian people."[28]

In Bucharest, the communists make their presence felt by acting as a fifth column behind the front. The intentions are clear:

"The Romanian communist collectives, meeting today, 5 April 1919, voted the following resolution: they salute the power of the Soviets and engage themselves in the common fight in support of the Russian Revolution, which will aid us in the common fight to enfranchise the Romanian proletariat. Long live the power of the Soviets! Long live the Russian Revolution! Down with the Romanian oligarchy! Long live the Romanian Revolution! Long live the International Revolution!"[29]

In Budapest, Béla Kuhn sends messages 'to the international proletariat', assuring them of his victory. In Paris, the former belligerents are drawing up the map of the new Europe. Kuhn refuses a mission of mediation presided over by General Smuts and begins a military campaign for the 'liberation of Transylvania' on the night of 15-16 April. The Romanian counter-offensive manages to drive back the Hungarian Army. The operations of

---

[28] Institute for Party History annex to the Central Committee of the Romanian Workers' Party, *Documente din istoria PCR, 1917-1922* [*Documents from the History of the Romanian Communist Party*], Bucharest: Editura pentru literatură politică, 1953, pp. 109-110.

[29] *Op. cit.*, p. 111.

the Romanian Army continue successfully, and it rapidly advances towards the Tisza and Budapest. Béla Kuhn is on the verge of losing power. The Red Army intervenes in his support. On 1 May 1919, Racovski, 'president of the Soviet of the Commissars of the Ukrainian People', sends the Foreign Minister in Bucharest an ultimatum in which he demands the evacuation of Bukowina within 48 hours (a region which is, according to Racovski, "under the yoke of the Romanian landowners and the Hohenzollern dynasty, prey to the insatiable Romanian military and civil oligarchy"). The motive is formulated explicitly in the document: "The Ukrainian working class cannot tolerate the fact that, between Soviet Hungary and Soviet Ukraine, Bukowina remains enslaved." On the same day, another ultimatum – this time signed not only by Racovski but also by Georgy Vasilyevich Chicherin, the Foreign Minister of Soviet Russia – demands that the government of I.I.C. Brătianu evacuate Bassarabia. The text says, "At the end of 1917, Romania perjuriously entered Bassarabia. … There [it abolished] the conquests of the Russian Revolution, restored the universally hated power of the landowners and strengthened the Romanian police and bureaucratic tyranny … The government of Romanian landowners, sensing that it is teetering on its own territory and that the workers and peasants will soon revolt, is trying to strengthen its power by means of a crime – pursuing the suppression of the power of the Hungarian Soviet. … Not wishing to shed the fraternal blood of the Romanian workers and peasants, who are compelled by force [*sic.*] to fight, both Soviet governments send the Romanian government the following ultimatums: The immediate evacuation of the Romanian Army, functionaries and agents from the whole of Bassarabia."[30] The deadline is the same: 48 hours.

A provisional government of Bassarabia is formed in Odessa, and on 11 May, the Red Army, at the orders of Racovski, begins operations along the Dniester. On 13 May, Lenin informs Béla Kuhn by telegram that Ukrainian troops "have defeated the Romanians and crossed the Dniester."[31] The two leaders are in permanent contact; the exchanges of messages are almost daily. Together they decide on a concerted military attack against Romania on two fronts. Attacked in the east and in the west by powerful forces, the

---

[30] *Ideologie și structuri comuniste în România* [*Communist Ideology and Structures in Romania*, vol. 2, INST: Bucharest, 1997, pp. 264-67.
[31] V. I. Lenin, *Opere complete* [*Complete Works*], vol. 50, Bucharest: Editura Politică, 1968, p. 337.

Romanian Army holds its positions. The situation on the Dniester is grave; the situation of Romania desperate. Racovski nevertheless halts the offensive. He is confronted with a critical situation on the Ukrainian front, where General Denikin is engaged in a vigorous advance on Moscow. In addition, the local conflicts of spring 1919 produce chaos. Racovski finds himself obliged to halt the advance westward across Romanian territory, aimed at joining up with the Hungarian Red Army. The dream of a world proletarian revolution is very close to being fulfilled. It would have been the end of Greater Romania. The situation was also complicated by the agitation kept up by the communist groups from Odessa, Moscow and Kharkov on the one hand and Budapest on the other. In Romania, the main 'revolutionary' focal points are in Bucharest, and, in the provinces, the cities of Oradea, Timișoara, Cluj, Jassy, Kishinev, Constanța, and Silistra. Bolshevik agents, Comintern activists, professional revolutionaries and emissaries bringing funds traverse the country, arriving from Russia and Hungary. Romania becomes a centre for Moscow-orchestrated subversion. The army is one of the direct targets for Bolshevik propaganda. The unions and workers are instigated to different forms of protest, from strikes to insurrections. The peasants are urged to revolt. Clandestine communist groups appear one after the other and organise with a view to decisive action. Their clients are above all former prisoners of war returning from Russia. In Odessa,

"the Red Armies are nearing our frontiers from every side. Sooner than we think, revolution will be unleashed in Romania. And this revolution will have to be a proletarian, not a bourgeois, revolution … And in order to avoid new bloodshed, it is natural that, from the outset, we should do a thorough job, enthroning the proletarian dictatorship at once, as it is enthroned today in Russia." The motion concludes: "The Romanian workers in Odessa, gathered here today, on 16 April 1919, salute the Russian Revolution, the revolutions in France, Austria, Hungary and Germany … they acknowledge that we have embarked upon the phase of international social revolution and express their wish to take up arms to fight for the overthrow of the feudal-capitalist regime in Romania and for the enthronement of a Soviet Republic of Romanian workers and peasants!"[32]

---

[32] *Ideologie și structuri comuniste în România, op. cit.*, p. 224.

A manifesto launched in Oradea on 29 March 1919 stated, "Rejoice all you peoples that dwell in this happy land, tremble you idlers who have pillaged the workers and peasants for so bitterly long! … Lift up your heart, brother Romanian! … All shout from the innermost depths: Long live the dictatorship of the proletariat! Long live the Hungarian Republic of Workers' and Peasants' Councils!"[33] A Romanian communist group from Budapest addresses the soldiers thus:

> "Comrade soldier! Now you have been sent here, to the Ardeal,[34] where the people, by means of revolution, have won all that you lacked, therefore your place is not here with us, to bring us your chains, which weigh heavily on you. No! Your place is at home, whereby means of revolution you will take mastery of everything … Have your healthy say at once, even with the weapon that your wicked masters have given you! … Long live the rule of the workers! Long live international socialism!"

Also in this interval, the spring and summer of 1919, the reports of the Interior Ministry and of the General Siguranţă indicate feverish levels of agitation, propaganda and subversion. In Bassarabia, there occur repeated attempts at insurgency, mounted by Red Army soldiers disguised as civilians. The feverishness and expectations connected to the revolution in Russia and Hungary can be seen in the activity of the PSD, which at the end of the month holds the conference of its organisations in a radical climate, which incites to revolt. The Hungarian scenario, combined with the intervention of the Red Army led by Racovski, promised the socialist leaders rapid seizure of power. Moreover, once the Versailles Peace Treaty was signed, the governments in Moscow and Budapest reject it. "Down with the Treaty of Versailles!" becomes the slogan of the Comintern. What was aimed at here was the disappearance of Greater Romania, as it had resulted from this treaty. In the vision of the Comintern, Romania was an imperialist state which had annexed territory that did not belong to it. The communists had to fight to tear back these provinces: Transylvania, Bassarabia, Bukowina. We rediscover the same perspective in all the documents of the Romanian communists.

---

[33] *Ideologie şi structuri comuniste în România, op. cit.*, p. 206.

[34] I.e. Transylvania, from the Hungarian name for the region: Erdély – *Translator's note.*

Against the backdrop of these developments, the Bolshevik regime of Béla Kuhn, failing to solve the problems that confront it, enters into crisis. The popularity of the regime falls rapidly and the only solution for survival is foreign action. On 20 July, the Hungarian Army attacks along the Tisza. On 25 July, the Romanian Army counter-attacks. Béla Kuhn requests assistance from Moscow. The situation on the front in southern Russia and Ukraine, where the Red Army was in difficulty, makes intervention impossible. The Romanian Army crosses to the western bank of the Tisza and advances on Budapest. On the evening of 1 August, the Magyar Bolshevik leaders flee the city by train. The Romanian Army enters Budapest and occupies the city on 4 August. The occupation will last until November. After a stay of about a year in Vienna, hidden in a hospital, the leaders of the 133-day Bolshevik regime arrive in Moscow. The fate of the world proletarian revolution was played out at the same time as that of Romania. The combined victory of Racovski and Béla Kuhn would have amounted to the disappearance of the Romanian State. "Many believed that the future of the European revolution would be played out in the eventual juncture of the revolutionary Red Armies from Ukraine and Hungary."[35]

Béla Kuhn vehemently accused Racovski of being to blame for the collapse of his government. The enmity between the two is notorious. The two leaders mutually detest each other. Both have close ties with Romania and see the perspective of installing a proletarian dictatorship in Bucharest as an immediate possibility. Like Racovski, Béla Kuhn envisaged himself as the dictator of the entire region. Hence the rivalry between them, notorious in the corridors and back rooms of the Comintern. With the failure of the Bolshevik regime in Hungary and of the putsch in Bavaria, one stage in the attempt to export what Lenin and Trotsky named the "proletarian revolution" comes to a close.

"If the actions of Romania had not crushed it at the Dniester and the Tisza, where would the expansion of the Revolution stopped? ... Had there not been this organised and conscious element of resistance and reaction, how easily the spectre of the universal Red Army, which disturbed the nights of Lloyd George, would have materialised on the banks of the Rhine! Between Bolshevik Russia and Spartakist Germany,

---

[35] Pierre Boue, *Histoire de l'Internationale Communiste 1919-1943*, Editions Fayard, 1997, p. 93.

an independent Poland would have been killed in the womb and the
armies of Tukhachevsky, which invaded a year later, would not have met
the victorious opposition that halted them. What a different turn events
in Central Europe would have taken!"[36]

After the onslaughts of December 1917, December 1918 and spring 1919,
Romania is threatened once more in the summer of 1920. A Polish Army
offensive in Ukraine is followed by a Red Army counter-offensive, advancing
on Warsaw. With Poland defeated militarily and a dictatorship of the
proletariat installed in Warsaw, the corridor towards Germany and Europe
would have lain open. The plan to wrench the Kremlin out of isolation
would have been achieved. Once again, the fate of Romania is at stake. Once
again, Racovski is involved, waiting at the Dniester frontier ready to pounce
at any opportunity for military intervention, with Bucharest his goal. In a
telegram sent to Stalin, Lenin writes,

> "23 July 1920 / Kharkov to Stalin / The situation in the Comintern is
> splendid. Zinoviev, Bukharin and I, too, think that revolution in Italy
> should be spurred immediately. My opinion is that to this end, Hungary
> should be Sovietised, and perhaps also Czechia and Romania. We need
> to think it over carefully. Communicate your detailed conclusion. The
> German communists think that Germany is capable of mustering three
> hundred thousand troops from the lumpen against us."[37]

In the summer of 1920, Lenin's plans to export the Bolshevik coup seemed
to be coming to fruition. The Red Army was advancing westward with the
aim of occupying Poland. Whereas the first Comintern congress of March
1919 had unfolded against the backdrop of the Bolshevik coup in Budapest,
the second congress takes place during the Red Army advance on Warsaw.
This should have been a triumph of Bolshevism. The Red Army was ready
to bring Poland to its knees and then move on to Germany in order to
unleash revolution throughout the whole of Europe. In Petrograd and
Moscow, festivities were organised on a grand scale, with tens of thousands of

---

[36] Gheorghe I. Brătianu, *Acţiunea politică şi militară a României în 1919*,
Bucharest: Corint, 2001, p. 141.
[37] Richard Pipes, *The Unknown Lenin – From the Secret Archives*, New
Haven and London: Yale University Press, 1996, p. 90.

participants, demonstrations, fireworks, and fiery speeches. A huge amount of resources was squandered in spite of the famine that was devastating Russia. Emigrants, adventurers, deserters, terrorists, professional revolutionaries, occasional theoreticians, left-wing journalists, madmen, déclassé bourgeois, idealists, naïve intellectuals, fellow travellers, delegates, spies etc. gather to debate the fate of the world revolution. The number of delegates had grown considerably in comparison with the founding conference of the Comintern. On a map in the congress auditorium was marked the advance of the Red Army. This time, Lenin was certain that his plan to emerge from isolation would succeed. It would be the salvation of his regime, he believed. As for Romania, Lenin believed that, after its occupation by the Red Army, it would be possible to install a Soviet regime. This plan would be achieved after a delay of 25 years, at the orders of Stalin, the addressee of the prophetic telegram. On the Vistula, a miracle occurred, however. When no one was expecting it, the Red Army was routed after almost reaching Warsaw. The calculations of a Bonapartist expedition across Europe, setting out from the East, come to ruin. Bolshevik Russia is forced to retreat. The Comintern is witness to a military and political disaster. The Polish offensive is halted with great difficulty. Racovski has to abandon Kiev. There follows a peace, in which Lenin's government cedes territory and has to pay large reparations. Racovski is made one of the scapegoats for this failure. Angelica Balabanova records:

> "When we were forced by the Polish offensive to evacuate Kiev and return to Moscow … we were surprised by the change in attitude to Racovski in official circles. He was put in the situation of having to defend himself. I was indignant that the socialist government could accuse one of its officials for a military defeat he could not prevent and I communicated what I thought to Lenin at the first opportunity."[38]

The revolutionary wave was thus ebbing, not to return, and along with it the scenario of the federalisation of the Balkans and the installation of a Bolshevik regime in Bucharest. Trotsky and Racovski, like Lenin, believed that it was only a strategic, temporary withdrawal, and that the Revolution would go on the offensive once more. However, Racovski's activities – subversion, financing, training, propaganda against Romania – do not cease.

---

[38] Angelica Balabanoff, *op. cit.*, p. 236.

In the autumn of 1920, in the weeks after the disaster in Poland, he brokers the Romanian socialists' affiliation to the Comintern. On 31 March 1921, a Court Martial of the Army 2nd Corps sentences him to death *in absentia*. As an effect of the Kremlin power struggles that erupted while Lenin was still in his death throes, Racovski gradually loses his influence. As one of Trotsky's lieutenants, he is marginalised among the Bolshevik leaders. In 1922, Racovski takes part in the Geneva negotiations, as an adjunct of Chicherin. In 1923, he is appointed ambassador to London. From 1925 until 1927, he occupies the same post in Paris. In autumn 1927, he is recalled. As a diplomat in the 1920s, he is also linked to the Romanian communists. The embassy in Paris is a revolving door for many operations. There is a post office box here, but also a till from which Comintern agents coming from Bucharest, or on their way back to the Romanian capital, collect sums of money, pick up instructions, report. Marcel Pauker, Al Constantinescu et al. all pass through here. Racovski is behind the scenes of press campaigns in the West, such as the one for the release of Mihai Gheorghiu Bujor, arrested and tried in 1920, the one connected to the rebellion mounted by the Soviets at Tatar Bunar in Bassarabia in 1924-1925, the one condemning the Romanian government for the 'assassination of Pavel Tkachenko', and the one demanding the amnesty of communist detainees. In the 1920s, many of the threads of subversive activities, assassinations and espionage aimed at Romania can be traced to Racovski.

III
A Popular Orator

In April 1904, Panait Istrati arrives in Bucharest. He gets a job at the employment agency of a certain Gheorghe Cristescu on Sfinților Street, behind the Colțea Hospital. The owner found work for unemployed, unqualified manual labourers from the lumpenproletariat, charging them a part of their earnings. Cristescu was neither a merchant nor a functionary. He was an erstwhile shop assistant who had learned the trade of quilt maker. He had not plied his trade for very long, electing to become a small-time capitalist and live off the back of the workers. He had a certain flair for petty wheeling and dealing. Above all he was preoccupied with elevating himself above his present status. When he meets Panait Istrati, Cristescu is already quite well-known as a socialist agitator. Istrati describes him thus:

> "The Eforie Auditorium was packed. The throng of workers was dotted with brawlers, brought in by the 'cops' to break our ribs. The sight of them made you want to seek safety in numbers. Gheorghe Cristescu, hefting a hefty club and rolling his eyes like a madman, was running hither and thither, elbowing his way through the crowd. He was zealously guarding the meeting room, inspiring respect. I was standing at the entrance to the hall, sticking close to him. Cristian Racovski had appeared on the podium, like a fireball, with the shaggy beard he had back then, his eyes flashing fire."[1]

Racovski had only just returned to Romania, after studying in France and wandering around Europe from one left-wing conference to another. His speech covered two topics: solidarity with the arrested Maxim Gorki and the reconstruction of the Social Democratic Party. Sticking close to his boss, Cristescu (who had supplied Racovski's bodyguards), Istrati is picked out by police spotters and arrested in the street after the meeting. A few years later, in 1909, Cristescu and Istrati will be arrested together, and then brought to trial for agitation in favour of the same Racovski, deported a year previously.[2]

---

[1] Panait Istrati, *Cum am devenit scriitor*, Editura Florile Dalbe, 1998, p. 205.
[2] C. Bacalbașa, *Bucureștii de altădată*, Editura Ziarului Universul, vol. 3, 2nd edition, 1936, pp. 189-191.

After 1905, Cristescu becomes one of the leaders of left-wing and trades union politics. He makes a name for himself thanks to the protest campaigns against the expulsion of Racovski, the strikes he instigates among the workers, and his oratorical talents. Racovski backs him for his loyalty, but also for the proletarian figure he cuts in a movement dominated by radical intellectuals, lawyers, professors, physicians, and journalists, all unpopular among the workers. Cristescu is a professional agitator. He addresses the strikers. He stirs up protests. He takes part in the conferences of the PSD (Social Democratic Party), re-established in 1905, of whose leadership he is a member. He becomes a popular figure. In the period of neutrality, from 1914-1916, he is a 'pacifist'. He opposes Romania's entry into the war on the side of the Entente, waging a campaign massively funded by Berlin and Vienna. During the occupation, he remains in Bucharest, and as early as 1918 he is accused of doing business with the German occupying authorities and of fraudulent management of Party funds. After the socialist movement is reactivated on the outbreak of the Russian Revolution and Racovski flees to Odessa, Cristescu, his favourite, becomes a kind of 'heir' to the leadership of the Party. Not the only one, but the most influential. In accordance with the Bolshevik template, the PSD operated legally, but also had clandestine networks. Some of them were not even subordinate to the PSD leadership, but acted independently, under direct orders from Moscow, Kharkov and Odessa. These networks, regardless of where they took their orders from, were plotting to overthrow the government in a revolution. To achieve this goal they launched acts of terrorism, subversion and espionage, they financed clandestine activities: the underground press, illegal demonstrations, and Bolshevik agitation. Since 1918, the leader of the clandestine communist groups had been Alecu Constantinescu. He and his friend, Cristescu, were loyal to Racovski, their unopposed leader. The two had been working with Racovski at the head of the PSD since 1905. From Odessa, and then from Kharkov and Moscow, Racovski sent them funds through couriers and agents to finance the overthrow of the 'oligarchy'.

The political and social climate in Romania was completely different to what Lenin imagined, however. Romania was not 'prepared' for a takeover of power on the part of the 'vanguard of the proletariat'. After unification with Bassarabia, Bukowina and Transylvania, Romanian society was preoccupied with many things, but not with a 'revolution' against the monarchy and capitalism. Russia was viewed with mistrust and aroused fear.

The Romanian Army, having been peacefully demobilised, had not gone on to form soldiers' committees against the officers, unlike in Russia. The army nurtured deep monarchist feelings. The peasantry seemed to have forgotten the traumatic experience of 1907[3] and was loyal to the Crown. Opportune agrarian reforms had ensured social peace. The industrial working class agitated, but its influence was limited. After the war, however, the wave of social demands often did take radical forms. Marches and strikes followed one another and exerted continual pressure on successive governments in Bucharest.

The agitation was kept up by the PSD leaders, prisoners of war formerly held in Russia, extreme left-wing clandestine groups, radical trades union leaders, and professional Bolshevik agitators sent from Russia. It was a motley world that brought together déclassé bourgeois, idealists, the dregs of society, union leaders, terrorists, the lumpenproletariat, the unemployed, demobbed soldiers, young people swept up by the fever of revolution, Western-educated social democrats, etc. It was a mix of many different traditions. One of those traditions was that of the Old Kingdom of Romania, linked to Dobrogeanu-Gherea and Cristian Racovski. Another was that of Bukowina and Transylvania, which recalled the Parliament of the Austro-Hungarian Empire, elections and ideological debates, and the spirit of Vienna and Budapest. Then there was the Bassarabian tradition, which originated in the Russia of the Okhrana and the Tsar, of Siberia and clandestinity. Finally, there was the tradition of the Quadrilateral, which recalled peasant uprisings, armed ambushes, and Balkan banditry. Many things could and did happen in this composite milieu. Where did the local Bolsheviks recruit adherents at the beginning of the 1920s and later? In the 1970s, Belu Zilber, who joined in 1918, writes, "The few who came over to our side were driven by the most divers motives, from simple curiosity about a mysterious organisation, glorified by partisans and cursed by enemies, to intellectuals convinced that here were gathered the earthly representatives of a happy future, one proven *more geometrico*, and in between the whole host of malcontents from factory, village, family and slum. Hungarians and Bulgarians who wanted independence from Romania, workers who saw themselves masters of the factory, Jews horrified by anti-Semitism, the unemployed of no fixed trade and mediocre professionals, aspiring

---

[3] The year of the large-scale peasant uprisings in Wallachia and Moldavia – *Translator's note.*

politicians unable to get ahead in any other party, plain housewives or those suffering from *Bovarysme*, children sick of school: this was the world from which Party activists were drawn before the war. Each felt himself a victim of injustice in one way or another, deprived of the goods he dreamed of. Attracted by the mystery of a closed world, in their minds they were entering a new life rather than joining a political party. ... They became important in their own minds, they began to acquire a heroic status. They stepped out of the skin of those disinherited by fate and entered that of an important person, a bearer of great secrets."[4]

To Zilber's minute and exact description we need to add yet another factor valid for the years 1917-1920. The explosion in Russia fuelled the imagination of an entire generation, radicalised by the squalor of the trenches and the 'failure' of the bourgeois world. Romanian society, lying on the border with Russia, was highly exposed to these influences. Industrial workers, intellectuals without a role, marginal politicians, militant socialists, trades unionists, and the masses easily manipulated by equalitarian demagoguery were overcome by the mystique of a new world. Moreover, the events in Russia seemed to herald these radical changes in a foreseeable future. Against this backdrop, there abound agitation, protests, every kind of conspiracy, strikes, noisy demonstrations, and calls to 'the great struggle'. It is a highly confused situation. Some call it a revolutionary crisis, from which the leaders of the movements hope to draw advantage, and which they hope to guide in this very direction. This direction seems to them to be that of history itself. They hope to set up a dictatorship in Bucharest, take power, and overthrow the monarchy and the democratic regime. "The weariness and disillusions of war, the ineffectuality of the bourgeois-capitalist system, guilty of having unleashed and perpetuated the war ... had exacerbated the revolutionary tendencies of the masses, which were returning from the front wholly radicalised. Fatally, the movement in our country had been subjected to these influences from abroad. It believed with all the firmness of sincere conviction that the time had come to bring about a socialist society."[5] The shifting fortunes of the civil war in Russia were followed with nervous tension, and some were given cause to hope that things would be repeated

---

[4] Belu Zilber, *Actor în procesul Pătrășcanu*, Bucharest: Humanitas, 1997, p. 25.

[5] Constantin Titel Petrescu, *Socialismul în România*, Bucharest: Editura Biblioteca Socialistă, 1940, pp. 313-4.

in Romania, that once the White Guard commanded by generals Denikin, Kolchak and Vrangel and the interventionist forces had been defeated, the Red Army would expand its operations beyond the Dniester. Depending on the evolution of events, and military ones in particular, "the proletariat will rise up to fight the bourgeoisie," under the command of its established leaders, of course.

The year 1920 was especially confused and murky for the Romanian Left. It was also the year when it unravelled as a unified movement for the rest of the century. The year commences with the secret arrival in Bucharest of Mihai Gheorghiu Bujor, with the mission of organising a decisive strike against the monarchist regime. Lenin and Trotsky regard the reformist Socialist Party as un-Bolshevik: it is 'opportunist', eaten away by internal strife, predisposed to compromises with the bourgeoisie, incapable of proceeding to any assault on the ruling powers. Bujor brings funds and is accompanied by other experienced agitators. The Siguranţă, through its informants, gets wind of his arrival and begins a hunt for the dangerous agent. Alecu Constantinescu – a Comintern representative and head of the clandestine Bolshevik networks – is waiting for Bujor. Any juncture between the two could be very damaging, but time is short. In April, Bujor is arrested. In Russia, the civil war is drawing to a close, with the Bolsheviks victorious. In the Kremlin, an incursion into Poland is being planned, and then, along the same corridor, into Germany. Rakovski is stirring up thousands of Red soldiers in Ukraine, as well as Romanian deserters and former prisoners of war. He is threatening to cross the Dnieper into Romania, to bring about a 'popular uprising'. His proclamations and ultimatums are followed nervously at the socialist/communist general headquarters on Sf. Ionică Street and in the editorial offices of the *Socialistul* newspaper. Couriers bring funds. The increasingly numerous clandestine groups are organising. The Siguranţă keeps a close watch on all these developments. On 13 June 1920, the police raid the headquarters of the Socialist Party. The documents discovered there reveal the extent of the plot, the existence of a vast plan of subversion. Likewise, evidence is discovered of massive funding from over the Dniester. Most of the funds come from Romania's national treasure, which has been in Moscow since 1917. Yet more communist agitators are arrested during the raid. They include Alecu Constantinescu, wanted since his disappearance in December 1918. He had subsequently been sentenced to death in March 1919. The others are Solomon Schein, Şmil Marcovici, and C. Agiu, all well-known Bolshevik agents wanted for terrorist activities.

Gheorghe Cristescu is no stranger to any of this, as is proven by the documents the police uncover in the raid on Sf. Ionică Street, the headquarters of the Socialist Party. As a deputy, a well-known public figure, he escapes arrest, however. In any case, three days later, on 16 July, he applies to the authorities for a passport. The next day, 17 July, Cristescu makes an interpellation in Parliament in connection with the arrest in Constanța of Georgi Dimitrov (the future head of the Comintern) and Vasil Kolarov, the two Bulgarian communist leaders, who were on their way to the congress of the Communist International. The congress will take place between 19 July and 7 August. Neither the Bulgarians nor the Romanians arrive in time. Gheorghe Cristescu is mixed up in it all, with his customary ambiguity, half public figure, half man of clandestine operations (and funds). He plays a double role, in accordance with the Bolshevik rulebook. He has an official political life, but also an underground life. He is in contact with the clandestine networks. He is close to Alecu Constantinescu and Mihai Gheorghiu Bujor. But he is also close to Ilie Moscovici and Constantin Titel Petrescu. Cristescu declares contradictory positions, now radical and extremist, now reformist. He makes numerous declarations in which he urges insurrection and the violent overthrow of the regime. At other times, he disavows such attitudes through calls to moderation. His typical position is one aimed at winning the goodwill of all factions, but also, paradoxically, that of the ruling power. He was a "practical joker lacking in convictions, who made use of the communist movement in order to go from being a quilt maker to being a politician. ... Blond, blue eyed, lithe, agreeable, as sharp-minded as a Parisian 'gavroche', he was the perfect physical and moral embodiment of the Figaro type, of the immortal barber: 'Figaro-si Figaro-la'. Cristescu was everywhere. He poked his nose into everything. He solved problems by means of a pirouette and shut you up with a jest. ... When you sought him in Bucharest, he was in Vienna; when you sought him in Vienna, he was in Moscow. And the very next day you would bump into him down the corridors of the Ministry. For, unlike 'his comrades', Cristescu frequented us, and often too! In front of his people, he wanted to pass himself off as a man influential with us, and in front of our people as a man influential with his people."[6] Argetoianu, as Minister of the Interior in the Averescu government, had negotiated with him on various occasions,

---

[6] C. Argetoianu, *Memorii*, Vol. 6, Editura Machiavelli, 1996, p. 170.

when collaborating with the socialists and when Cristescu had applied for permits for socialist demonstrations. Among his comrades, too, Cristescu was viewed in the same light as Argetoianu saw him. Marcel Pauker, in his autobiography, written in Moscow in 1937, regarded him as an opportunist. Alexandru Dobrogeanu-Gherea and David Fabian Finkelstein, answering questions put by Nikolai Bukharin in Moscow in November 1920, placed him in,

> "the group of leaders that ride two horses at the same time (Ilie Moscovici, Gheorghe Cristescu, Constantin Popovici) of which a part is capable of evolving to the point of genuine communism. This group, which today [November 1920 – *author's note*] holds the leadership of the Party, has conducted a politics of confusion, vacillation, whitewashing, hushing-up, procrastination, eternal compromises with social chauvinists, and secret fraternisation with the bourgeois parties, besides which it has indulged here and there in communist demagoguery so that ultimately it might enter the Communist International as a hero."[7]

Pauker and Ghera belonged to the extreme Left. Ilie Moscovici, a non-communist socialist leader as influential as Cristescu in those years, saw him no differently: "An ignorant and conceited practical joker, who has passed his life among a dozen ladies and a few bottles of brandy, has been able, on the basis of his mandate from Moscow, to terrorise the whole movement, to disorganise it and lead it to ruin."[8]

In an increasingly split movement, Cristescu (and not only he) attempts to keep everyone in line, although their positions are often irreconcilable. The congress of the Socialist Party is postponed a number of times, precisely in order to avoid a split. Things are unclear. It is decided that a delegation should go to Moscow to enter into direct contact with the Russian state of affairs and to hold talks with the Bolshevik leaders. The end of the war has precipitated this decision. In the summer of 1920, there are incidents on the Polish front. It seems that Europe is once more facing a revolution. The Romanian socialists do not want to be left out. The delegation from Romania sets off to Moscow in the first week of August 1920, travelling via Vienna and Berlin. Cristescu cuts a figure as the head of the small group. He

---

[7] *Ideologie și structuri comuniste în România*, Bucharest: INST, 2001, Vol. 3, p. 238.
[8] Ilie Moscovici, in *Adevărul*, 8 February 1922.

is accompanied by Alexandru Dobrogeanu-Gherea (for the Old Kingdom), Eugen Rozvany and Ion Fluieraş (for Transylvania), Constantin Popovici (for the trades unions), and David Fabian Finkelstein (fresh from Paris, a student, for socialist youth). They are men of the Left, but of differing outlooks. Their mission is to gather information, not to negotiate. They are forced to wait for a month in Vienna, because the authorities in Berlin deny them transit over German territory, in spite of the presence of three parliamentarians: Cristescu, Gherea and Fluieraş. In Vienna, they find out about the 21 conditions for affiliation laid down by the recent congress of the Comintern. But the first piece of bad news is the disaster suffered by the Red Army outside Warsaw. The context of their visit thus radically shifts. In Bucharest, too, the effect of the Bolshevik defeat in Poland is powerfully felt. Marcel Pauker recalls:

"I was waiting with great impatience to get home, to work there ... Bucharest was a great disappointment to me... I had naturally been thinking that I would find there a buzzing hive... Not a bit of it. I presented myself to the Bucharest Party organisation, to central office, etc. Everywhere, uninterested faces, living from one day to the next, without any drive, like in an office. ... So, the leadership of the Socialist Party continued its sleep, giving ground to the social democrat opportunists, without there anywhere appearing any trace whatsoever of a spokesman for the Comintern followers. And in this situation, the communists present busied themselves with the formation of illegal groups which did not do anything and which, as would be discovered the following year, were seething with provocateurs."[9]

The 'world revolution' had failed. The defeat of the Red Army meant the definitive closure of the corridor to the heart of Europe. The scenario of installing a Bolshevik dictatorship in Germany and thence the rest of Europe had come to an end. With the failure of the Soviet enterprise, the revolutionary wave ebbed everywhere else. Romania, in spite of Lenin's calculations, was not on the threshold of a 'dictatorship of the proletariat'. In Vienna, among the delegates, the atmosphere was the same. Their political future, so promising but a few days previously, had now become uncertain.

---

[9] *Lichidarea lui Marcel Pauker. O anchetă stalinistă, 1937-1938*, ed. Gh. Brătescu, Bucharest: Editura Univers Enciclopedic, 1995, pp. 35-37.

The final part of the Vienna sojourn of the group led by Gheorghe Cristescu coincides with the preparations the leaders of the Socialist Party are making to unleash a general strike. It was a trial of strength with the Averescu-Argetoianu government, and in the minds of the strike's organisers it corresponded to a new phase of the 'Revolution'. The paralysis of transport, the cessation of work in the factories, etc. ought to lead to a political crisis and the fall of 'military dictator' General Averescu. From here the crisis would evolve in various other directions, including insurrection. Things did not go according to plan, however. The socialists had miscalculated. On 11 October, the leadership of the Socialist Party and the trades unions vote to hand the government an ultimatum. The text of the ultimatum formulated economic and, above all, political demands, some of them unrealistic. Finally, it stated that if these demands failed to be met, "workers all over the country will be called to a general strike." On 19 October, General Averescu answers with an appeal for calm addressed to the populace, and gives assurances that things will not deteriorate. The next day, he orders the arrest of the agitators, union leaders and socialist politicians. The headquarters of the socialists and trades unions are searched and closed. On 21 October, a royal decree introduces a state of emergency and censorship. Worker participation in the general strike is desultory. Transport is not paralysed. Most factories continue to operate. On 28 October, the general strike ends in the defeat of its organisers. The trial of strength has not succeeded, and the Socialist Party and trades unions emerge greatly weakened. "General Averescu," writes C. Mille, director of the *Adevărul* newspaper, a man of left-wing sympathies, "has not wavered even today and has struck a pose as saviour of a moribund oligarchy. He did not even need to unsheathe his sword. The police, the Military Prosecutors, the Courts Martial, and mobilisation were sufficient for the general strike to falter, for the socialist movement to be destroyed once again, or at least set back 10 years … and subdued for a long time to come, to the detriment of public freedoms." The socialist leaders[7] "have given the oligarchy occasion to resurrect itself and to realise that it is powerful and does not need to fear the socialist spectre, which indeed has proven to be nothing but a spectre." The large-scale failure of the imprudent general strike was one of the causes of the Left's decline.

On 20 October (the very day the strike commenced), Cristescu, Ion Fluieraş and David Fabian Finkelstein, having been detained by the Russian authorities for a week in a train carriage on the border with Estonia, arrive in Petrograd. Gherea, Popovici and Rozvany are already there. When the authorities refused to issue them with visas, they crossed Germany clandestinely. The clash between government and strikers in Bucharest is followed by the delegates from Moscow, where they arrive two days later, on the 22nd. In the Kremlin, Lenin, Trotsky, Bukharin, and Zinoviev decide that negotiations should be conducted by Racovski, who is knowledgeable of Romanian affairs. In Kharkhov, Racovski's fief, the delegates arrive on the same day as the end of the general strike, 28 October. Racovski and Cristescu had last met in the autumn of 1916. They had known each other since 1905. Cristescu had always been a member of Racovski's inner circle. Racovski also knew Alexandru Dobrogeanu-Gherea, to whose father he had been close. For the visitors from Bucharest, Racovski was a 'legend', a protagonist of the great proletarian revolution, one of the leaders of the Comintern. He was their erstwhile political boss. But he was also the man who could have become dictator over Romania and the Balkans, had the Bolsheviks' plans succeeded. Moreover, there were many conspiracies and plots to which Racovski was linked. All the strands of the clandestine communist networks led to him. It was Racovski who was behind every subversive activity and terrorist attack. It was he who fed them funds. It was to him that couriers delivered reports, requests, etc. Racovski's main correspondent in Bucharest was Cristescu, an initiate in all these things, whether it was a question of funds smuggled over the Dniester, strikes, protests, demonstrations, or the Party.

The defeat of the general strike in Bucharest puts the delegation on the defensive. They were not the victors, the leaders of a numerous and organised proletariat. And nor was Racovski in the best of positions, after the Red Army's disastrous retreat from Warsaw and the surrender of Kiev. The atmosphere of the meetings is tense, not only because of the bad news arriving from Romania. The delegation is forced to listen to the reproaches of their hosts. Cristescu and the others are criticised for the socialists' position towards unification with Transylvania. But also for their support of the Treaty of Versailles.

These were not the only criticisms. The Romanians are vehemently condemned for not having supported Béla Kuhn and the Revolution in Budapest. Béla Kuhn was in fact present at the meetings. Cristescu and Popovici disagree with Racovski. The latter's perspective on Romania after the war is highly critical. The arguments almost lead to a split. The Romanians refuse to accept a list, laid down by the hosts, of those members of the Socialist Party that have to be elected at the forthcoming congress. Cristescu is the most adamant on this point of the negotiations. He rejects Racovski's criticisms and refuses to implement the list demanded. Mainly at dispute is the name of Alexandru Dobrogeanu-Gherea, rejected by Cristescu, but demanded by Racovski. Cristescu also makes objections to the demand to organise a parallel, clandestine party. Accompanied by Dobrogeanu-Gherea and David Fabian Finkelstein, Racovski abandons the discussions. The rest of the delegation returns to Moscow.

A week later, fresh discussions begin, at Comintern headquarters. On the other side of the table sits Nikolai Bukharin, "the favourite child of the Bolshevik Party," as Lenin will call him in his political will and testament three years later. Cristescu and the others listen to another set of accusations, formulated in the same terms. Bukharin demands that they accept en masse the 21 conditions for affiliation. The delegation is not in Russia in order to affiliate the Socialist Party with the Comintern: when they left Bucharest, the 21 conditions did not even exist. The mandate of the delegation was strictly limited to the gathering of information. The congress had yet to take a decision. The conditions for admission to the Comintern had been written up by Lenin in person, obsessed with the repeated failures of Bolshevik insurrections in Europe. The delegates to the Second Congress of the Comintern, held in Petrograd and Moscow in July and August 1920, find lists of the conditions in their hotel rooms, along with a brochure by Lenin (*Leftism, the Childhood Disease of Communism*) and another by Trotsky (*Terrorism and Bolshevism*), a gift on the part of the hosts. Lenin believed that hesitations, betrayals and capitulations to the enemy on the part of the social democrats, moderates and centrists were the cause of the defeats suffered by what he imagined to be the 'proletariat' and its political 'vanguard', the Party. Moreover, as he believed, these revolutionaries, scattered throughout all the countries of Europe, were in need of a single command centre. This had to be the Communist International. Lenin laid out 21 conditions that had to be met by any group wishing to become affiliated. Cristescu and the others were presented the list as if it were an ultimatum. The conditions were non-negotiable. The document's conclusion made it clear: "Those Party members that reject the conditions … shall be excluded from the Party." Let us review some of them. "The urgent dismissal from their posts of reformists and their replacement with experienced communists." "In almost every country in Europe," writes Lenin, "the class struggle is entering the phase of civil war. In such circumstances, the communist can have no trust in bourgeois legality. They are obligated to create by themselves a parallel, illegal organisational apparatus, which in the decisive moment will help the Party to fulfil its duty to the Revolution. In every country where the communists are unable due to the state of emergency and exceptional laws to conduct their entire activity legally, it is absolutely necessary that they combine legal with illegal activity." Other conditions stipulated "the duty to disseminate communist ideas … in the army. Where such propaganda is banned by exceptional laws, it must be carried out illegally. … Every party must recognise a complete break with reformism. … The Communist International requires absolutely the execution of this break in the shortest possible time. … The Communist Parties … must be built upon the foundation of the principle of democratic centralism. In the current period of fierce civil war, the Communist Party will only be able to fulfil its duty if it is organised in as centralist a way as possible, preserving at its heart iron discipline. … Any party that wishes to be part of the Comintern is obligated to provide unconditional aid to any Soviet Republic fighting against counter-revolutionary forces. … Likewise, legal or illegal propaganda must be carried out using every means possible among the troops sent to crush the workers' movements. … All the decisions of the congresses of the Communist International, as well as the decisions of the Executive Committee are binding upon all the parties that make up the Communist International."[10]

Grigori Zinoviev, the president of the Comintern, travels to Kharkhov to find out why there has been a split. Two weeks later, discussions are resumed, this time in the presence of Zinoviev. Trotsky also takes part in one meeting. Bukharin demands that Fluieraș leave Russia, accusing him of taking part in the reunification assembly in Alba Iulia and the Paris peace talks. The Versailles Treaty was despised by the Bolshevik leaders. Neither Cristescu nor the others object. The arrogance of the Russian leaders intimidates the Romanians. They are in the "homeland of the Revolution." The prestige of Bukharin and Zinoviev is huge. Although disappointed at the way they are being treated, Cristescu and the rest of the delegation continue to admire

---

[10] *Ideologie și structuri comuniste în România*, Bucharest: INST, 2001, vol. 3, pp. 176-180.

them. The core of the negotiations was the 21 conditions of affiliation. It was in fact a diktat that subordinated all the parties to the interests of the Kremlin. At first, Cristescu and the others reject the conditions. The delegates are subjected to pressure and the usual propaganda techniques, the sowing of discord, threats, and corruption. The documents reveal how they cave in, gradually, point by point. Cristescu vacillates for a while, as was his wont whenever he was trying to reconcile contrary opinions and attitudes. He even accepts the list demanded by the Comintern, over which he had quarrelled with his mentor, Racovski. On 3 December, Cristescu, as head of the delegation, signs the document demanded by the Russians, together with Gherea, Popovici, and Rozvany (David Fabian Finkelstein, who is not in Moscow, signs separately). It is a capitulation for which he has no mandate. He and the others undertake to abide by the conditions for affiliation and to get the Party to accept them. In addition, once they are back in Romania, they agree to eliminate from the Party all undesirables, i.e. social democrats, reformists, etc.

Besides the mistake of unleashing a general strike, the acceptance of the conditions for affiliation to the Comintern is a *coup de grâce* to the socialist movement in Romania. It is a blow from which it will never recover. Cristescu is one of those principally responsible, if not the sole culprit. His inconsistency, lack of firmness, duplicity, opportunism, unreliability, and corruptible nature led to the unexpected and fatal finale of the visit. A week later, on 10 December, Alexandru Dobrogeanu-Gherea and C. Popovici are received in Lenin's office in the Kremlin. The meeting is brief and strictly formal. At the end of the interview Cristescu also shows up, unannounced. After an exchange of words, the meeting with the Bolshevik 'god' comes to a close. One fact nevertheless remains: from Bucharest news has just arrived that a bomb exploded in the Senate on 8 December, at 3.45 p.m. "In the first moments it was thought that the radiator boiler had exploded in the basement. The senators threw themselves to the floor. A few seconds later, however, blood was flowing in abundance and screams of horror could be heard."[11] The shock could not have been greater, the feeling more widespread. Maz Goldstein, nicknamed 'Lop-handed', was a professional terrorist. He had been working in Romania for a number of years and was well-known to the Siguranța. The attack, coming after the crisis of the general strike and subsequent trials, was yet another blow

---

[11] *Adevărul*, 10 December 1920.

to the Left. Public opinion turned against the socialists. Maz Goldstein was part of a group made up of Saul Ozias and Leon Lichtblau. Gelbert Moscovici oversaw the execution of the attack. He was the brother of Ilie Moscovici. He had fled to Vienna after escaping from prison in the spring of 1920. He was the head of the clandestine communist networks after the capture of Alecu Constantinescu. "Colourless, devoid of enthusiasm, bureaucratic, sarcastic," as Marcel Pauker described him in 1937.[12] Gelbert Moscovici, Saul Ozias and Leon Lichtblau would take part in the Third Congress of the Communist International in Moscow between 22 June and 12 July 1921, a few weeks after the terrorist attack. In addition, Gelbert Moscovici (1899-1937, alias Al. Bădulescu, Ghiță Moscu) would be elected to the Executive Committee of the Comintern, as a reward for his success in Bucharest. Did Lenin know anything about the plot? Did the Romanian delegates? Did Cristescu, Gherea and Popovici comment on the subject during their meeting in the Kremlin on 10 December? It is hard to believe that they did not. On the same day, 10 December 1920, Grigori Zinoviev, president of the Comintern, will send a letter to the leadership of the Socialist Party in Bucharest, with a series of accusations that had also been heard by the delegates in Russia. Significantly, they include the following: "With the assistance of the police opportunism triumphs in the Romanian Socialist Party." The question of why he did not give the letter directly to the delegates present in Moscow and preferred a secret courier, who risked capture by the Siguranța, remains unsolved. Cristescu, Gherea, Finkelstein, Rozvany, and Popovici, the 'capitulators', would not read it until they were back in Bucharest.

Cristescu returned to Romania via the Odessa, Varna and Sofia route. Barely having arrived after his long trip (he had set off in August), he launched a splitting operation according to the Leninist pattern. The aim is to take over the Party headquarters and newspaper and to eliminate undesirable leaders. The socialist movement is on the ebb. Alecu Constantinescu and Mihai Gheorghiu Bujor are no longer active: Bujor has been tried and imprisoned, Constaninescu has escaped arrest and fled the country. The principal socialist leaders have likewise been brought to trial. The verdict in the trial of the trades unionists was as follows: "Yesterday evening, after two hours of deliberations, the Court Martial passed the following sentence ... applying article 53 in conjunction with article 61 of the military code

---

[12] *Op., cit.* p. 35.

of justice, the Court sentences Ilie Moscovici, Em. Socor, I. Petrescu Ghempet, Al. Pătrulescu, Al. Oprescu, Spiridon Calu and Paul Mare to five years, hard labour, and acquits Toma Dragu."[13] C. Mille, director of the *Adevărul* newspaper, a man of the Left, made the following observations in an editorial entitled 'The Socialists' Mistake': "This sentence was passed without any reaction from anyone. Not even from the Socialist Party. It did not make any move, it called no strike, proof that this time the government has hit the workers' organisation hard. … What should the socialists' attitude have been? Taking stock of the situation and their weakness, they ought to proceed in conformity with reality. … Without industry … socialist power is nothing but a shadow. On the other side there is the great majority of uneducated peasants, whose interests are inimical to the socialists. Without the peasants on their side, they do not have the army either, which is under the absolute command of the rulers. It is not only in Romania that the Russian Revolution has troubled the minds of some in the socialist movement. What will the workers think? We are weak, naturally. The majority is not with us, but with much courage and sacrifice we might lay hands on power, and thanks to the dictatorship of the proletariat we might rule for the time being and then transform Romanian bourgeois society into a socialist one."[14]

The failure of the general strike dealt a heavy blow to the Left. The terrorist attack of 8 December likewise produced an extremely negative effect on public opinion. In the absence of the more moderate leaders, now in prison, the extremist leaders with Cristescu at their head were able to operate unhindered. In the trades unions and the Party a process of radicalisation can be observed in 1921, as a direct result of the events of the later part of 1920. The delegates returning from Moscow provide an impetus for the reactivation of a Left that has taken the shock of defeat hard and is on the recoil. Then there was the prestige of those who had been to Moscow. They were validated by the fact that they had met Racovski, Bukharin, Zinoviev, Trotsky and Lenin. This was a strong factor of persuasion over the Party. The Left was fragmented into a multitude of groups: from social democrats and socialists to communists of every stripe, all of them dreaming of getting rid of the bourgeoisie. The Democratic Left was losing influence the more the movement as a whole became split. The

---

[13] *Adevărul*, 27 November 1920.

[14] *Ibid*.

controversies were unending. To imitate what had taken place in Russia was uppermost in the minds of many leaders. Some warned against the dangers of such a development. Others plotted to bring about a dictatorship of the proletariat. Among the latter, Lenin and Trotsky were the examples to be followed. The clandestine groups were increasingly aggressive, sustained by funds and agents from Russia. They were subordinate to the Comintern and Cheka much more than they were to the Party leadership. It was the police that dealt with these groups, dismantling them and infiltrating them with undercover agents. In 1921, the Party had a little over a thousand members. The socialists were more a movement than a party, a disorganised and quite anarchic movement. It was a movement that combined underground operations, espionage, provocations and sabotage with the traditional, 'open' political activities of 'agitation of the masses', organisation of strikes and protests, press campaigns, and participation in elections.

Barely having returned from Russia, Cristescu, Popovici, Finkelstein, Gherea and Rozvany called a National Council of the Socialist Party and the trades unions. Three factions were vying for supremacy. The Left demands affiliation with the Comintern and the transformation of the Socialist Party into a communist party, as the delegates to Moscow had undertaken. Em. Socor, Ilie Moscovici, I. Pistiner, Grigorovici, Fluieraș and Jumanca reject the idea, affirming social democratic values of the Western type. The centrists attempt to reconcile the two. The congress is convened on 8 May 1921, which is equivalent to a victory for Cristescu's faction. The reformists withdraw from the Socialist Party, and with that the split is final. The proponents of affiliation with the Comintern conduct a stealth campaign. They take the headquarters by storm. They eliminate delegates who are in disagreement with their point of view. The pro-Muscovites, or 'maximalists', take control of the congress. "The majority have fallen victim to the stupidity and ambition of Cristescu and the undercover agents [of the Siguranță – *author's note*] who were numerous among them ... Can we allow it [the socialist movement – *author's note*] to destroy itself completely, just because that is what the imbeciles and the police want?"[15] Thus wrote Ilie Moscovici from prison on 12 May. Subordination to a foreign organisation, which did not recognise the Versailles Treaty and was plotting to overthrow the government by terrorist means, was a direct threat to State Security. The then Minister of the Interior, C. Argetoianu, decides to arrest the congress

---

[15] CC of the PCR Archive, Fund 1, Dossier 63, p. 63.

participants as soon as they vote to join the Comintern. This happens on the last day of the congress, before the close of the ballot: "WRITTEN STATEMENT. Today, 12 May 1921, we, Lt. Colonel Georgescu Ioan, Royal Commissar of the War Council C 2 A … went to the headquarters of the Socialist Club on Sf. Ionică Street, No. 12, where we proceeded as follows. We entered the club premises, which we immediately placed under guard so that no one might leave the premises, and entered the club conference room."[16] The delegates that had voted to join the Comintern unconditionally were placed under arrest. Cristescu had dominated the proceedings with his repeated interventions. He recounts with a wealth of details his expedition to Russia and the negotiations. He describes the Kremlin leaders. The auditorium listen. The atmosphere is heated. The Romanian Bolsheviks mimic the gestures of Lenin, Trotsky and Zinoviev, in festive mood. They even imagine their factions in exactly the same way as in the Russian Bolshevik Party. They call themselves 'maximalists'. They attack the 'opportunists'. They talk about the dictatorship of the proletariat and revolution as something imminent. Eugen Rozvany takes the floor and demands a vote of censure against Cristescu, for having insulted the memory of Rosa Luxemburg and Karl Liebknecht, assassinated in Berlin in January 1918. Cristescu denies the accusation, saying that he merely meant to say that "even great men can make mistakes, not just pygmies like us."[17]

After repeated delays, the trial is held on Spirii Hill. In the dock: the congress delegates from Sf. Ionică Street, with Gheorghe Cristescu heading the bill. Alongside him is a small group headed by Max Goldstein. In the first two weeks of the trial, the deliberations of the War Council are taken up with the insistent demands of the defence to deal with the cases separately. On 9 February, in the sixteenth week of the trial, the War Council rejects the application. The Royal Commissar has proven with hundreds of documents "ties to socialist organisations in Romania, as well as with the Russian Soviets." In fact, Max Goldstein and Gheorghe Cristescu represent different facets of the same phenomenon. Cristescu represents the visible, political part, as a 'leader of the masses'. He is the leader of a party. He speaks at public meetings. He is a union agitator. He is a subject for newspaper articles. He is a Member of Parliament. Max Goldstein represents the

---

[16] CC of the PCR Archive, Fund 1/1921, Dossier 18, p. 1.

[17] CC of the PCR Archive, Fund 1/1921, Dossier 10, p. 21; see also C. Argetoianu, *Memorii*, op. cit.

conspiracy, terrorism, the underground, conspiracies, the bomb attack. Both sides are instrumental in the 'global proletarian revolution'. Gheorghe Cristescu and Max Goldstein are no strangers. They know each other personally. They have met many times. Among Goldstein's accomplices we find close associates of Cristescu: Gelbert Moscovici, Leon Lichtblau, Saul Ozias, et al. Like Max Goldstein, they travel to Russia in the period both before and after the bomb attack. Cristescu was in Russia in the autumn of 1920 at the head of a socialist delegation. On 10 December he was in the office of Lenin himself, just two days after the bomb exploded.

Are the general strike in October and the bomb attack on the Senate part of a two-speed plan to destabilise the regime in Bucharest? At the end of 1920, the Comintern was, for the nth time, in search of a 'revolution' to pull Russia out of isolation. If we look at the sequence of attempted putsches in Bavaria, Germany, Hungary, Finland etc., we can observe the same modus operandi: protest meetings, provocations, strikes, terrorist attacks, clandestine groups, and the immixture of Soviet agents and local loyalists trained in Russia. None of these elements is absent in Bucharest. The attack on the Senate was not an isolated act, caused by a madman or lone anarchist. Lawyer Eliad Românul says of Max Goldstein, "he is a neuropathological anarchist acting alone." Another defence lawyer declares, "There is no connection whatsoever between Goldstein and what is imputed to Cristescu, Popovici, and Dobrogeanu." The final ruling declares, "Max Goldstein and his comrades … believe that they will overthrow our homeland and transform it into a savage province of the Soviet Republic." The general strike of October and the terrorist attack had been planned at the same time. Racovski was the strategist in Moscow and Kiev. Involved were men who, in May 1921, were attending the congress, voting for affiliation with the Comintern. Max Goldstein and his accomplices missed the congress either because they were already under arrest or in hiding, or because they had fled to Russia. The Socialist leaders – Cristescu, Dobrogeanu-Gherea, Popovici et al. – were out of the country during the general strike in October. It was a precautionary measure given the events that were being prepared. The assassination of Roza Luxemburg and Karl Liebknecht in Berlin was an example to be avoided. The underground co-ordination of the strike was provided by Boris Ştefanov, a Bolshevik. On the surface, it was a legal movement, run by socialists and the unions. The protest was fuelled and guided by a network of clandestine groups tied to Moscow. Nor are Cristescu, Finkelstein, Gherea etc. in Romania on the day of the bomb attack. Once the two events have taken place, and after the interview with Lenin, Cristescu and co. return to Bucharest. Goldstein's accomplices are known to have been in Moscow in 1921, following which they return to Romania with new orders. And it is here that they are finally arrested. They appear together in the dock on Spirii Hill. Although the attempt to bomb the Senate was successful, Romania did not descend into chaos. The authorities reacted swiftly and calmly, managing to take control of the situation. We might wonder what would have happened if the general strike had gathered momentum and the populace had taken to the streets. What if Romania had entered into the "revolutionary crisis" planned by instigators? Who would have carried through the customary Bolshevik putsch to seize power? A putsch was avoided firstly because of the dismantling of the general strike in October. And secondly because of the restraint shown by the authorities in December, after the terrorist attack.

The trial of 1922 unfolds in a highly charged atmosphere. There are too many people – hundreds of accused, lawyers, spectators, families and journalists all in a cramped, airless, noisy room. "No sooner does the president of the council rise from his chair than two machine guns appear on the scene, their muzzles menacing the accused. In the street there are four or five infantry platoons. Fontăriei Street is completely sealed off. The accused are taken to the military prison. On the corners of the two streets a large number of residents of Spirii Hill stand watching this operation."[18] The proceedings begin at the end of January. It takes a week to read the 232-page final ruling, in Romanian, Russian and Hungarian. The treatment of the detainees is harsh. A number declare that they have been beaten. The reasons: communist propagandising, infringement of the rules of detention. Others have been kept in solitary confinement. A part of those accused engage in agitation, continual protests, ceaseless baiting of the War Council. It is also a battle of nerves. "The general order was given," reports *Adevărul* on 29 January 1992, "for the three hundred accused to do fatigues on Saturdays and Sundays … Without exceptions the accused are made to clean the latrines and soldiers' parade grounds." The authorities take a keen interest in the progress of the trial. A number of ministers visit the courtroom and take measures to improve conditions for the detainees. The lawyers are Take Policrat, Pompiliu Ioanițescu, Eliad Românul,

---

[18] *Adevărul*, 1 February 1922.

Constantin Titel Petrescu, N. D. Cocea, Osvald Teodoreanu, Basile Sepeanu, Dem. Dobrescu (dean of the Bucharest bar), Iorgu Petrovici, G. Clony, Mihail Mora, I. Vasilescu-Nottara, et al. They are also joined by a number of *ex officio* defence lawyers. The clashes between the Royal Commissar, Constantin Cernat, and the defence are frequent and pointed. The proceedings sometimes have the appearance of a comic and pathetic, rather than solemn, spectacle.

The first round of cross-questioning centres on Gheorghe Cristescu, the main figure in the trial. He steps up to the bar in elegant attire, wearing a red cravat. His deposition lasts two days. It is a work of pure mystification, by a skilled orator who knows how to create an effect on his listeners. "We communists do not demolish a social structure … All we do is to lead the workers towards something better. The commissar has accused us of wanting to change the social order through terror. I answer categorically: no. … We work using only legal methods. We are accused of wanting to bring the enemy into this country. I defy them to prove it with a single word." Cristescu then speaks about the Third International and says that the organisation rejects and condemns terrorist methods. "We who are part of the Third International have engaged only in legal propaganda, by organising the masses, and we have had no factual link with any terrorists," Cristescu lies. Questioned about the money he has received from Moscow, he serenely replies, "Labour organisations help each other. We are not saying that we have not received money from our comrades, on the contrary, but on this occasion we did not receive any money." He rejects the accusation that in Russia he signed any undertaking, even if adhesion to the Comintern under the 21 conditions it imposed was a well-known fact. Cristescu plays his role, he rejects the evidence and accusations, he mystifies. His rhetoric is in the spirit of the age: "Does the fact that we wish for the good of this nation, and therefore that of the country in which it dwells, constitute an act of social demolition? No, your honours. And if you wish to send us to prison only for this desire, then if the prison receives us, we will go, your honours, with a clear conscience and in the knowledge that our sacrifice has guaranteed others a better life." On 11 February, *Adevărul* reports: "The former deputy, his cheeks wet with tears, concluded his defence. The whole auditorium was moved. … The compassion was universal: the public gallery, all the defence lawyers, the *ex officio* defence, and even the soldiers guarding the court were weeping. When the session was convened, the civil and military lawyers surrounded Cristescu, shaking his hand and embracing him. Everyone was congratulating him."

The cross-questioning does not go as well for him, even though neither his aplomb nor his innate intelligence is overshadowed by anything. The Royal Commissar confronts him with the evidence – letters, receipts. Cristescu denies their authenticity and rejects every accusation. Where he does not succeed, his principal defence lawyer, N. D. Cocea intervenes. At one point, the president of the Court angrily interrupts, saying to him, "You do not have the floor. A serious matter is being cleared up here [about the money – *author's note*]." N. D. Cocea replies, "Yes, the situation is tragic, only to stop it becoming comical." We are quoting here from Cristescu's deposition and have compared it with the documents in the archive, some of them bearing his signature, which show that he was telling lies. He says, for example, that he had not made any undertaking in Moscow; he denies that his Party had received money from the Comintern, etc. When the Royal Commissar cites the depositions of witnesses from within the Party, Cristescu resolves the situation by declaring that they were all informers and agents provocateurs in the pay of the Siguranţă. Here ends the first act of the trial.

When the trial resumes, a few days later, the second act of the performance commences with the other protagonist: Alexandru Dobrogeanu-Gherea, a Bolshevik fanatic and absolute believer in the Red Revolution, of whom Cristescu once said, "he is a good soul, but is unmatched in his naïvety." Alexandru Dobrogeanu-Gherea was the eldest son of Constantin Dobrogeanu-Gherea, the tutelary figure of Romanian socialism, a literary critic, a Jewish refugee from Russia, and a naturalised Romanian citizen, who died in 1920. He was in close contact with Gheorghe Cristescu, whom he regards as hesitant and overly inclined to negotiate with the bourgeoisie. "Because of the persecutions, more than two hundred accused are on hunger strike. Not having eaten for three days, they are kept in the courtroom in chains day and night or in prison … Behold what is happening in a country that claims it is civilised! … The pen in which the women accused sit, gives the impression of a room in a hospital for cholera patients. Wholly isolated, the women, exhausted by hunger, have made from benches and overcoats makeshift beds, on which, during the session, they take turns lying down… "[19] One of the accused, Jenny Kipervaser, passes out. The physician who examines her determines that she is faking. The effect: more of the accused

---

[19] *Adevărul*, 15 February 1922.

faint during the same session. After three quarters of an hour, reports the journalist for *Adevărul*, they are brought back into the courtroom. "On the fifth day of the hunger strike, the accused give the impression of people sentenced to death."

The scenes are melodramatic. The press is taken in. The accused can barely answer the roll call. Their voices broken, they stretch out on the benches; they prop themselves up against one another. A few flagons of ether are unstopped and the courtroom immediately takes on the air characteristic of a hospital ward. "The desperate cry of an old woman draws all eyes to the public gallery ... What has happened? The mother of Timotei Marin [a student, executed in Moscow in 1937 – *author's note*], thinking that her son has passed out, wants to hurl herself from the balcony in desperation. Two soldiers pull her back. The old woman is clinging to the balustrade and struggling, emitting dreadful cries."[20] In fact, it was Niculescu-Mizil that had fainted, the same journalist drily notes. The scene does not end here. The widow of Constantin Dobrogeanu-Gherea, mother of Alexandru, cries out, "In the name of humanity, officers of the court, give assistance to the dying!" The pain produced by this spectacle squeezed tears from the accused and the public. At last, a physician enters the pen. Niculescu-Mizil is writhing on the floor, crying, "'Let me die! Let me die!' Five minutes pass. At the back of the room, the telephones are buzzing. The defence lawyers are conferring heatedly. The public is stirring, fettered. And while the members of the council take their tea in the deliberation room, there are more cries. ... A philosophy student, Miss Ida Pigo ... falls down in a faint... Not two minutes pass and one by one the other accused – four in number – fall down in a faint. They are carried out of the courtroom. The telephones keep ringing, informing the commandant of the army unit and the ministers of everything that is happening. Eventually, at a quarter to 12, the members of the council enter the chamber and reconvene the session." The next day, 18 February, after refusing food for five days, the hunger strikers cease their protest, following a visit to the prison by Generals Davidoglu and Mărgineanu. The exercise in revolutionary agitation has come to an end. Two days later, 37 of the accused are released and will be tried at liberty. They include Ilie Moscovici, Constantin Popovici, Ion Mirescu (later a PSD deputy), Elek Köblős (future head of the PCR, from 1924-1928, shot in Moscow in 1937), Berger Aladár and Moscu Cohn all well-known communist militants.

---

[20] *Adevărul*, 17 February 1922.

The cross-questioning continues to attempt to establish whether the accused are communists, are members of clandestine groups, signed/voted for membership of the Comintern, or were involved in the bomb attack on the Senate. "I am a communist," declares Alexandru Dobrogeanu-Gherea, "and communist ideas reject terrorist methods." Fifteen years later, he will be put before a firing squad in the Lubyanka, in Moscow. In the trial, he recognizes that he signed, together with Eugen Rozany, Gheorghe Cristescu and Constantin Popovici, the undertaking with the Comintern during his visit to Russia two years previously. Alexandru Dobrogeanu-Gherea's situation captures the attention of the press on a number of occasions. He goes on hunger strike. He has repeated conflicts with the administration, he is molested, whence more protests, articles, etc. The memory of his father, the socialist theorist, is still fresh, likewise the esteem he had enjoyed. This causes the press to treat him sympathetically, in spite of the public's general reservations regarding those in the dock, who are seen as agents of Moscow. Alexandru Dobrogeanu-Gherea is mentally unstable, as will be seen in the years to come. He is among the fanatical and intransigent communists, an extremist, an adept of demonstrative, spectacular postures. He is an adept of the hunger strike, for example, which he employs in any circumstances and on any pretext. In many situations, he refuses to speak, to answer questions, and so on, considering this to be a pure revolutionary attitude.

Ilie Moscovici, who had already been convicted in the general strike trial, says, "affiliation with the Comintern is deleterious to the interests of the working class," the opposite of what Alexandru Dobrogeanu-Gherea, Gheorghe Cristescu, Berger Aladár, David Fabian Finkelstein, Eugen Rozvany et al. say. Another of the accused, Constantin Popovici, denies that in 1918 a revolution had been plotted in Romania. "The Soviets in any case have no interest in requesting our collaboration with the Red Armies to bring them into the country. ... We would have to be naïve when we look at our minuscule forces to promise our support to the Soviets. ... With such forces we cannot think of revolution. In 1918, when the thrones were toppling, we had an opportunity to think of revolution. Then, the German, Hungarian and Austrian socialist parties were masters of the situation. Not even then did we make a revolution because we knew our forces were weak. Even less so today can there be any question of a revolution for the Socialist Party. Today, with the support of the bourgeois governments, Lenin is going to Genoa to consolidate the situation of the Soviets." It is also Popovici who claims that he has "never believed in the seriousness of the clandestine movement in Romania" and is "convinced of its failure." The Royal Commissar asks him to give a few names of "clandestines." Popovici refuses: "Don't ask me to do the work of an informant!" It is also he who says that he has signed undertakings towards the Comintern as a debt of honour and "with the determination to oppose the clandestinity" incumbent upon this affiliation. Heinrich Sternberg, a close associate of Cristescu, says, "We were not so naïve as to believe that the 34 communist groups with two hundred and eighty men could bring about a revolution. ... The clandestine action was the result of the regime of censorship, especially given that what we wanted to publish in *Socialistul* was banned. It cannot be said, however, that clandestine action is illegal. ... The masses cannot be won through illegal propaganda." The deposition of upholsterer Samuel (Sami) Margulies is just as ambiguous. During the investigation, he had become a Siguranță informer. He rejects the accusations that he has been mixed up in clandestine activity, saying that the strikes were not 'ordered' but spontaneous. He denies that he was involved in the attempt to assassinate King Ferdinand in Ploiești railway station in 1920. Boris Ștefanov also appears in court, albeit not charged with having been a delegate to the congress of May 1921, as he had been in gaol at the time for organising the general strike. Ștefanov, a nephew of Cristian Racovski, had been elected to Parliament, but had been invalidated by the Chamber of Deputies. Between December 1934 and 1939 he was to be General Secretary of the PCdR. Leonte Filipescu, a waiter by trade, was shot while trying to escape from under armed guard. His death was the subject of disagreement in the press, as well as at the trial.

The trial unfolds in parallel with the election campaign. Some of the accused take part in meetings: Constantin Popovici, lawyer Ionescu Gregorian (the son-in-law of Gheorghe Cristescu a few years afterwards), Ilie Moscovici, Elek Köblős, Ida Pigo, et al. Among the speakers we also find figures we shall encounter frequently throughout this book: Marcel Pauker, Petre Constantinescu-Iași, et al. The trial on Spirii Hill is one of the main topics of debate. Letters of protest are sent. Motions are passed, signatures are gathered. In the afternoons, the speakers address the adherents; in the mornings, starting at 9 a.m., they appear together before the War Council of the Second Army Corps on Fontăriei Street. It is a rather unusual situation.

In Moscow, during this time, events take place which seem at first glance wholly unconnected to what is happening in Bucharest. On 2 April 1922, Stalin is appointed General Secretary of the (Bolshevik) Communist Party. Three weeks later, Lenin suffers the first in a series of strokes which culminate in his death on 21 January 1924. Stalin engages in a wide-ranging campaign to win power for himself. The influence of the situation in the Kremlin and above all Stalin's victory in the struggle for supremacy against Leon Trotsky, Grigori Zinoviev, Lev Kamenev, and Nikolai Bukharin will be decisive for the next quarter of a century. We need only recall that many of the protagonists in the trial on Spirii Hill were to be executed at Stalin's order in the years of the Great Terror between 1936 and 1938.

Also interesting are the depositions of the Romanians who had been part of the 'revolutionary battalion' in Odessa, as well as other Bolshevik groups in Russia during the civil war. Cristian Racovski's name frequently comes up, as an instigator of the violent overthrow of the political regime in Romania, the abolition of the monarchy and the imposition of a 'dictatorship of the proletariat'. From cross-examination the full extent of the Bolshevik propaganda emerges. Some of the witnesses recount how emissaries and professional agitators were sent to organise trades union protest meetings, strikes and demonstrations. Another question is the financing of these clandestine groups. Funds were sent to pay local clandestine militants, to purchase paper and pay printers, to publish newspapers, pamphlets and manifestos, to buy safe houses and to pay lawyers.

When the trial comes to the terrorist attack of 1920, it is discovered that the plot was hatched by one of the clandestine communist groups, with close ties to the legal socialist movement and even to its leaders. Max Goldstein meets with Leon Lichtblau, Saul Ozias, Pavel Tkachenko, Timotei Marin, Heinrich Sternberg et al. in Jassy, at No. 2 Rîpa Street, a house bought using funds supplied by the Comintern. All are co-accused with Gelbert Moscovici, who has fled to Vienna. Max Goldstein was born in Bîrlad and became a Bolshevik in Russia. In 1919, he returned to Romania, as an agitator in the employ of the Comintern. The police also suspected him of being the author of other terrorist attacks. When he is arrested for the first time, in 1919, a search of his house finds guns, bombs, and explosives. He escapes, flees to Russia and then returns to Romania. He planted the homemade Senate bomb with the help of Leon Lichtblau (later, in 1928, a member of the PCdR Political Bureau based in Vienna; shot in Moscow in

1937). Saul Ozias, one of the accomplices, declares that the initial plan was for the bomb to be planted in the Capșa Restaurant, which was frequented by the political and intellectual elite. In the summer of 1920, Ozias and Lichtblau took part in the Second Congress of the Comintern, where the 21 conditions for affiliation were passed. They were arrested in October of that year, on their return to Romania. The story of the capture of Max Goldstein in Rusciuk/Giurgiu is epic. Soldiers and other witnesses are cross-examined. He was captured after an exchange of fire with the army, near Călugăreni, by night. Dr Nicolae Lupu and Nicolae Iorgu appear as witnesses. Their testimonies are not directly related to the case. Dr Lupu is of the opinion, for example, that the Siguranță ought to be abolished. Iorga says of Cristescu that he is "a decent man and a patriot." As for the attacks aimed at the King, Iorga further declares, "The King is only attacked by politicians when they have been too long in opposition. But you [Cristescu] never had any prospects of being in government, and so you had no reason to make such attacks."[21] Iorga goes on to say that Averescu and Cristescu organised the general strike together, but the General would have liked the strike to be "more extreme." As for the guilt of those who had been to Moscow, he says, "inasmuch the men on trial have not made any pact with the enemy during wartime, nothing can be imputed to the communists, even if they have made an arrangement with the Soviet Union, a state with which we are not at war."[12] Iorga defends Alexandru Dobrogeanu-Gherea, "a decent, rational and peaceful man," and also student Timotei Marin from Jassy. "It has been a bad day for the architects of this tragic but nonetheless comical trial."[22] The surprise comes on 1 June 1922, when the government grants an amnesty for political prisoners. The King travels to Belgrade for the wedding of his daughter Marioara to Alexander of Yugoslavia. Moreover, Russia had signed the Genoa Treaty with the Western powers, whereby the Moscow government was officially recognised. Racovski had also taken part in the negotiations on behalf of Russia. The context was thus favourable to such a gesture. The amnesty came after a number of years of high political tensions, conflicts and threats, lasting from 1916-1922. The domestic climate in Romania had changed, however. After years of war, it was now possible to hope for peace. Among those amnestied were strikers of every variety, communists, adherents of the Third International,

---

[21] *Adevărul*, 12 April 1922.
[22] *Adevărul*, 12 April 1922.

'clandestines', Hungarian and Russian plotters convicted in Transylvania and Bassarabia, those who had committed offences in the press or carried out civil espionage, and the organisers of clandestine border crossings to/from Russia and Hungary. Those who had taken part in conspiracies, uprisings and rebellions were likewise amnestied.[23]

Excepted from the amnesty were a number of restricted categories, including the perpetrators of the Senate bomb attack. For them the trial continued. There are 31 accused, seven of them minors. At midnight on 25 June 1922, after the Council had deliberated for 12 hours, the Clerk of the Court and the Royal Commissar read the sentence to the accused, over the course of two hours. Twenty of them are convicted *in absentia*. Among them are Leon Lichtblau, Gelbert Moscovici, and Paul Goldstein, all notorious communists, living abroad. Among those in the dock, Max Goldstein was sentenced to life, hard labour. He will be sent to Doftana, where he dies on 11 October 1925, six days after a hunger strike of 56 days. His brain is sent to the Mina Marcovici Coroner's Institute, as a curiosity, and is exhibited alongside that of Terente the bandit. Saul Ozias is sentenced to 10 years, hard labour. Leon Lichtblau, Gelbert Moscovici, Paul and Rebecca Goldstein and others are also sentenced to life, hard labour. All of them apart from Rebecca Goldstein will later be released, only to be executed in Moscow during the Great Terror. Constantin Agiu is sentenced to eight years imprisonment. He survives the inter-war period. In 1944, we find him at the head of the Union of Patriots, a communist front organisation. He subsequently has a long career in the Communist Party apparatus. Pavel Tkachenko, later a member of the Secretariat of the PCdR, and who will perish in 1926, is sentenced to one year in prison, along with Şmil Bubnovski and I. Kanner. Others, such as Solomon Schein (later head of the Secretariat of the PCdR in the late 1920s), are acquitted.

What were the effects of the trial? Marcel Pauker recalls in an autobiographical statement written in Moscow in 1937, a few weeks before his execution, "The majority of the leaders released in the amnesty had already left. The only ones that had remained were Cristescu and Sternberg. … It might be said that I begged the comrades on my knees to resume their work and not abandon the Party. In vain. It proved that the year … in prison as well as the lengthy trial had demoralised them. Rozvany, known back then as a tireless fighter for the Communist International, withdrew to his

---

[23] *Adevărul*, 6 June 1922.

law practice, refusing to remain in Bucharest to carry out the work of a member of the Central Committee. Dobrogeanu went to Berlin to start up a business. David Fabian Finkelstein went on holiday in the provinces and thence abroad. ... Comrade Macavei, who was a member of the provisory Executive Committee, fled to his estate in Mehedinți. ... Comrade Ştefanov returned to his estate in Dobrudja. ... Pătrăşcanu, who had been leader of the Socialist Youth, worked for a while longer ... but then, after gaining a law degree, went abroad, against our interdiction, to Leipzig, to study for the title of Doctor."[24]

After the trial, Gheorghe Cristescu gradually becomes a marginal figure. He continues to make public appearances. He is highly visible in the editorial offices and at the meetings of the socialists, in the trades union clubs, in the cellars and back yards of the Bolshevik sect. He is a 'pacifier'. He believes that through his ability and notoriety he will be able to bring all the factions together. The following is a description dating from November 1922, written by Gelbert Moscovici in Vienna at the request of the Comintern: "Gheorghe Cristescu, quilt maker, owner of a house and a shoe shop. A brilliant demagogue, he employs a turn of phrase that is radical, but from the theoretical point of view he is uninformed, in fact he is a petit bourgeois opportunist of the purest kind, nevertheless given appropriate leadership he works well and serves the Party thanks to his huge popularity and from time to time his diplomatic tact."[25] Cristescu is an orator. He is nostalgic for the mass demonstrations and revolutionary situation of 1918-1919, when his influence was at its height. The truth is that after the general strike of October 1920, after the split of 1921 and after the trial on Spirii Hill, but above all after affiliation to the Comintern, the 'movement' dissolves. The surviving fragments move to the periphery of Romanian public life. The time of the masses, strikes, demonstrations, threats against the government and King Ferdinand has passed. History casts Cristescu in minor roles and then bit parts. He shares the fate of the now fragmented socialist movement as a whole. He is elected head of the Party at the clandestine congress held in Ploieşti in October 1922. Conflicts arise between him and the other leaders. The core of the dispute is the question of the underground Party,

---

[24] *Lichidarea lui Marcel Pauker. O anchetă stalinistă, 1937-1938*, ed.
Gheorghe Brătescu, Bucharest: Editura Univers Enciclopedic, 1995,
pp. 58-59.
[25] CC of the PCR Archive, Fund 1, Dossier 78, p. 52.

insistently demanded by the Comintern. Marcel Pauker, David Fabian Finkelstein, and Alexandru Dobrogeanu-Gherea are proponents of the idea. Cristescu, the man of public speeches, a politician of the old school, hungry for popularity, rejects it. He had once accepted it, malleable as he was in Moscow under the pressure of events and above all the Bolshevik leaders. In Bucharest, he does not want to be the chief of a handful of clandestine agitators under surveillance by the Siguranţă. In any case, he was very well-known. He could not have vanished over night, becoming a shadow, a hero of the underground. This is the reason why he shows himself to be more and more reticent towards Comintern tactics. He is not the only one in this position. Paul Levi, the head of the German communists, also rejected the tactics of insurrection, splits, and the theory of the small vanguard of the Revolution, saying, "If a party loses touch with the masses, it becomes a political sect." The consequence: Levi was expelled in 1921, when he came into conflict with the Kremlin leaders. Also expelled was Valeriu Marcu, a German-language writer, a Bolshevik from the very beginning, born in Bucharest, who knew Cristescu and had been close to Lenin when he was a *lycée* student in Switzerland. He was the author, in 1924, of the first biography of Lenin. Such examples are numerous. Cristescu will suffer the same treatment in 1926.

The power struggle that commenced in Moscow during Lenin's death throes had an influence upon the small world of the Romanian Left. Cristescu had become obsolete in the eyes of those in the Kremlin. Within the PCdR he is a figure from an earlier age, surrounded by young men like Köblős, Gherea, Finkelstein, Pauker and Pătrăşcanu, who were eager for clandestine action, subversion and insurrection. The death of Lenin in January 1924 radicalises the situation. The Comintern is seeking leaders who are not so caught up in the past. The disquiet causes upheavals and anarchic actions. Prudently, the Siguranţă makes numerous arrests among the communists in April. Cristescu is one of those detained. A secret committee is formed to run the Party. In a letter written from Braşov and dated 9 July 1924, Marcel Pauker reports to the presidium of the Balkan Communist Federation in Vienna, "The replacement of Gheorghe Cristescu with a more courageous, more disciplined comrade was inevitable. Cristescu reacted weakly to this because ultimately, at this time, this situation of no responsibility suits him marvellously."[26]

[26] CC of the PCR Archive, Fund 1, Dossier 158, p. 3.

The Third Congress of the PCdR was meant to take place in Romania in February 1924. The authorities ban it and take drastic measures to keep all the members of the CC of the PCdR under surveillance. The congress is held in Vienna in December. Cristescu's replacement is ratified. Elek Köblős, a carpenter from Transylvania, takes his place. Cristescu nevertheless remains a member of the CC of the PCdR thanks to his great popularity. In fact, he seldom attended Party meetings, being more concerned with running his small businesses and with forging anew links with other leaders of the Left and trades unionists. He is even toying with the idea of a legal workers' party. He remains a man of the masses, of noisy public meetings, where he shines as an orator, in the Dacia, Tomis and Sotir auditoriums. He increasingly rejects political underground, subversion, and conspiracies.

"What have you done? (This is what you, the Lenin of Romania, said to Lenin himself in 1922 when you were in Moscow.) You, the leader of the Romanian working class, you, as a member of the CC of the PCdR and the Executive Committee of the Communist International, at whatever meeting of the Central Committee, conference or congress you presented yourself. And have you not been summoned time and time again? Which is the article where you have defended yourself against the accusations? What has been your answer to the insult made against you in Parliament by Dr Vaida Voevod, who declared that 'we ought to be very grateful that Gheorghe Cristescu is no longer a communist, that the prodigal son has returned to the parental home'? What did you say to this slur against you as a communist? You were silent and by your silence you confirmed that you had gone over to the camp of the enemy of the working class."[27]

The foregoing is part of a letter published in the clandestine communist press, signed by the Hoppe brothers (expelled from Romania in 1907 at the same time as Racovski, and living in Vienna, where, in the 1920s, they are agents of the Comintern).

Nevertheless, Moscow keeps him on PCdR representative to the Comintern. The argument was of course his popularity among the workers. After the Party is outlawed in December 1924 under the Mîrzescu Law, he is arrested. He appears with the other communists of Francmasonă

---

[27] CC of the PCR Archive, Fund 1, Dossier 265, p. 148.

Street in the trial of 1925. As usual, he is dapper, with an old-style red cravat, and speaks eloquently. He is acquitted. A rumour circulates about his collaboration with the authorities and his conciliatory attitude. He is increasingly isolated. In public, he frequently takes a line independent to that of the PCdR. As conflicts intensify in June 1926, the CC of the PCdR expels him from the Party, accusing him of "liquidationism." Cristescu opposes the setting up of an illegal clandestine party. The *de facto* banning of the PCdR in 1924 clarifies matters as far as he is concerned. An illegal party is nonsensical. The accusations against him are as follows: "This collaboration [between Cristescu and the PCdR – *author's note*] has become ever more untenable. Not only has Comrade Krilenko [Cristescu's codename – *author's note*] refused to carry out the mandate of the EKKI [Executive Committee of the Comintern], but also, seeking to establish and maintain factional relations, he has undertaken a systematic campaign against the Party, which has been thrust into illegality, against the CC and its representatives, seeking to discredit it in front of Party members and the working class. Among other things, in this context he makes use not only of financial questions, which are wholly fabricated, saying that fraud has been committed … but also he strikes a policeman's attitude, revealing them to the workers and even the authorities." Another accusation is that he has a hostile and even counter-revolutionary attitude towards Soviet Russia: "He has refused to stand for election on the list of the Peasant Worker Bloc … he has proceeded to open and public action against the Party's campaign … he has conducted a well-prepared action against the Communist Party, a stab in the back in the thick of very heavy fighting … Comrade Krilenko has categorically refused to appear before the CC to explain his attitude. The CC rules that Krilenko should be expelled from the PCdR."[28] At the meeting of 22 November – 16 December 1926, the Executive Committee of the Comintern ratifies the decision. Present are Elek Köblős, the General Secretary of the PCdR, and Gelbert Moscovici, the new PCdR representative to the Comintern, both of them adversaries of Cristescu. The document of the decision to expel Cristescu mentions the same accusation of "liquidationism": "Cristescu has not ceased to wage war against illegalism, against illegal work, against the illegal party, and for its replacement by a legal communist party such as would be tolerated by

---

[28] National Archives of Romania, *Copilăria Comunismului românesc în arhiva Cominternului*, Bucharest, 2001, pp. 185-186.

the bourgeoisie and suit him too … Cristescu who at one time enjoyed the greatest popularity in the bosom of the working class is today completely compromised and isolated … We should not underestimate the danger that his demagogic agitation might constitute, waged under the slogan of 'let us set quarrels aside, let us unite, let us become strong through unification as we once were'."

In 1927, Cristescu founds the Socialist Party of Romania, which unsuccessfully negotiates with the PSD and the Peasant Workers' Bloc, a buffer organisation of the PCdR, an electoral cartel. On 11 February 1928, Cristescu joins the Social Democratic Party at a turbulent meeting in the Tomis Auditorium, on Văcăreşti Avenue, at which Zaharia Tănase, Constantin Titel Petrescu and others give speeches. The *Socialistul* newspaper runs the following front-page headline: "Cristescu is back!" 1928 was the year of the attempted reunification of the non-communist left within a single party. It ended in failure. The splits and disputes are unending. On 9 January 1930, Cristescu makes his *mea culpa* for his Bolshevik past in *Socialistul*. A year later, he joins the Romanian Socialist Workers Party. The Party had been founded in 1928 by Leon Ghelerter, Vasile Anagnoste, Ştefan Voitec, Petre Zissu and C. Mănescu, and was critical of Stalin, aligning itself sooner with the positions of Trotsky. In February 1933, a group within the PSD led by Constantin Popovici, a former trades union leader, split away and formed the Independent Socialist Party. Popovici had, like Cristescu, been one of the negotiators for affiliation of the Romanian communists to the Comintern in the autumn of 1920. Cristescu – a friend of Popovici's – leaves once again. The Party, together with a group led by L. Ghelerter, later forms the Unitary Socialist Party. Cristescu also takes part.

The world of the Left is one of minuscule groups, of political sects. They are ephemeral, coalescing and dissolving depending upon interests and circumstances and according to the vanity of their leaders. Gheorghe Cristescu is one of the protagonists in these evolutions. His reputation as an established leader of the working class and the socialist movement guarantees him a place in all the presidia and leaderships. He appears at public meetings in various auditoria. He writes for Party publications. Meanwhile, he looks after his business affairs, making a small fortune. In 1928, he is elected as a councillor to Bucharest City Hall. He has long since abandoned the labour placement agency about which Panait Istrati wrote. He has a small shop in Unirii Square. He is the owner of a quilt making workshop, whence his nickname Cristescu-Plăpumaru [Quilt maker]. Then he opens a restaurant.

The second moment of his 'glory' is the trial of his daughter's murderer in 1936. Tita Cristescu was a woman of the demimonde, kept by a number of wealthy men. In 1926 she had been voted Miss Romania (*Dimineața* newspaper, October 1926) and in the mid-1930s she was regarded as one of the most beautiful women in Bucharest. She had unsuccessfully tried to pursue a career as an actress in Berlin for three years. In 1929-1930, she was cast in minor roles in two plays at the Queen Maria Theatre. At Christmas in 1935, she was found dead in her flat at No. 34 Brătianu Boulevard, poisoned with cyanide. Gheorghe Cristescu went to the police to accuse engineer Liviu Ciulei of the murder. Ciulei, a freemason and wealthy entrepreneur with whom Cristescu had otherwise enjoyed very good relations, had been Titi Cristescu's lover for many years. According to her father's wishes, Tita Cristescu is buried in Bellu Cemetery, without any religious ceremony. At the grave a brass band plays the International. While the band plays, Cristescu holds his fist aloft, the proletarian salute of the epoch. He will make the same gesture in 1960, when he attends the cremation of Ana Pauker. He had also wanted his daughter to be cremated, but his wife was against it. Tita Cristescu was a member of the minuscule Unitary Socialist Party. She was head of the women's section. During the murder trial, Gheorghe Cristescu's ambiguous position comes to light. Both he and his son-in-law, lawyer Ionescu Gregorian, the husband of Cristescu's other daughter, had taken advantage of Ciulei, who, on demand, used to transfer to them various sums of money. His daughter likewise used to provide for the family from the generous gifts she received. At her premature death, at the age of 28, she left a fortune estimated between three and five million lei, a huge sum, as well as furs and jewels. Her father used to close his eyes to all this and was uninterested in where the money came from. In any case, he knew. Cristescu himself was well off. He had a number of businesses, principally his restaurant on Carol Boulevard, which was frequented by high society, but also, above all, by left-wing sympathisers, lawyers, journalists, and militant socialists. Engineer Ciulei was also a frequent patron. Of course, nor was the Siguranță absent, always on the lookout for information direct from the source. Pamfil Șeicaru, in an editorial published in *Curentul* (13 January 1936), writes,

"A working man, a canny businessman, full of initiative and highly enterprising, Gheorghe Cristescu was careful not to mix up his ideological weaknesses with strictly economic realities. He had a quilt making workshop and ran it with great skill. He did not have a single vice. It is rare to find such a settled man, a man with such a sense of family honour as Gheorghe Cristescu. I knew him in the socialist movement as a man of steadfast conviction, and although he was not very familiar with Marxist dialectics … he brought in exchange a naïve energy, a passion that won over the simple man. During the German occupation, he had a courageous attitude and did not flinch on occasion from spending hours in prison for his restless socialist beliefs. In December 1918, after the attempt at a communist insurrection, Ghiţă[29] Cristescu resigned himself to endure all the violence of repression … He regarded himself as a rebel against the bourgeois order, but Ghiţă Cristescu was by his way of life a peaceful bourgeois … He was a merchant with a weakness for the revolutionary turn of phrase … To rebel against the capital order, to dream of the demolition of a social system, and not to be struck by the situation of your own daughter! … I did not understand what it was that rhymed with the *Internationale*, that hymn of the proletarian revolution, when played at the funeral of a beautiful girl who fully benefitted from all that the capitalist system has to offer: luxury, pampering, not having to work, being a goddess in the temple of love? The International, the revolutionary hymn, movingly evokes all the heroism of socialist fever and even an adversary feels obliged to respect the vibration of that insurrectional emotiveness: but what can socialism have in common with a drama of capitalist love? … Why this public spectacle? … I do not know whether in this event there is also mixed up some macabre theatricality."

The *Universul* newspaper of 11 January 1936 records the following among the hypotheses taken into account by the investigators: "Tita Cristescu, a beautiful woman with relations in high society, might have been tangled up with some spying organisation." The newspaper notes that the woman spent far too much and always needed more money, that she was a communist, a member of the Unitary Socialist Party, a radical left-wing group, which could pass as communist thanks to its leaders: Gheorghe Cristescu and Constantin Popovici, old-time Bolshevik militants. "Thanks to her political ideas, Tita

---

[29] Ghiţă is the diminutive of Gheorghe – *Translator's note.*

might have been in the service of some spying organisation, which at a given moment eliminates agents when they become a threat to the organisation as a whole." The Siguranţa, via its chief inspector in charge of investigating communist networks, Vintilă Ionescu, conducts its own inquiry. The documents in the archive today do not reveal the results of that investigation.

The affair stirred huge interest in its day. For a whole year, the press was full of the details of the murder and the trial. Gheorghe Cristescu was a civil plaintiff, accusing engineer Ciulei of the murder of his daughter and demanding millions of lei in compensation. After a long trial, widely reported in the press, the court acquitted Liviu Ciulei. Of Cristescu's court appearance, Constantin Argetoianu writes, "In May 1921 his role ended and no one mentioned him again until the murder of his beautiful daughter Tita and the trial of Ciulei – a trial in which he cut the sad figure of a father-pimp."[30] The last news of the affair appears in the press after the conclusion of the trial, in October 1936. It refers to the dispute between Gheorghe Cristescu and his brother, Dumitru, over the eternal resting place in Bellu Cemetery in which Tita Cristescu has been interred. It occasions a new trial, won by the communist militant.

After the war, Gheorghe Cristescu was a prisoner at the Danube-Black Sea Canal in 1949. In 1956, at the funeral of Constantin Titel Petrescu in Bellu Cemetery, Securitate agents record the following: "On this occasion, Gheorghe Cristescu-Plăpumaru intended to give a speech, but at the moment when he made his appearance he was met by the family and begged to refrain otherwise something would happen. All the same, Gheorghe Cristescu, in the moment when the body of Constantin Titel Petrescu was lowered into the tomb, said, 'You have been extinguished, great flame, we shall never forget you'."[31] It was an admission of his own failure and of the rightness of a democratic adversary, a firm opponent of the clandestine tactics and Bolshevik liaisons of Cristescu's early years. He makes another appearance in June 1960, at the cremation of Ana Pauker. He was the only communist militant of the old guard in attendance. Rehabilitated by Ceauşescu in the 1960s, he gives a speech at the PCR congress in 1969. He died in 1973 and was buried in the communist Pantheon in Libertăţii Park. After 1990, his remains were reinterred in the family vault in Bellu Cemetery.

---

[30] Constantin Argetoianu, *Memorii*, vol. 6, Bucharest: Editura Machiavelli, p. 170.

[31] *Cartea albă a Securităţii*, vol. 2, Bucharest: SRI, 1994, p. 590.

IV
Like Rats in the Underground

Go underground, fight from the darkness, because only thus will you grow
and gather the strength you now lack. Comrades, we will lurk ready to
pounce, stalking our enemy at every step, waiting for the right moment to
deal the final blow to the bourgeois greed that sows poverty and suffering.
Be and create fanatical communists! Long live the Russian proletarian
revolution! Long live the vanguard of the consciously Romanian
proletariat!

Local Committee of Romanian Communist Groups

One of the clichés about the 'history of the PCdR' is that it emerged as a
legal party in May 1921. That for a time it operated openly, but in 1924 was
forced to 'go underground'. Thus, its clandestine activity is supposed to have
appeared after 19 December 1924, the date on which it was outlawed under
the Mîrzescu Law aimed at "repression of infractions against the public
peace." It is a cliché, a counterfeit history. From the very first, Bolshevik
groups appeared in Romania as clandestine networks, based in Bucharest
during the occupation by the Central Powers in the summer of 1918.
These networks came into being as a result of a decision taken by a number
of Socialist Party leaders: Alecu Constantinescu, Gheorghe Cristescu,
Ilie Moscovici, Heinrich Sternberg, Constantin Popovici. Moreover, in
Romania, pro-Bolshevik groups had begun to form spontaneously, under the
impact of the coup carried out by Lenin and Trotsky in Petrograd. After the
collapse of the Central Powers at the end of 1918, they continue to exist and
evolve. They start to make direct contact with Russia, with the Romanian
Bolshevik committees that had appeared in Moscow, Kharkov, Odessa, and
Petrograd, as well as with Russian Bolshevik organisations. The Romanian
Bolsheviks imitate their Russian counterparts, enthused by the success of
the coup. The idea of repeating such a coup in Jassy, Bucharest, Bassarabia
or Transylvania is widespread among them, even a temptation. The road
to power seems short. All that is required is to arm a few hundred men,
to take government headquarters by storm. As there were discontented
soldiers and workers everywhere, easily spurred to anarchy and violence,
the accomplishment of such a scenario seemed feasible. The clandestine

experience of Lenin's men up to 1917 fits this formula of political success.

The clandestine groups appear not only spontaneously, but also as an effect of the sympathy for the collapse of the tsarist regime and as a result of egalitarian demagoguery. The formation of clandestine networks is also demanded by Moscow. The appeals of Lenin, Trotsky, Kamenev and Zinoviev point the way. The disturbances and chaos caused by such networks can only benefit the Bolshevik putsch. Some have agreed to 'make a revolution', to plot against the constitutional regime. Others oppose it. Some have not accepted the goals of such a government, others do not agree with violent, insurrectional tactics. According to Lenin, 'professional revolutionaries' were the only ones capable of preparing for and conducting the overthrow of the bourgeois regimes. Hence their mistrust towards those who act within the law, on the surface. Lenin wagered upon those who acted in secret. Clandestinity was obligatory for any revolutionary party. In *What is to be Done?* Lenin writes, "This organisation must necessarily not be too large and should be as conspiratorial as possible."[1] He demands the "concentration of all conspiratorial functions in the hands of a limited number of professional revolutionaries."[2] Furthermore, "Conspiracy is a necessary condition to the highest degree for such an organisation, so that all other conditions (number of members, their selection, functions, etc.) should be guided by that of conspiracy."[3] What is a "professional revolutionary"? He is not a political dabbler, to be found in clubs or newspaper offices, but someone who dedicates all his time to preparing a revolution. He has "acquired professional training in the art of fighting the political police."

Lenin sees such groups as strictly hierarchical and small in size. They are like sects. There is iron discipline, and anyone who breaks it is 'objectively' someone who harms the movement, and therefore a 'traitor to the cause'. The consequences are that he is eliminated, either politically or, where necessary, physically. Lenin also writes that in absolutist regimes this type of party is the only one capable of "leading the struggle of the proletariat" and seizing power. After 1917, Lenin regarded Bolshevik Russia as the only democratic political regime, while all the other regimes in Europe

---

[1] V. I. Lenin, *Opere alese*, 2nd edition, Bucharest: Editura pentru literatură politică, 1954, p. 220.

[2] *Idem*, p. 229.

[3] *Idem*, p. 237.

were absolutist dictatorships. As a result, he demanded and imposed that Bolshevik methods should be applicable everywhere. Lenin, together with Trotsky, Zinoviev, Racovski, Bukharin, Stalin, Sverdlov, and Kamenev were to impose these methods directly in 1918 and 1919 and then, after March 1919, through the Comintern.

Such a party was not a party properly speaking, one oriented toward society, but rather a group of plotters planning a putsch, whose goal was to seize power by any means possible. A large part of the Romanian leaders and militants refused to set up clandestine networks. They demanded action exclusively by the usual political means. Here is one such point of view: "In tsarist Russia there never existed any right to speak or write freely or to organise, and this is why all the good people who wanted to do something for the working class were forced to lead a clandestine life, to assume false names, to have false passports, to move from place to place to avoid police surveillance. The Russian Revolutionary movement, because of the special circumstances in which it developed, was unfamiliar with the public activity to which the workers' movements in Europe are accustomed. The lack of any public activity was a great evil for the development of the Russian Revolution. As Lenin himself acknowledges, almost all revolutionaries, leading a clandestine life and busying themselves only with small groups, are familiar with neither the spirit of the masses nor the life of the state and all its mechanisms, they are unfit for any kind of public activity. And also because of the clandestine life, where the party members do not know each other or even the leaders, all kinds of adventurers and men who are wholly dishonest and compromised were capable in the first moments of the Revolution of gaining important functions. Even though Lenin recognises these disadvantages of clandestine life, he imposes this activity on the workers' parties in Europe today [1920]. Point three of the conditions [for admission to the Third Communist International] imposes on all parties and in all circumstances clandestine activity. In Europe the party has at all times led a public life. All the leaders, from the greatest to the least, all the orators, all the theorists and journalists are known to the whole world, including the bourgeois police. How can Lenin imagine that at a given moment they could suddenly cease to be known to anyone and lead the clandestine life that the anonymous Russian revolutionaries were able to lead in the immensity of Russia? How can Lenin imagine that in the statutes of a party the obligation for clandestine activity could exist? That besides the public committees there could also exist clandestine committees? … However, if the official party does not recognise its clandestine activity in public – which is against the conditions and incompatible with affiliation [to the Third Communist International] – then this activity is worthless. An anonymous manifesto might be produced by a genuine communist, but it also might have been written by a police agent. … When you have newspapers and meetings, when you can gather together hundreds of thousands of workers … a clandestine manifesto … is educationally worthless, and constitutes at best a defiant challenge … But this has not been understood by others; some have made clandestine activity an ideal, others a trade. Incapable of carrying on public activity, because of a lack of education or an unwillingness to work, wanted by the police, or convicted *in absentia*, the clandestines have declared themselves the leaders of the movement on their own initiative, they have drawn to them a number of naïve elements and are set upon a revolution of spirits. … They have been encouraged in this clandestine calamity by the Third International … But this clandestine movement is also profoundly immoral. To occupy even the most minor place in a trades union organisation or a party section you have to be elected at a general meeting, your whole life and your whole activity is checked and followed by the members that have elected you and by the superiors that lead you. In clandestine activity, any young hothead, illiterate or adventurer thinks of himself as the sole leader of the movement, he dictates to the public movement and the masses, he engages the movement in actions and struggles without anyone knowing who he is, without anyone keeping a check on him. … Clandestine action is a danger for a mass movement … For, the clandestine is always an ultra-revolutionary, fleeing from one place to another, with fear in his heart, imagining himself pursued by the police even in his sleep, he can no longer keep a cool head or perceive reality, he is a dreamer, he wants a revolution as soon as possible to rid him of the police, he wants to make mankind happy and draw the masses into actions that become fatal. And clandestine action also presents another danger, that anarchists such as Max Goldstein and his ilk might muddle naïve heads, or even that agents provocateurs might hatch plots and attacks so that they themselves can then denounce them or reveal them. We cannot, in any shape or form, accept clandestine action as imposed by the International, and as practised by its representatives," the author concludes.[4]

---

[4] Ilie Moscovici, "Probleme actuale ale mișcării socialiste," *Adevărul*, 8 February 1922.

Constantin Popovici, a member of the Romanian communist delegation that signed the act of affiliation to the Comintern, relates that after the events of 13 December 1918, organised by the clandestine Bolshevik networks with the complicity of some socialist leaders, the leadership of the Socialist Party decided to give up underground activity.

"Extremists like Alecu Constantinescu did not want to take any notice and continued secretly to carry out clandestine activities. ... The revolutionary tactic of clandestinity took the form of clandestine manifestos, sabotage, provocations, army mutinies, caches of arms, attacks etc. ... And all this action ... was carried out in the name of the Communist International. In order to put a stop to the equivocation regarding the clandestines ... we sent a delegation to Russia. Both in Kharkov, with Racovski, and in Moscow, at the Committee of the International ... we revealed the danger, the immorality and the pointlessness of illegal and clandestine action, when a legal movement had full freedom to hold meetings and public demonstrations ... In spite of all the efforts I made there to protect the movement from the disaster into which it was being led by the reports submitted by Alecu Constantinescu, Sternberg and Ghiță Moscu and above all the written statements made by a part of the members of the delegation, such as Dobrogeanu, Finkelstein and Rozvany ... reports that demanded the removal of the Social Democratic parties and leaders and obligatory clandestine action to prepare for a revolution, Rakovski and the committee of the Communist International ... accused us of opportunism and called us cowards, traitors and careerists because we opposed a split in the party and above all because we opposed illegal action."[5]

Both Ilie Moscovici and Constantin Popovici were part of the radical wing, up to a point. They supported the parallel structures. Both of them revised their positions, however, when they realised that the socialist movement, the Left, had been ruined as a result of the Comintern's baneful diktat with regard to obligatory clandestine activity.

The clandestine networks, in accordance with the Bolshevik catechism, were the armed wing of the Revolution. They were small, disciplined, hierarchical paramilitary units made up of three to five persons. Their

---

[5] *Lumea nouă*, 17 February 1924.

mission was to organise diversionary activities, sabotage, acts of terrorism, to gather information about the army and security measures, to locate targets – official buildings and politicians. They existed behind a political façade. Everything was justified ideologically, according to a Jacobin pattern. The militants, especially when they were captured and brought to justice for acts of terrorism, used to speak earnestly about political liberty and freedom of conscience. They manipulated constitutional rights with the aim of destroying bourgeois democracy. The dawn of the 'new world' was heralded by bombs, espionage, subversion, murders and violence. One such underground structure included Max Goldstein, Saul Ozias, Leon Lichtblau, and Al. Bădulescu (Ghiță Moscu), who carried out the bomb attack on the Senate. It is to be understood that given such activities the Bolshevik networks were hunted by the Siguranța. Those mixed up in them were kept under surveillance; their networks were infiltrated by secret agents and police informers. The boundary between political activities (propaganda, electoral campaigns) and terrorism, subversion, and espionage was very blurred among the militants of the extreme Left. Such networks are very costly. The money was supplied from Moscow, via the Comintern and the GRU, the Soviet foreign intelligence service. The two institutions of world revolution worked together closely to organise and extend the networks. In that period, the export of revolution was official Kremlin doctrine and its main theorists were Lenin and Trotsky. The Romanian Bolsheviks were continuously financed from Moscow. Lenin wanted to replicate the model of his own coup: a handful of Bolshevik militants with foreign funding (German, in his case). He encouraged the existence of a small communist party and imagined that if he supplied sufficient funds and a few 'experts in revolution' his plans would succeed. He confiscates the Romanov treasure and makes it available to the Comintern in March 1919, so that its militants can export the revolution to their home countries. The huge amount of booty from the looting of the property of the aristocracy, bourgeoisie and Russian Orthodox churches is used to finance attempted coups in various other countries.

The Romanian national treasure, taken to Moscow for safekeeping by the Romanian government in 1917, was also looted. In July 1920, a police raid on the headquarters of the Socialist Party at No. 5, Sf. Ionică Street leads to the discovery of 72 sheets of banknotes issued by the National Bank of Romania, originating from the treasure in Moscow and brought back in secret. Their purpose was to finance clandestine activities. The newspapers recount a tragic-comic scene:

> "A large sum of money arrived from Moscow for Constantinescu this winter, but instead of going directly to him it went to the Socialist Club, where deputy Moscovici took receipt of the sum from a Bolshevik courier. After a time, Mr Constantinescu found out where the money had gone and sent Bujor to seize it from Moscovici. There was a scandal, for Mr Moscovici had spent a part of this sum of money to cover Party expenses … Given Moscovici's refusal to hand over the money … to its rightful recipient, Bujor threatened the socialist deputy with a revolver and in the end took away the money, which he surrendered to Cristescu."[6]

The cast of this dramatic scene topped the bill of the socialist movement. Alecu Constantinescu was the head of the clandestine networks, a dangerous terrorist. Mihai Gheorghiu Bujor is glimpsed here during the short interval between his clandestine arrival from Russia and his later arrest. He will remain in prison for 13 years. Ilie Moscovici, a deputy, was the number one figure in the party at that time, and Gheorghe Cristescu, also a deputy, was the future leader of the PCdR. The meaning of this scene is that the money sent from Moscow was meant to go to the clandestine network and not to the official Socialist Party. But all the leaders were up to date with the affair.

The secret funds were meant to ensure the victory of the dictatorship of the proletariat. The same scenario was repeated in other countries. The professional revolutionaries, those who had taken the path of the underground, were paid. The clandestines were wholly dependent on Moscow for money. Given that these networks controlled the legal party, the party as a whole was undermined, compromised, incapable of waging a real political struggle. Whenever the police broke up a clandestine group, it meant that the party as a whole was compromised. This is what happened in the case of the Socialist Party, which lost its popularity between 1920 and 1922. The clandestine groups, relatively numerous as they were up until 1920, eroded it from within. In 1921, the 'maximalists' tore the party asunder. It was in fact a victory for these extremist groups. Their leader was Alecu Constantinescu (born 1872). After 1908 he was elected to the leadership of the Social Democratic Party at every congress. Panait Istrati

---

[6] *Îndreptarea*, 14 July 1920.

paints his portrait as follows:

> "The only man who understood friendship in the same way as me and whom I love and treasure from the depths of my wounded heart, was Alecu Constantinescu. An upholsterer by trade, he had lived for about five years in Paris, and thanks to his sensitivity, culture and oratorical gifts he had become the only socialist militant with any influence over me ... Alecu was the archetype of the revolutionary ... He combined revolt with the tenderness of friendship ... Alecu was the bridge between the Party and myself. ... Alecu became my best friend."

Istrati also confesses,

> "When I was young, I sinned like you did. I believed in friendship, in art, in woman's faithfulness, and in the end I placed all my hopes in my child. Today everything is a graveyard ... Womanhood deceived me and I killed it. As for the child, my idol, well! In spite of a choice education, in the end he became a good-for-nothing, because he inherited the soul of his mother. Then I threw myself into the international socialist movement. I lived in Berlin, London and, mostly, Paris. ... For a man of awareness there is only one way to endure a devastating life: to do your duty and not to expect anything from anyone else."[7]

The portrait is generous, but false. Numerous historical facts contradict it. From 1918, Alecu Constantinescu led a clandestine Bolshevik network in Romania. He was an adept of terrorist methods, of political violence and insurrection. He organises repeated acts of subversion against the regime in Bucharest. From Russia he receives funds, comprising money and jewels; printing materials for propaganda; explosives; and guns. The police files reveal his close links with Racovski, in particular, and with other Bolshevik leaders. He was the leader of the clash of 13 December 1918, which resulted in 102 dead. In March 1919, he was sentenced to death *in absentia* at the trial brought against the instigators by the Court Martial of the Eleventh Army Corps. He is apprehended a year later, in July 1920, in Bucharest and arrested together with his nucleus of agitators. The Siguranţa thereby deals

---

[7] Panait Istrati, *Cum am devenit scriitor* [*How I Became a Writer*], Editura Florile Dalbe, 1998, pp. 214-216.

a heavy blow to the clandestine networks. They are left for the most part in disarray. Go-betweens, couriers and agitators are captured. Along with them, a printing press, guns and money. Alecu Constantinescu manages to escape on 2 December 1920 from Jilava prison with a group of communists. He flees to Russia. In the 1920s and 1930s he operates in the West, particularly in France, acting as an important Comintern agent. In 1935, he returns to Romania clandestinely. He lives in hiding until 1937, when he is arrested. Having been amnestied, in 1940 he is imprisoned once more in Caracal and Tîrgu Jiu. He dies in 1949.

With the arrest of Alecu Constantinescu in 1920, a chapter in the history of clandestinity comes to a close. Another similar moment is the arrest on 12 May 1921 of the delegates who voted to join the Comintern unconditionally at the congress to establish the PCdR. The hard core of the clandestine movement was annihilated for a time.

> "At the beginning of 1922, the illegal organisations no longer existed … in the Old Kingdom, and soon the final remnants of the political organisations in Bassarabia also ceased to exist. We were paralysed by a lack of money … In the area of the illegal movement we came back from nothing … we had to start everything again from scratch. We could no longer think about a serious new organisation until the legal one had at least been strengthened or, in principle, until we found the money required for the purposes of the illegal organisation."[8]

This was not only a consequence of the blows dealt by the Siguranţă. The revolutionary wave was now ebbing, after the failure of the Red Army in Warsaw in August 1920. The aftermath of the war was waning throughout Europe. The illusion nurtured by Lenin and Trotsky that a proletarian revolution would erupt outside Russia had quickly been shattered. Returning home, former soldiers and prisoners of war readapted to civilian life. The masses which the Bolsheviks had been able to manoeuvre – soldiers, prisoners of war – thus diminished radically. Deserters, the elements that had supplied the networks, were captured, tried and often amnestied. Against the grain of these changes, at the Second Congress of the Comintern in 1920, one of

---

[8] "Raport al Comitetului Provizoriu al PCdR către Comitetul Executiv Comintern, 1922," in *Copilăria Comunismului românesc în Arhiva Cominternului*, Bucharest: National Archives of Romania, 2001, p. 91.

the 21 conditions formulated by Lenin himself stipulated,

> "The class struggle is entering the phase of civil war. In such circumstances, the communists can place no trust in bourgeois legality. They are obligated to create everywhere and in parallel an illegal apparatus, which at the decisive moment will help the Party to fulfil its duty towards the Revolution."

Although he had lived in the West for 17 years, Lenin understood Europe very scantily and poorly. He wanted to exert strict control over the communist parties that were emerging and made use of his customary technique: splits. The groups that called themselves communist had to be completely separated from the old social democratic movement (which Lenin detested) and to adopt a 'revolutionary line'. This meant the use of violence to overthrow the 'rotten bourgeois regimes'. The operation had to be carried out strictly under his control and that of his men. With such goals, these groups came into conflict with democratic institutions and above all their instruments for self-preservation: the police, legal system, army etc. Hence Lenin needed to push them into the underground, where they would act clandestinely through conspiracies and terrorism. The professional revolutionaries acted in secret, controlled by the Comintern. To sustain such networks, with personnel of thousands of men in Europe alone, Lenin, Trotsky and Zinoviev allocated huge sums. Incapable of supporting themselves, the terrorists were financed from abroad. They were thus transformed into 'agents of a foreign power' – Russia – and no longer had anything in common with politics or political ideas, but rather with subversion.

In Romania things came about in exactly the same way:

> "Following the arrests [of 1921] it firstly came to light that all the so-called illegal 'party' groups had been trained for terrorism and secondly that they were in contact with illegal organisations in Bassarabia, where party activity, diversionary tactics and spying for the Soviet Union took place simultaneously ... Even to a child it was obvious that in all these terrorist organisations there swarmed a host of agents provocateurs."[9]

---

[9] *O anchetă stalinistă. Lichidarea lui Marcel Pauker, 1937-1938*, op. cit., pp. 140-141.

All the protagonists in the drama are present here. Firstly, there is an underground world, sparsely populated in spite of the Comintern's repeated attempts to expand it. The denizens of this world are reminiscent of Dostoevsky's *Demons*. They are political idiots, utopians, naïve idealists. But above all they are persons in the pay of Moscow, cadres whose wages are paid by the Comintern and GPU. For most of the agitators of these sects, revolution is a business. Instead of working in a factory or newspaper office, in a school or law firm, they prefer to become 'professional revolutionaries'. They integrate into various clandestine groups, because there are various sources of funding available in the field. For some it was not a business proposition but an adventure: a life of travel and danger. The Comintern provides political asylum elsewhere in Europe when the Siguranţă threatens them with arrest. It was a way of life, with safe houses, code words, aliases, forged passports, and secrecy. The following is a short commentary on the arrest of Alexandru Dobrogeanu-Gherea in January 1929, a few days after he had returned from Russia, a sign that the Siguranţă was perfectly informed. Gherea was apprehended in the Central Post Office, in disguise and carrying forged papers and letters in code. Again, the scene has its farcical elements.

"These last survivors of conspiracies, romantics rather than dangerous men, can no longer create a communist movement out of nothing. The workers have turned their eyes towards a paradise other than the red version across the Dniester. There is a difference of temperature between now and the climate of the years 1919-1923, when such delusions could still inflame spirits and the mood of the proletariat ... The agitators, with or without false beards, with or without glasses, and with their mysterious conspiratorial false names, operate within a closed circle, and they act out the comedy of conspiracy above all for themselves. They wave a red flag on the barricades their comrades have deserted. Obviously, Soviet Russia, for its proselytism, needs communist martyrs in Romania; it needs corpses and hunger strikes. Some volunteer out of self-interest, others out of revolutionary romanticism. Both categories are innocuous, however, for the agitators are concentrated in a closed circle. The arrest of Alexandru Dobrogeanu-Gherea and the eventual arrest of the other communists, Pauker, Finkelstein and co., ought not to exceed in importance any other act of police work. The government has no interest in manufacturing martyrs to the communist cause. It is merely a sundry news item and nothing more."[10]

Life in these secret societies was extremely difficult. Those in the underground have no identity. They are in permanent hiding. The rules of clandestinity are strict. They were in fact political sects eaten away by endless conflicts, by denouncements and provocations, by suspicions, by continual betrayals.

"I knew a few professional revolutionaries ... they are more elusive than the wind, more amorphous than dough, more unpredictable than chance, and more stupid than stones. They resemble religious fanatics, dogmatists. They are dogmatic, intransigent about trifles and lodestars that we laymen and free spirits cannot even see in the heavens ... These professionals are lethargic dogmatists and disagreeable fanatics. They have a head on their shoulders, but they don't use it to think, rather they use others' heads ... They have a soul, but they can become murderers however delicate and candid they might be."

Belu Zilber, a habitué of the underground, describes clandestinity and initiation into the world of the catacombs thus:

"The first step could be, for example, a small service performed for a friend, such as providing a house for a meeting with someone unfamiliar to the host, money to help people unjustly imprisoned, sending a parcel from one town to another, perhaps sheltering an innocent person wanted by the police ... These and other similar things, albeit requested in a whisper, under the seal of secrecy, gave the petty tradesman, the unhappy housewife, the young man sick of school and the petty functionary yearning for adventure the feeling that a door had opened on to a large and invisible power that was showing its trust in them, of whom no one had taken notice before. They became important in their own estimation, they began to acquire a heroic status. They shed the skin of those disinherited by fate and entered that of an important person, a keeper of great secrets ... After this beginning, there would follow an issue of the illegal *Scînteia*, read in a whisper and commented on by the emissary

---

[10] *Curentul*, 28 January 1929.

of the unseen power, then… the tale of heroic deeds, full of sacrifices, the grandeur of the five-year plan and magnificent victories. The more the person being worked on became separated from those around him thanks to the secrets he kept and the sense of his own importance, the more other tasks would follow, until his every free moment was taken up. Overwhelmed by the importance of his new persona, and without the habit of independent thought or other reading, the theses of the party, administered beneath the veil of conspiracy, became a treasure house of truths, entrusted not only to a reliable man, but to the hero he could admire in his own mirror. The ultimate truths were those revealed in the History of the Party (Short Course), typed up on yellowing paper and passed from hand to hand. By means of memorisation, the phrases glued themselves to his brain, becoming part of the cell tissue of the new man, who thereby possessed not only a heroic stature, but also the keys to the universe. It never crossed the mind of any of them that there might be other teachers apart from Stalin and the Party … With cast-iron logic it was proved to the aspirant that the deep illegality in which the Party found itself, surrounded by enemies that wanted to destroy it, obligated it to know everything about what each new tenant, each new Party member, did and thought. In the first place, it wanted to know the especially grave, criminal things which are confided neither to family nor girlfriend (murders, rapes, fraud, forgery, hidden vices, thefts, affairs). Not only those committed by aspirants, but also those concealed by people he was acquainted with… For how else could the Party defend itself? And the aspirant had to have more faith in the Party than he did in himself. Some hesitated or lied. The majority turned their souls inside out. They denounced themselves, their family and friends to the conspirators."[11]

What happened to the person who entered the underground? How did such a person change? What did he become?

"The frustrated man obsessed with his own advancement ceased to be anything other than a member of the great mystery. He dedicated himself to the Lord. He no longer had family or friends. He began a new life, without pity, without gratitude. He joined a community that could cast

---

[11] Belu Zilber, *idem*, pp. 26-27.

him into the rubbish or burn him at the stake. An ideologically motivated denunciation, in a gazette read by a few illegals and many policemen, or a mission to Moscow, used to put a stop to any velleity. The new persona of the man who had become a Party member was quickly consolidated by deeds whose meaning was known only to the invisible and unknown Party leadership … Politically, all these manifestations in general had as their effect nothing but arrests. But the arrests constituted a motive for another kind of mass activity. The assistance of those imprisoned was an activity that led only to fresh arrests and therefore gave rise to yet more activity … The man who had never in his life had a profession began to acquire one [that of professional revolutionary – *author's note*], and the one who had had a profession forgot it and retrained. He used to know a number of ideological formulas, rules of conspiracy; he knew how to organise a cell, how to control others' activity, how to receive and give orders, how to liquidate a competitor or opponent, how to behave toward superiors and inferiors, what to say and not to say. He had subordinates. He decided others' lives. Thus, he would become a professional of power and deteriorate the more he wielded it.

Even if before joining the Party he had been one of those in whom revolt against injustice and poverty seethed, perhaps also a love of his fellow man, the profession of activist would in time cause his sense of morality to atrophy. His peers would become objects. Something fundamental in his quality as a human would alter. His soul would be covered with a thick layer of insensibility towards other people, ideas, and feelings. He would become sombre, taciturn, unscrupulous, ruthless. Laughter changed to a hypocritical smile, humour to sarcasm, and criticism to mockery. They were like Dominican monks, ready to send people to heaven, to save their souls, ready sometimes even to be heroes themselves for the sake of this salvation. These were the professional revolutionaries. … These were the men educated to construct a world of happy people. They were devoid of any interest in abstractions or beauty. Innately bad and made worse by life, volunteers, without any profession, capable only of mental stereotypes, regardless of their social origins, they all felt frustrated within an open society.

The Party gave their life a meaning and certainty precisely like the Church once did. A small baggage of ideological formulas, the duty to hate, denounce and control minds and souls gave them a sense of success in life, of having power, of being what they wished to be: bearers of noble ideas and sentiments, important men. As in Biblical times, not all were called or chosen. Power has its own iron laws. Some lost patience; others were too vainglorious. Many were sent to the bottom of the ranks because others had risen. It happened that among them were also men who could not abide the absurdity and stupidity. They disappeared. Those who remained were the disinherited of the spirit, men obsessed with power. This breed of men has always existed... They did not arise, however, as a cruel force except when the new type of party was invented, which provided them with their ideological framework and the man to summon them to life. The Party was invented by Lenin. Stalin organised it and instilled discipline, and it was he that gave them power. He became their chief, and they became the new men. ..."[12]

The underground meant dehumanisation, alienation. It was a laboratory for producing hybrid humans, monsters, who went on to show what they were capable of after they seized power. For power was their obsession.

The orders came from afar. The local professional revolutionaries obeyed. Hierarchy and military discipline were the rule. At least in theory. Then there were the practical needs. All these operations were costly. Requests for money and expense claims sent to the Comintern are documents we frequently meet in the archives. Moscow maintained these networks at its own expense. The Party that was supposed to exist around these networks was in fact quasi-existent. The bills include the printing of manifestos and pamphlets, wages for the cadres, and the organisation of agitation. Legal, semi-legal and clandestine publications are bankrolled. Terrorist attacks are funded (the bomb in the Senate, the 'rebellion' at Tatar Bunar, train derailments, the blowing up of bridges or army munitions dumps). We discover Russian money involved in the strikes and protests orchestrated by the trades union leaders controlled by the Bolsheviks, as well as in the defence of communists brought to trial. The Comintern, whether directly or via other of its organisations – such as MOPR (Red Aid International) – hires lawyers, conducts press campaigns, pays for petitions, and organises protests and 'aid committees' both in Romania and abroad. Another aspect is that those who have worked for the Comintern are also connected to the GRU, the Soviet foreign intelligence agency. The

---

[12] Belu Zilber, *idem*, pp. 27-28.

Comintern is, from the very outset, the main centre for the recruitment of spies, agitators, terrorists, and experts in the proletarian revolution and for all kinds of conspiracies and diversions all over the world. In Moscow, they study in special schools, where they are instructed in the techniques of the putsch, terrorism, espionage, and propaganda. Then they are sent to their home countries, or other countries, where they operate from the underground to overthrow the democratic regime. The secrecy of these operations was illusory. In Bucharest, the Siguranța Generală has them under strict surveillance. They have lists with the names of agitators, their photographs and distinguishing features. In every city where they have been detected, there is a special bureau to keep track of them. Such groups are set up by individual Comintern agents arriving from Russia. As they emerge on the surface and reveal their presence, the Siguranța carries out raids and arrests. Printing presses are discovered, along with propaganda materials and/or stocks of arms and ammunition. Often, they identify persons who have been carrying out espionage in addition to agitation and propaganda. Painstaking investigations lead to the discovery of accomplices and the extent of the network is ascertained. The suspects are sent to military tribunals for trial. Thence they are sent to the prisons in Ocnele Mari, Aiud, Galați, and Doftana, after the obligatory stopover at Jilava or Văcărești. Dozens of clandestine groups, whether engaged in espionage, acts of terrorism, propaganda or Bolshevik agitation, were annihilated in this way. The authorities are well informed. Also because the communist networks are not numerous, and because the Siguranța has recruited many of the agitators in the pay of the Comintern.

The history of the inter-war Bolshevik underground is full of stories of betrayal to the authorities. None of the communists escaped the accusation of having worked for the Siguranța, of having been a traitor, of having sold out the comrades. The story of the assassination of Ștefan Foriș, head of the PCdR between 1940 and 1944, is one of betrayal. Gheorghiu-Dej and his acolytes – Bodnăraș, Maurer, Rangheț, Constantin Pîrvulescu, Iosif Chișinevschi and Teohari Georgescu – accused him of being a Siguranța informer. It was the gravest accusation that could be levelled at someone in the underground. The main charge in the indictment against Pătrășcanu and Koffler in 1954 was that they had been Siguranța agents and spies in the pay of the British intelligence service. In 1946 the PCdR was on the road to power. In 1954 it already held power. The reflexes acquired during the period of illegality continued to function. Conspiracy and secrecy were strong instincts. Although in power, Gheorghiu-Dej and the others acted as if they were still in clandestinity. No one could verify accusations of collaboration with the Siguranţă or espionage. And they were frequently employed against those who had fallen into disgrace. The unmasking of someone brought with it his exclusion or even murder. In 1946, at the headquarters of the CC of the PCdR, in the same room in which Foriş was murdered, Ion Zelea Pîrgaru, a former member of the Secretariat, proven to have been a Siguranţă informer, was also slain. Pîrgaru had provided information about the activities of Ana Pauker, Şmil Marcovici, and Dimităr Ganev, members of the Secretariat of the CC of the PCdR, which had led to their arrest in July 1935. Another informer with a lengthy career was Nicu Tudor. A participant in the Grivitza strike of 1933, during the investigation he agreed to pass information to the Siguranţă. He builds a career for himself in the PCdR apparatus, where he heads the Bucharest organisation, and later becomes a member of the Secretariat. Another informer was Petre Melinte, secretary of the PCdR Bucharest-Ilfov organisation, who in 1941 betrayed the Paneth-Kronhauser terrorist group. Ştefan Reich, a middle-ranking activist, hands over to the Siguranţă names and addresses which lead to the arrest in April 1941 of three of the five members of the Secretariat: Teohari Georgescu, Iosif Chişinevschi, and Gavrilă Birtaş, plus a number of members of the CC of the PCdR. An informer of long-standing was Sami Margulies. A communist from the early days, he was involved in a number of terrorist attacks, including a bomb planted in Ploieşti Station, intended for King Ferdinand. He is also mixed up in the bombing of the Senate. During the investigation, Margulies agrees to work for the Siguranţă. He is acquitted. He is a member of the PCdR leadership. He knows all the agitators in the upper echelons of the Party. In the 1920s, Margulies is the Siguranţă's most important informer within the PCdR. He writes for both the legal and the illegal communist press. After 1926, he is part of the leadership of the Peasant Workers Bloc, a legal organisation of the PCdR. He is one of the protagonists of the 'factional struggle' at the end of the 1920s, when he agitates the 'Otopeni group' (with Timotei Marin, Imre Aladár, et al.), independently of the two main rival factions, Marcel Pauker-Luximin vs. Vitali Kholostenko-Barbu. Margulies provides the Siguranţă with information about these disputes. In 1929, he is expelled from the PCdR, a punishment current in this period. It is also Margulies who provides information about the espionage activities of Victor Aradi and Belu Zilber in 1930.

There follows a trial, with harsh sentences. Belu Zilber, accused of espionage, also agrees to become an informer during the investigation. In return, he is acquitted. Margulies is arrested in 1948 on charges of having collaborated with the Siguranţă. When Belu Zilber is arrested, on the same charge, Sami Margulies is put in the same cell. Zilber's memoirs of this episode and the reports written by Margulies have been preserved. Similarly, Ladislau Ady had appeared in the dock in the trial brought against a group of 19 communists in 1936, with Ana Pauker topping the bill. Ady had been an important figure in the UTC networks and then among the communists in prison. He rose to the position of Deputy Minister of the Interior in the 1950s, only to be sacked in 1959. The reason: it was discovered that he had collaborated with the Siguranţă.

It should be mentioned that all the communists accused each other of being informers and provocateurs in the pay of the Siguranţă. No one escaped suspicion. The medium itself generated it. Pătrăşcanu was accused by Al. Mihăileanu and vice versa. Both of them were former leaders of the Socialist Youth Organisation. Ovidiu Şandor, a railway worker, Foriş's man in the Tîrgu Jiu prison camp, accused Pătrăşcanu of being a Siguranţă man while both were in detention. Later, he was brought forward as a witness for the prosecution in the trial of Pătrăşcanu in April 1954, repeating the same accusation. Ion Gheorghe Maurer, took the side of Ovidiu Şandor during the quarrel in the prison camp. Foriş, the head of the PCdR, was under suspicion by the communist agitators. In 1937, Elena Balogh, in charge of the Oltenia regional organisation, complained that she had been arrested as a result of betrayal by Foriş. The truth is that under interrogation she revealed everything she knew. In 1938, there are fresh allegations against Foriş. The proof was that he had been arrested and then released, after being taken into the office of Moruzov, the head of the special services, and invited to join forces in the fight against the Legionaries, 'our common enemy'. At that time, Foriş was working on the surface; he circulated freely. Moruzov had him picked up precisely in order to make this proposition to the communists.

The relationship between the communists and the special services was far from being clear. They were on different sides of the barricades. A strong ambiguity lingers to this day. Were there agreements and exchanges of information between the PCdR and Eugen Cristescu in the 1940s? There are contradictory accounts. Did Foriş make an agreement with Eugen Cristescu in July 1941, after the attack by the USSR, whereby Cristescu undertook not to send the communists to the front or to hand them over to the Gestapo? And did Foriş in exchange undertake not to carry out any terrorist activities behind the front lines? Foriş was never arrested in the 1940s, although a few times he was close to falling into the traps laid by the Siguranţă. Many saw in this proof that he was an informer, rather than that he was lucky or quite simply abided by the rules of clandestinity with the utmost strictness. He was accused that all the arrests of 1940-1944 had come about as a result of his treachery. The psychosis of betrayal, of infiltration by provocateurs, was extremely powerful. There was a host of informers, the networks were riddled with them, but no evidence of treachery on the part of Foriş was discovered, in spite of the meticulous investigations of 1946-1954, ordered by Gheorghiu-Dej after he had him murdered for the crime of collaborating with the Siguranţă. Nor did Gheorghiu-Dej escape from the suspicion of having been an informer. His exceptionally good relations with the authorities of the gaols through which he passed – Văcăreşti, Craiova, Ocnele Mari, Aiud, Galatzi, Doftana, Caransebeş, and the Tîrgu Jiu prison camp – caused him to be viewed with suspicion. Therein lay one of the sources of his power over other detainees. His recruitment, if this occurred, must have taken place in 1937, at Doftana, when Dej was convinced that the PCdR had abandoned him. We may never learn the truth. He personally destroyed his files in the archives at the beginning of the 1960s. Documents about Vasile Luca, a member of the Political Bureau and Secretariat between 1945 and 1952, have been preserved. Arrested in 1924, after the PCdR was outlawed, he agreed to collaborate with the Siguranţă. Like the others, he was given a salary. Luca had forged a career for himself in the unions controlled by the communists and in the PCdR. He had access to increasingly important information about Moscow's agents. He is placed under arrest for short periods, as a cover for his role, and then, naturally, released. After taking part in the organisation of the Grivitza strike, however, he is tried and handed down a long gaol sentence. The appeal did not result in an acquittal, as he had been expecting. His sentence was later reduced. On his release from prison, in the summer of 1939, he becomes a member of the Secretariat of the PCdR. To repay the Siguranţă, which had even made use of his services in prison, for its ingratitude, Luca refuses to play this double role any longer, arguing that he is 'too old'.

The tales of informers, betrayals and arrests are endless. The relationship between the Siguranţă and the communists is complicated. Officially, the two organisations hate each other, fight against one another. In reality, they intersect. Sometimes their interests coincide, sometimes not. The Siguranţă requires funds, and so it conjures up the spectre of Bolshevism, it uncovers plots, arms dumps, and large quantities of communist manifestos. The state of emergency imposed after the war extends into the 1920s and then 1930s. Domestic and foreign arguments are required in order to maintain it. The discovery of clandestine networks to overthrow the constitutional monarchy is always opportune. The communists also need the Siguranţă. First of all, because many of them are mere adventurers, ready to take payments from either side. They are financed by the Comintern and it is hard to check how these funds are being used. The Siguranţă is also prepared to pay, in return for information. The Comintern is always waiting for reports with information about underground activities. Arrests, heroic behaviour in prison, hunger strikes, and information slipped into the newspapers provide cover for the way in which the money sent by the Comintern via Vienna, Paris or Prague is being spent. This complicity characterised the relationship between the Siguranţă and the communists. Contrary to the myth of 'resistance on the part of the illegals' during Siguranţă investigations and the brutal treatment to which they were subjected by commissars, the truth is different. It was a close game in which each pursued his own interests. Take the following account, for example:

"Between the odious institution of the state Siguranţă and the Romanian communist movement there is an extensive bond of friendship … How otherwise can we interpret the fact that over the course of eight years of terror waged by Romulus Voinescu [the director of the Siguranţă – *author's note*], hundreds of anonymous workers have filled the prisons, serving 10-15-year sentences, accused of handing out clandestine manifestos, while notorious communist leaders such as Sternberg, Rozvany, Müller, and Mihăileanu have been unmolested by the repressive authorities? How are we to interpret the trial in Cluj [between September and October 1928, with 114 accused] where 40 simple workers were convicted, while the communist leaders got off with small fines? How are we to interpret the flight of the 10 communists headed by Pauker and Finkelstein [during the trial of 1926, when 16 communists were tried at liberty and fled abroad], when it is known that the Siguranţă accompanies you even to the toilet, not to mention when you try to cross the border clandestinely? Finally, how are we to judge the communist movement in Romania when ... every time a plot is uncovered, no matter how large or small, the communist bosses can be seen strolling down Calea Victoriei freely? When we claimed that the payrolls of the Siguranţă and the communists are muddled up, i.e. when we claimed that the Communist Party was not only on Moscow's but also Siguranţă's payroll, we knew that we were not committing calumny, we knew that we were telling the truth."[13]

The author of the article recalls the words of Virgil Madgearu and Alexandru Vaida-Voievod, both of them ministers. Madgearu had claimed that the Communist Party was a "wing of the General Siguranţă." "It may not have invented it," remarks *Socialistul*, agreeing with Madgearu and Vaida-Voievod, "but it did stimulate it; it did procure funds for it and men to carry out its 'plots'."

The PCdR existed in the form of small groups in one town or another, and these were ephemeral. The different centres had sporadic connections with each other and were rapidly annihilated by the Siguranţă. No sooner were the networks set up than they were discovered. The best-known communist leaders were wanted by various police forces throughout Europe. They were kept under strict surveillance. These leaders – Gherea, Ştefanov, Pauker, Pătrăşcanu, Finkelstein, Foriş et al. – travel frequently along the Moscow, Vienna, Berlin, Prague, Sofia, Bucharest route. They cross over frontiers clandestinely. They use assumed names and forged papers. On various occasions they are arrested and brought to trial. They are detained for short periods and freed by amnesty or after successive reductions in their prison sentences. The Siguranţă destroys all the networks in turn, in 1921, 1924, 1928, 1933, 1936, and so on. All these campaigns of arrests lead to the repeated disappearance of the PCdR. The Comintern makes new recruits, sends fresh agents, these too annihilated in a short space of time. Then everything starts all over again. At the Seventh Congress of the Comintern in 1935, Boris Ştefanov (who, under the name Draganov, was for a short time General Secretary of the PCdR), says,

---

[13] "Siguranţă şi comuniştii," in *Socialistul*, 16 December 1928.

"As regards the struggle against provocation and against infringement of the rules of conspiracy, only the initial steps have been taken. The comrades who are guilty of breaking the rules of conspiracy are brought to book and their mistakes are brought to the knowledge of all the members of the Party. Unfortunately, we have been forced to take severe measures against infringement of the rules of conspiracy and against members of the Party leadership. The rotten liberalism towards comrades who do not hold up well in front of the Siguranța and in court and who underestimate the importance of conspiracy has not yet been liquidated."[14]

In the underground, in the dark, dank labyrinth, in the clandestine networks, in fear of the lurking police, they nevertheless dream of the light of day. They see revolutions and hear explosions. They raise imaginary barricades. They unfurl fluttering red flags. Armed detachments of workers take the palaces of the monarchy and the bourgeoisie by storm. The crowds sing… To survive in the underground, such visions are imperative. From time to time, to rouse its agents from lethargy, the Comintern sounds the alarm and announces that the final hour of battle has arrived. Every few years, capitalism is on the verge of collapse and all that is needed is to lead the masses into the streets in order for the old world to come crashing down.

The Comintern fosters these illusions. It maintains a state of agitation. It gives the order to mobilise. The impression is that the working class, the same as in Russia, is on the brink of taking power, that democracy is in its death throes. Preparations for the great day are constantly being made. One example: in January 1934, the *Deșteptarea* (*The Awakening*) weekly in Detroit publishes a practical guide, with the title *The Fight to Conquer the Streets*, written by L. Alfred, translated from *The Communist International* (June 1931). It explains to the organisers of protest demonstrations what they have to do when confronting the police and crowds of extreme Right adversaries. It explains how and where to form columns, namely in working class districts, and whether or not barricades should be erected, and if so, how and where. It argues that the time for peaceful demonstrations is over. The bourgeoisie are arming in order to combat the proletarian masses, and the proletariat needs to do the same thing: "Demonstrations are exercises for civil war." The columns of demonstrators need to penetrate

---

[14] *Deșteptarea* (Detroit), 15 February 1936.

the bourgeois neighbourhoods, to reach the headquarters of power, not to scatter outside the city, through parks and green spaces, as happened in the past. The attention of the forces of law and order needs to be diverted. Demonstrations, although they are not yet armed insurrections, are a preparation for the demolition of the bourgeoisie and the seizure of power. A separate chapter is dedicated to the self-defence of the masses and their arming for the final battle.

In 1934, when this guide is published, in Bucharest there is no end in sight to the economic crisis that commenced in 1929, but rather a heightening of the crisis and of major social conflicts. 1933 had been the year of the Grivitza strikes, and the Comintern was hoping that this example would spread. It sends to Romania a detachment of a few dozen trained agitators, headed by Ana Pauker, Şmil Marcovici and Dimităr Ganev. This is also the reason for the publication of such instructions. The Siguranţă has been keeping a watch on this publication printed by Romanian communists in the USA, who are in contact with the Comintern, which also supplies them with funds. The paper regularly published official Comintern communiqués, PCdR documents, and texts by Romanian communists who have lived in the USSR. *The Awakening* is an "organ of revolutionary communist propaganda, prohibited from entering Romania."[15] This does not impede its distribution by underground or normal channels. Issues arrive in the post at the addresses of newspaper offices in Romania, whence they are collected by communist sympathisers.

---

[15] ANCR, Fund DGP/1936, Dossier 148, p. 27.

V
Campaigns

> Because ledgers are good only for recording the dead.
> *Panait Istrati*

Up until September 1924, when the newspaper headlines screamed "Terror in Bassarabia" and "Soviet attacks in southern Bassarabia[1]," Tatar Bunar was a Russian-majority fishing village in southern Bassarabia[1] no one had ever heard of what happened?

"In Tatar Bunar (Cetatea Alba County) gangs of bandits armed with rifles and machine guns entered the village during the course of the night between Monday and Tuesday, wreaking unprecedented terror. The bandits first of all went to the post office, which they set on fire, cutting all the telephone and telegraph wires. Then they began to roam up and down the village, firing in every direction. The doors and windows of numerous buildings were broken. The terrified population ran into the street shouting for help. The bandits fell upon the citizens, killing them and robbing them. Many citizens were wounded in their own homes. The village was under a siege of terror the whole night, during which time the bandits stole everything they could lay their hands on. The number of the dead and wounded is not yet known, because all communications with Tatar Bunar have been cut off and the authorities have not been able to relay details very quickly. What is certain is that the postmaster was killed. Towards daybreak the bandits' motor cars left the village, sowing the same terror in other villages as they went. … The latest version of events relates that some villagers in Tatar Bunar and Cișmea, probably accomplices of the bandits or foreign interlopers, are fraternising with them, helping them in the looting and destruction. In Cișmea, the bandits attacked the gendarme post with the assistance of the villagers. Up to now, it is not known where the bandits came from. Given the gravity of the situation, cavalry and infantry troops have been sent to Tatar Bunar."[1]

---

[1] *Universul*, 18 September 1924.

Two days later:

> "Cetatea Alba. Bolshevik bandits … it seems they were 40 in number. The bandits did not cross the Dniester by the ferry, but advanced along the coast and disembarked on the beach. Then, probably with the assistance of locals, they advanced in carts along the highway from Sagauna to Tatar Bunar via Tropocle. The bandits were armed with machine guns, rifles and grenades. The gendarmes, taking refuge in the neighbouring village of Sărata, informed the authorities by telephone of the attack under way. … A part of the population, Bulgarians and Russians, tried to fraternise with the Bolshevik bandits. A part of the bandits were arrested."[2]

On 26 September, in Berlin, the press agencies announced that Leon Trotsky, the commander of the Red Army, had given a speech to Soviet troops along the border with Bassarabia in which he threatened Romania, saying, "either the Romanians evacuate Bassarabia of their own free will, or they will soon feel the might of the proletarian regiments of the Red Army."

Romania was not the only country under attack by such commando units along its border. Estonia and Poland were also the targets of terrorist incursions. The scenario was identical. Armed Soviet agents in civilian clothes penetrated border areas. They were joined by Bolshevik cells already operating there clandestinely and formed especially for this purpose. They attacked administrative buildings and border and gendarme posts. They caused the maximum commotion, firing continuously. They raised the red flag over official buildings. Then the local population would "fraternise" with the Soviet agitators. In Tatar Bunar, it was announced that Bassarabia had gone over to the Soviets, that there was a revolution, and that the Red Army was on its way. The more victims the better. It was a demonstration of 'violent revolution in action' and the 'ferocity of the reprisals' unleashed by the authorities.

The incident was intended to provoke a precise response in the Western press. Moscow could claim that the local population had risen up against the authorities. Thus, there was an ethnic and territorial problem, and Moscow was justified in intervening to pursue its interests. As Moscow had not recognised the Versailles agreements, it had additional reasons for

---

[2] *Universul*, 20 September 1924.

these rebellions. Incidents of the Tatar Bunar kind were diversions that served pro-Soviet propaganda in the West. In addition, the creation of a Moldavian Soviet Republic on the east bank of the Dniester was a more precise indication of these interests.

The ultimate reaction of the Romanian authorities was to outlaw the PCdR in December 1924, under the Mîrzescu Law, and to arrest all known communist agitators in Romania, amounting to a few hundred persons, plus those operating in southern Bassarabia. In September, however, the authorities' reaction was late in coming, due to the isolation of the region. The five-minute Soviet Republic was nonetheless annihilated. Drastic security measures are taken. The area is cordoned off. The gendarmes, police and army bring the situation back under control. The advance party is pushed back over the Dniester. Most of the attackers are either killed or captured. Investigations are carried out in the villages where the mostly ethnic Russian and Bulgarian population revolted. In the climate of heightened tension, violence and abuse is perpetrated by the gendarmes and army.[3]

Five hundred persons are transported to Chişinău for interrogation. A year later there follows a trial, extensively covered in the press. 285 persons are accused. The verdict: 85 acquittals, 200 convictions, with punishments ranging from life imprisonment, hard labour (Justin Botishchev), 15 years imprisonment (Leonte Ţurcan, Nikita Lisovoy), 10 years (Petre Grozdiev, Grigorie Bunovski, Petre Kavalenko), etc. There are three months of deliberations, hearings, appeals. There is extensive coverage in the press. Also present are foreign journalists, Western intellectuals, and lawyers sent by various organisations. For Moscow it is another exercise in the propaganda war waged throughout Europe. Having been the victim of aggression, Romania now appears as a dictatorial regime and aggressor nation, a 'bloody oligarchy' against which the peasantry is rebelling. It appeared as a state that oppressed its ethnic minorities, an occupier of territories that did not belong to it, and became the target of a major campaign financed by the Comintern. Large sums are spent funding this campaign. Sympathy is purchased in the press and among politicians. Protests by various associations controlled by the communists – even if only temporarily, until the funds reached their destination – are bankrolled. A pamphlet by C. G. Costa-

---

[3] See *Documente străine despre Basarabia şi Bucovina, 1918-1944*, Bucharest: Vremea, 2003, pp. 50-70.

Foru, entitled *The Abuses and Crimes of State General Security* (1925) is funded, and quickly published in translation in Paris and Berlin. The pamphlet served as 'evidence' in the campaign. It is reviewed, disseminated, and cited by the entire pro-Soviet Left. It is published by the League for the Defence of Human Rights, whose Secretary General was C. G. Costa-Foru, and consists of a collection of depositions by the communists arrested in December 1924, when the PCdR was outlawed, who complain that they have been subjected to psychological pressures and even tortured. They include Ana Pauker, Vasile Luca, Elena Filipescu and Imre Aladár. The author collects this information during the enquiry. C. G. Costa-Foru presents no other position or official documents. The testimonies of the communists, made according to the Comintern rule book, were reproduced per se by foreign journalists and various committees controlled by the Soviets in Western Europe. They are used as propaganda material in the campaigns of disinformation required by Bolshevik agitation. One example: the communists accused were brought to trial after painstaking investigations, often arrested in flagrante and carrying as evidence against them large quantities of Bolshevik printed materials, clandestine printing presses and sometimes weapons and explosives. They are always defended by some of the best-known lawyers (Ella Negruzzi, Lizetta Gheorghiu, V. V. Stanciu, et al.). C. G. Costa-Foru mentions none of this. In a report addressed to the leadership of the Balkan Bureau of the Red Aid International organisation, we find the following:

"The executive committee accords great attention to the important trials in Romania. To the trial of the Central Committee of the Communist Party we have sent two defence lawyers from abroad. To the trial of the peasants from Tatar Bunar we have sent three lawyers, a Frenchman, an Italian and a Czechoslovak. During the trials in Bucharest and Chișinău, the Central Committee of the Red Aid International organisation printed two pamphlets (edited by Costa-Foru, a well-known social figure in Romania), and during the trial in Chișinău it printed a weekly bulletin."[4]

International Red Aid, founded in September 1924, was controlled and financed by the Comintern. It went by the name MOPR (Международная Организация Помощи Борцам Революции). At the date of the Tatar Bunar

---

[4] The National Archives of Romania, *Copilăria Comunismului românesc în arhiva Cominternului*, Bucharest, 2001, p. 172.

trial, it had between 1,200 and 1,500 members. It was well financed and operated clandestinely. It dealt with communist detainees, their defence in court, aid parcels for communist prisoners and their families, and campaigns for their release. In the same report it is mentioned that MOPR received 1,500 U.S. dollars a month from Moscow, "besides sums destined for trials, the printing of pamphlets, and bail for those under arrest."[5] In professional circles in Bucharest, it did not go unnoticed that Costa-Foru's pamphlet was more than a mere attempt to defend human rights. The Comintern, i.e. Soviet interests, lay behind this façade. The Journalists' Union expelled the author in December 1925, and so did the Society of Romanian Writers. Costa-Foru was a prominent public figure. He had made his debut in the 1880s as a journalist and lawyer. He had also been involved in politics, with various groups. Had he been won over by the Bolshevik cause? Was he a fellow traveller? Had he been bought? Today, it is hard to say. That the pamphlet was ordered and paid for by the Comintern is proven, however.

He was not the only one to get caught up in this dangerous game. Another example of an intellectual connected with and financed by the Comintern is N. D. Cocea (born 1880, in Bîrlad). His newspaper, *Facla*, appears on the list of newspapers published by the PCdR. Boris Ştefanov writes to the Secretariat of the Executive Committee of the Comintern on 21 October 1924 as follows:

"The Party's legal Romanian-language newspaper *Facla* is published under the guise of a republican newspaper run by N. D. Cocea. The publication of this newspaper demands many sacrifices, but they are absolutely necessary in a period when the poverty of the working class is continually growing and not one other newspaper cares about the interests of the working man. In order to make the publication of the Party's newspaper possible, capital of 200,000 lei had to be laid out, and besides this sum, around 50-60,000 lei are needed to keep the newspaper running."[6]

From Moscow, on 11 December 1924, Iosif Piatnitzki (secretary of the Comintern) writes to the presidium of the Balkan Communist Federation,

---

[5] *Idem*, p. 171.
[6] CC of the PCR Archive, Fund 1, Dossier 209, p. 2.

"The issue of *Die Fackel* (*Facla*). We are afraid that the position of the presidium, as expressed in written statement no. 50, has prevented the comrades from printing *Die Fackel* (*Facla*) newspaper. We likewise know who N. D. Cocea was and is and we know that the publication of the newspaper, as it is claimed under his direction, is continually exposed to danger. However, we are convinced that in today's conditions (terror and economic-political crisis) we are heading towards a greater danger if we (i.e. the Communist Party) are silent than if we speak in the name of N. D. Cocea. For the time being, the Central Committee of the PCdR should declare itself satisfied with the provision of editing and administration, which we have been informed is the case. If you are in agreement with this write immediately to Bucharest."[7]

N. D. Cocea, along with Gheorghe Cristescu (at that date PCdR representative to the Executive Committee of the Comintern) and others, was a member of the leadership committee of the Peasant-Worker Bloc (Blocul Muncitoresc-Ţărănesc–BMŢ), a legal front organisation for the PCdR. The BMŢ was set up in the autumn of 1925, while the trial in Chişinău and the Comintern campaign were still unfolding. In the pages of *Facla* we can find articles by many communist agitators. Throughout the campaign they supply pro-Soviet propaganda materials, whose texts are provided by foreign communist networks. *Facla* expressed the viewpoints of the Comintern and the PCdR. Ilie Moscovici, a social democrat leader and long-time acquaintance of N. D. Cocea, writes in one article,

"In order to have a daily gazette and to be able to wage campaigns against us, our communists have agreed to subsidise and work for N. D. Cocea's *Facla* and to co-opt him into the BMŢ committee, which today stands in for the Communist Central Committee. In this comradeship with N. D. Cocea, the masked collapse of the communists has become all the more profound. This man, who has lived his entire life by blackmail and fraud, who, without any positive labour, has possessed countless millions, placing that money at the disposal of greedy politicians and blackmailing public and society figures, could not be satisfied with the limited sums available from the communists to sustain the gazette. A man who lives a life of debauchery, with large outlays, Cocea has always

---

[7] *Idem*, Fund 1, Dossier 253, p. 43.

required larger and larger sums."[8]

N. D. Cocea was in very close relations not only with the communists, but also with Mihai Moruzov, the head of the army's secret service. He was on his payroll. It is not clear whether *Facla* received stipends or whether Cocea was paid only for specific services. In any case, he was the newspaper's owner. Let us say that he was perfectly informed about the situation of the Left, from the Social Democrats to communists of varying hues (Bolsheviks, Stalinists, Trotskyites). He knew all the leaders and many of the cadres personally. He had been a PSD member before the war, and for a while had even been in the leadership. He had made a name for himself with virulent newspaper attacks, aimed primarily against the Liberals, the Brătianu family and the monarchy. He had been convicted of *lèse-majesté* as a result of an article against King Ferdinand. In the mid-1930s, N. D. Cocea joined the National Liberal Party, and was close to the group led by Tătărescu, Prime Minister at the time, as well as to circles in the Royal palace. In the meantime he had become a sympathiser of the monarchy, or rather of King Carol II. How sincere he was in this we do not know. Anyway, he also received stipends from the palace. He frequented palace circles and those of Elena Lupescu, which did not prevent him from printing crypto- and pro-communist gazettes financed by the Comintern, such as *Chemarea* (*The Call*) and *Era nouă* (*The New Era*). He remains just as close to Mihai Moruzov, and the two visit each other. He is also close to the communist leaders, especially Ştefan Foriş, after his release from prison in 1935. Foriş is number two in the PCdR hierarchy, the head of the propaganda section, and is thus in charge of press operations. N. D. Cocea collaborates with him. In 1940, during the Soviet-German pact, the SSI has information that *Facla*, up until then a weekly publication, is going to be financed as a daily by the Soviet legation,[9] with Cocea to be director of the newspaper. In the 1940s, Cocea takes refuge in Sighişoara. As a man with close ties to the communists, Carol II and Mihai Moruzov (murdered in Jilava Prison in November 1940 by the Legionaries) – all of whom were despised by the Antonescu regime – N. D. Cocea is marginalised in this period. He is not interned in a prison camp, unlike many of his acquaintances. He returns to public life in the autumn of 1944. In 1945 he becomes president of the Journalists' Union, acting as the

---

[8] "Amoralitatea comuniştilor," *Socialistul*, 8 November 1925.
[9] ANC, CC of the PCR Archive, Fund 1, PCM, SSI, Dossier 51, p. 45.

communists' man. He will survive for a year after they take complete power. He dies on 1 February 1949.

The campaign organised by the Comintern in 1925 against the Tatar Bunar trial is of the greatest amplitude. In the West, that is, not in Romania. Romania was too small a world to be the real target of the campaign. In the West, signatures are gathered. Support committees are set up for 'the revolting peasants' who are protesting "against the terror unleashed by the Brătianu government." Thus, for example, on 15 September, in Berlin, Red Aid and the Human Rights League, two organisations controlled by the Comintern, assemble hundreds of people in the Friedrichshain Hall. It is in fact a ceremony of stigmatisation. The speakers deplore the situation in 'oppressed Bassarabia' and the conditions for minorities there. The ritual is the same and is orchestrated by the propagandists. German communist-controlled newspapers report the event, announcing that in other cities similar protest meetings will be held. The operation is co-ordinated by Willy Münzenberg. He has his headquarters in Berlin, whence he organises protest meetings using a vast network of agitators. 'Brătianu's regime of terror' is universally vilified by the Left, in the press and political circles. The letter signed by, among others, Romain Rolland, André Gide, Albert Einstein, Henri Barbusse and Panait Istrati has the greatest impact. It is not the only such letter. In Germany, Czechoslovakia, Belgium and Britain signatures are collected from intellectuals with Soviet sympathies. They deplore the fate of the 'revolting peasants of Tatar Bunar' and the repression ordered by the Bucharest regime. The signatories are politically naïve. They are unaware that Moscow agitators and funds are behind the campaign. Others quite simply have a vested interest; they have been bought or are 'fellow travellers'. They condemn the abuses of the Romanian authorities, the lack of any right to self-defence, the lack of democratic political rights, and the treatment of detainees in prison.

The same intellectuals so concerned about human rights and the infringement of civil liberties did not protest against any of the trials the Bolshevik regime brought against the Orthodox Church, intellectuals or opposition militants in the 1920s and again in the 1930s. It is paradoxical that many of those defended by such committees and protest meetings, convicted by the Romanian legal system according to democratic procedures and frequently amnestied, were later convicted in Soviet show trials and executed (Marcel Pauker, Alexandru Dobrogeanu-Gherea, David Fabian

Finkelstein, etc.). Naturally, neither Romain Rolland, nor Albert Einstein, nor any of the others wrote a single word in their defence. They did not travel to the USSR to investigate the manner in which the trials were conducted, to observe whether human rights were respected. The ideology of 'man's liberation by a worldwide proletarian revolution' and the cult of Stalin were far too powerful anaesthetics. The complicity, as well as the blindness, was vast and often not at all innocent. The Comintern spent enormous sums so that the 'fellow travellers' would remain anaesthetised.

One fellow traveller in this period was Panait Istrati. In the 1920s, Istrati was involved in all the protest campaigns against the Bucharest government. He presents himself as a Bolshevik and adversary of the Romanian oligarchy. The Tatar Bunar campaign is one example. In August 1925, before the trial commences in Chişinău, Istrati arrives in Bucharest. He had been out of the country since 1916.

When he left he was a nobody, a working-class drifter. On his return, he was a writer published in Paris, a successful man, regarded by Romain Rolland, in the catchphrase that made his career, as a 'Gorki of the Balkans'. Translations of his books began to be published in Bucharest, first of all those with Romanian subjects: *Old Man Anghel* and *Kira Kiralina*, which go through numerous print runs. For the Siguranţă, however, he is a "communist agent," connected since his early youth to Alecu Constantinescu, Mihai Gheorghiu Bujor, and Cristian Racovski.

As we have seen, Racovski was an implacable enemy of the Romanian constitutional monarchy and state. Alecu Constantinescu had been the head of the clandestine terror networks between 1918 and 1920. He was arrested, escaped, was sentenced to life imprisonment by a Romanian court, and lived in Paris, where he worked as a Comintern agent. Mihai Gheorghiu Bujor was sentenced to life and imprisoned at Doftana. In France, Istrati was the vice-president of an association financed by the Comintern, 'Friends of the Soviet Union', and frequently took part in protest meetings against Romania organised by left-wing groups. He was the author of countless articles vehemently attacking the 'oligarchy' in Bucharest. He had made his alignment with Bolshevism public as early as 1917, when he published an article entitled *Tolstoyism and Bolshevism* in *La Feuille*, a Swiss newspaper. The Siguranţă had information about his contacts with the Soviet ambassador to Paris, Cristian Racovski, as well as with other Romanian communists, for example Alecu Constantinescu.

He returns to Romania at the beginning of the 'Tatar Bunar Revolt' trial. The newspapers treat his visit as an important event – he was the most famous living Romanian writer. He is interviewed; reviews and articles are written about his work. Istrati is also incommodious. He makes declarations that provoke strong antipathy. In addition, he has the reputation of being a Bolshevik and an implacable foe of the Brătianu regime. For the Siguranță, he is not so much a famous writer as much as a dangerous communist agitator. As soon as he crosses the border, the reports start to come in:

"We have the honour to signal that communist writer (journalist) Panait Istrati, has lately arrived from Paris … According to our information, Panait Istrati's voyage to Romania has as its aim the creation of a close link between French and Romanian communists. In any case, the above-named has visited, since arriving in Romania, the cities of Buzău, Brăila, Galatzi, Focşani and Jassy, where he has made contact with all the communists there. To disguise the purpose of his visit to Jassy, he has had numerous meetings with novelist Mihail Sadoveanu and other writers. In Paris, where he has his domicile and where he will return, one month from now, he has carried on vigorous activity in the communist group there, being a member of the editorial board of the socialist-communist newspaper *L'humanité*. In the pages of this newspaper he has waged a violent campaign of denigration against Romania."[10]

General security keeps him under close surveillance. He is shadowed everywhere he goes. Today, it is possible to reconstruct, day by day, every meeting he had and everywhere he went. His visit is covered in detail by the press. For some, Istrati is a great writer, for others, a traitor, Bolshevik and communist agent. Istrati would have liked to be received exclusively as a famous writer, to enjoy his popularity. His violent articles against Romania published in the pro-Bolshevik press earned him enemies in various sections of society. The commentaries that accompany his visit to Romania are highly political, from right-wing nationalist to left-wing Cominternist. We find every shade of opinion, from *Universul* to *Adevărul* and *Dimineaţa*, to *Lupta* and *Curentul*. He also receives threats. The police consider it most prudent to provide him with an escort of two

[10] ANC, CC of the PCR Archive, Fund 95, Dossier 5, 796, vol. 1.

agents for protection. Any aggression against him would have provoked undesired reactions from Paris. Obviously, the agents also kept him under surveillance. The atmosphere surrounding him is inflamed. He is forced to cancel a number of public appearances. His situation causes him to cancel his trip to Chişinău to follow the Tatar Bunar trial, as he had planned. He cuts short his visit. On 3 October, he leaves Romania on the Orient Express, via the border crossing at Curtici. He had also come to Romania to see the grave of his mother, who had passed away six years previously. This was the official, humane reason. He failed to reach Chişinău, where he had been due to report on the trial for *L'Humanité*. He did, however, achieve another aim of his visit: Istrati had come to Romania not only to carry out the customary 'revolutionary agitation', but also to pave the way for the visit of Henri Barbusse, the president of the 'Association for the Fight against White Terror in the Balkans'. Istrati was an active and vocal vice-president of the association. The association was one of the many phantom organisations controlled and financed by the Comintern and was based in Paris. Most often, money and orders were sent through the Soviet embassy, from Racovski directly to Istrati. The two had known each other since their youth. Before his arrival in Romania, Istrati had spent three weeks at Miramar, Barbusse's villa on the Côte d'Azur, in order to finalise the details of the campaign and his trip.

Henri Barbusse was at that time a celebrated author. Having made a name for himself with his novel *Le Feu* (1917), he cut the figure of a militant for various benevolent causes. He was an influential intellectual. He was accustomed to getting involved in various pacifist protests and 'humanitarian' campaigns. He was a communist. We know today that he worked for the Comintern and was paid a stipend by Moscow. A few weeks after Panait Istrati's departure, Barbusse arrives in Romania "to investigate the situation for political prisoners in Romanian prisons, the judicial system" and the "progress of the Tatar Bunar trial." He visits a number of newspaper offices, including *Adevărul* and *Dimineaţa*. The Romanian authorities are intimidated by the writer's celebrity. Barbusse is received three times by Foreign Minister I. Gh. Duca, and by Gh. Tătărescu, Under Secretary of State in the Interior Ministry. A number of newspapers protest. The government is forced to answer questions in Parliament. Tătărescu declares to the press that he received Barbusse because of the poor impression it would have made on France if he had refused to meet him. Duca and Tătărescu provided him with information about Soviet activities along the Dniester, about infiltration by Soviet agents and the provocations in Bassarabia. Barbusse's show of being an independent, humanist intellectual there to investigate the human rights situation in a country 'under terror' was nothing but a façade. In fact, Barbusse was an agent of influence working for Moscow. He was in Bucharest on a mission paid for by the Comintern. The first item on his agenda was the propaganda campaign the Comintern was waging in the West. The hosts of adherents, fellow travellers, accomplices, and the gullible always had to have a cause to defend. Now it was Tatar Bunar. After his meetings with I. Gh. Duca and Gh. Tătărescu, Barbusse travels to Chișinău, where he attends a session in the Tatar Bunar trial. He returns to the capital, where he meets with the small world of the Bucharest Reds, at No. 10 Șelari Street, the headquarters of the (Communist) United Unions. Here he is greeted by Solomon Schein, at that time the number two in the PCdR hierarchy, by I. Kanner, recently released from Doftana Prison, after being involved in the Senate bomb attack and by Gheorghe Vasilescu Vasia, another well-known communist. After leaving a public auditorium on Calea Victoriei, accompanied by a group of sympathisers, Barbusse is confronted by passers-by and demonstrators (nationalist students) on Edgar Quinet Street, outside the Capșa Restaurant. The incident is provoked by Barbusse's companions, who start chanting communist slogans. Barbusse prefers to leave in a cab, rather than continue along Calea Victoriei on foot. That evening, there is a demonstration in front of the Athénée Palace Hotel, where he is staying. The demonstrators shout, "Down with Barbusse!" and "Leave!" The police intervene. Barbusse was particularly eager for his visit to cause uproar. Agitation was the main feature of Leninist propaganda. And it must be said he succeeded. Anonymity and indifference would have meant failure for Barbusse and his two companions (Paul Lamy, a lawyer from the Appeals Court in Brussels, and a certain Vernouchet, Secretary General of the Intellectual Workers International).

The reactions of the press are contradictory. A few journalists view the visit in a relaxed way. Most attack him, regarding the investigation as a slap in the face for Romania and immixture in domestic affairs. It does not escape others that, beyond his visiting card as a great writer, Barbusse was doing a service to the Soviets. For Ion Vinea, who interviews him for *Facla* (18 November), Barbusse is "a man without a face and without a body, he is an illusory column upon which rests not a mask but a nimbus. On seeing him you think of Da Vinci's *Last Supper* in which the visage of Christ is a faint light in which the human features have been erased."

In *Universul* (22 November), Romulus Şeişanu writes, in an article entitled *Who speaks in the name of public opinion in the West? The Barbusse case*,

"Who has authorised him to conduct an investigation in Romania? Western public opinion? World opinion? The Third International, whose principles he shares and whose methods he does not oppose? We know that the Russian Soviets are directly interested in the Tatar Bunar affair and desire to present the rebellion set in motion over the Dniester as a result of discontent directed against the Romanian regime."

In *Adevărul* (21 November), B. Brădişteanu writes,

"M. Barbusse is not the emissary of a foreign government. Behind him stand no battalions. He is a free writer. … We are not the only country where writers and journalists conduct such investigations … Such abuses and illegalities cannot compromise a nation, but only their perpetrators."

Also in *Adevărul*, (25 November 1925), Constantin Bacalbaşa responds,

"Why does he not investigate the country where for eight years there has been no freedom, no newspaper with opinions against the current rulers, no democratic institutions? Why does he not intervene when political prisoners are shot? Why does he not protest against the unjust system there? Why, today, does no member of any group of intellectuals go to Russia to investigate? For it is there where the real dramas are taking place."

Constantin Bacalbaşa goes further still. He demands that the Romanian Journalists' Union condemn Barbusse's visit. Although he is director of *Adevărul*, he publishes this call in *Universul*. The episode marks a rupture between Bacalbaşa and *Adevărul*, for which he had worked since before the war, at the time when it was run by Constantin Mille. On 26 November 1925, Henri Barbusse leaves Bucharest from the Northern Station on the train to Constanţa and boards the King Carol, bound for Constantinople.

"He was accompanied, from Bucharest to Constanța, by two inspectors from the Siguranță," a press communiqué drily reports.

A collateral effect of Barbusse's visit: long-standing lawyer C.G. Costa-Foru is made a scapegoat. The headline in *Universul*: "The Stool Pigeon." The article is a commentary on his pamphlet *The Abuses and Crimes of State General Security*. The Romanian Journalists Society (Societatea Ziariștilor din România–SZR) raises the question of C.G. Costa-Foru's attitude, taking into account the pamphlet and his 'anti-Romanian' attitudes in 1925 during the Tatar Bunar trial and Barbusse's visit to Bucharest. He is expelled from the SZR. The board of directors, which does not support the motion, resigns, not wishing to get mixed up in 'politics'. The atmosphere is tense. A group of extreme Right students beats up C.G. Costa-Foru in Cluj railway station. Reactions from the West are not long in coming. Protests are sent to Prime Minister Ionel I.C. Brătianu. On the other hand, on 16 December a number of newspapers publish a *Protest of the Romanian Writers Society addressed to the Public Opinion*. The text employs solemn, jingoistic rhetoric. Firstly it recalls the two thousand-year sufferings of the Romanian people and, naturally, the creation of Greater Romania in 1918. And then it comes to the point:

"Men posing as inspectors of humanity are roaming the length and breadth of Romania, and having received our generous hospitality, they disseminate abroad stories culled from agents of anarchy sheltering in this country. These bizarre inspectors have two measures: all-encompassing sympathy towards terrorists, rebels and conspirators and wilful ignorance towards the Romanian victims who are not lowered into their graves draped in the red flag."

The inspectors of humanity "did not have a single word of reproach to say when Soviet agents planted a bomb in the Romanian Senate ... likewise they could not find a single word whereby even to mention the thousands of Romanian soldiers villainously killed on the banks of the Dniester ... We the undersigned protest with the full indignation of our consciences against the campaign of methodical denigration that the centuries-old tools of the oppression of the Romanian people have been waging in the name of false humanitarianism against our nation. At the same time we make the warmest appeal to world opinion in the name of justice to reject all the biased machinations and infamous actions that have been attempting to alienate us from the sympathies of the rest of the world, in order to be able to make a direct assault on our independence."

The list of signatories is long. Just a few of the famous names: Liviu Rebreanu, Octavian Goga, Tudor Vianu, Camil Petrescu, Vasile Voiculescu, Nichifor Cainic, M. Sorbul. The naïvety of such an endeavour is obvious. Its results were negligible. Which public opinion did it address? The campaigns of which Barbusse was a part were conducted by the Comintern and strictly served the interests of the Bolshevik regime.

A year later we find the 'Tkachenko affair', and then, in 1928, the trial of communists held in Cluj. For 13 years, between 1920 and 1933, Mihai Gheorghiu Bujor was a good pretext for mobilising public opinion in Moscow's favour. In the 1930s, Bucharest is the setting for two major 'movement' causes: the trials of the CFR workers in 1933 and 1934 and the trials of Petre Constantinescu-Iași and Ana Pauker in 1935-1936. These causes were adopted by the Comitern's propaganda machine, run by Karl Radek, and manipulated for Western audiences by Willy Münzenberg and his men. The latter controlled a host of crypto-communist newspapers, publishing houses and associations. They carried on professional agitation, exercised by an experienced apparatus. In all these affairs, the name of Henri Barbusse continues to crop up, until his death in Moscow in 1935. His final work was a biography "about the greatest man history has ever known," i.e. Stalin. The Comintern paid him handsomely for it. Echoes of his 1925 trip to Romania can be heard a few months later in his book *Les Bourreaux* (*The Torturers*).[11] It is a work of pure Soviet propaganda, in which the Romanian constitutional monarchy and the Brătianu government are castigated. One sordid little detail given away by the book is that the printing of C.G. Costa-Foru's pamphlet was financed by Red Aid.

Another underground figure about whom Istrati writes is Pavel Tkachenko-Antip. Istrati did not know him personally, but a campaign on his behalf was organised in Paris in 1926. What was the reason? In Bucharest, Pavel Tkachenko had been arrested together with Boris Ștefanov. A third man, Timotei Marin, had been captured by the Siguranța but managed to escape. He then took shelter in the home of C.G. Costa-Foru. A fourth man, Elek Köblős, the head of the PCdR at the time, managed to elude the trap laid by the Siguranța. All of them were members of the Political Bureau

---

[11] Henri Barbusse, *Les Bourreaux*, Paris: Flammarion, 1926.

of the PCdR Secretariat. They were living clandestinely, receiving money from the Comintern, and were hunted by the Siguranţă. The arrests led to the unravelling of the PCdR for a long period.

Who was Pavel Tkachenko? He was a Ukrainian, born near Kiev in 1899. Tkachenko had studied philosophy in Petrograd. In 1917, he became a Bolshevik and after 1918 he worked under Racovski in Kharkov. He crosses the Dniester into Romania clandestinely, organises acts of subversion (he is part of the same terrorist group as Max Goldstein, the perpetrator of the Senate bombing) and is arrested. During his escape from prison in Chişinău he kills a soldier. He is sentenced to death *in absentia*. He flees to Kiev and then Kharkov, where he receives new orders from Racovski. He returns to Romania to lead the clandestine network in Bassarabia. He is arrested in Jassy in March 1920, when police uncover the printing press he has brought from Russia, along with explosives and large quantities of Bolshevik printed materials. Tkachenko resists arrest, firing shots at the prefect of police. Convicted in the trial of communists held on Spirii Hill in Bucharest, he does not benefit from the amnesty of 1 June 1922. In August 1923, his case is retried, and Pavel Tkachenko-Antip, alias Ivan Baranov, alias Vladimir, alias Naum Lichter, alias Abrikosov, alias Gaida, alias Haim Iankel, alias Kosov, alias Kalman Strahman, alias Bespiatti, alias Vlad, alias Stefan, is deported, not being a Romanian citizen. From 1924, he is a member of the PCdR Political Bureau, but lives in Vienna, operating as a Comintern agent. He returns to Bucharest in 1925. He is arrested again on 15 August 1926 and is transferred to Chişinău, where he is due to stand trial. At the end of August he vanishes. One version of events says that he was shot while trying to escape, another that he was shot by soldiers merely under the pretext that he was trying to escape. Yet another account says that he managed to flee to the USSR. A campaign of communist agitation is unleashed. In Romania, the Comintern allocates 50,000 dollars to this campaign. Leading left-wing journalists and militants are drafted in. They include Ilie Moscovici and Emil Socor. The whole set-up comes to light in February 1928, when, having been criticised by the Comintern, David Fabian Finkelstein, number two in the Party hierarchy at the time, defends himself by citing the manner in which the protest campaign in the 'Tkachenko case' was conducted. He will be sacked, together with the entire PCdR leadership. The truth is that the campaign got off the ground very quickly, at the beginning of 1927. This supports the hypothesis that Tkachenko managed to escape to the

USSR. According to another version, he is supposed to have been killed in 1937 during the Great Terror.

A terrorist, Pavel Tkachenko is the Comintern's most trusted man in the PCdR leadership. His arrest is a serious blow dealt by the Siguranţa. There follows a campaign, conducted throughout Europe by Karl Radek's men. The same recipe: demonstrations and petitions. Leading intellectuals send letters to Bucharest and publish exposés in the press. Panait Istrati is among them. On 5 October 1926, Istrati takes part in a protest rally held in Paris by the Committee for the Defence of Victims of White Terror in the Balkans, whose president is Barbusse. At the demonstration he reads out an indictment against what he, like Racovski, names the Romanian oligarchy:

> "And if the fate of the imprisoned seems to me worthier than that of free men; if I must yearn for the fate of Tkachenko, shot without trial merely for being a communist, or that of Mihai Gheorghiu Bujor, who is rotting in Doftana gaol for the same crime … then even now I am ready to say to the France that gives me hospitality and the opportunity to express my feelings: I am a communist, an anarchist, I am whatever you want! Here are my two wrists: handcuff them! Shoot me without trial, the same as they do every week in my homeland, your ally, the Romania of assassins!"

The text is later published as the preface to a pamphlet with the title *Au pays du dernier Hohenzollern. L'histoire d'un crime*, printed by the same committee, run by Barbusse with Istrati as his deputy. On the cover there are two portraits: Pavel Tkachenko and I.I.C. Brătianu, identified as victim and executioner. No author is specified. It is a Bolshevik propaganda text. The following are quotations:

> "The assassination represents the very foundation of the centuries-old regime … But this regime … with the king at its head … is nothing more than a catalogue of assassinations, lies and betrayals … Prostitution … is the very essence of the Romanian oligarchic regime … And not only prostitution, but also *backsheesh* [bribery, corruption]. And not only *backsheesh*, but also assassination, and every illegality, arbitrary justice, blackmail, beatings, torture, theft, forgery. And who is it that pays for

all of this? Who is it that maintains these *ciocoi*,[12] these landlords, these boyars, this Court? It is the worker, the petit bourgeois and above all the peasant. There are five million people in the ethnic minorities who are without protection. We can easily understand the danger that threatens the oligarchic scoundrel … The proletariat in particular is capable of achieving this union against the feudal and oligarchic forces that wage White Terror in Romania. Behold the great motive for the assassination of Tkachenko."[13]

In Panait Istrati's Siguranţă dossier we find an address to the Romanian legation in Paris announcing the publication of the pamphlet. In other documents in his file we find an order from Romulus Voinescu, the director of the Siguranţă, for measures to prevent the pamphlet's distribution in Romania. He also demands that the French authorities identify its authors. The pamphlet makes use of the 'revelations' provided by C.G. Costa-Foru and Barbusse in their own pamphlets. The man behind the publication of the pamphlet is Alecu Constantinescu. And behind the propagandistic operation as a whole is the Comintern. Cristian Racovski, the Soviet ambassador to Paris, assisted by his friend Istrati, had set up and financed the operation. Up until the late 1930s Tkachenko remains one of the most frequently invoked figures in campaigns of this type directed against Bucharest, along with Max Goldstein and Mihai Gheorghiu Bujor. Interestingly, all three were deserters.

Ultimately, Romanian communism existed during this period only through the campaigns waged by the Komintern. The Siguranţă had in effect annihilated the clandestine communist groups, dismantling the networks set up between 1918 and 1924. The agitation surrounding Bujor and a few others – Tkachenko, Ştefanov, and the Tatar Bunar rebels, for example – created the false image of a mass movement led by the Bolsheviks in Romania. According to the propaganda, the Bucharest regime was faced with an insurrection, with a 'proletarian revolution', such as the one that had occurred in Sofia. It gave the impression that the inexistent PCdR was 'at the head of the masses'. It was a typical campaign of misinformation and mystification. The trial of 1925, the capture of the PCdR leadership in 1926,

---

[12] Term of abuse for wealthy parvenu landowners, later used under communism as the equivalent of the Russian "kulak" – *Translator's note*.
[13] *Op. cit.*, p. 8-11.

and successive investigations and arrests had reduced clandestine Bolshevik activities to virtually zero. The communists survived as a presence only thanks to Siguranță provocations and in the articles of journalists obsessed with subversion exported from east of the Dniester.

Another name that the Comintern repeatedly throws into the fray during the period 1920-1933 is that of Mihai Gheorghiu Bujor. The campaign is launched in the Western press in December 1927, when the *Manchester Guardian* publishes an excerpt from the report of the Investigative Commission of the Trades Union International in Amsterdam on the situation for political prisoners. In the report, Bujor is presented as a persecuted political detainee. He is described as being held in solitary confinement in H Wing of Doftana gaol. His only contact is with a deaf-mute warder. He is allowed only 30 minutes exercise daily. He has no rights to written correspondence. There is no mention of his desertion, his terrorist activities, or the murders he ordered. His release is demanded. Other newspapers in the Comintern's network publish articles and appeals. In Bucharest the same thing happens. Bujor is once more thrust to the centre of public debate. He is portrayed by the Left as a victim of 'oligarchic terror'. The Comintern unleashes similar attacks at regular intervals, whenever the need to vilify the Bucharest regime arises. Bujor is 'living proof' that a 'regime of terror' exists in Bucharest, a regime that imprisons its political opponents. According to Agitprop, Bujor is a prisoner of conscience, not a terrorist who turned his gun on Romania; he is not guilty of the killings of numerous people in the Crimea in 1918; he is not guilty of treason and desertion during wartime.

We do not know how interested the Comintern really was in the fate of Bujor, but it did persistently use him as a subject of propaganda against the regime in Bucharest. Bujor was made out to be a martyr, a hero of Bolshevism, a victim of Brătianu's oligarchic dictatorship. 1928 was the year of a major campaign for his release. In Europe, communist networks, groups, newspapers, associations and parties mobilise. Bujor is a victim of the White Terror, a working-class hero kept in shackles. There was a need for such 'prisoners of conscience', capable of mobilising public opinion, be it that of the gullible or be it that of the complicit, a public opinion ready at any moment to place itself in the service of a 'pacifist', 'humanitarian' cause. The USSR thereby became the 'side of historical good', pointing the finger at the bourgeoisie as being an odious, anachronistic and corrupt class. The networks function like clockwork. The Soviets spend large sums of money on what they call 'agitation'. The actors have learned their parts well. Bujor receives visitors in Doftana; he gives interviews. Articles are written about him. Pamphlets are published. His release is demanded. One campaign is identical to the next, with the same script, playing in Berlin, Paris, Vienna and Prague simultaneously. The result of the campaign is that Romania has a poor image on the world stage. Brătianu, the Prime Minister, even drafts a pardon. But in Bucharest, Bujor has a very poor reputation, which makes any final decision difficult. The fact that he had deserted during wartime and that he had perpetrated murder and mayhem in Odessa remained in the memory. The reaction of the right-wing press and politicians blocks the pardon. Even when the USSR is willing to take him in an exchange of prisoners, Bujor remains in gaol.

Romania was also the setting for other major propaganda 'manoeuvres' orchestrated by the Comintern. For example, the trial of 114 accused (76 present in the dock), with 800 witnesses called (300 present in the stand), which was held in Cluj in the autumn of 1928. The authorities had hauled the clandestine networks of Transylvania into court. These networks were controlled from Vienna by the émigré heads of the PCdR, in fact the Comintern's South-Eastern Europe Bureau. Among those indicted were Ştefan Foriş, the future head of the PCdR, tried *in absentia*; Koloman Müller, Head of the (Communist) United Unions, tried *in absentia*; Alexandru Sencovici, later Head of the Unions in the 1960s; Imre Aladár; Haia Lifşiţ, who was to die in prison and become a cult figure for many decades; Solomon Schein, the Head of the (domestic) PCdR in 1926-1929; and Eugen Rozvany and Dezideriu Szántó, both lawyers from Oradea. Rozvany had been a member of the delegation that signed the PCdR's affiliation with the Comintern. The lawyers for the defence are L.D. Pătrăşcanu, Constantin Vicol, Petre Zissu, and also Dem. I. Dobrescu, the president of the General Union of Romanian Lawyers, later deputy mayor of Bucharest (1931-1933), and Aurel Lazăr, the PNŢ deputy for Bihor and vice-president of the Bar. Among others, Al. Vaida-Voievod and Iuliu Maniu testify at the trial.

The central figure in the trial is Victor Aradi. He held a Doctorate in Sociology from Budapest University. He was an ethnic Hungarian journalist, born in Turda[14]. He was the author of a book about Ecaterina Varga, the nineteenth century freedom fighter for the *Moți*.[15] Aradi was above all a communist of the old Left. A prisoner of war in Russia in 1915, he joined the Bolsheviks in 1918. He served as a volunteer in the Red Army. He returns to Budapest in 1919. He works in the Ministry of Foreign Affairs during the Béla Kuhn Government, as an expert on Russia. After the fall of the Béla Kuhn Government, he settles in Cluj. Aradi passes as a refined and erudite intellectual. He frequently publishes articles in the German and Hungarian press. He carries out sociological research and edits an academic journal. Victor Aradi leads a double life, however. He is also a man of the underground. Behind the façade of his public activity, his persona as scholar, researcher and writer, we discover a Bolshevik, a secret agent, a figure of the underground.

In November 1927, Aradi travels to Vienna and Berlin. Here he meets with Willy Münzenberg, the head of Workers International Relief (WIR), the most influential Soviet propaganda tool in the West. WIR had been founded in 1921, at the orders of Lenin, to relieve famine-stricken Russia. Münzenberg had met Lenin in Switzerland. In 1917, when Lenin and his group of loyal supporters leave Zurich in a diplomatically sealed train bound for Petrograd, Willy Münzenberg is among those who see him off. Thenceforth he takes care of underground operations throughout Europe on behalf of the Bolsheviks. After 1919, he is also a member of the Comintern leadership. He dies in suspicious circumstances in 1940. He is found hanged near the French border with Switzerland. After the signing of the Ribbentrop-Molotov Pact in 1939, Münzenberg had been reckless enough to distance himself from Moscow.[16]

---

[14] Torda in Hungarian, Thorenburg in German; a town in Transylvania, part of Greater Romania after 1918 – *Translator's note.*

[15] The Moți are a Romanian-speaking ethnic group living in the Carpathian Mountains in South-Western Transylvania. They were subject to conditions of serfdom under the Austro-Hungarian Empire – *Translator's note.*

[16] See Branko Lazitch, Milorad M. Drachkovitch, *Biographical Dictionary of the Komintern*, Hoover Institute, Stanford, California: Stanford University UP, 1986, pp. xxviii and 330; see also Stephen Koch, *Sfârșitul inocenței.*

In 1927-1928 he was at the height of his glory. With practically unlimited funds at his disposal, he had developed throughout the West a network of newspapers, publishing houses, film production companies, committees, and associations that supported Moscow's policy. Münzenberg was likewise a man of secret actions and semi-legal associations, half on the surface and half underground. One of his pawns is none other than Victor Aradi. In 1927, the WIR spent more than two million gold Deutschmarks (sixty million lei) in Romania, from a Comintern budget of forty five million Deutschmarks allocated to Eastern and Central Europe. Aradi had already been financed by the Comintern for a number of years, working as an agent in Cluj and later Bucharest. On the date of his arrest in summer 1928, he was the Secretary of WIR. He frequently received envelopes stuffed with cash. Three days before his arrest, for example, he had received 500,000 lei. In accordance with the technique he had picked up from Münzenberg, he opened a bookshop in Cluj, from where he distributed propaganda materials printed in Vienna, Moscow and Berlin. A communist nucleus formed using the bookshop as a front. Under the auspices of the WIR, similar bookshops were opened in Paris, New York, London, Warsaw and elsewhere. They were also mechanisms for the distribution of funds. When he was arrested, Aradi was in the process of opening another bookshop in Bucharest, on the pretext that it would distribute German-language books. Charged with clandestine activities, Aradi naturally shifts the focus to claim he is an innocent, 'persecuted' intellectual. Immediately after Aradi's arrest and indictment, the WIR network gears up. Münzenberg is called as a witness for the defence, but declines to travel to Cluj. Committees and associations send protest letters to Bucharest in solidarity with Aradi. Leading figures write to the authorities to demand his release. They include Oxford historian Hugh Seton-Watson, the author of the most important history of the Romanians to be published in the interwar period. Fridtjof Nansen, the Norwegian explorer, Albert Einstein and Romain Rolland also send letters of protest. It is the same list of famous persons as in every other Comintern-orchestrated campaign.

"I have been brought here before you charged with fictive deeds, for the sake of my beliefs. This trial of conscience shows just how far Siguranța

Intellectualli din Occident și tentația stalinistă. 30 de ani de război rece,
Bucharest: Editura Albatros, 1997, pp. 17-18, 23-29.

fabrications and reactionary terror are prepared to go in our country. Whatever your verdict, I shall continue to travel the same path, fearlessly and without hesitation."

In fact, Aradi had been a spy for many years, as will emerge later in his trial in 1931. In the Cluj trial of autumn 1928, Aradi is acquitted, however, after a propaganda campaign waged throughout Europe. He is given a fine for carrying an illegal weapon. Two years later, when he is arrested for espionage, he will once again be discovered to be carrying a pistol about his person.

Aradi has the same double face as many Bolsheviks. They are professional revolutionaries. They engage in politics, make propaganda, organise protests, strikes and marches, they take part in election campaigns. These men lead a normal, public life. They are professors, journalists, lawyers, engineers, etc. The Cluj trial concerns such open activities. But Aradi and others like him also have a hidden, secret, underground life. They receive funds from abroad. They are members of the Comintern's secret networks, preparing for a 'revolutionary' assault. Below the surface can be found sabotage, terrorism, and espionage. For a professional revolutionary there is no dividing line between these two different lives. Anything that hastens the downfall of democracy is permitted. Aradi is a typical case. He was tried in 1920 for 'political offences', and he was able to justify himself to the world as an intellectual persecuted for his beliefs.

Three years later, Aradi is implicated in an espionage case, as the head of a secret network operating in Romania. This time, Münzenberg prefers to abstain. He does not launch the usual campaign to support the 'victims of White Terror', as he had in the cases of Mihai Gheorghiu Bujor and the Tatar Bunar peasants, and so many other notorious cases: Sacco and Vanzetti in 1927 and Georgi Dimitrov in 1933. As he had done in the case of Aradi himself in 1928. It would have been compromising to him. There were great risks that the real activities behind the apparently 'pacifist' networks he conducted might be unmasked. Ultimately, who would have declared solidarity with a spy? In support of a revolutionary and intellectual he had found Barbusse, Einstein, Rolland and Istrati, regular customers for all the Comintern's appeals. But subversion, espionage and secret funds were the dirty side of politics. Willy Münzenberg, who in 1928 was vociferous in the campaign to free Aradi, prefers to remain silent in 1931-1932.

VI
The Renegade Istrati

It is 1927. The Russian ambassador to Paris is Cristian Racovski. In the summer, Moscow finds itself confronted with a vociferous campaign against Racovski led by the French press. After much hesitation, the Russian Foreign Minister, Chicherin, makes a declaration in which he thanks the ambassador for his services, but bows to the pressure. He announces Racovski's recall. On 15 October, Racovski leaves the embassy in a luggage-laden automobile, surprised that there is not a single policeman to be seen. He is accompanied by Panait Istrati. The paths of the two had crossed as early as 1905, in socialist and trades union circles. They met again in Paris, once Racovski had taken up residence in the Rue de Grenelle. They had many shared memories and common acquaintances. Istrati frequented the embassy and was, for example, on familiar terms with Racovski's adoptive daughter, who recalls him thus: "Panait Istrati often used to visit us for dinner and would sit for hours on end chatting in Cristian's office."[1] He was "a nervous man, as scrawny as could be, who used to say very interesting, cutting things, things often embarrassing to Cristian, who was nevertheless fond of him and valued him a great deal."[2] Racovski invited Istrati to visit Russia as early as 1926, but preparations were drawn out. For propaganda reasons, Moscow was keen to invite intellectuals. Istrati was ideal for this purpose, in view of his notoriety, as well as his Bolshevist sympathies. However, no one could have imagined that his visit would coincide with the twilight of Racovski's career. It remains unclear whether Stalin recalled his ambassador because he was getting ready to exile Trotsky and his acolytes, or whether it was because of pressure from the French press. However, the tension was there. Racovski and Istrati were abreast of the fact that something was afoot. Istrati asks him in the car, "Are you really being exiled by France or are you being destroyed by your countrymen?"[3] Racovski prefers to

---

[1] Elena Codreanu Racovski, *De-a lungul și de-a latul secolului (1908-1999) [The Length and Breadth of the Century]*. Bucharest: Univers Enciclopedic, 2002, p. 53.

[2] *Idem*, p. 77.

[3] Panait Istrati, *Spovedanie pentru învinși [Confessional for the Vanquished]*, Cluj: Editura Dacia, 1990, p. 39.

change the subject. When Racovski was appointed ambassador to London in 1923, Lenin was already ill and no longer ruled Russia, which had fallen into the clutches of Stalin. Racovski is removed from his post as Head of the Ukrainian Government, which conferred on him too great a power, and sent to London as ambassador. It was, in effect, a luxurious form of exile. Racovski protests, but submits. In 1927, things worsen for him. Lenin had died three years previously. In the Kremlin, the struggle for succession was at its height. Racovski's faction loses. His closest friend, Leon Trotsky, Stalin's number one enemy, is on the point of being deposed. At the same time, preparations were under way in Moscow for the tenth anniversary of Bolshevik accession to power.

This is the context of Istrati's arrival in Moscow. Three weeks later, on 14 November 1927, Trotsky and Zinoviev are expelled from the Party. Racovski, Kamenev, Shmilga and Yevdokimov, the leaders of the opposition within the Party, are excluded from the Central Committee of the CPSU. On 19 November, Adolf Ioffe, a proponent of Trotsky, is buried in Moscow. His suicide letter creates nervousness in political circles. At the funeral ceremony, we witness Trotsky's last public appearance in Russia. Racovski also attends the funeral. In December 1927, Racovski is heckled as he gives a speech at the Party congress. In January 1928, the leaders of the opposition are banished from Moscow and Leningrad, and sent into exile. Trotsky is forcibly transported to Alma-Ata, while Racovski is sent to Astrakhan, in the Volga Delta. Since Racovski's name is closely linked to that of Trotsky, his career is, in effect, over. The period Istrati spends in the USSR is full of events of this kind. The climate is that of a frenzied struggle for power. Stalin assails those who had opposed him in the operation to succeed Lenin. In January 1929, Trotsky is deported to Turkey. The date almost coincides with that of Istrati's departure from Russia. On 15 February, Istrati arrives in Paris, after having spent 16 months in the USSR.

So, early in the morning of 15 October 1927, the two leave Paris. The previous evening, in a restaurant, Racovski and Istrati had met Boris Souvarine, a former Bolshevik, expelled from the Comintern. In 1929, Souvarine, together with Istrati and Victor Serge, will write one of the books in the trilogy *Vers l'autre flamme*. In the mid-1930s, he will publish one of the best biographies of Stalin. He narrates the evening of departure as follows:

"That evening, Racovski was pensive, taciturn, from time to time he seemed distrait, although he was usually such a sparkling conversationalist. ... Istrati was talkative, euphoric, even exultant at the thought of the pilgrimage to the 'Mecca of communism' he was about to make and which he had dreamed of so long. So, Istrati kept heaping enthusiastic praise on the Revolution and the radiant future that lay before it. He was not a member of the Communist Party, but he shared the popular convictions regarding the 'great light from the east', as they used to say back then, due to his strong hostility to 'bourgeois' society. ... He did not know anything about Marxism but was not at all worried on that account; his feelings substituted for doctrine, instinct caused him to take the side of the poor, the exploited, the victims. And of rebels of every kind. ... His ideology sooner placed him in the ranks of a kind of humanitarian anarchism devoid of theoretical reasoning. Of the Soviet regime he knew nothing, apart from its hostility to the capitalist world ... Overcome by the joy of imminent departure, he did not sense the incompatibility of his behaviour with that of his travelling companion. He had no idea of the political tragedy upon which Racovski had embarked ... The ambassador, a disciplined militant above all else, complied to a strict rule that forbade him to speak of secret family problems in front of a stranger to the Party, even if that stranger was a declared communist [such as Istrati – *author's note*]."[4]

The journey to the USSR takes the two by automobile to Berlin, whence they take the train to Riga, and thence to Moscow. Once he arrives in Moscow, Istrati enthusiastically declares to *Pravda* that he is a Bolshevik, that he has left the West for good, that Russia is the only place where there is the freedom to create. He would like to be buried here, but he further desires that his body be taken to Romania once a Bolshevik regime is installed in Bucharest. Are there echoes here of conversations with Racovski, who dreamed of being a red dictator in Bucharest? In spite of all these customary declarations, Istrati notices how Racovski is received:

"We arrive in Moscow one beautiful morning (20 October). At the station, there is nothing to attest the slightest attention on the part of the government for a great ambassador, even one fallen into disgrace...

[4] Boris Souvarine, *Souvenirs*, Editions Gérard Lébovici, 1985, pp. 56-58.

None of those luxurious limousines that drive the bureaucratic rabble around … Nothing. And the hand of the former president of the Council of Commissars of the Ukrainian People, which signed so many documents in Geneva, London and Paris, was shaken by no one. Racovski's athletically built and highly intelligent attendant Lithuanian went to look for a taxi, while the newspaper photographers fixed their lenses on us. Cristian dodged them. I say to him, 'Why do you dodge them so maliciously? They are just doing their job'. 'In that case, they don't know what they are doing. I am sparing them from gaffes and threadbare clichés'."

Racovski knew what awaited him. The cold, even hostile, reception given to Racovski did not prevent Istrati from manifesting his enthusiasm for Russia and Bolshevism, even in the presence of his companion. In *Confessional for the Vanquished*, Istrati was to recollect: "Before leaving, I asked Racovski, 'What is going on in Soviet Russia?' And he gave me this diplomatic reply: 'If you look at the surface, you won't be satisfied. However, if you know how to look, you will love our Revolution'."[5] Paid by the Soviet press, Istrati had already written two eulogising articles about Racovski, which he had brought in his pocket. Neither of them would be published. Why? Between the date they were commissioned and the date of his arrival in Moscow, the fate of the former head of the Bolshevik Government of Ukraine, of the former ambassador to London and Paris, had been decided.

Istrati's relations with Bolshevism are not, however, as simple as they appear at first sight. Was Istrati won over by Bolshevism? Can we take his declarations at face value? Can we regard his enthusiastic words of autumn 1927 as merely a formulaic response to the hospitality of his hosts? The Kremlin propagandists desperately required famous writers to give their regime credibility. The scenario was relatively simple. Major figures from the West were invited and then given supervised tours of Russia. Large-scale ceremonies are laid on for them, receptions with flowers, celebrations; they are shown that they are popular. Back home, almost none of those invited bask in such glory. Moreover, they were paid royally. Their works were printed in millions of copies, and the royalties they received were to match. They were requested to contribute to magazines. They were interviewed. All expenses paid. Soviet propaganda was unstinting, especially when the

---

[5] Panait Istrati, *op. cit.*, p. 39.

person invited was someone famous. Returning to the West, after the adoring crowds, financial rewards and grandiose ceremonies, they carried out their task by 'remote control', won over by the manner in which they had been received. They wrote eulogising pages about the Soviet regime. Not necessarily because they had been corrupted, although this was also true, but because the manipulation had had its effect. They had not seen Russia so much as a series of choreographed performances, in which they more or less believed. Istrati was also one such pawn in the game played by the propaganda apparatus and the GRU. He was not naïve, but rather volatile in his options. He became easily enthused, shed his convictions just as easily, and would start over again. Istrati's itinerary in Russia is telling in this respect. We might say that he comes to Russia ready to see what lies hidden behind the veil of Bolshevik propaganda.

Panait Istrati's political experience was more than sufficient for him to understand the truth. He had been a militant socialist in his youth; he had worked for trades unions. He had organised strikes and demonstrations; he had worked as an editor for *Workingman's Romania*. He personally knew all the Romanian socialist and trades union leaders of the day. He was well acquainted with the conditions of the workingman, whose cause he championed whenever he had the opportunity. He goes to the USSR believing that he will find a dictatorship of the proletariat 'at work'. Instead, he encounters a venal bureaucracy and a working class exploited by brutal masters. Hence his disappointment, which, however, occurs later, towards the end of the journey, after his illusions have been shattered one by one. He sees the reason for the regime's failure as Russia's new rulers. The 'bureaucratisation of the Soviet regime' was the thesis of the Trotskyite opposition, with whom Istrati had close contacts. It should be remembered that in 1913 he had met Leon Trotsky in Bucharest, in a hotel room near the Romanian Athenaeum. Racovski is his closest link to opposition circles. On 6 August 1928, Racovski writes and sends his adherents an article/manifesto entitled *The Professional Perils of Power*. Six weeks later, Istrati is in Astrakhan. We have no direct evidence that Istrati had read the text, but it would be naïve to think that he had not, especially if we bear in mind the stir it caused. It was Racovski's succinct analysis of the regime. Istrati adopts its theses in the way he views the USSR, as is transparent in *Confessional for the Vanquished*. Accompanied by their girlfriends, Nikos Kazantzakis and Istrati arrive on 18 September 1928 in Astrakhan, "a malodorous city. Swarms of mosquitoes. Plague, malaria, cholera."[6] They stay in the 'best hotel' in town, the Коммунальная Гостиница. He finds bedbugs in his room. He goes out into the corridor and kicks up a fuss. "A door opens in the gloom of the corridor, a squat man comes up to me. 'Is it you who are doing all that swearing?' Racovski? How? You're living in a hotel with bedbugs?" The luxurious diplomatic residence in Paris was a distant memory. The reunion with the 'great outcast' seems unreal. The erstwhile leader of the Communist International is living in a filthy hotel, exiled from his fellows. "A single room in which it would have been difficult to fit five people, a screen hiding the bed and washstand. Suitcases stuffed with books. A table heaped with papers. Racovski is working on *The Life of Saint-Simon*. He is ill with malaria." They had last seen each other in Moscow in October. Almost a year had passed since then. Is the reunion between them an accident, as the description would have it? Did Istrati know that Racovski was in Astrakhan? He knew. Had he ended up in the city by chance? Hard to believe. Had he planned to go there in order to see his friend once more? Was there an understanding between them? Had he gone there out of solidarity, out of bravado? The pages of *Confessional for the Vanquished* do not tell us. But perhaps he did not write about any of these things in order to protect his host. "He has no dark ideas," Istrati assures us, probably for the ears of the GPU.

> "He is always ready to fight and more than ever convinced of … Of what? I couldn't say. From his words, well convictions, but to define them is time wasted. For even when they are friends, Bolshevik ambassadors remain diplomats. Thus he prefers to speak enthusiastically of the lotus … and he describes to us the melancholy existence of these flowers, harried by the cold. He extols to us a plan to fertilise the sands."[7]

Does Istrati refuse to write about what the two 'accomplices' have discussed in Astrakhan, or has Racovski lost trust in his visitor and prefers not to say anything risky, anything political? Istrati nevertheless cuts the figure of an unconditional enthusiast for the Soviets. He had made numerous press declarations to this effect. Racovski had reasons to be prudent and to view Istrati with suspicion. He had enough political experience not to be

---

[6] Panait Istrati, *Spovedanie pentru învinși*, Cluj: Editura Dacia, 1990, p. 88.

[7] *Idem*, p. 89.

taken in by someone like Istrati, who was always changing, always exulted, rebellious, unrestrained, angry at something, at someone. At the time, he was fascinated by what he saw in Russia. Racovski would have had a lot to say. He was one of the main leaders of the opposition. He was at the centre of a clandestine network, with which he corresponded and planned acts of political protest. He was under close surveillance by GPU agents. Did he impart any of this to Istrati? Did he give him any messages for persons in Moscow or for the foreign press? We shall probably never know. *Confessional for the Vanquished* maintains its silence.

On the other hand, we learn all about excursions along the banks of the Volga. Istrati, Kazantzakis and Racovski are accompanied, bizarrely, by two invalids, one missing a leg, the other paralytic. Both are 'supermen', fanatical about transforming nature. There is a hint of Bosch, of Breughel, in these pages. The only echo of Racovski's status as an exile, but also of the power struggle within the Kremlin, is captured by Istrati when he reproduces the words of an official, on a tugboat named '*Comrade Stalin*'. The latter admonishes his sympathy for the opposition, whose leaders are nothing but 'traitors'. After eight days of excursions in the Volga Delta, the small group parts. Istrati, Kazantzakis and co. leave Astrakhan for Georgia/ Tbilisi, Stalin's native turf. Istrati provides no details about his parting from Racovski. They will never see each other again.

A number of things took place prior to the reunion of Istrati and Racovski. In the USSR, Istrati was the official guest of VOKS (a GPU hotbed – the organisation ostensibly handled cultural relations with foreign countries). From the outset, he seems fascinated by the adventure he is caught up in. He makes and reiterates enthusiastic declarations about the homeland of the Revolution, about the workers, about Bolshevism. He vehemently attacks the West, especially France, and the "putrid and decadent bourgeoisie." Of course, Soviet propaganda records all such declarations and reproduces them word for word. Istrati plays his role well; he seems to have blinkers over his eyes. That was why he had been invited and paid – to be taken to different places under the strict supervision of the GPU, to be toasted at banquets, give interviews, watch parades, be greeted by brass bands, and travel in special trains and limousines, surrounded by activists ready to provide him with almost anything. The hosts' aim was to win him over, so that on his return he would become, willy-nilly, an agent of Soviet influence, and so that, ultimately, he would write works of pro-Soviet propaganda. He was not the only one. H.G. Wells, George Bernard Shaw, Henri Barbusse, Romain Rolland, Nikos Kazantzakis, Lion Feuchtwangler, Emil Ludwig and André Malraux also fell prey to the same treatment. Istrati is enchanted by his reception, by the money he is earning in abundance. Many of his books are translated, for which he earns copious royalties. He writes articles, gives interviews. He is treated like a dignitary, even though he is nothing more than a 'fellow traveller' from the West. Things go well for a while. Istrati does not see what is happening, or feigns not to see. He lets himself be carried away by success, money and ceremonials.

Let us compile a time-line of the journey. Having only just arrived in Moscow, he takes the train to Leningrad, where he arrives on 31 October. Here he makes the acquaintance of Victor Serge, a French translator living in Russia. He returns to Moscow and in Red Square on 7 November he attends an ostentatious parade on the occasion of the tenth anniversary of what the regime names the 'Great October Revolution'. He witnesses a counter-demonstration organised by the opposition and the reprisals that follow. Istrati does not react, although he personally knows many of the anti-Stalinist opposition leaders. One week later, on 13 November, he meets Nikos Kazantzakis, who from now on accompanies him. Kazantzakis had manifested Bolshevik ideas since as early as 1922. In 1927, he came to the USSR at the invitation of VOKS, like Istrati. He had also travelled in the USSR two years previously, in 1925. On 16 November, Istrati and Kazantzakis set out on an official excursion to the Black Sea and Caucasus.

In December, they both set out for Greece. Beforehand, they send a letter to Stalin, in which they express their admiration for the USSR. They embark at Odessa on the Chicherin, arriving in Piraeus on 31 December 1927. A confidential report sent to Bucharest by the Romanian legation to I. Gh. Duca, the *ad interim* Foreign Minister, noted: "Under close surveillance, the authorities realised at once that Istrati was a dangerous agent of Moscow."[8] He makes contact with the Soviet legation and Greek communist leaders. On 3 January, Istrati visits Singros Prison. What does he say to the political detainees, most of whom are communists? He shows them that he has two fingers missing and tells them that he lost them as a manual labourer. He is not "Istrati the writer" but "Istrati the worker." He recounts to them, "I too have been thrown into prison on many occasions," and they sympathise with him. Then he speaks to them about the USSR.

---

[8] ANCR, CC of the PCR Archive, Fund 95, Dossier 9796, vol. 1, p. 72.

"Something unrepeatable and wonderful is being accomplished there." He ends by saying, "Do not be discouraged in moments of affliction. Victory is ours. ... Istrati is yours. Istrati is no lickspittle. I shall not bow my head. No. The others are traitors... I am and remain in your ranks. I shall remain a soldier in your ranks."[9] He visits a hospital for consumptives. He is summoned by an examining magistrate to give an explanation for his speech at Singros. To the amazement of the Romanian diplomat, as noted in his report, Istrati is not deported. Moreover, on 11 January, he gives a lecture at the Alhambra, an auditorium in central Athens, with the blessings of the regime in the USSR, which is followed by scuffles with the police in the street. A report for the Siguranţă translates an article published in a pro-Bolshevik newspaper.

> "Yesterday evening, at seven o'clock, Panait Istrati spoke of his impressions of Soviet Russia ... The lecturer was greeted with enthusiastic applause and spoke in French, translated for the auditorium by an interpreter. The Soviet Union, as it is today, can be loved only by two social categories, by the workers and by those who are born courageous ... I shall divide the Soviet Union into two unequal parts, one the part is the living souls and the other the dead souls. The first part comprises that terrible organism that carried out the October Revolution and which now holds power. The second part comprises the parasites on this organism: a few kulaks, bureaucrats and professionals, they are tolerated by the new organism of the vigorous Russia. ... It is always good for a living soul to sense around it the cold breath of a dead soul, behold the spectacle of reality ... in the red democracy there is not enough work for all, nor food, nor abundant clothing, but what does exist is shared equally and fairly between the entire nation. BEHOLD GREAT JUSTICE!! The great power of communism. ... It is said that the Bolsheviks do not get on with each other and that very soon they will devour each other and this will be their end. You, miserable undertakers of Soviet Russia, must be out of your minds to believe such hopeless ideas ... The more they contradict each other, the more they will strengthen Soviet power, because in Russia it is the people that govern. ..."[10]

---

[9] *Idem*, pp. 73-74.
[10] ANCR, CC of the PCR Archive, Fund 95, Dossier 9796, vol. 1, p. 58-59.

On leaving the lecture theatre, the audience provokes incidents with the police, who:

> "try to break up the crowd, but the workers do not back down and chant, 'down with white democracy, down with the coalition government … long live the Communist Party'… Many were beaten and trampled. The crowd heads for the university avenue, motor cars and trams are stopped, nothing can be heard except the International and the protests of the crowd. …"[11]

Istrati is summoned before an examining magistrate. To the amazement of the Romanian diplomat filing the report, he is not deported. Or at least not for long. The press is unleashed against the two. Istrati's visa expires and he has to leave. Kazantzakis stays behind to face trial. "We inform of the following: On 23 February, at 14:00 hours, the communist Panait Istrati, expelled from Greece, boarded the Soviet ship Chicherin at Piraeus. He is heading to Odessa and Moscow, where he will stay for two years, after which he intends to return to Romania," notes a telegram addressed to the General Bureau of the Siguranţă.[12] The two writers' expedition to Athens was evidence of 'enthusiasm and sacrifice'. Both Istrati and Kazantzakis wanted to show their loyalty to the Revolution. It was a provocation, an agitator parachute-drop behind enemy lines.

While the two writers are in Greece, Trotsky and Racovski are sent into internal exile. The Greek press announces the event. No reaction on the part of Istrati. Moreover, he returns to the USSR. He meets up with Kazantzakis in Kiev. On the way north, they stop over in Leningrad, where they see Victor Serge again. At the end of March, they both go to Murmansk and Arkhangelsk. Istrati and Kazantzakis wanted to visit the 're-education camp' in the Solovki Isles. Gorky was to go there a year later and, to his shame, write a eulogy. The two, accompanied by their girlfriends, do not reach Solovki; they remain in Murmansk for a few days, waiting for the necessary permits. To this end, Istrati writes to the GPU. He also writes to Romain Rolland a letter enthused by what he is seeing, by the visit he is about to make … Istrati is still prey to the illusion and to his prejudices, fostered by the VOKS organisers of the trip. When the answer

---

[11] *Idem*, p. 61.
[12] *Idem*, p. 69.

from Moscow delays in coming and the accommodation is bad, he calls off the plan. It was only by chance that Panait Istrati did not visit the camp at Solovki, the first Soviet concentration camp. It is only a fortunate accident that shielded Panait Istrati from the shame of having numbered among the ecstatic visitors that were shown around the GPU's horrible 'achievement'. "To go over to the side of the executioners and to praise them for the suffering they inflicted on the people became a way of life (sometimes of death) for the proletarian revolutionary writers."[13] Our travellers change their minds and head south. In April, they arrive in the Crimea. A note by the Siguranţă reveals: "At Odessa he is working on the making of a cinema film about his communist ideals, and it is to be titled *The Haidouk* … From the information we have, the aforementioned is very interested in the fate of the communists imprisoned at Jilava, which causes him to publish in various foreign newspapers about the way they are treated in prison."[14] Istrati is still a devotee of the Comintern, for which he has performed many services as a propagandist and agent of influence.

He has health problems and stays in bed for around a month. At the beginning of May, Istrati is at Bekovo, near Moscow (one of the sites where victims of the Great Terror were executed between 1936 and 1938). From Bekovo, Istrati intervenes in favour of Victor Serge, who he discovers has been arrested. On 28 May, with Kazantzakis he meets Gorky, in the offices of a publisher. In July, the first article about Kazantzakis to appear in the West is published in *Monde*, a magazine published by Barbusse and financed by VOKS. The author: Panait Istrati. He then travels down the Volga to the south of Russia. On 1 August, Istrati meets Ecaternia Arbore, a militant socialist whom he knows from Romania, now Minister of Health in the Moldavian Soviet Socialist Republic (murdered in 1937 on the orders of Stalin). *Red Ploughman*, the local Romanian-language newspaper, publishes on 10, 14 and 17 August articles about Istrati's journey. Here is an excerpt from an interview published on 17 August: "As soon as I heard about Moldova, I decided at once to come and see what the Moldavians were doing … I have been down to the banks of the Dniester. Thence I gazed over to the other side for a long time. And on seeing the empty fields, the gendarme with a rifle over his shoulder, I was filled with pity. And how can you not

---

[13] Mircea Iorgulescu, *Dilema*, no. 64/1994.
[14] ANCR, of the CC of the PCR Archive, Fund 95, Dossier 9796, vol. 1, p. 76.

pity your brother, who you know is so sorely afflicted. You are especially filled with pity when you see how on the Moldavian side they are building socialism before your very eyes, while on the other side the greater part of Moldavians and Romanians are still under the yoke of the boyars. I came to Russia weary; I leave cheerful. And I shall be more cheerful still when the time comes and I shall see what I have seen here in the whole of Romania, that is, when the whole of Romania will be a free Soviet country."[15]

At the end of August, Nikos Kazantzakis and Panait Istrati, together with Eleni Samiou and Istrati's lover, Bilili Baud-Bovy, are already in the south. On 30 August, the two meet Barbusse, who is in hospital at Nizhny Novgorod. On 8 September, they arrive in Astrakhan, where Istrati sees Racovski once more. On 30 September, they arrive in Tbilisi. Thence by ship to Baku, Batumi, Sukhumi, Novorosisk. On 2 December, Istrati is in Rostov, then Kiev. On 19 December, he arrives in Moscow at last. On 30 December, he is in Leningrad with Victor Serge and Nikos Kazantzakis. It is here the two part ways. Kazantzakis does not support Istrati in the 'Rusakov Affair'. On 11 January 1929, Istrati is already preparing to leave. On 15 February, he is in Paris. Kazantzakis remains in Russia until April, when he departs, bound for Berlin.

Before leaving the USSR, Istrati sends two letters to Gerson, one of the heads of the GPU, in which he begs leave to criticise one per cent of the realities in the USSR as he has seen them. At the same time, he gives assurances regarding his loyalty. Is the idea that the GPU might solve such problems naïvety on Istrati's part? Or had he understood that the USSR was a police state and that everything depended on the special services? Had he understood that the GPU held the real power? We do not know. What is for sure is that instead of addressing himself to the Comintern, Agitprop, VOKS or directly to the Kremlin leaders, Istrati writes to the GPU, asking permission (with faux or genuine candour) to criticise the Bolshevik regime when he gets to the West. Istrati writes:

"There are three kinds of writers who may pronounce on the Soviet Union ... (1) The neutral, authors of books that are more or less acceptable ... (2) Our enemies, professional detractors of the Union. (3) Our friends, of the Henri Barbusse type ... professional apologists ... As for me, the Soviet issue is a personal drama. I am a born rebel and a long-

---

[15] *Idem*, p. 106.

time revolutionary. I did not come to the Union in search of subjects for books, but so that I could see for myself and be of use to the proletarian cause. Today I realise that I can be of use only on one condition: not to write like Barbusse. When a writer gives up all sense of criticism and becomes like the cracked bell for an idea, he is no longer a man who is listened to and he no longer serves the cause he thinks he is upholding. He compromises it. I do not mean by this that we should succumb to the babbling and prating that would submerge us in bourgeois chaos. But there are dangerous evils here, whose name should be uttered aloud. … then let me be permitted also to speak of what is bad, moderately, compassionately, gently, but to speak of it. I ask your consent, I ask for that of the Party. If you accord me it, I shall write about my impressions of the Soviet Union. If not, I shall keep silent in public and in private. Here as well as abroad. I shall live alone."

Once back in Moscow, he again writes to Gerson, the Secretary of the GPU:

"My definitive position (at least so I hope) can be summarised thus: (1) No willing return to capitalism and the bourgeoisie, which must be annihilated, in spite of the ideological and moral shortcomings of the Soviet regime. (2) The current evils of the Soviet regime are, in my eyes, remediable, on the condition that they are dealt with. (3) Absolute faith in the Soviet working class … (4) I do not believe that this rectification is incumbent upon the opposition … On the contrary, left to do as it will, the opposition is capable of even greater mistakes. (5) I can see only one means of escape from the current critical impasse: (a) to cease combating the opposition through terror; (b) to proclaim the right to criticise within the Party, for all members … (c) introduction of secret ballots, in the Party and trades unions … I should like to be such a communist and to fight using all the means at my disposal. Here it is impossible without the consent of the Party. And abroad – where my honest word might give rise to base polemic in the opposing camp – I should not wish to combat at all, except with your approval, since I am neither an oppositionist nor an anarchist, but a collaborator in the Soviet project. … This is my programme. I am ready to give my life to defend it."[16]

---

[16] Panait Istrati, *Spovedanie pentru învinși*, Cluj: Editura Dacia, (cont. 161.)

"Istrati is once and for all disillusioned, disabused, and in the end he no longer thinks in terms of deceptive formulas about the pseudo-dictatorship of the proletariat. ... He returns to Paris on 15 February 1929, broken, ill, disoriented, no longer knowing to whom or to what he should dedicate himself; he can no longer speak, but nor remain silent. He can no longer write, but nor refrain from writing," writes Boris Souvarine.[17] On 23 February, he makes his first declarations:

"Trotsky or the opposition represent the gold reserve of the Russian Revolution. Without this reserve, I do not know how there will be any revolutionary progress in Russia. ... It is a country that today permits every revolutionary hope. ... For me, Stalin and Trotsky are still two good revolutionaries. I have met no real counter-revolutionaries in Russia, apart from the ill-omened bureaucratic apparatus, made up of rodents, of communists without a party, who gnaw away and threaten to demolish the wonderful work that resulted from the October Revolution."[18]

Just two days later, Madeleine Paz,[19] a member of Parisian Bolshevik circles, publishes another interview in a small-circulation magazine, *Contre le courant*, which bore the stigma of opposing Stalin. Istrati explains the difference between his declarations at the beginning of his visit to the USSR, when he was an admirer of the Moscow regime, and those made on his return, when, disillusioned, he had become critical. In the meantime, he had travelled the length and breadth of Russia; he had made contact not only with officialdom but also with simple people. His previous image of the Revolution and the Bolshevik regime had changed radically. "In the last three months of my stay in Moscow and Leningrad, the enchantment faded, the veil suddenly fell away, and the real situation ... confronted me in all its cruelty."[20] He repeats the main thesis of the opposition in Russia – the bureaucratic deterioration of the Revolution – and he holds Stalin responsible. The most delicate subject of the interview is Trotsky, who was on the front pages of all the newspapers at the time, due to his expulsion

---

1990, pp. 136-139.

[17] *Op. cit.*, pp. 72-73.

[18] Interview in *Les Nouvelles littéraires*, 23 February 1929.

[19] See *Cahiers Panait Istrati*, no. 11/1994, pp. 147-150.

[20] *Idem*, p. 149.

from Russia. Istrati says, "The way in which the opposition and their leader Trotsky are treated in Russia is what caused me to leave Russia so quickly." He regards the act as barbarous. And he adds, "When I hear how Trotsky is branded a counter-revolutionary, I wonder whether he would have been treated the same if Lenin had been alive today. I am convinced that if Lenin had been alive to see what is happening in Russia now, he would have acted no differently than Trotsky."[21] With these words, Istrati becomes *persona non grata* for the Kremlin. When *Monde*, Henri Barbusse's magazine, interviews him, Isrtati's tone is milder; he sometimes contradicts himself. Istrati thus exposes himself to the ripostes of his former comrades. These are not long in coming. On 29 April 1929, *Literatrunaya Gazeta* publishes an article by Boris Volin, entitled *Two-faced Istrati*.[22] The author compares the differing positions taken by Istrati in *NRF* and in *Monde*.

The truth is that, only just having returned from Russia, Istrati was not yet decided on what to do. He was hesitating. The issue was not what he thought of the USSR, since on this matter he was clear, but whether he should make these opinions public. The blackmail according to which criticism of the USSR served the enemies of the Revolution was strong in left-wing circles. Hence, the way he puts things does not always get to the very bottom of the truth as he knew it. Volin accuses him of duplicity and wonders whether Istrati has ever been sincere. He accuses him of using typically Trotskyite phraseology and petty bourgeois idle talk. Likewise, he warns readers about Istrati's forthcoming book about the USSR. An anthropologist might say a witch hunt was being prepared. The dogs are about to be set loose. Istrati is dragged ever deeper. In Brussels he tries to obtain political asylum for Trotsky, but without success. Even though he meets with Belgian officials, he does not push the matter, because Trotsky in the meanwhile announces the formation of a fourth, Trotskyite International, in opposition to the Comintern. Istrati takes a step back. He does not want to be politically involved. He remains a loner. However, his endeavour did not escape the eyes of the Soviet authorities and he was put on a blacklist, if he was not on one already. Not only in his interviews but also his moves to secure political asylum for Trotsky, we can see that Istrati is hesitating.

His decision to break his silence was not at all simple. He was taking a number of great risks: that of not making himself understood, that of

---

[21] *Idem*, p. 150.

[22] *Idem*, p. 151.

irritating his readers, and in particular, that of provoking the ire of the Comintern's agents, the fellow travellers and the pro-Soviet press. This lobby was very influential in the West, especially in France. Moreover, it should not be forgotten that Istrati himself had been launched and supported by this lobby. He thus risked alienating his old friends, without any guarantee of gaining others. His revelations might have appeared to be nothing more than a family quarrel, one between Bolshevik sympathisers. This would have made the report of his transfiguration produce unconcerned reactions. Given that Istrati had loudly proclaimed his pro-Soviet convictions up to then, why should he be believed now? When had he been lying and when had he been mistaken? When he had declared his enthusiastic attachment to the Bolsheviks, or when he had become a critic of the USSR? For the Kremlin, the fact that an 'insider' was rebelling was extremely dangerous. He had to be liquidated morally, to be compromised and discredited. Did Istrati know what awaited him? Yes and no. In 1929, although the opposition had been defeated and Trotsky jettisoned in Constantinople, matters were still unclear. The USSR was still an ambivalent country, capable of going either way: either towards a fascistic regime, or towards an amplification of the NEP, a kind of semi-capitalism, à la Bukharin, or towards a harsh communist dictatorship, which is what indeed happened. Stalin is getting ready for forced industrialisation and the collectivisation of agriculture. It is a nefarious policy, which will leave millions dead in the famine of 1929-1931. It is a policy which will lead to the Gulag, to the Great Terror at the end of the 1930s. Russia is faced with a historical disaster. However, the terrain of 1929 was not as clear-cut as it would be later on. Moreover, illusions regarding the 'revolution' of October 1917 were still strong everywhere, both in the USSR and in the West. Numerous and influential left-wing intellectuals saw in the USSR the only salvation, the only exit from the crisis of capitalism.

Istrati operated within a political and intellectual climate which were full of uncertainties. We observe, throughout 1929, his hesitations, insecurity, and about-turns. He makes his mind up with difficulty, changes it, and then starts all over again. He receives contradictory pieces of advice from his entourage. Some warn him not to put himself in a bad light with the Soviets and their fanatics in the West. Others, fewer in number, encourage him. His correspondence with Romain Rolland is dramatic. From Rolland, Istrati was expecting clarification. He sends him the two letters addressed to Gerson, the GPU Secretary, in which he had undertaken not to write critically about the USSR. At the end he adds, for Rolland's eyes only:

"When I made this commitment, I imagined, in my naïvety, that the men of power are of good faith, that they are unaware of the putrefaction below them, and I believed that it would be sufficient for a powerful and friendly voice to alert them, in order for them to become aware and to take measures. After the 'Rusakov Affair', I became convinced that those in power were aware of the evil that was undermining the Revolution, and that they did not brook any criticism. This situation released me from the commitment I had taken, since there was no longer anything to be expected from those at the top. To proceed cautiously will not mean anything."[23]

Rolland answers him:

"The letters addressed to the GPU are perfect (I condone them in their entirety). ... She [Rolland's sister, Madeleine – *author's note*], like myself, thinks that you cannot, that you must not publish them at this moment, and in particular you must not let Boris [Souvarine – *author's note*] or the friends of Serge [Victor – *author's note*] publish them. That would be a terrible, bludgeoning blow whereby the wretches would strike at the whole of Russia, under the illusion that they were rooting out the putrefaction ... You have done all that you had to, all that you could. There is nothing more you can do. These pages are holy. They should be conserved in the archives of the eternal Revolution. ... We still love you and, moreover, we venerate you for what you have written. But do not publish them! It would not serve the Russian Revolution, but rather the European reactionaries, whose game the opposition blindly play. ... It is evident that those in power [in the USSR – *author's note*] are too compromised, that they depend too much on one another, on their material competition, to be able to take account of what you are saying. ... Unfortunately their force is spent, there is no one else capable of leading post-revolutionary Russia. It can only hasten the process of putrefaction ... It is your role to save the flames of heroic idealism from the ruins."[24]

---

[23] Panait Istrati, *Spovedanie pentru învinși*, Cluj: Editura Dacia, 1990, p. 139.
[24] *Idem*, pp. 115-116.

Panait Istrati replies impressively, two days later, on 30 May: "I am no longer writing *Vers l'autre flamme.*"[25]

At the end of August 1929, Istrati visits Romania again. Four years had passed since 1925. Istrati was a different man. In the meantime, he had completed his journey through the USSR. Shortly before taking the train to Bucharest, he leaves the manuscript of *Confessional* at the Rieder publishing house in Paris. The promise made to Rolland is not kept. On 18 August, he is already in Munich. On 20 August, one day before entering Romania at the Curtici border crossing, he writes to Rolland from Budapest: "My friend, I have poured out my anger! During 28 days of sciatica and toothache, I poured out all the hell that was poisoning my life ... There will be three volumes: one written by me, the second by V. S., the third by B. Suv. All three to be published provisionally under my name." So, there were to be three books, written by Victor Serge, one of the characters in Istrati's book; Boris Souvarine, an expelled communist; and Istrati himself. In order for the enterprise to produce a reaction, Panait Istrati was provisionally to sign the three volumes under his own name, since the others were virtually unknown at the time. This gesture clarifies the fact that he knew what he was doing. He did not wish merely to bear witness; he wanted to win the match. It was a kind of campaign, which he knew well how to unleash.

The reasons for his presence in Bucharest were not literary. At the beginning of August, there had been a miners' strike in Lupeni. The county prefect, Ștefan Rozvany, had given orders to fire on the strikers. Rozvany was the brother of well-known communist Eugen Rozvany, the lawyer from Salonta/Oradea. Even if his change of attitude regarding the Kremlin regime was known, Istrati remained a dangerous Bolshevik agitator as far as the Siguranță were concerned. His long trip to the USSR and repeated declarations of support for the Kremlin made him all the more suspect. The Communist Party from Romania (PCdR) was in a state of collapse. A number of factions were vying for power. One was led by Marcel Pauker-Luximin, the other by Vitali Kholostenko, nominated General Secretary in 1928 by the Comintern. Arrests and betrayals from within had completely annihilated the PCdR. Not by chance, Panait Istrati – arriving in Romania in the very midst of this crisis – is suspected of having arrived in order to rebuild the PCdR or else to "organise a new Romanian Workers' Party," as a note of the Siguranță claims. The press also act as scandalmongers for

---

[25] *Idem*, p. 117.

this information (*Curentul, Universul*). The truth is different, simpler, and emerges from the so-called 'clandestine scenario'. It relates to a tragedy.

On Sunday 4 August, the miners of Lupeni declare a strike. On 5 August, they occupy the electricity plant and begin to flood the tunnels. The army intervenes. The miners refuse to cease their actions. On 6 August, the army fires on the strikers. There are 21 deaths. The press devotes extensive coverage to the event. Istrati quickly makes a decision. On 8 August, he writes to Romain Rolland: "I am going to Romania for the sake of those massacred at Lupeni." He was impressionable by nature and a believer in the 'workers' cause'. Moreover, he had managed to finish *Confessional for the Vanquished*. He leaves Paris, where he has been hounded by the press. The tensions surrounding his manuscript increase. There was already talk of the book in newspaper offices, cafés, and political and literary circles. Many classed him as a suicide. Perhaps he wished to take account of the advice given to him by Rolland, who had asked him to leave Paris. There was another argument in favour of going to Romania: he was going to stand up for the workers in the trial of the communists in Timișoara. Then, he wanted to carry out an investigation, to write a reportage about the tragedy at Lupeni. With these two gestures, he wanted to counterbalance his anti-Bolshevik attitude. His former comrades' accusation that he had betrayed the 'cause' would have been diminished. He thus balanced his criticisms of the Kremlin with criticism of "the Romanian authorities guilty of the tragedy at Lupeni." He wished to underline that he was on the side of the workers, the strikers and the communists brought to trial in Timișoara. Istrati did not want to pass as a traitor to the proletariat, to the USSR, to the Revolution. He did not want to go over to the other side of the barricades, "to the bourgeois camp." He wanted to be an "honest critic of the Revolution" and the Bolsheviks. A spectacular gesture on behalf of the strikers arrested and investigated by the police, of the victims of 'bourgeois terror', would show the West, but also the USSR, that he had not changed his options. Another detail in this confused situation. A crossroads. Istrati continued to hold many of his old convictions. He had not abandoned his *sui generis* Bolshevism. For him, what he had seen in the USSR was still an authentic revolution, which had unfortunately fallen into the hands of corrupt and incapable leaders. Istrati was still a believer, one of the faithful. The heresy towards which he was now veering caused him much suffering. The break was not yet definitive. It would occur later, after the launch of the campaign of denigration orchestrated by Moscow. Only then would he understand the nature of the regime led by Stalin and sever the umbilical cord. In the summer of 1929, however, he still finds himself at a crossroads. He had not emancipated himself from communism, even if he was preparing to become a heretic.

On reaching the Romanian border (21 August) he is met by the Siguranță. "On 21 August, on the No. 24 International Train, writer Panait Istrati entered the country, travelling from Paris together with his wife, bound for the town of Brăila, where he will stay for six weeks. He possesses certificate 930 issued on 2 May by our legation in Paris."[26] Here is another note:

"Department of General Security, Brigade IV. Today, 28 August, he left the locality on the 8:40 express train, bound for Timişoara. The purpose of this journey is connected with the case of the communists brought to trial following the disorder at the funeral of the communist Fonaghy, deceased in hospital at Cîmpina, and transported by automobile to Timişoara. From Timişoara he is going to Lupeni in the Jiu Valley, where he will make contact with the workers and inform himself about the incidents that have taken place, with a view to an account that he is going to publish in pamphlets. After completing these enquires, he is going to return to Bucharest and stay there for a couple of days, after which he will go to Brăila, his birthplace, where he will stay for two weeks. On 5 October, he is leaving the country, bound for Paris."

As we can see, the agent is very well informed as to Istrati's plans. The writer is shadowed, watched, his correspondence is opened.

"General Department of Police No. 2751/29 August. Note. The Timişoara Regional Police Inspectorate reports: after being given permission by Mr Chief Prosecutor Nicolau to make contact and speak with those arrested on 7 April [when the incidents connected to the funeral of Fonaghy occurred – *author's note*] and after introducing himself to them, Mr Panait Istrati communicated to them that he had been sent by the French Government at the request of our government in order to make contact and to verify the disagreements between the workers and capitalists in Romania. In discussions, the aforementioned

---

[26] ANCR, CC of the PCR Archive, Fund 95, Dossier 9796, vol.1, p. 109.

said that, in fact, since he arrived in the country, he had ascertained that in Romania the working class is terrorised by the capitalists and had become convinced that this country is administered by bandits, promising those under arrest that on his return to France he would inform public opinion over there about the terror being exerted in these trials and about what had happened at Lupeni. When he leaves the country he will assist the workers and will discredit, as is only warranted, this country and its leaders. ... Before leaving the country, the aforementioned is going to inform Minister Vaida-Voievod of the latest events. The latter gentleman, thanks to promises made to those under arrest, is to a large extent agitating the spirits of the workers, compromising the leadership of the country and the entire administration. He has even dared to defame our Romanian women, saying that they are depraved. We have been informed that tomorrow he wishes to make contact with workers' leaders at various factories, something which is against our interests and will produce discontent in the ranks of the workers, encouraging them to continue the disturbances which have been repressed only with great difficulty up to now. The trial continues and will probably last another two days. We shall report in the morning to County Prefect Dr Țigăreanu who is similarly informed. We ask that you should give orders for the measures we are going to take."[27]

Istrati takes part in the debates at the trial in Timișoara. On 7 April 1929, a conflict had arisen between the authorities and participants at the Congress of the Communist United Unions. It was a provocation engineered by Comintern agitators. The body of Ion Fonaghy, a detainee from the Doftana Prison, is brought to Timișoara during the congress. There is a confrontation between police and demonstrators and shots are fired. There are dozens of arrests.

"What happened at Timișoara should come as no surprise. Hidden tools have been machinating everything. ... Everything was calculated. The stupidity of the police and the magistrates, always ready to light the fuse, counted for little. The communist leaders even thought of the consequences. The dispersal, the terror ... But this is precisely what they were after. Moscow has no need of unions, of democratic workers'

---

[27] *Idem*, pp. 113-114.

legislation. Moscow knows one thing and one thing only: there must be agitation at any cost – even at the price of innocent workers' blood; and as for the monitors with millions of *chernovetzi* [money – *author's note*], the only thing that suits them is clandestine activity. It's very profitable."[28]

"A ludicrous police provocation," notes Istrati (*Lupta* [*The Struggle*], 26 September). Against the background of these events, Istrati meets Lucrețiu Pătrășcanu, the defence lawyer, who offers him information and asks him to intervene on behalf of his clients. Which is precisely what Istrati does.

Panait Istrati arrives in Lupeni a month after the tragic events. On the night of 7-8 September, he stays in a hotel there. The next day, he visits the victims' widows and the hospital where there were still many wounded. He meets the miners' leaders. The authorities take special measures, fearing new disturbances. There is a state of siege in the Jiu Valley. Additional squads of gendarmes are allocated to the area. Before travelling to the Jiu Valley, Istrati is received in Bucharest by ministers Alexandru Vaida-Voievod and Ion Mihalache. He obtains a free-access permit to the area. We know his impressions from a series of eight articles published in *Lupta*. The 'investigation' conducted by Istrati runs parallel with the official enquiry. He does not have time sufficiently to inform himself, to gather impressions. His articles express revulsion at what has happened. He admonishes. He threatens that he will inform Western public opinion about what he has seen when he returns. From the series of articles published in *Lupta*, we shall transcribe a few notes about communism, a subject that preoccupies him:

"I too believed in such [revolutionary – *author's note*] enthusiasm, like so many heroes mixed up with the bandits, fanatics and bootlickers who fill the as-yet-unwritten history of Bolshevism. Today, however, the hoaxed and bloodied masses believe in nothing except the strength of their own hands."[29] "It is a matter of war. The communists have declared war on the capitalist bourgeoisie, throwing the pacifist, legal methods of social democracy onto the scrap heap. … The bourgeoisie had a right to defend its existence. And it did so, positioning itself very comfortably on the same

---

[28] *Socialistul* [*The Socialist*], 1 April 1929.
[29] *Lupta* [*The Struggle*], 24 September.

field of illegality to which its mortal enemy had made resort, even going beyond the right to self-defence, tying the tin can of communism to the tail of all those who inconvenienced it, imprisoning, beating, killing people. But the communists do not only use illegality in their struggle to lay hold of power. In non-fascist countries in particular, they agitate within the limits of the law. And thence one from two: either the law is the same for all, and in this case the communists are permitted to profit by it, or it is not the same for all, in which case one should say so decisively, eliminating any trace of legal communist agitation: newspapers, meetings, economic or political organisations. [A]nd I shall reveal these things [that he has discovered – *author's note*] to the eyes of the West, because the governments here get away with too much... determined as they are to do everything in their power to create fertile ground for Bolshevism."[30]

Naturally, rumours and suspicions regarding Istrati's journey to Romania abound. Some are fomented in Paris, in newspaper circles, others in Moscow. On 31 August, a Siguranţă report cites a news item from a Russian-language newspaper published in Paris, *Poslednaya Novosti*, according to which "Istrati is recommended to prepare for a renewal of diplomatic relations between Romania and the Soviet Union."[31] Other rumours speak of the mission he is supposed to have been given by the Comintern to organise a new workers party, which would replace or unify the various conflicting factions.[32] The Siguranţă is to follow whether Istrati makes contact with these groups and their leaders. He does not.

On 18 September 1929, a confidential report, sent to the General Police Department, reveals that on 13 September a parcel containing "72 typewritten loose leaves in French" was received at the Brăila Post Office.

> "[F]rom the summary examination that has been made it results that these loose leaves are part of a work by writer Panait Istrati, regarding his visits to various towns in Georgia and Soviet Russia and in which he documents the state of affairs in that country, the political turmoil and the means of organising the Russian proletariat in plants, factories and construction sites etc."[33]

---

[30] *Lupta*, 26 September.
[31] ANCR, CC of the PCR Archive, Fund 95, Dossier 9697, vol. 1, p. 129.
[32] *Idem*, p. 130.
[33] ANCR, CC of the PCR Archive, Fund 95, Dossier 9696, vol. 1, unspecified page.

Istrati was thinking of the book he was going to publish, *Confessional for the Vanquished*. He had asked the editor to send the proofs to Romania, in order to hasten publication of the book. Istrati stayed at home for a few days, reading the proofs. He could have waited until he returned to Paris. It is interesting that he had taken precautions for the operation not to be detected by the secret services. The envelope arrives in Timişoara, addressed to a friend, who in his turn sends it not to Istrati's address but to that of another friend in Brăila, who is to deliver it. It is possible that Istrati was afraid not of the Siguranţă but of the GPU, who were interested in reading the book in advance and attempting, as in other situations, to halt its publication. On 25 September, the General Police Department reports, "It would have been interesting for the Department to have copies of the letters addressed to the writer, or at least a summary of the findings made in Soviet Russia."[34]

The Brăila police inspectors send daily reports to Bucharest regarding Istrati's movements and conversations. Here is an excerpt for 29 September:

> "Panait Istrati shows himself to be a convinced partisan of the workers suffering as a result of the current social order and states that in his writing he will continue to support them, albeit solitarily, in isolation, unregimented by any party or left-wing or extreme left-wing group, of which he has a horror due to their narrow spirit and the compromises they accept. In this way, he criticises the Romanian Social Democratic Party, which has made a compromise with the government, as well as the communist regime in Russia … which he accuses of tyranny and narrow views."[35]

On 27 September, Istrati holds a conference in the local theatre. Nothing remained of his pro-Bolshevik, inflammatory discourse in the speech he had given in the lecture room in Athens.

> "Finally, speaking about what has been happening in Soviet Russia, which is to say the behaviour of the leaders, saying that they have done nothing short of banishing one social class and installing another, which is

---

[34] *Idem*, p. 136.
[35] *Idem*, p. 137.

heedless of even the most elementary humanitarian notions, proceeding more tyrannically with the people than the class deposed."[36]

Istrati's attempts to appear in public are obstructed by various groups. On 6 October, he was due to speak in the Tomis Room on Văcărești Avenue, a traditional left-wing meeting place. Socialist leader L. Ghelerter was organising the conference.

> "Ghelerter thought to obtain a victory thanks to the Social Democratic Party and thanks to Panait Istrati ... a writer of great talent, but ... a great muddlehead. He has remained the same muddlehead as before the war. Those of us who knew him then will not deny this. Moreover, he is a man of no character. He was in the service of the Soviets, but today he rejects them without having the courage to tell the whole truth about what he saw in Russia. The motive? He does not want to burn all his bridges with Moscow."[37]

The Istrati conference did not take place. Agitators belonging to other socialist groups, as well as nationalist students, protest both inside and outside the auditorium. Police agents stand by passively. Nevertheless, they bundle Istrati out of the theatre and protect him when the situation gets nasty. "The aforementioned Panait Istrati was notified by the Prefecture of the Bucharest police that he must leave the country on 2 October this year. On that date, Panait Istrati, in two motor cars, transported his luggage, which was searched, to the station ... The aforementioned and his wife have left the country..." At the Northern Station in Bucharest, there are likewise disturbances. Istrati takes the Orient Express to Paris. In the evening, he crosses the border at Curtici, as noted in another report by the Siguranță. He had received news that *Confessional for the Vanquished* was about to appear in the bookshops.

The Bucharest press treated him with suspicion; his recent past had not been forgotten. Nichifor Crainic[38]:

---

[36] *Idem*, p. 143.

[37] "The Panait Istrati Conference" (unsigned), in *Socialistul* [*The Socialist*], 13 October 1929.

[38] Nichifor Crainic (1889-1972) – Journalist, poet, and prominent anti-Semitic and extreme right-wing ideologue of the 1930s and (cont. p. 173.)

"Panait Istrati has resurfaced in Romania with his eternal hobby-horse: the persecuted masses. This too is a profession we all know about today. It has been practised by … Guernet, Torres and Barbusse, the famous Masonic comrades of Panaitache, impresarios of the 'venerable', no less famous Costa-Foru. You know the story: they came, they investigated us, they left, they cursed us for the whole world to hear. Romania was depicted as a country of gallows and bandit officials. Panait Istrati too has plied the trade of 'defender of humanity'. He investigated us; he cursed us thoroughly, with world-wide echoes, protected by his great, and justified, prestige as a famous and fashionable writer. … I saw him in Brussels, at the PEN Club Congress. Before the writers assembled from all over the world, he gave a lecture – about Romania, naturally; slanders, curses, lies, outrages. Our country was presented as an immense inquisition from whose cellars any innocent man would emerge tortured and disfigured – if he emerged at all! … Panait Istrati then spent a year in Soviet Russia borne in triumph and fed on the golden apples of the communist Paradise … Returning to Paris from Marxist Russia, Panait gave fresh declarations to the press, in which, this time, he renounced communism, cursed the Leninist regime … Such is the man!"[39]

Pamfil Şeicaru writes:

"The articles *What Lupeni Conceals* and *The Jiu Valley* are a disgusting accumulation of insolence, intended to disfigure the majesty of a drama provoked by politicising that had been converted into communist methods of agitation. … Panait Istrati's articles have convinced us that besides his confessions of pederasty, the narrator is a little thug with stumpy fingers who strains to appear violent, who yelps so as to appear rebellious. … Conventional, mediocre, vulgar and stupid – such is the impression given by Panait Istrati's articles. Poor humble poverty of the workers, how many pens sully you! … But did Panait Istrati really come to our country in order to portray the blood shed by the miners of the Jiu Valley in the sombre colours of tragedy? … Panait Istrati obeys orders;

1940s. Imprisoned by the Communists from 1947-1962. After his release he worked for *Glasul Patriei* (*The Voice of the Homeland*) newspaper, an organ for nationalistic communist propaganda – *Translator's note*.

[39] "Un om neserios" [An unreliable man], in *Curentul*, 29 September 1929.

he did not come at the call of any proletarian solidarity … Who are those who have deployed Panait Istrati? Who is so fervently interested in 'what is happening here in Romania? And what occult, irresistible, tyrannical force sent Panait Istrati, the poor little poet of deflowered bottoms? … Here is what Panait was assigned to present to the mysterious masters who sent him: the Romanian authorities and army as beasts crazed by alcohol and thirsty for warm, human blood. 'Those who have the right to rise up and to set the country ablaze', writes the servant of Racovski. … What a dangerous confusion – what an encouragement to all kinds of outrage! Panait Istrati the lyrical narrator of sexual perversions, the Marcel Proust of beer vendors, investigates us. Panait, Panait, was there any need to prostitute your writing, after you had defiled your body with so much voluptuous publicity?"[40]

Finally, from the *Universul* newspaper of 30 September:

"These are the words by which Panait Istrati, the slanderer of Romania and protégé of Minister Vlaida-Voievod, cynically adopts – in one of the enquiries he has published about 'Lupeni' – the sad tool of anti-Romanian interests. But not even the cynicism of these confessions, nor the shameless insults, with which, in the same enquiries, this sinister character has slung mud at the army, magistracy, police and the government of this country itself, could prompt the order of the interior minister to withdraw the blessing for him to continue his enquiry, at the same time as the hospitality which he saw fit to mock."

Istrati's isolation in Bucharest is a bad omen and foretells what awaits him in Paris.

On 1 October (while Panait Istrati is still in Romania) *L'Affaire Roussakov ou l'Union Soviétique* (a text included in *Confessional*) is published in *La Nouvelle Revue Française*. Romain Rolland's reaction: "I am consternated," as he writes one week later, on 7 October. "Nothing of all that has been written for the last 10 years against Russia, on the part of its inveterate enemies, has done so much harm as these pages will do. … The only ones who will gain any advantage from this crazed revenge: reactionaries. How could you not have realised?" Rolland again: "Istrati, I would have liked to spare you from this

---

[40] "Ah, Panait, Panait," *Curentul*, 30 September 1929.

ill-fated error … Now it is too late! Withdraw from politics. You can bring nothing but misfortunes!" The question would be, to whom? Istrati replies on 18 October:

> "We no longer have the same knowledge of Russia, nor the same feelings towards our political friends (I might say even towards the working class, as I saw it there, crushed by my countrymen). You hold me responsible for this act, as if it alone were capable of organising a capitalist crusade against the USSR. I am responsible only for a certain weakening of faith at the heart of the International. This is what I wanted and I should like to go all the way, annihilating this 'communist' party chock-full of charlatans."

Rolland's reaction is extremely negative: "I refuse you my name … My disapproval is next" (20 October 1929). In resignation, Istrati replies,

> "I was expecting your refusal. I accept it. … But if you are determined to sacrifice the best people in Russia today, not by defending the bad, but quite simply by refusing to make any distinction, taking Russia as a homogenous whole – then know that you are unintentionally supporting the destruction of hope and idealism in the world, which is now being perpetrated, both in Russia and in the International, by a generation of careerists."

Rolland replies (25 October): "I know very well that any revolutionary government swims in blood. Nor do I like bloodied hands (those of Danton, Marat, Trotsky, Lenin etc.)." Istrati writes from Strasbourg (three days later, on 28 October):

> "I shall not hide from you my amazement at seeing you become so officially Soviet. Or perhaps it is because you think me an anti-Soviet? … The question might be put to me now that I have returned from Russia: 'Were you not at all aware of what was going on over there before you left? For everyone knew you were a Bolsheviser. …?' I answer NO! … I know today that a majority of people from my class came to power, that they immediately started to stuff themselves, that they became distanced from the masses, allowing all those who were not on their side to die of hunger."[41]

---

[41] For the correspondence between Istrati and Rolland, see (cont. 176.)

The attack against Istrati is launched by Moscow. In its September-October 1929 issue, *Vestnik inostrannoy literaturny* publishes *Le grand bazar des idéologies*, signed by Bruno Jasienski. In a polemic against the interview given to Barbusse's magazine *Monde*, the author speaks of "Istrati the renegade" and a slanderous campaign against the Soviet Union. On 2 November, *Vechernyaya Moskva* publishes *The True Face of Panait Istrati*, signed by Béla Illés. It is a harsh attack, the subject is no longer limited to Soviet literary life; it turns toward the political. There is talk here of the fact that Istrati might be an agent of the Romanian secret police and that he has agreed to create an anti-communist party. Istrati is a 'writer-adventurer'. Béla Illés recalls Istrati's leftist stance and reproaches him for always having been dissatisfied with the money he received in the Soviet Union. Illés's conclusion: "Istrati quite simply wished to sell out the USSR. But since in the USSR people cannot be bought, Istrati found other buyers – the enemies of the USSR." We shall find the same accusations in 1935, signed by H. Barbusse. One week later, on 9 November, *Literaturnaya Gazeta* publishes a letter from a group of Soviet writers, including Leonid Leonov, Vladimir Mayakovsky, Valentin Katayev etc., which warns the West to be on its guard. The letter is in fact a denunciation. There is a list with the names of a number of writers who have viewed the USSR sympathetically: Theodore Dreiser, John Don Passos, George Duhamel, Stefan Zweig, H. Barbusse, Ludwig Renn. Then comes the denunciation proper. Panait Istrati, "whose very name sounds shameful" and who had come to the USSR as a:

"Determined apologist of the October Revolution," has profited from all the privileges "of his situation, which were offered him in good faith and in abundance. ... He considers himself a 'revolutionary', but he is an 'adventurer'. Istrati has demonstrated how convictions can change simply by crossing a border. After he had taken everything he could get, he abandoned his 'country of adoption' with the same ease, as can be seen, as he once abandoned the 'putrid West', whither he has now returned."[42]

Linkskurve, a left-wing publication, takes up the accusation: "With what rapidity Istrati has changed his point of view! It seems to us that the opinions

---

Les Cahiers Panait Istrati, nos. 2, 3, 4/1988.
[42] *Idem*, p. 166.

of this independent left-wing intellectual depend too often on the opinions of those paying him."[43] The line of attack for the campaign is to discredit Istrati. It was not a case of a crisis of conscience, of a lived experience, of the fact that he had understood that the Bolshevik Revolution was something other than the Kremlin claimed. Istrati was portrayed as an adventurer, a mercenary who, dissatisfied with how he had been treated and paid, had sold his services to the enemies of the USSR, the Western bourgeoisie. Behind the scenes, we discover Agitprop, the propaganda section of the Comintern and GPU. Newspapers financed by the latter take part (in France, *L'Humanité*, *Monde*), as well as subservient intellectuals and fellow travellers. There are brief lulls in the campaign, but it will not cease until after the death of the author. Istrati is mentioned in pro-Moscow left-wing circles only in a negative context. Otherwise, his name is ignored. It is a conspiracy of silence, compounded with repeated campaigns of defamation.

Under these circumstances, Istrati prefers to return home. *Confessional for the Vanquished* can be found in large Bucharest bookshops after January 1930. It is a refuge. Present in the political, newspaper and cultural media of the West, in Paris especially, where he had been launched and achieved literary fame, he could have defended himself. By returning to Romania, did he give up? Is he overwhelmed, vanquished? In any case, even at home he finds no peace. The Siguranță continue to keep him under surveillance, suspecting him of communist activities, as is revealed by the reports in the archive. The polemics surrounding him, connected to his change of attitude to the USSR, were well-known, but might be a diversion, they might be a myth created by the Soviet special services in order for him to operate more effectively as an agent of influence. In Bassarabia, the authorities ban sale of *Confessional* (the Romanian-language edition, published by *Cugetarea*) in March. A few days later, at the beginning of April, a telegram from the police at Curtici reports, "he has entered the country on No. 24 Express Train ... declaring that he is heading to Bucharest." The next day, 6 April 1930, a note from the police and Siguranță reveals: "Agitator Panait Istrati, former honorary member of the USSR [*sic!*], has been expelled from the Third International, due to his attitude towards the latter, which culminated in the issue of the volume entitled *Confessional for the Vanquished*/Soviet Russia."[44] The same report recapitulates his trip of 1929 and his relations with Dr

---

[43] *Idem*, p. 168.
[44] ANCR, CC of the PCR Archive, Fund 95, Dossier 9697, vol. 1, p. 179.

Leon Ghelerter, the president of the small Socialist Workers Party. Likewise, the report records his daily movements. It is reported that "he appears to be an inveterate enemy of the Soviet regime and describes the life of the Russian people in the blackest colours. Panait Istrati upholds that if the borders of Russia were not guarded with such severity by the Soviet authorities, a large part of the populace would emigrate to other countries."[45]

"Panait Istrati recently received from France a voluminous mailbag among which there are a few letters from Russia posted to his address in France, by the writer Victor Serge (pen name), who is in Moscow with his family and of whom Panait Istrati makes mention in his recent book 'The Rusakov Affair' [sic!]. In these letters Victor Serge gives a detailed description of economic life in Russia, and in order to characterise better the state of affairs in that country, he expresses himself in the words 'When you were in Russia in 1928, it was a paradise, but today it is a hell'. Panait Istrati, reading the letters, remarked 'In 1928, when I was in Russia, it was already a hell, so what must it be like today?'"[46]

On 17 June, a report reveals that he has not made contact with any suspicious left-wing organisations, that he has refused to give any more lectures in union circles, that he receives 6,000 French francs every month from Reider publishers in Paris, that he is ill and is going to Cîmpulung to take the air and for treatment. Other notes record the foreigners who visit him. Arriving in Bucharest, he meets Nina Arbore, Dr Ghelerter, and George Costa-Foru. On 10 July, when he leaves Romania, also via Curtici, a note demands, "the person in question should immediately be notified to the Department on his return."[47] The conscientious functionary does so on 17 July. Istrati goes to Brăila, comes to Bucharest, whence he goes to Cîmpulung etc. He receives foreign guests, publishes some works in the press, is signalled in reports by the Siguranţă, looks after his health. Istrati gives the impression of a man who cannot find a place for himself. Which is true.

Willy-nilly, he provokes disturbances, quarrels. He does not have the peace he desired, if he ever desired such a thing. One example: in January 1931, at the conference in Jassy, the followers of Alexandru C. Cuza and

---

[45] *Idem*, p. 185.

[46] *Idem*, pp. 186-187.

[47] *Idem*, p. 197.

militant communists separately agitate to prevent him from speaking. The police take drastic measures to maintain order. Here is an excerpt from the Cuzist manifesto disseminated in the city:

"A new crusade by the 'advocates of humanity' is venting its fury in our native Romanian lands. The Communist International, hand in hand with occult freemasonry, the author of all the infernal plots to destroy Christianity, royalty and constructive nationalism, has this year sent the most odious scoundrel, the abortion that answers to the name Panait Istrati. In Jassy, the pederast cur was embraced with the utmost warmth by his brothers in Judas ... The miscreant who abroad made the most injurious slurs on our dear monarchy, our Church and Romanianism in general, the scoundrel who, in collusion with all the internationals in the world, has caused the country the greatest evil is now coming to Jassy, sent here by occult Judaeo-Masonry, under guise of literature, to apologise for destructive communism ... he thinks that in Yiddified and Masonised Jassy there is no longer a Romanian consciousness to nail him to the post of infamy ... We shall teach the miscreant a lesson."[48]

Nor do the communists treat him any better. Alexandru Sahia writes on 30 January 1932, in *Floare de foc* [*Flame Flower*] (director: Sandu Tudor):

"What a great scoundrel you are, Comrade Istrati! I remember your glory days, when all you had to do was announce you were working on a book for all the Western publishers to fall over themselves making you offers. What was this down to? Talent? Let's be honest! It was the red trampoline that bounced you so amazingly high. The two fat cows, Racovski and Trotsky, proffered you their teats, to suck your fill like a frisky colt. Racovski, representative of the Soviets in Paris at the time, was happy to meet the comrade again; he offered you roubles. Away in Russia, recommended by Racovski to Trotsky – the latter divined in you a fresh element for his permanent revolution movement. But Trotsky has been thrown overboard in the meantime, Racovski scuppered in Astrakhan. And in Russia, formidable industrialisation and reconstruction of the economy begin in earnest. Who would think that in a corner there still exists Panait, the bard of the 'taverns'! But things

---

[48] *Idem*, p. 197.

might still have been confused if the one who today curses communism had not come up with meddlesome financial claims ... As his reward, Panait, a follower of Trotsky, was shown to the Dniester. The Bolsheviks were unaware of any way to pay you except with bread, the same as any other worker, and on top of it all they gave you the freedom to roam. You couldn't understand. You refused indignantly; you wanted money and blood. You feel good now ... among the Danube cesspools, providing for the King's dictatorship... lover of tyrants."

On 15 November 1932, *Şantier* [*Building Site*], a left-wing weekly run by socialist Ion Pas, translator of the first version of *Confessional*, published an article by Sandu Eliad (himself a man of the Left, a journalist and film director, the discoverer of singer Maria Tănase, and later one of the founders of the 'Friends of the USSR' association): *Panait Istrati: The Globetrotter of Beliefs*. It is a personal attack: "Panait Istrati has flown banner of every belief according to the fashion of the time, according to how much he expected to get paid." Another attack came from a friend of his youth, also a communist, who lived in Paris and whom he also used to meet at the USSR embassy, at gatherings hosted by Racovski. On 7 February 1932, his old friend Alecu Constantinescu breaks with him, publishing in Detroit, in the Romanian communist weekly *Desteptarea*, a long article entitled *A Necessary Explanation. My Friendship with Panait Istrati*. It is a late reaction to *Confessional for the Vanquished*. "I have known Istrati since 1909. During the period when the union and socialist movement headquarters were situated on Victory Avenue, opposite the White Church, a tall, slim young man, with a greedy mouth but gentle, obedient eyes, introduced himself to me. ..." Constantinescu wanted to turn the decorator, who had only four years of primary schooling, into a theoretician of Marxism. He introduces him to left-wing circles, discusses with him, helps him to get to Paris, and initiates him into the mysteries of the doctrine. Then their paths separate. Constantinescu adheres to Bolshevism, becomes head of the clandestine movement in Romania, is condemned to death, arrested, escapes, emigrates to Russia, subsequently living in Paris, as a Comintern agent. Istrati goes to Switzerland in 1916. He too is full of enthusiasm for what is happening in Russia, for Bolshevism. Before becoming a well-known writer, he attempts suicide. Istrati, the "born revolutionary" (his words), could find nothing better to do in Nice than to slit his throat when four or five white armies surrounded Soviet Russia, ready to slice into the living flesh of the Russian people. Istrati is also guilty of revering Trotsky. "Trotsky is the only leader capable of illuminating the opinion of the masses," he believes, while Constantinescu believes that Trotsky tried to obfuscate it. For Istrati, "these communists are inferior beings who have lost any notion of individual liberty, puppets moved by the strings of the Comintern and the Russian Party." We discover that Istrati threw his French Communist Party membership card into the Seine when Trotsky was expelled from the Comintern. His old friend disapproves of him and says that he is a "thoughtless anarchist, for anarchy at any price." He also reproaches his opinion that there is no proletarian class awareness, writing of the latter that it is "nothing but appetite to get their hands on the bourgeoisie's turkeys and geese! Nothing more. Panait Istrati could see nothing more in Russia and Marx." And he concludes: "The difficult times my class are undergoing has opened a gulf between myself and the writer Istrati."[49] Their split did not prevent Alecu Constantinescu writing to Istrati, who was in Filaret Hospital, one month later:

> "For all the deep differences between our views and the bitterness your apolitical capers have provoked in me, the news that you too have arrived in the last palace of Gheorghiu [Ștefan Gheorghiu, militant socialist, friend of Istrati in his youth, died of tuberculosis in Filaret Hospital in 1914 – *author's note*] and perhaps even in the same bed, has touched me … I have received the parcel of newspapers and thank you."

Further on, the text seems to be rather a secret, ciphered message, such as those which old, clandestine friends used to send each other.[50]

In 1935, the anti-Istrati campaign erupts once more. This time, it is connected to the trial of a university professor from Cernăuți, Petre Constantinescu-Iași. After his arrest in November 1934, the Comintern organises the usual agitation. The Moscow-financed press comes to the defence of the arrested professor, claiming that he is not a communist agent, but an anti-fascist intellectual. Various (crypto-)Bolshevik associations from Europe join the campaign. Naturally, a group of 'independent' intellectuals

---

[49] *Deșteptarea*, 7 February 1932.
[50] In Panait Istrati, *Pagini de corespondență* [*Pages from the correspondence*], Brăila Museum, Galați: Editura Porto Franco, 1993, pp. 114-115.

come to Romania in order to conduct an investigation. At their head, we find a well-known figure, architect Francis Jourdain (1876-1958). He is the vice-president of the Les Amis de l'URSS Association. In 1927, he is part, together with Panait Istrati and others, of the French delegation that attends the tenth anniversary of the Bolshevik Revolution in Moscow. The French Communist Party daily *L'Humanité* (31 October 1927) even runs the front-page headline *"Panait Istrati et Francis Jourdain à Moscou,"* in an article illustrated with colour photographs of the two. They knew each other well. After 1929, ties between them are broken. On 14 January 1935, Petre Constantinescu-Iași is released on bail to await trial. On the same day, the French delegation arrives in Kishinev. On 17 January 1935, Panait Istrati publishes in *Curentul* an "Open letter to my friend Francis Jourdain, vice-president of the French Friends of the USSR, and currently their moral delegate in Romania." A few excerpts:

"You should understand how unsuitable it is for a man of your moral worth to play the role of communist investigator in a communist affair, a role you have accepted to play in the country most exposed to communist terror. ... You admit that in the investigation you are conducting you are accompanied by two Soviet stooges of more than dubious morality ... you should ask yourself whether it is honest to patronise moral investigations only when a communist is arrested in a bourgeois country, and on the contrary to remain tight-lipped whenever, in Soviet Russia, legions of young idealists are exiled to the icy wastes and summarily executed, idealists that have included my personal friends ... Professor Constantinescu-Iași was neither exiled nor martyred, but was quite simply arrested for communist agitation ... I presume that you are not so naïve as to believe that the situation in Romania, here on the Dniester, is the same situation as in France, between the Rhine and the Atlantic, or that the bourgeois government could have been moved by this whole sentimental comedy [Petre Constantinescu-Iași's hunger strike – *author's note*], when they have to deal with an adversary that promises to put them up against the wall on the very day a Soviet regime is installed here. I read in the papers today that, arriving in Kishinev, you had nothing better to do than make contact with two communist Jews, which unleashed the legitimate fury of those nationalist strata that have a thousand reasons not to share your sympathy for the communist regime.

Well, dear Jourdain, you will not know the consequences of this exploit of yours, because you are going away, protected by those Romanian soldiers that the theology professor's comrades shoot year after year on the Dniester and who don't really know what to make of you when they are fighting communist banditry."

Istrati resumes two days later, in *Universul*: "I no longer believe in communism, which, especially for the vanquished, I regard as the greatest danger that threatens humanity today."

These two articles unleash a frenzied campaign in *Monde*, a publication financed by the Comintern. But before that, in Bucharest, Mihail Sebastian writes of Istrati in *Rampa*: "Rhetorical, sentimental thinking, quite gross in its theories, but lyrical, animated, made to warm simple hearts. ... Bolshevik or Nazi, Mr Istrati is innocent. ... What Mr Istrati says on the subject of political doctrine is hilarious, pretentious, mediocre and – let us state it clearly – stupid ... The theory of a semiliterate, limited man, a closed mind."[51] Mihail Sebastian was not lacking in left-wing sympathies. Sahia, in *Bluze Albastre* [*Blue Shirts*], 1 July 1932, sharply reminds him of his communist sympathies, already abandoned at that date, and the fact that he had become a member of the bar on the recommendation of two communist lawyers. Sebastian had a marked awareness of his own status as a Jew. As such, he was disturbed by Istrati's membership of the *Crusade of Romanianism*. The attack in *Rampa* may be a coincidence, not necessarily an episode in the anti-Istrati campaign.

The leader of this campaign was Henri Barbusse, director of *Monde*. Barbusse was a militant communist. A Kremlin favourite involved in all the Comintern's agitation and propaganda activities in Europe. He was to be found more often in Moscow than in France. His relationship with Istrati dated from 1919, when the Romanian had addressed a letter to him, *"Lettre d'un ouvrier à Henri Barbusse,"* published in *La Feuille* in Geneva. In the 1920s, the two collaborated. In 1928, Barbusse publishes *"Istrati est des nôtres,"* in defence of Istrati, attacked for anti-Sovietism in the German communist press. After publication of the *Vers l'autre flamme* trilogy, the two part ways. The new anti-Istrati campaign is launched under the heading *"Les victoires du capitalisme"* in *Monde*, with an article signed by Francis Jourdain himself:

---

[51] "Panait Istrati, ideolog politic" [*P. I. political ideologue*], *Rampa*, 30 January 1935.

"Réponse à Panaït Istrati," dated 1 February 1935.[52] A few quotations:

> "Since we arrived in Romania, the reactionary press has treated my comrades and myself as agents provocateur, thugs disguised as 'intellectuals', OFF WITH THE MASK! it cries ... You [Panait Istrati – *author's note*] willingly lend them the support of your talent, you place at their disposal the authority granted to you by your supposed acquaintance with us ... since you are afraid that, from an excess of modesty and discretion, I might forget to tell your anti-Soviet government that I am an active friend of the USSR, then you pre-empt me, with a generous and chivalrous initiative, presenting me as the vice-president of an association whose activity is banned in your country, and whose members your fascist friends have undertaken to exterminate ... Sincerely, such sentimentalism (?) might naturally have forced a number of errors: BUT NOT CAPITULATION. I no longer believe in the sincerity of your deranged ardour. I do not incriminate you for what you were unable to be, for what you in any case have never pretended to be: A MARXIST. I impute to you that you are not what you claim to be: a rebel, a refractory. Rebellious, braggart but sincere, you would have wept for admiration before the courage and abnegation of the likes of Dimitroff, Thaelmann, Rákosi – likewise before the likes of Constantinescu-Iaşi, at whom you bark like a cur. ... Anarchist, rebel, unyielding? Let's be serious! Patriot, anti-Semite, fascist!"

In the same issue, Louis Dolivet publishes *Le loup devenu mouton ou Panaït Istrati fasciste*. There follow others – authors Charles Vidrac and lawyer J. Ferucci (the latter of whom comes to Bucharest) under the title *Le cas Panaït Istrati*. The subject is the same: Istrati's fascism. "You are neither a democrat nor a communist. All that is left is for you to be a fascist," J. Ferucci tells him. In a long article for *La Commune* (March 1935), entitled *Un traître*, Vladimir Pozner reminds Istrati of his erstwhile opinions about the USSR and publishes a letter sent to Francis Jourdain in 1928, from near Moscow, in which the Romanian is very critical of the West and displays his enthusiasm for the USSR. "Friends, believe steadfastly in the red star that rises over the horizon of communist humanity!" wrote Istrati then. After returning

---

[52] The text was published in Romanian translation in the gazette of L. Ghelerter *Proletarul* [*The Proletarian*], on 4 March.

from the USSR, Istrati became "a professional of oaths, a recidivist of good intentions, a hysterical man of letters, he declaims, he foams at the mouth, he spits out his lungs." Pozner accuses him of Trotskyism and fascism: "The ambivalence did not last an eternity. There followed a brutal descent into chauvinism, anti-Semitism, fascism: the 'other flame' of Panait Istrari." Istrati is a "corpse." We shall also encounter this double accusation, of Trotskyism and fascism, in the trials of the Great Terror.

The most significant text of the campaign is signed by Henri Barbusse, on 22 February: *Le Haïdouk de la Siguranţă*. We also find here the themes with which we have been dealing in this book: collaboration with the security, denunciation, betrayal and money. Thus, Istrati is an agent of the Siguranţă and has become a critic of the USSR for financial motives. Barbusse writes, "Panait Istrati made his debut in life as a poor man. Crushed by social injustice, needy, a vagabond, porter, vendor of postcards and itinerant photographer, one fine day he was washed up on the Côte d'Azur, with his belly empty and his literature drowned." After being saved by Rolland, "he knew satiety, fame, almost glory … moreover, in our half of humanity [the communist half – *author's note*], we saluted him as a rebel." Then Istrati, writes Barbusse, referring to *Confessional for the Vanquished*, published books which did not live up to the hopes placed in him. And he adds: "The decline of Panait Istrati the writer and Panait Istrati the man are not two different stories, but one and the same story. For him, the man has ended up demolishing the artist." The two had known each other for almost 15 years. What he recalls now, in 1935, is that "Istrati was infatuated and displayed an air of superiority, that he hated Gorky because he had been compared to him and the latter earned more money. In any case, Istrati used to talk only about himself and about money." "The dithyrambic praises of the USSR … the solemn oath … to be buried in Soviet soil" were nothing more than a business deal for Istrati. Barbusse tells us that Istrati told a mutual friend that if the USSR had treated him better, he would have had a different attitude. Naturally, Barbusse does not tell us who has given him this information. He knew perfectly well that VOKS, Agitprop, Comintern and the GPU paid cash for the many image-building services that various journalists and writers agreed to perform for the Soviet Union. He himself received stipends from Soviet funds, and he was adept at making propaganda and taking part in campaigns such as the one launched against Istrati. Istrati too had received large sums in royalties for the many editions of his books translated into Russian. He had also received money for articles and interviews. The Russians had paid for his hotels, train fares, meals etc. for the entire duration of his trip. This is true, but it did not prevent him, once he had become aware of what was happening in the USSR, from keeping his distance, even if he knew that he would lose all these advantages. Barbusse did not do likewise, and remained until his death, in August 1935, on the payroll of the Comintern.

After finishing with the accusations regarding money, Barbusse moves on to accusations regarding morality. He claims that at Lupeni in 1929 Istrati took part in a 'government investigation', he travelled around with official investigators, he was in agreement with the authorities that had ordered the miners to be fired on and were guilty of the massacre of the union that called the strike. Denunciation, slander and blatant lies were part of the techniques frequently used by the Comintern when someone had to be destroyed. Barbusse manipulated them dextrously and unscrupulously. Then, Istrati is supposed to have taken part at a congress of the (communist) United Unions in 1932 and to have demanded that it should be outlawed and a large number of its militants arrested. Furthermore, Istrati is supposed to have denounced to the press a number of communists who were living clandestinely in Brăila and played the 'role of provocateur'. The Siguranță made many arrests, writes Barbusse, after these denunciations, approved by Istrati in an article for *Curentul*. The episode is entirely invented. For six months, continues Barbusse, "Istrati has been officially attached to a faction of the Iron Guard, an armed, pogromist and terrorist faction, controlled by the Hitlerite government." Barbusse mentions that it was the Iron Guard that assassinated Prime Minister I. Gh. Duca. Istrati is supposed to belong to the Mihai Stelescu group and is one of the group's three leaders. He mentions that he writes for *Cruciada Românismului* [*Crusade of Romanianism*], the group's newspaper, and that it has dedicated many articles to him.[53] Barbusse accuses that on 19 January 1935 Istrati wrote in an article for *Universul* that the wider interests of humanity were threatened by communism and revolution. "Behold the writer, behold the man!," exclaims Barbusse, overcome. Istrati "presents himself as an apostle and even as a martyr, when in fact he is the lackey of the reactionary hangmen, the holders of secret funds, and the police torture chambers. Panait Istrati, rabid dog

---

[53] This episode in the career of Istrati requires separate analysis, which we do not propose to make here.

of the pack that hunts down revolutionaries. Panait Istrati, bought by the enemy to betray his former brothers in poverty and his former comrades in the struggle, to betray his own cause. Panait Istrati, handsome ornament of Panurge's flock of mangy sheep." In his indictments, prosecutor Andrey Yanuarevich Vyshinsky will also dub Kamenev, Zinoviev, Bukharin Rykov and Rakovksi as "rabid dogs" and demand their extermination. As he was writing these lines, Barbusse was negotiating the royalties and expenses for his work on Stalin. And he was paid handsomely.[54] Barbusse had a sumptuous villa on the Côte d'Azur, and practically unlimited sums from Soviet sources. The "venal Istrati" remained poor. The accusations bore no relation to reality. The attack was strictly a propaganda exercise, intended to destroy the adversary.

The article was a public execution. Who could check the truth of the affirmations made by Barbusse and the others in *Monde*, *La Commune*, and *L'Humanité*? The silence surrounding Istrati is remarkable. No one came to his defence. He was also far from Paris, in Bucharest. He was ill and had no means of intervening. He also had a reputation for inconstancy. He passed as an erstwhile, vociferous Bolshevik, who had betrayed his old beliefs. He was viewed with suspicion by apolitical intellectuals. To them, Istrati was far too mixed up in political disputes and had once adhered to a dubious cause. The politicised, but with other allegiances, viewed him as a former communist. In any case, Istrati did not hesitate to criticise capitalism and Western democracies in harsh terms even after 1929. In this context, it is no wonder that Istrati is isolated, put up against the wall of infamy by Barbusse and co., morally assassinated, annihilated. Many preferred to view the campaign passively, seeing it as a 'family' quarrel. The 1936-1938 trials in Moscow will be viewed in the same way. The death of Istrati, on 16 April, puts an end to this campaign.

The 1930s were a decade of Manichaeism, of fascism versus communism. Any 'midway', independent position or nuance was neither understood nor followed. Changes of attitude were even less appreciated. Hitler's accession to power in Germany had simplified the terrain and reduced the options.

---

[54] See the details in Dmitri Volkogonov, *Lenin. O nouă biografie*, Orizonturi-Lider, 1999, p. 435 and in Arkadi Vaksberg, *Hotel Lux. Partidele comuniste frățești în slujba Internaționalei comuniste* [*Hotel Lux. The Fraternal Communist Parties in the Service of the Communist International*], Bucharest: Humanitas, 1998, pp. 74-77.

The criticism unleashed by Istrati's travel diary, which under normal circumstances ought to have become broader, more focussed, and to have provoked a debate (as happened in the 1970s when Alexander Solzhenitsyn published *The Gulag Archipelago*), is reduced to silence. After January 1933, the USSR is perceived as a hope, an alternative to the Nazi regime in Germany. For a time, Europe had to choose between two dictators, Hitler and Stalin. The democracies seemed weak and lacking in any political will to confront their adversaries. Istrati had been a proponent of the cause of revolution and Bolshevism who, disillusioned by what he had encountered in the USSR, broke the silence. He was regarded as a traitor. The *Greater Soviet Encyclopaedia* (1937) writes: "Istrati manifests himself [in his novels – *author's note*] as an anarchist extremist and individualist. In 1928, he visited the Soviet Union. In collaboration with counter-revolutionary Trotskyites he wrote a series of revolting caricatures about the Soviet Union." In the same year, 1937, the *Lesser Soviet Encyclopaedia* noted: "His works are coloured by facile romanticism and a spirit of petty bourgeois revolt. He likewise manipulates this mediocre ideology in his description of the *haidouks*." After he had made a journey to the USSR, "he spread venomous slanders against the Soviet land and out of compliance with the international counter-revolution spread propaganda hostile to the USSR."[55]

---

[55] *Cahiers Paniat Istrati*, no. 11/1994, pp. 187-188.

VII
The Heroes of the Proletariat (1)

On 32 July 1963, Vasile Luca dies in Aiud Prison. "Myocardial infarction, against a background of generalised arteriosclerosis and viscerotropic hypertonic disease," states the death certificate. Luca had been syphilitic since early manhood, and died in the terminal phase of the disease. He was not the only communist leader to be infected with syphilis. Chivu Stoica and Remus Koffler suffered from the same disease. Clandestinity also meant promiscuity. In prison, Luca lost his mind. He could no longer speak and was capable only of emitting unintelligible grunts. He could not wash himself; he soiled himself. He was delirious. He was a human wreck. During his imprisonment he had not had access to any medical treatment. Gheorghiu-Dej watched him with hatred until the day of his death. The press wrote nothing about the death of Vasile Luca. Nevertheless, he had been a communist militant in the 1920s, one of the emblematic figures of the years leading up to the PCR's seizure of power.

In those years, Luca cut the figure of a working-class hero. He had served 10 years in prison. He had taken part in numerous class struggles. He had been an important union leader. During the war, he had worked in the USSR. Therefore, he had a 'heroic' past. After the war, he was vice-president of the Council of Ministers and Minister of Finance. However, he derived his real power from being a member of the Political Bureau and the influential Party Secretariat, alongside Gheorghiu-Dej, Ana Pauker and Teohari Georgescu. Luca was, for a time, one of the most powerful men in Romania. In 1952, he was deposed and arrested. He was brought to trial two years later and sentenced to death. No one could have imagined that he would die in the way he did.

Vasile Luca (Luka László) was born in 1898, in the village of Catalina, near Brașov/Kronstadt. His parents were Szekler Hungarians. He had a sister: german, seven brothers: german and four stepbrothers. His mother was thrice married and twice widowed. In 1905, Luka László was taken to the Maria Thereza Hungarian Catholic children's home in Sibiu. He never spoke Romanian fluently. He left school after only finishing sixth form. In 1910, he learned the trade of locksmith in a small workshop. "I grew up in a petit bourgeois setting and dreamed of becoming somebody by having adventures like in the novels I read."[1] In 1915, he gets a job as a porter at a railway depot in Brașov, then as a railway station porter. He is caught stealing. As he is a minor and the amount small, he is sentenced to remain under his parents' supervision. Although still a minor, he prefers to volunteer for the army. "In October 1915, I joined the army in Prague, Czechoslovakia, and after two months of instruction I was sent to the Russian front. From 1915 until the collapse of the war effort in 1918 I was at the Russian front twice and once on the front against the Romanian Army, in Slănic Moldova, once in Italy and Albania, where, sick of the war, I deserted a few weeks before the outbreak of Károly's bourgeois-democratic revolution in Hungary, and in Budapest I took part in the popular demonstrations for peace, for Hungary to leave the war, to separate from Austria and declare a republic. I was demobilised and went home to my parents' house in Lemnia. In the First World War I obtained the rank of sergeant at arms and two medals. A medal for bravery and the Cross of Karl (former King of Austria-Hungary). The First World War had a disastrous effect on my morale. I had become a drunkard, and a lecher in relation to women. In the city of Lugoj, where my Division was stationed for a few months in 1916, and in Volhinia (on the Russian front) I contracted syphilis in contact with prostitutes. I continued to lead this decadent life even after my return home. I did not seek to return to honest work."[2]

Like many other communist leaders he began his political career in the opposing camp. In 1919, a Bolshevik Revolution broke out in Hungary. Demobilised, unemployed, without any income, Luca joined the 'national guard' as a paid volunteer, with the task of maintaining law and order locally. Then he volunteered for the Szekler Division, a paramilitary organisation with a dual orientation – anti-Bolshevik and anti-Romanian – to fight 'for the salvation of Transylvania from Romanian invasion' and to halt the eastward spread of the 'Bolshevik Revolution in Hungary'.

In 1919, during the Russian offensive to reach Budapest, part of the illusory scenario of a world proletarian revolution led by Lenin and Trotsky, Luca deserted as the front came closer and tried to join the Reds. He was rejected because of having been a member of the Szekler Division. He was always on the lookout for better-paid jobs, watchful of how the balance of forces was shifting. He returns to the Division and takes part in the forcible

---

[1] ASRI, Fund Y, Dossier 40005, p. 244.

[2] *Idem*, p. 246.

removal of a number of local Soviets. The Division is dissolved by the Romanian authorities and Luca goes into hiding, waiting for the 'Hungarian Red Army, believing in its victory and the Revolution in Hungary and thus the liberation of Transylvania'. Béla Kuhn is defeated in Budapest after the invasion of Romanian and Czechoslovak troops. Later, in search of a heroic past, Luca will claim to have fought in the Hungarian Red Army.

In September 1919, Luca is a civilian once more, working as a locksmith at the CFR Brașov depot.

> "I was at the forefront of them all as far as a debauched life of drunkenness, card games and parties with prostitutes went. A lad of 20, I was becoming more and more degenerate [...] I did not manage to rid myself of this lumpenproletariat degeneracy for a long time, not even when I was elevated into the workers' movement, and my whole life I have never had any genuine morals."[3]

Luca is thus a semi-qualified lumpenproletarian, in an exigent, disciplined working-class environment dominated by Germans and Hungarians. Thanks to his biography, Luca belongs to the periphery, to the dregs of the working class, to the déclassé. By temperament, he is choleric, restless, ever in search of a better, more secure position. He does not like the factory. He changes his place of work frequently, at intervals of a few weeks or even days. He prefers taverns, brothels, discussions, parties. He likes meetings where he can speak to the crowd and show off as a leader. He discovered this liking on the occasion of the unrest of 1917-1919 among the soldiers, when he was chosen to represent the men in front of the commandants. He likes to have power. He likes meetings, demonstrations where he can take the floor and be applauded. The trades unions offer him the opportunity to 'elevate himself', as he puts it, to be a 'gentleman', to exchange his overalls for a white shirt and tie, to sit at the table with the factory owners (for negotiations), to be noticed. He does not have any 'class consciousness' properly speaking, any working-class pride, otherwise widespread in an area where the worker has a tradition behind him and a trade is often handed down from generation to generation.

Luca is a peasant by origin, and he adapts to his new circumstances as he goes along. The cause of the working class is alien to him. He is an outsider,

---

[3] ASRI, *idem*, p. 251.

a newcomer. The same pattern is repeated in the case of Nicolae Ceauşescu, also from a non working-class background, without any trade, a déclassé, a marginal. Luca has the smatterings of a trade. He was an apprentice in a small workshop for four years. He quickly gives it up to dedicate himself to union agitation, a more lucrative occupation in his eyes, one which also advances his social status. The more alien and lacking in tradition, the more radical and fanatical.

> "Being highly active in the workers' movement and combative in the working-class cause, the union and the Party promoted me very quickly to union leadership and then the leadership of the local organisation of the Romanian Communist Party, even though I was very young both in terms of my age and how long I had been in the movement. I also had great personal ambitions to get ahead, to become a noted leader of the working-class movement. The more I rose in the movement the more my pride grew, and I was aiming to increase my popularity at the heart of the working masses […] For me, however, the movement – I mean the period of the legal movement up until the illegal clandestine movement – was my salvation from falling once more into drunkenness and debauchery [he had married in 1922 – *author's note*] of the lumpenproletariat. For me the movement was everything. I could not live without the movement. I could not live the monotonous life of a petit bourgeois."[4]

He quickly builds a career for himself in the 1920s. In 1922, he becomes a member of the PCdR. He climbs the hierarchy of the Red unions and the PCdR. On 1 July 1924, he becomes Regional Secretary, after the Fourth Congress of the PCdR, held in Vienna, at which Elek Köblős also becomes Secretary General, replacing Gheorghe Cristescu-Plăpumaru. It was an important position, given that he was running the party organisations in Braşov, Trei Scaune, Tîrnava Mică, Sibiu, Hunedoara and Valea Jiului counties at the age of only 26 and after just three years in the party. "I thought a lot about the good salary I was offered, about the title of Secretary, about my importance in the movement, about my easier life, about travel, adventure, etc."[5] Circumstances are not in his favour: the PCdR is outlawed under the Mîrzescu Law. The Siguranţă proceeds to make arrests. The

---

[4] ASRI, *idem*, p. 254.

[5] *Idem*, p. 261.

communist militants and leaders had acted in the open up until then, and as such they were well-known to the Siguranță. There followed a wave of arrests. Luca, accused of printing and distributing irredentist manifestos addressed to the Hungarian population of Transylvania, was arrested. He played an important role, as he was in direct contact with the Secretary General of the PCdR, Elek Köblős, who was in hiding near Brașov, in a house provided by Luca himself. He was also in contact with other communist leaders, likewise in hiding: Alexandru Dobrogeanu-Gherea, Marcel and Ana Pauker, and Ștefan Foriș, whom Luca had known since 1922. Beaten during interrogation by the Brashov police, Luca capitulates. "I behaved in a way unworthy not only of a communist but also of a simple worker with class consciousness. I behaved in a traitorous way. I betrayed the Party and with it the working class,"[6] he writes after his final arrest on 18 February 1953. In addition, he accepts, in return for payment, to become a Siguranță informant. "He [the commandant] promised me money, producing from a drawer a wad of banknotes. He promised me a good job after my release or if I wanted to join the Siguranță with a decent wage, etc. I capitulated."[7] The enthusiastic proletarian, the defender of the exploited worker, begins to play the game of the Siguranță and is an extremely dangerous agent, because "I knew very many of the Party's secrets."[8] It is the turning point in his career.

In March 1925, Vasile Luca is released, after a hunger strike, together with other detainees. He then vanishes, at the orders of the Comintern, along with Alexandru Dobrogeanu-Gherea, Marcel Pauker, David Fabian Finkelstein, et al. They will each receive 10 years imprisonment. Luca hides for a time, but is captured in September 1925. He is already suspected of being a Siguranță agent. The internal inquiry, conducted in its entirety inside Jilava Prison by Marcel Pauker, reaches no conclusion. Luca denies any agreement between the Siguranță and himself. In 1957, he sends Gheorghiu-Dej a memorandum from Rîmnicu Sărat Prison in which he admits, "I fell into the hands of the Siguranță through my own stupidity the first time, as an informer, but I broke off this connection quickly. And then, in 1925, when I was sentenced *in absentia* to 10 years, I betrayed, I fell. I thought that I had been abandoned by the Party, and I sought to save myself through betrayal, i.e. through an arrangement I made with Inspector

---

[6] *Idem*, p. 264.

[7] *Idem*, p. 267.

[8] *Idem*, p. 264.

Zahiu [...] But the truth is that I did not fulfil the wishes of the Siguranță, but made use of the respite gained through compromises with the Siguranță to carry out revolutionary activity. I sincerely recognise today that it was a perfidious, villainous game, but at the time I saw things differently and I believed that I would be able to deceive the Siguranță for a long while and they, using information received from other informers and provocateurs, forced me to confess to a number of things."[9] This 'game' was widespread in the communist networks. The same as wherever conspiracies, plots and the underground are to be found, the secret services infiltrated the networks with their agents and recruited informers. The Okhrana and the Bolsheviks had had similar relations.

In 1928, after three years of detention, Luca is tried anew, in a large-scale trial of communists, in which he figures as Boris Ştefanov's second-in-command. There are numerous convictions. Boris Ştefanov is handed the heaviest sentence: eight years. Luca is acquitted. No sooner has he been released than he crosses the border into the USSR clandestinely and takes part in the Fourth Congress of the PCR, near Kharkov, in June and July. Luca's protector, Elek Köblős, accused of Trotskyism, is ousted from the position of Secretary General. David Fabian Finkelstein, the number two man in the PCR hierarchy, is also ousted. The Comintern imposes Vitali Kholostenko as Party leader. He is a Ukrainian activist, a former student of veterinary medicine in Bucharest. Vasile Luca abandons his former boss and joins the camp of the victors, proof of his instinct for political survival. He is a member of the Congress Presidium. He heads the committee on peasant issues. Finally, he is elected as a member of the Central Committee of the PCdR. In addition, he is a member of the Political Bureau and the Party Secretariat. In 1929, when the leadership abroad, based in Vienna, and the leadership in Romania merge, Luca is also part of this clique.[10]

Among all these professional revolutionaries, he cuts the figure of a worker, of a union leader. In the late 1920s, the PCR was dominated by intellectuals and petit bourgeois converts to Bolshevism, lured by the mirage of the 'Revolution of 1917'. Luca is one of the few who come from a working-class background. And this also explains his rapid rise in the communist hierarchy. Having become an influential leader of the Red trades unions

---

[9] *Sfera politicii*, no. 33/1995.

[10] Marin C. Stănescu, *Moscova, Cominternul, Filiera comunistă balcanică şi România, 1919-1944*, Editura Silex, 1994, pp. 103-105.

and the clandestine communist networks, Luca is also caught up in wide-ranging actions. At the beginning of April 1929, the Congress of the United Trade Unions is held in Timișoara. Behind the congress is the PCdR. Luca directs operations from the shadows. Dumitru Grofu is elected President, Luca Secretary General. Having been informed of communist infiltration, the authorities take measures. It is in fact a provocation prepared by the Agitprop section of the Comintern. The corpse of a communist detainee in Doftana Prison, Ion Fonaghy, is brought to Timișoara for burial. It is the pretext for agitators from all over the country to clash with the authorities. This was the goal. Incidents take place. The police make arrests. A trial follows in the autumn. Lucrețiu Pătrășcanu is the lawyer for the defence. Panait Istrati, who is in Romania, intervenes on behalf of the accused. The sentences are light. Luca, at the orders of the PCdR, does not show up for the trial and is sentenced *in absentia*. It was not the only violent incident in which he was involved that year. Luca was in charge of operations in a number of counties on behalf of the PCdR. They included Valea Jiului (the Jiu Valley). A crisis had been smouldering here for a long time, caused by low wages, broken promises on the part of the administration, and conflicts between the various unions operating there, some of which were instigating the miners to radical protest. At the end of July, Vasile Luca was in the Jiu Valley to prepare for 1 August, declared by the Comintern 'a day of struggle against war'. On 6 August, the miners attacked the power station and then tried to organise a general strike.

The vulgate of the history of Romanian communism ascribes to Luca various roles. For a time he is the hero of these 'strikes, which he led in the name of the PCR', later he is a 'traitor', who prevented the miners from organising and abandoned them in a cowardly fashion. During the whole of his career as a union agitator and Comintern agent, Luca roused controversy. The roles he played were viewed differently, even in opposite ways. From hero to traitor was but a single step in the underground. As he himself was to realise in 1930, when he was deposed from all his functions in the CC of the PCdR, and above all in 1953, when he goes from being number three in the PMR hierarchy to being just another prisoner in a Securitate cell. In 1930, the reason he is ousted is his participation in the factional struggles between various groups vying for power. Vasile Luca positions himself on the side of the faction led by Marcel Pauker-Luximin, along with Dori Goldstein. All of them are members of the Political Bureau. He also supports Ştefan Foriş and Alexandru Dobrogeanu-Gherea, members of the CC. The opposing camp – led by Vitali Kholostenko, the head of the PCdR appointed by the Comintern in 1928, and other members of the Political Bureau, for example Alexandru Nikolski, Constantin Pîrvulescu, and Dimităr Ganev, members of the CC of the PCdR – in effect disappears as an organisation. In 1930, the Comintern decides to sack them all and sends them to do 'spadework'. Luca, a member of the Political Bureau and the Secretariat, is sent to the provinces, to a minor posting in the apparatus. Not even now does he escape arrest. He is detained in 1929 and again in 1931, being released on each occasion. At the Fifth Congress of the PCdR in 1931 he is not elected to any function.

In the same year, the Comintern orders a change of tactics. The order is to turn to the unions. The PCdR activists have to operate in direct contact with the workers, within the unions and inside the factories. The industries targeted are of strategic interest to the USSR: petroleum, the railways, armaments. The tactic is to infiltrate the official unions and then to take over their leadership or, failing that, to provoke splits. Luca becomes head of the clandestine united revolutionary unions. It is now that Luca discovers and promotes within the hierarchy a certain Gheorghe Gheorghiu, an electrician, sacked from the CFR Workshops in Dej. Vasile Luca is his mentor. He introduces him into the Party. Luca pits Gheorghiu against Ilie Pintilie, another, rival communist leader. It is Luca who will work behind the scenes during the Grivitza strikes. On behalf of the Comintern, he supervises the progress of the strike, alongside Lucreţiu Pătrăşcanu and Moscu Cohn (Gheorghe Stoica). After the strike, Luca disappears. He is convicted *in absentia* at the trial in Bucharest to 20 years, hard labour. Betrayed by an informer, he is arrested on 27 August 1933. "The aforementioned has been living clandestinely all the while in various locations around the country, and is paid by communist organisations between 4 and 10 thousand lei monthly, and at present is ready to cross the border into Soviet Russia permanently, having been sentenced to 20 years hard labour," a Siguranţă report notes.

Even now his double role remains ambiguous, full of unknowns and ambiguities. Was he left at liberty in order to inform the Siguranţă about the reaction of the PCdR apparatus to the repression? Did Luca try to wriggle out of the agreement that bound him to the Siguranţă? The heavy sentence – 20 years, hard labour – had to make an impression on the communists, because Luca had long been suspected of being an informer. Or was he no longer working for the Siguranță? His depositions during the investigation of 1952-1954 incriminate him.

Although it exonerates him, the report of 1968 leaves a number of matters unclarified. The facts show us that once captured in August 1933, he was tried separately and sentenced to five and a half years. He completes the whole sentence and is released on 4 April 1939. A year later, on 4 April 1940, he is once again arrested while attempting to cross the frontier into the USSR clandestinely, together with Ştrul Zigelboim. He was denounced by a Siguranță informer: Nicu Tudor, a member of the Secretariat. He had been summoned to Moscow by the Comintern to be appointed head of the PCdR. Boris Ştefanov had been dismissed from the post. Béla Breiner, who had been the interim head of the PCdR, died in March in a Bucharest hospital. Had he not been captured, Luca would have become head of the PCdR in 1940. Foriş – together with Teohari Georgescu – managed to cross the frontier a few months later and take up the post offered by the Comintern. Luca is tried and sentenced to eight months imprisonment. He is held in Cernăuți/Czernowitz and freed by the Red Army when it invades Bukowina in 1940. Luca continues his career in the USSR. He is awarded Soviet citizenship. He becomes a member of the Communist Party of the Soviet Union and in 1941 a deputy of the Supreme Soviet of the USSR. He is drafted into the Red Army as an officer in the political section on the Southern front until March 1943. We then find him in the camps for Romanian prisoners of war, alongside Ana Pauker, conducting Soviet propaganda and recruiting men. The Kremlin was preparing for the occupation of Romania. Luca is mentioned in the diary of Georgi Dimitrov, in his entry for 7 September 1944. He is sent with Ana Pauker to Bucharest to take over power. Luca becomes the number two among the Romanian communist émigrés in the USSR, rising higher than Constantin Doncea, Petre Borilă, Gheorghe Stoica (Moscu Cohn), Valter Roman, and Mihai Burcă, members of the international brigades that fought in Spain. Doncea had also been the leader of the Grivitza strike, and he too was a worker, trades union leader, and the central figure in a famous trial.

In the USSR, before his return to Romania, Luca agrees to work for the Soviet secret services, to pass on information from the upper echelons of the PCdR, to locate the old spies in order to rebuild the pre-war networks and to recruit new agents. He was not the only one to work for the Soviet secret services. Iosif Chişinevschi, Teohari Georgescu, Petre

Borilă, and Emil Bodnăraş, to mention only the members of the Political Bureau, were also at one period or another Soviet agents. It was part of the Bolshevik revolutionary catechism to place the interests of the USSR above those of one's own country. Ironically, after his arrest in 1953, he was accused of remaining on Soviet soil between 1940 and 1944 in order to spy for Romania. Once he arrives in Bucharest in September 1944, Luca remains Ana Pauker's second-in-command. During the whole conflict in the upper echelons of the PCdR he remains loyal to her. He is a member of the Secretariat and the Political Bureau after the congress of 1945. His portrait is carried by the crowds at all the demonstrations organised by the communists and hangs on the walls of trades union and Party offices. His name is chanted at mass meetings. A slogan of the time was, "Luca, Pauker şi cu Dej/Bagă spaima în burgeji" (Luca, Pauker and Dej put fear into the bourgeoisie). The propaganda had turned him into a demigod of the proletariat.

On 16 August 1952 he is arrested. Within six months, starting in February, he had lost all his functions: member of the Political Bureau and Secretariat, Minister of Finance. From working-class hero he is transformed in the space of a day into a pariah, a non-person. He is accused of having been a Siguranţă informer and of undermining the national economy. He himself had contributed to the transformation of others into political corpses. Foriş, for example, whom he had met in Braşov in 1922, and with whom he had worked throughout the clandestine years. Luca was one of those behind his assassination, together with Gheorghiu-Dej, Ana Pauker and Teohari Georgescu. Pauker and Georgescu fell into disgrace at the same time as Luca. Dej had won the match. Luca had made an enemy of him not only by the fact that he had placed himself in the Pauker camp, but also by his attitude. When they quarrelled, he used to remind him that it had been he who had launched him in politics. He would remind him of the strikes of 1931-1933, when he had been his boss in the union. Dej saw his authority dented by the outbursts of the choleric Luca. He had no patience whatsoever with anyone who contradicted him. He was a man of resentment. He would patiently isolate his victim and annihilate him when he decided that the risks were minimal. Luca was one of them. In the autumn of 1954, after a four-day trial, the Supreme Court, military section, sentenced him to death. He appeals for clemency. The execution was supposed to take place the next day, as happened in the case of Pătrăşcanu and Koffler. It was postponed. A few days later, Luca learns that the Great National Assembly has commuted the sentence to life, hard labour. It was yet another example of Dej's sadism. Luca serves another 11 years in prison, to add to the 10 before the war. In 1957, from Rîmnicu Sărat Prison, Luca writes a memorandum to Gheorghiu-Dej, his former protégé:

"Everything has been taken away from me. I have lost my honour as a worker, my Party membership card, my family, friends, everything; everything that made up part of my life and was dear to me, love and the esteem of the working people. [...] I have suffered too greatly and I still suffer today both from the moral and from the physical point of view, having been imprisoned for five years already and held in dreadful conditions, isolated from the whole world, locked up alone day and night in a cell, completely isolated, with no one to talk to, I am isolated from family, relatives and friends, I receive no letters from them, I suffer from hunger and cold, I have heart problems and am in danger of dying like a dog, abandoned in the darkness of this prison..."

VIII
Belu Zilber

"He is to blame! He is the guilty one. This monster invented it all!"
Lucreţiu Pătrăşcanu, during the trial of April 1954

Belu Zilber was a very well-known figure in the world of Bucharest newspaper offices. An unmistakeable figure. In appearance he was almost a midget (5'1"), and had a complex about his height. He was garrulous, timorous, rapid in movements, always in a hurry. A contradictory figure. A man of contrasts. Born Herbert Zilber (in 1901, Tîrgu Frumos), he becomes a Bolshevik in early manhood. In 1918, he is expelled from college for having taken part in the print workers demonstration of 13 December. He continues his lycée studies in Paris and enrols at a polytechnic in Grenoble, but returns to Romania in 1922 without having managed to obtain an engineering qualification. In Bucharest he claims to have completed his studies, but never provides any documentary proof. It is a serious imposture, but without practical consequences, because it does not hinder him from pursuing a career as an expert in the War Ministry. Beginning in 1932, he works at the Institute for International Affairs, run by Virgil Madgearu. Zilber ends up the *de facto* director of the institute. Emil Cioran once said that Belu Zilber was the most intelligent man in the Bucharest of his youth, in the 1930s. He could be spotted in newspaper offices and at cafés – wherever journalists, intellectuals and high society gathered – at conferences, *vernissages*, and premieres. He is to be seen at the Criterion conferences held in the Athenaeum. Without suffering any complexes, he frequents right-wing, non- or anti-Marxist intellectuals and aesthetes, something unheard of for a communist. For example, he was frequently seen with Mihail Polihroniade, a historian and journalist, member of the Criterion group, ideologue of the extreme Right and leading member of the Legionary movement, assassinated in Rîmnicu Sărat Prison in September 1939, on the orders of King Carol II and Armand Călinescu. Mihail Sebastain, who was a fellow student of Polihroniade at the Lycée School in Brăila, observed, "Mişu[1] Polihroniade a martyr to a political cause? Nothing destined him for this. It is a mistake, a *mal entendu*, a poor

---

[1] Mişu is a diminutive of Mihail – *Translator's note.*

joke. … All the lad wanted was a seat in Parliament … And here he is, dying like a revolutionary. Up until the very last, I do not think he understood what was happening, why things had taken such a turn, and at what point they began to go awry."[2]

So, Belu Zilber eats out with Mihail Polihroniade and they engage in debate. Each is aware that should either of their parties come to power, it would mean the extermination of his interlocutor. The scene is described by Mihail Sebastian in 1935. Pierre Quint, a French writer staying in Bucharest, meets the pair at the Capşa restaurant and cannot understand how two men with such differing opinions can be friends.

> "Pierre Quint could not understand how such a friendship could be possible between two men who ought theoretically to be 10 worlds apart. I recall very well the candid reply of the two extremist friends: 'You see, we are nothing but friends. This does not engage one in anything else'. This 'nothing but' is a psychological catch-all in Bucharest. It explains very many things; it excuses everything. *'Comment ça ne vous engage à rien? Mais un seul geste engage, Monsieur'*."

And Sebastian elsewhere makes the following observation:

> "These men are not indeed engaged in anything else: love, life, or death … Rigour, in any form, is outside their competence. They are free men. Perhaps the only free men in Europe, because deeds do not bind them together and nor do ideas place any obligation upon them."[3]

Belu Zilber was always to be found wherever there was something interesting going on. He was perfectly informed, always available, a man of contacts and schemes. He used to spread information wherever he went, and in this respect he was the personification of indiscretion. He was a blend of prattle and secretly hatched coups.

> "Belu Zilber … has become a popular figure in Bucharest. He is a voluble young man, who gossips about international politics at the Corso,

[2] Mihail Sebastian, *Jurnal, 1935-1944*, Bucharest: Humanitas, 1996, p. 235.
[3] Mihail Sebastian, *De două mii de ani*, Bucharest: Humanitas, 1990, pp. 237-238.

putting Europe to rights, violently holding forth about governments, shaking states to their foundations, and setting continents at enmity."[4]

He is a figure who leads a double life, which is probably his most enduring vocation. He is a conspirator who is working to demolish bourgeois democracy, but he also leads a 'normal' existence, at the surface of social life. He seems an eloquent *causeur*, a man who displays his radicalism as a fashionable accessory. He is not the only one. Most look on them as 'decent fellows', who are trying to make an impression on the gullible. Few take them seriously. They were living in a well-educated society, one tolerant of eccentrics. In the communist milieu could be found other socially well-connected people: Anca and Mihai Magheru were descendents of the General Magheru of 1848 fame; Scarlat Callimachi, the 'Red Prince', had as his ancestors a number of Wallachian princes; lawyer Mihai Macavei was a rich landowner; Victor Aradi, inculpated in the Soviet espionage trial, was a baronet; N. D. Cocea and Lucrețiu Pătrășcanu were of Moldavian boyar stock; I. Gh. Maurer and Athanasie Joja were from wealthy families; Constanța Crăciun was the daughter of a banker. And the list could go on. It includes Romanians, Jews and Hungarians, educated, well-off people highly placed in the social hierarchy. The idea that these communists originated exclusively from the ranks of the ethnic minorities or that they were mere lumpenproletarians is, to a large degree, false. What is true, however, is that Moscow preferred to promote those from the margins within the hierarchy of the PCdR. It was a tactic aimed at keeping the PCdR under Moscow's control, with isolated, ethnically and socially marginal, poorly educated leaders. Nevertheless, at the middle level and, above all, at the bottom, the situation was different. In spite of the fact that it remained a tiny minority in Romanian society, in this utopian political milieu we can meet the progeny of the petit and haute bourgeoisie, aristocrats, intellectuals, and well-connected professionals. Some were members of the PCdR, others, the majority, were not. Adventurers, idealists, idlers, con artists, professional revolutionaries, spies. ... What set people like Belu Zilber apart from the ordinary, 'bourgeois' context was the fall of tsarism in Russia in 1917. This was a 'revolutionary' generation, with a intense anti-bourgeois and anti-democratic spirit. The members of this generation

---

[4] Mihail Sebastian, *Cum am devenit huligan*, Cultura națională, 1935, p. 174.

dreamed of revolution, until their usually dramatic demises. Just when their enthusiasm was beginning to wane in the 1920s, the crisis of 1929-1933 came along, and then the Nazi peril, which once again mobilised those born at the turn of the century. A turbulent European generation that had seen the trenches of the First World War and the ruin of Europe. Some fell prey to the temptation of the extreme Right, others to that of the Left. They all despised bourgeois democracy and the liberal spirit, which they regarded as anachronisms. They were fanatics, dogmatists, inclined to violence, thirsty for power, scornful of democratic processes, intolerant by the very nature of their beliefs. Whoever sees Zilber as a 'salon communist' is mistaken. This was the label Pătrășcanu applied to him. Why did Belu Zilber become a spy? Why did he not limit himself to Marxist propaganda and the role of deliberately provocative intellectual of the Left, albeit in its radical form? Why did he not remain a *causeur* of Bucharest's cafés and newspaper offices?

> "Regardless of the communist fanatics' country of origin, they were convinced that, by carrying out the missions entrusted to them by the secret services in Moscow, they were doing nothing more than fulfil the duties of a party member, selflessly serving the cause of world revolution and the universal triumph of Marxist ideas."[5]

A poor reputation clung to Belu Zilber: that of being a Siguranță agent. He had made a name for himself when he had appeared in the dock of the military tribunal at what the press called the 'Soviet espionage trial'. The trial was front-page news for three months, from April until June 1931. There were 36 accused in the dock, aged between 25 and 35. A further 20 persons managed to disappear before they could be arrested. They were engineers, businessmen, functionaries, officers, and journalists, Romanian and foreign. They were handed down heavy sentences, between five and 10 years imprisonment, some with hard labour, for treason and espionage, under the new espionage law of 1930. According to his own testimony, Belu Zilber became a Soviet spy in 1928 while in Vienna, where the PCdR leadership was based, and at the invitation of David Fabian Finkelstein, a member of the PCdR 'external' Political Bureau, and Moscu Cohn (Gheorghe Stoica), a member of the PCdR 'internal' leadership.

[5] Arkadi Vaksberg, *Hotel Lux. Partidele frățești în slujba internaționalei comuniste*, Bucharest: Humanitas, 1998, p. 37.

"I could not refuse to take part in the defence of the first socialist state. As ever, like so many others, I told myself that if it was demanded of me then it was necessary. In any case, the new party assignment, as orders were and are still called, was not unpleasant to me. It promised to give more range to the imagination than the ritual cell meetings. I became a free man to a certain extent, without ceasing to be a communist. At the time, not to be a communist or not to love the Soviet Union seemed to me something inhuman, unworthy, lowly, absurd."[6]

On 15 October 1930, the Siguranță proceeds to make arrests, after months of surveillance, when Cilly Auslander, carrying funds and new instructions, arrives from Vienna. She was a doctor of chemistry, born in Rădăuți. Just two hours after her arrival, she is arrested. The others are rounded up during the course of the same day. They are taken to Văcărești Prison. The ramifications of the networks are more extensive than had been believed. Engineer Paul Solomon controls dozens of agents, organised into four autonomous cells, one of which he headed himself, while the others are led by Victor Aradi, Klauda (a.k.a. Gustav Matta), and Manhofer Hugo. "The spies in Romania were working under guidance of the Soviet espionage central office in Vienna, and their operations were aimed at the army in particular."[7]

The following are among the central figures. French engineer André Prot passed on information about the IAR aircraft plant in Brașov, where he worked and spied beginning in 1928. A communist since his student years, he had been recruited by the GPU while working in Le Havre as an engineer for a Soviet naval company, the Transatlantic. He dies in the rubble of Doftana Prison during the earthquake of 10 November 1940. Major Grigore Vărzaru was an officer in the Austro-Hungarian Army, taken prisoner by the Russians at the Battle of Lemberg in the First World War. He escapes and wanders through Russia, China, Japan and Mexico before returning to Europe. In November 1918, when the Austro-Hungarian Empire disintegrates, he forms a Romanian regiment. Enrolled after the war in the Romanian Army, he is recruited in Vienna in the summer of 1929 by a Soviet agent, Sikora Hugo, also inculpated in the trial, but who

---

[6] Belu Zilber, *Actor în procesul Pătrășcanu*, Bucharest: Humanitas, 1997, p. 37.
[7] *Universul*, 29 April 1931.

vanishes. In court Vărzaru claims that he wanted to infiltrate the network in order to denounce it to the authorities. The court does not believe him and hands him the heaviest sentence of all those convicted: 20 years, hard labour, and demotion to the lower ranks. He had received large sums of money. For the codes of his regiment in Alba Iulia, he demanded 100,000 lei. For his services, the GPU paid him a further 20,000 lei monthly. In the 1940s, in Caransebeș Prison, he was isolated and viewed with contempt by the other inmates, as one witness recounts.[8]

The head of the network was Paul Solomon, an engineer from Oradea. He did not speak Romanian very well. In court, he requires an interpreter, as do many of the other accused. He studied at polytechnics in Berlin and Gdansk. Recruited in 1928, he received a monthly salary of 12,000 lei. All the agents in the network were paid large sums. Solomon organises the network under the guise of a small company, which engages in commerce, opens technical offices and branches, repair shops, etc. Behind this façade there unfolds a spying operation, involving the massive collection of data from all over the country. Engineer Paul Solomon presents himself before the court not as a communist, but as a man lacking in political convictions. He was merely doing business. He gathered and sold information. The documents in the archives present him as a dangerous communist agent, however. One amusing detail is that on the second day of the cross-examination he appears in court with his moustache shaved off. He admits that he has been a spy and in his final word to the court takes all the blame upon himself. His is an exceptional position, given that all the other accused have pleaded "not guilty."

Another leading figure was Szántó Dezideriu, a lawyer and communist journalist from Oradea. At Paul Solomon's request, he organised together with two accomplices clandestine crossings of the (then) border with Czechoslovakia, through Crăciunești village in Maramureș, for agents and couriers. Szántó Dezideriu was a well-known communist. He had been tried in Cluj in the autumn of 1928 along with another 110 persons. These included Ştefan Foriş, Eugen Rozvany, Imre Aladár, Alexandru Sencovici, Haia Lifşiţ, Solomon Schein and Victor Aradi. Another person involved in this major trial was Vasile Şaio, an engineer and director of the Grivitza Workshops in Bucharest. During the Bolshevik republic in Hungary

---

[8] Pavel Câmpeanu, *Nicolae Ceauşescu. Anii numărătorii inverse*, Jassy: Polirom, 2002, p. 54.

he had been director of transport in Budapest. After the fall of the Béla Kuhn Government, he was convicted and fled to Romania. A communist and Soviet spy, he passes on information about the state of the transport network, about the railways and rolling stock. In the trial of 1931 he is acquitted due to a lack of evidence. After the trial, in the summer of 1932, he flees to the USSR. He becomes the director of the Ukrainian Railways. In 1938, he is tried for espionage, convicted, and executed.

One unusual case was that of Petre Zissu, a communist lawyer. He discovers that he is about to be arrested for espionage and prefers to flee to the USSR. Accounts differ as to what happened after that. Some say that Zissu was shot by border guards (whether Russian or Romanian is unknown) as he was trying to enter the USSR clandestinely. Others say that he reached the USSR, but the Soviet secret services did not believe his story, or perhaps he knew too much. In any case, it seems he was sent to the Gulag, where he vanished.

Another of the accused was Moise Kripper, from Soroca. He studied at polytechnics in Germany and worked in France, firstly on the railways and then in Le Havre, for the Transatlantic Soviet transport company, where he was a deputy director. It was here that he met André Prot. After four years in France, he was exposed as a Soviet spy and deported. He returned to Romania via Berlin and continued his espionage activities, first in Cernăuți then in Bucharest. Boris Vîlcev, a chemical engineer from Silistra, ran a photographic workshop, which he Calea Griviței is a turn plate for couriers and letters.

Friedrich Klauda, who went by the name of Gustav Matta, was the head of one of the network's four cells. Originally from Vienna, he came to Bucharest in April 1930, under the pretext of opening a business there. In fact, he was sent by the GPU to consolidate the network. He has direct contacts with Aradi and Solomon. Theodor Gaudig passed himself off as a German businessman. He did not speak Romanian. In 1930 he arrives to open a photographic workshop, where he took pictures of stolen documents. Klauda pays him 16,000 lei a month. Klauda and Gaudig are sentenced to 15 years hard labour. We meet them again in the 1940s, in Caransebeș Prison.

"Theo Gaudig was to return after 1947 as Ambassador of the German Democratic Republic to Bucharest, a post he gave up soon thereafter, as well as GDR citizenship, in order to return to his home town of Hamburg.

Fritz Klauda, the pro-Soviet spy, impressed by the initial defeats suffered by the Red Army during the Second World War, suddenly becomes an enthusiastic supporter of anti-Soviet Nazi aggression. He vanishes from Caransebeș before 1944."[9]

Andreas Koscher, an Austrian, was the network's courier for the Bucharest-Vienna route, under the guise of a carpet salesman. Leopold Katz, a writer and well-known journalist, vanishes. Ștefan Teodorescu, a journalist who worked for newspapers including N. D. Cocea's *Facla*, gathers information in newspaper circles. Engineer Eduard Hrușcă, from Cernăuți, a Slovak, the only old man among the accused, was a member of the Austro-Hungarian Parliament in Vienna during the war. He sends reports to the Soviets on the minorities in Romania and the economic situation. He is recruited by Manhofer Hugo, who presented himself to him as a businessman, authorised by the German Foreign Ministry. He travels frequently to a number of cities in order to gather information, under the pretext of opening company branches. He also recruits his own son to the network, a sub-lieutenant in the army. Manhofer Hugo, the head of one of the network's cells, has time to vanish and is tried *in absentia*. Iosif Kaliș, a spy, has contacts with officers and policemen, whose company he keeps. He was close to Israel Averbuch, another important figure in the network, who also manages to disappear. Averbuch was the only one to be in direct contact with Vienna, rather than through engineer Paul Solomon. He is sentenced to 20 years, hard labour, *in absentia*. Kaliș tried to persuade a Siguranță agent, a good friend, to help him to free Moise Kripper, one of the arrested spies. Iosif Kaliș had already served time in Czechoslovakia in the 1920s, after being convicted of fraud. He deals in the same business while a member of the Solomon-Aradi network: traffic of influence, con tricks. Belu Zilber paints the following portrait of him in his memoirs:

"During the course of my trial in 1930-1932, I met a man who possessed to the absolute degree that quality which propelled Gheorghiu-Dej [to power – *author's note*]. His name was Iosif Kaliș. He was a Jew, originally from Soroca. In appearance, something between *Pithecanthropus erectus* and the higher lemurs, with a vocabulary of a few hundred words in a language that resembled neither Romanian, Russian nor any other language. As flighty as

---

[9] Pavel Câmpeanu, *op. cit.*, p. 54.

a monkey. Amoral and illogical."[10] Kaliş has a 'hallucinatory career'. Taken prisoner by the Austrians in 1915, he becomes director of a sanatorium in the Tyrol in 1916, rather than being interned in a camp. In 1917, he is the Italian consul in Odessa. In 1919 he comes to Romania. In 1921 he is at the centre of a scandal involving espionage, forgeries and fraud that breaks out among the Prague elite. After 1924, in Bucharest, he works for a number of generals, without giving up his spying activities for the Soviets. One of them is General Mircescu, the Minister of War, who commits suicide after it is discovered that the mobilisation plans for the Romanian Army have been stolen.

The 'Soviet spy trial' of April-June 1931 did not elucidate all the aspects of the affair. A number of secret sessions were held. Many key witnesses managed to vanish. Sometimes the accused refused to answer questions. Sometimes they blatantly lied. There was also complaisance on the part of the court. Some truths must never be uttered in public. For example, the name of the country for which the network was working was never mentioned, although the speech for the royal prosecution did identify it as the USSR. There were also other, ramified groups complicit with the spies, which were not brought to trial. Thus, for example, in February 1933, there is another trial, a continuation of the first, in which another 31 accused appear in the dock. Among them are Saul Ozias and Constantin Agiu, the perpetrators of the Senate bomb attack of December 1920. Also present are the lawyers from the PCdR legal office, all of them members of Romanian Workers' Aid, a Comintern organisation: Paul Moscovici, Stelian Niţulescu, Marcu Witzman, and Petre Grozdea. Also implicated is lawyer Petre Zissu, who vanishes in the USSR during the investigation.

What was Belu Zilber's role? He was arrested in Bucharest in 1930, immediately after returning from Paris. He had stopped over in Vienna on the way, where he met with the network's bosses abroad. The news of the arrests had been published in the press, and Zilber already knew what to expect. All the same, he decides to go back to Romania. He was an expert at the Ministry of War and had been passing military and economic secrets to the GPU for more than two years. The cell to which he belonged was run by Victor Aradi. As we have seen, Aradi was a sociologist, with a doctorate from Budapest, and he passed as a refined and erudite intellectual. He had been tried in 1928, accused of 'communist agitation and carrying an

---

[10] Belu Zilber, *op.*, *cit.* pp. 207-208.

illegal weapon'. The trial was held in Cluj, following the discovery of an underground pro-Soviet organisation in Oradea. More than 100 people were brought before the court. He was acquitted, thanks to his reputation as a journalist, his social standing, the interventions of the Justice Ministry and also the appearance as witnesses for the defence of leading public figures such as Alexandru Vaida-Voievod, one of the leaders of the National Peasants Party. Important persons from abroad, such as Seton-Watson in Oxford, wrote to the authorities to demand his release.

In March 1927, for purposes connected with the espionage ring, Aradi moves to Bucharest. Under the pretext of writing reportages and articles for a press agency in Vienna, he travels around the country. He establishes contacts and gathers information, which he sends abroad in letters written using invisible ink. In Bucharest he runs an association that is a nothing more than a front for the spy network – Romanian Workers' Aid (AMR) – and which in fact handles funds sent by the Soviets. The AMR is funded by the Comintern, the same as in every other country where there is an association linked to International Workers Aid exists. To allay Siguranţă suspicion, known communist militants are not allowed to be members of the organisation. The exception is lawyer Petre Zissu, also implicated in the investigation, and another lawyer, Petre Grozdea. Aradi's activities do not pass unobserved. In his entourage can be found one of the Siguranţă's informers, Sami Margulies, a militant communist since 1918 and on the police payroll since 1922. Zilber says of Aradi at the trial, "Ardi is a kind of expressionist artist. He juxtaposes a fiddle, a boulevard, a rainbow … The way he has presented things here during the trial I am convinced that he only remembers fragmentary and sometimes distorted things." Zilber seems to be enjoying himself. His playful, clownish nature never lets up. He is too intelligent to put up with the ceremonial of a major public trial. Moreover, there is, as usual, a hidden side to things. Corruption and secrecy. Aradi declares at the hearings that Zilber is a "man of the theatre wings, of the back corridors." The president of the court promptly rejoins, "'Of the back corridors and the back yard toilets!' Aradi (laughing), 'Yes'."

At the date of the trial, Belu Zilber is 29, Aradi 49. The former was the latter's liaison. It was via Zilber that Aradi passed military and economic secrets to Vienna, where the organisation's headquarters was located. It was also here that the Political Bureau of the PCdR was located, in close contact with Soviet agents controlled by 'Colonel Martin', who remains unidentified.

Victor Aradi and Belu Zilber were long-standing communists and members of clandestine cells. In addition, both were spies. They dedicated themselves to the 'Bolshevik Revolution'. Their image of themselves was not one of traitors to their country, but rather of heroic fighters for the victory of the world proletariat, conducted from Moscow by Stalin, the incarnation of the Revolution. Passing on national secrets and the trial that followed were for them episodes in the 'final struggle against the bourgeoisie'. It is a blend of *roman noir*, full of conspiracies and secrets, preposterous scenarios, and abjection. A mixture of vaudeville, *opéra bouffe*, Offenbach and Sade. It is somewhere between the burlesque and Dostoevsky's underground, between tawdry idealism and human squalor. From this mixture is born betrayal, murder and violence, however. Belu Zilber was to experience it for himself in 1948, when he was arrested and not released until 1964, 17 years later.

As one of the network's leaders, Aradi was sentenced to 15 years hard labour in 1931. Belu Zilber receives five years reclusion. All those inculpated appeal. The court agrees to only two appeals: those of Aradi and Zilber. In April 1932, their appeals are heard in court. Aradi says of Zilber, "Belu Zilber is innocent. He is a bourgeois who has nothing in common with the communist movement." The pair's lawyers are Petre Zissu, Lizetta Gheorghiu, Constantin Solomonescu, Gh. Banu, and Iosif Șraier. The last of these, head of the PCdR Legal Office, deplores what he sees in the case of Aradi as being "the injustice of convicting a man for espionage when he was doing the work of a journalist."[11] Belu Zilber is acquitted. Aradi's sentence is reduced from 15 to 12 years, and he is ordered to pay the sum of 1.2 million lei, a very large sum at the time. Aradi makes another appeal. The trial is moved to Jassy. This time, in 1933, he is acquitted, represented by Lizetta Gheorgiu and Iosif Șraier. Aradi flees to the USSR with his family the same year. This was probably part of an understanding between the Romanian and the Soviet secret services for his release. Aradi was too important an agent for the GPU to allow him to languish in a Romanian gaol. His fate is grim. He does not survive Stalin's Terror. He is accused of 'spying for Romania', sentenced to death and shot in 1940, according to the information available. The clemency of the bourgeois justice system – a system he had criticised during the trials in both Cluj and Bucharest – did not exist in Moscow. David Fabian Finkelstein, who recruited Belu Zilber, was to share the same fate: he was tried and executed in 1937.

---

[11] *Universul*, 15 May 1931.

Half of Zilber's being was to be found in the Bucharest high society as we have seen. The other half of his existence was spent in the underground. Zilber was in fact a dedicated 'professional revolutionary', a Bolshevik, as theorised by Lenin in *Kto Kogo*: disciplined, unscrupulous, obsessed with the destruction of the bourgeoisie and the political regime it patronised. He was a soldier of the proletarian revolution. Let us not be deceived by his *boutades* and humour in the cafés and newspaper offices. Zilber is a man of secrecy, with a taste for conspiracy. A spirited man, an unsurpassed *causeur*, like Petre Țuțea, with whom he vied for supremacy in the salons, he led a double life, as laid down by the canons of the Comintern, in which legal was to be combined with illegal work. In plain view were to be seen anti-fascist activities, the mobilisation of public opinion, and the use of 'fellow travellers' – professors, journalists, naïve lawyers – in various campaigns. But his involvement was not merely general, that of a sympathiser of the cause. On the contrary. Zilber and some of those in his entourage carried on illegal activities, actively taking part in the underground communist networks. Their work was to undermine the democratic regime, using diversionary tactics, espionage and hostile propaganda. Zilber also had a precise mission in these disciplined and hierarchical networks controlled by the Comintern and infiltrated by the Siguranță. In principle, Zilber was an agent of influence, a formidable one. He worked efficiently in the press and intellectual circles, as well as in business circles, thanks to his position at the Institute of Foreign Affairs, financed by Nicolae Malaxa and headed by Virgil Madgearu. Zilber was perfectly informed about the Romanian economic situation and was in contact with bankers and industrialists. He also made use of his strategic position in order to adjust his own income. He was not ruled by a working-class attitude of poor but honest. His lifestyle remained bourgeois. He liked the finer things in life: limousines, expensive furniture, comfortable flats, chic clothes. He frequented the most expensive restaurants in search of discussion partners as intelligent and informed as himself. Did he not realise that the communist victory he was plotting would lead to the disappearance of the world he liked to frequent?

The reappearance of Zilber in the newspaper offices and cafés of Bucharest as a free man after such a high-profile trial raises many questions.

"When I was released in 1932, I was in effect déclassé. On the one hand, no one wanted to employ a man accused of spying for the USSR, even if he had been acquitted. On the other hand, the Party no longer wanted to have anything to do with me ... and in addition it was rumoured ... that I was a Siguranță agent," he will later write while under investigation as part of the Pătrășcanu case.[12]

People were wondering how he had managed to get off scot-free. Had he become a Siguranță man in the meantime? There are a number of testimonies to bear this out. Sami Margulies, a confidant of Aradi, imprisoned after the war for being a notorious Siguranță agent, is placed in the same cell as Belu Zilber in Aiud Prisscon for three and a half months in 1948. The two had known each other well since the 1920s, a circumstance upon which the investigators were wagering. What does Margulies declare in his report?

"Silber [*sic.*] was a willing informer, i.e. he did not receive any payment for his services to the Siguranță. Silber was part of the category of occasional informers. At intervals, when special circumstances arose, he was called upon to write reports ... Neither V. I. nor M. [Vintilă Ionescu, Moruzov] demanded or expected Silber to reveal safe houses, to hand over to them any *gestetner*, or to provide information about any cell meetings in the suburbs of the capital. For this kind of information, the Siguranță had plenty of paid informers. Silber was not employed in petty matters ... And if Silber did not demand or receive any salary ... it is because he knew that any expense, salary etc. outlaid by the authorities would necessarily be on a payroll and booked in the accounts, and in this way there would remain material proof of his activity as an informer."[13]

"All of us avoided Belu Zilber like the plague. He was known to be a Siguranță informer ... In the working class world the term 'agent' was a stamp of *summa cum infamia*. The agent was ... a moral degenerate, a leper with whom you had no contact of any kind, not even to say 'good day'. Belu Zilber found himself in this moral situation from 1932-1944 because of the espionage trial ... I didn't know Aradi ... I met Petre Zissu on three occasions. He was a lawyer with a nebulous clientele and a dwelling place terrifying in its filthiness. He used to emerge from

---

[12] ASRI, Dossier 40002, vol. 12, p. 254.

[13] *Principiul bumerangului. Documente ale procesului Lucrețiu Pătrășcanu*, Bucharest: Vremea, 1996, p. 267.

that pigsty wearing a stiff, white collar, ironed clothes, and a dirty shirt, shaved, powdered and perfumed. He died on the Dniester, as he was trying to cross the frontier, he was shot … Is Belu Zilber an Asew[14] of Romania? … I talked with Belu Zilber at length, amicably, just once, on my arrival in Germany [in 1932 – *author's note*] … Later, Sahia told me he was an agent. I stopped saying hello to him after that."[15]

The same author also asks, "What was Belu Zilber? Can he have been a pathological case, a typical case of mythomania, a man tangled up in his own lies?"[16] The author, Petre Pandrea, was the brother-in-law of Lucreţiu Pătrăşcanu. In the inter-war period, he appeared as a witness for the defence in many of the trials brought against the communists. Belu Zilber was the closest associate of Lucreţiu Pătrăşcanu. Pandrea also gives different accounts of Belu Zilber's situation after the trial. One such account is that Belu Zilber claimed that the judges were bribed two million lei by a rich uncle. Pandrea does not believe this version. Another is that the spy was saved thanks to the influence of Zilber's cousin Mihail Sebastian, who interceded for him with Nae Ionescu, at the time the main adviser to King Carol II. Acquitted and released from prison, Zilber proceeds to make a virulent attack on Nae Ionescu in the press. By chance, the two meet at the Capşa. Nae Ionescu admonishes him thus: "Belu, I've forgiven you. But the communists won't forgive you so easily. They're going to hang you."[17] Mihail Sebastian, who was close to Nae Ionescu, writes of Belu Zilber in the preface to *How I Became a Hooligan* (1935), "A little bit Siguranţă agent, a little bit martyr, he has the flexibility of the first trade and the vehemence of the second, which otherwise produces an alloy of genuine humour." Writing "a little bit Siguranţă agent" he adopts the formula used by Zilber himself in an article in which he accuses Mircea Eliade of being a Siguranţă man. Eliade was close enough to Zilber to be able to spend New Year 1933-1934 with him.[18] Also at the party were Camil Petrescu, Mircea Vulcănescu, Dan Botta and

---

[14] Allusion to German spy film *Lockspitzel Asew* (1935) – *Translator's note.*

[15] Petre Pandrea, *Memoriile mandarinului valah*, Bucharest: Albatros, 2000, pp. 12-13.

[16] *Ibid*, p. 22.

[17] *Ibid*, p. 23.

[18] Petru Comarnescu, *Jurnal. 1931-1937*, Jassy: Institutul European, 1994, p. 103.

Ionel Jianu. This was the set with which Belu Zilber mingled. When Eliade reproaches him for such a serious accusation, Belu Zilber serenely replies, "They were nothing but words on the wind. It's part of the Marxist turn of phrase. I am, of course, duty-bound to combat your ideological positions and can only do so by resorting to the traditional clichés."

What kind of clichés? The accusation of being a Siguranţă agent is part of the stage props of the class struggle. This means that Eliade is an agent of the Siguranţă by virtue of the fact that his ideological position is diametrically opposed. Whoever thinks differently than us is an agent, is sold to the enemy. Being a Siguranţă agent was the most infamous thing possible. This kind of reasoning was to cost Belu Zilber dearly in the period 1948-1954, when he was under investigation. The principal accusations were that he was an agent of the Siguranţă and a spy in the pay of the Americans and the British. In fact, the aim of the accusations was to liquidate him politically and physically, at the same as his friend Pătrăşcanu. By attacking Eliade, Zilber had wished to destroy him, starting with his reputation. The hellish noose is tightening. Zilber falls victim to the same type of mechanism he had merely sketched out while Romania was still a democratic country. Defended by Mircea Eliade and Nae Ionescu, he attacks them in order to justify himself before the leaders of the PCdR. He would have become suspect if he had had sympathies towards the extreme Right. In order to rid himself of such an accusation, he preferred to attack the two in public. Here we have the whole personality of Belu Zilber: a man of contradictions, entangled in the thickets of his own lies, fictions and duplicities. How does Mircea Eliade recall Belu Zilber, decades later? Describing the beginnings of the Criterion Group, where Zilber and Pătrăşcanu were invited to speak about Lenin and Bolshevism, Eliade recalls, "We wanted to have two Marxists alongside Mircea Vulcănescu and Mihail Polihroniade … I had met Zilber some time previously in the offices of the *Cuvîntul* newspaper. He had befriended Gh. Racoveanu since the time when he wrote … an article taking his side in an espionage trial. Belu Zilber was extremely moved by this, and as soon as he was acquitted he went to thank him. Back then he was always coming to the newspaper offices. In particular, he was a friend of Mircea Vulcănescu, Ion Călugăru and Paul Sterian. He was short, brilliant, highly cultivated, and although he kept repeating that he was a Marxist, he did not seem either dogmatic or intolerant."[19]

---

[19] Mircea Eliade, *Memorii*, Bucharest: Humanitas, 1991, p. 224.

Eliade does not seem to remember their angry exchange and ignores the suspicion hovering over Zilber that he was a Siguranţă agent. In any case, such a suspicion also hovered over Eliade in the 1930s and 1940s. Both the extreme Right and the extreme Left were carefully monitored by the authorities. The most efficacious method was to plant informers within the two movements, the higher up the better.

The Bolshevik Revolution was not Zilber's only passion. He liked women, but had countless complexes because of his height. The zigzags of his love affair with writer Henriette Yvonne Stahl were the talk of Bucharest in the early 1930s. But his main obsession, equal to his passion for revolution, was to make a fortune. In this respect he resembles Parvus (Alexander Helphant), a close associate of Trotsky and Lenin, whom we met in an earlier chapter. An initiator of the concept of 'permanent revolution' adopted by Trotsky, Parvus dreamed of overthrowing the Tsar and making a huge fortune. Thanks to his imaginative mind, he managed to achieve both ends. Zilber desired the same things: to get rich and to demolish the 'bourgeois-boyar regime'. The contradiction is obvious, but Zilber was a man of all contradictions. He felt comfortable within their framework. He saw them as something normal, a manifestation of the Marxist dialectic he preached to whoever would listen. That his fortune would be confiscated by the communists as soon as they reached power seemed to him a secondary matter. It seemed to him a safer bet to get rich than to wait for the coming of a communist regime, an extremely unlikely prospect in the 1930s. The prospect of a Soviet occupation was tantamount to fantasy up until 1938. He felt comfortable in the bourgeois milieu of Bucharest, playing the role of a left-wing radical. Zilber was a second-hand communist. He was too intelligent not to doubt the truths of Stalin's *Short Course in Marxist-Leninism*. He was not cut out to be a fanatic, a dogmatist. He was also a second-hand businessman. His method of procuring money was just as dubious as his way of doing politics. We find the same amorality.

"In 1967, Zilber admitted that in the period 1932-1940, when he was a functionary and then secretary of the Institute of Foreign Affairs, he made use of blackmail in order to obtain money. Given his opportunity to discover that various clerks in commercial and industrial companies or state functionaries were embezzling money, he forced them to pay him sums of money – sometimes in the order of hundreds of thousands of lei – not to divulge the matter. He also managed to find out about the dishonest business affairs various Siguranţă employees were involved in, and when the need arose he would threaten them with exposure."[20]

The reputation of being a Siguranţă informant and spy followed Zilber his entire life. What does Lucreţiu Pătrăşcanu say? Did they ever discuss the subject? They had known each other since their early youth, when they were classmates in the same lycée and shared the same political sympathies. They were both fascinated by what was happening in Russia and became Bolshevik supporters as early as 1917. Did Zilber tell Pătrăşcanu about the Siguranţă investigation and the circumstances of his acquittal for espionage? It would be interesting to know how Zilber explained all these. Pătrăşcanu was certainly abreast of the suspicions hovering over his closest friend. He was a prudent man, initiated in all the machinations of clandestinity. If Zilber had a reputation among the communists of being a Siguranţă agent, then by maintaining relations with him Pătrăşcanu was consciously putting himself in an extremely dangerous position. Nevertheless, he defied the situation. He worked with Zilber in various public contexts. They published together legal and illegal communist materials. They wrote for these publications under their real names and pseudonyms (Ion D. Ion, Andrei Şerbulescu, etc.). The links between them were even closer in 1936 and 1937, when both the one and the other were deeply shocked by the Moscow show trials.

When Pătrăşcanu becomes active in the movement once more, in the winter of 1943-1944, his party contact is none other than Belu Zilber. Each member of the PCdR had a single contact person in the party, for conspiratorial purposes. Zilber played this role for Pătrăşcanu. At that time, although he was not part of the PCdR hierarchy, Zilber nevertheless played an important role. He raised funds for Red Aid from rich donors such as Alexandru Ştefănescu and Max Auschnitt (both non-communists), and Emil Calmanovici and Jacques Calman (both communists). The money went to prison inmates and the few militants still at large. Pătrăşcanu was one of them. The head of these operations was Remus Koffler. Zilber was not the only one to engage in this, but he was among the most influential. His access to business circles, the bourgeoisie and intellectuals meant he was effective. How much secrecy was involved remains an open question.

---

[20] Grigore Răduică, *Crime în lupta pentru putere, 1966-1968: Ancheta cazului Pătrăşcanu*, Editura Evenimentul Românesc, 1999, p. 10.

The Siguranță was abreast of the operation. It preferred to close its eyes. It is to be supposed that the pact from the early 1930s was still operational. Zilber defended himself during the Securitate investigation by saying that no communist had ever been arrested as a result of any denunciation made by him. It is also true that Vintilă Ionescu, the commissar who headed the anti-communist brigade and with whom Zilber had made an agreement to provide information, died in 1940. Zilber must have been assigned to someone else, of this there can be no doubt. The fact is that in the 1940s he was not brought to trial, convicted or sent to a prison camp. And nor was he in 1940-1941, when General Antonescu gave orders for all the communists to be rounded up and imprisoned, or later. All the same, it was a time when the communists were frequently arrested and imprisoned. See, for example, the cases of Teohari Georgescu and Iosif Chișinevschi, members of the CC of the PCdR, arrested in April 1941, or the fall of the Paneth group, the arrest of Petre Gheorghe, leader of the PCdR in Bucharest, the arrest of the leadership of the Patriotic Union in 1943, the discovery of the PCdR archive, followed by further arrests. Sami Margulies, a Siguranță informer, arrested in 1948 and placed in the same prison cell as Zilber in order to spy on him, writes as follows in his report to the investigator:

> "Given that he was a major donor to the Party and MOPR and was well-known as a communist in newspaper and political circles, often undertaking missions of trust among intellectuals and politicians on the side of the party such as Pătrășcanu, Foriș, and Ilie Pintilie, is it possible to accept Zilber's argument that he was overlooked by accident?"[21]

The Siguranță kept a close watch on the activities of the communists still at large. It was not difficult, because they were few in number. In any case, Zilber did not encounter any problems. It is possible that he provided information. Just as it is possible that the Siguranță kept him under continual surveillance in order to observe his contacts.

The tolerance of the secret services increased after the fate of the war turned in the Allies' favour after Stalingrad. Through Zilber information was obtained from an area to which they did not have much access. Ștefan Foriș was not discovered for four years. The Siguranță did not know who

---

[21] *Principiul bumerangului. Documente ale procesului Lucrețiu Pătrășcanu*, Bucharest: Vremea, 1996, p. 265.

the leader of the PCdR was. As for Foriș, it was thought that either he was dead or had fled to the USSR. Of course, we might suspect that the secret services knew where Foriș was, but left him at liberty for various political motives. There was also the accusation launched by the Dej group that Foriș was an agent of the Siguranța, and therefore it had no reason to arrest him. Belu Zilber knew who the head of the PCdR was. He also knew that Foriș was hiding in Bucharest. He was able to make contact with him. The most direct route was via Remus Koffler, with whom he collaborated. They had known each other well since the 1920s. Koffler was the number two in the PCdR hierarchy, Foriș's right-hand man. Zilber was up to date with the plot to eliminate him. He had been informed by Pătrășcanu. Nevertheless, it was not until August 1944 that the Siguranța discovered Foriș had been sacked in April of the same year. This tells us that Zilber was selective about the information he passed on to the Siguranța. He was playing his own game. There was also a negotiation at stake. At one time, the Siguranța had done Zilber a service; they had got him out of gaol in 1932. Especially after the winter of 1942-1943, Zilber was a useful contact. The closer the Red Army advanced, the more obvious it was that the PCdR would play an important role in the period to come. Many of the Siguranța bosses saw him as a bargaining chip. Zilber was in a position where he could facilitate the negotiations that would ensue after the fall of the Antonescu regime. This tolerance explains why in April 1944, when Zilber was collecting signatures for the intellectuals' memorandum addressed to Antonescu demanding Romania's withdrawal from the war, the Siguranța did not react. Belu Zilber was the organiser of the initiative, almost entirely conducted from his flat on Dionisie Street. After 1944, while under investigation, Eugen Cristescu, the director of the SSI during the period 1940-1944, is asked, "Besides Zilber, who else did you have [as informers]?" He answers, "I know Zilber from the General Siguranța. He is exceedingly intelligent and cultivated. … I would have liked to get my hands on Zilber. There must be something on him in Vintilă Ionescu's counter-intelligence section. For us, the communist problem was a social problem and did not fall within our remit [that of the SSI – *author's note*], but rather under that of the General Siguranța and the Bucharest police. If the communist organisation had attempted a coup, it would have come under our department."[22]

---

[22] Cristian Troncotă, *Eugen Cristescu, asul serviciilor secrete românești*, Editura Roza Vînturilor, 1994, p. 310.

Thus we learn what Cristescu thought of Zilber, but also that Zilber was an agent of the General Siguranță rather than the SSI. Given that the communist organisation organised a coup in 1944, albeit under the directions of King Mihai and the army chiefs of staff, it is worth asking whether Zilber, a participant in this plot, then came to the attention of the SSI.

The intellectuals' petition addressed to Antonescu is not the only major action in which Zilber takes part during 1944. In July and the beginning of August, he organises the prisoners' escape from Caransebeş Prison. The escape was ordered by the Bodnăraş, Pîrvulescu and Rangheţ triumvirate. Without orders, a 'disciplined soldier of the Revolution' like Zilber would not have acted. The idea occurred after the massacre of 17 March 1944 at Rîbniţa, Transnistria, when retreating SS troops massacred dozens of Jewish communists. In Caransebeş there were around 150 communists and Soviet spies. As the front was moving closer, the situation might reoccur. The Party cell was led by Teohari Georgescu, seconded by Pantiuşa Bodnarenko. The plan was for all the prisoners to escape and cross the border into Yugoslavia. The situation was critical. The coup against Marshal Antonescu being prepared in Bucharest might inspire reprisals on the part of the authorities or the Germans. The idea bears the hallmark of Bodnăraş's adventurism. Bodnăraş had become leader of the Party in April. Two men close to Zilber – Nicolae Betea and Anton Raţiu, from the Statistics Institute (a hotbed of communists, including Mihai Levente, Corneliu Mănescu, and Ştefan Popescu) – are sent to Caransebeş Prison, with the approval of Anton Golopenţia and Sabin Manuilă. On arriving there, Betea and Raţiu manage to make contact with the prisoners without any difficulty. Prison conditions were not harsh. For example, Teohari Georgescu is discovered by the two emissaries strolling down a street in the centre of the town, peddling items made in the prison workshop. Betea and Raţiu pass on a million lei to the prisoners, a very large sum at the time. The prisoners' reaction is paradoxical: they refuse to leave the gaol. They preferred to be guarded by the authorities than to run the risks of an escape. They were waiting for events to unfold according to the plan about which they had been informed. "We spoke with Belu on the telephone and he told us that things were on the right track, and so we could leave Caransebeş immediately," recalls one of the two participants.[23]

---

[23] Anton Raţiu, *Cumplita odisee a grupului Lucreţiu Pătrăşcanu.* (cont. p. 220.)

There is, however, another explanation. In Tîrgu Jiu, the escape of Gheorghiu-Dej was being planned for the middle of August. In case the authorities got wind of an escape of such proportions, something that was highly likely, then political prisoners would be kept under closer guard. This would have made Dej's escape impossible. After consultations between the two communist cells, the prisoners in Caransebeş rejected the plan. Nevertheless, we have to bear in mind that the Siguranţa was following closely communications between the Royal palace, leaders of the historical parties, army and communists. There was, as always in the case of a coup d'état, complicity. The secret services were playing their own game, wagering on the Allied card. In the investigation that followed his arrest in 1948, Zilber will be accused of having organised the escape – at the orders of the Siguranţa, of course – not in order to shield the prisoners from being killed, as happened at Rîbniţa. The Securitate will accuse him of trying to organise the escape in order to provoke a massacre of the communists. In the sentence handed down by the Military Tribunal in April 1954, the same accusation is made. Thus, the prisoners had not been lacking in courage, but rather Zilber was a 'provocateur' who consciously endangered the lives of the communist prisoners.

In 1944, Zilber is feverishly at work. This time it is no longer a matter of a petty intrigue at the margins of Romanian society or shady intelligence gathering. He is involved in a far-reaching plot to overthrow the dictatorship. Also involved are the King and his entourage, the army chiefs of staff, and respected political leaders. Zilber is thus mixed up in a veritable coup, the dream of every Bolshevik. The feverishness with which he takes part in all the preparations of spring and summer 1944 is understandable. Situated at the centre of the web of this plot, Zilber feels in his element. His long experience as a conspirator and spy makes him useful. He is skilled at it. He likes what he is doing. It is the happiest period of his life. Constantly flanking Pătrăşcanu, Zilber is preparing the publication of *România liberă* (*Free Romania*) newspaper. Together with Grigore Preoteasa, Ştefan Popescu, Mihail Sebastian and Anton Golopenţia. He is directly involved in the coup of 23 August. He is in charge of printing the royal speech and the first issue of *România liberă* on 24 August. The text of the royal declaration, read over the radio on the evening of 23 August, was written by Zilber and approved by Lucreţiu

Adevăruri dureroase, vol. 1, Editura Gestiunea, 1996, p. 86.

Pătrășcanu. The newspaper includes the royal speech, a list of the members of the new government, the decree of amnesty for political prisoners, and the declaration of war against Germany and alignment of Romania with the Allies. A. Rațiu describes it as follows:

> "On the afternoon of 23 August 1944, as evening fell, I did my usual rounds of the printing press. All the men were at their posts … I didn't know what was happening at the palace or elsewhere. At a given moment, on Latină Street … a small motor car appeared. It came to a sudden stop in front of the building at No. 8. Belu Zilber, the contact between Lucrețiu Pătrășcanu and ourselves, alighted. Seeing me in the yard, he rushed up and joyfully embraced me, kissing me, saying, 'It's over! We did it! The Antonescu government have been arrested. Now, let's get to work!'"[24]

Antonescu had been arrested. Belu was one of the few people in on the secret. He supervised the printing of *România liberă* during the night that followed. For someone who had been tried for espionage, for a Siguranță informer, it was a reversal of destiny.

After 23 August, Belu Zilber's position is paradoxical and brings together all the contradictions of the man. He becomes director of the Institute of Foreign Affairs and a university professor, head of the Political Economy Department of Bucharest University, after which he writes a doctoral thesis on *The Imperialism of the Backward Nations*. It is a good feeling. He has an affair with Nuțu Fuxman (Ana Naum), with whom he had worked in Red Aid. Zilber's five-year affair with Henriette Yvonne Stahl had been a disaster. He had recovered from it with difficulty. Nuțu Fuxman offered him the affection he needed. They get married. Zilber is earning a lot of money. He is mixed up in all kinds of wheeling and dealing. His political clout opens every door for him. It might be said that he is a successful man. His dream of taking part in a proletarian revolution and of getting rich has been fulfilled. He is the bourgeoisic and its enemy all rolled up into one. He becomes the director of the CEC (National Savings Bank). The Soviet occupation and the increasingly prominent position of the PCdR bring him multiple social advantages.

---

[24] Anton Rațiu, *op. cit.*, p. 93.

"In the spring of 1945, I met him on Calea Victoriei … he was shopping for some items of furniture he still needed for his home. On the way to the centre of town, I went into a couple of furniture and antiques shops and a carpet dealer's shop with him. He spoke with pleasure about the art of creating a tasteful interior from unmatched items,"[25] an acquaintance recalls.

The same Anton Golopenția, under investigation in 1950, will characterise Zilber as follows:

"He made a mark and stuck in the mind thanks to his conversational verve … He was not a literary man in the proper sense. He applied ready-made formulas mathematically, without seeking to make discoveries … It would sometimes seem to you that he was merely playing and that he was amazed at really having succeeded. He took an interest in the fate of the people he worked with, being a good comrade. He had a feeling for the good things in life, for fine food and a tasteful home. The defect he sometimes revealed was a slight lack of proportion, reserve, tact."[26]

He is sought-after and praised in the press. As a Bolshevik since the early days, close to Pătrășcanu, the most popular of the communist leaders, he becomes increasingly influential in the public sphere. But his ambiguous, duplicitous pre-war situation reveals its hidden edge. He is recruited by Petya Goncharuk, a GPU agent assigned to Romania, who obliges him to pass on information. In other words, he is reactivated as a Soviet spy. Goncharuk himself had been arrested for espionage in the 1930s, tried and sent to prison. He passes through Doftana, Caransebeș and Tîrgu Jiu, where he is close to the communist group led by Dej. Goncharuk is Bodnăraș's adjunct in the Government Special Service. At the same time he is Zilber's Party contact. As an old Bolshevik, Zilber cannot refuse an order coming from his Party superior 'to serve the homeland of communism'. Devotion to the USSR was decisive in defining a Bolshevik, and he had known this for a long time. He had done the same in 1928 when David Fabian Finkelstein had demanded it. This dual condition of communist and Soviet spy was

---

[25] Anton Golopenția, *Ultima carte*, Bucharest: Editura Enciclopedică, 2001, p. 30.
[26] *Idem*, p. 31.

natural for Zilber. The secret services were now working for the Soviets, and so things were simpler. Up until 1944, as a Siguranță informer, Zilber had to be an anti-communist and a communist at the same time. Now subordinate to the Soviets, the secret services no longer contribute to the inner turmoil of our hero. He is no longer the servant of two masters who wish for each other's destruction. He is working for the same master. His mission is to spy on diplomats, officers, and British and American journalists in Bucharest. It is a Party duty, assigned by Petya Goncharuk. Zilber carries out his duty. He cultivates relations with foreigners in Bucharest. He gathers information. He reports his conversations with Western emissaries.

But did he report everything? In the investigation of 1967, Petya Goncharuk declared that "Zilber was an agent whose work was honest."[27] In the autumn of 1945, in October, Mark Ethridge, an American journalist came to Bucharest on a fact-finding mission. He talks with all the political leaders. Among them, the only one who prefers to maintain anonymity is Belu Zilber. The reason he gives is that he is not reproducing the Party line but rather his own point of view. This is heresy. The analysis he makes is not at all one that comes from a communist in power. He is subject to scepticism, a cardinal sin for a Bolshevik. From the viewpoint of a militant it is in fact treason to the cause. In the Ethridge report we find the words of Zilber, hidden beneath the anonymity of 'a Romanian communist'. On 24 November 1945, Zilber tells Ethridge that the Romanian government is controlled by Moscow. He proposes a government with Pătrășcanu as leader, who is more acceptable to him than Petru Groza as Prime Minister. He tells him that the PCR has 8-10 per cent of the vote, the PSD 20-25 per cent, and that the PCR is better organised than the PNL and PNȚ.[28] We can imagine him then going to Petya Goncharuk to report the conversation. However, we must wonder how exactly he did describe it. Certainly, he will give his impressions of the journalist and the questions he had to answer. But he will pass over other things in silence; he will lie about his own statements. How could he have done otherwise when he had adopted a double attitude? We have definite data[29] that tell us that his relations with westerners were

[27] *Principiul bumerangului. Documentele procesului Lucrețiu Pătrășcanu*, Bucharest: Vremea, 1996, p. 329.
[28] Ulrich Burger, *Misiunea Ethridge în România*, Bucharest: Editura Fundația Academia Civică, 2000, pp. 210-211.
[29] Edward Mark, "The OSS in Romania 1944-1945: An (cont. p. 224.)

very close. Luis Madison, an officer in the US intelligence services, a name that crops up frequently in Zilber's trial, writes, "We met with him, officially, probably more than a hundred times … I cannot remember him ever having deliberately given us any false information." The author of the article, Edward Mark, comments on this paradoxical situation as follows: "Zilber became the advocate of a firm American policy of resistance to the Soviets in Romania. The Secret Intelligence reports present the strange spectacle of a prominent communist persistently asking the US to support free trade, free elections and the free press in Eastern Europe." What is interesting here, beyond the change in Zilber's attitude, is his ability to convince both his superiors and the Americans – neither of them naïve in such matters – that he is honest. The plasticity of his personality is extraordinary. Once again, he enters this dangerous game and becomes a double agent.

From October 1944 onward, he is sent by Goncharuk to meet officially with the representatives of Western secret services. Instead of fishing for information and spreading misinformation, he conveys alarm signals about the situation in Romania, about the dangers of exclusive Soviet domination in Romania. He passes on confidential information. Zilber is perfectly informed. He explains, analyses, requests Western assistance. He is a very good source for the British and Americans, who thereby find out what is happening in the upper echelons of government, which has been pro-communist since 6 March 1945. He does not do so for money. But why? With the Soviet occupation, his illusions about the 'liberation of man by means of a proletarian revolution' seem to have unravelled. The homeland of equality reveals itself to be merely a great power, an empire that is pursuing its own interests. It is not at all a case of the liberation of man, quite the contrary. His intellectual inclinations towards tolerance and dialogue make themselves felt strongly. Soviet brutality and looting, the censorship diktat, the conditions laid down by the armistice, and the memory of the trials of 1936 and 1938 nourish the presentiments he has had since before 1944. He seems to remain a Bolshevik, but Stalin's policy in Romania causes him to have doubts. His ideological options and loyalties are no longer clear. In 1946, he reads Arthur Koestler's book *Zéro et l'infini* (*Darkness at Noon*) in

Intelligence Operation in the Early Cold War," in *Intelligence and National Security*, no. 2/1944. See Fl. Constantiniu in *Curierul Naţional Magazin*, July-August 1995 and the afterword by G. Brătescu to Belu Zilber, *Actor în procesul Pătrăşcanu*, Bucharest: Humanitas, 1997, pp. 242-243.

English, brought to him from Paris by Pătrăşcanu. The book causes him a shock that he will recall until his dying day. The experience of old man Rusakov, a Bolshevik leader of the old guard, arrested, investigated, tried and convicted, who, out of devotion to the Party, ends up testifying falsely that he has committed treason, will haunt Zilber during his own trial.

In 1946, Zilber goes to Moscow for the first time, accompanying the economic delegation to take part in negotiations. The impressions with which he returns reinforce his opinion that the Soviet model is not applicable to Romania.

"In the SU, [Soviet Union] the working class is more exploited than in capitalist countries. … The workers are not free to organise or to fight to improve their lives … Workers refractory to Party orders are expelled from the workplace, which is equivalent to their and their family's death from starvation, or else they are deported to Siberia. Workers and functionaries supplement their meagre wages by theft. They all steal, from the workers to the directors. In the SU, worker productivity is far lower than in Western Europe, given the dreadful physical exhaustion to which they are subjected. The Soviet worker receives a much lower wage than his counterpart in the capitalist countries for the same amount of work. The peasantry is exploited even more bloodily. The peasants pay feudal tithes! … The Soviet statistics that announce progress in various fields are false. … Soviet production is greatly outstripped by American production in oil, steel, coal etc. … Some progress has been made … But at what cost? The modest progress of the Soviets has been paid for by the working class with tides of blood … Agrarian collectivisation has also been paid for with the death or deportation to Siberia of twelve million peasants."[30]

From August until November, Zilber is in Paris, with his wife, Nuţu Foxman, as part of the Romanian delegation to the Paris Peace conference. He leads a comfortable life, going to the theatre and cinema and attending high-society events. He had not been to Paris since 1939, when he accompanied Virgil Madgearu, then director of the Institute of Foreign Affairs, to a congress. Paris had recovered from the war and was in full political and cultural bloom.

---

[30] *Principiul bumerangului. Documente ale procesului Lucreţiu Pătrăşcanu*, Bucharest: Vremea, 1996, pp. 270-271.

Zilber meets up with old friends. Among them are intellectuals from the Criterion Group, now refugees in France. He does not hesitate to seek out Emil Cioran. On the other hand, he refuses to meet with Mircea Eliade. "Both of them Legionaries, but the first is honest while he [Zilber] has evidence that the second denounced men of the Left."[31] The old conflict between Zilber and Eliade was still smouldering. Zilber, as it would seem from this passage, still felt rancour towards Eliade.

A close associate of Pătrășcanu, Belu Zilber finds himself isolated, at a time when Pătrășcanu himself is isolated and viewed with mistrust, in addition to being kept under surveillance at the orders of Gheorghiu-Dej, who is also in Paris. Zilber, subordinate to Petya Goncharuk, who is close to Dej and also present in Paris, has a mission here, too. He is to gather information from the American delegation. He attends a number of meetings in order to gain an impression of Western points of view. Here, too, he plays a double game: he alerts his interlocutors to the danger of Romania being swallowed up by the USSR. He asks for help in tempering the Soviets' position. His appeals are in vain, however. The West abandons Eastern and Central Europe for decades to come. A serious incident takes place, which will cost Zilber dearly. An article in the *New York Times*, published during the conference, provides plentiful details about the Romanian economic situation, many of them confidential in nature. Zilber is suspected. He is supposed to have passed on to a journalist a secret report of the economic commission of the Romanian delegation. The suspicion is due to his close relations with the Americans. Which is true. The situation causes a scandal within the delegation. Zilber's attempts to exculpate himself fail. In his defence, he says that he is in contact with the Americans at the orders of the PCR, and, moreover, he is working for the Soviets. In vain. He is isolated. On his return from Paris, Zilber asks Goncharuk for an official document to prove that he met with westerners as part of a mission ordered by the PCR leadership. In response to such an unorthodox request, Goncharuk takes the appropriate measures. He breaks off relations with Zilber as an informant.

Not long after, Zilber is expelled from the PCR. He had not been a member for long, only since 1945, although he had been an activist since its formation in 1921 and had taken part in the actions of the radical wing

---

[31] Aron Golopenția, *Ultima carte*, Bucharest: Editura Enciclopedică, 2001, p. 29.

of the Socialist Party since as early as 1918, while he was still a lycée student. He appeals, unsuccessfully. On 20 May, *Scînteia* announces, "Herbert Zilber (Andrei Șerbulescu) has been expelled from the Party for having maintained links with elements at enmity with the working class," as he recalls 20 years later.[32]

> "Friends and foes, each did everything not to be suspected of solidarity with the man expelled for such nebulous deeds. Some out of the conviction that someone like me must have done something serious, others because, given that I had been expelled, there was nothing else that could be done."[33]

An empty space forms around Zilber. Non- and anti-communist milieus did not allow themselves to be frequented by one of the best-known 'Reds'. The Soviet occupier was hated by the traumatised population, as were its local tools, the Romanian communists. Zilber is rejected, viewed with resentment, isolated. The communists in their turn, knowing he has been expelled, treat him like a pariah. It was better to be outside the Party, as a bourgeois, even as an opponent, than to have been a member of the PCR and then to be expelled. You were treated twice as badly. Zilber does not doubt the Party's judgement; he doubts himself. The following is a page that might have been taken from Kafka's *The Trial*:

> "Perhaps I had done something without realising it, for example an indiscretion towards some foreigner or agent, somehow reported and then finding its way into a file. It is the original sin beneath whose burden we live. We always feel guilty towards someone, towards an unseen God, who never tells us what crime we have committed, towards the dead who depart without explanations, towards an unknown file. Neither family nor friends, even if they told me otherwise, imagined that I could have been cast out among the lepers without having done something."

Zilber continues,

---

[32] Belu Zilber, *Actor în procesul Pătrășcanu*, Bucharest: Humanitas, 1997, p. 22.
[33] *Ibid*, p. 19.

"The sight of the mystery in print makes them all shudder in horror. In vain did I try to explain to Pătrășcanu that everything seemed to have been covered ready for a Pătrășcanu trial... His reply was invariable: 'Who knows whom you talked to and what you said! It must have been something!'"[34]

"I thought that after my expulsion they would leave me in peace. On the contrary, it was not until then that the real call to the hunt was sounded. Pressures on my wife, orders for me not to be visited, pressure on Ștefan Voitec [the Minister of Education – *author's note*] to sack me from my university post, orders not to finance the research Institute I had recreated in 1944, orders to the functionaries of this Institute to resign. I wished for one thing, to be left in peace ... The farther I wanted to stay away from them, the more oppressive the harassment became ... Hence begins my civil death ... Apart from my family, the last person who started to abandon me was my wife ... For the salvation of her soul were mobilised all her friends and superiors. Each in his own way told her that she had to separate from me, because 'you separate from whoever the Party is separated from', ... The last attempt before starting to separate from me was an audience with Ranghet, the head of the cadres, to ask him what was behind the mysterious communiqué of expulsion, as she was determined to divorce me immediately if he could provide her with a single proof that I had committed treason. The result of this audience was astonishing even to me, who was ready for anything. As soon as he found out what it was she wanted to know, Ranghet expelled her on the spot for not having faith in the Party!"

In the summer of 1947, he is forced to close the Institute for Foreign Affairs, due to a lack of funds. The communists, in control of all the levers of government, refuse to go on funding him. In autumn, he is banned from teaching at the University, by order of Minister of Education Ștefan Voitec, an acquaintance of Zilber's, a social democrat and former Trotskyite. His attempts at reconciliation with the PCR all fail. Pătrășcanu was still Minister of Justice, but he was unable to help him. In addition, he advises him to flee the country. Zilber refuses, arguing that on his arrival in Vienna he would be intercepted by the secret services and forced to tell everything

---

[34] *Ibid*, p. 23.

he knew, to become their man, in return for permission to go to the West. He knew very well how the secret services operated and what was the price of collaboration with them – betrayal. This argument, not a very strong one in his case, given that he was a habitué of all kinds of secret agencies, was overshadowed by another, impossible to contradict for a Bolshevik:

> "I was unable to tear myself away from the Party, just as some men cannot tear themselves away from the woman in their life, even if she is a whore, a thief and a liar. He's fallen for a woman, as the saying goes. Marxism practised since youth becomes a vice. I had fallen for the Party. I sensed what awaited me, but I could not tear myself away from that abstraction named the Party."[35]

Zilber advises Pătrășcanu to save himself by fleeing the country. Pătrășcanu refuses. Harried, with no escape, Zilber concocts all kinds of plans, for himself and for Pătrășcanu, without ever making up his mind. Flight to the West had become an obsession in many circles. The Tămădău incident in August 1947, when a number of PNȚ leaders were caught trying to board an aeroplane and flee clandestinely to Turkey, discouraged him. The fact that the whole episode had been a provocation mounted by the SSI and conducted by Petya Goncharuk did not escape him. The atmosphere in Romania was increasingly oppressive. Things were going in the direction he had been afraid of, and it meant that he would be convicted of treason, betrayed by his own comrades.

In November 1947, the trial of Iuliu Maniu and Ion Manolache is held. At the end of the year, King Mihai is forced to abdicate. A few days before this, Zilber sends a letter to Ana Pauker. He wants to know what he is accused of. Above all he desires an end to his state of uncertainty. He had been accused without any charge; he was a free man, but at the same time a prisoner. He wanted the Party to take him back. His existence outside the Party seemed meaningless to him. He writes to Ana Pauker that he places himself at the Party's disposal for investigation. After close surveillance lasting a few months, he is arrested by the SSI. Up until then, the special services, under the control of the PCR, had dealt with 'class enemies', 'reactionaries', the bourgeoisie, politicians of other opinions, and capitalists. Zilber's arrest was a sign that the Party was preparing to settle accounts within its own ranks.

---

[35] *Ibid*, p. 45.

Arrested by the SSI, Zilber is firmly convinced that a war is about to break out between the USSR and the USA. The USA possesses a formidable weapon: the atomic bomb, against which there was no defence. To the objection that Russia too might have an atomic weapon, given that it has the raw materials, Zilber answers that the Soviets do not have the technical or industrial capacity to build the bomb. "I want the war to find me outside. An atomic bomb will burn us all up like mice. Or if we're not all deported to Siberia, they'll shoot us like dogs," he declares to an informer in his cell.[36]

During the investigation, Belu Zilber lies to everyone, convinced that thereby he will survive. Caught up in his own contradictions, the great schemer, who emerged from beneath the overcoat of Karl Radek, the Bolshevik ideologue, and Ostap Bender, the Ilf and Petrov character, prepares for the denouement step by step. His double game does not escape the secret services. Zilber finds himself expelled from the Party in 1947, accused of spying for the British and Americans. The accusation is accurate, but incomplete. The accusation of spying for the USSR, likewise correct, should also be added. A year later he is arrested and embroiled in the masquerade of the Pătrășcanu trial. In August 1967, he will be the last prisoner to be released from Dej's gaols.

---

[36] *Principiul bumerangului. Documente ale procesului Lucreţiu Pătrășcanu,* Bucharest: Vremea, 1996, p. 273.

IX
Portrait of a Spy

> Where do these people come from? From the void.
>
> *Petre Pandrea*

In the 1920s and 1930s, the USSR waged through the GPU an offensive in which it infiltrated spies into capitalist countries, viewed as targets of the world revolution. While espionage and subversion involved typically Bolshevik underground, illegal activities, there was also massive action on the surface, through the control, infiltration or corruption of movements against the extreme Right or for human rights, and through the manipulation of trades unions and various protest groups. Let us not forget that in some countries the communist parties were legal, which broadened the scope for Bolshevik political manoeuvre, as well as spying and terrorist operations. All these parties, whether legal or not, were in fact bases of operations for numerous spy networks. There follow a few brief examples.

In France in 1924, the 'Tommasi affair' occurs, named after a prominent union leader and member of the Central Committee of the PCF, caught spying for the USSR in the French aeronautics industry. In 1927, the Crémet Network is broken up, consisting of around 100 persons co-ordinated by Jean Crémet, a member of the PCF Political Bureau and union leader in the naval and steel industries. The network gathered information for the USSR from the arms industry about new types of weapons, tanks, cannons, aeroplanes, warships, etc. In 1931, the year of the Solomon and Aradi trial in Bucharest, the network led by Jean Muraille is broken up. Muraille was a long-time Bolshevik and chief of Soviet espionage in France. In 1932, another network falls, headed by Jacques Duclos, a prominent figure in the PCF, who in the 1940s will lead the communist resistance against the German occupation. At the beginning of the 1930s, newly appointed to the Political Bureau, Duclos ran the Party's clandestine structures. Using a network of thousands of 'correspondents' for *L'Humanité* newspaper, Duclos gathered the information demanded by the USSR. To escape arrest, he flees from France.[1] There are numerous examples in every European country.

---

[1] Thierry Wolton, *KGB-ul în Franța*, Bucharest: Humanitas, 1992, pp. 20-26.

In *KGB: The Inside Story of its Foreign Operations from Lenin to Gorbachev* (1990), Cristopher Andrew and Oleg Gordievski list no fewer than eight Soviet espionage plots that were exposed in eight separate countries in the spring of 1927 alone. These include: in Poland, a spy ring led by former White Russian General and GPU agent Daniel Vetrenko; in Turkey, a high-ranking functionary of the Soviet-Turkish commercial corporation, arrested for spying on the border with Iraq; Soviet espionage documents uncovered by a police raid on the Soviet consulate in Beijing; the eight members of the Soviet spy ring controlled by Jean Crémet arrested by the Sûreté; a number of functionaries in the Austrian Foreign Ministry, caught supplying secret information to the OGPU; an extensive spy network uncovered during a raid on the All-Russian Co-operative Society in London.

Romania was one of the main targets on this map. The trial of 1931, described in the previous chapter, was not a rarity. Since 1918, the communists had been operating on two levels. One was intelligence gathering, subversion, and terrorism, the other politics, essentially agitation and propaganda. The Comintern and the GPU vied for influence in the underground networks. Espionage was a priority for the Kremlin, but also propaganda. Both were part of the script for exporting revolution. A report sent by the communist leadership to the Comintern in August 1922 observes,

"Since we are talking here about the main difficulties which the Communist Socialist Party of Romania has to overcome, we should mention spying. It seems to be an acknowledged fact that Russian espionage in this country is rather poorly organised. Nevertheless, there is quite a clear tendency on the part of Razdevot [Razdevka, the Soviet spy service in 1922 – *author's note*] to make use of our organisations as a means of gathering information, and herein lies a great danger. Not only because many of our best comrades have found themselves yet again in trouble with the law and have had to go into exile etc., but also because there is an increasingly imminent danger of a direct link between our organisations and the spying organisations being discovered ... The requirement for money further heightens the attractiveness of the extraordinarily large sums from Razdevot, where it is to be remarked that not only the comrades are functionaries of this institution, but also Romanian detectives. ... The comrades from Bassarabia admonish us for not wanting to have relations with the Russian military authorities … Lately, on repeated occasions, bosses [of the PCR] have been arrested on charges of espionage … It has been proven that our relations with the other side of the Dniester are a continual danger for the existence and unity of the Party … The necessary documents arrive here more easily from Western Europe. This is why we request that our Ukrainian budget should be sent via Vienna. … In Romania there is almost no legal, or illegal, organisation and what remained recently fell into the hands of the government. None of the comrades who had, in one way or another, been a 'boss' now remain out of gaol."[2]

The Army counter-intelligence service and the Siguranţă had no qualms about prosecuting communist agitators for espionage, even if the latter claimed to limit themselves strictly to political activities. Proof of this is the frequent capture of networks of agents in the pay of Moscow who were involved in both communist agitation and espionage. The following is a list of examples. In 1924, the press reported the dismantling of a large-scale network based in Cernăuţi/Czernowitz and operating in Dobrudja, Bassarabia and Bukowina, controlled by a certain Lago Kolpatov (pseudonym Oscar Spacek). The memoirs of spy Boris F. Lago, who survived and emigrated to the West, provide interesting information about his career in Romania between 1923 and 1925. He confirms the information to be found in press reports of the time (presented by Florin Constantiniu in *Privirea*, nos. 6-7, 1996). The aim of the network was to gather military information. It had contacts in Vienna, Berlin and Prague. The accomplices included Victor Tomashevsky, an air force officer, and Kalcev, a student, who committed suicide after his arrest. Lago was sentenced to five years imprisonment and taken to Doftana, where he met up with numerous other Soviet spies. He was amnestied in 1929.

Also in 1924, the members of a group led by Stefan Petrov were captured in Constanţa. The group passed on information via Constantinople, where the CPU centre of operations for the Middle East and the Balkans was located. A search uncovered large sums in foreign currency and secret documents relating to port activities in Constanţa. But the major discovery of 1924 was the exposure of a network whose members included the former

---

[2] ANR, *Copilăria Comunismului românesc în arhiva Cominternului*, 2001, p. 95.

Ukrainian Minister to Bucharest, Count Georges de Gasenko, lawyer Vasile Didushchuk and G. I. Gruglyov. The network was based in Berlin. Its head was Vasile Didushchuk, born in Russia and recruited by his brother, the GPU's resident agent in Germany. The sentences ranged from one to five years, in accordance with the law. The trial had barely ended when another network was discovered in Cernăuți. The leader was Soviet Lieutenant Colonel Maxim Sulak. There were 20 arrests in total. Another network was uncovered in Tighina, led by Constantin Plămădeală, a former officer of the Russian Army under the Tsar, who fled to Romania in 1917. A secret organisation was discovered in Galatzi in October 1924. In November of the same year, 35 members of a single network were arrested. They included a Bulgarian diplomat by the name of Kisseloff, Lieutenant Teodor Niță, a Romanian officer, and Margareta Arvala, a variety singer. A certain Major Ceaikovski was in charge of the group. As in other affairs of this kind, a lot of money was involved, sent from Moscow via Vienna, where the Comintern's bureau for South-Eastern Europe was based. The trial takes place in December. Major Ceaikovski, Lieutenant Niță, Alexandru Kisseloff, Captain Widman, Kapel, Oscar Singer, and Al. Zarvodin are given the maximum sentence of five years imprisonment. Another nine people are convicted *in absentia* and handed down the same sentence. A further 16 persons receive prison sentences of between one and four years.

In February 1925, 45 people were tried for espionage and terrorism in Cernăuți. The network had been operating since 1920 and was controlled from Odessa. The leader was a certain Alexander Gurov, an engineer. He dealt in military espionage and organised terrorist attacks, blowing up bridges and public buildings. They were all Russians. The same as in other cases, caches of guns, ammunition, grenades, and dynamite were discovered, as detailed in the indictment of over 100 pages. In 1926, Eugenia Novak is arrested. She was part of the Ceaikovski-Kisseloff network. Another agent, Alexey Kutsulab, regarded as highly dangerous, is arrested in Soroca. In 1926, the Soviet secret services manage to steal the mobilisation plan of the Romanian Army. General Ludovic Mircescu, the Minister of War, making his resignation, declares, "When I came to the Ministry of War I prayed to God that I should preserve a healthy body and mind. On leaving now, I thank God that he answered my prayer."[3] A strange declaration. It was the General who was to blame for the disappearance of the documents. The

---

[3] *Universul*, 8 June 1927.

GPU had managed to lay a trap for him, using a female agent with whom the minister had an affair. In Vatra Dornei with his mistress, the general requested the documents from Bucharest. The next day, they were gone, and with them the agent. Later, when the whole story is exposed, General Ludovic Mircescu commits suicide.

In February 1927, there is a conference of the Balkan Communist Federation in Constantinople, dedicated to espionage. Measures are taken to establish in Constantinople a Secretariat for counter-intelligence. The members appointed to the Secretariat include Georgi Dimitrov and each Party has a representative. The conference demands the organisation of spy cells in the army, the printing of a propaganda leaflet to be disseminated among soldiers, and the training of informants and provocateurs among the civil and military institutions of the state. It also requests a "special loan from the Comintern" for these activities.[4] What information had to be gathered? The following is a quotation from the same Siguranţă report sent from Constantinople: "Army and fleet positions, arms dumps, infantry and marine general staff, superior officers." Constantinople, along with Vienna, Prague and Berlin, a very important point on the GPU's map of subversion.

In 1927, the trial of a spy network from Gorj takes place. All three members are sentenced to six years imprisonment. Also in 1927, at the time of the resignation of the Averescu government, five accused of espionage in the Bukowina region are tried in Jassy. A month later, another network, led by painter Mihail Maţisin, is brought to trial in Chişinău. In February 1928, three persons are indicted for espionage: Maria Löbel, Paul Schor, and Dr Tikinovski. The last of these three had denounced the network and was acquitted. The network was much larger, however. One of those not captured was Iosif Kaliş, who would later be implicated in the major trial of 1931, along with Paul Solomon and Victor Aradi. In the summer of 1928, a journalist named Iacobovici, the director of Russian-language newspaper *Utro*, is murdered in Chişinău. The murder was in fact a GPU execution, carried out by a Soviet agent who had crossed the Dniester. Also in 1928, a network of spies is discovered in Constanţa, where they had been gathering information from the naval base and sending it across the Dniester by courier. A certain Tibacu, who held a high-ranking position in the Siguranţă in Chişinău, was also captured at this time. He was in fact a GPU agent. In May 1929, there is an exchange of fire between the banks of the Dniester.

---

[4] ANCR, CC of the PCR Archive, Fund 50, Dossier 2231, pp. 70-71.

Arrests ensue: engineer Sergey Burlachenko and Mikhail Stoikov, the GRU resident in Cetatea Albă. The third person arrested, the network's courier, Grigori Grishchenko, escapes and either flees to Russia or is killed by border guards. Burlachenko and Stoikov admit to having spied for the USSR since 1927. In December 1929, three soldiers are tried in Galatzi, charged with spying for the GRU. In 1931, the trial of another network is held (Vasile Dobrescu, Boris Vîlcev, Gh. Rusescu). Also in 1931, the Solomon-Aradi trial is held, in which 63 people are implicated.

An annual report of the Siguranţă on communist activities states,

"In 1931, 50 communist organisations were discovered, including 12 spying and 38 propaganda and agitation organisations. Twenty two attacks on the national railways were attempted or committed ... 1,097 communists were arrested and 244.convicted. 86,615 manifestos were confiscated ... In 1932, up until 1 October, 45 communist organisations were discovered, including 10 involved in espionage and 35 in propaganda and agitation activities, and four terrorist attacks were committed or attempted. Eight hundred and seventy seven communists were arrested and 396 convicted. Forty thousand eight hundred and seventy seven communist manifestos were confiscated."[5]

On 29 January 1932, *Universul* and *Dimineaţa* newspapers announce the arrest of 20 persons from a Soviet cell operating in the Central Post Office. They are under investigation by the Siguranţă accused of "the theft of official documents and correspondence, which they transmitted over the border." The investigation is conducted by Eugen Cristescu of the Interior Ministry, later head of the SSI, and Vintilă Ionescu, the number one specialist in communist activities, an inspector general in the same ministry. The network was made up almost exclusively of Bulgarians and was part of the DRO (Dobrudja Revolutionary Organisation), a branch of the Balkan Communist Federation. The head of the network was Ivan Dimitrov Tevekelev, "a clandestine agent for communist instigation and intermediary for the international espionage bureau in Vienna. The above named came to our country with the task of intercepting telegrams sent by the state to legations abroad, various orders regarding national defence and communiqués between Romanian legations and the respective states,"

---

[5] MAN Archive, SSI Fund, Dossier 182, p. 57.

as the indictment states.[6] He had arrived in Romania in 1931, bringing money and collecting information from the other agents in order to send it abroad. In November 1935, he was sentenced to eight years imprisonment. He was released in 1940 and deported to Bulgaria. The network had been operating since 1927. A number of its members had been imprisoned for offences under the Mîrzescu Law. Danciu Voicu, a member of the German Communist Party, had already been sentenced to 18 months imprisonment at the Gustav Arnold/Lucrețiu Pătrășcanu trial. Mihail Ignatov had another conviction for espionage under the new law of 1931. Most of the members of the network worked at the Central Post Office as functionaries or clerks. They were each paid around 20,000 lei a month by the GRU. Another nucleus of spies operated in Constanța under the leadership of veterinarian Boris Makedonov. In 1933, engineer Alexander Rubinstein is arrested in Chișinău for espionage and communist activities. In September, Romanian counter-intelligence arrests seven agents. They were based in Odessa, from where they crossed over the Dniester. In November 1933, Soviet spy Boris Taratuta is captured. He hangs himself while under arrest at the inspectorate of gendarmes in Chișinău. He had crossed the Dniester from Romanian to Soviet soil a number of times and had been trained as a spy by the GPU.

In January 1934, the trial of the Central Post Office spy ring commences, causing a great public stir. Some of the accused held key positions, while others were telegraph clerks or telephone operators. In 1934, an organisation based in Kiev is discovered to be operating in Bukowina and northern Bassarabia. Secret documents, encrypted correspondence and lists of addresses are found. Fifteen people are arrested. The head of the network, a Dr Brakharin, was paid the equivalent of 20,000 lei in hard currency per month. In February yet another Soviet spy ring is broken up. Dozens of people are arrested. Radio apparatus and secret codes are confiscated. In September 1934, a network with ramifications throughout the country is discovered in Soroca. Raids lead to the discovery of radio transmitters. In August 1934, an espionage organisation is uncovered in Jassy. In Cluj in September 1934, the War Council of the Sixth Army Corps passes sentence in another espionage case. Two of the accused are sentenced to 10 years, the maximum punishment in accordance with the new espionage law. A third is sentenced to five years imprisonment. Also in September, in the port of Constanța, four spies are unmasked and deported by sea on The Romania.

---

[6] *Universul*, 30 October 1935.

In December 1934, a Soviet spy ring is uncovered in Austria. One of the network's principal agents was Isidor Simon Reiss, a Romanian citizen from Rădăuți, trained by the GRU.

After the re-establishment of diplomatic relations between Romania and the USSR, the Soviet legation installs in Bucharest an undercover agent for all its intelligence operations in Romania: G. M. Eremin. Up until 1931, Soviet agents were tried under the espionage law of 1913, which stipulated a maximum of five years imprisonment. The new law of 1931 introduces heavier sentences. More often than not, terrorism, intelligence gathering and extremist militancy went hand in hand. At trial, the indictments often refer to the espionage law and at the same time the Mîrzescu Law of 1924, which covered plots against national security and collaboration with foreign extremist organisations. The capture of such clandestine groups always leads to discovery of printing presses or simpler copying apparatuses, large quantities of pro-Soviet propaganda materials, and large sums of money. Often, caches of guns, ammunition and explosives are found (especially in Bukowina and Bassarabia). Terrorism was part of the vast operation to undermine the Romanian State that was conducted and financed from Moscow. In December 1920, as we have seen, Max Goldstein, a Bolshevik from the Odessa group, together with a number of accomplices from clandestine communist cells, planted a bomb in the Romanian Senate, killing three. This was not the only such attack. The Arsenal of the Romanian Army in Bucharest was blown up, an operation carried out by the GRU in 1924, working through Boris F. Lago, mentioned above. Lajos Palaghy, sentenced to 10 years imprisonment, was caught with six accomplices – Soviet spies – digging an escape tunnel in Craiova Prison. All seven are moved to Doftana. In 1925, Palaghy had attempted to plant a bomb in the Hippodrome on Derby Day, attended by the Royal Family and members of the government. A similar attack was successful in Sofia, when a bomb exploded in a church during a service attended by Bulgarian state officials. In Bucharest, however, the plot was foiled in time and the perpetrators arrested. During the entire inter-war period, numerous munitions dumps were blown up, railway bridges were sabotaged, and trains derailed.

In 1935, 46 were arrested for spying in Bassarabia. The maximum sentence of 10 years imprisonment was handed down to Sara Sukhoy (a GRU agent who led the organisation under the cover of working as a French teacher), Petre Oskopenko, Maria Ruga, Mikhail Protopopov, Peretz Dorfman, Gers

Ferklandarski, Ivan Galuzinski, Petre Schwartz and Mikhail Kalavenko. The group's clandestine activities were a mixture of terrorism, espionage and clandestine Bolshevik militancy.

Inter-war Romanian communism is closely tied to the question of Soviet espionage, subversion and terrorism, organised on a large scale by the GRU and Comintern. The PCdR was an agency of these operations to undermine the Romanian State more than it was a political movement. The networks were usually directed from Vienna, where GRU central and the Comintern's South-Eastern Europe bureau were based.

> "From the very beginning, the Comintern had close ties with the GRU, which created the USSR's foreign intelligence service. Links were established with the Comintern's sections, operations were funded, personnel were recruited … The national sections of the Comintern, i.e. the non-Russian parties, had not only the task of recruiting new members and making propaganda, but also that of organising strikes, demonstrations, protest marches and uprisings whenever the opportunity presented itself."[7]

The Comintern, as a tool of the GPU, was involved in all the subversive activities carried out by local communists in the inter-war period. It was also mixed up in other, camouflaged operations to protect the local communist parties.

> "A short time after the death of Lenin, the Comintern was transformed into a servile executant which could be called upon for special services … the foreign parties were subsidised only via the NKVD, circumventing the Comintern. … NKVD expenses for the Comintern were processed according to a sophisticated system, in that party matters were no longer at stake but rather matters of espionage and terrorism. The Comintern had become more useful to the NKVD as a human resource for diversionary operations in capitalist countries than the communist movements … The Comintern was vegetating, because Stalin had increasing doubts with regard to its reason to exist and only the NKVD still used it as a breeding ground for the recruitment of its future agents for foreign espionage."[8]

---

[7] Dmitri Volkogonov, *Lenin. O nouă biografie*, Editura Orizonturi-Lider, 1999, pp. 424-425.

[8] *Ibid*, pp. 435, 437-438.

In any case, the leaderships of the communist parties were imposed by the Comintern on the basis of reports from the cadres section, which was exclusively made up of GPU/NKVD agents. They appointed to leadership positions only people who had been their subordinates, and whom they could control through their intelligence network or using money.

From its very inception, the Comintern was in essence an organisation dedicated to espionage and subversion more than a political movement. The Soviet special services made use of Comintern agents. Their mission was to gather information and to carry out attacks and assassinations – anything that might undermine the democratic regimes. Beneath the disguise of the Comintern lay Soviet imperial ambitions. It was not so much a hypothetical 'revolution to liberate the proletariat' that was pursued as much as the national interests of Bolshevik Russia. This did not come about after 1927-1928, as is believed, but from the very beginning of the Comintern in March 1919. The undermining of democratic regimes and organisation of coups and putsches to overthrow them were the Comintern's defining purpose. The stipulations of its programme and other official documents obligated members to organise clandestine networks and to undertake any action that might undermine those states where communist parties were operating. These parties were often illegal (as in Romania) and existed only as underground networks, funded and controlled by the Comintern. They were far from being political parties in the proper sense. As soon as they were set up, they began to engage in clandestine, illegal activities, as laid down by the Comintern. The PCdR did not become clandestine until 1924, when it was outlawed. The clandestinity of the Romanian communists is consubstantial with the activities of all the groups that appeared after 1918. The clandestine communist networks were all directly financed from Moscow, via the GPU and Comintern. The money was delivered by couriers or sent via the 'post office box' system under the guise of legitimate businesses, or else through MOPR as aid for political prisoners. In 1932, Lucrețiu Pătrășcanu, for example, was implicated in the trial of a communist network whose head, a certain Gustav Arnold – a Comintern agent, German citizen from Berlin, and member of the German Communist Party – had been captured in Romania with a large sum of money, 1.2 million lei, intended to finance a clandestine printing press and set up a post office box system. Arnold was to send the money, in British pounds or German marks, to a certain Paul Hollinger, a jeweller. The latter was to change it into lei and hand it over to Pătrășcanu or Béla Breiner. The lawyer defending Gustav Arnold, the very well-known V. V. Stanciu, says during the trial, "The bourgeois societies of today are becoming neurasthenic because of their obsession with communism."[9] He knew what he was talking about. In 1946, he would defect to the West. Another defence lawyer at the trial, Iosif Șraier, also fled to the West in 1947. In spite of an array of leading lawyers (Paul Moscovici, Constantin Vicol, I. Vlădescu, Stelian Nițulescu and the two already mentioned; Lucrețiu Pătrășcanu provided his own defence), the accused were convicted. Gustav Arnold received two years imprisonment, increased to four years after appeal by the prosecutor's office. Thanks to his social standing and connections, Pătrășcanu was acquitted. Béla Breiner was sentenced to three years imprisonment. The trial proved that the communist militants had links to Soviet spy agencies, not always via the Comintern.

Political militancy, espionage and provocation were impossible to contain. Loyalty to Moscow obliged the communists to carry out whatever mission was entrusted to them. These missions involved the gathering of military, political and economic intelligence as part of the communists' struggle against the bourgeoisie and to foster the world proletarian revolution. The press of the time carried frequent bulletins about the capture of new Soviet spy networks and agents. Bucharest was a turning plate for the whole region. The Balkans, the Bassarabia question, Hungarian and Bulgarian irredentism, and the encouragement of separatist movements were priorities for the CPU and Comintern in Romania. A huge stir was created by the 'Agabekov affair'. In January 1932, the Siguranță arrests a number of GPU agents in Constanța and Arad. They are Geno Tsonchev, a Bulgarian; Alexandre Lecocq, a Frenchman; Sava Samuridis, a Greek; Grigori Alexeyev, a Soviet citizen; and Spiru Catapodis, a Greek. The indictment accuses them of plotting.

> "The GPU is seeking to capture G. S. Agabekov. [GPU] Central in Paris has received orders from Moscow for Agabekov to be brought to Romania, and for GPU Central in Constantinople to take him to Russia. The GPU agents in Paris are Jean Panaiotti and Serge Meinz. In Constantinople the affair is conducted by Iosif Mikhailovich Kaminsky, the GPU resident for South-Eastern Europe and the Middle East, and Nikolai Ivanovich Dnieprov, Head of the Soviet Commercial Representation."

---

[9] *Dimineața*, 21 December 1932.

The five are accused of infringing Article 1 of the Mîrzescu Law: "The association of persons for the purpose of preparing crimes against persons or property." The punishment varies between five and 10 years imprisonment. Who is Georghi Agabekov, the target of this plot hatched by the GPU? Agabekov, whose real name was Arutunov, was the GPU resident for South-Eastern Europe and the Middle East. In 1930, he had defected and was living in Brussels. In 1931, he published two books *The GPU* and *The Cheka at Work*, in which he unmasked the subversive activities of the Soviet special services against the West. Stalin demanded he be liquidated. In autumn-winter 1931-1932, a number of agents lured him to Constanța. He was to be captured, put on a ship and taken to Odessa. Failing this, he was to be killed by an assassin sent for this purpose, Grigori Alexeyev.

Detecting the trap into which he was being lured, Agabekov, knowledgeable of GPU methods, makes contact with the Romanian security services. Following a six month surveillance operation, the members of the gang are arrested. The Romanian and foreign press publish numerous articles about the affair. *The Guardian* and *Le Journal* follow the progress of the investigation and the trial. The investigation brings to light GPU procedures, the extent of subversive operations throughout Europe, the large number of agents and accomplices, and the sources of the money for these activities. The trial begins in May and ends in August. The lawyers for the defence include V. V. Stanciu, Constantin Solomonescu, Petre Sadoveanu and C. Răileanu. In August 1932, the court rules the case out of its jurisdiction, and the five are acquitted "for lack of evidence." The plotters are deported to their home countries: the USSR, Turkey, Greece and France. Georgi Agabekov, the hero of this convoluted affair, did not escape the vengeance of the GPU for long. Six years later, he was lured into a trap in Paris and murdered. His body, sliced into sections, was found in a suitcase that had been tossed into the sea.[10]

Such affairs were a small part of all that went on in Romania during the period between the wars. The Siguranță captured only a part of the networks. And few cases ever made it into the press. One such case, for a long time unknown, is that of artillery Lieutenant Emil Bodnăraș, who deserted on 1 February 1932 and crossed over to the other side of the

---

[10] Cristopher Andrew and Oleg Gordievski, *KGB. Istoria secretă a operațiunilor sale externe de la Lenin la Gorbaciov*, Editura ALL, 1994, p. 116. Pavel Sudoplatov, *Special Tasks*, Little Brown and Co., 1994, pp. 47-48.

Dniester. This was in the period when the Agabekov affair was front-page news, and only a few days after the extensive spy ring in the Central Post Office had been discovered.

***

Emil Bodnăraş is the most enigmatic figure among all the Romanian communists. The adventure of his lifetime begins in the depths of a harsh winter. "On 13 February 1932, Lt. Bodnăraş Emilian requests leave and on the evening of 15 February 1932 sets out from Sadagura to Hotin, arriving the next day at 12 p.m. Wearing a military cape and a fur hat, he enters the Patria Hotel in Hotin, where he registers under the name of Lt. Iliescu Gr. from Bucharest. After reserving a room he goes to the restaurant where he stays in the company of a woman until 5 p.m., when the officer goes to the border post at the Cetatea Hotinului frontier point. Here he reconnoitres the border and asks the soldiers on guard where guard posts have been placed, where the Bolsheviks' posts are, and finally how thick the ice is. At 8 p.m. he returned to the hotel where he paid for his room and then together with his female companion he moved to the Dacia Hotel. Here Lt. Bodnăraş informed the owner that he would be leaving at midnight, and that the woman, whom he presented as his wife, would remain in the room he had paid for until the next day. Lt. Bodnăraş went out of the hotel, entrusting to a waiter a letter to be posted. In these circumstances the officer left without being seen by anyone else. The next morning, the border patrols inspecting the bank of the Dniester found a lieutenant's cap and a revolver holster, and on the ice, tracks leading towards the left bank of the Dniester were visible."[11] The letter was addressed to his host in Sadagura, Dr Ioan Ştefanovici. "Investigations have not been able to establish whether Lt. Bodnăraş was assisted by anyone else in his crossing of the Dniester or to identify the woman who accompanied him in the day preceding his desertion, because the next day, after Lt. Bodnăraş's flight, she departed without leaving any trace," writes Royal Commissar Palade, in charge of the inquiry.

The case caused a great stir among the military. It was almost unprecedented for an officer to desert to the USSR. The army took care that the information should remain a secret and, above all, that it should not

---

[11] MAN Archive, Fund 983/3, Dossier 4, p. 92.

reach the press. "Please take measures that the press in the capital should not make this public."[12] The depositions in the dossier allow us to construct a psychological portrait of the young Lieutenant Emilian Bodnăraş, born on 10 February 1904, in Colomea, at that time part of Poland, and called Cîmpulung after 1918. He graduated from the Artillery School in Timişoara on 1 July 1927. Can dissatisfaction with the poor report the ambitious young officer received for the year 1931 have caused his desertion? He was upbraided for "lack of tact, drunkenness and frequenting persons lacking in patriotism." In a note dated 7 February, just a week before he crossed the Dniester, Bodnăraş complains, "I am all of a sudden vilified for being a drunkard and for not loving the homeland."[13] In reply, two days later, Colonel Ioan Rizescu, the commandant of the Twelfth Artillery Regiment, in a report to his superiors, observes Bodnăraş's "weakness for strong drink and his lies in various situations." He continues, "The officer is from Bukowina. His mother is German in origin. Having come high in his class at school he is rather conceited. ... His judgement is still a little childish, and his actions towards superiors are violent ... a recalcitrant temperament." The report likewise notes Bodnăraş's quality as officer material and his desire to pursue a career. Thus, the frustrated Bodnăraş had demanded that the unit commandant, Colonel Ioan Rizescu, explain the reasons for the report. On 11 February, Bodnăraş appears in front of the brigade commandant. The conclusion is that if the lieutenant changes his behaviour he will be given a better report. On 13 February he requests leave. Two days later, on the night of 15 February, he disappears in Hotin. So much for the facts.

There were also other cases of Romanian officers who deserted to Soviet Russia. The following is just one of them. On 17 November 1925, an air force lieutenant, C. Brăiloiu of the Galatzi garrison, takes off in a Brandemburg 34 aircraft, flies over the Black Sea and lands in the centre of Odessa. Six months later, the *Krasnaya Gazeta* publishes an interview with the deserter, reproduced in *Facla* (20 May 1926), in which he explains the reasons for his act and announces that he is going to become a communist. But how many officers deserted because they received poor marks in their reports? Bodnăraş was not mentally unstable and nor was he a man to take rash decisions. As the above facts demonstrate, his desertion was calm and well planned. Bodnăraş did not cross over to the USSR because he was

---

[12] MAN Archive, Fund 983/3, Dossier 59, p. 11.
[13] MAN Archive, Fund 948/3, Dossier 4, p. 337.

unhappy with his superiors. His quarrels within the garrison must provide a more plausible explanation for his desertion. Bodnăraş had been sent to Sadagura only recently. On 24 February 1932, a confidential report signed by the commandant of the Eighth Artillery Brigade states,

> "The causes that determined Lt. Bodnăraş to desert to Soviet Russia can only be the pathological mental instability that strikes anyone who comes into contact with him. Eternally discontented by his current situation, he thought he was a genius who ought to rise to the highest ranks as quickly as possible. He was never embarrassed to say within his circle of comrades that he wanted to be a general for the Russians or Chinese. To this can be added the influence of the communist company he kept, which his sick and susceptible nature could not resist. According to the declarations of his comrades he did not like to listen to the radio except to Soviet propaganda speeches. ... I think that he intended to carry out espionage, to serve the country that was his ideal in life (Soviet Russia) ... thus everything passed beneath his eyes and, intelligent and capable as he was, he was able to copy everything he wanted at leisure. ... Then, besides what he sent via Soviet couriers, on his departure he took with him a briefcase which he had been keeping at the house of a communist comrade and which evidently contained important documents. ... He moved in places where he met with persons suspected of being communists ... He stood in for an officer with the codes ... He worked alone in an office and so he was able to make as many copies as he wished, without needing to arouse suspicion."

Was Bodnăraş a spy? Had he been recruited by the GRU before his desertion? If so, when was he recruited? Perhaps as early as when he was still a student at the artillery school in Timişoara. The GRU lured capable young men from all over Europe. A famous example is that of British spies Kim Philby, Anthony Burgess, Donald Duart McLean and the others unmasked in the 1950s and 1960s, who were recruited when they were still students at Cambridge or young graduates, in the early 1930s. Recruits went on to rise through the military, scientific, political and business hierarchies of their home countries. Called 'moles' in secret service jargon, they had access to top-secret documents inaccessible to ordinary agents. Some even ended up running strategic institutions and taking important decisions. It was a long-term plan, which, when it came to fruition, would have devastating results.

Why then did Bodnăraş desert? He would have been of more use to the Soviets as an active officer in the Romanian Army. Once he was in the USSR, a precious source of information would be lost. It is possible that he was summoned by the Soviets in order to be trained as a spy and then be sent to other countries. A man with military training and a German education could be highly useful in an increasingly turbulent Europe. Was he called to the USSR for the obligatory indoctrination, training and verification? What is certain is that in the USSR he graduated from an espionage school and became a Soviet agent, if he was not one already. Another reason might have been his imminent exposure as a spy in Romania. Bodnăraş knew that he had blown his cover and that he would shortly be arrested. His own commandant, Colonel Ioan Rizescu, wrote in his report that he had not suspected him of spying. But can his activities and contacts have eluded the secret services? Was the USSR for Bodnăraş merely an ideological attraction or did he desert because he had secretly joined the communist movement, something banned by military regulations? Did Bodnăraş see in the USSR the homeland of communism, a place where he desired to live? Did he hate Romania and the bourgeois political regime? Communists generally chose to flee to the USSR for ideological reasons. Intoxicated by the propaganda, they saw in the USSR the homeland of triumphant communism and the future of mankind. But there were also personal motives: money, a career. The communists were people at the margins of society, adventurers, terrorists, lunatics, idealists. Others, because of criminal law or political offences they had committed in their home countries, were seeking to escape punishment. Was Bodnăraş one such case? It should be remembered that Bodnăraş became a member of the PCdR in prison, many years after his desertion. Numerous westerners agreed to spy for the USSR for ideological rather than pecuniary reasons.

The investigation into Bodnăraş's desertion was carried out by the Inspectorate of the Siguranţă in Cernăuţi/Czernowitz. The first report from the Intelligence Office in Cernăuţi, signed by a certain Anagnastopol, dates from 20 March. The following are excerpts:

"In Cîmpulung he had a borderline reputation, being by nature closed, selfish and tormented by the idea of getting ahead more quickly, regarding himself as an exceptional element. He had few friends and then only in order to have someone to rely on in case of need … The material circumstances of the Bodnăraş family are extremely precarious. His mother receives a pension of 550 lei a month in the name of her deceased husband, a former clerk of court. She recently found a job at the Cîmpulung Hospital with a wage of 1,400 lei a month. From this income she supports two sons, Aurel, aged 17, a pupil in the fourth form at a lycée, and Ervin [in fact Emanoil and Manole – *author's note*], a photographer by trade, currently unemployed and thus not earning. The latter, after finishing his national service, joined the Social Democratic Party, and not holding any job he looks after the Party club."[14]

The homes of Bodnăraş's relatives and acquaintances are searched, as well as his own digs, naturally. Bodnăraş rented a room in the house of Ioan Ştefanovici in Sadagura. In his room were found a portrait of Lenin and a painting depicting a Bolshevik soldier holding a machine gun. Is this sufficient to say he was a communist? Various secret regimental documents were also found. The investigators also find a number of letters received from his best friend at the time, Titus Cristureanu, sent from London. Cristureanu was suspected of having communist sympathies. Who was this friend, singled out in the report as "the one who to a large extent instilled extreme left-wing political convictions in him"? He is an extremely interesting character. He was born in the same year as Bodnăraş, in 1904, in the village of Iţcani, where the two spent their childhood together. He graduates from the Faculty of Commerce and Law in Cernăuţi/Czernowitz. He has a short career as a public functionary. His contacts with the communists do not pass unobserved. SSI reports reveal that he was kept under close surveillance from the 1920s onward. When Bodnăraş deserts, he has been at the London School of Economics since 1928, where he is studying for a doctorate. Like Bodnăraş, he goes through a brief fascist phase. Both of them were members of the Romanian National Fascia. During his short stint as a student in Jassy in 1924-1925, Bodnăraş was a member of A. C. Cuza's group. Because of his excesses he was expelled. In February 1932, according to a SSI report, Cristureanu was in Tiraspol, in the USSR, where he met up with recent deserter Bodnăraş. He returns to Romania, stopping off in Prague and Vienna, well-known turning plates for the Comintern. He writes articles for the left-wing press – *Dimineaţa* (*Morning*) and *Adevărul* (*The Truth*) – on

---

[14] MAN Archive, Fund 983, Dossier 4, pp. 39-40.

economic subjects, presenting the USSR. He publishes two pamphlets: *The Soviet Union and Romania* and *Romania's Static and Dynamic Borders* (Editura Adevărul, 1934 and 1935 respectively). In 1934 he joins the Friends of the USSR association. A SSI note reports that he is a frequent visitor to the USSR embassy. In 1938, Titus Cristureanu becomes the first director of the Romanian Economic Agency in Moscow. Grigore Gafencu appreciates him for his competence. In 1940, he is transferred to Ankara to occupy the same post, whence he returns in 1943, having been dismissed by Antonescu on suspicion of spying for the Allies. In Turkey he has links with British diplomats, according to another Siguranţă report. Arriving in Bucharest, he resumes his friendship with Bodnăraş, who has been out of prison since November 1942, and also with the leaders of the PNŢ. In autumn 1944, he becomes economic adviser to Gheorghe Gheorghiu-Dej, on Bodnăraş's recommendation. In April 1948, he is arrested. This was the man who had a strong ascendency over Bodnăraş in his adolescence and youth and whom the future communist leader saw as an example of success in life. For the ambitious Bodnăraş this was no small thing. It was enough to guide his most important decisions. When Cristureanu joined the extreme Right, Bodnăraş followed him; when he went to the other extreme, Bodnăraş did likewise.

Let us go back to 1932, to the garrison at Hotin. Was Bodnăraş's passage to the USSR desertion? Was Emil (or Emilian, in the official documents) Bodnăraş already a spy at that date? Or had he been enthralled by Bolshevik ideology, by a mental image of the USSR as a land of equality, of contented workers and peasants? The following is the conclusion of the royal report:

> "Although from the documents drawn up by the Security Inspectorate in Cernăuţi and from the incriminating evidence found in Bodnăraş's domicile there is sufficient proof that he nurtured communist sentiments, nevertheless there is nothing to prove that, guided by these political beliefs, he was a member of any subversive organisation or that he made propaganda for this movement."

In other words, even though he displayed communist sympathies, Bodnăraş was not a member of any organisation. He did not behave like a communist activist. He did not take part in the meetings of any clandestine communist cell. He sooner behaved like a lone spy, who conceals his real activities. The Intelligence Office in Cernăuţi reports that in the autumn of 1931 Bodnăraş made a number of long motorcycle trips through northern Moldavia, where he made notes of distances, roads, bridges, important landmarks. Typical intelligence gathering, one might say. If he was not a spy, and if he was not threatened with exposure, why then did he flee? Did Bodnăraș hope to have greater career opportunities in the USSR? He was probably frustrated because of his humble social background and poverty. He saw his way to the upper echelons of Romanian society and the army barred by those with a good family name, with wealth and relations. Another version of events is possible: in his youth, Bodnăraș, influenced by Titus Cristureanu, his intellectual and social superior, became a communist. There exists the hypothesis that, as a member of the PCdR, his party superiors gave him the mission of defecting to the USSR. This was common among PCdR members. For example, in order to be promoted within the apparatus, a candidate had to undergo a period of training in the USSR. "When he took this step [i.e. desertion], Bodnăraș did not leave the PCR in order to dedicate himself to spying for the Soviets, but rather he dedicated himself to spying for the Soviets because the PCR gave him that mission," writes an author who was in Caransebeş Prison with Bodnăraș.[15]

What other reason might have caused him to desert? Dishonour. The embezzlement of a large sum of money or some similar affair. However, the inquiry does not discover any money missing. The sins described by the investigation are different: arrogance, lack of discretion, discontent at his slow advancement, drunkenness, womanising. What else, then? There is a suspicion, without definite evidence, that Bodnăraș crossed over into the USSR as part of an operation organised by Army counter-intelligence. If his crossing of the Dniester was not desertion, then Bodnăraș might have been a Romanian spy sent on a mission to the USSR. In this case, his desertion is nothing but a cover story, and he was in fact an agent with Romanian military counter-intelligence."[16] The superficiality of the SSI investigation of 1932 justifies this hypothesis. But if so, why then was he later convicted and sentenced to 10 years imprisonment? According to this hypothesis, Bodnăraș is supposed to have been recruited as an agent by the Romanian intelligence services, a legend is created about him being a communist, and

---

[15] Pavel Câmpeanu, *Ceauşescu, anii numărătorii inverse*, Jassy: Polirom, 2002, p. 56.

[16] See G. Iavorski, "Pentru cine a lucrat « inginerul Ceauşu » ," in *Magazin istoric*, no. 9/1994.

he is sent on a mission to the USSR. Here, he was turned by the Soviet special services. His recruiter is supposed to have been Florin Becescu (Georgescu), the head of counter-intelligence.[17]

The question of Bodnăraş's time in prison arises. Can the SSI have wished to send a career officer to the USSR in order to penetrate the Soviet intelligence services? Did the SSI want to obtain information about the capabilities and preparedness of the Red Army? Or did it want to infiltrate someone into the entourage of the communist leaders in order to gather information? The hypothesis is weak. Counter-intelligence did not need to carry out such a complicated manoeuvre or to keep a precious agent in gaol for eight years. A large part of the communist leaders were informants for the police or SSI. Who was Bodnăraş working for? As an agent of the Romanian secret services, Bodnăraş gave himself up (if he was a communist) once he reached the USSR or was captured (if he was a spy). In that case, he did not complete his mission for the SSI. Moreover, he was obliged to work for the GRU. Therefore, he was detected as being an agent not a deserter by the Soviets. It is possible that, given his communist sympathies since the late 1920s, and unhappy with the slow rate at which his career was progressing, Bodnăraş accepted to work for the Romanian secret services. He had another plan in mind, however: to cross over into the USSR and give himself up. Naturally, in order to obtain the best conditions for himself, he took with him various regimental documents. Whatever the case, Bodnăraş was an adventurer. The whole episode provides the measure of his ambiguous personality, of the secret man behind the military uniform.

Following his desertion, Bodnăraş was tried *in absentia*, after a long investigation carried out by the War Council of the Fourth Army Corps in Jassy. Presiding was Colonel Constantin Eftimiu. The charges were four in number: (1) desertion to a foreign country in peacetime; (2) an offence against national security; (3) theft of public acts; (4) insulting a superior. Sentence was passed almost two years after the desertion, on 8 December 1933. Why it took so long to decide such a simple case is another of the mysteries in this story. The punishment: 10 years imprisonment, dismissal and a fine of 6,000 lei. At this time, Bodnăraş, having stayed in Astrakhan for verification,

---

[17] Se Cristian Troncotă, *Istoria Serviciilor secrete româneşti*, Editura Ion Cristoiu, 1999, pp. 141-142; Dennis Deletant, *Teroarea comunistă în România. Gheorghiu-Dej şi statul poliţienesc, 1948-1965*, Jassy: Polirom, 2001, pp. 49-51.

was studying at the Comintern's espionage school in Moscow, located in the Podlipki suburb. The school had been established a year previously and was strictly controlled by the GRU. This is the moment when the Comintern goes from being a platform for 'world revolution' to being a nexus for anti-Western subversion. The school's pupils were communist militants and spies, mostly from abroad – Germans, Americans, French, Asians, Chinese, Indians, etc. In January and February 1933, Bodnăraș follows the Grivitza strikes, analysing newspaper reports for the Soviets. It is possible that in June 1933 Bodnăraș met Willy Münzenberg, who was visiting Podlipki and whom we have met previously in the pages of this book. Since its foundation in 1932, the school had produced thousands of extremely dangerous, qualified spies, provocateurs and terrorists, who went on to operate in the USA, Britain, Germany and France. The names of some of them appeared in the press following the discovery of their networks, public scandals and the ensuing trials. Can Bodnăraș have been sent to the USSR by the PCdR or summoned by the GRU precisely in order to attend the Comintern's new one-year espionage course in Podlipki? In the meantime, he corresponds with his family through intermediaries, writing to his mother in particular. We are able to read this correspondence today because it was intercepted by the SSI. Bodnăraș feels happy in the USSR: "I am at peace here ... Please don't worry about me. I'm in my element here and I feel happier than ever before in my life." He receives the news of his conviction as follows:

> "I got 10 years. I was elated and I was congratulated here about it because of its importance. To be honest, lately I was ashamed, living here without any 'success'. Even now I still feel like a 'snotty-nosed kid' because there are men here who have [prison sentences] two or three times longer than that. So we should be thankful for it. They'll not have the satisfaction of having me there. Then again there's also a slight miscalculation, because if they think all this filth will last another 10 years then they're badly mistaken. Let's leave joy aside for a moment. As our peasants say, 'don't count your chickens before they're hatched'."[18]

He promises to send his mother money regularly (15 U.S. dollars monthly, around 1,500 lei), through contacts in Czechoslovakia, a turning plate for the Romanian communist underground networks. He also describes his

---

[18] MAN Archive, Fund 948/3, Dossier 56, p. 10.

visits to the Volga and Caspian Sea and how he is planning a trip to the Caucasus. The letter – which Bodnăraș knew would be read by Siguranță agents – was a red herring. The aim was to lull the Siguranță into a false sense of security by means of his assurances to his family that he had no intention of returning to Romania. It is dated 9 June 1934. Six weeks later, Bodnăraș is arrested on the platform of the Northern Station in Bucharest. A year had passed since the SSI got wind of his intention to return. The following is a top-secret note, dated 6 August 1933: "Former Lieutenant of the 12th Reg. Emil Bodnăraș is intending to return to Romania." Frontier posts were alerted, and police divisions all over the country had orders to arrest him on sight.[19] One might say he was expected.

Why did he return to Romania? Why did he not remain in the USSR? Why did he return after only two years? He had graduated from the GRU school for spies and was being sent back. Normally, the GRU would have sent him to a different country, where the risks of capture were infinitely less. GRU agents crisscrossed Europe. A fluent speaker of German, Bodnăraș could have been sent to Germany as an agent. Romania was the most dangerous place on the continent for him to be. That it was a mistake can be seen from the fact that he was arrested as soon as he stepped off the train. Might he have surrendered? Might he have allowed himself to be captured, in order to be sent to prison to join the communist leaders? Or were the SSI waiting for their agent to report to them?

Another hypothesis takes the facts at face value. A deserter from the Romanian Army, trained as a spy by the Soviets, returning to Romania to gather military intelligence, he is caught. A second trial is held on 13 October 1934, in Jassy, also at the War Council of the Fourth Army. It was the result of the contestation Bodnăraș had submitted on 27 September against his conviction *in absentia* and sentence of 10 years imprisonment. His lawyer is Nicolae Rodoș from Jassy. In court, Bodnăraș declares that he has no domicile in Romania, he lives in Moscow, and is an economic statistician by profession. The court rejects the action and confirms the sentence handed down in December 1933. Within 24 hours, as required by the regulations of the Court Martial, Bodnăraș appeals. The High Court Martial allows the appeal on 5 December 1934. The grounds were that he had not been informed of the conviction, as required by the law, either at his domicile in Sadagura or by its publication in the Official Monitor,

---

[19] MAN Archive, Fund 948, Dossier 56, p. 10.

as should have occurred, given his absence from the country. Two quite important names are to be noted in this trial. One of the members of the Council of Judges is Horia Măcelariu (1894-1989), at the time a lieutenant colonel, later a rear admiral, Commandant of the Maritime Fleet. He was imprisoned in 1948 and released in 1964. The Royal Commissar was Major Alexandru Petrescu, who held a Law Doctorate from the University of Paris. He tried many cases involving communists in the 1930s and 1940s. After the war, he becomes the communists' main tool for convicting their political enemies. He was rewarded with the rank of General, president of the Military Tribunal. He was the judge in the War Criminals Case, the Iuliu Maniu Case, the Canal Case, etc. He gained a grim reputation due to the extremely harsh sentences he handed down.

The case is heard two months later. The final sentence is passed on 19 February 1935. Three years had passed since Bodnăraş's desertion. The War Council of the 21st Infantry Division, presided over by Traian Smeu, upholds the sentence: 10 years imprisonment. On the same day, the sentence is read out by the Clerk of Court for the War Council in front of the Division and in the presence of the convicted man. He is stripped of his rank in front of the soldiers and officers in the barracks, in Jassy. Bodnăraş will not forget this ceremony of humiliation until his dying day. The resentment will eat away at him for the rest of his life. He craved social retribution, rehabilitation honours, power. On 18 May 1935, he is transferred to the penitentiary in Galatzi. Ten days later, he is informed that he has been stripped of his Romanian citizenship. Bodnăraş, having become a stateless person, applies to the Soviet authorities, via the legation in Bucharest, for citizenship of the USSR. He receives it within a short time. It was recognition of his status on the part of Moscow. In February 1937, the USSR requests the Romanian Government make an exchange of prisoners. The name demanded by Moscow was Emil Bodnăraş. In 1938, he is tried once more, with his brother, Manole, and an otherwise unknown person, Demény Akó, who had attempted to steal official army documents at his instigation. A year is added to Bodnăraş's sentence. His brother receives three years, Akó, five.

What is Bodnăraş's version? Who was he working for? Was he a communist summoned to the homeland of the Revolution, or an agent of the Army secret service? In May 1961, in a session of the Political Bureau of the CC of the PMR, he confesses. Bodnăraş claims that in 1932 he was not a member of the PCdR, but held communist beliefs.

"The Soviet Union received me with friendship, comradeship, with much care and attention, although I was there as a fugitive, a man without an organisation ... If Luca [László] and Simu hadn't been in Cernăuți at the time, who can be accused of anything but qualified leadership, I would have found another contact here [in Romania] and not have had to cross the Dniester to make contact with the movement there. But they were very little concerned about influence in the ranks of the intellectuals, in the ranks of the army ... Even though I showed up as a man without any organisation it is clear that the Soviet secret services did their research quickly, and after a short time, but especially after I was sentenced to 10 years *in absentia*, they had a particularly attentive attitude towards me. ... Towards the end of 1933, Menzhinsky was still alive, he ran the special department where I worked ... He sent word to me that it would be well for me to think about carrying out a mission that would take me abroad. I accepted happily and after some two months of preparation ... I asked – given that I hadn't gone to the Soviet Union to keep myself out of harm's way, to conserve myself until after the Revolution – how the matter of my joining the Party was viewed by the comrades. I raised this question before leaving on the mission and after a few days I received an answer – Menzhinsky was a man who was very attentive to details, very cultured – and then it was communicated to me: comrade, don't concern yourself with that, what you are doing is the direct route to the Party ... for the cause we serve. And with that I departed."[20]

So, Bodnăraş's request to join the Party was turned down by the Soviets. He did not offer sufficient guarantees.

"In July 1934 I was discovered here in Romania and I fell. At the Galatzi trial I was unable to make contact with the comrades ... in my declaration, when asked by the investigators whether I was a communist, I proved that I wasn't a communist, but I had faith that, in the years to come, and in the trials I would have to undergo, I would become worthy of this title of Soldier of the Comintern. So, at the trial I was honest. I

---

[20] CC of the PCR Archive, Political Bureau, MTG, 12-14 March 1961, p. 157.

did not attempt to claim for myself a quality I did not possess. Why, on reaching Brașov, did I not maintain the same line, why was I not honest there?"

In Galatzi Prison, according to his own account, Bodnăraș had observed that there were two categories of political prisoners, members of the PCdR and the rest. The few communists were organised, they enjoyed certain privileges in relations with the administration, they had connections outside the prison, they received letters, visits and money, they had jobs in the workshops, they occupied various positions in the prison administration, canteen, baths, offices.

"Arriving in Brașov, this pride of mine, which was somehow also affected by a slight inferiority complex ... caused me to say 'Yes!' when Leib Nahman asked me, 'Are you a communist?' And so there I was, thought of as a Party member, and because they didn't do much research or many checks at the time, that was how I joined the Party, dishonestly. The years passed. I went to Aiud. I met the comrades who are here now [Gheorghiu-Dej, Chivu Stoica, Alexandru Drăghici, Alexandru Moghioroș, Dumitru Coliu] and I presented myself in the same capacity. I went to Doftana. It weighed on my back, because only I can remember how heavy that boulder was. In the Soviet Union I hadn't known the Party, in gaol before arriving in Doftana, in closer relations [with the communists] I had little knowledge of it, and in 1938, around the summer, when, thanks to the attitude of the comrades, in particular Comrade Gheorghiu [-Dej], whom I got to know very closely, I had the opportunity to discover its way of thinking, I realised that the Party was different to how I thought it was and that it is not right to reckon yourself a member of its ranks merely on the grounds that you've let slip a 'yes'. That question had a very precise meaning, it didn't have a general meaning, but nonetheless I answered 'yes'. I led people astray."

So, Bodnăraș is an imposter, passing himself off as possessing a quality he did not in fact possess. He does not hesitate to lie if this can assure him of a particular status. He is a mystifier. And it is not the only such example during his career. "What was behind this mystification?" he himself wonders during this confessional in front of the Political Bureau in 1961. The lie was discovered by another communist detainee, Nicolae Goldberger, who realised that Bodnăraș claimed to have joined the Party in a period when the PCdR had suspended new memberships. An activist accused him of claiming to be a member out of careerism, and Bodnăraș, in 1961, agrees: "But all this, the pride and tendency to be a parvenu, did not stop me, after healthy deliberation and much anguish, to write that letter which no one forced me to write and send it to Colev." Dimităr Colev was the leader of the communists in prison between 1935 and 1940. He succeeded Boris Ștefanov and Ștefan Foriș, the second of whom was released from Doftana in 1935. Unmasked in prison as a liar, Bodnăraș confesses. We can imagine a session during which his case is discussed after he delivers his self-denunciation. He is eliminated from the Party cell. It happens that Colev is released from prison at this very moment. Gheorghiu-Dej becomes the leader of the communist detainees. It is his good relationship with Gheorghiu-Dej, whom he teaches Russian, German, and Yiddish, as well as military knowledge, that saves him. Under other circumstances, he would have been treated as a traitor, as a provocateur sent by the SSI, as a foreign body within the Party. The changes at the top are useful to him. "The comrades had a lot of understanding and benevolence towards me, seeking to maintain relations with me. I didn't have the feeling of being banished from their ranks"[21] Bodnăraș is now indebted to Gheorghiu-Dej. Instead of being banished, isolated, he continues to be a member of his entourage, to have influence. This time, however, it is not as a Party man, but as Dej's man, as his protégé.

> "In Caransebeș, the communist who enjoyed the greatest authority after Gheorghiu-Dej was not his comrade in the trial and his secret cell, Chivu Stoica … or Teohari Georgescu … or Chișinevschi, but Bodnăraș. The impression he made was not due to his extraordinary past … but to the presence of three factors: his martial bearing combined with a remarkable elegance; the obvious respect he inspired in the management of the penitentiary in his capacity as quasi-official representative of the organisation; and, in particular, his just as obvious friendship with Gheorghiu-Dej," recalls one eye witness.[22]

---

[21] *Ibid*, p. 159.

[22] Pavel Câmpeanu, *Ceaușescu, anii numărătorii inverse*, Jassy: Polirom, 2002, p. 126.

His release from Caransebeş Prison presents a number of unclear aspects. The same question arises: who was Bodnăraş working for? For the Army secret services? For the SSI? Was he a Soviet agent, a spy who enjoyed the clemency of the authorities? In September 1940, Bodnăraş is given a reduction in his sentence, like all political prisoners. The regime's practice was to intern communists in camps once their sentences expired. On 7 November 1942, however, Bodnăraş is freed and settles, according to his own wish, in Brăila. Why did the Siguranţă proceed in this way? Was he a Siguranţă man? Was Bodnăraş working with the authorities? If so, in what capacity? Was this part of an understanding? Traian Borcescu of the SSI declares under interrogation after the war that the Germans demanded the arrest of Bodnăraş, who was in Brăila at the time, having only just been released from Caransebeş. Cristescu opposed those who were in agreement with this demand, on the grounds that "he might be useful if Romania leaves the war, an argument borne out by events."[23] The SSI was also interested in observing whom Bodnăraş would contact. A few months later, in 1943, when Gheorghiu-Dej and Chivu Stoica were due to be released, the Siguranţă refused, citing the danger the two would present. Bodnăraş – a deserter, Soviet spy, and former officer – was no less of a danger. The same argument ought to have applied to Dej and Stoica. Once released, both of them would have contacted the Party, and the Siguranţă would thereby have been able to capture other communists. Moreover, Gheorghiu-Dej was known to be an important person. In 1940, the Soviets had demanded him in an exchange of prisoners. So, what special interest did the Siguranţă have in Bodnăraş?

After the Battle of Stalingrad the authorities would have been expected to keep the communists locked up, far away from the front line, or to use them as bargaining chips. The fact that Bodnăraş was at large did not change the situation. He could be arrested and sent back to the camp at any time. Pătrăşcanu was sent to Tîrgu Jiu in January 1943, two months after Bodnăraş was released from Caransebeş. He goes to Brăila, where he joins his brother Manole, who has a photographic workshop there. His relations with the authorities in Brăila are curious. It may be that he was subject to the usual requirement of those recently released from prison to report to the authorities. But it may also have been something else: he had resumed his relationship with the Romanian secret service. He is frequently seen in

---

[23] Cristian Troncota, *Eugen Cristescu, asul serviciilor secrete româneşti*, Editura Roza Vînturilor, 1994, p. 84.

the company of the town prefect. It is not the first time he has dealings with high-ranking officials. Before arriving in Brăila, he stays in Bucharest for a few days, during which time he has discussions with Ion Rînzescu, Eugen Cristescu's adjunct. These contacts show us that Bodnăraș was under special supervision. It is hard to determine today what role he played. According to one account, he refuses Rînzescu's offer to settle in Bucharest, preferring Brăila. Was he thinking of attempting to cross the frontier during wartime? Did he have a secret mission? He gets a job as a representative for a timber company. This is quite strange if we bear in mind the fact that he was considered to be a 'dangerous communist'. In Brăila he establishes a cell and sets about acquiring arms. Bodnăraș has access to substantial funds. The Romanian police notices nothing, or pretends not to notice. After Bodnăraș vanishes from Brăila, the affair is uncovered by the German Gestapo, and Bodnăraș's accomplices are arrested. The Gestapo demands a warrant for his arrest be put out, but the SSI refuses.[24]

There was another suspect affair linked to the name of Bodnăraș: at the end of 1943 a great stir is caused by a major discovery made by the Siguranţă in the house at No. 5 Crîngului Street, the residence of Etty and Paul Wexler. The archives of the CC of the PCdR, other top-secret documents, large sums of money and two gold ingots are found during the search. The house, thought to offer the greatest secrecy, was frequented by a number of the PCdR leaders, including Foriș and Koffler. Its discovery led to the arrest of dozens of communists and a trial. There was much talk of treachery, of a denunciation from someone in the upper echelons of the Party. For the PCdR it was a disaster. In the trial of April 1954, Remus Koffler was accused of this betrayal, and was sentenced to death and executed along with Pătrășcanu. Koffler did indeed frequent the Wexlers' house. However, he had been doing so for a very long time without anything of this nature happening. The guilty person must have been someone who had been going there for only a short time. One such person was Bodnăraș. On the evening when the Siguranţă raided the house, Bodnăraș was supposed have gone there for a meeting, but he did not turn up. The house was being kept under surveillance. Did Bodnăraș know this? Did he fail to show up in order not to give himself away?[25]

---

[24] G. Iavorski, "Pentru cine a lucrat « inginerul Ceaușu »?" in *Magzin istoric*, 9/1994, pp. 18-19.

[25] SRI Archive, Dossier 40002, vol. 28, pp. 119.

In March 1944, a hidden cache of explosives set up by Bodnăraș was discovered by the Siguranţă in Rîșnov. A coincidence? Foriș gives him a warning over the incident. A few days later his dismissal supervenes, executed by Bodnăraș himself. There are thus grounds for suspecting him of collaborating with the Romanian secret services. In a clandestine environment, exchanges of information and complicities are inevitable. All the protagonists know each other, police and plotters alike. They met during investigations, during trials. It is not a fractured space, separated by a wall, but rather a continuum. The boundaries between the conspirators and the secret services are never immutable, especially during murky periods of crisis. Many conspirators play a double game; they are informants, agents and provocateurs. But the reverse is also true. In the case of Romania, especially after the defeat at Stalingrad in the winter of 1942-1943, the authorities sought, both as individuals and collectively, to make contacts among the communists. Bodnăraș was in an ideal strategic position to play such a double game. To be noted is the tenacity with which Bodnăraș later pursued the disappearance of the few persons who knew various things about him: Koffler, Foriș, Calmanovici.

The mission Gheorghiu-Dej gives him on his release from Caransebeș is suited to his adventurous spirit. He was to remove, by any means possible, Ștefan Foriș, the official head of the PCdR, appointed by the Comintern in the autumn of 1940. It could be a non-violent dismissal, a sequestering, or an assassination. Bodnăraș promises Gheorghiu-Dej to fulfil the mission. It was to be carried out in conditions of conspiracy, isolation and a chronic lack of resources. He now has an opportunity to utilise the training he received in Moscow, in the schools for subversion and espionage. It would be the first time. In 1934, he had not had the chance to try out his skills, because he had been arrested as soon as he arrived in Romania. Another story is that he organised Gheorghiu-Dej's escape.[26] Bodnăraș, too, later backed up this story. It is false or at least incomplete. Likewise the legend of him being parachuted in by the Soviets in 1943. In November 1942, when Bodnăraș was released, Gheorghiu-Dej and Chivu Stoica were also awaiting their own release. It was due in the summer of 1943, when their prison terms expired. Given the attitude of the authorities in the case of Bodnăraș, they had no reason to believe that they would not receive the same treatment.

---

[26] Pavel Câmpeanu, *Ceaușescu, anii numărătorii inverse*, Jassy: Polirom, 2002, pp. 124-128.

Thus, waiting to be released, Dej had no reason to give Bodnăraş the order to organise his escape. It was one of the legends spread by those involved, by Dej and Bodnăraş. The legend presents two courageous militants, in control of the events that were to occur: the sequestering and dismissal of Foriş on 4 April and the Royal Coup of 23 August. Bodnăraş is not for the first time involved in such mystifications of history. He applied one of the techniques for creating legends that he had learned in the schools for espionage and subversion in Astrakhan and Moscow. Teohari Georgescu was present at the final discussion between Dej and Bodnăraş before the latter's release from Caransebeş.[27] He says that Bodnăraş's mission was "to make preparations for the escape of political prisoners (high-ranking Party members)." Dej intended, looking forward to his release, due in 1943, to have alongside him the men with whom he had surrounded himself in the prisons during the power-struggle within the PCdR. Hence the paradoxical order to Bodnăraş: not to make contact with Foriş and the clandestine network. It was a secret operation. Foriş was not to get wind of what was being planned.

In Brăila, kept under close surveillance by the Siguranţă, Bodnăraş remains for almost one year. The historical backdrop: the Battle of Stalingrad, the Battle of Kursk, and the British and American landings in Sicily. The balance of forces is rapidly changing. Bodnăraş makes contact with the communists still at liberty, and then vanishes without trace. He enters the clandestine world, installing himself in Bucharest. He re-establishes contact with the Party through Colonel Victor Precup and Iulian Orban, whom he met in gaol. The two had been involved in the plot against King Carol. Like Bodnăraş, Precup is an adventurer. In contrast to Bodnăraş, who is anonymous, Precup is highly well-known. In November 1918, in a Farman aeroplane piloted by Ştefan Niculescu, he crossed the Carpathians, from Bacău to Blaj, in Transylvania, with the mission of delivering documents to those who were preparing the gathering at Alba Iulia (on behalf of the Romanian Government). En route, he scatters manifestos over a number of towns in Transylvania, that announced the Romanian Army was going to cross the Carpathians. Four days later, he returns to Jassy with messages in reply. Captain Victor Precup becomes a national hero. In the 1920s, we find him in the entourage of Prince Carol. He becomes one of the architects of his return to the throne. He is responsible for maintaining the channel of communication between Prince Carol in

---

[27] ASRI, Dossier 40009, vol. 1, pp. 433-434.

Paris and Prime Minsiter Iuliu Maniu in Bucharest. In 1930, Precup plays an important role in the restoration. Once Carol becomes King, Precup enters into conflict with the Court clique, and above all with the King's mistress, Elena Lupescu. He supports Iuliu Maniu in his demand that the King drive out 'Lupeasca'[28] and resume his marriage with Queen Elena. The King refuses and banishes Precup from his entourage. Victor Precup is implicated in the Skoda Affair, the greatest political and financial scandal of the inter-war period. His reputation is damaged during the trial. In 1934, he hatches a plot against Carol. The King was to be assassinated on Calea Victoriei, outside the Boulevard Hotel. Another assassination attempt was to take place in the Bălașa Church, when members of the government and other leading political figures would be present. The plot also involved acting officers and civilians, dozens of people in all. Discovered following a denunciation, the plot fails. Precup is arrested. His trial is front-page news for a number of months in 1934. Precup denied wanting to take the King's life, but he admitted to a plot against Carol's clique, primarily Elena Lupescu. Anti-clique and anti-'Lupeasca' feelings were running high at the time. Tried in Bucharest, Precup is sentenced to 10 years imprisonment and a dishonourable discharge. A description of the dramatic scene:

"5 May. Today, the officers convicted in the Precup affair were stripped of their ranks. In fear of demonstrators, the ceremony of dishonourable discharge was held on the parade ground of the Malmaison Barracks. The convicts entered the courtyard shouting, 'Hoorah! Long live the King!' Once they had been lined up and General Ionescu, the commandant of the Army Corps, began to speak, Colonel Precup and Major Nicoară started yelling, 'Down with the Yid bitch and those sold to her! Death to the Yid bitch!' Then, drowning out the voice of the general and addressing the officers and functionaries present, 'Vile scoundrels! Wretched sell-outs! Scoundrels!' … The order was given for bugles to be blown next to Precup in order to drown out his voice and

---

[28] 'Lupeasca' would literally mean 'wolfish (woman)'. The termination '-escu' (a compound of the masculine adjectival suffix '-esc' plus an elided form of the masculine definite article: '-ul') is used in Romanian surnames for both men and women, but the feminine suffix '-ească' (definite article: '-a') is sometimes used in ironical or derogatory contexts, as here. – *Translator's note.*

the dishonourable discharge proceeded apace. As he left, Precup threw his cap in the air above the ranks of soldiers and shouted to them, 'Have no fear, we shall be avenged!' Very few soldiers shouted 'Boo!' when the discharged officers filed past, as they had been ordered."[29]

In February 1935, after the trial in Jassy, Emil Bodnăraş had also undergone the same ceremony of humiliation, on the parade ground of the Fourth Army barracks. Precup and Bodnăraş shared the humiliating memory of being paraded in disgrace in front of the troops. Former Lieutenant Colonel Precup becomes a communist in prison. Precup and Bodnăraş are close in Aiud, Doftana and Caransebeş Prisons. Precup is released a few months before Bodnăraş and makes contact with Foriş. During all this time, Bodnăraş was not busy planning the communists' escape from Caransebeş. Dej and Chivu Stoica were not released on time, but rather transferred in January 1943 to the camp at Tîrgu Jiu. In February, Bodnăraş leaves Brăila for the first time since his release. In Bucharest, he makes contact with Victor Precup. Precup alerts Foriş to the presence of Bodnăraş. The two meet in June 1943. On finding out, Gheorghiu-Dej reacts badly. Bodnăraş was supposed to be planning the escape and keeping away from the 'group of traitor Foriş', but instead he agreed to work for the PCdR military department. Bodnăraş was not a Party member and, in the plan to capture and depose Foriş, this detail counted. Foriş had to be deposed in a manner more like a settling of accounts between gangsters than the way a political party obliges an unpopular leader to step down. Dej was conducting a plot against the leadership appointed by the Comintern, and the risks were great. Bodnăraş was a tool of this plot. They were both staking their careers and, in the case of failure, their lives on it.

Why did Dej choose Bodnăraş, who was a known Soviet spy and thus connected to the Comintern? Did Dej take into account Bodnăraş's loyalty to Moscow? Bodnăraş had signed an agreement in 1932 and was bound by oath to the comrades who had trained him. It had also been Moscow that appointed Foriş as head of the PCdR. In the first place, Dej did not have anyone else. Dej and Bodnăraş were friends and accomplices. Moreover, Bodnăraş could lay no claim to the Party leadership. He was not a Romanian but a Soviet citizen, and he was not even a PCdR member. In Dej's eyes,

---

[29] Constantin Argetoianu, *Memorii*, vol. 10, Editura Machiavelli, pp. 300-301.

Bodnăraș was perfectly placed to eliminate Foriș from play and to set up a new leadership until he himself could become boss. Dej sends word to him that he is in disagreement with him and breaks off contact. Bodnăraș, in repeated letters, tries to justify himself and begs for a meeting. Dej declines, maintaining his silence for a long time, until he eventually summons him to Tîrgu Jiu to explain. An initial exploratory meeting takes place between Bodnăraș and Chivu Stoica, Dej's lieutenant, in August. There follows a meeting with Dej himself in October 1943. The meeting takes place in a hospital. Gheorghiu-Dej has been admitted for a haemorrhoids operation. The camp administration is complicit. The two talk throughout the night in a private room in the hospital. Dej questions Bodnăraș about his intentions and whether he has betrayed him in favour of Foriș. Why had he not taken care of his escape from Caransebeş? Bodnăraș informs him about what he has been doing on the outside, about his contacts, and about the political situation. He gives explanations for his collaboration with Foriș, the 'traitor' to the Party. In 1960, Bodnăraș recounts that it was on that night that the plan to remove Foriș was discussed in detail. He is not giving the whole story. The Party was convulsed by conflicts. The detainees – the majority of the communist militants – were in conflict with Foriș. The mutual accusations were the usual ones: splittism, collaboration with 'Auntie Varvara', rupture from the masses, passivity in the face of the German war machine. After Stalingrad and the German retreat from the Eastern front, after the Allied surge in southern Italy, the direction of the war had changed. The communists understood perfectly that the parameters were different now. Sooner or later, the victorious Red Army would have a role to play in post-war Romania. In the upper echelons of the PCdR tensions heighten. Dej has been in the Tîrgu Jiu camp for two months. He is in conflict with Pătrăşcanu, who arrived in January. Dej sees him as a rival to his supremacy. There are also other rivalries and conflicts. Dej and Bodnăraș analyse them. The key question is how to seize control of the Party. However, the main subject probably concerned relations with Moscow.

In May 1943, Stalin decided to dissolve the Comintern. Like the show trials of the Great Terror in 1936-1938, like the Ribbentrop-Molotov Pact, and like the war, in particular the one on the Eastern front, the dissolution of the Comintern was full of consequences for the hundreds of communists in Romania. The Comintern had appointed Foriș as head of the Party in the autumn of 1940. Dej and Bodnăraș could consider themselves to have a free hand as far as their plot went. Foriş's legitimacy as Party leader had been diminished. 'Internal forces' were entitled to make their own decisions. Another factor: with the advance of the Red Army westward, it was to be expected that the group of Romanian communists who were refugees in Russia – Ana Pauker, Luka László, Constantin Doncea, Dumitru Petrescu, et al. – would arrive in Bucharest with claims on the leadership. Amid all these factors, the scenario of deposing Foriş arises. Bodnăraş is assigned to the operation. He has a chance to redeem himself in Dej's eyes. Dej had accepted him as a 'member of the PCdR', in spite of his imposture. He has the upper hand over him. Bodnăraş is in his debt. To carry out his mission, Bodnăraş resorts to mystification, as was his wont. He pretended that he had been contacted by a messenger from Moscow. Foriş had been seeking to re-establish contact with Moscow since 1941. Bodnăraş presents himself as the providential man to solve the key problem of the PCdR. His Khlestakov-like comical imposture in the situation is to be underlined. The whole thing is a farce, but with a tragic outcome for Foriş, murdered two years later. Bodnăraş is an imposter. He is not a member of the PCdR. He has no mandate from the Comintern to sack Foriş. All the same, he presented to Foriş documents he himself has forged. Bodnăraş is an actor. He has set in motion a lie. Even in the gravest situations, he does not flinch from lying. Here we have the entire mystique of the Comintern, 'revolution' and 'conspiracy'. Here we have above all the feeling of belonging to an elite. Foriş and Bodnăraş were 'initiates'. They were playing a game according to special rules, understood only by those in their own circle. The proof is the ease with which Foriş accepts the situation. His instincts for self-preservation were completely abolished as soon as he saw the piece of paper with the Comintern's 'decision' to dismiss him. He hands himself over without suspecting anything. He puts up no resistance. He does not check the document. He does not ask any questions. The pistol Bodnăraş places on the table to intimidate his victim enhances the melodramatic effect. Foriş takes Bodnăraş at his word; he capitulates before this "extraordinary and plenipotentiary emissary from Moscow." Events are reminiscent of the scene when Vodă Hangerly allows himself to be strangled after the emissary from Istanbul shows him the Sultan's signature on the *firman*[30] to depose him. He is removed from the throne of Wallachia and murdered. At least it was an authentic written order. In Bucharest in 1944, we are dealing with a fake messenger and a fake document.

---

[30] *Firman*: edict issued by an Ottoman sovereign. – *Translator's note.*

In the months up to the Royal Coup of August 1944, there are many episodes that have a vaudeville feel to them. The rival camps follow each other closely. The plotters and the authorities know everything about each other. Everybody is negotiating by every available channel with the Allies. In Cairo, Ankara, Stockholm, Lisbon, and even directly across the front lines. In Bucharest, conspiracy is all the rage. They are dancing on top of a volcano that is about to erupt. Of the members of the troika set up on 4 April, Bodnăraş is the most influential. He is a factotum. Nevertheless, it is not Bodnăraş who is assigned to take care of the plan to spring Gheorghiu-Dej out of Tîrgu Jiu, but I. Gh. Maurer. This was at the express wish of the prudent Gheorghiu-Dej, who had begun to have doubts about Bodnăraş. An important detail: it was not Dej who requested the escape plan, but the PCdR, with Dej making it a condition that Maurer, who had been with him in the camp since 1943 and supported him in the quarrel with Pătrăşcanu, take care of it.

> "When we talked to each other in Bucharest about Dej's escape, it was Bodnăraş who offered to provide me with 20 men armed with machine guns for the breakout. With these men – in the mind of Bodnăraş – I was to attack the prison camp and get Dej out. I got annoyed and told him, 'If you, officer, are capable of thinking that a man leading 20 men armed with machine guns is capable of successfully attacking 400 armed men, then I don't know what can be said about your training as an officer…' Dej, aware of Bodnăraş's organisational talents, didn't think he was capable of organising the escape."[31]

Nevertheless, it was Bodnăraş and Pătrăşcanu who represented the PCdR in negotiations with the palace, not Maurer. Bodnăraş had the mission of seconding Pătrăşcanu, who did not enjoy the trust of the new communist leadership. They take part in conspiratorial meetings in various houses around Bucharest, with generals and emissaries of King Mihai and with the leaders of the PNŢ, PNL and PSD. The secret services are abreast of the plot, but look the other way. The situation is highly complicated. Everyone is thinking about the future. The official version during the communist period painted Bodnăraş as the mastermind of the Royal Coup of 23 August. This was far from the reality. General Sănătescu records in his diary that he

---

[31] Lavinia Betea, *Maurer şi lumea de ieri*, Cluj: Editura Dacia, 2001, p. 66.

needs Bodnăraş and Pătrăşcanu in order "to organise the factory workers I am counting on to supplement my lack of troops." The General was labouring under an illusion. Even according to its own leaders, the PCdR was incapable of organising anything. Its contacts with the workers were highly tenuous. It was the advance of the Red Army that determined the palace, as well as also Antonescu, to seek to make contact with the communists. The communists negotiated with both the one and the other. They were a bit-part player, who both the palace and the leaders of the historical parties understood was required for reasons of opportunism.

Bodnăraş presents a report during the negotiations of summer 1944 in which he gives entirely fictional figures. The PCdR is supposed to have 12,000 armed men in Bucharest, 90,000 in Galatzi, 120,000 in Ploieşti, and 70,000 in Braşov. These figures were intended to impress the military men, palace emissaries and leaders of the traditional parties who were present. We do not know how much credence they lent to such fabrications. What would have happened if the Royal Coup had come up against greater resistance than anticipated and General Sănătescu had called upon Bodnăraş to lead his tens of thousands of armed men on to the streets? There would have been a bloodbath. The drama of Warsaw would have been repeated in Bucharest. Fortunately, Antonescu did not put up a fight. The Germans were taken by surprise and their reaction was weak. As Belu Zilber recounts,

"In the morning I went to Pătrăşcanu; it was 24 August. He tells me, 'Go to Emil. We haven't got anything. If that lot fall upon us we couldn't even say boo'. I caught a taxi on the street and went to Alexandru Lane [the headquarters of the 'patriotic guards' led by Bodnăraş – author's note]. Bodnăraş was standing in front of the gate. I told him to give me four revolvers so that we could have something to shoot with. It was around nine in the morning. At that moment Dej gets out of a DKW with Maurer [having escaped from Tîrgu Jiu a week earlier, Dej had just arrived in Bucharest – author's note] ... On 25 August, when I went to fetch the revolvers, at Bodnăraş's place I saw a crate with a whole range of revolvers – from 1848, 1870, 1920 – and he rustled up four for me. I tell him, 'So, these are the 12,000 armed men, are they, Emil, what the hell?' That's what it was like."[32]

---

[32] Belu Zilber, quoted in *23 August 1944 în arhivele comuniste*, Editura Majadahonda, 2000, pp. 134-135. See also the account of the (cont. p. 267.)

On 24 August, after their discussion, Bodnăraş solemnly hands Zilber a visiting card, printed in advance, bearing the inscription, "Emil Bodnăraş, commandant of the patriotic forces." The scene epitomises the man. Bodnăraş is to the same degree conceited, dangerous and serious. He is eaten away by the ambition to play a major role on the historical stage. A typical mystifier. A failed dictator.

With 23 August comes a radical change in the status of Bodnăraş.[33] The PCdR emerges from clandestinity. Bodnăraş is a NKVD resident in Romania, a Soviet citizen, as are Ana Pauker, Vasile Luca, Constantin Doncea and many others in the upper echelons of the PCdR. He takes charge of the secret services. Surrounded by Soviet spies from the 1930s – Pantiuşa Bodnarenko, Petya Goncharuk, Vanya Didenko, Sergey Nikonov, Alexander Nikolsky, Sergey Babenko – he forms the hard core of the PCdR, grouped around Gheorghiu-Dej. He is the 'armed wing' and takes care of many shady matters. Using his men – communist militants, naturalised NKVD agents, prisoners of war returning from the USSR – Bodnăraş establishes a network to infiltrate the areas of maximum political interest: the political adversaries of the PCdR, the leaders of the historical parties, the entourage of King Mihai, and the army. Within the PCdR, too, Bodnăraş is called upon, by Gheorghiu-Dej in particular, to do the dirty work, ranging from surveillance of rivals to their liquidation. It is he who arrests Ştefan Foriş on 15 September, on the eve of Ana Pauker's arrival in Bucharest. It is he who guards Foriş, interrogates him, and, together with Dej, decides to assassinate him in the summer of 1946. In the whole dirty business, Bodnăraş was an important pawn. It was Bodnăraş who deposed and sequestered Foriş, and it was also Bodnăraş who had every reason to want him to disappear. And this is what he made sure happened. Foriş knew too much about Bodnăraş and the pasts of the PCdR leaders to be spared. He was an inconvenient witness and, under certain circumstances, given the extremely fluid situation, he could become a dangerous rival. Bodnăraş was Dej's closest accomplice in the affair of Foriş's liquidation. For Dej, it was primarily a vendetta, a result of his inferiority complex, and a political move. For Bodnăraş it was above all a matter of preserving a secret, of liquidating a witness.

---

same episode in Belu Zilber, *Actor în procesul Pătrăşcanu*, Bucharest: Humanitas, 1997, p. 188.

[33] On Emil Bodnăraş during those days, see Rolf Pusch and Gerhardt Stelzer, *Diplomaţii germani la Bucureşti*, Editura ALL, 2001, pp. 198-200.

But Bodnăraş is also mixed up in another affair. As early as the autumn of 1944, he gives the order for Pătrăşcanu to be kept under close surveillance. The order had come from Dej, who was jealous of Pătrăşcanu's popularity, which he sensed imperilled his ambitions for supremacy. The following is an account of the business:

"On 8 October 1944, around 10-10:30, I was in the office of Emil Bodnăraş. After a while, Vanya Didenko shows up … the head of Section 7 of the General Espionage and Counter-espionage Command, Intelligence and Counter-intelligence. The two start talking in Russian, without knowing that I speak Russian quite well … 'Did you see who was with Pătrăşcanu yesterday at the ANEF? The Prime Minister! That man is getting above himself. We need to do something about him. Get Misha, Vanya, Petya, Sergey to follow him'. Those were Bodnăraş words … What had happened? The day before, i.e. 7 October 1944, Lucreţiu Pătrăşcanu speaks to the crowd at a popular meeting at the ANEF stadium … The crowd applaud him tumultuously. Chanting, '*Pă-trăş-ca-nu prime mi-nis-ter!*' for minutes on end."[34]

It is highly likely that it was not only an order from Dej but also from the Kremlin, unhappy with Pătrăşcanu's attitude during the signing of the armistice. Bodnăraş, as the NKVD resident at the top of the PCdR, was the most capable of carrying out this order.

And so Bodnăraş remains at Dej's side, but his importance wanes. Between 4 April and 23 August he had been a factotum, the most influential member of the troika that replaced Foriş. In the foreground were Ana Pauker, Gheorghiu-Dej, Teohari Georgescu, and Vasile Luca, the strongmen in the Party hierarchy. Bodnăraş was also overshadowed by Pătrăşcanu's notoriety. He is not a political leader, but rather an executant. His area of expertise is the secret services. Beginning from 6 March, when the Dr Petru Groza government is installed, he runs the Special Intelligence Service. His name is rarely mentioned, but he is a constant presence in the upper echelons of government and the PCR. His influence derives from his links with Moscow. We know little about his part in the power struggle. It is possible that the backroom intrigues of the PCR were of little interest

[34] Anton Raţiu, quoted in *23 August 1944 în arhivele comuniste*, Editura Majadahonda, 2000, pp. 137-138.

to him, due to his military rather than political temperament. He passes as one of Gheorghiu-Dej's trusted men. Their friendship in prison is well-known. He also cultivates a friendship with Ana Pauker, whom the Soviets had sent to run the Party. He is on best terms with Kavtaradze, the influential Soviet ambassador, but also with Molotov, Georgi Dimitrov and Manuilsky in Moscow. In June 1947 Bodnăraș writes a report that he gives Susaikov to pass to Mikhail Suslov, the head of propaganda and relations with the communist parties.[35] The report is highly critical of Gheorghiu-Dej. Had Bodnăraș disowned his friend and protector? Had he betrayed him? Was he plotting to take his place? Had Gheorghiu-Dej's position weakened? Was Bodnăraș disassociating himself from him to protect his own career? Was it the reaction of a proud man, frustrated that his influence in Gheorghiu-Dej's entourage was waning? It was a little of all these things, but there was also cold calculation at work. That summer, Gheorghiu-Dej was not looked on favourably by Stalin, who had criticised him. In addition, Bodnăraș, hesitant, possessing little political flair, not knowing which way the balance was going to swing, had been frequenting Ana Pauker. Later, in March 1961, Bodnăraș would recall Ana Pauker as a person who shone. Bodnăraș was drawn to her entourage of writers, including Sadoveanu, intellectuals, such as Mihai Ralea, and generals. He frequented this circle, where references to Gheorghiu-Dej were condescending. Dej was a proletarian, nondescript, uncultivated. Bodnăraș had been an officer, at the top of his graduating year. It seems he felt more comfortable in this milieu than around Dej, who was frequented by ex-convicts from Caransebeș – Chișinevschi, Chivu Stoica, Apostol, Drăghici. Dej also had a few intellectuals at his service: Maurer, Simion Zeigel, Gh. Gaston Marin. In the report to Suslov, Bodnăraș ascribes Dej's 'deviation' and closeness to the British and Americans, to their bourgeois influence. After 23 August, Dej displays mistrust in Bodnăraș. In his eyes, Bodnăraș was "guilty" for his part in preparing the Royal Coup. He had in effect run the Party after April 1944. He had deposed Foriș. These circumstances nevertheless conferred upon Bodnăraș political stature and authority within the Party. Dej rebuked him for disloyalty when he had made contact with Foriș in 1943, in spite of his order not to. Dej was suspicious of Bodnăraș's adventurous spirit. Bodnăraș was also a bit of a braggart, hungry for glory.

---

[35] Robert Levy, *Gloria și decăderea Anei Pauker*, Jassy: Polirom, 2002, p. 72.

The "heroic" episode of 23 August was at the core of the tension. Bodnăraș was inclined to show off about the role he had played. A few years after the war, a documentary film was made, in which Bodnăraș appears dismounting from a motorcycle in the courtyard of the Royal palace on the afternoon of the coup. Another sequence shows him leading his imaginary Patriotic Guards into an equally imaginary battle at the edge of Bucharest woods against a German armoured division.

"On 23 August 1945 … I saw the commander of the patriotic forces wrapped in a tricolour flag, at the head of a magnificent column of workers in overalls armed with *balalaikas* [Soviet AKM machine guns] parading in front of Marshal Tolbukhin. In the following years he began to lead the parade of the 23 August fighters mounted on a grey horse, while Gheorghiu-Dej, dressed modestly, wearing a coat unbuttoned to the neck, looked on [from the official stands – *author's note*]."[36]

Gheorghiu-Dej saw all this as a threat to himself, because of his own insignificant presence during those days, when he had preferred to converse – prudently waiting to see how events played out – with I. Gh. Maurer in a village near Rîmnicu Vîlcea. Bodnăraș's thirst for glory was displeasing to Dej. He saw it as a danger to himself.

Bodnăraș was politically powerful, thanks to his direct links with Moscow, over Dej's head. He could thus be useful as a friend, but dangerous as an enemy. Dej was unable to remove him, but nor did he grant him his maximum trust, preferring Maurer, Zeigel, Gaston Marin, and a few of the CFR workers and former political prisoners. The friendship from their days in Doftana and Caransebeș cooled, but did not evaporate. Dej calculatingly made Bodnăraș Minister of Defence in November 1947. Stalin had decided to install communist regimes in Eastern Europe. In Bucharest the forced abdication of King Mihai was being prepared. A trustworthy man was required to command the army at this critical moment. He was the man with the longest career in their service. General, minister – Bodnăraș had achieved the ambitions of his youth. But in a secondary role. He had reached his furthest limit. He would never be a Bolshevik Antonescu.

---

[36] Belu Zilber, *op. cit.*, p. 90.

X
Grivitza

The strikes at the CFR Grivitza Workshops in February 1933 were a turning point in the career of Gheorghe Gheorghiu, alias Ivanov, Dej, Comrade X, Feraru. The legend of these strikes lived on throughout the post-war period, especially in the years from 1948-1965, when Gheorghiu-Dej was dictator of Romania. Today, after so many myths, rumours, mystifications and guilty silences, it is difficult for us to reconstruct events and place them in their proper context. Whereas the proletariat was seen by the communist regime as the 'vanguard of the communist revolution', the railways workers were the 'vanguard of the proletariat', "the most self-aware and disciplined detachment of the Romanian working class." "From 1921 … until 1944, in the West there were thousands of strikes, involving millions of workers, some peaceful, others bloody. In Romania one strike took place, the one at Grivitza. Gheorghe Gheorghiu-Dej was part of the strike committee. For that he was imprisoned for 11 years."[1] What in fact happened in the Grivitza Workshops?

The winter of 1933 was extremely harsh. Ice floes blocked the Danube. A blizzard from Siberia caused devastation. So much for the winter. The political situation was complicated. In the middle of January, Prime Minister Iuliu Maniu resigned from the government. The PNȚ had been in power since the elections of 1928. A number of cabinets had come and gone, led by Iuliu Maniu, Alexandru Vaida-Voievod and G. G. Mironescu. During this interval the restoration had taken place; Carol II had returned to the throne of Romania. The Iuliu Maniu Government had survived for only a few months when he resigned on 12 January 1933. Carol II entrusted the presidency of the Council of Ministers to Alexandru Vaida-Voievod.

From the economic point of view, the situation was bad. The economy was undergoing a prolonged period of crisis, which had led to increased unemployment and poverty among the general population. In order to balance the budget, the PNȚ governments had resorted to so-called 'sacrificial curves', drastic reductions in salaries. Public functionaries, railway workers and teachers had been the hardest hit. Their wages were

---

[1] Belu Zilber, *Actor în procesul Pătrășcanu*, Bucharest: Humanitas, 1997, p. 206.

slashed by half as a result of the sacrificial curves. On 25 January the government signed the so-called 'Geneva Plan', which was equivalent to fresh wage cuts. The government's decision provokes discontent among an already impoverished population. Reactions soon appear. The hardest hit – public functionaries, teachers, railway workers – hit back. Meetings are held at the national level. The trades unions mobilise. Demonstrations are planned. Petitions and delegations are sent to the ministries responsible. The press takes note. The atmosphere is tense, in places incendiary. On 29 January a few thousand CFR workers meet in the Marna auditorium. The motion of the meeting: "CFR personnel warn the government of the land that they know how to defend their rights to life at any cost. …"[2] On 2 February disturbances break out in Ploiești, in the oil industry. The army intervenes. In Bucharest, Cluj, Galatzi and Jassy, in the CFR Workshops, there are protests with workers, more often than not, laying down their tools. Negotiations take place between a delegation of CFR workers and the Minister of Communications, Eduard Mirto. A part of their demands are met. On 3 February, the majority of the 6,000 workers at the Grivitza Workshops in Bucharest demonstrate their lack of faith in the accord ever being implemented. The cause is that such understandings had never been stuck to before. On the other hand, this success, albeit partial, encouraged the workers to radicalise their demands. Thus, they now demand that the central action committee elected at the Marna Auditorium should be recognised as their sole representative. They put forward fresh economic demands: inflation allowances, a 40 per cent wage rise, etc. There is also something new: the workers occupy the workshops and refuse to leave until Minister Eduard Mirto comes to hold talks with them. *Universul* newspaper reports, "The demand to establish Soviets in the state workshops, as well as the pretension to increase salaries and abolish taxes [the workers had not demanded this – *author's note*], is abundant proof that elements alien to the working class, extreme Left agents provocateurs, have begun to operate among the railway workers."[3] On 4 February, the government passes a law declaring a state of emergency. After the war, the government of General Averescu had declared a state of emergency in 1920, which was maintained by the PNL government until 1928, when the incoming PNȚ government repealed it. Laying out the motives for the state of emergency

---

[2] *Universul*, 31 January 1933.
[3] *Universul*, 4 February 1933.

before Parliament, Interior Minister G. G. Mironescu declared, "Recently, concerted movements of a communist nature have disturbed the peace in various regions, with the obvious tendency to destabilise the country. In order to keep the peace and to avoid any unfortunate need for harsh repression, the government believes that it shall be forced to take exceptional measures to prevent disturbances. Such exceptional measures can only be taken within the framework of a state of emergency."[4]

This reaction is disproportionate. The haste to impose a state of emergency throws into question the parliamentary regime. In opposition, the PNȚ had opposed the state of emergency, but now, in government, it is imposing it. Instead of negotiations and measures in favour of those affected by poverty, the government prefers a show of force. In opting for authoritarian measures, the cabinet led by Alexandru Vaida-Voievod not only reveals its fragility but also points to the looming end of four years of PNȚ rule. It also reveals the weakness of Romanian democratic institutions. The state of emergency is imposed for six months in the cities of Bucharest, Jassy, Timişoara, Galatzi, Cernăuţi/Czernowitz, and Ploieşti, and in the county of Prahova. It does not defuse the crisis. On the contrary, it steers it towards a confrontation. Prime Minister Vaida-Voievod says in parliament, "We wish to avoid bringing out the machine guns and shedding blood. In order for it not to come to street fighting, unleashed by a clan whose strings are pulled from abroad, we must vote for this law." On 6 February, the royal decree is published and enters into vigour. Censorship of the press is introduced. Meetings and demonstrations in areas subject to the state of emergency are banned. Publications, leaflets etc. instigating disorder are likewise banned. The wearing of uniforms, badges or flags other than those in official use is outlawed. Gun owners are to surrender their weapons to police commissions by 10 February. Military tribunals are set up in order to try anyone guilty of infringing the state of emergency. On 11 February, orders are given to the Command of the Second Army Corps to break up any associations involved in the protests at the CFR Workshops or the Prahova Valley. The PCdR, UTC, Red Aid etc. remain outlawed, in conformity with the Mîrzescu Law of 1924. Associations of communist origin formed after this date, for example the Peasant Workers Bloc, are likewise banned.

On the night of 14-15 February, those suspected of having instigated the strike are arrested. They include Constantin Doncea, Dumitru Petrescu,

---

[4] *Universul*, 5 February 1933.

Gheorghe Gheorghiu, and Chivu Stoica. Those who have links with the communists are targeted in particular, but social democrats, anarchists, those without political convictions, and crowd agitators are also rounded up. The next day, Wednesday, 15 February, the workers, having been informed, try to hold talks with the management. The director of the workshops, Athanasiu, refuses to receive the delegation. Around 6,000 workers mass in the yard of the workshops and declare that they will not go back to work until their leaders are released. In the government, an emergency meeting is held, attended by Minister of Communications Eduard Mirto, Secretary of State in the Interior Ministry Armand Călinescu, Minister of Defence General Samsonovici, Commandant of the Second Army Corps General Uică, and Eugen Bianu, on behalf of State Security. Alexandru Vaida-Voievod proposes application of the decree declaring a state of emergency. A military command unit is installed in the administrative offices of the Grivitza Workshops. Confrontation is looming. It is ineluctable. The measure taken by the authorities is to concentrate the workers militarily, on the grounds that "a large number of workers from the Grivitza Workshops are Soviet agents, remunerated with large sums of money. The persons in the pay of the Soviets have been identified." There were, without doubt, instigators in the pay of the Comintern among the strikers. But this merely provided the government with an excuse to ignore the demands of the strikers more generally. After four years in power, the PNȚ no longer had any authority or sufficient political capital for a negotiated solution. The politicians that made up the government were not on top of the situation, and above all they did not want to take any responsibility for it. Hence they call in the army. *Universul*, which was far from having any sympathy for the strikers, describes the situation as follows:

"In the course of the afternoon the situation remained unchanged. Thousands of workers are massed in the northern wing of the yard. A few hundred have climbed on to the roof of the workshops, from where they vociferate. Other groups are walking up and down the length of the roof. The workshop gates are closed and guarded by gendarmes. Gendarmes are patrolling the pavements in front of the workshops, the St. Vineri Cemetery and beyond, towards Bucureștii Noi. The pavements in front of the workshops on Calea Griviței, as well as a part of the road for vehicles, are full of thousands of men, who are circulating slowly, moved along by the patrols. They are idlers, workers from other factories, the unemployed, and women: a motley crowd that stands around quietly or shows its sympathies for the strikers. Sometimes there are exchanges of acclamations between those in the yard of the workshops and those standing outside. The more time passes the more the number of those in front of the workshops swells. All the railway worker neighbourhoods and those populated by various other factory workers have begun to stream towards the workshops. In the neighbouring yards are massed companies of public guardians and gendarmes."[5]

At lunchtime, a delegation of strikers is received by Minister Eduard Mirto. The talks last two hours, until 3 p.m. The minister demands that the delegates should not allow themselves to be instigated by the communists. The strikers demand the release of those held under arrest and the recognition of the strike committee. The minister draws their attention to the fact that these grievances are a matter for the Interior Ministry, not for him. "At six in the evening," the newspaper report continues, "the patrols of gendarmes began to disperse the crowd. At the same time, the strikers, as well as those blocking the street, threw stones and chunks of ice at the army, wounding a number of guardians." Up until this point things had been unfolding more or less peacefully. The sequence of events had been clear. Henceforward, reports of what happened are confused. The crowd puts up a fight. "During the course of the evacuation of the street in front of the workshops a number of revolver shots were fired at the guardians and gendarmes."[6]

The episode remains murky. Was it a provocation mounted by the police with a view to justifying the repression they were preparing? The enquiry that followed was unable to answer this question. Let us trace the course of events. The operation to evacuate Calea Griviței, along the section adjacent to the CFR Workshops, lasts an hour, between 6 and 7 p.m. The police report numerous people wounded and vehicles and buildings hit by flying bullets. The strikers and the crowd on the street are supposed to be guilty. Twenty guardians were wounded during the clashes and 13 civilians. "All this was carried out by gangs of young communists, which were dispersed with great difficulty, inasmuch as they were firing from hidden positions."

---

[5] *Universul*, 17 February 1933.
[6] *Universul*, 17 February 1933.

There is one fatality: Sergeant Ion Chiriță. The police will claim that he was killed by a bullet fired from the direction of the workshops. At the appeal heard in court in the summer of 1934, the defence brings forward witnesses who prove that the sergeant was accidentally killed by one of the guardians. After the street was evacuated, the workers barricaded themselves in the workshops. Tension mounted during the course of the night. Groups of persons unknown devastate Calea Griviței, along the section of the road between the Northern Station, St. Vineri Cemetery, Chibrit Square and the Bucureștii Noi district. They break the windows of the shops. The enquiry was unable to elucidate who these 'persons unknown' were, preferring to label them agitators, communist gangs etc. Many aspects remain obscure even to this day. During the course of the evening, the authorities gave the order for the CFR Grivitza Workshops in Bucharest to be closed from 16-19 February. On the basis of this order, the army surrounded the workshops in the wee hours of the morning, starting from 4.30 a.m. At 5.40 a.m., Royal Commissar Hotineanu gave the workers an ultimatum to evacuate the workshops. The police report, quoted by *Universul*, notes, "the strikers responded with gunshots ... When the deadline expired [five minutes – *author's note*] a number of machine gun salvoes were fired, mostly at the walls of the workshops and into the air. The strikers in front of the gate, caught in the hail of bullets, collapsed to the ground. At that moment, the soldiers stormed the gates, demolishing them and entering the yard. A part of the frightened workers fled across a field, where they were surrounded by soldiers, and the others lay down on the ground, surrendering. The workers who surrendered were loaded into requisitioned buses and taken to the headquarters of the Second Army Corps. ... The wounded were taken by ambulance to hospital. ... At 9 a.m. the entire operation to evacuate the workshops was completed."[7] Armand Călinescu, Secretary of State within the Interior Ministry, the *de facto* head of the operation, wrote in his diary,

> "In the workshops the workers turned off the electricity, so that the street, supplied from there, was thrown into darkness. All the manifestations were visibly revolutionary in nature ... We eventually evacuated the street and kept the workshops under guard through the night, with the evacuation to be carried out at 6 a.m. the next morning. The operation was executed. Ultimatums. Bugles. The workers fire shots. A long burst

---

[7] *Universul*, 18 February 1933.

of machine gun fire in reply (mostly into the air), and then the troops advance. Among the workers, three dead and 40 wounded fall. There are no army casualties. The soldiers fix bayonets and the workers surrender. I arrived there at 6.30. Everything was over. 1,200 workers lying face down on the ground, leaning on their elbows, with their hands behind their heads, like prisoners. They are taken away to Malmaison."[8]

Parliament holds an urgent debate on the situation. What is to be noted first of all is that the government does not resign. It had demanded a state of emergency in order to take measures to prevent disturbances and avoid 'harsh repression'. The disturbances had not been prevented, and the repression was as harsh as could be. The final toll was seven dead and 44 wounded. There were almost three thousand arrests. The government was well enough informed about the mood of the workers. If it had been informed of communist infiltrators, why did it not take measures to isolate and arrest them earlier? How many communists had been operating in the workshops? They were a minority. After the disaster of the morning of 17 February, 'communist provocation' was an alibi. It would be inexact to explain the tragedy of that February morning as a confrontation between a rebellious mass manipulated from behind the scenes by communists on the one hand and a government overtaken by the unfolding events on the other. Political calculations, vested interests, and a poor understanding of the core of the dispute worked together to cause the tragic denouement. Much more was at stake: the democratic regime itself. The violent repression of the CFR strikers was not merely a marginal episode, a conflict between a few thousand workers and the forces of law and order. The manner of solving the crisis showed the limits and weaknesses of the Romanian democratic regime. The question was whether that regime would crumble in the case of a major clash. Almost no one seemed interested in analysing events seriously. In his report, G. G. Mironescu, the Interior Minister, says,

"it was obvious that we were dealing with armed insurgents, who were seeking to provoke a revolution ... and then I gave the order to fire. They fired into the crowd. ... After a few salvoes had been fired, the workers also stopped firing, probably because they had run out of bullets. Then

[8] Armand Călinescu, *Însemnări politice*, Bucharest: Humanitas, 1990, pp. 147-148.

the army stopped firing and went inside, clearing a way with their rifle butts and bayonets. Within an interval of approximately 20 minutes, the workshops had been entirely evacuated. Two thousand workers surrendered and were detained for questioning ... We must firstly point out, with especial satisfaction, that the army and police force displayed an attitude worthy of all praise ... We find ourselves ... confronted with a tenacious attempt to bring about the disintegration of this country by means of violence, by means of a communist revolution, for they have been working for some time to break up this country clandestinely."

Dr N. Lupu replies to this, claiming that not the communist leaders but the delegates who were negotiating with the CFR Workshops' management and Minister Eduard Mirto were arrested:

"The families and children [of those arrested – *author's note*] went to the workshops and complained to the mass of workers reminding them that these men had defended them, they were their spokesmen ... This was their demand: the release of those arrested. ... Did they demand those things the minister claims, i.e. cessation of the state of emergency, re-establishment of the communist organisations and inspection of the management? No. The workers quite simply demanded the release of those arrested. ... The government used excessive force."

Dr Lupu demands: (1) the replacement of the prefect of the Bucharest police, Gabriel Marinescu, responsible for the repression and (2) repeal of the state of emergency, which, in his opinion, does not calm spirits but is leading towards disaster. In the name of the PSD, Ion Mirescu declares,

"the agitation at the CFR was set in motion by a few communists known to State Security but in spite of this they were released to mingle with the workers ... They worked hand in hand with the communist agents, assisted by the agents of those interested in proclaiming a dictatorship, with the direct help of the organs of the Siguranţă. With the help of agents provocateur, workers' blood has once again been shed."

By this declaration Ion Mirescu follows the current trend of mutual social democratic and communist accusations of 'fracturing the workers' unity'.

In the CFR Grivitza Workshops there had long been conflict between the workers unionised by the Social Democrats and the others, some of them communists, others not. In 1932, their coalition led to the Social Democrats losing influence, whence the resentments and accusations in the speech of Ion Mirescu. In the name of the PNL, Richard Franasovici says, "Responsibility for the bloody events of this morning remains entirely yours. For, either because of incompetence or a wretched spirit of demagoguery you have always denied the existence of this danger [communism – *author's note*]." It is no secret that the Liberals are preparing for government. They will come to power in the autumn of that year, 1933.

The oratorical duel in the Chamber of Deputies reaches no conclusion. In fact, under the pretext of a communist plot, any real debate was rejected. The incidents at the CFR Grivitza Workshops ought to have been occasion for a debate about the way in which democracy and its institutions functioned. The bugbear of the 'Bolshevik peril' functioned efficiently. Romania was threatened by Soviet expansion. Any social protest or proposal for radical reform was regarded as communist in inspiration. This blocked many much-needed debates within Romanian society, as well as the measures required for the consolidation of democracy and more rapid progress. Of course, with historical hindsight, these 'efforts' seem futile. No one at the time suspected what was to come. Hitler had come to power on 30 January 1933. It was the opening scene of a drama that would end with the Red Army occupying Romania and the communists in power.

On 1 February 1933, two weeks before the strike a police report[9] reveals communist infiltration of the railway workers. Constantin Doncea was a member of Romanian Workers' Aid (AMR), a branch of International Red Aid, which was a Comintern organisation. Doncea ran an AMR canteen for railway workers on the other side of the road from the Grivitza Workshops. The money for the rent, staff and food came from the Comintern. It was the perfect place for spreading propaganda among the workers. The AMR had already been involved in two major trials at that point: the trial of the Victor Aradi group for espionage and subversion, and the one involving a number of lawyers who were members of the AMR, on similar charges. The organisation was outlawed. As early as November 1931, Imre Aladár had set up an independent trades union, controlled by Profintern, the Red unions, based in Moscow. Imre Aladár succeeded Aradi as the head of the AMR.

---

[9] MAN Archive, Fund 948/3, Appendix, Dossier 2, p. 28.

Aladár, elected as a deputy in 1931, only for the vote to be invalidated, was deported for communist activities and espionage in 1933. He took part in the Fifth Congress of the PCdR in Gorkovo. In 1937, he was executed by firing squad in Moscow. Among the strike leaders we find many communists, conspirators and professional revolutionaries, trained in Moscow and Berlin. They make up the Red opposition – a tactic demanded by the Comintern was infiltration of the trades unions. Where the communists managed to place their own men, they took over the leadership. Where they did not succeed, they engineered splits and set up parallel unions. This is what happened in Grivitza in the summer of 1932.

In Grivitza, the same as everywhere else, there was a conflict between the social democratic and communist unions. In the tense atmosphere of the early 1930s, a part of the workers became radicalised. Negotiations with the workshops' management or the minister in charge did not bring any positive changes. The workers were assailed by falling wages, poverty and insecurity. A part of them had gradually moved towards more aggressive tactics. At the Grivitza Workshops, moreover, a deficient, often corrupt, management cultivated poor relations with the workers. This aspect was emphasised at trial by ministers Mihail Maoilescu and Eduard Mirto themselves when testifying. Long working hours, frequent punishments and fines, and sackings heightened the tension. It was natural that against this backdrop the radicals gained a larger audience. The workers were not united, however. Two unions were vying against each other for influence. It also came to physical violence between the militants of the two groups. The difficult economic situation fuelled the growth of communist and non-communist radical influence. The reality of the working-class milieu was highly complex. There was no ideological, organisational or political unity.

In 1932, Moscow is the venue for the congress of the International Red Unions, Profintern. Earlier, in December 1931, the Fifth Congress of the PCdR was held in Gorkovo, near Moscow. It was attended by numerous leading figures in the Romanian communist underground: Imre Aladár, Ecaterina Arbore, David Pastilică-Avramescu, Petre Borilă, Alexandru Buican, Béla Breiner, Georgi Krosnev, Elena Filipovici, Petre Gheorghe, Nicolae Goldberger, Dori Goldstein, Dumitru Grofu, Emil Haliţki, Eugen Iacobovici, Alexandru Iliescu, Lucreţiu Pătrășcanu, Alexander Ștefanski

Danieluc-Gorn, S. Tinkelman Timov, et al.[10] However, a number of major clandestine figures are absent: Moscu Cohn, Al. Dobrogeanu-Gherea, David Fabian Finkelstein, Ștefan Foriș, Elek Köblős, Vasile Luca, Constantin Pîrvulescu, Marcel Pauker, Eugen Rozvany, Solomon Schein, Boris Ștefanov, et al. Some are in prison in Romania, others are out of favour with the Comintern. Nevertheless, never had so many spies, terrorists, professional revolutionaries and provocateurs been gathered together in one place. And nor would there be until September 1944, except in the prisons any other gathering of such size of Aiud, Galatzi, Ocnele Mari, Doftana, and Caransebeș. Presiding are their patrons: Dimitrov, Manuilski and Béla Kuhn. One of the central decisions of the congress was to infiltrate communists into industries where there was a high concentration of workers. It was a task of the utmost urgency. The targets were transportation, oil, large factories, the war industry, and ports. Lucrețiu Pătrășcanu, a member of the Political Bureau, is the most powerful communist leader to return to Romania after the congress. The others remain in Moscow or go to Prague, where the PCdR has its headquarters. The Party is behind everything that happens in the first part of 1933. The Grivitza strike reveals it as a mastermind of subversion. Pătrășcanu is accompanied by two 'professional revolutionaries', experienced 'clandestines': Moscu Cohn and Vasile Luca. The two co-opt Gheorghe Gheorghiu into a CFR 'action committee' in March 1932. Gheorghiu is unemployed and already on Moscu Cohn's payroll.

> "Moscu was an accountant in a vague way, having taken three evening school classes. He knew a little German and some Russian and came directly from Moscow, because he had become a 'professional revolutionary' … He had a wallet full of banknotes … He was the Profintern representative from Moscow and all the Romanian intellectuals hankered for silver, while the workers were ready to leave their jobs to become professional revolutionaries."[11]

1932 was the year of Gheorghe Gheorghiu's emergence in the hierarchy of

---

[10] See their Comintern cadre files in *Copilăria Comunismului românesc în arhiva Cominternului*, ANCR, 2001, pp. 282-315.

[11] Petre Pandrea, *Memoriile mandarinului valah*, Bucharest: Albatros, 2000, p. 282.

the 'revolutionary unions'. He had been recruited a year previously, on the recommendation of Ilie Pintilie, a well-known CFR union leader from the Socolo workshops in Jassy. It is the beginning of a career that will culminate with Gheorghiu-Dej as Dictator of Romania. He was the third generation of a working-class family. A working-class mentality is discernable in him, even much later, when he is in power. In 1932, Gheorghiu-Dej is described in a report by the police in Galatzi as follows: "We suspect him of being a dangerous communist agitator and have information that he has also received sums of money for clandestine propaganda." Arrested in Jassy after a union meeting in the CFR Socolo workshops, under interrogation he declares that he was born in Bîrlad, Tutova county, that he is an electrician and has worked for the CFR since 1926. He had done his military service in 1926, with the Third Sapper Regiment in Focșani. His parents, Anica and Tudose, are deceased. He married in Galatzi and has two daughters. He lives in Bucharest, on 10 May Street, in the Grant district. Asked whether he is a communist, he replies, "It's true that I've been suspected by the police of being a communist, but it isn't true because I'd have had some connection with the communists. I've never done propaganda like that."[12] The answer is in accordance with the Comintern rulebook, which demands, in the case of arrest, denial of everything. Gheorghe Gheorghiu was one of the militants chosen to contribute to the reorganisation of the unions and to bring them under communist control. In the operation are also involved Luka László, Marin Ionescu, and Gheorghe Vasilichi, on behalf of the pro-communist unions, and Moscu Cohn (Gheorghe Stoica) and Dumitru Petrescu, on behalf of the PCdR. Gheorghiu-Dej worked directly from within the PCdR. He was a paid agitator, financed by Profintern, the International Red Unions. A police report of 8 October 1932 concludes, "Not employed in any job and not plying the trade he knows, Gheorghe Gheorghiu-Dej is subsidised by the Communist Party from Romania."[13] In 1931, after the union protests in which he had been involved, Gheorghiu was transferred to Dej. As a police report of 24 September 1932 points out, up until 1931 "he was a worker at the CFR Galatzi Workshops and was part of the workers' movement without being mixed up with the clandestine organisations."[14] He was recruited from the communist-oriented unions

---

[12] MAN Archive, MStM, Fund 948/3, Dossier 177, p. 132.

[13] MAN Archive, MStM, Fund 948/3, Dossier 2, p. 18.

[14] MAN Archive, MStM, Fund 948/3, Dossier 24, p. 17, 24 September 1932.

in the winter of 1932. He was arrested for the first time on charges of communist agitation. In March, he is a member of the nationwide CFR Action Committee. In April 1932, the CFR Workshops in Dej are closed down and Gheorghiu-Dej remains unemployed. "Since this date the above-named has been responsible for propaganda among the workers at the CFR Grivitza Workshops in Bucharest, carrying out intensive propaganda in the CFR communist union that has lately been set up ... and contributes to the *Lupta CFR [CFR Struggle]* newspaper,"[15] a police report five months prior to the Grivitza strikes notes. As can be seen, the police had him under surveillance. A week after this report, he was arrested in Jassy and detained for a week. In July he had been arrested and held in Văcărești Prison, during the election campaign, when he worked for the Peasant Worker Bloc. But it was not Gheorghiu-Dej who was the prominent figure of the Grivitza strikes. In the two trials, the prosecution identified Constantin Doncea as the strikers' leader. He was the dominant figure among the accused in the dock. The story of the two's rivalry begins here. What was the relationship between them in 1933? Doncea worked at CFR Grivitza in Bucharest, Gheorghiu-Dej did not. The uncontested and popular leader of the workers there was Doncea. Gheorghiu-Dej was the delegate from 'central'. He was known to the instigators, to the underground. Up until the trial, he remained an unknown figure on the factory floor, among the six thousand strikers. His wages came not from Grivitza but from Moscu Cohn, therefore from Profintern. In the speech for the prosecution, the Royal Commissar states, "Gheorghiu-Dej alias Ivanov is the liaison agent between the various communist CFR unions and the Communist Party. It is he who roams the length and breadth of the country and he who brought word from Doncea to the safe house on Giulești that 15 February 1933 was the day decided upon by all to unleash the general strike." They failed to achieve this goal. They did not succeed in unleashing a general strike. The scenario attempted in 1920 was aborted before it could be unleashed. About Doncea, the prosecutor says, "His orders brooked no disagreement, no interpretation. Prodigious in his activity, we see him during the days of the strike now in court ... now in the midst of the workers gauging their morale and the effects of his words, now giving orders ... now inspecting the guards at the gates, only to mount the podium once more with furious voice. ... If Doncea is not the creator, then he is the admirable tool of the Comintern,

---

[15] *Idem*, p. 18, 2 October 1932.

guided, controlled and checked by Gheorghiu-Dej, Moscu Cohn and the other superiors acknowledged by him."[16]

The CFR workers were the oldest segment of the working class in the Old Kingdom. They had organised as long ago as the 1860s. There was a proletarian tradition and ethos here, as well as an extensive network. A railway strike could paralyse the entire country. The economic crisis of the beginning of the 1930s caused additional solidarity in the face of the threat of unemployment and repeated wage cuts. A diffuse and then clearly outlined discontent emerges. A number of figures make a name for themselves among the workers. A Siguranță report of 1 February 1933 notes,

> "any arrest will not only fail to temper or demoralise the masses but will rather make them all the more determined, because today's leaders are not the professional instigators of former times, but rather simple workers who have emerged from the ranks of the many, and the question that is causing the agitation is the discontent of the CFR employees and as such, if they are arrested they can easily be replaced at any time. Moreover, these measures will further agitate the masses, who will end up believing that the government is hostile to their interests, and this is why it has arrested their spokesmen, instead of satisfying their grievances."[17]

Radicalisation of the workers went hand-in-hand with worsening standards of living. The Social Democrat leaders who had up until then dominated the CFR unions – and who pressed for negotiations and avoided any direct confrontation with the management – were gradually losing their influence. They were blamed for lay-offs and wage cuts. Against this background, the more radical elements, some of them communists, gained in influence. "The activity of the communists, according to the fixed directives, is a crowning success and an initial result is the takeover of the Social Democrat CFR Union, which was even forced to abandon its office on 10 October 1932."[18] On 29 January, the previously mentioned meeting of CFR union

---

[16] ANCR, CC of the PCdR Archive, Fund 96, Dossier 5487, pp. 97-98.

[17] MAN Archive, MstM, Fund 948/3, Appendix 2, Section 2, Intelligence, Dossier 2, p. 38.

[18] MAN Archive, MstM, Fund 948/3, Appendix 2, Section 2, Intelligence, Dossier 2, p. 31.

associations is held in the Marna Auditorium, next to the Northern Station. The ever watchful police note,

> "In summary, due to the mood of the CFR employees who on the one hand have to a large extent lost confidence in the leaders of the moderate legal associations, and on the other hand despair of the fact that they have not received any satisfaction for the grievances they presented to the management and now they declare themselves ready to take action, saying that the time for words has passed. The communists have managed to achieve the two main points of their programme, namely: (a) the creation up to a certain point of a single front of all CFR employees … (b) popularisation of the word 'strike'."[19]

The communists were involved in all the protests at Grivitza. Behind the radical union leaders there were professional conspirators orchestrated by the Comintern. At the beginning of February 1933, Béla Iacobovici (née Rabinsohn, the sister of Ana Pauker, married to Eugen Iacobovici, a member of the PCdR Political Bureau) is arrested in Berlin. The German police discover about her person documents with instructions for the Grivitza strike from the Soviets. Béla Iacobovici is extradited and placed under house arrest in Bucharest. She manages to escape, but the documents confiscated by the German police will be used as evidence in court. Many of the accused were known to the police as communist agitators. A few of them – Dumitru Petrescu, Gheorghe Vasilichi, Marin Ioan-Ionescu – had travelled in 1931-1932 to Moscow, Berlin and Vienna, where the headquarters of various Comintern organisations were based: WEB (West-Europäische Büro) and the Political Bureau of the PCdR. Of the PCdR leaders, Lucrețiu Pătrășcanu and Moscu Cohn are the most deeply involved, and of the union leaders, Vasile Luca. Moscu Cohn (Gheorghe Stoica) is elected an alternate member of the CC of the PCdR at the plenary of April 1933 for the role he played in January-February. The immixture of the communists in the Grivitza strikes does not mean that they controlled those protests, however, and nor does it mean that they managed to guide them in the direction they wanted, i.e. towards a general strike. A number of groups were vying for influence over the

---

[19] MAN Archive, MstM, Fund 948/3, Appendix 2, Section 2, Intelligence, Dossier 2, p. 33.

workers. The role of the communists was certain. In the speech for the prosecution, Royal Commissar Romulus Hotineanu says, "the whole action at the Grivitza Workshops was the work of Moscow." But things were not quite so simple as to be a plot hatched and executed by a handful of communist agitators in the pay of the Comintern. The Grivitza protests were a result of worsening standards of living, on the one hand, and of disputes between various political and union groups, on the other. The legend of a communist plot was transformed into one of 'the PCR leading the masses'. The Grivitza strike provided a source of legitimacy for the group led by Gheorghiu-Dej. A number of leaders vied for supremacy over this source of legitimacy. Above all Constantin Doncea and Gheorghe Gheorghiu-Dej, but also Pătrășcanu and Vasile Luca.

A 'strictly confidential' report to Mihai Moruzov, the head of the SSI, probably from an informant in the upper echelons of the PCdR, reveals the following:

"In Moscow the failure of the communist movement in Bucharest is attributed to lack of preparation and the premature eruption of the movement. Stalin seems to take a personal interest in the situation in Romania and in order to demonstrate the continuing success of 'Red activity' he is supposed to have given orders that all available propaganda means should be directed towards Romania. Significant sums of money will soon be delivered, fresh agents will be sent, under various disguises – false passports, refugees from Transnistria, etc. The movement will also target student circles. It is necessary to double surveillance everywhere."[20]

On 18 July, the CFR workers trial commences during a heat wave – 40°C in the shade near the site of the strike, by the Northern Station. "It cannot be said that the location of the War Council on Calea Plevnei excels in its physical appearance. A more pleasing setting would have been appropriate, not this limestone architectural behemoth, with its cold and ugly rooms and the reliefs of its whitewashed walls. It gives one the impression of an improvised Algerian fort, like one sees in certain films."[21]

[20] MAN Archive, SSI Fund, Dossier 182, p. 257.
[21] *Dimineața*, 19 July 1933.

So much for the décor. In the courtroom, besides the members of the court, there were 125 accused and 20 lawyers. During the 30 days of the trial, more than 400 witnesses pass through the courtroom. "In this trial," remarks the same journalist for *Dimineaţa* (*Morning*), "everything is on a large scale. The principal accused are Panait Bogătoiu, Constantin Doncea, Dumitru Petrescu, Gheorghe Vasilichi, Gheorghiu-Dej, and Chivu Stoica. The list of the accused also includes Lucreţiu Pătrăşcanu, Moscu Cohn, and Luka László (Vasile Luca), well-known communists. The last two disappear and are tried *in absentia*. The 125 accused are divided into two lots. Placed in the second lot, Pătrăşcanu will not be tried until 1938, after numerous postponements. In 1933, he wisely leaves the country.

Many of the 125 in the dock do not have any connections with the communists, some of them not even with Grivitza or the strike. The accused are mostly young men between 19 and 25, almost all of them unemployed. The lawyers reflect the composition of the accused in the dock. Some were communists (Iosif Şraier, Petre Grozdea, Grigore Conduratu), others were 'bourgeois', defenders of human rights (V. V. Stanciu, Lizetta Gheorghiu). Lawyer I. Emilian was part of LANC, the extreme Right group led by A. C. Cuza. The defence rarely manages to find a consensus. A number of incidents stand out. The first is the application for a postponement of the trial, tabled by the defence. To this, Royal Commissar Romulus Hotineanu (who will die in a communist prison in the 1950s) remarks that the real motive for the application is that money to pay the lawyers has not yet arrived from Moscow. The defence vehemently protests. The debates were closely followed by the press, enjoying almost the same level of interest as the Skoda trial, a major corruption case. In his closing statement, Gheorghiu-Dej (and not only he) claims "he is neither a communist nor an agent provocateur" and declares himself "in solidarity with all the CFR strikes. It is not by petitions and negotiations that the workers' grievances can be addressed."[22] Nicu Tudor, a future member of the PCdR Secretariat, from 1939 to 1940, and an informant working for the Siguranţă, says that he has been accused of going to Russia, but in fact "he went to Germany to treat an incurable disease." He claims that he is "not a communist and is not involved in politics." The truth is that he had indeed been to Russia. What is interesting here is the fact that a number of the strike leaders connected to the PCdR disown communism. This was a ruse laid down by the Comintern.

---

[22] *Facla*, 21 August 1933.

Things will be completely different at the second trial, in Craiova, a year later. Another interesting detail is that Gheorghiu-Dej was arrested in the house of Nicu Tudor, who, after the trial, will be his connection with the CFR Grivitza Workshops in the 1930s.

Sentence is passed on 20 August. Constantin Doncea and Dumitru Petrescu are sentenced to life, hard labour. Gheorghe Vasilichi is given 20 years, hard labour. Gheorghe Gheorghiu-Dej and Chivu Stoica are each given 15 years, Marin Ioan-Ionescu 12 years, hard labour, Richard Wurmbrand 10 years, Nicolae Tudor two years, etc. Others among the accused are sentenced to 20 years, hard labour, *in absentia*, including Vasile Luca and Moscu Cohn. The others are acquitted, including communists Constantin David (killed during the Legionary uprising of January 1941), Vasile Bîgu, Ovidiu Șandor, Paulina Doncea, et al.

There is a retrial one year later, in Craiova. Of the 125 accused involved in the first trial, only eight, those with the heaviest sentences, appeal. They are defended by a group of lawyers from the PCdR Legal Office, headed by its director, Iosif Șraier, assisted by Petre Grozdea, Victor Gherasim, Radu Olteanu et al. "The first to open fire was lawyer Șraier from Bucharest, energetic, with a humour that demolished everything in his path, as much a master of the law as Doncea of his hammer, lawyer Șraier blazed the trail, intuiting the entire trial."[23] Iosif Șraier was head of the PCdR Legal Office from 1935-1944. He represented the communists in numerous trials. His clients included Ștefan Foriș, Gheorghiu-Dej, Constantin Doncea, Constantin Pîrvulescu, Vasile Luca and Teohari Georgescu. He defended Victor Aradi and Belu Zilber at the 'Soviet espionage trial'. In 1944, he was Secretary General of Patriotic Defence, a PCdR front organisation. In 1945, he became a Secretary of State in the Interior Ministry. On 27 November 1945 he gave an interview to American journalist Mark Ethridge. His judgements about the situation in Romania were highly critical. He says, "If free elections were held today, Maniu and his party would win a sure majority ... as an expression of the population's current anti-Russian feelings. ... The Romanian communists do not make any move without complete approval from Moscow."[24] Two years later he flees to the West, crossing the frontier clandestinely. There are documents that indicate he

---

[23] *Reporter*, 20 July 1934.
[24] Ulrich Berger, *Misiunea Ethridge în România*, Bucharest: Fundația Academia Civică, 2000, pp. 229-230.

was a Siguranţă informant. During the war, he was accused of getting rich by doing business with Jews whose companies had to be 'Romanianised'. Iosif Şraier was the first defector from the communist elite of an Eastern Europe under Soviet occupation. In 1950, two years after he vanished from Bucharest, he was found dead. We also know that in the mid-1930s he fathered a child with Lotti Foriş, at the time married to Ştefan Foriş, whom Şraier had represented in court and who was in prison at the time.

The context of the 1934 trial was different. In Germany, after Hitler came to power, the trial of the Reichstag arsonists had provided a model of what the Comintern intended in cases involving communists. These trials had to be propaganda spectacles, in the first place. In addition, the identification of Social Democrats with the class enemy, with traitors and 'social fascists' had been changed by Moscow in the meantime. In the first trial, the 125 accused represented every union and political tendency. This time, those in the dock are exclusively communists: Constantin Doncea, Dumitru Petrescu, Gheorghe Vasilichi, Gheorghiu-Dej, Chivu Stoica, Alexandru Rosenberg and David Korner. The last two are accused and then convicted of having made contact with and received money from the Comintern in the period prior to the strike. They were proof of Royal Commissar Vasile Gelep's thesis that the strike had been an international communist plot. This time, the script of the defence and the prosecution is clearer. This time, too, Gheorghiu-Dej is a secondary figure. He is overshadowed by Constantin Doncea, Dumitru Petrescu and Gheorghe Vasilichi. Among the witnesses we meet other communists, including Gheorghe Cristescu, the first General Secretary of the PCdR; Mihai Gheorghiu Bujor, sentenced to 13 years imprisonment in 1920, released in 1933 and now treated as a Siguranţă agent by the communists, which he was not; and Ilie Pintilie, whom Gheorghiu-Dej cross-questions during his testimony.

Ştefan Foriş, a member of the CC of the PCdR, is brought from Văcăreşti Prison to testify. He was sentenced to five years imprisonment in 1931. Gheorghiu-Dej and Foriş met in Văcăreşti Prison in 1932. It did not take much to create enmity between them. The reason was Gheorghiu-Dej's pretensions to supremacy. Another witness for the defence is Vasile Luca, the leader of the Red 'unified unions', which had been dissolved when the state of emergency was declared in January 1933. He had been tried *in absentia* at the first trial and sentenced to 20 years, hard labour. Having been captured, he is brought to the Craiova trial from prison. Luca was a long-standing militant and much better known. He was in a hierarchically superior position. Dej was new in the movement, having joined in 1931, and newer still to the upper echelons, to which he had been promoted by none other than Vasile Luca. Dej will later detest Luca precisely for this reason.

The debates during the trial revolve around the same questions as in 1933. The prosecution tries to prove that the strikers were armed, that they organised a rebellion backed by the Comintern, and that they murdered gendarme Ion Chiriță. The defence denies these accusations, arguing that the gendarme had been killed not by the strikers but accidentally by the soldiers. Their thesis is that poverty brought people out onto the streets spontaneously. During the debates, references are made to the Leipzig trial brought against the 'Reichstag arsonists'. Constantin Doncea, quoting Marx, without remembering his name, says that history repeats itself, the first time as tragedy, the second time as farce. The first trial, the one in Germany, was the tragic one. Doncea can in no way be suspected of ever having read Marx. The accused were actors reciting lines written by PCdR agitators outside prison. Their script differs from that of the previous year. 'Revolutionary Bolshevik' discourse is now dominant, employed by the defence and a part of the witnesses. The protagonist for the defence is Iosif Șraier. Alexandru Sahia, for *Dimineața* (1 July 1934) describes his summing-up as follows:

"This young man of overwhelming energy gave rise to moments of the highest humanity. His attitude was reserved, clearly. With a profound knowledge of the events, over the course of six hours he presented before the council the most vital problems of the Romanian proletariat. He spoke of the unbelievable restraint of the workers, who, provoked countless times and exasperated by their life of struggle, only reacted when the last chances of legality had been exhausted. The cry of the workers was too late and their voice, which demanded only bread, was reduced to silence by death. The defence described down to the last detail all the dramatic moments of the days of the strike, highlighting the spirit of sacrifice of those who fell on the sand banks, at the factory gates, true martyrs of the proletariat. Sixteen eyes of flame, gleaming with tears, tirelessly watched the young man of 30 who for the second time conjured up the surging struggle of the strikers ... Marin Ion wept. Vasilichi Ghiță also wept ... while Gheorghiu-Dej, Petrescu and Doncea continually smiled with a luminosity that overwhelmed you. ... The defence caused the point of view of the Romanian proletariat to resound powerfully. Only the two soldiers on guard were unable to comprehend the boldness of this young man in black clothes and probably from Bucharest, to whom their colonel was listening."

The fact that during the trial Romania signed a friendship accord with the USSR did not prevent the judges from handing down heavy sentences, albeit lighter than in the previous year. Constantin Doncea and Dumitru Petrescu were given 15 years, hard labour, Gheorghe Vasilichi, Gheorghe Gheorghiu-Dej and Chivu Stoica 12 years, hard labour, Alexandru Rosenberg five years imprisonment, and David Korner 18 months. The higher military court rejected any appeal. The Court of Cassation likewise. The sentences were final. The Court of Cassation passed judgement in the absence of Doncea, Petrescu, and Vasilichi, however. They had escaped in the meantime.[25] The escape was organised by the PCdR with the intermediation of the lawyers for the defence. Marcel Pauker, on behalf of the Comintern, supervises the whole operation, including the removal of the three out of the country.

---

[25] *Universul*, 28 March 1935. See also Gheorghe Vasilichi, in *Arhivele totalitarianismului*, magazine published by the Romanian Academy and the National Institute for the Study of Totalitarianism, nos. 3-4, 2000, pp. 113-118.

XI
The Heroes of the Proletariat (2)

1. *Mihai Gheorghiu Bujor*

Panait Istrati once called Mihai Gheorghiu Bujor "the gentle apostle." They were colleagues working for *România muncitoare* (*Workingman's Romania*). Bujor was a lawyer and journalist. In 1910, on the re-establishment of the Social Democratic Party, he is one of the leaders, alongside C. Rakovski, Alecu Constantinescu and I. C. Frimu. After Romania's entry into the war, he is mobilised with the rank of sub-lieutenant, in the 54th Infantry Regiment. An opponent of Romania's war on the Entente side, a 'pacifist', he deserts in December. He is captured, tried, convicted and imprisoned. On 1 May 1917, he is liberated by Russian troops in Jassy, together with Cristian Rakovski. He reaches Odessa where, together with other deserters, Romanian prisoners and refugees, he forms the Romanian Social Democrat Action Committee and later the Romanian Revolutionary Battalion. He is seconded by Racovski in these actions. He gives orders for Romanian refugees to be arrested, including parliamentarians, politicians, dignitaries and diplomats. He sacks the headquarters of Romanian institutions and, 'in the name of the Revolution', requisitions their goods. He engages in looting against Romanians sheltering in the Crimea. He carries out Bolshevik propaganda in articles in the gazette he runs – *Lupta* (*The Struggle*), and in the meetings he organises in Odessa, Sevastopol and Feodosia. He prints anti-Romanian manifestos and distributes them in the trenches. He instigates the Romanian Army to overthrow the monarchy. He leads his Romanian Revolutionary Battalion against the Romanian Army on the Dniester. He confiscates the Romanian Black Sea fleet and places it under the Russian flag. On his orders 14 Romanian soldiers are killed in the port of Feodosia. Bujor, as Racovski's adjutant, is the one who negotiates with Colonel Boyle of the Red Cross, an emissary of Queen Maria, for the release of Romanian prisoners.

In March 1919, he opposes the foundation of the Comintern. His argument is that such an organisation will cause a split in the socialist movement. But this is exactly what Lenin wants. He constantly promoted splits in the 'movement', aiming for a small, disciplined and closed party of professional revolutionaries. Lenin detested social democracy and reform. On this subject, Bujor was at odds with Lenin, Trotsky and Racovski. He conforms, but he gradually loses influence. The idea of organising a general staff for the world revolution of the proletariat was highly popular among the Kremlin leaders. For Lenin, Trotsky and Racovski it was even an obsession.

The Comintern sends Bujor to Bucharest at the end of 1919. He arrives clandestinely in the first week of January 1920. His mission is to prepare a Bolshevik Revolution. In the eyes of the Comintern, Romania was in the same situation as Russia in the summer and autumn of 1917. In his first report back to Moscow, Bujor says,

> "I am organising communist and Soviet groups … We are setting up arms dumps. I am collaborating with the Party newspaper. Agitation in the Party. A communist congress. Discussion between myself and the Party committee. Criticised for moderate activity. … Received report and money from Moscow. … Money and jewels entrusted to the official Party. Romanian Tiraspol transport arrived. For our work … a lot of money [needed]. Courier with calculations soon. M. Gh. Bujor."
>
> (document reproduced in *Universul*, 8 February 1928)

During a quarrel over the money that has arrived at the headquarters of the Socialist Party, Bujor 'the dreamer' does not hesitate to draw his pistol. He lives clandestinely in Bucharest for around three months, plotting, buying guns, printing manifestos, training agitators. He is arrested in a beer hall, eating a turkey dinner.

> "He tried to protest, but did not make a scene. … From the information in the possession of the Siguranţă, Bujor was assigned by the Grand Revolutionary Collegium in Odessa to prepare a revolution in Romania. To this end, numerous propagandists have been working in various regions of the country, preparing a revolution."[1]

Two months later, in May, he is brought to trial. After five days of deliberations, the Military Tribunal sentences him to life imprisonment, hard labour, and strips him of his rank. The charges were "desertion

[1] *Îndreptarea*, 17 and 19 March 1920, quoted in *Ideologie şi structuri comuniste în România*, INST, vol. 3, 2001, pp. 62-63.

during wartime, repeated calls to rebellion addressed to Romanian soldiers, the crime of high treason, and endangerment of national security." The sentence will be commuted to 20 years imprisonment.

He is imprisoned at Ocnele Mari and then Doftana. He is the object of numerous campaigns for his amnesty. The Comintern makes use of him for agitation and propaganda. In 1924, for example, when the Bucharest government is negotiating with Russia in Vienna, the Comintern unleashes a campaign for the release of Bujor the 'prisoner of conscience'. He gives interviews to the press throughout his imprisonment. Journalists visit him and write about him. He is also visited by lawyers, left-wing militants and foreign delegates interested in his fate. He is a 'prophet of the working class', a 'martyr', a 'victim of government terror'. In his cell, Bujor writes poems and his impressions of prison life.

> Lights out. Now the old gaol
> With its hoary walls of stone,
> Worn by snow and hail,
> To the clank of keys does groan.
>
> In the watchtower,
> The changing of the guard.
> The sentinels glower
> As they scan the yard.

The same poem compares the "throngs of sad prisoners" to flocks of sheep harried in the fold by hungry wolves. In the darkness of "cyclopean" Doftana, time is "distorted." In other poems he compares himself with Jesus Christ. His supporters continually deplore his prison conditions, the fact that he is kept in a dark cell, that he is not allowed to exercise in the open air, that he cannot receive visits, parcels or letters, that he is gravely ill, that he is often kept in solitary confinement, that he has attempted suicide, that the prison administration has tried to kill him. They were lies and rumours, part of the Comintern campaign.

The truth is that Bujor, the most famous political prisoner in Romania, enjoyed special treatment. He even has a garden plot, where he cultivates flowers. In his cell he has writing materials, books and newspapers. He is not kept in solitary confinement. He is allowed to exercise in the open air for three hours every day. When Ilie Moscovici and Em. Socor visit him in Doftana in 1928, Bujor complains about being disturbed by "nocturnal noise." "I am a soldier fallen in battle," he says. "I can have no other hope than death. I await it calmly." He speaks like a prophet, like a hero and martyr, whenever he is interviewed by journalists. He situates himself above all parties and trends. The Left, fragmented into dozens of groups, communists of every hue, and the socialists all vie for him. Both the Comintern and the Socialist International lay claim to him. Bujor refuses to make any judgements on their disputes or to get mixed up in polemics. He is untouchable, above criticism. A 'working-class hero, who languishes in a damp, dark cell, guarded by the tyrants of reaction'. It is a powerful image, one highly useful for propaganda purposes. Every cause needs such a figure to serve as an example for the masses. His sentence of life imprisonment, hard labour and his participation in the Russian Revolution gain him respect. His stature in those years was far greater than that of any other left-wing leader. Moscow was very interested in Bujor. In exchange for Bujor and three other Romanian prisoners, the Russians offer to return the archive and treasure of the Romanian Academy.[2] The Romanian government declines. In 1926, an exchange of prisoners is negotiated via the Swedish legation. The talks fail. The reason is that the USSR demands Bujor. Racovski, the Soviet ambassador to Paris, makes efforts to secure the release of his erstwhile collaborator. The I. I. C. Brătianu government refuses to bargain, regarding Bujor as 'extremely dangerous'.

He is released from Doftana in the summer of 1933, after 13 years of imprisonment. The authorities make this gesture two weeks before Titulescu and Litvinov sign the Romanian-Russian Treaty. Was it a sign of goodwill on the part of the Romanian authorities, or was it at the express demand of the Soviet government? We do not know. There were plenty of negative reactions in the press. "The Bujor case. It is rumoured that dangerous revolutionary Bujor is to be pardoned. … He was in the service of the Soviets. He terrorised Romanians in Odessa in 1918. He commandeered Romanian Black Sea vessels and replaced the Romanian with the Red flag."[3] The newspaper opposes his release. On 15 June, it publishes another article, with the title *The pardoning of M. Gh. Bujor. An unjustified and condemnable act.* Paradoxically, the decline in Bujor's status as uncontested leader of the left-wing movement commences with his release from prison.

---

[2] *Adevărul*, 12 January/24 February 1928.
[3] *Universul*, 11 June 1933.

He settles in Cîmpina, near Doftana, where the leaders of the Left, both communist and non-communist, make pilgrimage. The Siguranţa keep him under observation and record all his meetings. There are informants among Bujor's visitors. Many of them write reports and provide summaries of conversations. All the left-wing groups try to annex him, to make use of his famous name, to get him to make statements in their favour. Bujor wants to place himself above them and unite them. His decline has begun. He is no longer a prisoner of conscience, a living legend, a victim of the dictatorial regime of the bourgeois oligarchy. He is an ordinary man. The fact that he spent 13 years in prison is at most a detail, an accident of biography. The 'god' who descended among mortals has himself become a mortal. Bujor awakens strong resentments and irreconcilable enmities. Between the communists and Social Democrats there is a schism, engineered by Lenin. This rupture was not solely a Romanian problem. Bujor risks going from working-class hero to politician, a commonplace agitator, exposed to attacks. And this is what happens. The following is from a long, anonymous article, *On the road of Bujorism or on the road of Leninism*, published over a number of issues of *Deşteptarea*, between February and March 1934 (*Deşteptarea* was the weekly newspaper of Romanian-American communists in Detroit, which strictly towed the PCdR or rather Comintern line, that of Romanian communist refugees in Moscow, and published PCdR official documents): Mihai Gheorghiu Bujor is attacked for being "in cahoots with social fascists, opportunists, social monarchists, social traitors, social policemen." The reference is to the Social Democrats. The anonymous author wonders why Bujor was pardoned by the hangman king. The fact that he accepted the pardon made him guilty.

> "Bujor thinks that his historic mission is to revive the unity of the working class ... what a great joker you are, citizen Bujor! ... Bujor's role is ... to crush the working class ... such is the megalomania Bujor displays at every turn. ... Your release has not proved to be a victory for the working class. It has been shown to be a cunning and bold manoeuvre on the part of the enemy of the working class and the deadly enemies of communism and the USSR."

Bujor is a "tool to crush the proletarian movement and an enemy of the Communist Party." Why? Because he desired co-operation between the communists and the Social Democrats, at a time when Moscow forbade it. This policy paves Hitler's way to power. Stalin realises the new situation and makes one of his political about-turns. He demands the collaboration of all political forces against fascism. Naturally, in Bucharest the communists no longer reject any collaboration with the Social Democrats, but rather seek it. Talks are held, in which Bujor takes part. But a united Left front is not achieved. The communists were an illegal party. They were organising to overthrow the regime by violent means. Nor had they relinquished the slogan, "the right of the peoples of Romania to self-determination, as far as separation from the state."

The Social Democrats operated legally. They wanted reforms and recognised democratic institutions. It was an unbridgeable gulf. Caught between the two groups, Bujor loses stature. Unexpectedly, he is invited to the Kremlin. From November 1935 to January 1936, he travels around the USSR. He crosses the border at Tiraspol and reaches Moscow in time to attend the 7 November parade in Red Square. His itinerary takes in the palaces of the Tsars at Tsarskoe Selo, Peterhof, Moscow, and Leningrad, and then on to Minsk, Kiev and Gomel. Everywhere he sees 'signs of plenty' and 'the working class dictating and ruling'. He visits Kharkhov, Grozny, and Baku. Everywhere he goes he sees Stalin's name. He has a number of meetings at Comintern headquarters. He is received by Stalin and other Soviet leaders. Communist legends tell that thanks to him putting a word in with Stalin, Sahia was released from the Lubyanka.

A Siguranță report[4] reveals how "having arrived in Moscow, Bujor proceeded to the home of Racovski. This fact, constituting solidarity on the part of Bujor with Racovski, who is currently in disgrace, almost caused conflict between the Romanian socialist and the Soviet authorities that continually supervised his correspondence. … Racovski received instructions from the Central Committee of the Russian Communist Party to convince Bujor to accept the eventual position of leader of the Popular Front in Romania. Bujor avoided such discussions, explaining that he was on a fact-finding mission. … As for the efforts made by Racovski to get him to acccept the leadership of the Romanian Popular Front, the Russian Politburo thinks that the former Soviet ambassador to Paris was not insistent enough, because it is Bujor's opinion that a strong anti-fascist front cannot be achieved except

---

[4] ANCR, CC of the PCR Archive, Fund 95, Dossier 9/524, vol. 6, pp. 69-70.

with the collaboration of the Trotskyite Fourth International. Bujor argues that inasmuch as the Third International is bound to the life of the Soviet State, it ought to make use of the Fourth International for the success of anti-fascist propaganda. ... in Moscow, Bujor had a second meeting with Stalin, who reproached him for being able to endure 'the Romanian prison regime' but then being won over by 'Trotskyite phraseology'."

Racovski knew Bujor well, from before the war. Bujor had been his second-in-command at Odessa. Why did Stalin want to meet him? Firstly, because he was curious to meet a legend. He also had the Asiatic habit of wanting to 'touch' his adversaries, their glories, those he thought might count. Much had been said about Bujor. Bujor's formulation, "a single working class, a single party, a single union," interested him. This is the era of the Popular Front. The Seventh Congress of the Comintern, which launched this policy through the speech of Georgi Dimitrov, had recently ended, in August 1935. Was Bujor the man they were looking for in order to give him a role in this about-turn? Stalin and the Comintern leaders were still looking, after so many failures, for a solution to the chronic weakness of the 'workers' movement' in Romania. He could be summoned to Moscow, to the Comintern, as an exponent of the new non-sectarian line. He could be exhibited throughout Europe, at congresses. He could be made to take the podium at anti-fascist meetings, which propagated the Comintern's new policy. Bujor did not convince them, since his situation remained unchanged.

After his return to Romania, he is increasingly isolated, a figure who attempts to reconcile left-wing groups with each other, nothing more. His return from the USSR is pounced upon by the press. "Bujor arrived this morning from the USSR and commenced with his Bolshevik propaganda," writes Octavian Goga's newspaper, *Țara noastră* (*Our Country*). Nor does the event elude *Universul* (*From Unamuno to Bujor*). Bujor is preparing to publish a book entitled *The USSR, Impressions of a Journey*, but the censors ban it. It will not printed until 1944. We know how Bujor viewed the Moscow show trials in which his comrades, Russian and Romanian Bolsheviks, were exterminated. Racovski is one of the victims, but there are also other famous figures: Al. Dobrogeanu-Gherea, Al. Nicolau, Al. Bădulescu, Ion Dic. Dissescu, Leon Lichtblau, Saul Ozias, and Alter Zalic, all of whom are executed. Bujor frequently publishes in the press poems and memoirs of prison. He translates from Russian. He writes pamphlets. His presence, in spite of calls for unity, is losing its clout. He is forgotten. From being a 'prisoner of conscience', with the aura of a revolutionary – a propaganda myth disseminated by the Comintern – he becomes a commonplace militant who cannot find a place for himself. We meet him most often at gatherings of the Socialist Party, led by Constantin Popovici, also frequented by Gheorghe Cristescu. A police report notes that he gave a speech in a meeting held at the Party's headquarters at No. 13 Smîrdan Street on 17 February 1937. In his speech he explained that the Moscow trials were caused by old rivalries between the leaders of the Revolution. Trotsky had lost and then dedicated himself to subversion and terrorism. His agents had been captured and punished by Stalin. Here we see Bujor adopting the official Kremlin line. In the autumn of 1937, during the election campaign, he surfaces again, calling for unity against the PNL. The communists rehabilitate him. Bujor takes part alongside Pătrășcanu in the negotiations with the PNȚ and PSD. C. Titel Petrescu's PSD and L. Ghelerter and Șt. Voitec's Unified PSD reject any collaboration with the PCdR, as well as with the PNȚ, giving as their reason the non-aggression pact Iuliu Maniu had signed with the Iron Guard. This is what Bujor writes concerning Ilie Moscovici, an opponent of collaboration between the PNȚ and the PCR:

> "Thanks to his rancour, capriciousness and conceitedness, the Romanian workers' movement remains split. … He is a liability to the workers' movement in Romania. The sick man needs to be taken to a sanatorium. … Ilie Moscovici is an old and incorrigible recidivist when it comes to insults and lies … Who is it that has not been splashed by his laundry tub?"[5]

The language is extremely harsh. Bujor seems to have forgotten the campaigns Moscovici conducted for his release from prison, or that he was waiting for him at the prison gates when he finally was released.

The royal dictatorship supervenes. Mihai Gheorghe Bujor is arrested once more and convicted of Bolshevik propaganda. Sentenced to a year in prison, he arrives in Doftana once more, where he is held from June 1938 to August 1939. In 1940, he is interned in the prison camp at Miercurea Ciuc, and then the one in Caracal. In 1941, he is moved to the camp at Tîrgu Jiu, where he is held until August 1944. After 1944 he holds various honorary positions. He is often made use of in official propaganda. He lives on until

---

[5] *Adevărul*, 19 December 1937.

the 1970s, forgotten. He sometimes publishes memoirs, which are heavily censored.

2. *Alexandru Sahia*

Alexandru Sahia dies in August 1937. He was 29 (born 1908, real name Alexandru Stănescu). A few newspapers publish obituaries. Ion Călugăru, in *Reporter* (22 August), writes,

> "With Sahia a martyr of our guild has passed away, a typical representative of martyred Romanian intellectuals. ... He was a gentle lad, nondescript, not brilliant in his speech and clumsy in his movements. ... He did not seem to be passionate about general ideas ... on the contrary, he seemed destined to make his way through the crowd at the periphery of our intellectual life with modesty and humility."

Constantin Noica writes,

> "If he did not persuade you of the justice of his cause, he impressed you by his capacity for suffering and compassion. Perhaps there was something romantic concealed in Sahia's social struggle. For this young man from the country to stand in the midst of the workers at the few factories in Bucharest, participating in their sufferings ... – if it was to the class struggle that he felt the call – ... required much idealism, decidedly more than his cause deserved. ... In his bearing could be seen something of what we imagine today must have been primitive Christianity."

Arşavir Acterian writes,

> "He was as good as a wholesome loaf of bread and worn down by a poverty he did not know how to cope with. ... From being a disillusioned monk, he became a communist. ... In the end, the villains who had used him, his revolt and his naïvety, sacked him."[6]

In Detroit, *Deşteptarea* dedicates a page to him. The Romanians of the international brigades in Spain pay him homage. A Siguranţă report observes,

---

[6] *Vremea*, 22 August 1937.

"The communist journalists, who are part of the legal press college of the Communist Party, intend to give a political character to the funeral of communist journalist Alexandru Sahia, author of the book *The USSR Today*, which will take place today, 13 August, in the village of Mănăstirea, Ilfov county. To this end, the Communist Party has taken the decision that the entire press corps should travel to the village to attend the funeral. … Al. Sahia made a name for himself above all thanks to his articles on the CFR Grivitza trial and the Ana Pauker trial. The death of journalist Alexandru Sahia will be exploited by the communists for propaganda purposes."[7]

The situation is paradoxical, absurd. Only a few days before his death, Sahia was classed as an 'enemy of the Communist Party'. The reason for the conflict between him and the other tenants of the underground seems to have been the Great Terror, and in particular the orders from the Comintern on the subject of what propaganda should be issued about the Moscow show trials. In the months before his death, in the first part of 1937, Sahia was expelled from the PCdR by a number of his friends: firstly, Ștefan Foriș, head of PCdR Agitprop, to whom he was close, then Leonte Răutu, Sorin Toma, and Aurel Rotemberg (Ștefan Voicu after the war). Nor was Lucrețiu Pătrășcanu a stranger to the affair. Among the journalists in the communist cell headed by Sahia were Gheorghe Dinu (who wrote surrealist poetry under the name Ștefan Roll), Gherasim Luca, Miron Radu Paraschivescu, George Macovescu, Ion Călăguru, and Gheorghe Ivașcu. There was another reason for his exclusion. Sahia had travelled around the USSR. Suspected of espionage, he was arrested and sent to the Lubyanka. Like in Kafka, the repercussions were soon felt in the world of secret files where nothing is ever lost. He is released, but the fact that he was not investigated places him among those tainted by suspicion forever. In the first purge he is expelled from the ranks of the Comintern. This was the logic of the system: "The GRU does not make mistakes." Fortunately for him, he was in Bucharest when he was expelled, not in Moscow, where he would have ended up in front of a firing squad in the Lubyanka. Still alive, Sahia was banished from the underground as a pariah. Dead, he could be used as a 'martyr of the proletariat' or a 'working-class intellectual', 'murdered by the wretched world of the bourgeoisie'. PCdR propaganda, conducted by

---

[7] ANCR, CC of the PCR Archive, Fund 95, Dossier 131, p. 64.

Ștefan Foriș, who had expelled him, does not hesitate to make use of Sahia's corpse. A year later, the PCdR exploits the anniversary of Sahia's death. The same communist journalists, at the orders of the Agitprop section run by Foriș, try to organise a pilgrimage to his grave. It was an opportunity for pro-Bolshevik speeches and invectives against capitalism, as well as to mobilise the workers to be brought by truck to Mănăstirea Cemetery, the local peasants, and the deceased's relatives. After a number of delays and unsuccessful attempts, Gheorghe Dinu (Ștefan Roll) is forced to call off the pilgrimage. The manoeuvres are kept under close surveillance by the Siguranță.

Sahia travelled to the USSR not as a privileged guest or a famous writer. VOKS and Comintern did not lay on ceremonies. He was not interviewed by the press. He did not receive royalty payments. He was a nondescript journalist from a small country. What interest could the Comintern have in him? Yagoda's men, however, were interested in him. In fact, Sahia was a communist, a clandestine. But it was the clandestines who were suspected most of all. What if they were double agents or provocateurs? What if he had come to the USSR using the cover of journalist and communist sympathiser, but in fact was a spy? These questions cost him an interrogation in the Lubyanka. He was released without explanation and sent back to Romania. He takes the first train, via Warsaw, stops over in Paris, and returns to Bucharest. We find nothing about this dramatic experience in his book *The USSR Today* or in his press articles. Sahia did not repeat the mistake Istrati made. A few references in others' memoirs record Sahia's shock. Petre Pandrea writes, "Al. Sahia … was held under arrest in Moscow for a few weeks, as a Romanian spy. It was winter. He caught a cold. This developed into tuberculosis. Late on, he received a sweater from Pătrășcanu, who was in Moscow. At least this is the version that has remained in my mind. In any case, after his arrival from Moscow, Al. Sahia had dinner at my house one evening and told me his impressions. His book had been published. It was written before he visited the earthly paradise he was expecting. He realised that it was not a paradise, that Panait Istrati and André Gide were right. Al. Sahia returned from Moscow disillusioned. He wept in our arms … Here was a man in search of ardent, absurd ideals… and he did not find them. We, the anti-fascists, were alarmed. We implored him not to share the fate of Panait Istrati. To be disillusioned, but not a renegade, especially given that his apologia for Soviet achievements had been published. … Al. Sahia died disillusioned. There are streets named after him, statues, and poems. If he had lived, he would have ended up in prison with us, the sympathisers of Bolshevism and the planned economy."[8] Sahia preserved his silence. His interrogation in Moscow was known only to a few. It remained a secret.

Whereas alive he could no longer be of service to the 'cause' – whence his expulsion from the PCdR – dead he was still useful. He was made use of after 1945 in order to consolidate the regime he had dreamed of. The propaganda made use of his corpse, his memory, in order to construct a myth. He became an object of worship. He was presented as a great writer, living in poverty, a saint who sacrificed himself to the cause of the proletariat. He was included in literature textbooks and presented as a model. He was obligatory reading, one of the classics of Romanian literature. He was the true type of the writer and journalist who describes the misfortunes of the many and the struggle for their cause. He showed intellectuals "the true path," that of fraternity with the working masses. He was presented as a victim of the bourgeoisie. It was the bourgeoisie that was responsible for his premature death. Dozens of editions of his few novellas were printed, in millions of copies. Books were published about his life and 'work'. Thousands of articles were dedicated to him. His birth date was always marked by propaganda conducted by Iosif Chișinevschi and Leonte Răutu. He was elected to the Romanian Academy post mortem in 1948. Streets, schools, villages, collective farms and various institutions were named after him. The Romanian Academy and Writers' Union dedicated commemorative events to him. Why such zeal for an obscure writer? Because his writing satisfied the demands of the official ideology. It was useful to the rewriting of inter-war history and, above all, the history of the communist movement. In his prose, Sahia describes the workers, the harsh life in the factories, industrial accidents, merciless exploitation by the bosses, strikes, conflicts with management, and repression. Here we find all the Bolshevik clichés. The communist press of the 1920s and 1930s did not describe the workers' situation otherwise. Sahia includes in his writing the slogans and watchwords of the manifestos and pamphlets clandestinely published by the PCdR. This was the material used by the propagandists to create the 'Al. Sahia' legend, after 1945. They exploited his life, but also his prose. He was depicted as a working-class intellectual, a radical, devoted

---

[8] Petre Pandrea, *Memoriile mandarinului valah*, Bucharest: Albatros, 2000, p. 345.

to the cause, poor, sleeping on the floors of newspaper offices, going to the factories and workshops to talk to the workingman. He died of tuberculosis contracted as a result of poverty. This was the official portrait, the myth.

His biography reveals to us a different story and a different man, however. He did not come from a poor family. He was born in the village of Mănăstirea, on the Danube. He studied at the military lycée in Craiova, preparing for a career as an officer. Barracks life leads to his first existential crisis. He abandons his military career. He completes his studies at the St. Sava Lycée. He enrols in the Law Faculty. His second crisis ensues, this time religious. He abandons worldly life and becomes a monk. He joins the Cernica Monastery, at the age of 21, where he takes the monastic name Sahia, which he will preserve as his pen name. Monastic life is similar to that of the military boarding school, with its closed walls, and Sahia fails to adapt. He loses his faith. He begins to read Marxist literature. Prey to another crisis, he abandons the monastery. In 1932, he gets a job at the *Vremea* newspaper, and works in the press until August 1937. The *proletcult*[9] myth says that he gave up his studies due to poverty. His family was well off. His father was a wealthy peasant and a former Liberal mayor. His brother was a prosperous innkeeper, his sister a teacher. Sahia worked for two newspapers, *Vremea* (*Time*) and *Dimineaţa* (*Morning*), and was well paid. He also ran a small taxi company, financed by the Soviet legation.

"When Al. Sahia fell ill with TB, there were not the medicines that there are today and treatment was long and costly … he was interned, at the expense of the newspaper office on Sărindar,[10] in the Dr Popper Sanatorium in Bucegi, the most expensive in that day. The Donescu brothers [the owners of *Vremea* – author's note] leapt to his aid, his parents and friends also, but there was no longer any need. Al. Sahia was a sober man, who was able to dress elegantly from his two salaries, like a dandy. He did not have the vices of heavy drinking, or smoking,

---

[9] Russian portmanteau word, shortened from 'Пролетарская культура' (Proletarian Culture), a propaganda movement active in the USSR from 1917 to 1925. So-called 'proletcultism' was an aspect of the hard-line Stalinist ideology of the Dej period in Romania. – *Translator's note.*
[10] The "Sărindar press" was the left-wing press in Bucharest between the two world wars. It was named after the street where the left-wing newspapers' printing press was located – *Translator's note.*

or gambling, or motor-racing. Al. Sahia loved, and was loved, by many women, two of whom were superior, literate women. He was likeable, pleasant, amiable, like a fairy-tale prince … His parents were kulaks, innkeepers and Liberals. How could such a *dynamitard* and communist come from such a background? Come he did, all the same. Because Al. Sahia was not cut from the same cloth. He possessed fine antennae and intuition. He lived the problematic of the times. Al. Sahia is problematic man *per excellentiam*," writes Petre Pandrea in January 1968.

The famished figure of the myth is absent here. Sahia frequented the most exclusive circles; he was in contact with the most influential intellectuals. "Şuluţiu and then Sahia tell me about Lovinescu's memoirs."[11] In his diary, Petru Comarnescu describes him a number of times. Once was as a participant at the author's conference of January 1932, where he "applauded the passage about Russia, although it did not suit him." On another occasion they attend a dinner together, in January 1932. On 29 March, Sahia visits him to fetch an article for the crypto-communist *Veac nou* (*New Age*) magazine. On 3 April, he meets Sahia, Ghiţă Ionescu (a close friend of Sahia's according to a Siguranţă report), Zaharia Stancu and others. The next day, Sahia and Comarnescu go for a nocturnal stroll together.[12] In his circle of close acquaintances are to be found Eugene Ionesco, Ghiţă Ionescu, Radu Popescu et al., men of the Left, but also Mihail Polihroniade, Arşavir Acterian and Constantin Noica, from the other side of the political spectrum. He also knows Barbu Brezianu and Mihail Sebastian, whom he admonishes (in *Floare de foc* (*Flame Flower*), 30 January 1932) for having abandoned his previous communist beliefs. Sahia was also secretly connected with communists Ştefan Foriş, Lucreţiu Pătrăşcanu, Moscu Cohn and Alexandru Mihăileanu, as well as the lawyers and journalists who defended them at their trials. He is close to N. D. Cocea and Petre Pandrea. In 1933 and 1934 he reports on the CFR trials. In 1936, he sends daily reports about the Ana Pauker trial in Craiova to the *Dimineaţa* newspaper. The police catch him taking secret messages to the accused, concealed in an apparently inoffensive parcel.

---

[11] Camil Petrescu, *Note Zilnice* (10 September 1931), Editura Gramar, 2003, p. 41.

[12] Petru Comarnescu, *Jurnal, 1931-1937*, Jassy: Institutul European, 1994, pp. 16, 22, 42, 43.

"Inspecting a parcel brought by Sahia, an editor for *Dimineața*," the police report states, "we ascertained that (1) there was a message written on a matchstick in a box of Atentt matches and a number of signs on the bottom of the box, (2) there was a leaf of cigarette paper with pricks made by a needle hidden in the heel of a shoe, (3) almost the whole of the wrapping paper had pricks made by a needle. On one of the eggs in the parcel sent to detainee Estera Radosoveschy [*sic.*] we discovered written the words TOT and DUE. The writing appeared when held to the flame of a candle."

Likewise, a blouse brought for Ana Pauker bore inscriptions and a note found by a Siguranța agent contained a list written in German containing the names of the members of the War Council.[13] He is not arrested or tried only thanks to Emil Pauker and Constantin Graur, the owners of the press in Sărindar, who intervene. Sahia was not only a journalist. He was a communist agitator. He belonged to the underground. He was not merely a 'fellow traveller', but a communist, a 'professional revolutionary'. The following is an excerpt from a Siguranța report of 1936:

"On the occasion of the Luka László trial, communist Ana Pauker ... was brought to the War Council to testify. ... From Văcărești Prison, Ana Pauker was escorted on foot by a single warder. Her return to Văcărești Prison took place on 11 December, in the same way, and Alexandru Sahia appeared on the street, and the guard escorting her allowed him to take her the rest of the way by taxi. Given that by such procedures a detainee might very easily escape, being able to vanish by motor car, rescued by the communists ... we have the honour to request that you should be so kind as to take measures."[14]

Sahia also writes for a number of publications financed by the PCdR: *Veac Nou, Floare de foc, Buletin, Bluze albastre* (*Blue Shirts*), *Reporter, Șantier* (*Building Site*). He takes part in all the campaigns ordered by the Comintern in the 1930s. In 1932, he launches a bitter attack on Istrati in an article entitled *What a scoundrel you are, Comrade Panait!* He writes in defence of Mihai Gheorghiu Bujor, the Grivitza strikers, Petre Constantinescu-Iași,

[13] *Universul*, 14 June 1936.
[14] ANCR, CC of the PCR Archive, Fund 95, Dossier 12316, p. 128.

etc. He does not limit himself to writing articles. He is one of the campaign organisers, working for Agitprop. The underground activities of Sahia the journalist do not elude the Siguranţă. They keep him under surveillance; they intercept his mail. Sometimes they follow him. They report his relations with the Soviet legation, his trip to the USSR, his entourage made up of communists. A file on him is kept. Nevertheless, he is never arrested or interrogated by the Siguranţă. All the same, he is marked down as an editor of a number of communist publications financed by the Comintern. The police confiscate these as soon as they leave the press, before they can be distributed. Once such a publication is banned, another is printed a few months later, under a different name, but with the same editors. Sahia is always among them. He is seen spreading communist propaganda among soldiers when he is called up in 1932. He is investigated by the counter-espionage service. A report presents him as,

> "a communist sympathiser … he shares communist principles, which he has expressed in the communist magazine *Bluze albastre*… the same principles he has exposited verbally among his student colleagues at university. Inasmuch as the above-named expresses his communist convictions in a doctrinaire form, with the content of the magazines being drawn from various communist authors and news originating from the global communist press, the Department has not taken any measures against him, but a file is kept on his activity. The above-named is to be kept under surveillance during his military service and not to be assigned any duties of trust."[15]

He does not give up communist propaganda even at university.

> "Gathering information in the Law Faculty in Bucharest in order to identify student Isaiah … who, in the class of Professor Istrate Micescu, conducted communist propaganda and who claimed he was a reporter for the *Facla* (*Firebrand*) newspaper, I established that at the Faculty there is no student named Isaiah. It is known, however, that in the Law Faculty in Bucharest there is to be found a third-year student by the name of Alexandru Sahia."[16]

---

[15] ANCR, CC of the PCR Archive, Fund 95, Dossier 131, pp. 34-35.
[16] *Idem*, p. 30.

After his return from the USSR, the Siguranță is alert to the fact that he frequents the Soviet legation and to his links with various Soviet couriers. They intercept his correspondence with Moscow. The activities that precede the launch of his book about Russia, as well as its contents, press reviews etc., are likewise recorded by the Siguranță. A report requests that the Interior Ministry should answer the question of whether,

"this book is going to be allowed to be distributed in bookshops ... because it is nothing more than an apologia for the people and new times in the USSR ... The unhindered publication of such books, the reading of *Izvestia* and above all, given it is in an accessible language, *The Moscow Journal* [on sale in a number of Bucharest bookshops – *author's note*] today completes the education of youth and the documentation of older people, not to mention the highly successful clandestine infiltration of communist propaganda literature from abroad. We repeat: this is how propaganda is conducted and this is how ideological intransigence is reached."[17]

His book, *The USSR Today*, is published in the autumn of 1935. It is a mixture of clichés, lazy thinking and Agitprop slogans. A conformist book. His friends Ghiță Ionescu, Radu Popescu (in *Cuvîntul liber* (*The Free Word*)), Al. Robot (in *Reporter*), and Alecu Constantinescu (in *Credința* (*The Faith*)) write favourable reviews. The book is a faux reportage, garnished with official statistics and figures. These alternate with prudent personal observations. A throwback to his time in Cernica Monastery, he frequently observes the religious situation, the large number of churches, their demolition. Like Istrati and Mihai Gheorghiu Bujor, he takes part in the 7 November festivities in Red Square. There are no incidents. The opposition has been crushed. Stalin is absolute master. "A twelve-storey building, covered with a panel showing Stalin wearing a soldier's greatcoat, with jackboots as tall as one storey, with a worker's cap on his head, with his left hand in the pocket of his greatcoat and his right held over his heart." Sahia finds out that Kirov has been murdered while he is in the USSR. He dedicates a single sentence to this huge political event. On the other hand, he dedicates dozens of pages to enthusiastic descriptions and official statistics. The trip lasts three months, for one and a half months of which, writes Sahia, "I wandered the streets of Moscow at will." In fact, he had been imprisoned in the Lubyanka. He

---

[17] *Idem*, pp. 55-57.

visits Leningrad, Nizhni Novgorod, the Volga region, Ukraine, and Soviet Moldavia (Tiraspol). He travels alone, unaccompanied by any officials, as he reminds us with suspicious frequency. He is at pains, he assures us, not to be shown any Potemkin villages. Everywhere he takes note of the churches and the official anti-religious propaganda. He is interested in the condition of women and intellectuals. He bumps into Henri Barbusse and Boris Pilnyak, who is also a figure in Istrati's book. Pilnyak even describes to him the conversations he had with Istrati. Pilnyak was to have a tragic end, placed in front of a firing squad in 1938.[18] Sahia is in no hurry to return to Bucharest. He makes a detour through Warsaw, Vienna, Paris, Milan, Venice, Trieste and Belgrade. He needs time to recover. Sahia maintains his silence. He does not recount the experiences he underwent in the USSR. Not even after he is expelled from the PCdR does he protest. Has he abandoned his revolutionary ideals? Does he remain loyal to Stalin? His premature death prevented him from going through another of his existential crises, which for him were cyclical and ineluctable.

> "Alexandru Sahia had a large heart and a bird brain. He was as uncultured as a boot and as enthusiastic as a boarding-school girl. Nae Ionescu was right when he advised us to avoid *Schwärmerei. Al. Sahia war der typische Schwärmer.* He felt an imperious need to believe in something profound and great. He tried to believe in God and took refuge among the monks of Cernica for two years. He did not succeed. He fell out with them. Divine grace did not descend upon him … He was a lazy man, fantastically indolent. Instead of buying a few hundred kilos of firewood for the winter, he would dress up as a dandy and shiver in the centre of town, hanging around the self-service canteens, newspaper offices and printing presses. He was a mystical snob. He swallowed aspirins to keep warm. … Sahia did not attend university courses regularly, because he would have liked to make two revolutions in five years. First a moral revolution, with the priests, then a communist revolution, with the workers. … He greatly needed to do the work of an apostle and thought he would find it in the Left. … Sahia's pilgrimage to Mecca ended in an ideological catastrophe, similar to Istrati's. … Sahia was desolate and disoriented. … He did not have the intellectual courage of Panait Istrati to spit on what he had once worshipped. He was also a sick man."[19]

[18] Al. Sahia, *URSS, azi*, Editura Librăriei Ion Creangă, 1935, p. 234.
[19] Petre Pandrea, *Turnul de ivoriu*, Bucharest: Vremea, 2004, pp. 56-58.

Had he survived, perhaps after the war he would have fallen victim to the purges. He had been guilty of friendship with Foriş and Pătrăşcanu, both of them slain by their comrades. Or perhaps he could have become, like so many others, one of the officials in charge of propaganda, the author of socialist realist prose, in which he would have praised the regime's achievements and the new workers' paradise to the skies. There was a time when "the restless and implacable ghost of Sahia used to haunt the RPR."[20]

Today, Sahia is forgotten. His myth, created after the war by the propaganda section run by Iosif Chişinevschi and Leonte Răutu, has likewise been forgotten.

3. *Constantin Doncea*

The Romanian-language communist weekly *Deşteptarea* (*The Awakening*), which was published in Detriot between the First and Second World Wars, announced on the front-page of its 17 March 1934 issue that the Mihai Gheorghiu Bujor Society was changing its name to the Constantin Doncea Society. It had adopted the name of Bujor in the 1920s because "he was a symbol of the working class in Romania. We were proud of him, we revered him, we glorified him … Bujor was sentenced to life imprisonment. …" Bujor's sins were his reprieve in the summer of 1933 and, above all, the reconciliatory line he had adopted after his release. Bujor wanted to unify the working class. As a result, the obdurate Romanian-American communists of Detroit, on the barricades of the class struggle, adversaries of social democracy and reformist trends, decided to choose a new patron.

Who was Constantin Doncea? Royal Commissar Romulus Hotineanu says,

> "He is one of those who have sought to stand out from the rest. A brawny man. Not very intelligent. A man of preconceptions. He has a single aim, that of causing disturbances, whenever and wherever. He wants to be at the forefront of the unions, as a new man, as a Messiah. For the working class, Doncea is a calamity, a disaster. … Lacking in any kind of intelligence or talent, Doncea has imposed himself upon the leadership in a brutish way, carried there by other interests, of course … Consequently, Doncea, on every occasion, through both legal and

---

[20] *Idem*, p. 55.

illegal acts, machinates against the national security, in preparation for the fatal day."[21]

Constantin Doncea dominated the Grivitza strike and the two trials that followed. All the other accused in the dock are secondary figures. Doncea is perceived as the leader of the strikers by the judges. He receives the heaviest sentence. The press takes note of everything he says and does. In his defence, he speaks for four hours during a nocturnal session of the court. For a simple worker, he is impressive. Gheorghiu-Dej is a colourless figure in comparison. Dej is neither an orator nor a leader of the masses. Doncea spoke like a typical union demagogue. He agitated the workers with his raucous radicalism. He was "the feared and uncontested leader of the communists at the CFR Bucharest Workshops."[22] From 1933 onward, he is the centre of press attention. Committees in his support are formed and protests for his release are held. A Doncea myth is born. In the 1930s, he becomes the most famous figure of the Romanian working class. He is popularised by the Left as a working-class hero.

In January 1935, together with Gheorghe Vasilichi and Dumitru Petrescu he makes a spectacular escape from Craiova Prison. He fires the imagination of many people. They are on the side of the victims, of those who defy the authorities. Doncea is at the apogee of his notoriety. He is a kind of folk hero. We find reports of his escape in many European newspapers. After a while, he is said to have reached the USSR, which is true. The shadowy organisers of his escape were Marcel Pauker and Moscu Cohn. Doncea reaches the USSR in June. He studies for two years at Lenin's school for cadres. He becomes a Soviet citizen and a member of the CPSU. He learns Russian. From the autobiography[23] he writes in Russia we learn that he was born in Cocu, Argeş county, in 1904. A smelter by trade, he did only five years of primary schooling. A member of the PCdR since 1931, he has no position in the hierarchy. He has not been a member of any other party. His rise was strictly through the trades unions. He claims repeatedly that he led the Grivitza strike.

The Bolsheviks were obsessed with finding leaders of the masses, to

---

[21] *Universul*, 12 August 1933.

[22] ANCR, CC Archive of the PCR, Fund 96, Dossier 5485, p. 94.

[23] Gh. Buzatu, *Românii în arhivele Kremlinului*, Bucharest: Editura Univers Enciclopedic, 1996.

organise strikes, to make themselves heard. Doncea was such a figure. He is a proletarian who has risen from the bottom, a man heard by 'the many'. His influence over the workers was real, where the PCdR had only failed. This, too, arouses the communists' interest. He is drawn into the underground networks. Doncea, like Luca, is a worker. His two trials allow the Comintern to carry out agitation and to present the 'proletariat' as a united force opposing the bourgeoisie and the oligarchic regime. Doncea and Luca come from the world the Bolsheviks needed in order to legitimise themselves, the world they claimed to represent: the proletariat. Luca did not organise any large-scale protests. He was more a man of underground conspiracy, after having been a man of public meetings and speeches. Doncea was a man of action. He imposed his will at Grivitza by means of his energy and even the violence with which he led the CFR workers and incited them to strike. After the crushing of the strike, the Comintern transformed him into a hero of the proletariat. He met all the requirements. The 'workers' cause' had found a concrete, flesh-and-bones figurehead. The Agitprop quickly embraces him, constructing his legend and promoting him by its channels. Doncea becomes a very well-known figure, one popularised at every opportunity by the Left. His heroic image flows from the drama of the conflict at the CFR Workshops, the dead and the wounded, the arrest of Doncea and his comrades; then the dramatic, spectacular trials, and the very heavy sentences handed down. All these ingredients make him a dramatic figure, one easily peddled by an expert propaganda apparatus.

After studying at the Comintern's school for cadres, Doncea trains with the GPU and becomes an agent. In March 1937, a Soviet newspaper in Odessa publishes the news of his murder. Doncea had been trying to cross the Dniester into Romania, but was caught by Soviet border guards and taken to Odessa Prison, from which he tried to escape, being killed by GPU agents in the attempt.[24] A Siguranță report observes,

"the matter of him being shot has not been verified among the communist leaders in Romania, and this system is one of the Comintern's procedures so that news of the death of important communists will be published in the press, and so that they can then be sent abroad to operate clandestinely, because Doncea enjoyed great popularity among

---

[24] ANCR, CC of the PCR Archive, Fund 95, Dossier 790, p. 27.

the CFR workers, as is known from the past, a case similar to communist Ana Pauker."[25]

Doncea is sent not to Romania, but to Spain, where civil war has broken out. He is a member of the international brigades. His name is already circulating. Sent by the NKVD, he is a political commissar, the best-known figure among the Romanians. His legend precedes him. In 1939, he is interned in the St Cyprien camp in southern France, where he runs the Party cell, with around 100 men. Relations between the members of the international brigades are tense. There are personal and ethnic conflicts, mutual suspicion, splits. The failure in Spain gave birth to demoralisation, in contrast to the enthusiasm of 1936. There is also physical deprivation: makeshift, chilly huts on the seashore, scarce rations, lack of clothing, complete isolation. After the international campaign of mobilisation between 1936 and 1938, the Comintern lost interest, and the anti-fascist movement grew weary. In addition, NKVD agents and political commissars kept watch over ideological purity and loyalty in the ranks. The Trotskyites and anarchists who broke ranks were purged, often physically liquidated. Doncea, as a political commissar (all such commissars were NKVD agents), played such a role. He was the eyes and ears of the NKVD and Comintern among the brigade members, both at the front and in the St Cyprien camp. He is an important leader and zealously carries out the mission entrusted to him in Moscow. It is the only subordination he can tolerate. His prominent position and the role he has played cause him to be listed among the important prisoners. This is why he is taken from the camp to Moscow. Thousands of other brigade members remain in the French camps. Doncea arrives in the USSR by ship, together with a few hundred Spanish officials and high-ranking brigade members. He disembarks at Odessa. In Moscow, Dimitrov regards him as the most important of the Romanian communist refugees in the USSR. Although Ștefanov was head of the PCdR at that time, Doncea, given his international renown, justified Dimitrov's appreciation.

His star begins to wane after his return to the USSR, however. His difficult temperament and the disordered life he led both contributed to this. He was comfortable in the midst of a conflict, leading the 'masses'. He was not at all a politician, a man of behind the scenes intrigues – essential qualities inside the Comintern. His rudimentary schooling did not help

---

[25] *Idem*, pp. 28-29.

him to ascend the hierarchy of the cosmopolitan and ideologically educated apparatus made up of the guests at the Hotel Lux.

After his return from Spain and France, Doncea has problems with the Soviets, who view the brigades with suspicion. Given his indomitable character, he had caused plenty of conflicts at the front and in the camps. In the USSR we do not find him in the upper echelons of the Comintern, as he had been expecting, but in the lower ranks. War breaks out and he is not among the privileged persons evacuated to Ufa, near the Urals, on Stalin's orders. He has no political work to do. The arrival of Ana Pauker, who was not at all sympathetic to him, is the real beginning of his decline. Pauker and Doncea were the acknowledged figureheads of the Romanian Communist Party. They had been the protagonists in two highly publicised trials, and had been transformed into cult figures by Agitprop. Pauker was the favourite of Molotov, Dimitrov and Manuilski. Doncea took second place. He writes to her many times, begging her to find him a different role, one worthy of his merits and stature. He saw himself playing an important role. He does not manage to convince her. Pauker preferred Vasile Luca when she needed a Romanian worker to enhance the social make-up of the 'new leadership'.

Doncea spends the war first in a military school then on the Crimean front. On 19 August 1944 he is parachuted into Romania. After the war, the legend of a so-called group of partisans in the Carpathians, led by Doncea, was created. In fact, he was parachuted behind German lines, as a Soviet soldier, to carry out a reconnaissance mission. The 'heroic history of the PCdR' required that he should be the organiser of 'armed resistance against the Nazi occupier'. Doncea was injured during the parachute jump, landing badly. The only thing left for him to do was wait for Soviet troops to arrive. Thus the legend of Doncea the partisan is born.

His post-war career is equally tangled, but less glorious. His name is connected with the demolition of the statues in central Bucharest, during his stint as deputy mayor. The statues of Kings Carol I and Ferdinand, and of former Prime Ministers I. C. Brătianu, I. I. C. Brătianu and Take Ionescu are bulldozed. Ana Pauker dislikes him. Doncea was the only one who overshadowed her thanks to his 'revolutionary' past. Gheorghe Gheorghiu-Dej dislikes him for the same reasons. Nevertheless, Dej and Doncea join forces to depose Ana Pauker. Doncea hated her for sidelining him in the USSR. He hoped that with Ana Pauker gone he would return to the forefront. Others, with a less glorious past than his, were members of the Political Bureau or the Secretariat. At the congress of February 1948, he is not elected to the CC of the PMR; at the congress of 1955 he becomes an alternate member. He is given secondary positions. For this reason, Doncea is frustrated. He frequently complained to his old comrades who were now his hierarchical superiors. He made repeated requests for his merits to be recognised and for him to be rewarded with higher positions. He did not succeed. Dej was jealous of his past. And it was not merely a question of jealousy, but also legitimacy: who was more entitled to lead the Party? As Dej drew his legitimacy in the apparatus from the Grivitza strike, Doncea, the real leader of the strike, was an embarrassment to him. Doncea viewed Dej as a usurper. In comparison, Dej had a colourless political biography. One mysterious episode remains the critical situation in which Dej found himself in the summer of 1948, when the Soviets had isolated him and seemed to be preparing his downfall, suspecting him, as a result of a denunciation, of Titoism. Doncea, in Grivitza, mobilises the workers, which causes the 'plotters' to free Dej. How much of this is legend, is hard to determine today. A number of sources confirm it. Other sources remain silent. What is for sure is that in the 1950s and 1960s Doncea claimed the merit of having saved Dej in the summer of 1948.

On the other hand, Doncea does not hesitate to criticise Dej in any situation, to claim that he was the protagonist of the "heroic struggle of the CFR workers in 1933," a hero of the Spanish Civil War, etc. Others would have been gaoled for less. Gheorghiu-Dej could not arrest or imprison him. Doncea was genuinely popular among the CFR workers. Most of the six thousand participants in the 1933 strike were still alive. The strike was the foundation of Gheorghiu-Dej's legitimacy. He therefore limited himself to keeping him away from power, not allowing him to take root in any position. Of all the figures in the upper echelons of the regime, he is the one who is most often dismissed, transferred, 'rotated'. Moreover, Dej orders his telephone to be tapped and plants informants in his entourage.[26] Gheorghiu-Dej is given reports about what he says, what he docs, whom he meets. In the 1950s, an exotic fauna gravitates around Doncea, made up of critics and malcontents, many of them former illegals, CFR workers, etc. Likewise, he maintains good relations with cultural figures, artists, and bohemians. Corneliu Baba paints his portrait (Dej had been painted by

---

[26] SRI Archive, Dossier 9604, vol. 23, pp. 1-3.

Iser). Miliţa Petraşcu (a pupil of Brîncuşi) made a bust of him. For this, he is severely criticised in the plenary of June 1958, as proof of the personality cult he is supposed to be encouraging. To have a statue of oneself made was the strict preserve of the established pantheon. "It's true I had a bust of myself in my house, made by sculptor Miliţa Petraşcu. Before this plenary it was taken away by some blokes holding pistols, who informed me that they were carrying out orders from above… This seizure of the goods that belong to me took place while I was an alternate member of the CC of the PMR, a deputy, a minister," writes Constantin Doncea, in a memorandum addressed to Nicolae Ceauşescu in 1966.[27] He buys paintings, but also receives gifts. He has a large art collection. Dej is determined to break up the group around him. Especially after the Hungarian Uprising of 1956, Dej understood the role that intellectuals could play, even those close to the regime. For purposes of intimidation, he orders people to be unmasked. Intellectuals were paraded in front of crowds of hundreds of workers, who jeered them and demanded they be punished, even executed. This was how they were "unmasked for their crimes against the regime." Then they would be sacked, evicted from their homes, fined, banned from meeting with each other. The most significant of these sinister sessions was held in the assembly hall of the Law Faculty in 1957,[28] when a number of cultural figures from Doncea's entourage were the target of "proletarian stigmatisation and fury."

In June 1958, it was Doncea's turn. His crime: he continued to contest the role Gheorghiu-Dej attributed to himself. After the events of 1958, Dej decides to purge the Party and to put a stop to the thaw. Doncea denied Dej's legitimacy as head of the PCdR. Foriş and Pătrăşcanu had been killed for this. Ana Pauker and Teohari Georgescu had been deposed. Luca would die in prison. Miron Contantinescu and Iosif Chişinevschi had lost their positions. Dumitru Petrescu, who had been involved in organising the strike and escaped from prison with Doncea and Vasilichi, likewise. In 1958, festivities are planned to celebrate the 25th anniversary of the strike. Doncea refuses to take part, saying, "Have your symposium, but I led the strike!" Gheorghiu-Dej reckons the time has come to get even with Doncea, as well as with the old guard, the CFR strikers who still saw Doncea as their uncontested leader. Dej and Doncea were old rivals.

---

[27] *Idem*, p. 6.

[28] See Stelian Tănase, *Anatomia unei mistificări*, Bucharest: Humanitas, 2003, pp. 167-180.

A plenary is staged, carefully orchestrated by Dej's henchmen. Dozens of CC members are unleashed on Doncea. They demolish the 'Doncea myth', even though some of them were its authors. Everything that the Comintern had constructed via Agitprop in the 1930s is negated, contradicted. Doncea and his deeds were nothing but a propaganda fiction. The official document of the plenary considered that Doncea was an "individualist, anarchic and disruptive element, imbued with petit bourgeois conceptions, dominated by petty, careerist ambitions, a limited man, with a reduced level of class consciousness … As long ago as the Grivitza struggles, he manifested his opportunist, anarchic-peasant habits."[29]

> "Insufferably conceited, attributing to himself merits that do not belong to him, in prison he continued his individualist, disruptive outbursts … Doncea behaved in the same way in the Soviet Union … Doncea's position and activity caused serious damage in Spain … After 23 August he continued with his anti-Party line of placing his own person above the Party and was a element that attracted and polarised all kinds of anti-Party elements, alien and inimical to the working class."[30] "Doncea, disregarding real facts, trampling underfoot the historical truth, has for many years been busy distorting the history of the Grivitza struggle, attempting for purposes of self-glorification to minimise the role of the Party leader, as well as the role of the Party cadres, with Comrade Gheorghiu-Dej at their forefront … In his lack of any common sense and his hatred of the Party's best cadres he goes so far as to slander those who endured the harsh conditions of Doftana. In Doftana Prison and in the camp, he says, it was easy, you had a bed, a bowl of soup … it was harder in Spain where you can take a bullet in the back at any moment."[31]

His old comrade from the international brigades, Mihai Burcă, says at the plenary, "Doncea … worked to undermine us. It is very hard for me to speak here about his dirty deeds … Speaking of heroism … Doncea fled."[32]

---

[29] Alina Tudor, Dan Cătănuş, *Amurgul ilegaliştilor. Plenara PMR din 9-13 iunie 1958*, Bucharest: Vremea, 2000, p. 17.

[30] *Idem*, p. 19.

[31] *Idem*, p. 41-42.

[32] *Idem*, p. 66.

Burcă is awarded on the spot with a place in the CC for this declaration. Part of the Doncea myth, his 'heroism' was contested. Not even Gheorghe Vasilichi, with whom Doncea escaped from prison in 1935, has anything good to say about him: "Limited, exceedingly conceited, arrogant, vain and ambitious … hence too his underestimation of the role of the Party leader. … His claims to have been the leader grew later and he was eternally dissatisfied." At this point, Dej interrupts, saying, "It seems we popularised him too much!" Vasilichi goes on, saying, "What characterises Doncea is his anarchic and dictatorial attitude … I've never met a more resentful man … Doncea has never studied in his life. … he's incapable of leading even himself, he doesn't have the qualities of a leader, but neither does he allow himself to be led by others." The uncontested leader of the CFR workers in 1933-1934 is completely negated, even by his erstwhile accomplices, Gheorghiu-Dej and Gheorghe Vasilichi. They had stood in the dock and been in prison together. He had escaped and fled to the USSR with Vasilichi.

For five days, Doncea was subjected to this process of vilification. He became a non-person. One of the myths of the proletariat, employed by the communists for reasons of power, was demolished by the very same people who had invented it. History is rewritten during the course of the plenary. The script remained the same, only the cast changed. Gheorghiu-Dej, the usurper of Doncea's position as leader of the CFR workers in 1933, presided over the operation. Everything that Doncea had ever done, his 'heroic past', was minimised and then negated. At the end of the plenary, Doncea was expelled from the PMR. He had been a member since 1931. He was taken to the Bărăgan Steppe, where he was made the director of the collective farm in the village of Ograda. A few years later, he was sacked and pensioned off. He was kept under surveillance. His telephone was still bugged. Informants reported on his everyday movements. Doncea did not cease to contest Gheorghiu-Dej and to speak about the role he had played in the 1930s. He survived Dej. On the death of his enemy in March 1965, he was sincerely jubilant. In front of the television, watching the funeral, he danced and laughed, shouting, "You've croaked! You've croaked!" He died in 1973.

XII
The Popular Front and the Great Terror

We communists are like dead men on holiday
Marcel Pauker

In August 1935, the Seventh Congress of the Communist International, the Comintern, is held. It is the first congress since 1928 and the last before the organisation is dissolved in 1943. The congress takes place between 25 July and 20 August, with 510 delegates from 65 countries. On behalf of the PCdR, Boris Ştefanov, Nicolae Goldberger, Marcel Pauker, and Şeila Averbuch participate. The congress legitimates the new policy, launched in December 1933 at the plenary of the Executive Committee of the Comintern (when Lucrețiu Pătrășcanu took part). From the point of view of the Comintern, the main dangers to the Bolshevik Revolution had, up to that time, been the bourgeoisie, fascism and 'social-fascism', i.e. social democracy. This policy split the forces of the Left and paved the way for Hitler to come to power. Stalin makes a U-turn, demanding that the communist parties should form anti-fascist coalitions, so-called 'popular fronts', with the Social Democrats.

> "Hitler replaces the powers that benefited from the Treaty of Versailles as the main adversary of the USSR and of peace. He is the vanguard of counter-revolution ... In this way communism and fascism clash head on within the revolution/counter-revolution dichotomy. ... Let the Popular anti-fascist front unite around the unique front of the working class, the backbone of the coalition. ... This is a new tactic proposed at the Seventh Congress. The final objective remains the dictatorship of the proletariat, the overthrow of the bourgeoisie all over the world. ... The Popular Front has taken the place of the 'class against class' struggle."[1]

The government in Moscow abandons its isolationist hard line and anti-Versailles diplomacy. The USSR signs accords with many European governments. The popular-front policy was dependant upon those accords.

---

[1] François Furet, *Trecutul unei iluzii. Eseu despre ideea comunistă în secolul XX* [*The Past of an Illusion. Essay on the Communist Idea in the 20th Century*], Bucharest: Humanitas, 1996, p. 240.

On the orders of the Comintern, the communist parties had to integrate themselves into the official political life of their countries. The means whereby to this was to attract various political groups into 'anti-fascist alliances'. Stalin did not trust the Comintern. He saw the Communist International as a network of foreign spies, who served not the USSR but the West. For Stalin, the Comintern was too undisciplined as an army in order to serve the Revolution. Given that he was xenophobic and suspicious of spies being everywhere, he did not view kindly the presence of thousands of foreigners in Moscow. In the period 1927-1928, Stalin succeeded in driving out Trotsky sympathisers and in deposing Grigori Zinoviev (the first president of the Comintern, in 1918), Lev Kamenev and Nikolay Bukharin, who had been close to Lenin. Subsequently, however, the organisation sank into lethargy. Stalin dedicated himself to "the construction of socialism in a single country," and was little interested in the scenario of 'world revolution'. The organisation was tolerated, without having any established objectives or any precise activity. It was a dinosaur of the Bolshevik Revolution and the civil war, unable to find a place or a role for itself. Stalin ignored the Comintern; he was suspicious, still undecided. However, during the same period, 1928-1935, he makes sure that it is subordinate to the Agitprop, the propaganda section of the CPSU and, above all, to the GPU, the political police. The old militants are replaced by new people, the Lenin generation, launched by Stalin in 1924. From now on, the Comintern is viewed as an annex to the activities of the USSR in the area of propaganda and espionage. "Stalin promoted a policy of NKVD and GPU penetration of the Comintern, but not the other way round. Up until 1935, the top leadership of the International had been an independent entity, but the differentiation lost any significance."[2] "This distinction between the NKVD and the Comintern ... was in effect nothing but an illusion."[3] The Comintern would have died a natural death, as a useless appendage, had Hitler not come to power. Hitler did not conceal that his mission was to revise the Treaty of Versailles, to redraw the borders etc. As Stalin was fearful of a war, his idea was 1) to provoke a conflict between Britain and France, on the one side, and Germany, on the other, as a step towards world revolution; and 2) to play for time. The aim was to mobilise public opinion

---

[2] Stephen Koch, *Sfîrșitul inocenței* [*The End of Innocence*], Bucharest: Albatros, 1997, p. 123.

[3] *Idem*, p. 122.

and to bring about a firm reaction against German rearmament on the part of Western governments. The Comintern finds a new use for itself after the fatal day of 30 January 1933. Once Joseph Stalin and Karl Rudek, the head of Agitprop, take it off the back burner, the Comintern emerges from isolation and the wilderness of sectarian politics to preach the alliance of all those who oppose Nazism: associations, parties, the press, trades unions, cultural figures. The essential aspect of this mobilisation was that it had to remain under the strict control of Moscow, through its undercover agents and the funds it supplied. The old Leninist principle of combining legal and illegal activities is hereby revived. On the surface, there is a magnanimous pacifist discourse of 'democracy under threat from fascism'. Below the surface, there can be found clandestine networks of spies and agents of influence, supplied with secret funds. "The new period that commences in 1934 provides it with a popular slogan and a political space whereby a vast apparatus of revolutionary subversion can be implanted throughout Europe."[4] The Comintern Congress of August 1935, in particular the speech delivered by Georgi Dimitrov, consolidates this new policy.

In order to achieve this about-turn imposed by the Comintern at the plenary of December 1933 in Moscow, Ana Pauker returns to Romania four months later. By various channels, activists trained in the schools of the Comintern arrive at the same time. The about-turn had to be accompanied by a reorganisation of the Party, which found itself in a critical situation. What was the situation of the clandestine PCdR networks? A report by the Siguranță provides a detailed description:

"As in 1933, 1934 has been a year of heavy defeats and retreat for the Communist International. To the defeat in Germany in 1933 can be added this year the defeat of the revolutionary movement organised in Austria (February), Latvia, Bulgaria (August/September) and Sarre, a few weeks ago. ... In Romania, the Communist Party, which had succeeded, in February 1933, during the strikes by the railway and petroleum workers, in raising itself to a height never before scaled and in leading the major deployments of the workers in their actions, has not yet regrouped after the defeat it suffered then, it has not succeeded since then in launching any important action. The movement has been reduced merely to verbal and written propaganda in various revolutionary

---

[4] François Furet, *op. cit.*, p. 244.

publications. ... Here in Romania, the communist movement has gone from around 1,200 members, as many as were registered as due-paying members in February 1933, to around 650 members. ... This failure of the united political front has had unimaginably large repercussions on the communist movement and on the workers in general, because it has caused disorientation to increase in their ranks and has enormously diminished the communists' prestige among the revolutionary masses. The organisational state of the Communist Party in Romania is much worse than that of the other sections of the Communist International."[5] "In its resolutions, the Communist Party recognises that its wretched organisational state cannot be attributed only to anti-communist repression. While this indeed resulted in serious damage in 1934, the deeper cause of the extreme organisational weakness of the Communist Party from Romania resides in the state of mind of the workers, who, although agitated by their professional grievances, are not, however, willing to adopt the communist ideology and to join revolutionary organisations. ... The party has decided that in its future propaganda it will display its own name as little as possible and disguise itself as much as possible, this is because a certain repulsion towards the communists has been observed on the part of the workers, after the disaster to which the communists led the railway workers at Grivitza."[6]

This crisis corresponds to a large-scale operation organised by the Comintern. The PCdR has to be reorganised, because it is in panic and disarray. The mission of the new leadership was to achieve a popular front. In March 1934, Ana Pauker arrives in Romania to lead this operation. At the same time, by various channels, as part of this Comintern deployment, there arrive around 50 trained activists, educated in the Party schools: professional revolutionaries. They are in the possession of significant funds to pay Party members, rent houses, print manifestos and posters, and finance various crypto-communist associations. They also bring funds to bribe various officials, especially in the police and judiciary, and pay lawyers representing communists brought to trial. The resumption of diplomatic relations with the USSR creates new opportunities. Propaganda materials proliferate, as well as actions to co-opt figures from public life: intellectuals

---

[5] MAN Archive, SSI fund, Dossier 67, vol. 1, pp. 29, 30, 33.
[6] *Idem*, pp. 36-37.

with left-wing sympathies or those predisposed to corruption and the usufruct of secret stipends.

In this new context, in 1934, Alexander Danieluc Stepanski-Gorn, the Secretary General of the PCdR, is dismissed. Besides a resolution of the crisis in the Party, the Comintern is also seeking the answer to another question. It needed someone determined to apply the new directives to achieve a popular front – someone not compromised by the sectarian tactics prior to 1934. In December 1934, Boris Ştefanov, a Bulgarian, nephew of Cristian Racovski, is designated. He is close to Georgi Dimitrov, the former leader of the Balkan Communist Federation. Once appointed president of the Comintern, Dimitrov, as soon as the matter of identifying another chief arises, chooses his old acquaintance and fellow Bulgarian. Paradoxically, Boris Ştefanov was excluded from the PCdR at the time. Although Bulgarian, Ştefanov had been a PCdR militant from its very foundation. He had been a Member of Parliament after the 1920 elections. At the Seventh Congress of the Comintern in August 1935, Boris Ştefanov was elected to the Executive Committee and was the PCdR representative at the Comintern. Having been expelled, ejected from the party, he now becomes its head. The 1934-1935 period is characterised by frequent changes in the upper echelons. Names such as Moscu Cohn (Gheorghe Stoica), Lucreţiu Pătrăşcanu, Nicolae Goldberger, Alexandru Sencovici, Ştefan Foriş, Marcel Pauker, Şmil Marcovici, Dimităr Ganev, Ana Pauker, Şeila Averbuch, and Dori Goldstein come and go. Besides the General Secretariat, which operated in Bucharest, there were other centres of decision in Vienna, Prague and Moscow, a situation that further complicated matters. The process of reformation demanded by the Comintern is difficult. Adherence of the workers to the policies of the PCdR is minimal.

With the new tactics of the Popular Front, the USSR embarks upon a different policy towards Romania. In the summer of 1933, the two countries sign a treaty and exchange legations. Mikhail Ostrovsky is the plenipotentiary Prime Minister sent to Bucharest by Moscow. Zaharia Stancu anticipates the fact in his article *The Non-subversive Red Flag*: "Mr Ostrovsky, the Soviet minister to Romania, will present letters of accreditation to H. H. King Carol II in Bucharest. Above the old and rambling house on Calea Victoriei [where the USSR legation was to be found – *author's note*], tucked away between the Alcalay Bookshop and the Prefecture of the Capital, the Red Flag will flutter day and night, without concealment or subversion. Our derisory patriots will protest ... the Soviets present no danger to Romania, either now or in the future ... The road to the Bosphorus? The Soviets have renounced this old Russian dream. For the love of a few tens of thousands of square kilometres [Bassarabia], the Soviets will not risk a conflict [with Romania]."[7]

Lothar Rădăceanu, a Social Democrat leader, writes in his article "Citizen Ostrovsky in Bucharest":

"Mikhail Ostrovsky will present his letters of accreditation to the King of Romania ... Impelled to have relations with all states – Soviet Russia ... must, whether it likes it or not, accept all the rules and forms common today in international diplomacy ... Mikhail Ostrovsky will not cease to be a communist by the simple fact that, in fulfilling his mandate from the Soviet State, he has bowed before the King and held banquets or receptions for gentlemen in coat-tails and ladies in evening wear. ... So, citizen Mikhail Ostrovsky will come. He will symbolise the disappearance of the so-called 'danger on the Dniester' that served so many Romanian governments as a diversion or as a pretext for terror ... the theme of world revolution has been abandoned and that of building socialism in a single country adopted with a frenzy."[8]

Ostrovsky arrives from Vienna at the Gara de Nord [Northern Station] in Bucharest on 2 December 1934. Together with his wife, he proceeds to the Athénée Palace Hotel. The same evening, he has a two-hour interview with Foreign Minister Nicolae Titulescu.

The ceremony for the presentation of his letters of accreditation is held, in accordance with protocol, at the Royal palace, where Comrade Ostrovsky arrives in a Daumont carriage. The arrival of the Soviet minister to Bucharest causes universal excitement. He is kept under close surveillance by the Siguranța, although this is by no means simple, given that Ostrovsky is a very active diplomat, desirous to make many contacts from the very first. On 13 December, he is already visiting the Colțea Hospital, with his wife, a doctor. The press follows him everywhere, interested in him as a character. Ostrovsky visits the *Universul* daily, where he has his picture taken with Stelian Popescu, to the surprise of the left-wing press. Stelian

---

[7] *Credința* [*Faith*], 16 May 1934.
[8] *Șantier* [*Building Site*], November 1934.

Popescu was an adversary of Bolshevism of every hue, be it Russian or native. The game was thus complex. Soviet diplomacy wanted to present a respectable façade for USSR policy. The precepts of the class struggle and world proletarian revolution were abandoned. The Kremlin negotiated and co-operated with bourgeois governments. In the eyes of some Bucharest radicals, it had even become pro-government. Moscow makes gestures of courtesy. It returns the earthly remains of Dimitrie Cantemir.[9] Ostrovsky is, of course, in attendance at the ceremony in the port of Constanța – with the agents of the Siguranța and the press hot on his heels. "Ostrovsky is not a photogenic figure, but this does not prevent him from allowing himself to be photographed at various meetings and in the company of the most various figures from Romanian high society. It seems that 'his lordship' is a *charmeur*, a demolisher of bourgeois resistance, for the photojournalists from the newspapers have captured him alongside, arm in arm, or at table with gentlemen who until not so long ago used to impale at least one Bolshevik a day on their pen nibs, convinced that Bolsheviks, when they dine, also thrust their forks into bourgeois meat."[10]

Soviet encouragement of the PCdR to prepare an insurrection fades away. The USSR has an interest in maintaining good relations with the government, the same as it does in France and Britain. The three-way game of 'clandestinity/subversion/official policy' continues, albeit within different parameters. The arrest of Secretariat members Ana Pauker, Șmil Marcovici and Dimităr Ganev in 1935 was tantamount to Moscow's failure to organise a new underground network. Moreover, after 1933, the Comintern lays the emphasis on the development of communist activities in the open, via legal groups with a democratic, 'anti-fascist', 'pacifist' semblance. Behind the scenes, however, the communist activists are present and control all the operations. Likewise, the funding comes from Comintern sources. One

---

[9] Dimitrie Cantemir (1673 –1723). Prince of Moldavia (1685-1693). Philosopher, historian and writer. His *Historia incrementorum atque decrementorum aulae othomanicae* (1714-1716) was known throughout Europe. After the victory of the Mohammedan Turks at Stănilești in 1711, Cantemir, together with his family and four thousand Moldavians, settled in Russia, where he was to remain for the rest of his life. He had considerable influence at the court of Peter the Great and gained a reputation as the most learned man in Russia – *Translator's note*.

[10] Unsigned article, *Șantier*, January 1935.

example is the Friends of the USSR, in the summer of 1934. The association was not a Romanian initiative. Such associations, formed at the instigation of Comintern agents, existed throughout Europe and were linked together in a network. On the list of founders can be found the names of well-known communists such as Petre Constantinescu-Iași, Alexandru Sahia, C. Paraschivescu-Bălăceanu, Al. Mihăileanu, Scarlat Callimachi, and C. Vicol; and fellow travellers such as Radu Olteanu, Ștefan Roll, Mac Constantinescu, Sergiu Dan, Radu Boureanu, Ion Iancovescu, Octav Doicescu, Cicerone Teodorescu, Dida Solomon Callimachi, F. Brunea Fox, and C. L. Vâlceanu. Besides these familiar public figures there are also the names of ordinary workers. There is also a Legionary, film director Haig Acterian, who will later take part in the Iron Guard uprising. Acterian will die on the Russian Front in 1943. The association is dissolved on 25 November 1934, by order of the commandant of the Second Army Corps, Division General Ion Prodan, only a week before Ostrovsky's arrival in Bucharest. It should be pointed out that on 30 December 1933, following the assassination of I. Gh. Duca, a state of siege was declared in a number of cities. In September 1934, the state of siege was extended for a further six months. The organisations that were banned included the PCdR, UTC, Red Aid, the Legal Bureau of the PCdR, the Council of Revolutionary Unions, the Circle for Marxist Studies, the League of Labour, the Friends of the USSR, the National Anti-Fascist Committee, a number of trades unions, the United Workers Front, and the DRO (Dobrudja Revolutionary Organisation). All were communist organisations. Their headquarters were shut down, propaganda materials were confiscated, their bank accounts were frozen, and a number of their leaders and agitators were arrested. The Siguranță had been keeping their activities under close surveillance. When things got out of hand, the Chief Prosecutor would intervene. Trials would be held. Two trials in particular caused a great stir at the time: that of Tudor Bugnariu, in Cluj, and that of Petre Constantinescu-Iași, in Kishinev.

Petre Constantinescu-Iași was a professor in the Theology Faculty of Kishinev University. Not alone among the communists, he was a freemason. He earned a high salary, 20,000 lei a month, and lived in a comfortable flat in the grounds of the university itself. What such a (presumably religious) character can have had in common with atheist communism, for which religion was the "opium of the people," is hard to guess. He is arrested at the end of 1934 and handed over to the War Council of the Third Army

Corps. He was charged with "links to persons abroad who want a Bolshevik Revolution." During the search of his flat on the night of 25-26 November, documents are found proving his connections with Moscow and groups and persons from the West under the control of the Comintern. Applying the usual Bolshevik methodology for such situations, Petre Constantinescu-Iași goes on hunger strike. In the middle of June 1935, the court passes final sentence on Petre Constantinescu-Iași, 42, professor in the Theology Faculty of Kishinev University, David Feuerstein, 31, teacher from Soroca, Paulina Rozenberg, 36, lawyer from Kishinev, Diner Etea, 25, lawyer from Kishinev, Mihail Brașoveanu, 56, livestock inspector from Kishinev and former people's commissar, in Russia in 1918, Ipolit Derevici, 38, physician from Kishinev, Grigore Zoltur, 31, agronomist from Kishinev, and Feiga Rabinovici, 34, mathematics teacher from Bălți. The final ruling asks, "Why is there an anti-fascist movement in Romania when Romania is not a fascist regime? … Unfortunately, this movement had completely different aims. The accused believe that the only means against the fascist regime is the establishment of a communist regime like that in the USSR. By this fascist regime they understand the current regimes of all monarchies and republics, with the exception of Russia. … The movement had a subversive and internationalist character." The arrested were members of the National Anti-Fascist Committee, yet another organisation funded from Moscow. The organisation's leaders were Iorgu Iordan, a professor at the University of Jassy, in the capacity of president, and Petre Constantinescu-Iași, in the capacity of vice-president, but in fact the real leader. The National Anti-Fascist Committee had a number of secretaries: Victor Gherasim, a lawyer, Ilie Cristea, a teacher from Brașov, who was also later brought to trial, Mihail Brașoveanu, a former commissar in the Romanian Revolutionary Battalion in Odessa in 1918, Tudor Bugnariu, a teacher from Cluj, Zoe Frunză, a journalist, Matei Socor, a musician, Scarlat Callimachi, a historian, and a handful of workers. Petre Constantinescu-Iași is accused of organising a clandestine congress in Bucharest on 9 September 1934. Such 'anti-fascist committees' had sprung up all over Europe after 1933. The World Anti-Fascist Committee was based in Paris and run by Henri Barbusse. As usual, behind the anti-fascist façade the Comintern could be found lurking. The themes of the anti-fascist campaigns were identical in Bucharest, Paris, Brussels and Prague: demands for the release of Ernst Thaelmann, the head of the German Communist Party, prison conditions, and so on. There were also a number of Romanian campaign issues: protests against the conviction of Scarlat Callimachi, demands for the release of the Grivitza strikers, etc.

"Petre Constantinescu-Iaşi's anti-fascists have done no more than change the name of the banned Communist Party," declares the final sentence. Petre Constantinescu-Iaşi had been a communist since 1918. He wrote for the left-wing press. He began his professional career in Bîrlad, as a lycée college teacher, where he was involved in a scandal as a result of an amorous liaison with an underage pupil, who subsequently committed suicide. He was transferred to Lăpuşna as a disciplinary measure. In 1920, he stood for election on the Socialist Party list, alongside Gheorghe Cristescu, Boris Ştefanov, Alexandru Dobrogeanu-Gherea, and Eugen Rozvany. In October 1920, after the general strike, he was arrested for having instigated the workers. He stood for election on the list of the Peasant Workers Bloc on numerous occasions, without success. On 23 October 1933, *Universul* runs a story with the title *Both a communist agent and immoral*, which reports, "The latest exploit of professor Petre Constantinescu-Iaşi, caught in a public park with a prostitute, Evdochia Burnozova, at midnight … He attempted to bribe the three guardians, then insulted them. At the police station, he threatened the commissar …" Whether Burnozova was really a prostitute or an agent from across the Dniester is impossible to establish today. The theology professor's nocturnal dalliance may have been merely a cover. Of course, the woman may have been both a prostitute and an agent. This is not the only information we have regarding Constantinescu-Iaşi's loose morals. During the trial that follows, witnesses speak of Constantinescu-Iaşi's habit of cohabiting with female students. In August 1932, Petre Constantinescu-Iaşi takes part in the World Anti-Fascist Congress Against War in Amsterdam, the largest gathering of left-wing and pacifist organisations. The delegates are more than two thousand "trades unionists, pacifists and veteran traditionalist socialist militants, anarchists, idealists and agitators … The whole thing was financed in secret and run by the Communist International."[11] Petre Constantinescu-Iaşi has the appearance of being a 'fellow traveller'. He is a university professor, a bourgeois professional, a left-wing journalist. But in reality he is something else entirely. He was one of the 'clandestines' who had been operating in Romania since 1920. In 1934, he was picked by the Comintern to head the legal 'anti-fascist movement'. In parallel, an illegal, strictly communist network operated, under the leadership of Ana

---

[11] Stephen Koch, *op. cit.*, pp. 65-7.

Pauker. In the mid-1930s, Pauker and Constantinescu-Iași were the heads of the Comintern's two agencies in Romania, the clandestine network and the legal front organisation respectively.

The trial took place in Kishinev in March 1936. As usual, the defence called a long list of witnesses – more than five hundred. They were a motley crowd, from celebrities to illiterate peasants, who knew nothing about the trial. More than 40 defence lawyers were announced. Those who actually took part in the trial were Lucrețiu Pătrășcanu, I. Gh. Maurer, C. Paraschivescu-Bălăceanu, and Stelian Nițulescu, well-known communists. Also taking part were Grigore Iunian, the head of the Radical Peasant Party, Dem. I. Dobrescu, a former mayor of Bucharest, and Al. Mîță. The indictment was based on documents that proved the group's links to Moscow, especially Constantinescu-Iași's. For example, there were two letters found on Mihai Gheorghiu Bujor in customs when he was crossing from Romania into the USSR. Other documents revealed the itinerary of Constantinescu-Iași during the summer of 1934, when he met with Comintern agents in the West and took part in communist demonstrations disguised as pacifist and anti-fascist events. In Paris, on 20 July, he was at a public meeting in the Wagram Hall, with eight thousand participants, including Henri Barbusse and Marcel Cachin, one of the leaders of the French Communist Party, at which the release of Constantin Doncea, the leader of the Grivitza strikers, was demanded. In London, he takes part in a demonstration in Trafalgar Square. On 29 June, he is back in Paris, where we find him at a demonstration held in memory of Jean Jaurès, attended by fifty thousand people. Two days later, he presides over a meeting of the World Anti-Fascist Committee. At the beginning of August 1934, he takes part in a meeting of the Committee for Anti-Fascist Unity. On 3 August, he is at a meeting of the executive committee of the International of Communist Educators, on whose board he sits. Between 4-7 August he is at a congress of communist women (!), where he successfully tables a motion 'against the terror in Romania'. The details of this itinerary, laid out in the indictment, show that the Siguranța had been keeping him under close surveillance. Constantinescu-Iași's trip to Europe was a Comintern operation. A report of the General Department of Police reveals, "in Brno there took place a secret meeting between Romanian communists and Comintern functionaries. To this end, eight illegal delegates travelled from Romania under false names … including Petre Constantinescu … This meeting was presided over by Willy

Münzenberg, a German communist … arriving from Moscow. The meeting was also attended by two Comintern functionaries … It should be especially emphasised that Willy Münzenberg arrived in Brno on the special orders of Béla Kuhn, the head of the Romanian section … The Red Aid central office for Romania was moved from Poland to Prague on 1 December last year and by the decision of the international presidency of Red Aid, 175,000 Swiss francs were allocated to the Romanian section on 9 December. By decision of the Executive Committee of the Third International the sum of half a million gold roubles was allocated to the organisation of communist actions in Romania … The leader of this organisation is Constantinescu Petre."[12]

Another aim of the Comintern, besides funding and organisational matters, was to create for this humble teacher from Kishinev a Europe-wide standing. Returning to Romania with the assistance of the Communist Party, always remaining in the underground, he organises 'anti-fascist' committees in Jassy, Cluj, Bucharest and elsewhere. These were diversified groups, which brought together PCdR members and sympathisers, and left-wing journalists, intellectuals and lawyers who opposed the regimes in Germany and Italy, as well as the Romanian extreme Right. The latter were not always aware that the operation was controlled and funded from behind the scenes by the Comintern. The situation does not escape the attention of the authorities, who arrest Constantinescu-Iași at the end of November 1934. In Bucharest, other 'militant anti-fascists' and 'pacifists' are likewise placed under arrest: Victor Gherasim, Matei Socor, Scarlat Callimachi. In Cluj, Tudor Bugnariu is arrested. They are all brought to trial. The arrest of Petre Constantinescu-Iași and, in particular, the ensuing trial triggered a campaign for his release, organised by communist networks in the West. Behind the campaign was Willy Münzenberg, the man who had invented Constantinescu-Iași. A number of committees send letters of protest and memoranda. They gather signatures. All according to the long-established ritual in such cases. We find the same names, the same associations. The pro-Moscow press in the West publishes articles, reproduced by the left-wing Romanian papers. The usual suspects sign petitions: Romain Rolland, André Gide, Albert Einstein, Henri Barbusse, André Malraux. In court, Philippe Lamour takes the stand. He is a member of the French Radical Party and Popular Front. Two militants from the League for the Defence of Human Rights, based in Prague, also testify. In Romania, too, there were reactions in favour of Petre Constantinescu-Iași.

---

[12] ANCR, Fund 50, Dossier 2315, p. 56.

Andrei Oțetea, Iorgu Iordan, Mihai Ralea, and Petre Andrei, professors at Jassy University, protest against the trial. The left-wing press (*Adevărul, Dimineața, Zorile, Cuvîntul Liber*, etc.) publishes fervent articles. Emil Socor:

> "For 10 days we have been witnessing this ugly spectacle. I cannot understand how the higher authorities tolerate it. Do they wish that Mr Constantinescu and the others should be punished? They could have done in a more decent manner, demanding that the judges abide by all the norms laid down by the law and display an attitude that did not betray the political end pursued so blatantly. In particular, the president of the court ought not have made of every question, every gesture a fascist display … For many reasons, the trial of the anti-fascists should not have been brought … Reasons for its suspension might still be found."[13]

The right-wing (*Universul, Curentul, Vremea*) and extreme right-wing press (*Porunca vremii*) makes its riposte. Pamfil Șeicaru:

> "That Professor Constantinescu-Iași has continued to receive a salary from the bourgeois state, while pining for a communist revolution, because, until he is appointed a people's commissar, a nice salary won't go amiss; that the same professor has not considered his position at the Faculty of Theology unsuitable, even though he has not the slightest glimmer of a belief in God – this we can explain; the poor man accepts from the current order everything it can give him, until his dream will come true … We are in the period of communist incubation. The Kishinev trial is merely an opportunity to make an inventory of how widely the evil extends; in the end, everything will settle down once more, until the secret operation to recruit loyal revolutionaries will have reached its limit. Let us follow closely what is happening in Spain. A recent telegram informs us, 'Popular Front unleashes violence. A newspaper office and three churches burned down'. Against these altars of the human spirit the guttersnipes have been unleashed. An armed insurrection is being orchestrated … The trial in Kishinev we should regard as a welcome warning … The exploits of the Popular Front in Spain foretoken the exploits of the Popular Front in Romania."[14]

---

[13] *Zorile*, 17 March 1936.
[14] *Curentul*, 19 March 1936.

The accused were tried at liberty, apart from Dr Ipolit Derevici, who had already been convicted in another trial and was brought to court from Tîrgu Ocna Prison. Petre Constantinescu-Iaşi frequently wrote for the press. His favourite topic was the Popular Front. Throughout the course of the investigation and the trial he was a cult figure in the left-wing press. There was barely a single issue that did not contain articles about or interviews with him. The trial lasts for a month, following the usual pattern in such cases. There is a muffled conflict between the 10 defence lawyers and the Royal Commissar. The defence is raucous, wagering upon propagandistic spectacle. There are hundreds of witnesses, of whom many have no idea why they have been called. Others have been sent by Agitprop, the propaganda wing of the PCdR. The witnesses include well-known communists such as Constantin Mănescu (indicted in the Spirii Hill trial of 1922), Constantin David (one of the CFR Grivitza strikers in February 1933, murdered by the Iron Guard in 1941), Vasil Bîgu (a trades union leader), Gogu Rădulescu (president of the Romanian Democratic Student Front, a communist organisation), Ilie Constantinovski (a communist student, leader of the UTC, émigré to the USSR in 1941), Scarlat Callimachi, the 'Red Prince', an historian (who says, "the convicted communists are victims of the Romanian regime of terror"), and Athanasie Joja, the secretary of the Democratic Bloc. There appear defence lawyers from other communist trials: Victor Gherasim and Petre Grozdea. Sympathisers and fellow travellers also testify: professors Iorgu Iordan and Andrei Oţetea, lawyer Constantin Nădejde, and Roman Stere (the son of C. Stere). To be noted is the aggressiveness and confrontational attitude of defence lawyer I. Gh. Maurer. Also to be noted is the conflict between Maurer and Lucreţiu Pătrăşcanu. The latter abandons the trial and goes back to Bucharest, where he prepares for the trial of the Ana Pauker group.

The speech for the prosecution, delivered by Royal Commissar Manea, denies that the trial is politically motivated, as Pătrăşcanu claims. The charges are disturbing the peace and infringement of the Mîrzescu/Mironescu Law. "It is not a political trial. They are common criminals." The Royal Commissar attacks the claim made by the accused that the "only anti-fascist country is the USSR" and their conclusion that all other regimes, being fascist, should be overthrown. "Why do the anti-fascists consider that Soviet Russia is the only anti-fascist country when it is known that the most dreadful dictatorship of the proletariat exists there?" The major accusation:

those in the dock "have made contact with foreign organisations, from which they have received instructions to prepare a communist revolution in Romania." In his summing up, the Royal Commissar says, "The accused deserve no pity, because all of them have sought to destroy the Romanian State." The speech for the prosecution lasts for one and a half days. The case for the defence lasts for one week. It is delivered by Grigore Iunian, the head of the Radical Peasant Party, and his close associate Ion Gheorghe Maurer, a member of the leadership of the same party. C. Paraschivescu-Bălăceanu, Al. Mîță and Osvald Teodoreanu argue that the accused have no links to any communist organisations. Stelian Nițulescu (the future Minister of Justice during the Dej regime) says that those in the dock are not "eight criminals, but rather eight intellectuals, eight martyrs, who are suffering for their ideas." The sentences are light. Two are acquitted: Paulina Rozenberg and Ipolit Derevici. Petre Constantinescu-Iași, Mihail Brașoveanu, Feiga Rabinovici, and Etea Diner are sentenced to two years six months imprisonment. David Feuerstein is sentenced to two years, Grigore Zoltur to three months. The press reaction: "Fascism has scored a success. Six of the eight accused from Kishinev have been convicted and sentenced to prison and court costs," writes Emil Socor.[15] Toma Vlădescu: "The sentence from Kishinev answers the imperious need to protect the public conscience of this country from ideological vagabonds who paint lipstick on criminal slogans using the latest dictionary of mystification manufactured in Comintern meetings. It is known today … that 'anti-fascism' is the transparent cloak that clothes the communist hyena in its desperate attempts to undermine our State."[16]

Petre Constantinescu-Iași serves his two and a half year prison sentence. On his release, he settles in Bucharest, living in a flat at No. 190 Calea Victoriei. He frequents the Soviet Legation daily, where he teaches Romanian. The Siguranță suspect him of conveying information to, and receiving orders from, the Comintern and of passing on those orders to communist agitators. The surveillance operation reveals that he is in contact with a number of Soviet diplomats and various communist suspects: Mihai Gheorghiu Bujor, Ștefan Voitec, Athanasie Joja, Constantin Popovici, et al. In 1941 he is interned in the Caracal Prison camp, and then in Tîrgu Jiu.

The light sentences at the Kishinev and Cluj trials gave cause for hope to the defence lawyers preparing for the trial in Craiova. But the standard

---

[15] *Zorile*, 2 April 1936.

[16] *Porunca Vremii*, 3 April 1936.

was to be set by another trial, also in March 1936, in Constanța. Here, the leaders of the DRO (Dobrudja Revolutionary Organisation, banned since November 1934) were handed heavy sentences, of between five and 10 years imprisonment; 1936 was a year of trials. An ill-omened year for the communists. The two major trials – those of Constantinescu-Iași and Ana Pauker – were followed by others. Nineteen UTC members were convicted in Brașov on 5 June, among them Nicolae Ceaușescu (sentenced to two years, a fine of 2,000 lei, and forbidden from leaving his parents' house for a year). In Kishinev, another 24 communists were tried in July. The sentences were heavy: between two and 10 years imprisonment. Twenty seven 'Democratic Bloc' members were tried at the end of August. They had been arrested during a clandestine meeting. They were defended by the usual lawyers: Iosif Șraier, I. Gh. Maurer, Victor Gherasim, Al. Mîță, Athanasie Joja, et al. The Royal Commissar argued that the organisation had been banned, because it was operating in a zone (Bucharest) that was under a state of siege, and demanded that "the council remove from the ranks of society the 27 accused, because wherever the sentence might be compared, the judges were, first and foremost, Romanians."[17] Athanasie Joja, for the defence, argued, "The Democratic Bloc is not a communist front." He was lying. Joja himself was a member of the PCdR at that time. Al. Mîță, Iosif Șraier and I. Gh. Maurer present the same argument. The play, the roles and the actors are the same. What are different are the masks in the dock, on this occasion mere anonymous bit-players, caught red-handed by the Siguranță. Their names say as little today as they did then. The instigators, as usual, were elsewhere.

The Tudor Bugnariu trial in Cluj caused quite a stir, as did the appeal. Support committees, intellectuals and petitions arrived at the Court Martial in Cluj from all over Europe. A sentence of 10 years imprisonment was handed down on 25 November 1935. The reaction of the right-wing press was vehement. N. Crevedia:

> "Who is it that is doing communism in Romania, if the Siguranță and military courts are so busy? Some young aristocrat or other, more from snobbery than deep-seated belief, a handful of Romanian workers – and, unfortunately, aimless Jews. Mr Constantinescu and his ilk, who are not content with subsidies from Moscow and a salary as a professor

---

[17] *Dimineața*, 30 August 1936.

of theology, are not communists, but mere charlatans. And nor is the other gentleman, Gheorghe Cristescu, a communist, but merely an unnatural (bourgeois) parent. … Then there are the communists who call themselves something else. One is Bujor, the traitor from Odessa who has lately left for Moscow. Then there is that little Romanian as green as goose droppings, who has the name of a cocotte, lawyer Titel Petrescu. Then there is Mr Ghelerter, a Romanian, who as you can see is also head of the great Socialist Unity Party! But what about old Ilie Moscovici? Is that lousy old man still alive? War is knocking at the door and we're all tied up with communism. The Jews have sold us to the Germans, tomorrow they'll sell us, all tied up, to the Russians."[18]

After the trial of Bugnariu, C. Clonaru writes, "In 1935, on 25 November, the democratic regime was buried in Romania."[19] The scissors of Left/Right are opened wide. Europe is being thrust towards conflict. And Romania is caught in the middle.

***

On the evening of 12 July 1935, a little after 10 o'clock, following a lengthy surveillance operation, the police arrest three people on the street. The three were leaving a meeting of conspirators. A police report states:

> "On the occasion of the arrest of the above-named, Colev Iordan resisted arrest and detective Belderof Dobre, scuffling with him, managed to draw his revolver from his pocket, in order to intimidate him and place him under arrest. Colev was lightly wounded in the head during the struggle, when the revolver went off, and the ricocheting bullet hit communist Ana Pauker in the left leg, as she was climbing into a motor car, in order to escape with Colev."[20]

The Kaufmans, who live at the house, are also arrested. It was the second major capture in the space of only a few days. On 8 July, the leaders of the youth organisation had been arrested as they were leaving a conspirators'

---

[18] *Porunca Vremii*, 23 February 1936.
[19] *Credința*, 27 November 1935.
[20] MAN Archive, SSI fund, vol. 1, p. 33.

meeting – Bernat Andor, Sandor Mogyorossy, Estera Radosovetşki, Liuba Chişinevschi, Alexandru Drăghici et al. On 14 July, there was another capture: a group of Communist Youth, caught at a clandestine printing press.

There follows a seven month investigation into those arrested. The enquiries reveal an extensive underground network. The documents seized by the authorities lead them to conclude that the persons in custody are important members of the PCdR, which had been banned in 1924. At the same time, the cache of documents reveals close and extensive ties to the Comintern. Most of those arrested deny belonging to the PCdR or the Comintern. The investigators found themselves confronted with a double-edged situation: 1) Ana Pauker, Iordan Coleff et al. insisted that they were 'anti-fascists' and that this was nothing culpable; 2) In Europe, the left-wing press, numerous human rights, civil liberties, anti-fascist and pacifist organisations mounted campaigns to support those arrested in Bucharest. The arrest of three members of the PCdR Secretariat had come about due to an informer, a graduate of the Lenin School for Comintern cadres in Moscow, and himself a member of the Secretariat: Ion Zelea Pîrgaru. He was to be assassinated in 1945, in the headquarters of the Central Committee of the RCP, an order carried out by Pantiuşa Bodnarenko. His skeleton, like that of another informer, Petre Melinte, will be found in 1967, in an unmarked grave, along with that of Ştefan Foriş.

In Bucharest, the trial of the 19 arrested communists commenced on 27 February 1936, at 9.30 a.m., at the War Council of the 2nd Army Corps. The trial was not conducted in a civil court of law, because, since 1935, a number of cities in Romania, including Bucharest, where the arrests had taken place, had been under a state of siege. This meant that certain offences, including that of agitating public opinion, were deferred to the military courts. A police report describes the atmosphere on the day the trial began:

"In front of the War Council, on the streets and in courtyards, approximately 800 workers had been assembled since as early as eight o'clock, cited as witnesses, among whom there were also communist propagandists, who encouraged demonstrations. At 9 o'clock, i.e. before the court session opened, there was a scuffle between the army and the workers called as witnesses, who were demanding that they be allowed to enter. During this scuffle, permanent agent Nicolae Gușă of the Municipality of Bucharest Prefecture of Police was attacked by the communist Șloim Moili, unemployed, from Bucharest. The agent was struck and managed to fire a shot into the air, as a warning, and order was restored ... The Municipality of Bucharest Prefecture of Police deployed a platoon of gendarmes under the command of an officer in order to keep the peace."[21]

There are more than 100 defence lawyers representing the communists at the trial. These include Ella Negruzzi, V. V. Stanciu, I. Gh. Maurer, L. Pătrășcanu, Ghiță Ionescu, Radu Popescu, Radu Olteanu, Alfons Nachtigal, Constantin Paraschiveschu-Bălăceanu, Alexandru Mîță, Petre Grozdea etc. We can distinguish three types of lawyer among those involved: 1) communists; 2) fellow travellers, men of the Left, or those belonging to various associations for the defence of civil rights; 3) ordinary 'bourgeois' lawyers, hired for a fee. Alfons Nachtigal alone received 120,000 lei.[22] The lawyers were paid from Comintern funds, channelled through Red Aid (МОПР). Some of them were singled out by the Siguranța in the entourage of the Soviet Embassy in Bucharest, such as Iosif Șraier, the head of the PCdR legal office, Paul Moscovici and Lascăr Șaraga. The press publishes numerous articles on the build-up to the trial. On 13 February, Lucrețiu Pătrășcanu gives an interview to the *Dimineața [Morning]* newspaper. On 20 February, none other than Ana Pauker appears in an interview in the pages of the *Adevărul [The Truth]* daily. Constantin Argetoianu records in *Însemnări Zilnice [Daily Observations]*: "The said lady is the wife of the nephew of Emil Pauker, Marcel Pauker, whose father, Simon Pauker, is the brother of Emil ... Emil Pauker is not at all a communist. The communists are Marcel Pauker and his wife Ana. The matter is of no importance to Marcel Pauker: he's in Russia, where he plays quite an important role; he doesn't have any connections with his family or any influence over it. It is an entirely different matter with Ana Pauker, who has got under everyone's skin."[23] Emil Pauker was one of the owners of the *Adevărul* and *Dimineața* newspapers. The right-wing press – *Universul, Curentul* – and the extreme

---

[21] MAN Archive, SSI fund, Dossier 42, vol. 2, p. 88.

[22] Petre Pandrea, *Amintirile mandarinului valah [Memoirs of the Wallachian Mandarin]*, Bucharest: Albatros, 2000, p. 179.

[23] Constantin Argetoianu, *Însemnări zilnice*, p. 387.

right-wing *Porunca vremii* [*The Commandment of the Time*] publish frequent hostile commentaries. The atmosphere is heated.

At the international level, the Comintern orchestrates the mobilisation – unprecedented in Romania – of European pro-Soviet public opinion. Many intellectuals, lawyers, writers, left-wing politicians, anti-fascist and civic activists, and foreign journalists are invited to take the stand as witnesses. Among them, we find major figures. The best-known figure from Britain was George Bernard Shaw, who had made a trip to Moscow, met Stalin and been charmed by him. Then there were André Gide, André Malraux, Paul Langevin, Paul Daladier, Pierre Cot, Jacques Sadoul, Marcel Cahin, Léon Blum, and Romain Rolland, all connected to the French Popular Front, manipulated by Comintern agents, some of them serving as agents of influence for Moscow. None of them attended. Most were busy with the congresses in Paris and in Moscow, events of greater importance than the trial of the 19 communists. A report by the Siguranţă identifies more than 70 organisations from France alone that sent protests and appeals to Bucharest. The names cited were to be found on all the lists approved by the Comintern in Europe for propaganda actions; these were people with Moscow's seal of approval in the campaign launched after Hitler came to power. From the Soviet Union too, a number of major figures are asked to testify: Georgi Dimitrov, I. Tanef and L. Popov, who were also involved in the Leipzig trial; Ilya Ehrenburg, a writer who travelled around Europe in the service of the NKVD and the Comintern; and Mikhail Koltsov, with the same status. The list included Karl Radek himself, the grey eminence of Agitprop and at the same time the Comintern (he was shot in 1937, following a show trial), and Nikolay Bukharin, another victim of Stalin in 1938. The latter had been Lenin's favourite, and, in 1936, although in decline, enjoyed influence in Moscow as editor-in-chief of the daily *Izvestiya*.

From the outset, the defence pleads for an adjournment of the trial, claiming that it has not had enough time to study the case files. After two hours of debates, the Council of War accepts the plea. It is a victory for the defence. The trial is rescheduled for 14 May, but it not will open until 5 June 1936, after further postponements, and will be held in Craiova, where the Grivitza group had been tried two years earlier. The agitation kept up by the left-wing press and various organisations connected to the PCdR is unrelenting. As the date of the trial draws near, preparations for a large-scale mobilisation intensify. Ştefan Foriş, the new head of Agitprop in the

CC of the PCdR, recently released from Doftana Prison, handles the entire campaign. Organisations of communist provenance spring into action. Support committees are formed. A great deal of money from Comintern sources is squandered. Manifestos and leaflets are printed. Meetings are held. An SSI report on the situation singles out a clandestine leaflet which writes:

> "Their conviction would mean yet another blow to the working masses in Romania, it would mean yet another blow to democratic liberties, it would mean encouragement of the liberal government and the Romanian fascists in crimes against all that is democratic, and the introduction of a fascist dictatorship, provoking hunger, poverty and imperialist war. ... You in the factories, businesses, villages, estates, universities, schools, form committees to defend them and all anti-fascists, collect money to help them, gather in solidarity to protest, leave work, strike in protest, demand their release ... Down with the liberal government of hunger, high prices and fascism!"[24]

The result is that the authorities are visibly nervous in the face of this unanticipated pressure. The fear that some of the prisoners might escape is apparent. Exceptional security measures are taken. On 12 May, they are taken from Jilava (the men) and Văcărești (the women) and transported to the prison of the 1st Army Corps in Craiova.

> "Before embarkation, both the men and the women will be handcuffed in a line. The most dangerous, Ana Pauker, Estera Radosovetșki, Colef, Marcovici, Bernat and Moghioroși, will be placed in the middle of the line and have both hands handcuffed. ... During the court sessions, 10 guards will remain by the accused, forming a cordon to isolate them from the public and with instructions not to allow anyone to come near the accused. Two sentinels will be stationed by the entrance door and two by the door to the courtroom. ... After the close of the court sessions, nine sentinels will enter the room with one or two NCOs and after the court is cleared, the arrested will be taken out one by one ... For number ones, the men will be taken to the latrines of the troop of Division 2, only two at a time, handcuffed together by one hand. For

---

[24] MAN Archive, SSI fund, Dossier 42, pp. 203-204.

number twos, the individuals Colef, Marcovici, Bernat and Moghioroşi will be taken individually with two wardens and in leg chains, the others individually with two wardens each and in handcuffs. The women will use the latrine of the officers in the Council of War where they will be conveyed individually by two wardens to the door of the latrine, who are to have their weapons loaded at all times when in the presence of those under arrest."[25] "The Fourteenth Artillery Regiment will station a battery (to sound the alarm) tomorrow 5 June at 7.30 hours in the courtyard of the military hospital, ready to intervene in aid of the sentry posts ... in case crowds of civilians try to break through to the First Pioneers Regiment ... the First Călăraşi Regiment will tomorrow 5 June at 7.30 hours ... have a mounted squadron at the ready with sabres and a platoon with lances ... in order to repel any eventual attack that might be made against the guards. ... Each man shall have 20 cartridges about his person. The Inspectorate of Gendarmes will place at the disposal of the Police Station a Detachment of 50 gendarmes to maintain order in the city, and the rest of the 100 gendarmes at the disposal of the president of the Council of War."[26]

Another document reveals the exceptional security measures implemented in Craiova with a view to the trial. The communists and their sympathisers had to be kept under constant surveillance, and were subject to repeated searches and checks. Hotels, taverns and inns were similarly kept under close watch by the police. At the train station and at the entrances to the city, checkpoints were set up for travellers. Raids were ordered and suspects detained. The head of the Siguranţă and the chief of police request information from factory directors, and for functionaries and, above all, workers to be kept under surveilance. For the entire length of the trial, taxi drivers and coachmen were obliged to report any strangers in town and the addresses whither they had taken them.[27] As for the accused, the police took extraordinary measures: all correspondence was censored, and visiting hours with relatives was reduced to a minimum, strictly in the presence of an officer. Parcels of food or clothing, letters, newspapers and books were closely checked.

[25] MAN Archive, SSI Fund, Dossier 32, p. 114.

[26] *Idem*, SSI Fund, Dossier 32, p. 121.

[27] *Idem*, Dossier 42, vol. 2, p. 315.

"Via food, items of clothing, books and newspapers sent to the detainees it is likewise possible to send secret correspondence. In bread, butter and soap, in tubes of toothpaste, in a piece of fruit, oranges, apples etc. it is possible to secrete a small letter, twisted around a needle, a toothpick or a matchstick. ... In the collar of a coat, in the hem of underwear, the seam of trousers, the cuff of a shirt etc. it is likewise possible to insert a letter written on thin paper. In the text of a book or of a newspaper, on certain pages inside it is possible lightly to underline or prick ... letters which when read in order will spell out the text of a letter. Permits for visiting should be limited as much as possible. Visits should be made in a room arranged in such a way that the visitor will not be able to come into contact with the accused. During a kiss, the visitor might easily and unobserved pass into the mouth of the prisoner a letter transformed into a small pellet of paper concealed in his mouth between the lip and gum. Similarly, during an embrace, a letter turned into a pellet might be slipped into the hair or the collar of the prisoner."[28]

It all looks as if it had been lifted from a nineteenth century pulp novel of conspiracy, plots and intrigue. Such intrigues, which are comical if anything, make the authorities even more cautious. Exceptional measures are taken. The 1st Army Corps, within whose circumscription the trial is being held, forbid anyone to come within two metres of the accused. Rifles are aimed at relatives, lawyers and journalists. Any kind of communication, whether verbal, written or in signs, is forbidden, "in order to prevent them adopting a common stance or executing any deleterious action." The number of guard posts is increased, a special telephone line is installed, and measures are taken to prevent arson in the prison, which would have provided an opportunity to escape. To the same ends, the prisoners' cells were to be searched day and night.[29] The disproportionate security measures reveal just how concerned the authorities were about the eventuality of a provocation or escape. It was the opposite of the spectacle organised by the Comintern, which was mobilising an important sector of public opinion in Europe. The authorities reacted, organising strict surveillance of the accused. The instructions are ridiculous, but for one of the prisoners to escape would have made the authorities look just as ridiculous. Just how valuable the group of

---

[28] *Idem*, D 42, vol. 2, p. 318.
[29] MAN Archive, D 32, p. 115.

19 was to the Comintern – in the eyes of the Romanian authorities – was betrayed by the amplitude of the demonstrations in their support. These demonstrations were unprecedented for a trial in Romania. Ana Pauker and the other accused became famous overnight, a subject of press interest. Had they been ignored by the Comintern and the trial had taken its course without all the fuss, the authorities would have been calmer. Given the amplitude of its campaign, the Comintern was signalling that the accused were very important persons in the clandestine communist networks (some of them indeed were) – not only in Romania. The authorities concluded that exceptional measures had to be taken. Another conclusion was that, when dealing with such dangerous agents, professional revolutionaries deployed and paid by the Comintern, exemplary punishments had to be meted out. The truth is that the Comintern did not place any great value on Ana Pauker and her comrades. The PCdR was an insignificant party. In the scenarios being acted out, the role of the PCdR was minimal. However, a price was placed upon the propaganda spectacle that could be staged with them in the leading roles. There was no direct link – as the Siguranță imagined – between their importance as Comintern militants and the amplitude of the demonstrations. The Comintern was engaged in an operation to mystify public opinion. In Bucharest, however, it was difficult to decipher such sophisticated manoeuvres. Ana Pauker & co. were utilised as instruments in a campaign aimed at rallying anti-fascist public opinion on the same platform, albeit not so much Romanian public opinion, which was negligible and without influence at a continental level. The target was public opinion in Western Europe and Western governments, especially the French and British. These were the weeks leading up to the outbreak of the Spanish Civil War. In addition, it was only a few until the Kamenev-Zinoviev trial, on which the GPU was working intensely in June. That it was nothing more than a propaganda operation is demonstrated by the simple fact that even as early as the summer of 1936 Stalin did not hesitate to order the assassination of many of the actors and directors of the manipulative operation known as "the policy of the Popular Front." The August trial in Moscow and the one that followed were a hecatomb in which the Bolshevik old guard, the initiators of the Popular Front policy, Comintern activists, and the heads of the European communist parties all perished. In 1936-1938, thousands of militants were executed in the USSR. Most of them had been implicated in operations of the same kind as that surrounding the trial

in Craiova. In 1939, in contempt of the cause for which millions of people had mobilised and which the Comintern claimed to represent, Stalin signed a pact with Hitler.

In 1936, however, the Comintern considers it to be in its own interests to turn the insignificant trial of a handful of Romanian communists, who had been caught red-handed, into a grand anti-fascist trial. It was an opportunity to organise a media show which would pay propaganda dividends. It was a technique that had been perfected by Karl Radek and Willy Münzenberg, an operation already tried and tested in other 'anti-fascist' trials in Europe. The best known was the Leipzig trial of 1933 – the trial of the Reichstag incendiaries. Georgi Dimitrov – president of the Comintern at the time of the Ana Pauker trial – had been top of the bill then. According to this scenario, scripted in Moscow, those in the dock were to be transformed from accused into accusers of the political regime in the Romania of the 1930s. For an anaemic, unknown, unpopular party at the margins of society, it was an unprecedented opportunity to make itself known. The financial and logistical support of the Comintern was likewise obligatory and welcome. By itself the Romanian Communist Party could never have mobilised the resources placed at its disposal by the Comintern, whether directly or through the various organisations under its control. Up until then, the Comintern had neglected the minuscule PCdR, which was regarded as too small to be capable of major actions. It was the first time assistance of such magnitude had come from the Comintern. The aid partly consisted in the costly orchestration of the international campaign to support the accused and partly in financing the domestic operation: lawyers' fees and other expenses relating to the trial – secret subsidies to sympathetic newspapers and journalists, the printing of clandestine literature and leaflets occasioned by the trial, the financing of actions organised by various associations. These aspects did not escape the notice of the police and the Siguranță, as is revealed by many reports to be found in the archives. Moreover, the act of accusation and the case presented by the Royal Commissar insistently recall the links between the communist networks in Romania and the Comintern, whether directly with Moscow, or via the Vienna office, where the WEB (West Europäische Büro) operated. In Bucharest and Craiova, we can observe the presence of a number of delegates from associations that are part of the networks organised by the Comintern in the West. For example, Martha Jeanne Stodel and Martha Chabrun, on behalf of the Global Committee for the Fight against Fascism, Stéphane Freund Priandel, a French journalist, Lucas Peereboam, a Belgian lawyer, and Isabelle Blum Grégoire, a Member of Parliament in Brussels, secretary of the Association of Socialist Women, who meet Ella Negruzzi, Athanasie Joja, head of the Bloc for the Defence of Democratic Liberties, one of the PCdR's camouflaged associations, Lucrețiu Pătrășcanu et al. In the Moulin de la Galette auditorium, during a meeting of the Popular Front, the release of Ana Pauker and Ernst Thaelmann, head of the German Communist Party, is demanded. A group of 50 Bulgarian lawyers sends a petition from Sofia on 4 June, which demands a halt to the trial and the release of the 19 etc. etc.

The best-known figure in the group was Ana Pauker, née Hannah Rabinsohn, born in Corlăești, near the city of Vaslui, in the province of Moldavia. She was 42 at the date of the trial. As a child, she had learned the trade of seamstress and graduated from a Jewish college as a teacher. At a very early age, she had entered the socialist movement, whose leader was Cristian Racovski at the time. She had taken part in the demonstration of 13 December 1918, which had culminated in dead, wounded, and arrests. She had been a member of the PCdR since 1921. In the same year, she married Marcel Pauker. She studied medicine for two years in Switzerland (1919-1921). In 1922, at the second PCdR Congress in Ploiești, she became a member of the Central Committee. In 1924, after the PCdR was outlawed, she was arrested. In the trial that followed, she was sentenced to 10 years imprisonment (June 1925) as a 'dangerous communist agitator'. The trial was held with the accused at liberty. Ana Pauker absconded and took refuge in Vienna. Here, she gave birth to a second child (her first, born in 1921, died a year later). She stays in Europe for two years, carrying out together with Marcel Pauker various missions entrusted to them by the Comintern, WEB and BCF (Balkan Communist Federation). In 1928, she was admitted to the V. I. Lenin Comintern International School, which trained cadres for the communist parties. She remained for three years, until March 1930. She thus became what was known in Bolshevik parlance as a 'professional revolutionary'. After graduation, she was delegated by the Comintern to the French Communist Party. In 1929, she was in Romania for a short time, where another trial was brought against her in Bucharest, at which she was sentenced to 20 years in prison on 15 April. Three weeks later, on 8 May 1929, she was given an amnesty, together with other communists, and left Romania on a Nansen passport. The Paukers separated. After a few months in Moscow, she goes to France, where she has a relationship with Eugen Fried,[30] a Comintern delegate to the Political Bureau of the PCF, entrusted with advising Maurice Thorez, the Secretary General of the French Communists. Eugen Fried, a Slovakian Jew, was the grey eminence of the PCF. From the union between Ana Pauker and Eugen Fried, a child was born in Moscow in 1932.[31] Ana Pauker plays an important role in the French communist networks. At the beginning of the 1930s, she was part of the Comintern's Latin bureau, which shows the importance of the role she had to play. After a few months in Moscow, between September 1933 and February 1934, Ana Pauker arrives in Romania in March 1934. She has dual Romanian and Soviet citizenship, and is member of three communist parties: the Romanian, Soviet and French. Her mission was to reorganise a Party that had been infiltrated by Siguranţă agents, and most of whose militants had been scattered or were in gaol.

A report entitled *The Clandestine Movement of the Communist Party from Romania, 1934* records the following:

> "In Romania, the Communist Party, which in February 1933 had managed to reach a pinnacle it had never previously attained and, in effect, to command significant numbers of workers, has still not recovered from the defeat it suffered. Since then it has not managed to unleash any major action, the movement having been reduced to mere verbal and written propaganda in various revolutionary publications."[32]

Since the Comintern regarded the Grivitza strike as the beginning of a revolution, the assessment made a year later underlines the failure. "Here in Romania the communist movement has gone from 1,200 members, as many as were registered and paid dues in February 1933, to around 650 members today."[33] The attempt to organise a common front with other left-wing parties had also ended in failure. The release from prison of Mihai Gheorghiu Bujor in the summer of 1933 and the appeal for unity had

---

[30] Annie Kriegel, Stephane Courtois, *Eugen Fried, le grand secret du PCF,* Editions du Seuil, 1997, pp. 174-187, 199-220.

[31] In 1931, Marcel Pauker also had a child from a relationship with a communist from Bassarabia.

[32] MAN Archive, SSI Fund, Dossier 32, p. 22.

[33] *Idem*, p. 23.

given risen to hope. There had been talks, but without any outcome. The communists rejected reformist tactics and demanded that the other parties adopt their clandestine tactics and the principle of 'class against class'. The failure of these endeavours led to,

"profound disillusion in both the ranks of the communists and the working class ... This failure of the united political front ... has caused disorientation to increase among their ranks and enormously dented the communists' prestige. ... Not even the insignificant number of members, as I have shown above, is made up of workers from the large industrial plants, as would be in the Party's interests. The majority is made up of ethnic minorities and individuals without any connections with the industrial proletariat, men who have no direct influence over the workers."[34] "The fluctuation of members within the Communist Party is extremely large, most workers, having stayed for a while in the Party, abandon it if they are not caught in the meantime, and the majority is made up of new members, without any revolutionary training ... without any conspiratorial training. ... In its resolutions, the Communist Party itself acknowledges its miserable state of organisation cannot be ascribed to anti-communist repression alone. ... Whereas this did indeed cause serious damage in 1934 in terms of personnel and technical equipment, the deep cause of the extreme organisational weakness of the Communist Party from Romania resides in the morale of the workers who, although agitated by their industrial discontent, do not, however, adopt the communist ideology or join revolutionary organisations. ... the PCdR has decided in its future propaganda to display its own name as little as possible and to disguise itself as much as possible, the reason being that a certain repulsion towards the communists has been observed in the workers ... henceforth they are going to agitate using revolutionary slogans without making a show that they are communists, so that workers of good faith will be deceived in their political orientation ... there is no panic or discouragement, as might have been expected in the leadership of a party that after 16 years of activity has been reduced to 650 members. This phenomenon can be explained as follows: in the first place, the communist leaders consider that the worldwide victory of communism will not be the result of a proletariat led by the

---

[34] *Idem*, p. 24-26.

communists in the capitalist countries but of a victorious war waged by the Soviet Union against the other states … the Soviets' current policy to consolidate the peace is considered to be a transitory tactic … after which there will be a policy of open hostility and declared war… The role of the communist parties is – in the Stalinist view – to be reduced to the auxiliary role, one nonetheless very important, of assisting a Soviet war victory from behind the front."[35]

This situation corresponds to the Kremlin's decision to send Comintern agitators, funds and a printing press to Romania. A Siguranţă report reveals:

"In Moscow the lack of success of the communist movement in Bucharest is put down to the premature and unprepared launch of the movement. Stalin seems to take a personal interest in the situation in Romania and in order further to demonstrate the success of 'Red activity' he is supposed to have ordered that all available means of propaganda should be directed to Romania. Soon, significant sums of money will be sent, together with agitators under various guises, false passports, refugees from Transnistria, people repatriated from Russia, etc. The movement will also target universities. It is necessary to double surveillance everywhere."

Professional agitators, trained in the USSR, are sent to Romania. A clandestine printing press is set up in Bucharest (confiscated during the course of the investigation). Significant funds are made available. Some of this money is also discovered during the investigation and confiscated. Likewise, from the materials discovered on those arrested, the same thing results: financing from the clandestine communist networks abroad. This will be one of the main counts in the indictment at trial. On the basis of these documents, it was possible to prove a connection with the Comintern. Not by chance, the lawyers for the defence systematically attacked the veracity of these documents. They demanded an expert graphologist's report. They raised points of procedure. The aim was to negate the authenticity of the incriminating documents and also to deny any connection between them and the accused. As the documents indicated, Ana Pauker was at the centre of this network. It was she who managed the funds. It was to her

---

[35] *Idem*, pp. 27-31.

that the communist networks were subordinate. It was she who handled the documents from the CPSU and Comintern.

Her return to Romania was meticulously prepared in advance by the Comintern and GRU. *Universul* was the victim of a diversion when it reproduced, on 15 May, a news item according to which Ana Pauker had been poisoned in Kharkov. As a Siguranță report reveals, the false information was meant to confuse the counter-intelligence services. The truth is that in the period when the story appeared, the 'deceased' Ana Pauker was in Moscow training a number of apparatchiks ready to be sent to Romania. The fact that the highly experienced Ana Pauker was being sent to Bucharest shows just how desperate the situation in the PCdR really was. In any case, she was not the only one to be sent. The Comintern sent 40-50 persons, in order to bring the PCdR back to life. The Comintern agents with this mission were Dimităr Ganev, Șmil Marcovici, Alexandru Moghioroș, Estera Radosovețki and Bernat Andrei. They were to appear together in the dock at the trial of the 19. With their arrest in July 1935, yet another attempt to reorganise the PCdR failed.

Who were the other protagonists? Iordan Coleff (1898-1975). Among the Bolsheviks there was a real passion for false names, disguises, pseudonyms, nicknames. Iordan Coleff was also Vasilieff or Verbanoff. In fact, his real name was Dimităr Ganev, a Bulgarian citizen. He was a member of the Secretariat of the PCdR.

> "He is the archetype of the terrorist. Conceited, stubborn and coarse. Coming to Romania on the pretext of furthering his education, in reality … he was active in the Dobrudja Revolutionary Organisation. He was discovered and deported in 1931. … But he returned to Romania … In 1932, he was sentenced to five years imprisonment *in absentia*. … He carried about his person at all times two revolvers and was guarded by adepts, in order not to fall into the hands of the police."[36]

On being sent to Doftana, Dimităr Ganev becomes the leader of the prison communists, until his release and departure for the USSR in 1940. After spending a few years in Moscow, he returns to Sofia. He is the first post-war

[36] Col. Magistrate P. Cetate, *Conspirația comunistă în România și evreica Ana Pauker în fața justiției militare*, 1941, no publishing house given, pp. 24-25.

Bulgarian ambassador to Moscow. When arrested in 1935, he drew his pistol and threatened the police. There was a scuffle. One of the policemen's guns went off and wounded Ana Pauker in the thigh, just as she was climbing into a taxi to make her escape. Ganev was a well-known Comintern and GRU agent, as the Bulgarian police described him in a report requested by their Romanian counterparts. He specialised in clandestine networks and was accustomed to carrying out dangerous missions.

Şmil Marcovici, aged 42 (a.k.a. Carol, Samy, Moraru, Schwartz, Groper, Ilie, etc.). Army deserter in 1917. He flees to Odessa where he joins Cristian Racovski, Mihail Gheorghiu Bujor et al. in the Romanian revolutionary battalion. Sent to Moscow as a courier, he travels back and forth, bringing printing presses and substantial funds to finance communist groups with the Socialist Party in Romania, as well as Bolshevik terrorist groups. Arrested as a spy in May 1920, he was sentenced to 20 years, hard labour. He escapes from Jilava Prison and flees to Russia. In Moscow, he completes the Comintern course and then becomes a teacher at the same school for communist cadres. Amnestied in 1929, he returns to Romania on the orders of the Comintern and GPU. He was a member of the Secretariat of the PCdR, the head of the Central Committee apparatus. He organises the PCdR's clandestine networks. He supervises printing presses and distribution of propaganda materials. He is the head of the internal police of the CC of the PCdR. He checks the circumstances of arrests. He keeps under surveillance those suspected of being Siguranţă informants. He distributes funds. He verifies the clandestine operations of paid activists. He also had a similar role in the Red Aid, looking after the parcels of money, food, clothing and newspapers sent to those in the prisons, as well as liaisons with various 'anti-fascist' organisations, which were funded by the PCdR and acted as a front for its activities. He died under the rubble in Doftana Prison during the earthquake of 9-10 November 1940.

Alexandru Moghioroş (a.k.a. Tell), aged 36. Locksmith. 'Professional revolutionary'. Graduate of the Comintern School for Communist Cadres in Moscow, in 1930. Sent to Romania by the International Union of Communist Youth. Arrested in 1931, he is tried at liberty but absconds. Arrested in January 1934 while travelling from Vienna to Kosice, where he was to deliver a report from IUCY central. Returned to Romania by the Czechoslovak authorities, he manages to escape yet again. Dangerous terrorist. Up until his arrest in 1935, he lives clandestinely, all the while trying to rebuild the UCY organisation in Romania. After the war he is a member of the Political Bureau, replacing none other than Ana Pauker in 1952. He is one of Dej's most trusted henchmen. In 1965, when Nicolae Ceaușescu comes to power, Moghioroș loses his position in the Political Bureau.

Estera Radosovețki. Graduate of the Literature Faculty of Bucharest University. A Siguranță report informs us, "she has a prominent role in the revolutionary communist movement and serves as a liaison with communist organisations abroad, being a member of the Political Bureau of the so-called Romanian Communist Party, for the transmission of reports to and reception of instructions from the Comintern." A member of the Political Bureau of the UTC, connected with the West-Europäische Büro, which directed the activity of a number of communist parties in Central Europe and the Balkans. Between 1931 and 1933 she was in Berlin, where she worked for Willy Münzenberg, alongside well-known German communist Walter Liestke, with whom she cohabited. In Berlin, she established connections with, among others Ștefan Foriș and Lucrețiu Pătrășcanu. In 1933, after Hitler comes to power, Münzenberg moves to Paris and the WEB, along with Estera Radosovețki, to Vienna. She is arrested in Prague the next year, together with two Comintern agents, also, like her, members of the PCdR: Dori Goldstein and his wife Șeila Averbuch (a.k.a. Vanda Nicolski). Dori Goldstein had been sentenced to 20 years in prison, having been convicted of spying for the USSR. Prague was a important junction for the PCdR. The Party had a secondary headquarters there, with direct links to Moscow, Vienna and Paris. At the date of the trial Estera Radosovețski was 27. She was responsible for UTC links with the Comintern, via the International Union of Communist Youth. After the war, she married Alexandru Moghioroș.

Liuba Roitman-Chișinevschi, aged 24. Like Estera Radosovețski, she was born in Tighina. A bookbinder by trade. In 1930, she served one year and eight months in prison in Ismail, in 1934, a further three months, also in Ismail, and in 1934, seven months, in Bucharest. A member of the Secretariat of the 'revolutionary unions', run by the communists. The wife of Iosif Chișinevschi. Liuba Chișinevschi played an important role in the 1950s, but later fell from grace together with her husband.

Bernat Andor, aged 28. Deserter. Carpenter by trade. He had already served two short prison sentences in 1930 and 1934. In 1930 he travelled to Moscow clandestinely. He studied at the Comintern School. The Comintern appointed him head of the UTC on his return to Romania. He set up the printing press discovered by the Siguranţă. Imprisoned at Doftana and Caransebeş, from where he was deported to Transnistria in 1942. He was executed on 17 March 1944 in the concentration camp at Rîbniţa by retreating SS troops.

Grimberg Leizer, aged 24. A soldier at the date of his arrest. It was not his first arrest for communist activities. Alexandru Moghioroş was hiding in the house where he lived. "His situation is all the more serious given that, being a soldier, he has infringed discipline and his oath of loyalty by operating in a revolutionary organisation whose aim is to overthrow the government." He is imprisoned at Doftana and Caransebeş in 1941. He is transferred to the concentration camp at Vapnyarka in September 1942. On 17 March 1944, he is executed at Rîbniţa by retreating SS troops.

Herbach János. Member of the UTC leadership. He dies of tuberculosis in prison. There was a factory named after him in Cluj in the 1950s.

Alexandru Drăghici, aged 22. The only ethnic Romanian at the trial. A labourer at CFR Grivitza. Communist agitator. Member of the UTC leadership. After the war, he was Minister of the Interior (1952-1965), one of the pillars of the communist regime, as well as one of the initiators and executors of repression in the 1950s. Feared and detested by the populace, he was Lavrenti Beria to Dej's Joseph Stalin.

Ladislau Ady, aged 24. Print worker. Communist agitator. Recidivist. Arrested together with Alexandru Moghioroş in 1932 for distributing manifestos. In charge of the UTC printing press at No. 36 General Cernat Street. Recruited as an informant by the SSI in 1936. Deputy Minister of the Interior from December 1953 to July 1955. Unmasked as a former Siguranţă informant, he is sacked.

Vilma Kajeso, aged 20. UTC printing press operative.

Donca Simo, aged 24. Communist agitator. Recidivist. Imprisoned together with her husband, Iuliu Simo, in 1933. UTC printing press operative. She died in Văcăreşti Prison in 1937. In the period from 1948-1965, she was transformed into a martyr for propaganda purposes, a Romanian equivalent of Zoya Kosmodemianskaya.

Nagy Stefan, aged 29. Host for conspiratorial meetings, in the pay of Red Aid. "Nagy Stefan was the intermediary between the Central Committee of the so-called Romanian Communist Party and various communist agitators." He was, above all, Ana Pauker's liaison man, setting up contacts for her and organising conspiratorial meetings in the house he rented using money he received from the Comintern via Pauker.

Samuel Kruck, aged 26. Communist agitator. As a cover for the illegal printing press, he rented a building, in which he opened a grocer's shop in April 1935. The money came from the PCdR via Bernat Andor.

Emanoil Kaufman, aged 42. It was at his house that Ana Pauker, Iordan Coleff-Verbanoff and Şmil Marcovici met immediately before their arrest. The house was rented using Comintern money. Kaufman had previously organised other safe houses.

Ana and Stefan Csacsar, aged 28 and 36 respectively. Like Kaufman and Kruck, the providers of a safe house. Members of the PCdR apparatus. Their names can be found in the documents of the CC of the UTC plenary of July 1935, when part of the group had been arrested. Likewise, forged documents used by PCdR activists were discovered (for example, the identity card used by one of the communist leaders, Alexandru Sencovici, when he had gone to Moscow in August 1935 to take part in the Seventh Comintern Congress). "The rent on the house where the Csacsars lived was paid from the funds of the so-called Romanian Communist Party."

Ernest Schoen, aged 23. Carpenter. Previously sentenced *in absentia* to five years in prison in 1934.

The trial of the 19, arrested 11 months previously, commences in Craiova on 5 June. All the actors in the tragedy into which Romania will be plunged 10 years thence were present. Firstly, the 'bourgeois' justice system, an ambassador of liberal democracy, an institution under siege, one which still bears the hallmarks of a parliamentary regime, but with one nuance: this is not a civil but rather a military court. Then there are the communists, both in the dock and among the defence lawyers. Among them are figures who will be the protagonists in the history that unfolds 10 years later: Ana Pauker, Alexandru Drăghici, Alexandru Moghioroş, Lucreţiu Pătrăşcanu, Ion Gheorghe Maurer. Nor is the extreme Right absent, even if it plays a peripheral role during the trial. The extreme Right is present inside and outside court, demonstrating in counterpoint to the groups mobilised by the communists. The play can now commence. The War Council of the First Army, the Royal Commissioner – Petre G. Popescu-Cetate – the lawyers for the defence, the accused – 13 men and six women – and the public, take their places on the stage.

From the outset, the defence's tactic is one of tergiversation. On the first day of the trial, after the pleas of the accused, a list of witnesses proposed by the defence is read out. It contains more than 6,000 names, 95 per cent of whom do not know the defendants. Their purpose was to be summoned to court so that, on returning home, they could become unwitting agents of communist propaganda. Another important moment was the defence's complaint that there was not free access to the courtroom. Not all those who wished to do so were able to enter, and hundreds of persons had been shut out. The court rejected the complaint as unfounded, given that the courtroom was not big enough to accommodate everyone. In the afternoon session, the defence demanded the postponement of the trial because not all the witnesses had been summoned. The first serious incident occurred on 6 June, when a lawyer contested the competence of the council of judges.

"Lawyer Nachtigal, demanded that he should be given the floor in an arrogant tone of voice and banged his fist on the table. The presiding judge denied him the floor and on this account there arose an incident involving the defence and the council, with all the defence lawyers vociferating in protest at the council, agitating the courtroom and even interrupting the presiding judge, shouting and gesticulating. Four of the accused joined in the shouting and were removed from the courtroom. The presiding judge called upon the guards for assistance. As a result of these undisciplined acts, the presiding judge ordered Mr Nachtigal to be removed from the courtroom, and this was carried out. The other lawyers resumed their protests, vociferating loudly, until the whole courtroom had to be cleared. Fifteen minutes later, the session resumed and the presiding judge ordered that the defence of the accused be provided by officers appointed *ex officio* for this purpose, on the grounds that the civil lawyers had not followed the Code of Military Justice and had engaged in acts of insubordination. He ordered the accused to be brought into the courtroom, and all were brought in, with the exception of Ana Csacsar, who refused claiming that she did not feel well after having been physically maltreated (so she claimed) and as a result the presiding judge once again adjourned the session for half an hour, during which time a physician was brought in to examine the accused, concluding that she had not been physically maltreated. When the session resumed, lawyer Mihail Macavei took the floor and said that the removal of the accused from the courtroom had been carried out in a brutal way, and that they had been physically maltreated and beaten. He demanded that the decision to exclude lawyer Mihail Nachtigal from the courtroom should be reconsidered. ... Lawyer Maurer protested against the exclusion of lawyer Nachtigal from the session. ... During the speech of the aforementioned lawyer, prisoner Estera Radosoveţki was taken ill and fainted, and so the session was adjourned."[37]

It was all a provocation. The image we get is of a well-planned performance, meticulously directed and cast. The public are the audience. The accused, the lawyers, the president of the War Council, the Royal Commissar, and the magistrates each play their role. What is surprising is the cohesion of the accused. It was natural that the authorities should go through the same ritual gestures, utter the same time-worn phrases, stipulated by the law and procedure. But what is astonishing is that the 19 accused, a part of whom claim not to know each other, can act out the script with the unison of a choir. It is not only their discipline that is amazing, but also their acting talents. The lawyers are also caught up in the farce. A part of them are connected to the clandestine communist network. The script had been written elsewhere, in Moscow, long ago. It had first been acted in Leipzig by Georgi Dimitrov and co. The reason for the courtroom outbursts, which resemble collective madness, affecting both lawyers and accused, is the presence of a TASS correspondent, Vladimir Bobrov, in the courtroom. He is also the Soviet legation's press attaché in Bucharest. One thousand copies of *Izvestia* were sold daily at the Hertz Bookshop. The buyers, as noted in a Siguranţă report, were communist sympathisers. Bobrov's article appears in the 9 June issue of *Izvestiya*, the newspaper run by Nikolay Bukharin (shot two years later on Stalin's order). He recounts an apocalyptic scene in the courtroom: the prisoners are beaten by the gendarmes, and as a result of the beatings two are taken ill, with Ana Pauker passing out twice. The defence is supposed to have sent a protest against the massacre to the Prime Minister. On 11 June, Bobrov publishes another article along the same lines: "Around the court are posted military patrols with machine guns. The accused are beaten during the court session. Bands of hooligans in uniform swear at them under police protection." The incident on 6 June, involving lawyers and the accused together, was aimed at causing a stir, provoking a

---

[37] MAN Archive, *idem*, p. 227.

drama to make headlines worldwide, and in the USSR above all. There was consistent reporting about the abuses of the Romanian justice system, about the 'revolutionary' atmosphere in the courtroom. Many of the lawyers were communists (Lucrețiu Pătrășcanu, Ion Gheorghe Maurer, Petre Grozdea) or had links with the clandestine communist networks (Ghiță Ionescu, Radu Popescu). They were thus able to anticipate the reaction. Moreover, via *Izvestiya*, the Comintern was able to find out that its operatives were doing what was required.

Up until 12 June, the defence did not make a single statement that did not conclude with the words, "I demand a postponement of the trial." The reasons given were various in the extreme. A number of times each session, through one or other of the lawyers, there are incidents of this kind. The most active in coming up with objections and all kinds of other chicanery were Ion Gheorghe Maurer and Lucrețiu Pătrășcanu. It takes a whole week to finish reading out the act of indictment and finally proceed to the cross-examination of the accused, beginning with none other than Ana Pauker. Șmil Marcovici and Iordan Coleff-Verbanoff are then examined. Pătrășcanu demands a postponement of the trial on the grounds that Estera Radosovețki is ill. The Royal Commissar objects, saying that he has the impression that the accused is faking. However, the council agrees to seek an expert opinion. Proceedings are adjourned. The physicians called upon to examine Radosovețki conclude that there is nothing wrong with her. During the afternoon session on 15 June, the presiding judge orders journalist Ștefan Voicu (Aurel Rotemberg) of the *Zorile* daily to be removed from the courtroom, on the grounds that he has "reported the debates in this trial in an inaccurate way." *Zorile* was published in the period between 1934 and 1936 and was run by lawyer Emanoil Socor.[38] Although he was a well-known left-wing sympathiser, Socor demands money to publish articles favourable to the accused when Lucrețiu Pătrășcanu goes to him to

---

[38] Emanoil Socor, sentenced to five years, hard labour, for crimes against the state on 25 November 1920. A sub-officer, on 24 January 1921, he is stripped of his rank in front of the troops in Jilava Fort (*Universul*, 12 April 1930). In 1930 he runs as a candidate for Parliament in Cernăuți/ Czernowitz. He loses to extreme Right candidate A. C. Cuza. In 1930, Ion Dumitrescu bombs the editorial office of *Adevărul* newspaper, whose director is Socor. He is sentenced to three years in prison in 1931 for the attack.

ask that he accredit Ștefan Voicu, a communist journalist, to cover the trial. Socor asks for 50,000 lei, but Pătrășcanu haggles him down to 30,000.[39]

On the same day, Alexandru Moghioroș and Bernat Andrei are cross-examined. They are both alumni of the Comintern's school for cadres in Moscow, tasked with rebuilding the UTC. Bernat Andrei causes a scene, refusing to answer questions. He verbally abuses the council. He yells in court. The session is adjourned while the rowdy prisoner is bundled out. The lawyers object and demand that he be brought back into the courtroom. The president of the council refuses. Bernat Andrei will not appear in the other sessions. In *Izvestiya* another article is published about brutality on the part of the authorities and the accused being deprived of the right to a defence. The article is reproduced by Comintern-funded Western newspapers, directed from Paris by Willy Münzenberg. The next day, another journalist for *Zorile*, Paul Samoilă, is expelled from the courtroom, on the grounds that he has reported that Estera Radosovețski is in a coma, something that is "a patent lie," as the Royal Commissar remarks. Lawyers Petre Grozdea and Lucrețiu Pătrășcanu demand that the *Universul* reporter be expelled for "mendacious reporting of the trial." The president of the Court rejects the demand, arguing that the journalist's accounts are in accordance with the facts. In any case, this incident follows the cross-examination of the 'comatose' Estera Radosovețski. The conflict between the Sărindar press and *Universul* had gone from the pages of the newspapers out onto the street and now into the courtroom. *Universul* was favourable to the court, wrote constantly about the communist threat, conducted a large-scale anti-Semitic campaign, and viewed both lawyers and accused with hostility. The Royal Commissar Petre G. Popescu-Cetate and the magistrates were described favourably and urged to hand down heavy sentences. *Adevărul*, *Dimineața* and *Zorile* – the Sărindar papers – took the opposite stand.

Because the accused and their lawyers talk among themselves in languages other than Romanian, in Hungarian and German in particular, an interpreter is brought in to report on the nature of these exchanges. He also has to translate the statements of those witnesses and accused that do not speak Romanian. The cross-examination of the accused concludes in the afternoon session on 16 June without further incidents. The next day, the questioning of the witnesses begins. More than six thousand have been summoned. Lawyers accustomed to defending communists had

---

[39] MAN Archive, SSI Fund, pp. 41-49.

ready-made lists of witnesses. At the Kishinev trial and the trials of Tudor Bugnariu, Grigore Preoteasa and Ofelia Manole, thousands of witnesses had been called, 90 per cent of them the same ones. Likewise, there was also a list of witnesses from abroad, always the same: Romain Rolland, André Malraux, Paul Langevin, Léon Blum, Georgi Dimitrov, et al. Moreover, associations, lawyers, journalists etc. were also invited to take the stand. The foreseeable non-attendance of these witnesses gave the defence extra reasons to demand a postponement of the trial. The lists did the rounds of every trial. With regard to the witnesses invited from abroad, the public figures and associations integrated into the policy of the Popular Front, orchestrated by Karl Radek and Willy Münzenberg, we can find them at trials involving communists in all the countries of Europe. All courtesy of Comintern funds. At the Craiova trial, too, we encounter numerous foreign journalists, lawyers there to observe, and civic and anti-fascist associations. Wherever in Europe communists are on trial, the same names crop up time and time again.

The cross-examination of the witnesses lasts until 30 June. More than 50 take the stand daily. Of the six thousand summoned, a few hundred turn up. Most of them have nothing to do with the trial and do not know the accused. The accused also ask them various questions. Similarly, these questions have nothing to do with the case. Ana Pauker, who is highly active in this part of the debates, asks the witnesses about their families, how much they earn, where they work, how many children they have, whether they own land, and so on. It is a propaganda exercise. During this cross-examination she is backed by Estera Radosoveţki, who has given up fainting at every opportunity, and Alexandru Moghioroş. Two witnesses – Constantin Rouă and Constantin David – are sentenced to six months in prison for grave offences against the Council. David had been tried for taking part in the Grivitza strikes and acquitted. He was assassinated during the Iron Guard rebellion of 21-23 January. There are incidents between the prosecutors and the defence. The president of the Court has to intervene, especially on the subject of shortening the discussions and focussing them on the subject at hand. In the same period, the press loses interest in the trial. The defence, too, begin to lose interest, with only one of them turning up to one of the sessions. Apart from this, to be noted is the fact that many of the witnesses do not speak Romanian, or speak the language poorly, and that not one of them knows why he has been summoned to court. Many of the courtroom exchanges are comical. From time to time, the accused make communist speeches. Almost all the witnesses are unfavourable to the 19. A few stand out for declaring that they support the 'anti-fascist' cause. The press records the unexpectedness and the humour of many courtroom scenes. The trial takes on the appearance of something risible and interminable. The Council seems to have allowed the situation to get out of control. The proceedings drag on unjustifiably. The pathos and sombre air of the first days of the trial has given way to an almost vaudeville, situation-comedy atmosphere. The attempt to transform the witness stand into a tribune, the accused into accusers, and the witnesses into pilgrims there to display the devotion of the masses to the anti-fascist cause and their attachment to the accused, has been a failure. As Belu Zilber said, Romanian communism will be a mixture of Stalin and Caragiale. It was a saying that was illustrated in this trial, long before Pauker, Pătrășcanu and Maurer came to power.

In the middle of the hearings, on 26 June, lawyer Lucrețiu Pătrășcanu was expelled from the trial as a result of a notification from the Ilfov Bar saying that he had been suspended on the grounds that he was under penal investigation by the War Council of the Second Army on the same charges as the 19 defendants in the dock, "infraction under the law for the public peace," in the trial brought against him for the role he had played in the Grivitza strikes. On 30 June, the cross-examination of the witnesses came to a close. The prosecutor's summing-up commenced in the morning session of 1 July.

> "Off with the mask! Now, I ask you to gaze upon them. Beneath the democracy, terrorist conspiracy, corruption and intrigue, the most determined enemy of the Cross, of freedom and of civilisation, the hatred and revenge of enemies of the nation, paid instigators and profiteers of mystification, proletarian idleness kindred to cunning, army deserters with the hearts of traitors and sullied hands, despoilers and dues-takers to fill their bottomless stomachs, veterans of the prisons with parvenu wiles, the lackeys of humiliated enemies," perorates Lieutenant Colonel Petre Popescu-Cetate.[40]

The accused are charged with "infractions against the public peace" according to the new law, which treats as a delict

---

[40] *Idem*, pp. 39-40.

"(a) maintaining links with any foreign person or association with a view to receiving instructions or assistance of any kind in order to prepare a communist revolution; (b) working by terrorist means to change the social and political order in Romania; (c) intentionally assisting in any manner a foreign association that aims to attack Romanian institutions or state order using the means under letter (b); (d) intentional membership of any association stipulated under the foregoing letter."

To these are added the provisions of the Journal no. 1544/30 December 1933 of the Council of Ministers with regard to the state of siege, which referred all such cases to military tribunals. The stipulated prison sentences were between five and 10 years. The Royal Commissar demands the maximum sentence for all the accused.

The speeches for the defence began in the afternoon of the same day. Only two lawyers presented themselves in court. Stelian Nițulescu was defending Bernat Andrei, Ernest Schoen, and Ladislau Ady. Lazăr Șaraga was defending Șmil Marcovici. Alexandru Mîță, a PNȚ deputy, was defending Ana Pauker. Tuna Lerner-Joja was defending Estera Radosovețki and Liuba Roitman-Chișinevschi. In the 1950s, Petre Pandrea recalls: "Tuna Lerner, the wife of Nachtigal, is a long-time communist militant, quite a libertine in her youth. She was the mistress of Lucrețiu (Pătrășcanu – *author's note*), then the wife of Athanasie Joja. When Joja went to prison, she divorced and took Nachtigal."[41] Lawyer Petre Grozdea was defending Alexandru Moghioroș and Herbach János. Because of "insulting remarks about the members of the War Council, we are, after repeated calls to order, withdrawing lawyer Petre Grozdea's right to address this court." Iancu Vasiliu-Galați was defending Emanoil Kaufman. Ghiță Ionescu[42] was defending Ștefan and Ana Csacsar. Ilie Raicu was the counsel for Vilma Cajeso, Donca Simo, and Liuba Roitman-Chișinevschi. V. V. Stanciu was the lawyer for Alexandru

---

[41] Petre Pandrea, *Amintirile mandarinului Valah*, Bucharest: Editura Albatros, 2000, p. 179.

[42] Ghiță Ionescu emigrated to Britain in 1946, where he became head of the Romanian section of Radio Free Europe at the end of the 1950s and, in the early 1960s, a professor of political science in Manchester, the editor of *Government and Opposition* review and author of the first history of the PCR, published in 1964.

Drăghici. Radu Popescu[43] was defending Ana and Stefan Csacsar and Leizer Grimberg.

On the morning of 6 July, Maurer began his speech for the defence. He was speaking for Ana Pauker, Alexandru Moghioroș, Nagy Stefan, and Herbach János. The next day, Stelian Nițulescu and Ion Gheorghe Maurer spoke in the name of all the accused. The accused were then allowed to have their say. Everyone was expecting the 19 to make communist speeches, with heart-rending accusations against the regime, with calls to join the proletarian revolution, with warnings against imminent war and a fascist takeover of Romania. Not a bit of it. There were no speeches in the heroic style of Dimitrov. The accused seem resigned and await the verdict. The jury withdraws to deliberate. The 19 are found guilty on all counts, with no attenuating circumstances. The verdict is unanimous. The sentences are heavy. This is to a certain degree surprising, because in the trial of communists held in Kishinev in March-April, the sentences had been light. The ringleader, Petre Constantinescu-Iași had been given only two and a half years. What counted for the jury in this case, however, was the campaign orchestrated by the Comintern, which magnified the importance of those in the dock, and also the pressures exerted by the press, especially on the Right. What also tipped the scales was the belief that Ana Pauker and the others were heads of clandestine communist networks in Romania (which was true: Pauker, Marcovici, and Ganev were members of the Secretariat of the PCdR, and Andor, Moghioroș, Radosovețki and Roitman-Chișinevschi were also Comintern agents, schooled in Moscow), that they were funded by the USSR. The materials confiscated during their arrest and during searches were sufficient evidence not only of their political affiliations but also of Comintern funding. All these circumstances aggravated the situation for the accused. The sentence specifies for each of the convicted "infractions against the public peace whereby in the year 1935, with forethought and culpable intention, he/she made contact with agents of the Third Communist International abroad willingly becoming a member of that association with the aim of receiving and in fact receiving instructions and pecuniary assistance to prepare a communist revolution in Romania."

---

[43] Arrested in 1948 and then released. He became an ideologue of the Dej regime and theatre critic. He played a nasty part in a number of political trials brought against intellectuals in the late 1950s, such as in the Noica-Pillat trial of 1960, where he testified as a witness for the prosecution.

The sentences: Ana Pauker, Dimităr Ganev-Verbanoff and Şmil Marcovici: 10 years; Moghioroş Şandor, Bernat Andor and Ladislau Ady: 9 years, 11 months; Ernest Schoen, Estera Radosoveţski and Leiser Grimberg: 9 years, 10 months; Liuba Roitman: 9 years, 9 months; Alexandru Drăghici: 9 years, 3 months; Herbach János: 9 years; Donco Simo: 8 years, 11 months; Emil Kaufman and Wilma Kajeso: 6 years; Ana and Stefan Csacsar, and Nagy Stefan: 5 years; S. Kruck: 2 years, 6 months. To each sentence was added a 10 year correctional interdiction, which meant they were denied the right to vote, be elected, occupy public office, or carry weapons. In addition, the convicted were obligated to pay fines of between 70,000 and 100,000 lei, which in 1936 was equivalent to an average-to-good yearly salary today.

The courtroom greets the sentence favourably, as reported in a number of newspapers. There are cries of "Down with communism! Down with Maurer! Down with Ana Pauker!" We must ask ourselves who were the people in the public gallery, and whether their support of the War Council was spontaneous or orchestrated by the extreme Right. The blue shirts of the supporters of A. C. Cuza and Octavian Goga were frequently to be seen during the course of the trial. They had threatened the lawyers for the defence and left-wing journalists. They had made aggressive declarations. "I cannot be suspected of any sympathy for communism or communists, but all the same, this delirious joy at 155 years in prison handed down for human deeds has a note of cannibalism about it. The extremes to which passion can go!" noted Constantin Argetoianu in his diary.[44]

The trial of the Reichstag arsonists was a success for the accused and their supporters. Georgi Dimitrov and two Bulgarians were acquitted. The first clash between the two dictatorships, the red and the brown, had been won by Stalin. Dimitrov made a good impression. On 28 February 1934, a year later, he was to arrive in Moscow by aeroplane. Two months later, in April, he would become leader of the Comintern, after an interview before the Politburo in the Kremlin. The Ana Pauker trial turned out very differently. In Leipzig there had been acquittals. In Craiova, the sentences totalled 155 years in prison, 190 years of civil interdiction and 1,475,000 lei in fines. Those in the dock failed to turn their accusers into the accused, where Dimitrov had succeeded. The propaganda war had not been a triumph for the Comintern, in spite of extensive mobilisation of anti-fascist

---

[44] Constantin Argetoianu, *Însemnări zilnice*, Bucharest: Editura Machiavelli, 1998, vol. 1, p. 389.

European public opinion. The immediate effects of the trial are described in a Siguranță report, which utilised information received from informants in the upper echelons of the PCdR. The report says,

"the great majority of people approve of the guilty verdict and even in the ranks of the industrial workers no protests have been reported, although the communist organisations are continuing their propaganda and agitation. The working masses in general view the guilty verdict as a powerful blow against the Communist Party from Romania ... The left-wing workers ... realised during the debates at the trial that there are only people from ethnic minorities in the leadership positions in the communist revolutionary movement and that these people displayed a frivolous attitude in court. ... The masses have realised the weakness of the Communist Party ... The leadership of the Communist Party, from the political viewpoint, interprets the guilty verdict as an act of a government that has begun to turn the country into a fascist regime ... In Jewish circles, opinions are divided. More than ever before there are many Jews that approve of the sentences handed down to the communists given that the attitude of the accused and of Ana Pauker in particular has contributed to a rise in anti-Semitism, and they ascribe all the incidents that have taken place recently to this cause. Of course, a very large number of Jews who hold democratic, anti-fascist, socialist or communist views are on the side of the convicted."[45]

Another SSI document, also from July 1936, reports,

"They (the upper echelons of the PCdR – *author's note*) are afraid of the criticisms their superiors abroad are going to make and of the consequences of these. The question arises: given the funds from abroad that have been made available to the Party and MOPR, given the manner in which the Comintern organised the defence, protests and all the international agitation, what were the Party and MOPR doing throughout the trial, if this is the known outcome?"[46]

---

[45] Siguranță report dated 12 July 1936, MAN Archive, SSI Fund, Dossier 43, pp. 371-376.
[46] MAN Archive, SSI Fund, Dossier 43, p. 347.

The political outcome of the trial was, for the PCdR, negative. The effect on the clandestine communist movement was major. Due to the actions of the Siguranța in 1935, the PCdR and Red Aid suffered a blow. The deployment of Comintern agents in 1934-1935, which ought to have meant a change for the better in the communists' fortunes, was a failure. Read today, the official reports show that the Siguranța was well informed.

> "The Central Committee of the Communist Party gave the order to transform the trial of Ana Pauker, Berat, Mogyorossy [*sic*.] and the other communists, brought to court for proven subversive, clandestine activity, into an anti-fascist trial. The reason for transforming a communist trial into an anti-fascist trial is that the communist leaders have realised – in carrying out the Comintern's change in tactics – that a communist trial has no effect on public opinion, whereas the slogan and the ideas of the anti-fascist struggle, regarded as a new trend, might mobilise the masses to greater effect, agitating them and channelling them gradually towards the platform of revolutionary communist struggle."[47]

Ștefan Foriș, the head of the PCdR Agitprop section at the time, organises protests, petitions and vigilantes to guard the defence lawyers. Likewise, sympathisers with the accused keep up agitation via a number of communist front organisations. The left-wing press carries favourable articles, in contrast to *Universul*. *Dimineața* publishes an interview with Lucrețiu Pătrășcanu, a lawyer for the defence, and *Adevărul* another with Ana Pauker. Pătrășcanu says (*Dimineața*, 13 February 1936), "Ana Pauker, Coleff and all the other anti-fascists arrested and brought to trial have been active against the establishment of a dictatorial regime in Romania, and for the daily bread and freedom of the Romanian people, for the democratic rights of the popular masses in Romania against the bellicose threats of Hitlerist fascist dictatorships. This is the activity of Ana Pauker and the others accused of anti-fascism." Lucrețiu Pătrășcanu was lying. He knew Ana Pauker personally, and also her husband, Marcel Pauker. They were all founder members of the PCdR. In 1934, they had all met at the Comintern headquarters in the Hotel Lux in Moscow.

Pătrășcanu knew that they were not anti-fascist militants, but Comintern agents. Likewise, he knew that Ana Pauker and the others, the same as

---

[47] MAN Archive, SSI Fund, Dossier 42, Vol. 2, p. 6.

himself, were engaged in clandestine activities, activities banned since 1924, and that 'anti-fascism' was nothing but a façade. In October 1936, Pătrășcanu writes a letter to the Political Bureau of the Secretariat (at that time made up of Boris Ștefanov, Ștefan Foriș, Constantin Pîrvulescu, Vanda Nikolski, Nicolae Goldberger, Gheorghe Crosnev, Moise Dubinski, Alexandru Sencovici, Ilie Pintilie and Ion Popescu-Puțuri). In it he analyses the trial from the viewpoint of its utility to communist activities. He regards postponement of the trial, demanded by the defence on the orders of Moscow, as a "political and tactical error." Pătrășcanu had even been threatened with a vote of censure if he opposed the idea. The public campaign has been weak, he writes:

> "The guilty verdict, which ought to have given rise to a storm of protest, has been received in total silence and passivity … The Right was able to turn the indictment and debates in Craiova into a tool for agitation and propaganda, to mobilise in Craiova and other urban centres combative fascist forces and to organise street demonstrations. To these right-wing campaigns around and against the trial, in fact against the revolutionary movement, our response, precisely because of the lack of a mass campaign, proved to be more than weak … and necessarily culminated in failure."

Pătrășcanu wonders whether the real cause of the failure should be sought only in what he calls "objective conditions" and concludes that it should not. Those responsible should be sought among the members of the Political Bureau and Secretariat, who quite simply vanished for the length of the trial. "To Craiova … no delegation was sent. There was no solidarity with those in the dock. Absolutely none. And we ended up with the paradoxical situation in which four delegates arrived from abroad, but not one from Romania … no guidance, criticism, or effective support was received from the Secretariat. Throughout the trial, the Secretariat was as good as non-existent. … Throughout the trial, hooligans (the extreme Right – *author's note*) ruled Craiova."[48] The trial of the 19 was one of the few major public events in which the communists were enmeshed. The Political Bureau and the Secretariat were non-existent, and likewise the Party they imagined they

---

[48] ANR, *Copilăria Comunismului românesc în arhivă Kominernului*, 2001, pp. 384-386.

led. The Comintern, too, in spite of a few outbursts in the Western press, seemed wholly uninterested.

***

The year 1936 was a crossroads. On 3 May, the Popular Front in France, bringing together socialists, radicals and communists, won the elections. On 4 June, Léon Blum formed a government. On 18 July, troops under the command of General Franco revolted against the Madrid Government. Civil war breaks out in Spain. Six weeks after the close of the Ana Pauker group trial, in Moscow the first major trial of the Great Terror commences. Five days later, on 23 August, sentence is passed. Stalin begins to decimate the Bolshevik old guard. On 2 September, Yagoda is replaced by Yezhov. The period that follows – up until 1938, when Yezhov is replaced by Lavrenti Beria – is called the Yezhovchina, the period in which repression reaches its pinnacle in the USSR. On 7 October, *Pravda* announces the arrest of Karl Radek, the erstwhile comrade of Lenin, head of the Kremlin's propaganda section, a Bolshevik Goebbels. On 22 October, the Spanish Government agrees to the formation of international brigades. On 7 November, the first units arrive on the Madrid front. At the first major show trial in Moscow those in the dock include Lev Kamenev and Grigori Zinoviev. They had been close associates with Lenin since before 1917. In the former ballroom of the Noblemen's Club, there are "150-odd Soviet citizens and 30-odd foreign journalists and diplomats. The foreign audience was crucial to the show. Unanimously hostile criticism might have prevented further performances. Too many of these privileged witnesses allowed themselves to be taken in by an improbable plot and incredible details. The Soviet spectators were all selected by the NKVD and were, in fact, mainly NKVD clerks and officials."[49]

Stalin was removing his adversaries, or whom he believed to be adversaries, but the trial was also a propaganda operation. This time we no longer have 'bourgeois' or 'fascist' tribunals trying Comintern agents, as was the case in Craiova and Bucharest. This time the Bolsheviks are settling accounts among themselves. They are doing so publicly, in a studied and bloody spectacle. The death sentences come thick and fast. Stalin destroys

---

[49] Robert Conquest, *The Great Terror: Stalin's Purge of the Thirties*, Penguin, 1971, p. 152.

all those who contest his power or who might potentially do so. His victims are Bolshevik chiefs, functionaries, diplomats, officers, and also Comintern cadres. For Stalin, the Comintern represented a branch of Western espionage. It was a hotbed of agitators who, given their contacts with the outside world, might at any time turn into heretics. They were a mixture of believers in the Revolution, adventurers and those in it for the money, in the pay of Moscow. Not one of these categories was trusted by the Kremlin. Around 20,000 Comintern agents were executed over the course of three years. They included many of the Comintern leaders. Grigori Zinoviev had been the Comintern's first president. He was sacked and replaced with Bukharin in 1928. Bukharin, too, was executed. Cristian Racovski, the author of the Comintern programme in 1919 and a member of the first leadership (alongside Lenin, Trotsky, Zinoviev, Platten and Bukharin) was another victim. Béla Kuhn, the leader of the Hungarian Bolshevik Revolution, who replaced Racovski in the Comintern presidium, was killed, accused, among other things, of spying for Romania.

In 1927, Racovski, lately having returned from Paris, was expelled from the CC of the CPSU and exiled to Astrakhan. Panait Istrati goes to visit him there. Racovski is staying in a hotel crawling with bedbugs and is sick with malaria. He is one of the leaders of the anti-Stalinist opposition. He is writing articles and manifestos, and keeps up an extensive correspondence with other opposition figures. Thousands have been deported, exiled, and dismissed from their jobs. In 1928, Racovski writes *The Occupational Hazards of Power*, which caused a great stir in the USSR. Trotsky is in Alma-Ata. In 1929, he is expelled and goes to live on Prinkipo Island in Constantinople. As a former supporter of Trotsky, Racovski remains head of the opposition that purports to be "on the Left," together with Preobrazhensky, Radek and Shmilga. At the end of October 1929, he is transferred from Astrakhan to Saratov. Here, he is visited by American journalist Louis Fischer, a Bolshevik sympathiser at the time and later author of one of the best biographies of Lenin. He writes that here Racovski was "saluted respectfully by people, because this political criminal was the most famous and respected inhabitant."[50] Racovski tells him, "Stalin has betrayed the Revolution." These opinions, once shared with others, reach the ears of Stalin. Racovski is writing an essay about Saint-Simon and a history of his

---

[50] Related by Pierre Broue, *Racovski, ou la Révolution dans tous les pays*, Fayard, 1996, p. 308.

own career as a revolutionary socialist, in which he portrays the leaders he has known personally: Engels, Lenin, Roza Luxemburg, Jules Guèsde, Jean Jaurès, Victor Adler, Karl Kautsky, Karl Liebknecht, Trotsky. He is also writing a history: the Bolshevik Revolution in Ukraine, which he ruled as a Bolshevik dictator from 1918-1923. In autumn 1929, he is deported to Barnaul, an even more desolate spot, where contacts with his supporters are practically impossible. He is to remain here for five years, until the winter of 1934. The conditions are harsh. He has to endure the Siberian frost. He also has a heart complaint. He is interrogated and searched at regular intervals. Thanks to his notoriety, he manages to avoid being sent to a labour camp. He was much too well-known in the USSR and abroad. Some of his friends were the leaders of influential parties in the West; some were even in government. Stalin had not yet decided what to do with the 'historical' leaders of the Revolution (Kamenev, Zinoviev, Bukharin, Rykov, Tomsky, Racovski, Radek etc.), and he had not yet gained a total monopoly on power. He preferred to employ corruption and all kinds of pressure. In the ranks of his opposition colleagues, Racovski proved to be among the most intractable. One by one, Radek, Shmila, Preobrazhenski, Kamenev and Zinoviev capitulate. They publish texts in *Pravda* recognising their 'errors' and unconditionally supporting Stalin's policies. Racovski is the last to take this step, in February 1934. He receives permission to return to Moscow. He is appointed Deputy Minister for Health. He is visited by Alexandru Dobrogeanu-Gherea, whom he has known since his time in Romania. Gherea had been living in Moscow since 1932. He is sometimes accompanied by Lucrețiu Pătrășcanu, the PCdR representative to the Comintern. He is visited by Romanian militants of the 1918-1920 period, as well as by Russians of the old guard.

1934 is the year of the assassination of Kirov, Stalin's main rival for the CPSU leadership. Stalin orders his killing. The deed is carried out on 1 December. It is the pretext to launch the Great Terror. Kamenev (Trotsky's brother-in-law, but also Stalin's fellow prisoner in Siberia) and Grigori Zinoviev, Lenin's main collaborator in the years before he seized power, are both implicated. They are unmasked as the perpetrators of the assassination. Stalin decides to destroy the old guard. Racovski is also on the list. Meanwhile, he disavows his past opinions in *Pravda* on repeated occasions. Even during the Kamenev/Zinoviev trial, in August 1936, he demands that an example be made of the two as traitors to the Revolution. He anticipates his own fate, in fact. In January 1937, he is arrested, held at the Lubyanka and interrogated. He is beaten, tortured and forced to make false confessions that he spied against the USSR, in the pay of a number of countries; that he plotted to assassinate Stalin. The trial takes place a year later, in March 1938. He takes his place in the dock next to Bukharin, 'the Party's favourite son'. as Lenin named him in his political last will and testament, and who later became the leader of the 'right-wing' opposition in the 1930s. Nikolay Rykov was there also, a former Prime Minister and close to Lenin; so too was Genrik Yagoda, former head of the NKVD. Racovski appears at trial as an aged man, his face once more concealed by the beard he had given up in his youth. He seems a different man. He acknowledges all the accusations. The Soviet press unleashes a campaign of accusations and demands for the 'plotters' to be sentenced to death. In the courtroom, there are foreign correspondents, diplomats, and secret police agents. Andrey I. Vyshinski, the Soviet chief prosecutor, demands the death sentence for the accused. He demands 'only' 25 years for Racovski. The verdict: Racovski is sentenced to 20 years imprisonment. Given that he is 65, the sentence is equivalent to life imprisonment. Three months later, on 21-22 June, Germany attacks the USSR. The Red Army retreats with heavy losses. Stalin decides to kill all the survivors of the political trials. Racovski was executed on 11 September 1941, in Orel Prison. His body was cut into pieces and dumped in the forest near the place of execution.

In the small world of the Bucharest Communists, the Great Terror had devastating effects.

"The Moscow trials (1936-1937) split my life in two. I read and reread the shorthand reports. It was clear that they contained not a single word of truth. However, I could not understand how Bolsheviks who had endured Siberia, heroes of the civil war, men with nerves of steel, could declare such absurdities. After the first telegrams, I did not believe that the trials had taken place. Then I refused to believe that men such as Bukharin and Zinoviev could have been executed. Then I believed it, but imagined that there had indeed been plots whose success would have led to a Soviet Thermidor,[51] and Stalin seemed to me like a Robespierre who had

---

[51] Thermidor – the eleventh month in the French Republican Calendar (19 July-17 August). 9 Thermidor of the Year 2 (27 July 1794), was the date when Robespierre and the other radicals came under attack in the National Convention, in a reaction against the Reign of Terror (cont. p. 369.)

decapitated the Thermidorians. Before the war, I suddenly realised that all the people together with whom I had embarked on life were gone [on 23 August 1940, Trotsky had been assassinated in Mexico, on Stalin's orders – *author's note*]. Had they all deceived themselves? Had they all betrayed? Was there not even one of them who had not deceived himself and betrayed? It was impossible to believe and I no longer believed anything, not even the truth. … Since then, I have had a physical, political and moral horror of Stalin."[52]

The effects were not only moral and ideological. The PCdR lost almost all the cadres who had taken refuge in the USSR. Stalin, Georgi Dimitrov and their puppet, Boris Ştefanov, decimated the PCdR. Today, it is hard to reconstruct the exact number of the victims. The PCdR was not the only Communist Party to fall victim to such treatment. The greatest pressure was borne in particular by the Communist Parties that were illegal in their home countries.[53] The leadership and cadres of such parties were, in particular, hunted under suspicion of treachery. The parties that operated legally, in France and in Czechoslovakia, were to suffer less. The reverberations of the massacre might appear in the press there, or might arouse reactions in political circles. For the illegal parties, dependence on the Comintern and the Soviet secret services was much stricter. Consequently, the chances of falling victim to the Terror were greater. Those targeted had nowhere to appeal. Public opinion in the various countries viewed events in Moscow with indifference. The Great Terror gave rise to satisfaction for many:

"The Bolsheviks are killing each other. The few Western reactions have prompted nothing but scornful silence from Moscow. Sometimes harsh replies were published in *Pravda* or *Izvestia*, on the topic of 'non-interference in domestic affairs'. The Comintern, which had orchestrated many campaigns for the defence of communists on trial in Europe, allowed its own militants to be massacred in the USSR. The

---

(the "Thermidorian Reaction") which brought to a close the most violent excesses of the French Revolution – *Translator's note*.

[52] Belu Zilber *Actor în procesul Pătrăşcanu* [*Actor in the P. Trial*], Bucharest: Humanitas, 1997, p. 67.

[53] Robert Conquest, *Marea teroare* [*The Great Terror*], Bucharest: Humanitas, 1996, p. 473.

leaders of the Kremlin and the Lubyanka exercise their right to dispose of the lives of not only their enemies, but also their supporters, and they do so without caring about public opinion."[54]

The Bolsheviks had always displayed their contempt for justice and bourgeois values. Now, in the 1930s, they proceeded in the same way. For them, once you had entered their secret world, you were subject to special laws, applicable strictly within the Party. The Comintern was a party that brought together 'professional revolutionaries' from outside the borders of the USSR. "Not one Comintern leader, not one leader of any of the fraternal parties ever cast into doubt the right of the Soviet authorities (the prosecutors, courts, secret police) to try and punish foreign citizens using the Penal Code, on the basis of formal accusations that related to problems in the internal life of the Party. They thereby tacitly and unreservedly recognised that all those who had adhered to the 'great family' of communists were subjects of the communist empire, represented by the rulers of the Soviet Union. ... There was not one trace of protest against the cynical arbitrariness to which they had fallen victim."[55]

The clandestines were more exposed, more vulnerable than those in the legal communist parties. Once you had gone underground, everything marked you out as a potential police informant, a *provocateur*. Moreover, it made you exclusively dependent on the Comintern, which appointed you, gave you missions, recalled you, expelled you, rewarded you. The Comintern could use you; it could also kill you if need be. Moreover, those involved in underground actions, acts of sabotage, diversion, terrorism and espionage knew too much. They operated from the shadows, in the interests of the USSR. Any defection in this area brought grave consequences. As was seen in the case of Ignacio Reis, Antonov Ovseenko, Agabekov et al. The massacre of the cadres from the illegal communist parties, of the networks of clandestine agents and propagandists, meant getting rid of inconvenient witnesses, cleaning up, erasing the tracks.

On 5 February 1937, the Comintern Presidium decided to set up control commissions in the communist parties and to proceed to make purges. "Those who have violated the unity and cohesion of Party ranks, who have been in

---

[54] Arkadi Vaksberg, *Hotel Lux. Partidele frățești în slujba Internaționalei Comuniste* [*Hotel Lux: The Fraternal Parties in the Service of the Communist International*], Bucharest: Humanitas, 1998, p. 90.
[55] *Idem*, p. 120.

violation of Party discipline and secrecy, who have displayed insufficient class vigilance, who have displayed a lack of Bolshevik firmness before the enemy" were to be investigated. "They have concealed their hostility to the Party under seeming loyalty (duplicity); they are agents of the class enemy who have infiltrated the ranks of the Party."[56] There was no need for the illegal communist parties to set up such control commissions since their role was already fulfilled by the Central Committees. The Central Committee of the PCdR was not functional, however. Its members were scattered throughout Romania (most in prison and a lesser number at liberty), abroad, in Vienna and Prague, or refugees in the USSR. Authority was exercised almost exclusively by Boris Ștefanov, who had been running the PCdR leadership since December 1934. Georgi Dimitrov trusted him.

> "Boris Ștefanov was a Bulgarian from the Quadrilateral, with the physical appearance of a butcher, with the square head of a brutish fanatic who could understand neither jokes nor compromises. It was not possible to converse with him, not only because he spoke Romanian poorly, but also because there was nothing to be got from him. Clandestine action was his speciality and he never appeared anywhere openly. ... He was the kind of man who would kill his father and mother without hesitation, if Moscow demanded it."[57]

In 1937, Ștefanov was a member of the Executive Committee of the Comintern, elected at the Comintern Congress of summer 1935, and the PCdR representative there. He was the PCdR's strongman, the one who decided everything. In 1937, he was summoned from Vienna, where he was to be found at the Political Bureau, in order to lead the operation to purge the Romanian communists. A highly disciplined man, he does so methodically and cruelly. Here is how another communist characterises him: "Comrade Boris was obsessed with the idea that people were working to undermine him. In my opinion, however, he proceeded very sketchily in this matter. He regarded any critical remark as baseness, being unable

---

[56] ANR, *Copilaria Comunismului românesc în arhivele Cominternului* [*The Childhood of the Romanian Communist Party in the Archives of the Comintern*], edited by Alina Tudor Pavelescu, p. 387.

[57] Constantin Argetoian, *Memorii*, vol. 7, Bucharest: Editura Machiavelli, 1996, p. 169.

to appreciate the gravity of the accusation, and the easiest thing was to speak to him confidentially, drawing to his attention that someone was undermining him."[58] Ștefanov had not succeeded in imposing himself as leader of the Romanian communists. In 1933, he had been released from prison, benefitting from a reduction in his sentence (he had been sentenced to eight years in 1928) and improved relations with the USSR. He was then expelled from the PCdR. At the plenary that had designated him leader in December 1934, Ștefanov said, "The Romanian communists were unable to appreciate me in the manner that was fitting, but the Comintern recognised me as an international leader and appointed me leader of the Communist Party from Romania."[59] The man was a fanatic; he was rigid, bigoted. This is what Gheorghe Vasilichi has to say:

> "He [Boris Ștefanov – *author's note*] believed and preached that a man should sleep with his wife only when he wanted to have children and, to go by what they used to say, he put this theory into practice. Later, around 1935, when he was in Moscow, after we had escaped from prison in Craiova, he called all of us who were from Romania (some seven or nine persons), men and women, and asked us to give him a list of the women and men respectively with whom we had had relations and namely: who, when, where. ..."[60]

In 1937, Ștefanov had occasion to avenge himself for the coolness with which he had been received as leader. All those with whom he had been at odds were to disappear in the years 1937-1940. More often than not, they fell victim to the firing squad. Ștefanov ratified the demands made by the Comintern and the NKVD. In order to be referred to the courts, the procedure required that the victim should undergo a Party investigation and be expelled. Ștefanov was the one who identified the 'enemies of the people', the 'traitors', the 'Trotskyites'. the 'spies'. His arrival in Moscow was the signal to unleash the great purge of the PCdR. There follows an

---

[58] *O anchetă stalinistă, 1937-1938. Lichidarea lui Marcel Pauker* [*A Stalinist Investigation. The Liquidation of M. P.*], Bucharest: Univers Enciclopedic, 1995, p. 186.

[59] *Idem*, pp. 187-188.

[60] Gh. Vasilichi, in Romanian Academy/INST, *Arhivele totalitarianismului* [*The Archives of Totalitarianism*], nos. 3-4, 2000, p. 112.

excerpt from a letter sent by Gelbert Moscovici on 11 June 1937. Gelbert Moscovici (known as Ghiță Moscu or Alexandru Bădulescu) had been part of the clandestine Bolshevik network since 1918. He was the brother of social democrat leader Ilie Moscovici. Hunted by the police, sentenced in contumacy he takes refuge in Vienna, from where he runs a number of illegal operations. One of them is the Senate bomb attack. In the 1930s, he was living in Moscow. It is here that, beginning in 1936, he is investigated and then expelled from the Party for 'opportunism', links to Trotskyites (the Köblős group) and to his brother, Ilie Moscovici, who was branded as a 'fascist'. He writes to Ștefanov:

> "To this crime you too are party, you are all party to it, it is true, by your silence (or perhaps even your consensus). Don't protest that we cannot interfere in the internal affairs of the CP of the USSR. It's a lie! There is no statutory formality to prevent you from unmasking a falsehood (I am convinced that it is a conscious falsehood) and re-establishing truth and justice, saving a man, even if he had never had anything to do with the PCR. ... I have the right to demand of my comrades in the struggle that they defend me against lies and intrigue... I have the right to defend myself, but nobody wants to speak to me. ... Comrade Boris, I have written to you because thereby I steal some of your time and so that it will remain on paper ... and inasmuch as I am prepared to shout until I am heard or until they gag me, it is much better that I write. I hope that it will not be in vain. Communist greetings, Al. Bădulescu. 11 June 1937. P.S. Comrade Dimitrov is also abreast of this."[61]

Gelbert Moscovici is one of those caught in the trap. He had come to Moscow in order to save his liberty. Here he finds prison and the firing squad. He is not the only one. Elena Filipovici and Marcel Pauker were members of the Political Bureau in 1937. Arrested, investigated, killed. The same fate was shared by three of the former general secretaries of the PCdR: Elek Köblős (1924-1928), Vitali Kholostenko (1928-1930), a Ukrainian, and Alexander Danieluk-Stepanko-Gorn (1931-1934), a Pole. There is then a long list of former members of the Political Bureau, of

---

[61] ANR, *Copilaria Comunismului românesc în arhivele Cominternului* [*The Childhood of the Romanian Communist Party in the Archives of the Comintern*], edited by Alina Tudor Pavelescu, p. 393.

the Secretariat, of the CC: David Fabian Finkelstein, Eugen Rozvany, Alexandru Dobrogeanu-Gherea, Gelbert Moscovici, already mentioned, Dori Goldstein, Leon Lichtblau, Izo Itzcovici, Emil Hmelniţki, Timotei Marin, Dumitru Grofu, Imre Aladár, Berger Aladár. Other victims: Gheorghi Ganev, Jacques Konitz, Moise Dubinski, Manea Erlich, Vasile Popovici, Dumitru Chelerman, Iohan Heigel, Petre Zissu et al. Besides the high-level PCdR cadres, also targeted were those connected to Cristian Racovski and the 1918 Bolsheviks, those nostalgic for Lenin and Trotsky, for revolutionary rhetoric, members of the Odessa group: Ecaterina Arbore, Alexandru Nicolau, Alter Zalic, Ion Dic. Dicescu et al. Others are suspected of various forms of 'deviationism', whether right-wing ('Bukharinism') or left-wing ('Trotskyism'). Others because they had taken part in various conflicts within the communist movement, or were personally disliked by various leaders of the CPSU or Comintern. Some because they were mixed up in various dirty work conducted by the secret services. They had to disappear as inconvenient witnesses. However, above everything else there hovers the suspicion of Stalin. Foreigners were, for him, danger incarnate. The Comintern was a wasps' nest of spies, of Western agents, of dubious individuals, who could betray at any time. The accusations brought against them were mere details, post hoc arguments for Stalin's decision to liquidate them.

Why did these people allow themselves to be slaughtered? Some were on Soviet soil and had no escape. So why did Marcel Pauker return to the USSR? He arrived in Moscow at the beginning of October 1937, via Prague. He was accompanied by Şeila Averbuch. Both had been arrested in Vienna on 29 October 1936. In June 1937, they were released. He had been invited to Moscow in September 1936. His arrest in Austria postponed his investigation and execution for a year. In October 1937, Elena Filipovici, who had requested that the Comintern bring Marcel Pauker to Moscow a year previously, was in the Lubyanka Prison and would soon be executed. Why did Marcel Pauker agree to undertake such a perilous journey? Had he refused, he would have saved his life. However, there were few who had the courage to do this, to come to their senses. Why? The reason was that such a gesture would have been tantamount to admitting failure and the meaninglessness of their lives. They would have had to accept that the 'revolutionary spirit' and the 'liberation of mankind' were illusions, that they were serving a dictatorship, that they had deceived themselves.

In the autumn of 1937, when Marcel Pauker returned to the USSR, the Great Terror had reached its peak. In spite of this, he docilely obeys orders and goes to Moscow "to report." Death awaits him. It is a trap laid by the Comintern and NKVD. In the autumn of 1937, the Kamenev/Zinoviev trial was underway. Thousands of Bolsheviks, diplomats, officers, and activists were killed. Pauker knew what awaited him. He was not the only one to proceed in the same way. They preferred to let themselves be interrogated, tortured, put on trial, and killed, or sent to a Siberian labour camp if they were lucky. Why did these men go like lambs to the slaughter? Why did they not protest? Why did they not prefer quite simply to remain in the West and save their lives? Did Marcel Pauker believe in the accusations against Kamenev and Zinoviev, against Radek and Tomsky? Did he believe in the accusations of betrayal, espionage, and anti-revolutionary plotting, in the attempts to assassinate Stalin? A death wish drew all these professional revolutionaries to the firing squads. They were creatures of the darkness and the underground, conspirators scattered throughout Europe. Did they believe they were innocent? In the labyrinth of clandestinity, no one is innocent, no one can claim they are without guilt. They had taken part in acts of terrorism and plotting. The life of concealment, secrecy and conspiracy was the air they breathed. These are the sins of which they are accused in Moscow, sins which are this time directed against the 'dictatorship of the proletariat', against Stalin himself. The language is the same, and they understand it well. The rules of the game are the same. Somewhere, at the end of the game, death awaits. All had sworn an oath and, when accused of having broken it, they knew what to expect.

When he arrives, on 8 October 1937, Pauker checks in to the Hotel Lux, where a number of important Comintern members are staying. The atmosphere is very grim. The Terror unleashed by Stalin is at its zenith. Moscow's resident aliens do not know whether they will be free or alive the next day, whether an NKVD team will arrive in the night to take them away. They all have their luggage packed ready by the door. The tension is at a maximum; intrigues and scandals are the order of the day. Many prefer to unmask others, in an attempt to save their own skins. The denunciations flow. They hope thereby to demonstrate their loyalty to Stalin and to be shielded from repression. In the world of the Hotel Lux there are no innocents. Of those who perish during Terror, Bertolt Brecht cynically says: "If they are not guilty then they all the more deserve to die." All the communist parties are represented in Moscow. Thousands of communist cadres live in the USSR, having fled their own countries. "In the purges, those who suffered the most were the émigré communists, the members of the illegal parties, because they had no one to intervene for them. The Bulgarian émigrés were lucky that Dimitrov was secretary of the Comintern, and it was his authority that saved many. There was no one to concern themselves with the Yugoslavs; they dug each other's graves vying with each other before the party authorities and proving their devotion to Stalin and Leninism."[62] The situation in which Marcel Pauker finds himself is disastrous and bodes even worse. The PCdR militants had almost all been arrested, and many of them had been executed. The PCdR, an illegal party, with no protector at the head of the Comintern, was one of the main targets. The threat of death wreaked havoc. But who was this Marcel Pauker? He came from a Romanianised Jewish family. His father, Simon, had worked as an editor for the *Dimineaţa* and *Adevărul* newspapers. He was the proprietor of the most influential economic newspaper of the epoch: *Argus*. Marcel Pauker was born in Bucharest in 1896. In Bucharest, he studied at the Evangelical School. "I was an eminent pupil at school," he writes in his autobiography, in November 1937.[63] He graduated from the Zurich Polytechnic in 1921. He joins the Socialist Party in 1918, positioning himself on the radical Left, pro-Bolshevik wing. He is an adept of affiliation to the Comintern. He marries Ana Rabinsohn-Pauker in 1919, with whom he will have three children, one of them dying prematurely. He rapidly forges a career for himself in the PCdR. In 1922, he is already one of the leaders, a member of the Political Bureau. He represents the PCdR at the Balkan Communist Federation. After the Vienna Congress of 1924, he loses his positions. His relations with the new leader, Elek Köblős, are tense, the same as they had been with the former leader, Gheorghe Cristescu. He is arrested in December 1924, and appears in court a few months later, in 1925, in the trial of the communists of Freemason Street. Along with the other 15 accused – tried at liberty – he absconds and is condemned *in absentia* to 10 years imprisonment. He goes abroad, arriving in Moscow in December, where he will stay until April.

---

[62] Milovan Djilas, *Întîlniri cu Stalin* [*Meetings with Stalin*], Editura Europe, *no date*, p. 23.

[63] *O anchetă stalinistă, 1937-1938. Lichidarea lui Marcel Pauker* [*A Stalinist Investigation. The Liquidation of M. P.*], Bucharest: Univers Enciclopedic, 1995, p. 24.

Then he is in Paris, as a Comintern agent. There, he is in contact with Cristian Racovski, who is the Soviet ambassador. On behalf of the PCdR, he organises the protest campaign in favour of Pavel Tkachenko. He has connections with the Association for the Struggle against the White Terror, led by Henri Barbusse and Panait Istrati. In 1927, as a result of differences with Racovski, who withdraws his subsidies, he goes to Vienna, where he is to be found in the Political Bureau of the PCdR. He works for Red Aid, continuing the campaign against the 'oligarchic regime in Bucharest'. The aim: the release of Boris Ștefanov, who is in prison, awaiting trial in front of a military tribunal. In 1928, at the PCdR Congress in Kharkov, the Comintern sacks the entire leadership. "The Communist Party had reached the lowest level of its disorganisation. An unbelievable hatred dominated"[64] Marcel Pauker returns to Bucharest. Here he runs the press section. Elek Köblős, David Fabian Finkelstein and Leon Lichtblau had been replaced by Vitali Holostenco-Barbu, a Ukrainian; Dori Goldstein; and Alexandru Nikolski. Marcel Pauker enters into conflict with Holostenco too. He becomes the leader of a faction. Pauker operates under the name Luximin. This is how he signs his articles in *Înainte* [*Forward*], the newspaper of the Peasant Workers Bloc, which he controls. The conflict propels the PCdR to the brink of extinction. The two groups vehemently dispute each other's power. They denounce each other to Moscow and Vienna. The leaders of both groups are dismissed by the Comintern in the summer of 1930. Marcel Pauker is summoned to Moscow. He works as an engineer in Magnitogorsk. In 1932, he undertakes a self-criticism and is reintegrated into the cadres of the PCdR. He returns clandestinely to Romania in 1933. In 1934-1935, he is a member of the Secretariat, the PCdR leadership in Romania. In the winter of 1934-1935, he organises the escape of Constantin Doncea, Gheorghe Vasilichi and Dumitru Petrescu, subsequently getting them out of the country. He becomes a member of the Political Bureau once more, as he had been in the 1922-1924 period. In October 1936, he is arrested in Vienna, where the WEB was based, the Comintern's Western Europe bureau. The Political Bureau of the PCdR was also located here. He is released in June 1937 and summoned to Moscow. He arrives on 8 October. The investigation is launched the very next day. Interrogations and declarations follow. On 26 January 1938, Wilhelm Pieck, secretary of the Comintern, informs him that he has been expelled from the PCdR. This

---

[64] *Idem*, p. 86.

was equivalent to a guilty verdict. The accusations? "Comrade Pauker has led a struggle against the line of the Communist International, and a faction of the Communist Party of Romania, he has clearly infringed the rules of conspiracy and maintained links with Trotskyite elements."[65] On 21 March, in room No. 10 of the Hotel Lux, at 36 Gorky Street, he is arrested by the NKVD and charged with spying for a foreign power. There follows another series of interrogations. Pauker, during questioning by NKVD officers, admits that he is guilty of links to Trotskyite elements Elena Filipovici, Alexandru Dobrogeanu-Gherea, Leon Lichtblau, Vitali Holostenco, and Manea Erlich. At the date of the interrogation they had already been executed as enemies of the people and therefore Pauker too was fated to die. On 31 March, he declared under interrogation: "I recognise I am indeed guilty of being a spy and of having conducted, on USSR soil, counter-revolutionary espionage activity for the Romanian secret services.[66] On 29 July, he is tried and sentenced to death by firing squad. He is executed on 16 August 1938.

The hunt for Trotskyites was the main pretext for repression. The label could be applied to anyone. Saboteurs, be they real or fictive, paid assassins, personal rivals, ideologues, the naïve, inconvenient fellow travellers, Bolsheviks of the old guard. A document sent probably by Boris Ştefanov himself from Moscow to Ştefan Foriş, secretary of the PCdR, in Bucharest, says:

"Trotskyism has become the advance guard of the counter-revolution ... together with German imperialism and global financial capital, it is taking an active part in the preparation of war against the USSR. ... Financial capital has entrusted the assassination of the USSR leadership to the Trotskyites, to Trotsky, Zinoviev, Kamenev and company. ... In Romania, the defenders of Trotskyism are the right-wing Social Democrats, the fascists and their press. The campaign they are waging in the press is closely tied up with preparations for war against the USSR."

The Comintern asks Foriş to publish materials from the trial brought against Kamenev and Zinoviev, to bring to the awareness of the masses the declarations of self-accusation made by those convicted, "so that none of

---

[65] *Idem*, p. 222.

[66] *Idem*, pp. 248-9.

the lies of the reactionary press against the USSR and its leaders will remain unanswered [in the press – *author's note*] for the masses ... the Trotskyites must be unmasked, the documents of the trial should be reworked within the Party, and the heightened vigilance of the entire Party is demanded, as well as its strengthened ideological unity."[67]

***

The following are some of the Romanian communist figures executed in Moscow. Many of them we have already met in the preceding pages.

Ecaterina Arbore (born 1875, in Switzerland). The daughter of a Russian political émigré, Zamfir Arbore. Expelled from Russia in 1909. Physician. Joins the Social Democratic Party. She is part of the leadership between 1910 and 1918. In 1918, she is arrested following the disturbances of 13 December. After the trial, she is forced to leave the country. She takes refuge in Russia. She works for the Executive Committee of the Comintern. In 1923, she returns to Romania, and is deported in 1924. Between 1925 and 1929, she is a member of the so-called Moldavian Soviet Republic, created by Moscow in 1924. She takes part in all the congresses of the Comintern. In 1931, she is a delegate to the Fifth Congress of the PCdR. Shot in 1937, having been accused of ties with Racovski.

Alexandru Dobrogeanu-Gherea (born 1879, Ploiești), the second son of Constantin Dobrogeanu-Gherea. He studies at a polytechnic in Germany. In 1916, he is mobilised. In 1920, he is elected to Parliament on the Socialist Party list. He is a member of the delegation of Romanian socialists who sign the document of affiliation to the Comintern. He takes part in the congress of communists in May 1921, and is arrested. He is one of the central figures in the trial on Spirii Hill in February/May 1922. He is amnestied. In 1923-1924, he is part of the first Central Committee of the clandestine PCdR, in the capacity of secretary. He is arrested once more and implicated in the Freemason Street trial of 1925. He is one of the 16 accused who abscond during the trial. He lives in the West. Sentenced to 10 years *in absentia*.

---

[67] NR, *Copilăria Comunismului românesc în arhivele Cominternului* [*The Childhood of the Romanian Communist Party in the Archives of the Comintern*], edited by Alina Tudor Pavelescu, pp. 419-421.

He takes part in the PCdR Congresses in Poliești (1922), Vienna (1924), Kharkov (1928). At the end of 1928, he returns to Romania and, in January 1929, he is arrested. After 35 days hunger strike he is released, in May 1929, and later amnestied. In 1932, he emigrates to the USSR. Here he translates the works of Lenin into Romanian. In Moscow, Gherea frequents Cristian Racovski, whom he had known in Romania. He becomes mentally ill. He is arrested in the autumn of 1937, and held at the Lubyanka at the same time as Racovski. He is executed there in December 1937.

Eugen Rozvany (born 1878, in Salonta). He studies law in Bucharest and Berlin. Beginning in 1900, he is a lawyer. At this time, he joins the socialist movement. He was in attendance at the Congresses of the Socialist International in Stuttgart (1907) and Basle (1912). He is taken prisoner during the First World War. He is repatriated in 1919 and settles in Romania. After February 1920, he is the secretary of the Transylvanian Socialist Party. It is in this capacity that he goes to Russia in August 1920. He signs, together with Cristescu, Finkelstein, Gherea and Popovici, the act of affiliation to the Comintern. He takes part in the congress of May 1921. In 1922, he is elected candidate member of the CC of the PCdR. He forges a career for himself as a lawyer in Salonta and Oradea. After 1926, he is a member of the Peasant Workers Bloc. He is arrested many times. In 1928, he is implicated in the trial at Cluj and acquitted. Expelled from the PCdR by the Political Bureau in Vienna, in February 1929, charged with 'opportunism'. In the autumn of 1931, he emigrates to the USSR. He works in the Comintern apparatus. He is a researcher at the Academy Institute of Economy. He becomes a doctor in juridical sciences in 1937, the year in which he is arrested and placed under investigation. Executed in 1938.

David Fabian Finkelstein (born 1895, in Huși). He attends the Higher School of Commerce in Jassy. A participant in clandestine Bolshevik groups from as early as 1918, in Bucharest. After the events of 13 December 1918, he is sought by the police and goes to Italy and France. He is part of the delegation that goes to Russia in 1920 and signs the affiliation with the Comintern. On his return to Romania, he is arrested. He takes part in the First Congresses of the PCdR. At the Third Congress in Vienna, August 1924, he becomes a member of the Political Bureau. From autumn 1925, he is an émigré in Vienna and Berlin. Between 1924 and 1928, he is the PCdR's second in command. In 1928, he is sacked, together with Elek Köblős. After 1933, he lives in the USSR. He works at the Lenin School for Party Cadres, part of the Comintern. He translates the works of Lenin into Romanian. He is shot in December 1937.

Elek Köblős (born 1887, near Tîrgu Mureş). Carpenter. Fights in the Red Guards during the Hungarian Bolshevik Revolution. He returns to Romania after the fall of Béla Kuhn. He takes part in the general strike of October 1920. He is a delegate to the May 1921 Congress, where he is arrested, indicted in the trial on Spirii Hill, and amnestied. Secretary General of the Lumber Industry Trades Union. He is editor-in-chief of the Hungarian-language magazine *Munkás* (*Worker*), which is published by the PCdR. At the PCdR Congress in Vienna, October 1924, he is appointed Secretary General to replace Gheorghe Cristescu. In December 1924, the PCdR is banned under the Mîrzescu Law. Arrests take place. He goes into hiding. After the autumn of 1925, he lives in exile. Firstly in Vienna and then in Moscow. After 1927, he is the head of the Political Bureau, the PCdR leadership abroad. He is arrested in Košice, Czechoslovakia, in the same year. Romania demands his extradition. A campaign led in the West by Henri Barbusse and the Committee for the Defence of the Victims of White Terror saves him. He is released and takes refuge in the USSR. In 1928, at the PCdR Congress in Kharkov, he is sacked, together with the entire leadership. He is then expelled from the Party. On 8 October 1938, he is tried by the Military Tribunal of the USSR, accused of Trotskyism, and sentenced to death.

Elena Filipovici (born 1902, Bucharest). Worker. In 1919, she joins clandestine Bolshevik groups. Between 1923 and 1925, she is secretary of the CC of the Union of Communist Youth. Arrested for the first time in 1921. She is implicated in the Spirii Hill trial, and amnestied. Arrested a number of times. She is a member of the editorial staff of *Socialistul* until it is banned in April, and then the editorial staff of *Facla* [*The Torch*], during the time when the newspaper was financed by the Comintern. An autodidact, she speaks a number of languages. Close to Lucreţiu Pătrăşcanu and Ana Pauker in the 1920s. From 1925, after the PCdR is outlawed, she lives clandestinely, continuing to be active in the communist network. She attends the Seventh Comintern Congress in 1935. She attends the Fifth Congress of the PCdR in 1931, when she becomes a member of the Secretariat (the leadership in

Romania) and of the Political Bureau. For a time she is the leader of the Party from the shadows, being the mistress of Alexander Stepanski-Gorn, who was head of the PCdR between 1932 and 1934. Even after the latter is sacked in December 1934, her influence is not much diminished, as she remains in the leadership, from where she opposes Boris Ștefanov. She falls victim to the latter's vengeance. In 1937, she is arrested, tried and executed, the same as Gorn.

Dumitru Grofu (born 1876). Worker in the metallurgy industry. After 1919, secretary of the Trades Unions. Attends the congress of May 1921 and is arrested. Tried in the Spirii Hill case, he is amnestied. He is one of the most influential union leaders. From 1926, we find him in the Peasant Workers Bloc. At the Congress of United Trades Unions in Timișoara, 1929, he is elected president. In 1931, he attends the Fifth Congress of the PCdR, held in the USSR. He is arrested many times in Romania. He is arrested in the USSR in 1937, investigated, and falls victim to the Stalinist terror.

Imre Aladár (born 1900, Bucharest). Carpenter. He joins the Socialist Party in 1919. In 1928, at the Fourth Congress in Kharkov, he is elected a member of the CC of the PCdR. He attends the Comintern congresses. Arrested more than 20 times, for short periods. In total, he spends 150 days on hunger strike. Head of the United Trades Unions. He was elected to Parliament in 1931, on behalf of the PWB, along with Lucrețiu Pătrășcanu and another three. The Chamber of Deputies invalidated all five mandates. Subsequently, a trial was brought against him and, under the pretext that he was not Romanian, he was deported (August 1931). Aladár leaves Romania the same year (1932). At trial, he was defended by Petre Pandrea. Pandrea writes in his memoirs:

> "Imre Aladár was my first communist friend ... He was invalidated at the instigation of Pamfil Șeicaru so that his editor, Cezar Petrescu, could take his place. Aladár was invalidated as a deputy for being Hungarian. Cezar Petrescu took his place with satisfaction. Later, Cezar Petrescu aligned himself with the communist regime. ... What happened to Imre Aladár? He had done his national service in Bucharest. His mother was Romanian (Maria Boeru). His father was a Hungarian carpenter who had settled in the capital. In order to forestall a correct decision in the law courts, Imre was deported to Hungary. ... I saw him again in Oradea Mare, in the vineyard

of communist lawyer Rozvany (killed by the Stalinists in the USSR). Imre was born and raised in Bucharest, a gifted autodidact, a carpenter, a fervent communist, an intellectual by vocation, a great orator."[68]

We find a note in Camil Petrescu: "Interesting conversations with Sebastian, Nae Ionescu ... Petru Marcu Balş [Petre Pandrea] goes to him to plead for Aladár's life. – Very well, but then give us another. – !?... – Of course... you still have to give us one! – !?... – It is in your interests and ours. If not Imre Aladár, then another ... It doesn't matter to us. You [communists] need a martyr, we need to show a strong hand."[69] An émigré to the USSR, Aladár is tried in 1937, sentenced to death and executed in Moscow under the accusation of "Romanian chauvinism." "Not Romanian enough in Bucharest, much too Romanian in Moscow," as Petre Pandrea ironically remarks.

Another target for repression was the Romanian revolutionary battalion that had seen action at Odessa in 1918. Cristian Racovski and Mihai Gheorghiu Bujor were central figures. The others were Gelbert Moscovici, Ion. Dic. Dicescu, Alexandru Nicolau, Alter Zelic, Leon Lichtblau et al.

Gelbert Moscovici (born 1889, near Tîrgu Frumos, Jassy). Graduated from the upper commercial school in Jassy, 1910. Beginning in 1906, he is part of the Romanian Workers' Circle, later renamed the Social Democrat Party. Arrested in Bucharest in 1918 by the German Administration and sentenced to four and a half years imprisonment for clandestine activity. Sought by the police, he takes refuge in Vienna in 1919. In the autumn of 1920, he is in Bucharest once more. Here, after the arrest of Alecu Constantinescu, he leads the clandestine Bolshevik networks. He organises the bomb attack on the Senate in December 1920. He takes part in the Third Comintern Congress, in June 1921. In 1922, he is a PCdR representative to the Balkan Communist Federation. After 1923, he is in Moscow, as a PCdR representative to the Comintern. His career is in decline by the end of the 1920s, when Stalin purges the old guard. Beginning in 1929, he no longer works for the Comintern. In the 1930s, he is a functionary in various Soviet institutions. A Soviet citizen. From 1934, he works in a publishing house. In the summer of 1937, he is executed.

---

[68] Petre Pandrea, *Reeducarea de la Aiud*, Bucharest: Editura Vremea, 2000, pp. 155-6 and 404-409.

[69] Camil Petrescu, *Note zilnice*, Editura Gramar, 2003, p. 45-6.

Ion Dic. Dicescu (born 1893, Bucharest). He studied at a school of commerce, graduating in 1910. In 1914, he is the editor-in-chief of *România muncitoare* [*Workingman's Romania*], a newspaper of the Social Democratic Party. After the beginning of the war, in August 1916, he is a correspondent for *Adevărul*. In 1917, he is wounded and evacuated to Russia. The abdication of Tsar Nicholas II finds him in Petrograd. A month later, in April, he joins the Bolshevik Party. He writes for *Pravda*. In October 1917, he is a member of the Red Guard in Petrograd. Between 25 October and 7 November, he attends the Second Congress of Soviets, when Lenin announces he has seized power. From February 1918, he is in Odessa, as secretary of the Romanian Revolutionary Military Committee. Henri Stahl, the parliamentary stenographer, who is a refugee there, meets him on the street, at the time when Dicescu is one of Racovski's seconds: "middling height, black beard, hooked nose, lively dark eyes, dressed in a green Russian uniform, red shirt, a revolver tucked into his belt."[70] In autumn 1918, he is part of M.V. Frunze's army, fighting on the Dniester against the Romanian Army. He prepares cadres for Soviet espionage in Romania and the Balkans. Beginning in 1927, he is a teacher at the Military Academy. He published more than 50 scholarly articles. Arrested on 5 April 1937 and executed on 4 January 1938.

> "There was a Jew from Bucharest, Isidor I. Kantor ... An adventurous spirit, unscrupulous, a swindler when need demanded, pathologically ambitious, he had been a journalist for Cocea's *Facla* before the war, and for *Adevărul*. From having been Isidor I. Kantor he became, successively and at lightning speed, Dore I. Kantor, Dic. Dicescu, and even, at a given moment, at the time Dissescu was minister, C. I. Dissescu. Now he is in Odessa [in 1918 – *author's note*] as part of the revolutionary assembly named Rumcherod, which rules the entire south of Russia, taking the law into its own hands, and this young tyrant stands out for his cruelty towards the hapless Romanian refugees."[71]

Alexandru Nicolau (born 1889). He studies law, and is granted a doctorate in Paris. He writes for *România muncitoare*. Tried in 1912 at the Ilfov tribunal, for an article entitled *To the Recruits*. He is defended at trial by Constantin

---

[70] Henri Stahl, *Parlamentul în URSS*, Editura Domino, 2003, p. 183.
[71] I. Gh. Duca, *Memorii*, vol. 4, part 2, Bucharest: Editura Machiavelli, 1994, p. 60.

Mille and Mihai Gheorghe Bujor. Acquitted. In 1916, in Paris, he publishes a brochure entitled *L'oligarchie roumaine*. In the summer of 1917, he goes to Odessa. He is part of the Social Democratic Action Committee. He is an editor for *Lupta* [*The Struggle*], run by Mihai Gheorghiu Bujor. He is a member of the Romanian Revolutionary Battalion. In 1919, he publishes a pamphlet entitled *The Socialist Revolution in Romania*. He returns to Romania in 1920 and is arrested. Imprisoned at Jilava, he escapes on 2 December 1920 together with Alecu Constantinescu and other inmates. On 31 March 1921, he was sentenced to death *in absentia* in Romania. He works at the Communist University in Moscow. In 1937, he is tried, sentenced to death and executed.

Timotei Marin (born 1897, in Bassarabia). In 1913, he is expelled. He takes a Degree in Literature at Jassy University. In 1919, he is the secretary of a clandestine Bolshevik cell. He is arrested for being a member of the terrorist group that planted a bomb in the Senate. Tried in the Spirii Hill case of 1922. One of the most dangerous of the clandestine agitators. He runs networks, co-ordinates couriers who come from Russia, and distributes funds and propaganda materials. He supervises the technical apparatus of the PCdR. He attends the Second PCdR Congress in Ploiești, October 1922. He writes for various communist newspapers. He is involved in the activities of Red Aid and the United (Communist) Trades Unions. Arrested in 1925 for his part in the Tatar Bunar rebellion. He is a member of the PCdR Secretariat. In August 1926, he escapes arrest and takes refuge in the house of G. C. Costaforu, who hides him on his estate. Boris Ștefanov and Pavel Tkachenko are captured during the same episode. He goes to Czechoslovakia in 1927. He is arrested in Košice, and flees to Vienna. From April 1928, he lives in the USSR. He publishes in various communist publications. He makes a name for himself as an ideologue on the left flank of the PCdR, arguing that "Romania is faced with a proletarian revolution." He takes part in the Fifth Congress of the PCdR in 1931. In 1937, he is arrested, investigated and executed.

Leon Lichtblau (Cristin) is part of the first wave of 'clandestines', the Bolshevik agents who utilise terrorist methods. Together with Max Goldstein, he plants a bomb in the Senate in December 1920. He is a student at the time. He flees to Russia. He occupies posts in the clandestine communist technical apparatus. During the period 1928-1930, he is a member of the Political Bureau. Alongside Vitali Holostenko, he takes part in factional fighting against Marcel Pauker/Luximin. In 1930, he is sacked. He settles in the USSR. He is a teacher at the Comintern's Lenin School for Cadres. He returns to the Political Bureau in the second half of the 1930s. Shot in 1937.

Victor Arcadi. Sociologist. Arrested in 1928, tried in Cluj for communist activities. Acquitted following a campaign organised by the Comintern in the West. Arrested again in 1930, accused of spying for the USSR. Sentenced to 15 years. Acquitted in Jassy in 1935, following an agreement between the governments in Bucharest and Moscow. He emigrates to the USSR in the same year. Shot in 1937 after being accused of spying for Romania.

Dori Goldstein (Rudolf, Dori). Beginning in 1928, he is a member of the Political Bureau. In the period of factional fighting, 1928-1930, he supports Marcel Pauker. He is sacked in 1930. He is a member of the Comintern apparatus and works as an agent all over Europe. He was married to Șeila Averbuch, also a militant communist. Dori Goldstein is shot in 1938.

Nevertheless, there were a few who managed to survive.

Șeila Averbuch, also known as Vanda Nikolski, a Comintern agent. Arrested together with Estera Radosovetsky in Prague, 1932, she is sent back to Romania. She gives her guards the slip. She is arrested again in Vienna, in July 1936, at the same time as Marcel Pauker. In 1937, she returns to the USSR. After 1938, she is imprisoned in a labour camp. For a short time, she looked after the children of Ana and Marcel Pauker, while the latter was under arrest in Moscow. She is released during the war, and takes part in the Red Army's westward campaign, until 1945.

Eugen Iacobovici (Marosi) (born 1902) – married to Ana Pauker's sister, Bela Rabinsohn. Tinsmith. In 1929-1930, he studies at the Lenin School for Party Cadres in Moscow. Beginning in November 1930, he is a member of the Political Bureau. He is accused of having suspect connections and ideological deviations. He is punished, stripped of his rank and sent back to Romania. This saved his life. He is expelled from the PCdR for not recognising his errors, but does not end up in front of the Lubyanka firing squad.

Alexandru Iliescu – in the USSR after the Fifth Congress of 1932, to which he was a delegate. A graduate of the Comintern School, he is sent to Romania in 1936, and thereby escapes execution.

Gheorghe Vasilichi – having escaped from Craiova Prison in January 1935, together with Constantin Doncea and Dumitru Petrescu, he arrives in the USSR via underground routes. Since the escape had been supervised by Marcel Pauker, and Marcel Pauker was under arrest for Trotskyism, the three Romanians are investigated, under house arrest. Vasilichi recalls: "Because of that I often regretted having escaped and would have preferred to stay in prison ... Before finishing the two and a half year [Comintern] school course in 1937, the school was abolished ... In 1936, Petre Borilă, who was with us, had been sent to Spain, where the civil war and foreign intervention had begun. We all asked to go, but we weren't given permission. It was not until the spring of 1938 that Doncea and I left the USSR for France. ..."[72] Those who escaped the slaughter later claimed they had been lucky not to be in the USSR during the Great Terror. Among them were Emil Bodnăraş, Lucreţiu Pătrăşcanu, Gheorghe Cristescu, Ana Pauker et al. For those who were in the USSR, to 'volunteer' to fight in the Spanish Civil War was their salvation. The alternative was to wait until a death squad knocked on the door, in the middle of the night, to arrest them, throw them into a cell in the Lubyanka, subject them, after a few weeks, to a brutal interrogation, and then to the firing squad. From whom could these communists hope to receive help? From the Romanian Government? No, since they had declared themselves its open adversaries, ready to use violent means to overthrow it. Many were Soviet citizens, having renounced Romanian citizenship. Others had been reported missing and had fled to the USSR clandestinely. Might help come from Romanian society? No, since, the communists were militating to break up the Romanian State whose new boundaries had been established by the Treaty of Versailles. Public opinion was anti-Bolshevik and anti-Soviet. The communists massacred in Moscow had been given genuine trials in Romania, with the right to a defence and appeal. The press

---

[72] Romanian Academy and INST, *Archives of Totalitarianism*, nos. 3-4, 2000, p. 119.

had written about them. They had sometimes received long sentences, but more often than not, the prison terms were insignificant. Their sentences were always later reduced, and many of them were pardoned or amnestied. In the trials in the USSR, any elements of real justice were absent. In Moscow, what occurred was in fact a series of conspiracies, which were thinly veiled political executions, with spectacular staging, for propaganda purposes. Intellectuals, lawyers, civic militants, journalists and left-wing figures mobilised when the communists were tried in Cluj, Timişoara, Jassy, Kishinev, Bucharest, Craiova and Brashov. However, the same figures remained silent when confronted with the Moscow trials. The Romanian Left, the democrat intellectuals, the militants for every humanitarian cause, the pacifists, and the anti-fascist journalists shared the same complicit behaviour as those in the West. Romain Rolland, Léon Blum, George Duhamel, Albert Einstein, André Malruax, Leon Feuchtwangler et al. kept silent. They accepted that the Bolsheviks and Comintern agents, whether Romanians or not, should be judged and executed in Moscow, since they had refused to be tried according to the legal system of their own countries. They mobilised in the cases of Boris Ştefanov, the Grivitza railway workers, the Ana Pauker group, and Petre Constantinescu-Iaşi. Not a word of protest, however, when Cristian Racovski, Alexandru Dobrogeanu-Gherea, Marcel Pauker, Ecaterina Arbore, Elena Filipovici and the others were slaughtered in Moscow. In the anti-Comintern operation, Stalin had enjoyed greater success than the Romanian Siguranţă. The Siguranţă arrested them, they were imprisoned for varying terms, the justice system released them after reducing their sentences, and the game resumed all over again. Stalin used the radical method: liquidation. It is an irony of history.

The question is why, after such unequivocal situations, the communists remained zealous executors of Comintern and GPU orders? Why did none of them, although perfectly informed about what was going on at the Lubyanka, publicly denounce these practices? What was the drug? Belu Zilber's saying might be an explanation: "they had fallen for the Party." The Bolshevik, anti-bourgeois, egalitarian world revolution fascinated the first generation Romanian communists. The shock of 1917 still reverberated. They were unable to understand any other reality, to adjust to normal life. For them, plotting and conspiracy had become second nature. They were prisoners of Stalin and Yezhov not just physically but also mentally. Regardless of whether they were in Moscow or somewhere in the underground of Europe, they were zealous prisoners, commissars of the revolution in training. They let themselves be slaughtered like cattle. They died convinced even in their final hour that they were serving the cause of the liberation of mankind. This utopia was the drug that annihilated their natural instincts. "They all disappeared without trace, and no embassy took any steps to discover anything about their fate. This discretion was favoured by the fact that, more often than not, they arrived as spies, under false names and with false documents ... clandestinity turned against the internationalist militants."[73]

---

[73] Arkadi Vaksberg, *Hotel Lux. Partidele frățești în slujba Internaționalei Comuniste*, Bucharest: Humanitas, 1998, p. 238.

XIII
Comintern Kaput

On 23 August 1939, Ribbentrop, the Foreign Minister of the Third Reich, alighted from his aeroplane at Vnukovo Airport, Moscow. He was greeted by his Soviet counterpart, Vyacheslav Molotov. At the Kremlin the following day, in the presence of Stalin, the two sign the Soviet-German Pact. The shock is immense. The policy of the Popular Front comes to an end. The implacable enemy is no longer fascism, to be opposed by the coalition of all political forces. The leaders of the Comintern were not abreast of affairs.[1] Dimitrov requests an audience with Stalin the very next day, on 24 August. Three days later, together with Manuilski he sends a letter in which he requests explanations. Stalin does not find time to answer him until 7 September. In the meantime, war breaks out. On 1 September, Germany attacks Poland. On 3 September, Britain and France declare war on Germany. On 17 September, the USSR invades Poland. All the communist parties had identified a grave threat in Hitler's regime, and the only force capable of combating it was the USSR. In the new circumstances, they are overwhelmed by panic and chaos. Their obedience to the Comintern was absolute. However, the Comintern remained silent, completely taken by surprise by this turn of events. It is not until 8 September, the day after Dimitrov's audience with Stalin, that the Comintern manages to formulate an official point of view – Stalin's.

In Bucharest, what remained of the PCdR after the decimation of its members in Moscow, after the arrests carried out by the Siguranţă, is deadlocked. It takes weeks before it can react. Discipline means unconditional acceptance of the Soviet line. In autumn 1939 and the first part of 1940, meetings are frequently held. A few expulsions at the top are dictated: those expelled are found guilty of Trotskyism, deviationism, whether to the Right or Left, and opportunism. A number of the 'tovi' (as they are designated in the documents),[2] compromised by their association with the Popular Front policy, are expelled, and all Party ties with them are broken. They are accused of 'collaborationism' with the bourgeoisie,

---

[1] *Dimitrov & Stalin, 1934-1943. Letters from the Soviet Archives*, ed. Alexander Dallin and F. I. Firsov, Yale University Press, 2000, pp. 148-163.
[2] Short for *tovarăşi* ('comrades') – *Translator's note.*

with its parties, with the Social Democrats, defined once again as "traitors to the cause of the proletariat and agents of the Siguranţă." Many of them make self-denunciations. There is no dissidence, no open criticism of the Ribbentrop-Molotov Pact. The atmosphere, in any case extremely tense, deteriorates even further. Accusations of 'provocateur' and 'traitor' abound. Suspicions are also fuelled by the numerous arrests. The Siguranţă had informants at the top. The most active among them is a member of the Secretariat, Nicu Tudor. He reports on all the discussions within the PCdR leadership and supplies addresses of the printing presses and safe houses. The Siguranţă is up to date with what is happening. They intervene only when a situation starts to coalesce. They make arrests, carry out searches, and confiscate printing presses and stocks of propaganda literature.

Internment in prison camps, arrests and close surveillance paralyse the Party. In 1939-1940, a marked thinning of the already slender PCdR ranks can be observed. Some of the intellectuals who had aligned themselves with the anti-fascist policies of the 1930s distance themselves from the Party. Many observe that the Pact also has an anti-Romanian edge, that it puts Romania in an extremely difficult position as regards the territorial claims of the USSR. The PCdR had managed to emerge from isolation in the period 1934-1939, when it had waved the 'banner of anti-fascism'. The trial of Dimitrov, the Popular Front, and the Spanish Civil War had all offered opportunities and a favourable background. On 23 August 1939, simultaneous with the close of this period, the PCdR once again becomes a sect, isolated from society. The pre-1933 Comintern slogans were re-adopted. Moreover, their stance toward the national problem, which had been played down for a period, was opposed to the sentiments of the general populace. Fascism and Berlin, the new ally of the USSR, vanished from the new agenda. The PCdR leaders inside Romania, at that date Béla Breiner, Ştefan Foriş, Teohari Georgescu, Iosif Roitman-Chişinevschi, Gavrilă Birtaş, Vasile Luca and Ştrul Zigelboim, who are at liberty, and those in prison (the majority), Ilie Pintilie, Gheorghiu-Dej and Ana Pauker, align themselves, as always, with the Comintern policy. Hitler's Germany and Nazism are now no longer the main adversaries of communism. The Pact is hailed and presented to the public opinion as a success for the USSR, as a weakening of the forces of imperialism, represented by Britain and France. The communist clandestine press gives up its attacks against the extreme Right. A rapprochement with the Iron Guard can be observed. King Carol is attacked, as well as his "terrorist government, which is preparing an attack against the USSR," as one manifesto puts it.

The Moscow group, led by Boris Ștefanov, has a delayed reaction. In an article published in the review of the Communist International, Ștefanov rehashes the old theses. Moreover, the reaffirmation of the principle of self-determination, to the point of the breakup of the Romanian State, prompts the Soviet Foreign Minister to issue a refutation. Ștefanov is obliged to publish another article, in which he toes the official Soviet line. He is sacked, and only thanks to Dimitrov's protection is he saved from the Gulag. Béla Breiner is made Secretary General. He was in Bucharest and had been running the Party since 1938. His death in hospital in March 1940 causes the Comintern to summon the members of the Secretariat – Vasile Luca, Ștrul Zigelboim and Nicu Tudor – to Moscow. It is highly likely that the Comintern intended to appoint Luca as head of the PCdR. Luca had been released from prison in the summer of 1939 and was seen as the most significant of the Romanian communist leaders not in gaol. The attempt on the part of the three – Luca, Zigelboim, Tudor – to cross the Dniester fails. The first two are arrested, denounced to the Siguranța by the third. Ștefan Foriș and Teohari Georgescu, also members of the Secretariat, are summoned to Moscow. They manage to cross the frontier into the USSR via Cernăuți/Czernowitz at the end of May. Teohari Georgescu remains in Moscow until October, Foriș until the end of December. With its leaders either arrested, in prison, or in Moscow, the PCdR is decapitated. It is a general staff without a commander, but also without soldiers.

The second part of 1940 is a tragic period for Romania. After the fall of France in June 1940, the USSR makes an ultimatum, demanding that the government in Bucharest should abandon Bassarabia and north Bukowina within 24 hours. King Carol consults the Crown Council and orders the retreat of the Romanian Army to the River Prut. There follows the cession of the Quadrilateral, and then the Vienna Diktat. In the course of three months, Romania loses around a third of its population and territory. Confronted with such a disaster, King Carol is no longer able to control the situation. At the beginning of September, he leaves the country. He is succeeded on the throne by his son, Mihai. General Ion Antonescu installs an authoritarian regime, in which the army collaborates with the extreme Right. The communists, scattered and few in number, are conspicuous by their absence throughout this period. During the crisis of summer 1940, the Romanian authorities took measures against the PCdR. "Arrests, internment in prison camps. Almost the entire legal membership was interned in camps all at once. Daily raids, night patrols. On the other hand, general mobilisation. All these things dealt the Party of the proletariat extremely heavy blows."[3]

The occupation of Bassarabia draws away many members from the PCdR. They see crossing the border into the USSR as an escape from their status as social pariahs. For the communists, the USSR was the homeland of the dictatorship of the proletariat, for which they were ready to sacrifice themselves. There was an exodus of members, which the heads of the PCdR were unable to stop. Further losses were caused by the cession of the Quadrilateral. Numerous members were active there, combining, as in Bassarabia, irredentist activities with communism. In the Quadrilateral, Bulgarian members were in the ascendant, thanks to the influence of the 'Bulgarian group' headed by Dimitrov within the Comintern. Cristian Rakovski, Boris Ștefanov, Dimităr Ganev, Gheorghi Krosnev, Petre Gheorghe, Petre Borilă, and Dumitru Coliu are just a few of the more well-known Romanian communists of Bulgarian origin. The Balkan Communist Federation was likewise dominated by Bulgarians. The PCdR was part of this structure and subordinate to it. After the Vienna Diktat, the Party members in northern Transylvania were stranded in what was now part of Hungary. The PCdR was better represented in the border regions, with their numerous minority populations, whom it encouraged "to liberate themselves from the terror of the landowners and the Romanian bourgeoisie." In December 1940, Ștefan Foriș, only lately appointed head of the PCdR, returning from Moscow, writes in his report to the Comintern: "The class enemy has not been able to annihilate our Party. However, after the liberation of Bassarabia and northern Bukowina and after the events of September, the royal dictatorship and the Iron Guard dictatorship respectively dealt heavy blows … the Party lost almost half its members."[4]

Apart from the losses of personnel, the PCdR also has serious political problems. After the Ribbentrop-Molotov Pact, the Comintern tries to discipline its troops, who are everywhere in disarray. Orders are lacking.

---

[3] ANCR, *Partidul comunist din România în anii celui de-al doilea război mondial, 1939-1944*, 2003, p. 145.

[4] Dan Cătănuș, Ioan Chiper, *Cazul Ștefan Foriș*, Bucharest: Vremea, 1999, p. 17.

The PCdR is too small a Party to be noticed in Moscow. When orders nonetheless do arrive in Bucharest, they are contradictory. The occupation of Bassarabia and northern Bukowina is hailed enthusiastically in Moscow, a position which isolates the Party yet further in Romania. The Romanian population had entirely different feelings. Many communists were expecting the Red Army not to stop at the Prut. The unanimity of this attitude contrasts with the confusion provoked by the cession of northern Transylvania. Slogans appeared militating for "Independent Transylvania," as a phase preparatory to a regime that would be ushered in by the Red Army. However, the USSR is no longer interested in any military incursion west of the Prut. The Comintern orders the Romanian communists to give up agitating for the Transylvanian independence. And this is what they do, accompanying their change of position with self-denunciations, sanctions and purges. Now, they protest against the concessions made at Vienna and condemn them, attacking King Carol. The zigzags of the PCdR also arise from the confusion sown by the Comintern. After the alliance between Hitler and Stalin, the Comintern does not manage to adapt to the new situation. The Comintern had identified fascism as the number one enemy, but after 23 August 1939 fascism had become an ally.

The Ribbentrop-Molotov Pact, the cause of this about-turn, also led to collaboration between the communists and the Legionaries/Iron Guard. The intersections between these two extremist groups go back longer. In the 1937 elections, the communists collaborated with the National Peasants Party, which had signed a non-aggression pact with the Iron Guard. The underground networks met, and there were negotiations and common actions against the royal dictatorship during the period 1938-1940. Communists joined the Iron Guard movement. Their anti-democratic spirit, hierarchy, and paramilitary formula made them akin to each other. The PCdR also lost the minuscule influence it had once enjoyed among the workers. One example: the sympathies of the railway workers were divided between the Communists and the Social Democrats at the beginning of the 1930s. In the December 1937 elections, a majority of railway workers vote for the Iron Guard. Another example: the members of the Workers Corps of the Iron Guard are mainly former communists. In the Caracal prison camp, where communists were interned, an Iron Guard group arrives in December 1940. There are no violent outbreaks, rather the contrary. The Iron Guard invite the communists to collaborate, in the name of their shared interests, their common anti-bourgeois spirit. One member of the Iron Guard says that the two ideologies are similar, the only difference being that "the Communist movement is based on atheism," and appears ready to join them (the communists). As an argument, he puts forward the fact that 20,000 workers from the Grivitza and Malaxa plant had gone over to the Iron Guard. Petre Constantinescu-Iaşi, when invited to give a lecture to his fellow prisoners in the Caracal camp, refuses, saying that after he is released he will reflect on the proposal. Mihai Gheorghiu Bujor adds, with reference to workers converted to the extreme Right, "if they wear the green shirt, they are doing it for the sake of form, for in their souls they are all Reds," as recorded in a report to the General Police Department.[5] Another episode of this kind is that which takes place on the night of 26-27 November 1940 in Jilava Prison. After an Iron Guard death squad shoots 65 former royalist dignitaries, the massacre comes to a stop when it reaches the cells where the communists are held.

After 21-22 June 1941, when Germany attacks the USSR, the PCdR position changes radically. It becomes anti-fascist once more, even attempting to be the sole legitimate claimant to such an attitude. After June 1941, and especially after the communists take power, in the middle of the 1940s, their closeness to the Iron Guard movement becomes a secret and forgotten chapter in the annals of communist agitation. In 1946, when a number of communist leaders appealed to Iron Guard members to join the PCdR, there was already a shared past. The gesture did not seem exotic or out of place. The Iron Guard supplied members and know-how to a party that did not have sufficient members to seize power, as Moscow demanded. In the summer and autumn of 1940, its leaders were either in gaol or prison camps, having been interned at Miercurea Ciuc in particular since May to June. The very few who were still at liberty were under strict surveillance. The Secretariat gives the order for members to remain hidden and not to circulate or agitate, in order not to provide any grounds for arrest. The Siguranţă is abreast of matters, thanks to surveillance and, in particular, its informants. Clandestinity is illusory. PCdR activity can be reduced to a few manifestos, which are in any case confused and without any impact. On 21 January, the Iron Guard rebellion breaks out. It remains a nebulous episode. There had long been connivance, partial collaborations, and complicity between the two groups. A police report recorded that in

---

[5] *Idem*, pp. 124-25.

November 1940, during a meeting at a hideout on Roma Street, the central headquarters of the Iron Guard movement, Dumitru Groza, the Head of the Iron Guard Workers Corps, had been accused of the massacres in Jilava Prison. Groza was also accused of taking part in the Grivitza protest, thus of being a communist. The incident was closed when Horia Sima backed Groza, saying that Zelea Codreanu supported the February 1933 protest. After the rebellion, the press as well as political circles claimed that there had been major communist participation and even that the rebellion had been incited by the communists with backing from Moscow. Ion Antonescu claimed likewise. The PCdR, after waiting a few days, riposted with a communiqué in which it denied any involvement. Nevertheless, a report of the General Police Deptartment, dated 27 January 1941,[6] stated that, "the Soviet Legation agrees that there are very many communist elements in the Iron Guard movement and they are well appreciated, and on the occasion of the rebellion many of them stirred up spirits provoking disorder and even taking part in robberies." Another note, of 1 February, reports:

> "The communists who are signed up in Iron Guard nests have received an order from their leaders … no longer to function in the nests in which they are signed up. … The Communist Party has sent a report to Moscow about the way in which events have unfolded in connection with the Iron Guard rebellion and the looting of shops, showing that this might be regarded as a first attempt at revolution in Romania with the support of the Party."[7]

After the rebellion,

> "the communist leaders maintain that the actions of General Antonescu in excluding the Iron Guard from Romanian political life … will create a favourable set of circumstances for the PCdR as it will be able to channel Iron Guard elements into the Communist movement … given that each Iron Guard member will sign up to the PCdR, where their demands ought to merge with the class interests of the proletariat."[8]

---

[6] *Idem.*
[7] SRI Archive, Dossier 40002, vol. 5, p. 165.
[8] *Adevărul literar și artistic*, 21 July 1998.

At the same time, other PCdR documents for public eyes condemned the rebellion and rejected the objectives of the Iron Guard movement, once it was clear that the uprising had been a failure and sufficient time had passed in order for the Comintern to elaborate an official line. The USSR had good relations with Germany and did not want to upset Berlin. The PCdR attacks against the Iron Guard in February to March 1941 should be understood as attacks against those who had opposed Antonescu, Hitler's favourite in Bucharest.

The situation in Europe, the tensions on Romania's borders, and the crisis in the regime lead the Siguranţa to make fresh arrests. The Party is swarming with informers who supply names and the addresses of safe houses. One police agent alone, Ion V. Taflaru, recalled in 1963[9] no less than 21 informers who, between 1939 and 1944, spied on the few dozen communists at liberty in Bucharest. How many could there have been in the prisons and in the provinces? One of the main informers was Iosif Şraier, the head of the PCdR Legal Office. As early as the 1920s, he had defended communists at trial: the Grivitza strikers, Ana Pauker, Petre Constantinescu-Iaşi et al. He knew the underground networks in detail, and all the communists personally. He had contacts with the families of those sent to trial, of those in prison. He was directly linked to Eugen Cristescu, the head of the SSI. He had business dealings with Jews trying to emigrate to Palestine and also those in concentration camps. In the 1940s, he made a fortune. He was a special informer. In exchange for information, he demanded services for his clients: reductions in prison sentences, lesser punishments at Court Martial, release from prison camps, better treatment. It was a barter in which both parties stood to gain. The Siguranţa was kept informed, while the communists obtained various improvements in their conditions. He was imprisoned in the prison camp at Tîrgu Jiu for a few months. The PCdR had its own intelligence service, which was meant to protect members and root out informers. It was not a very efficient safeguard. There are documents proving that there were relations between the Siguranţa and this safeguard of the PCdR. From Nuţă Natansohn, a communist tradesman, Lucreţiu Pătrăşcanu receives a list of informers within the PCdR drawn up by the Siguranţa. A Party inquiry certifies the validity of the list. The list came

---

[9] International Red Aid: Международная организация помощи борцам революции (International Organisation for Aid to Revolutionary Fighters), a section of the Comintern – *Translator's note.*

from an informer, a figure well-known for links with the Siguranţă: Zaharia Haimsohn, who wrote for the left-wing press in the 1930s.

Another high-level informer was Nicu Tudor. He was a railway worker, who had appeared in the dock at the Grivitza trial. He was replaced in the summer of 1939 by Constantin David as secretary of the Bucharest-Ilfov PCdR organisation. The motive for this replacement was the suspicion that David was an informer. We do not know whether he was or not, although Nicu Tudor certainly was. Tudor became a member of the CC Secretariat as a replacement for Béla Breiner, deceased in March 1940. A few months later, Nicu Tudor died of septicaemia, following an operation on his haemorrhoids. He had had sufficient time to relay the most confidential information and to trigger dozens of arrests. It was he who supplied the information that led to the capture of the two PCdR printing presses in 1940, and of those who operated them, led by Eugen Müller. In the investigation, Müller surrendered the archive to the Siguranţă, having taken possession of it from Béla Breiner. Arriving in Caransebeş, in order to mask his treachery, he accuses Foriş of being a Siguranţă man. Did he do so on the orders of the Siguranţă, as part of a sophisticated game, or was he merely frustrated at having been captured? Another source placed at the top and unidentified to this day appears in the archives under the code name '101'. During the period 1941-1944, 101 gave very well informed reports. He kept the Siguranţă up to date on the conflict within the PCdR. Among other things, he reported on the effect that the breakup of the Comintern in May 1943 had had on the PCdR. For a better understanding of the scale on which the PCdR was infiltrated by informers, the following is an excerpt from a declaration by a Siguranţă agent in 1953:

> "[I]n 1941 I shadowed Costel Dumitrescu from Leonida who was an informer for the Prefecture of the Bucharest Police, and after him I started shadowing Rech Ştefan. Who I later found out was an informer for Tâflaru from the General Siguranţă. In 1942 ... Sava Dumitrescu [a commissar – *author's note*] was holding Marcu Schon in a safe house on St. Constantine Street, using him to identify the contacts he knew ... Also in 1942, I shadowed Tunsoiu C[onstan]tin. from the STB, who was Sava Dumitrescu's informer ... In 1943, I shadowed ... Maria Iliescu who was later arrested with the organisation ... I think the organisation was given away by Marcu Schon..."[10]

---

[10] ANCR, *Partidul Comunist din România în anii celui de-al doilea război mondial, 1939-1944*, 2003, pp. 174-178.

The atmosphere of clandestine life can be reduced to suspicion, resentments and sectarian infighting. The PCdR meant a few dozen militants at 'liberty', plus a few hundred agitators in the prisons and camps.

On 22 April 1941, at Easter, the Siguranță made a large-scale capture. Fifteen were arrested, including Iosif Roitman-Chişinevschi, Gavrilă Birtaş, Teohari Georgescu, who were three of the members of the Secretariat, plus other high-ranking members, including Parascheva Abraham Breiner, and Melita Sharff. The Siguranță's source, a certain Ştefan Rech, mentioned above, was a middle-ranking member. After months of surveillance, the Siguranță managed to capture the entire network. For the PCdR, it was a catastrophe. For the third time in its history the Secretariat had been arrested en masse. Pavel Tkachenko and Boris Ştefanov were arrested in August 1926; Ana Pauker, Şmil Marcovici and Dimităr Ganev in July 1935. Behind all these cases, there was a denouncement from inside the Secretariat. In the 1941 inquiry, the Siguranță obtains other precious information, especially from Parascheva Breiner and Gavrilă Birtaş. The communist apparatus ceases to function for a while; connections with the provinces are lost. Foriş, the only one not to be arrested, is isolated. This arouses suspicions and later open accusations against him. The launch of the military campaign of 21-22 June 1941 prompts another wave of arrests and internment in prison camps. There are 250 in Bucharest alone: high or middle-ranking members, lawyers, journalists, and hardened agitators. All those who appear on the lists of the Siguranță as having been involved in communist activities in the past are arrested. The PCDR is in effect dismembered. There remain only scattered groups, with tenuous links to the centre. Foriş and his general staff do nothing except hide in order not to be captured.

The attack against the USSR that Germany and its allies, including Romania, launched on 21-22 June 1941 takes the PCdR by surprise, leaving it prey to even more violent splits. It is a group that is historically out of kilter, always trying to make up lost ground, always overtaken by the march of events. The PCdR does not operate in real time. It is absorbed in internal disputes, in reciprocal accusations of having betrayed the cause, of having worked for the Siguranță, of having formed factions against the legal leadership. The frequent arrests aggravate the situation. The political atmosphere is radicalised by the fact that war is being waged against the USSR. The communists were, objectively, enemies. Their unconditional affiliation with the Comintern and their subordination to Soviet interests transforms them quite simply into enemy agents, into a fifth column. War legislation prescribes Courts Martial and the maximum punishments, including death, which massively discourages action. In November, the Party's terrorist section is captured: eight persons. At trial, five sentences of death are handed down to Lilli and Francisc Paneth, A. Kornhauser, Ada Grünberg-Marinescu, and Elisabeta Nagy. The Siguranță obtained information about the group from two informers: Petre Melinte, a leading activist in the Bucharest organisation, and a certain Valache, a railway worker. The game of 'clandestinity' was not without its perils in a country at war. In March 1942, another two communists are executed: Ștefu Pompiliu and Nicolae Mohănescu, both print workers. In October, Schmuck Anton and Perl Simion are executed at Jilava. They were part of a network of 34 communists, tried in August. Six were sentenced to death, 20 to life, hard labour. On the same day, Suciu Ion, from another group, is also executed. In March 1942, the Siguranță sends a group of pupils from the two 'Cultura' Jewish lycée colleges to trial by Court Martial. They are charged with having stamped communist slogans on banknotes. Three of them (Zalman Leon, Moscovici Iancu and Elias Corneliu) are sentenced to death, another nine to hard labour for life.

These arrests, the smashing of the communist networks, and the heavy sentences exacerbate old conflicts and ignite new ones. At their source are not only the reciprocal accusations and suspicion of collaborating with the Siguranță, but also the differing attitudes in relation to the military and political situation. Foriș, prudently, imposes a strategy of survival. Others respond to the calls launched from beyond the front line by Free Romania radio and demand a partisan war; sabotage; assassination of Antonescu regime leaders, German officers and diplomats; and the blowing up of official buildings. Foriș's tactics took into account the weakness of the PCdR. The conflict flares up simultaneously with the attack on the USSR. It embroils the Party leadership and the Bucharest-Ilfov branch, pitting Ștefan Foriș against Petre Gheorghe. Around them, a sum of activists: Remus Koffler, Petrea Nicolae, Constantin Pîrvulescu, Ana Toma, Constantin Hagiu, Iosif Rangheț, on the one side, and Ilona Popp-Răceanu, Ștefan Pavel, Ioan Mețiu, Vasile Vîlcu, Anton Moisescu, Grigore Răceanu on the other.

The communists are more preoccupied with annihilating their Party adversaries than combating the Antonescu regime. The groups alter their configuration over time; alliances are formed and broken. When some of them are arrested, the opposing camp is accused of having provoked the collapse by collaborating with the Siguranţă. Petre Gheorghe ("Iancu") was Bulgarian by origin. As we have seen, the PCdR had an influential Bulgarian grouping, especially under Boris Ştefanov (1935-1940). In 1939, Petre Gheorghe has ambitions to be appointed to the Secretariat, but does not succeed. In December 1940, on the return of Foriş to the USSR, he nurtures the same ambition. He remains in the CC, as head of the Bucharest-Ilfov organisation, but it seems insufficient to him. In his political stance too, he is at odds with Foriş. He calls for assassinations and sabotage against the military machine. He accuses Foriş of being a Siguranţă man. The Bucharest-Ilfov organisation is insubordinate. Foriş reacts by dissolving it. Meetings follow, and an exchange of letters full of invective and accusations. The PCdR is deadlocked. Given that arrests ensue, the atmosphere becomes ever more venomous. In the gaols and prison camps – at Caransebeş, Văcăreşti, Mislea, Tîrgu Jiu, where the majority of the communists are held, kept up to date by couriers, visits from relatives and clandestine correspondence – the communists split, backing one camp or the other. Petre Gheorghe, in contrast to Foriş, is not a conspirator by nature. He is imprudent, he exposes himself; he works in the open. This greatly eases the mission of the Siguranţă, who are, in any case, up to date with the affair. Petre Gheorghe ends up being arrested by the Gestapo. He had tried to re-establish the link with the Comintern, through the Bulgarian Communist networks with which he had connections. He is accused of spying for the enemy during wartime and executed. After the war, Petre Gheorghe was to become the object of a cult, fabricated for propaganda purposes. The story had all the necessary ingredients. He was a communist, a proletarian, captured by the Gestapo and executed – it proved the entire myth of the Romanian proletariat, "devoted to communism, heroic, confronting Hitlerist terror." The PCdR needed to fabricate an imaginary past in place of the real one. Petre Gheorghe was an example that perfectly illustrated the official version of history. One of the few examples. To Gheorghe there cannot be ascribed any heroic deeds or acts of sabotage. On the contrary, his clumsiness and gaffes led to the arrest of dozens of communists. The network he led was copiously infiltrated by informers. The arrests numbered in the dozens.

In fact, the PCdR tactic was not to make its presence felt. It is a policy of 'wait and see' that defines this period. The objective was not to overthrow the military regime, but rather altogether more prosaic – that of survival until the arrival of the Red Army. The scenario did not foresee any proletarian insurrection in Bucharest. The communists were waiting for a Soviet military victory, followed by an occupation that would impose a Communist government made up of local agents. The PCdR did not organise any assassination attempts against superior German or Romanian officers; it did not blow up any trains, bridges, or buildings occupied by the military. There was no 'resistance' against the German war machine. The apparatus had to be conserved. As they were few, scattered and unorganised, this was the only tactic to hand. As regards this point, the communist groups both inside and outside prison were in agreement. Gheorghiu-Dej and Foriș promoted the same policy of conservation, of survival. They were waiting for a different political context. They knew very well, both the one and the other, how weak the PCdR was. Naturally, the most devastating accusation in the conflicts between the clandestine sects is "collaboration with the enemy." The presence of the Siguranța is, in fact, the obsessive preoccupation of the entire clandestine history of the PCdR. In a perverse way, the Siguranța was the supreme authority for the communists. How a communist thwarted secret police surveillance, how he conducted himself during interrogation, and whether or not he refused to co-operate were all decisive factors for his career and even his life. It was the most infamous of all the accusations that could be brought against someone in this labyrinth of clandestinity. Paranoid suspicion and the fear of being denounced or captured were dominant. Against this background, the conflicts are ever more violent, inside a party on the verge of extinction. Splits, ruptures, rivalries, accusations and reciprocal expulsions are part of everyday clandestine life. The conflicts paralyse what had remained of the Party, sap it of any political will or capacity to act. In effect, in 1941 the PCdR existed only as one of the official statistical fictions of the Comintern.

"*Procès-verbal*. 3 May 1941. Drawn up by the representative of the USSR border authorities, Lt. Dokalin, and Pavel Ghica, the head of the Ugheni repatriation commission, on behalf of the Romanian government. Today, at the Ugheni border crossing, political detainee Moș Ion Codreanu was surrendered to Romania from the USSR, and political detainee Ana Pauker from Romania. The present *procès-verbal* has been drafted in two copies, in Romanian and in Russian. We have received and surrendered. Signed on behalf of the Soviet authorities: Dokalin. We have received and surrendered. On behalf of the Romanian authorities: magistrate Ghica."

An inspector of police notes in his report the following:

"[Ana Pauker] has the proud bearing of the ardent communist, which characterises her. In her words, she has expressed her joy at departing for the USSR, where she will arrange her situation to her own liking, inasmuch as she feels capable and energetic enough to occupy a position of command ... She is a rather intelligent, cultivated woman, a doctrinaire of the communist idea, and very dangerous. We reckon that once she has entered Soviet territory, she will seek to denigrate the Romanian State."[11]

Five years had passed since the trial of Ana Pauker in 1936. Up until 1940, she was incarcerated, together with her co-accused, Liuba Chișinevschi and Estera Radosovețski, in Dumbrăveni Prison. Here, she was head of the Party cell. She wielded great authority over the other prisoners. Contributory to this was the celebrity that her trial at Craiova had brought her, but also her discipline. Among all the detainees, Ana Pauker held the highest position in the Comintern. She had studied in Moscow, at the Lenin School for Cadres, and then operated as a Comintern agent in France. All this gave her an undeniable ascendancy. Even while in prison, she is not forgotten. Signatures are gathered in memoranda that protest against the treatment to which she is subjected to in prison. Her release is demanded. The USSR exerts official pressure. In Spain, a detachment of a Romanian brigade (under political commissar Valter Roman) is named after her. Dolores Ibarruri-Passionara writes to her in 1937, likewise Aurora Thorez, the wife of Maurice Thorez, the head of the French Communist Party. She is looking after the child Ana Pauker had with Eugen Fried, whence also the rumour that Thorez was the father of the child. Poems are dedicated to her. Here is one, from the *Deșteptarea [The Awakening]* newspaper of 1 May 1937, published in Detroit, entitled *Ana Pauker* and signed by a certain N. Albu (excerpt):

"Your courage, O Sister Ana Pauker / Is an inspiration to the masses. / Into dreary houses, hidden and dark, / You have brought the light of

---

[11] ANCR, CC of the PCR Archive, Fund 50, Dossier 6, pp. 23-24.

a new spring. // In the vanguard of the masses you led / The struggle against the landowners, / With your brow aloft and your head raised high. / Let me paint you in the list of Heroes, // With my chisel, let me carve your portrait / On the highest crag, let me sing of you / In the plain words of the workingman, / Spreading the news of your valiant deeds / To every nation on earth, brave hero!"

The penitentiary regime is not very harsh, as a report of 1937 reveals:

"In the Dumbrăveni penitentiary there are currently 85 female prisoners. ... The incarceration of these detainees is among the most commodious, because they are repartitioned in three dormitories and enjoy an exceptionally lenient regime, being in permanent contact with each other throughout the day. The manner the detainees comport themselves ... gives the impression of a miniature communist republic organised and run by committee ... at the head of this committee is enthroned Ana Pauker."

A number of sections are operative. There is the educational section, which "holds lectures, and chairs discussions among the inmates about the situation in Russia, Spain and Romania. Under Ana Pauker's mattress was found a map of Spain with all the up to date markings of the battle front ... according to the accounts of the *Universe* newspaper as well as the *Morning* newspaper." There is the financial section, which keeps "a record of the sums of money arriving from different places and of the foodstuffs arriving from relatives of the inmates and the MOPR."[12] The report records the large quantities of foodstuffs that arrive for the communist inmates. Everything that is received in food parcels is shared jointly. They work in their own workshop, which they fit out using their own money. Then there is the GPU security section. The head of this section is Ana Pauker "who at every moment knows everything that is happening among the inmates and inside the penitentiary." Letters are read with all the inmates present. Whoever goes to the visiting room reports what was discussed and with whom. The communist nucleus forms "a perfect school from which emerge the most ardent communists ... each of them returns to society with the unshakeable conviction that the communist idea must be spread even at risk of their own

---

[12] CC of the PCR Archive, Fund 1, Dossier 353, p. 546.

lives."[13] Another official report, addressed to the Council of Ministers, two weeks before Ana Pauker arrives in the USSR, records: "At Dumbrăveni there are 90 detainees in total, including 30 [for criminal offences – *author's note*] and 41 communists, 11 Iron Guard members, seven spies and one common-law female prisoner … Of the 41 communist women … 33 are Jews, seven Hungarian and one a Romanian from Bassarabia … Until 1936, these communist women were serving their sentences at Deva, but in 1936 they were transferred to Dumbrăveni, where they remained until March 1940. Since that date they have been transferred to the special Interior Ministry penitentiary at Rîmnicu Sărat where they are subject to a harsher regime, being held in completely separate cells and receiving punishments more often. They don't have workshops here. On 5 October they were sent to Caransebeş, and on 30 November 1940 they were transferred once more to Dumbrăveni. … Ana Pauker, in conformity with Law Decree no. 3351 of 5 October 1940, has had a quarter of her sentence reduced, and her sentence, which was due to end in 1946, now expires in 1943 … The 41 communist women are detained in one wing of the prison, they have shared dormitories sleeping 10-12 to a room … Previously, they used to cook meat three times a week, now it is only twice a week, they receive a half kg of bread a day, and in the morning a half kg of milk … The inmates are entitled to receive up to 20 kg of foodstuffs sent by parcel per month. As regards sums of money … these funds come from two sources: 1) 75 per cent is from the value of their work in the workshops … 2) Money sent by their families … Investigating the postal register, I ascertained that Ana Pauker had received from Simon Pauker [Ana Pauker's father-in-law – *author's note*] in Bucharest, Pache Boulevard No. 15, on 4 March this year, 1,800 lei, and on 5 March 1,000 lei … The women prisoners are entitled to limited correspondence, three letters per month, and visits … They have a library … they are allowed to read the *Universe* newspaper … On a visit to the workshop I found prisoner Ana Pauker smoking, in a very irreverent, even impertinent, manner, she enquired as to the nature and purpose of our visit. Our impression is that this prisoner, who is regarded as the mentor and spiritual chief of the others, and in this capacity enjoying much consideration from the comrades, does not work … Thus, on the work roster for the month of February 1941, I did not find any objects made by Ana Pauker."[14]

---

[13] CC of the PCR Archive, Fund 1, Dossier 276, p. 103.

[14] CC of the PCR Archive, Fund 1, Dossier 353, p. 614.

In the prisons, the communists formed a closed group with its own rules. The leadership of the Party cell ruled the other inmates. The hierarchy and discipline were strict. Ana Pauker, like Gheorghiu-Dej, enjoyed not only an incontestable prestige, by means of which they dominated their fellow prisoners, but also exclusive privileges as regards work, food, and duties. The dominant figure at Dumbrăveni is undoubtedly Ana Pauker, something which can only be said of Gheorghiu-Dej starting from 1940, after all the important detainees had left Doftana Prison: Vasile Luca, Petre Constantinescu-Iași, and above all Gheorghi Ganev, the recognised leader of the communists in prison. In May 1944, it is rumoured that Ana Pauker was supposed to have asked "the Allies, over Radio Moscow, to bomb the town and penitentiary of Dumbrăveni, because she had been subjected to inhumane treatment there." The local authorities make a note: "As regards the manner in which the communist leadership has been treated, the following things are being said amongst the inhabitants of the town: the whole time she was imprisoned, Ana Pauker enjoyed exceptionally good treatment. She had six women at her disposal, four of them Jewish, who were like ladies' companions and who procured from the town or elsewhere everything she wanted. In one room of the penitentiary, she had installed a seamstress's workshop in which, along with her personal work, were made various items of embroidered lingerie and lady's dresses, which were then sold in town. From the money resulting from these sales, Ana Pauker claimed to support herself, although in reality she was sent tens of thousands of lei each month from all over the place. Likewise, it emerges that on certain days, Ana Pauker would leave the penitentiary, going for a walk through Hoghilag village and the surroundings, accompanied by two or three of her lady companions."[15]

Ana Pauker is faced with a critical moment in the autumn of 1938, when she discovers from the *Scînteia* [*The Spark*] newspaper, smuggled into the prison, that Marcel Pauker has been executed in Moscow. Even if they both had children from other relationships, the two remained married. In 1934-1935, they had collaborated in the Secretariat of the PCdR, run by Marcel Pauker, in Bucharest. A legend circulates according to which Ana Pauker denounced her husband to the Soviet authorities. This is incorrect. She receives the news of his execution at Dumbrăveni. According to the

---

[15] Report of the General Department of Police dated 29 May 1943, CC of the PCR Archive, Fund 1, Dossier 348, p. 201.

procedures imposed by the Comintern, communist detainees had to debate the case, condemning the victim and approving the measures taken against the 'Trotskyite traitors'. Ana Pauker limits herself to affirming that if he has been convicted, then the Party is right. In March 1940, she is moved to the prison at Rîmnicu Sărat (the Axis powers had exerted pressure on Bucharest to re-address the issue of Transylvania, and the authorities prudently transfer communist detainees to the Old Kingdom). It is here that she receives a visit from Ştefan Foriş, the highest ranking communist after the death of Béla Breiner. Foriş is accompanied by Tatiana Popovici, his second wife after he divorced Lotti Foriş. A number of questions remain unanswered. Why did the authorities allow a notorious communist to visit Ana Pauker? The Siguranţă knew that Foriş was one of the leaders of the PCdR. A few weeks later, Foriş left the country clandestinely, headed for Moscow, in order to be named head of the PCdR. The purpose of the visit to Rîmnicu Sărat Prison was to sound out Ana Pauker's position. It was not only her health or spirits that were of interest to him, but also her opinions. What was of interest to the Comintern were above all her points of view with regard to the killing of Marcel Pauker and the latest political developments: the Ribbentrop-Molotov Pact, the outbreak of war.

Foriş reports as soon as he arrives in Moscow, in the summer of 1940. It is likely that his answers were favourable. What is certain is that in 1941 the USSR, requested an exchange of prisoners. On the list appear Ana Pauker, Gheorghiu-Dej and Chivu Stoica. Ion Antonescu approves only Ana Pauker, justifying his refusal of the others as follows: "There will be too many communists gathering in Moscow." The second episode: on 22 September 1940, a year after the assassination of a number of Iron Guard leaders (Alexandru Cantacuzino, Alex. Cristian Tell, Mihail Polihroniade etc.), a pilgrimage to the Rîmnicu Sărat Prison is organised. The inmates were expecting the worst. The Iron Guard limit themselves to taking photographs, partying, and discussing political topics with Ana Pauker and the other inmates.[16] The Iron Guard intended to close down the prison and transform it into a museum. The explanation: after 23 August 1939, the fascists and the communists were working together. From Rîmnicu Sărat Prison Ana Pauker is transferred to Caransebeş at the beginning of October. Gheorghiu-Dej – along with the others from Doftana – is brought here after the earthquake of 9-10 November. The two were the best-known

---

[16] CC of the PCR Archive, Fund 1 Dossier 365, p. 560.

communist figures among the inmates. Each was head of a communist cell in prison: Pauker since as early as 1936, Dej for a few months, since Dimităr Ganev, who had seconded Pauker in the trial, had been released and left for the USSR. Dej and Pauker talk for around two hours. The same week, the communist detainees are transferred back to Dumbrăveni, and no further discussions take place between the two. They will meet again, four years later, in September 1944, in a Bucharest now occupied by the Red Army.

On 6 May 1941, Ana Pauker arrives in Moscow, and is greeted as a heroine. She is saluted at official ceremonies. Many Comintern leaders salute her in the press, including Maurice Thorez and Dmitri Manuilski. Doleres Ibarruri-Passionaria writes in *Pravda*: "Ana Pauker has been freed. Ana Pauker, the experienced Romanian revolutionary, is again among us. … We hail Ana Pauker here on Soviet soil, our Ana who has returned to the ranks of the fighters for revolution and the labour for freedom, she has returned to that which is the sole meaning of her existence" (article reprinted by *Scînteia* on 15 December 1944). She is not the only one in this situation. Toivo Antikainen, a Finnish communist, sentenced to life imprisonment, is the object of a similar barter. Likewise, in October 1941, Mátyás Rákosi, a Hungarian communist sentenced to life imprisonment in 1934. Once in Moscow, Ana Pauker finds few Romanian communists of the old guard, as many as had not escaped the firing squads. Gherea, Köblős, Finkelstein and Elena Filipovici were all dead. Cosmopolitan, ambiguous Moscow, the city of the NEP she had known in the 1920s, was now gone. The fear provoked by repression and the tense wait for the USSR to enter the war provide the backdrop. PCdR survivors are few and far between. Those who had been in Spain, or came from Romania later, after 1938, secretly crossing the Dniester, escaped the firing squad. Ana Pauker is appointed PCdR representative to the Comintern, replacing Boris Ştefanov, who has fallen into disgrace. During the period between 1941 and 1944, she is the dominant figure among the Romanian communist exiles in Moscow. Her international stature and her connections, dating from the 1920s, gain her recognition. Maurice Thorez, whom she knew, was also in Moscow at that time. Also to be found were Dolores Ibarruri-Passionaria, Wilhelm Pieck and Klement Gottwald, all in the Comintern leadership. She is close to some of the survivors as well as the instigators of the Great Terror. First of all, to Georgi Dimitrov, the president of the Communist International, who, in his diary, says she is "an enchanting woman." In particular, she has links with his adjunct, Stalin's man, Dmitri Manuilski. She is friends with the latter's sister, Varya, and with Polina Zhemshuzhina, the wife of Vyacheslav Molotov, a member of the Politburo, Foreign Minister at the time. Stalin's shadow. She is given a flat in central Moscow, whither she brings her children, Tania and Vlad Pauker, raised until then in an orphanage. She tries to find out about the fate of Marcel Pauker. She is advised by her protector, by none other than Dmitri Manuilski, to give up. Which she does.

By the beginning of the 1940s, the Comintern has been reduced to insignificance – a handful of refugees in Moscow, tolerated by Stalin and living under the threat of the fury of a dictator who might send them to their deaths at any moment. Stalin had not hesitated to hand all the German communists on USSR soil over to Hitler. Stalin kept Dimitrov, Thorez, Dolores Ibarruri, Palmiro, and Togliatii alive because they were symbolic figures, products of Kremlin propaganda. They had survived due to their 'international stature', their 'popularity', whether real or fictitious, in their own countries. They were the "symbols of the worldwide proletarian revolution." From time to time, they were wheeled out, as a means of keeping the Communist Parties under control. The Great Terror and the pact with Hitler had dissipated any lingering illusions.

On 21-22 June 1941, Germany invades Russia. All links between the communist refugees and their parties, small or large, clandestine or legitimate, are severed. The residents of the Lux Hotel no longer serve any useful purpose. Dimitrov no longer has any real connections with the masters of the Kremlin. The Comintern personnel are evacuated eastward. The Germans advance rapidly. The Soviet regime is on the verge of collapse. The Red Army retreats to the suburbs of Moscow. Ana Pauker is evacuated to Ufa together with the Free Romania Romanian-language section of the Comintern's radio station. The people around her belong to the communist new guard: Petre Borilă, Valter Roman, Leonte Tismeneţki, Leonte Răutu. There are also Dumitru Coliu, Vasile Luca, Dumitru Petrescu and Constantin Doncea, who have a longer record of service. Doncea, the leader of the Grivitza strikers and their figurehead in the trials that followed, a former fighter in the international brigades in Spain, was regarded by Georgi Dimitrov as the most important Romanian communist until 1941. The arrival of Ana Pauker sidelines him, the same as it does Boris Ştefanov, the old Secretary General, who was still working for the PCdR within the Comintern. In the spring of 1942, Ana Pauker returns to Moscow, where, together with Vasile Luca and other Romanian communists, she sets up the Romanian National Democratic Front, a political fiction convenient to the Kremlin. It was an organisation intended to rule Romania after the victory of the Red Army. Similar Polish, German, Hungarian etc. groups are formed, on the orders of Moscow.

The political destiny of Ana Pauker had been linked to the Comintern since its very foundation in March 1919. Almost none of the original Comintern was still alive. Lenin had died a natural death in 1924. Trotsky had been assassinated in Mexico, in August 1940, on the orders of Stalin. Zinoviev and Rakovski, from the original line up, had been tried and executed, Bukharin, who had succeeded Zinoviev as head of the Comintern, likewise. Fritz Platten, from Switzerland, had been one of the original five in 1919. He had organised the departure of Lenin's Bolsheviks from Zurich to Petrograd in March 1917. He died in the Gulag in 1942. Béla Kuhn, who had replaced Rakovski in the Presidium, was shot. The massacre of the historical leaders of the Comintern is preliminary to the disbanding of the organisation. The dénouement comes in May 1943. Dmitri Manuilski and Gheorghi Dimitrov are summoned to the Kremlin by Vyacheslav Molotov. To their surprise, they are informed of Stalin's decision to dissolve the Comintern. The two have to draft the wording of the decision, as if they had come up with the proposal themselves. Stalin reads the document and, after making a few modifications, signs it.

On 11 May, three days later, a meeting of the Executive Committee of the Communist International decides to dissolve the organisation. On 15 May, the Comintern leaders sign the document of disestablishment, after a meeting of the Executive Committee, the only one to have taken place for a long time. Stalin was in a hurry to bring this chapter of history to a close. In its 22 May edition, *Pravda* announces the event.[17] The shock is just as great as the one that had been felt on the announcement of the Ribbentrop-Molotov Pact. The links of the communist parties with Moscow were in effect broken off, because of the war. The immixture of the Comintern in the activities of the communist parties had been much reduced after June 1941. The Comintern had been a political cadaver since as early as the 1920s, brought back to life in the 1930s. It had been a scarecrow aimed at the democratic regimes. The Moscow trials in 1936-1938 and the Ribbentrop-

---

[17] SSI, 25 March 1944, CC of the PCR Archive, Fund 1, Dossier 378, p. 441.

Molotov Pact dealt it blows from which it was never to recover. Stalin vacillated for a while, forestalled by the war, but in 1943, he ascertained what had already occurred: the Comintern was an empty shell. Thus, when the Allies raise the matter of the Comintern, Stalin agrees to dissolve it. The political price was derisory and, in one spectacular gesture, he managed to placate the Americans and British. Since Stalin required massive aid from the Allies and was pushing for a second front in the West, it was a good bargain for him. None of the established Comintern leaders opposed the decision. A legend of the Communist movement faded away, the ghost of what was meant to be global Communist Party. On the act dissolving the Comintern (15 May 1943) we also find the signature of Ana Pauker. On its constitutive act (March 1919, we find the signature of another Romanian: Cristian Rakovski. Next to his signature appear those of Maurice Thorez, Ercoli (Palmiro Togliatti), Dolores Ibarruri-Passionara, Wilhelm Pieck, Vasil Kolarov, Klement Gottwald, Gheorghi Dimitrov, Dmitri Manuilski, Mátyás Rákosi, Walter Ulbricht, and André Marty. The *Kommunisticheskiy Internatsional* magazine publishes the documents. Stalin gives an interview. The Western press publish it in its entirety, plus commentaries hailing the decision. In reality, the structures of the Comintern are preserved. They become subordinate to the Kremlin, as departments of the Central Committee of the CPSU, masked as so-called institutes, designated nos. 99, 100, and 205. The Comintern apparatus, its leaders, retain their positions, preserve their privileges, and continue to control the communist parties, but hide their presence from the Western Allies. The Comintern has not been scuttled. Nor is it not a case of suicide. Ironically, the entire organisation becomes "clandestine." It is something its members are accustomed to.

In the summer of 1943, after the dissolution of the Comintern, Ana Pauker visits the camps for Romanian prisoners in order to recruit volunteers. The message is: whoever agrees to become part of the Division that is being organised will cease to be a prisoner. Six of the 12 generals captured by the Soviets accept. After the battle of Stalingrad, Stalin was confident of victory and was preparing to occupy a part of Europe. Together with Colonel Nicolae Cambrea and other officers, Ana Pauker organises an 'anti-fascist' committee at Suzdal, in a camp for Romanian prisoners. In September 1943, at Krasnogorsk, near Moscow, a congress of Romanian prisoners of war is held. From here, Ana Pauker sends a letter to Stalin requesting that he allow the formation of a Romanian Division to fight against the Axis. The Kremlin gives its approval on 2 October. On 15 November 1943, the Tudor Vladimirescu Division is founded, with 9,000 men and Ana Pauker as their political commissar. From now on, we find her wherever the Division goes. In April to May 1944, she is at Klembovska, in Ukraine. Her dominant position among the Romanian communist émigrés in the USSR can also be felt in Bucharest. In April, a note by the Siguranţa signalled that Ana Pauker's relatives were receiving financial assistance from MOPR (International Red Aid).

The Royal Coup of 23 August 1944 finds her in Bălţi, in Bassarabia. The plan devised by Stalin and Molotov foresaw that Romania would be 'liberated' by the Red Army and, simultaneously, an occupation government of 'Moscovites', plus a number of the Bucharest faithful, would be installed. The arrest of Antonescu and the participation of the local communists in the anti-fascist coalition take Ana Pauker and the leaders of the now defunct Comintern by surprise. She is summoned from Bălţi to Moscow by Georgi Dimitrov.

"I have been to Moscow. Comrade Dimitrov summoned me and told me: 'You're going to Romania', he also gave me two women radio-operators and told me: 'Take over the leadership in Romania and see what's going on, because we haven't got a clue'. Comrade Borilă, who was there, knew that that there wasn't any link with Romania and didn't know anything. And then on the spot I said: 'Comrade Dimitrov, I am a woman. I wasn't in Romania during wartime. I was in prison and I have no idea how things stand, 10 years have passed and it is hard to do this thing. I am a woman, a Jew, an intellectual'. – 'But who is there to take command there?' I told him that there was a popular comrade, a worker, Comrade Gheorghe Gheorghiu-Dej. I didn't know him very well. I had met with him for two hours at Caransebeş, but I knew that he was a very popular comrade, a railway worker, an experienced man. 'Look, he could be Party leader', I said. Dimitrov said, 'We haven't had any information from Romania for four or five years. We don't know anybody. It is you we know'. Comrade Borilă knows that the group had also been told: See what is going on over there and take over the leadership, because they didn't know what was happening in Romania. 'Go with two radio operators, announce to me what exactly is going on. You can communicate a number of times a day on how things stand. We're also going to send Luca to be of assistance and mind how you go'. And with that, I left," declares Ana Pauker on 8 May 1956 to the commission of inquiry, comprising Gheorghe Apostol, Constantin Pîrvulescu, Alexandru Moghioroş, and Ion Vincze, appointed by Gheorghe Gheorghiu-Dej. On 7 September, Dimitrov notes in his diary: "Arranged with Cherbakov to have Luká Laszló (member of the CC of the RCP) released from military service to work in Romania." On 11 September, Ana Pauker meets Georgi Dimitrov once more, as recorded in his diary, and together they discuss her departure to Romania. On 16 September, Ana Pauker lands at Băneasa airport in a Soviet aeroplane.

***

The dissolution of the Comintern is announced by Radio Free Romania on 22 May 1943. The few hundred communists, whether imprisoned or at liberty, take the news badly. Their mental dependence on the Comintern was absolute. It was their political, if not personal, reason to exist. They lived in expectation of orders, couriers, and funds from the USSR. The PCdR was confronted with an unforeseen situation. An unidentified SSI informer writes in his report, a few days after the announcement: "The dissolution of the Third Communist International has produced confusion in the ranks of a large part of the communists, the other part continuing to believe that in the future the Communist Party will also continue to act according to directives from Moscow. The communists in the second category assert that the dissolution of the Third Communist International is only formal in nature, dictated by the momentary necessities of foreign policy."

Via their informers, the police monitor the situation. On 30 May, a report reveals:

> "The Party's transition to a new organisational position following the dissolution of the Third Communist International is encountering difficulties due to permanent police surveillance and in consequence abidance by the rules of conspiracy is becoming the movement's greatest problem. Likewise, Party members and sympathisers cannot understand the need for the dissolution of the Third International. The more initiated see in the dissolution … an arbitrary act on the part of the

Executive Committee of the Third International and at the same time a renunciation of the Party's revolutionary principles. The movement's theoreticians argue that the Executive Committee has proceeded erroneously ... and that it should not have taken such an important decision without prior consultation with the members of all the sections of the International. The prominent members of the movement are threatening to create a committee of initiative in order to reorganise the Party on the basis of true revolutionary principles."

The PCdR is in a state of shock. Any official position is late in arriving. When it nevertheless does appear, it does nothing except repeat Stalin's declaration, word for word. As usual when faced with a sudden change, the PCdR is on the verge of schism. Factions are ready to form. Reciprocal accusations abound. The conditions of clandestinity make the situation dangerous. Correspondence between detainees in the camps and prisons and those 'outside' reveal that matters had reached boiling point. No one can rely on anyone else. Those in prison reproach those at liberty for having abandoned them and, in particular, for sending insufficient aid (money, food, clothing, printed propaganda). Likewise, they make secondary accusations of erroneous doctrine and political orientation. The phenomenon also takes place in reverse. The mistakes of those in prison are highlighted with the same vehemence. In fact, no one knows what is to be done, what is to follow. After a few weeks have passed, towards the end of summer, each grouping, in accordance with its own interests, with its own understanding of the consequences of Stalin's new position, asserts various positions as to what has in fact taken place. This time, the rupture between the leaders at liberty in Bucharest – Foriş, Koffler – and those in prison is definitive. The dissolution of the Comintern was the final blow for 'unity in the Party ranks'. It was perceived by the camp inmates as a de-legitimisation of the leadership, of Foriş himself, since the latter had been appointed by the Comintern. The severance of communications in June 1940, the isolation produced by the shift in the German-Soviet front further east, accentuated the rupture, which was now reaching its culminating point. The position of Foriş has been seriously shaken. The communists, his adversaries in the Party, see the new situation as an opportunity to get rid of him. It is a question of time. The detainees at Caransebeş break off correspondence with him and no longer recognise his authority. When Gheorghiu-Dej and

Chivu Stoica are transferred to Tîrgu Jiu on 26 June 1943, things move in the same direction here too. It is also now that Dej comes into conflict – on the subject of removing Foriş – with Lucreţiu Pătrăşcanu, interned on 3 January. On 6 June, Pătrăşcanu had become the leader of the 'camp communists' in the context of the shock produced by the dissolution of the Comintern. The change had occurred in spite of the support Foriş gave to Ovidiu Şandor, the leader of the communist cell up to then. Gheorghiu-Dej, having arrived in Tîrgu Jiu, reinstates Şandor, following Pătrăşcanu refusal to join the anti-Foriş plot. After Pătrăşcanu leaves the camp, at the beginning of August, Dej takes over the post, deposing Şandor. Factions are forming and unravelling in the fight for supremacy. The conflict is intensified by the urgent need to adapt to the new circumstances created by Stalin's decision.

Naturally, appeals to maintain discipline and abide by the rules of conspiracy abound. As if that were not enough, on 28 May, Constantin Pîrvulescu, a member of the Secretariat, takes a taxi at midnight from outside the Romanian Athenaeum, accompanied by a woman, heading for one of the communists' safe houses. His romantic fling causes him to relax his vigilance. After alighting, on Parfumului Street, he leaves behind a packet of PCdR documents in the taxi. "The taxi driver surrenders the packet to the police the next day. The capture is substantial: numerous activity reports from different clandestine organisations in the capital, manifestos and propaganda brochures, as well as the biographies of Communist Party members. …" Lists of names and addresses, archives, correspondence. In the following months, there are dozens of arrests and a number of networks are annihilated. Safe houses are discovered, as well as the treasury (foreign currency, gold ingots) and the central archives of the PCdR, in a house at Crîngului Street No. 15. It is a disaster. Constantin Pîrvulescu is sequestered in one of the safe houses and suspended indefinitely. The atmosphere of suspicion, natural in such an environment, intensifies. The arrests increase; dozens of persons are investigated, tried, and sent to gaol in the autumn and winter of 1943-1944. The Siguranţa comes very close to capturing Ştefan Foriş and Remus Koffler. Nervousness in the minuscule Party turns to panic. "The leadership Committee of the PCdR is at present discreetly following the activity of its members, through certain of its delegates," we learn from a note of the SSI dated 24 June. Expulsions, punishments, reciprocal denunciations soon follow.

The dissolution of the Comintern was news that was hard to digest in that small, closed world.

"As a result of the dissolution of the Comintern, there have been a series of upheavals inside the Romanian Communist movement, with some of the front-rankers agreeing to accept the consequences of this act, and others interpreting it to their own ends and attempting to undertake action independent of any future directives from Moscow. These upheavals have created a state of confusion, still not eliminated, within which a communist faction, representing the majority of the Marxist front-rankers, has attempted to collaborate with democratic bourgeois groups," notes the same SSI informer at the top of the PCdR (codename '101'), on 15 October 1943. Once the dissolution of the Comintern has been announced, the emphasis of party propaganda shifts from the 'class struggle', 'proletarian revolution' and 'Stalin and the USSR' to other topics: 'patriotism', the 'anti-fascist war', the need for a 'coalition of democratic forces' and 'taking the country out of the war'. The PCdR prefers no longer to operate under its own name. It uses the name of one of the organisations under its control, the Union of Patriots. It thereby offered an attractive image to those who did not wish to collaborate with a 'fifth column', but had anti-Hitler viewpoints and believed in an Allied victory. The 'communist' cells change their name to 'patriotic', 'anti-fascist', in order to attract leading political figures, intellectuals, the bourgeois etc. The manoeuvre also allows a settling of accounts. The Siguranță knows that on 7 June 1943

"this dissolution provided Communist Central with the opportunity … to eliminate weak and dubious persons, who were moved to the new anti-fascist and peace committees, while the capable, determined and devoted elements were left to lead, within the old communist organisations, the same life of revolutionary conspiracy. These elements form the backbone of the Communist movement in Romania and it is from their ranks that people will be recruited to carry out, at the opportune moment, acts of destruction and terror."

Once the Comintern is dissolved, the PCdR reverts to its Popular Front policy of the 1930s. Back then, the coalition had not been perfected because of subordination to the Comintern. Under the new circumstances, such a policy was reinstated.

> "They [the communists – *author's note*] are in fact rejoicing that they have got rid of a bureaucratic impediment, which the International represented, and that now they will have more freedom of action to organise their political activity and to adapt their tactics to the particular requirements of Romania ... they will no longer have to wait for the approval of the Third International before taking any step."

A series of figures involved in the anti-fascist campaigns, having been eclipsed after the signing of the Ribbentrop-Molotov Pact, are now once more moved up into the front ranks of the PCdR. Lucrețiu Pătrășcanu, Petre Constantinescu-Iași etc. are among them. A report by the SSI dated 27 June 1944:

> "From an anti-fascist intellectual, with links to extreme left-wing circles, we have the following: ... Neither Pătrășcanu nor Constantinescu-Iași represent the Communist Party, and are only elements used by the latter for the sake of various contacts and who cannot determine an extreme left-wing orientation, their only political potential being that of implementing a mandate."

Their past as former political detainees, as 'democratic' intellectuals, adversaries of the regime, gave them legitimacy. In the case in which Antonescu was ousted, men of this sort would have a role to play. Notoriety made them more credible than the anonymous agitators who operated underground. The latter usually came from the lumpenproletariat, deserters, or the Jewish petit bourgeoisie, areas from which the communists recruited personnel in the 1940s. The PCdR rediscovers and thrusts to the fore the protagonists of the anti-fascist campaigns of the 1930s. The real leaders remain behind the scenes in Moscow, in Bucharest, in the camp at Tîrgu Jiu, and in various gaols, biding their time. For the time being, in the second half of 1943, the drama is unfolding on a smaller stage. The situation is still ambiguous, militarily and politically. Emissaries are sent to the leaders of the PNȚ, PNL and PSD. With many reservations, contact is nevertheless made. The USSR was to have a decisive influence in post-war Romania, and consequently, the communists had to be taken into consideration. The dissolution of the Comintern opened the way for such a scenario. The tipping of the balance in favour of the Allies, after the battles of Stalingrad and Kursk, made decisive contributions to the change of attitude. The communists became more and more interesting partners the more the front drew closer.

In March 1944, the scenario of a Bolshevik putsch, with barricades controlled by detachments of workers and soldiers defecting to the side of the Revolution, was taken into account by the communist leaders.

"On 16 March 1944, the local organisation in the capital held a meeting at which was present a person who presented himself as the Secretary General of the CC of the CP. The latter brought to the knowledge of the members the following. In relation to military and political events, the CC of the CP ordered all members to act in the strictest secrecy in order to give the authorities the impression that the movement is all but non-existent following the arrests and detentions made. At an opportune moment, action will be taken according to the pattern of the Iron Guard rebellion of January 1941."

On 4 April, Foriş is sacked. The arrival of the Red Army in Bucharest is a matter of weeks away. The triumvirate instated on 4 April, to which were added Gheorghiu-Dej and Lucreţiu Pătrăşcanu, men of the greatest influence among the communists at that time, sends the following warning to its own ranks, on 1 August 1944:

"Let us not expect the PCdR to come to power immediately after the Russian occupation of Romania ... the capitalist regime will last for another two years after the end of the war. After the Armistice, Romania will be led by a democratic government drawn from the so-called National Committee ... as soon as it is legalised, the PCdR will commence action to win over the proletarian and petit bourgeois masses. ... General elections will follow, the PCdR will have a great chance of success but will not assume power alone, inasmuch as, in conformity with the accords made by the USSR with Britain and America, it will not be possible to force the instatement of an exclusively communist regime in Romania by revolutionary methods, and the take-over of power will have to contain a democratic and parliamentary evolution. … The PCdR gives its members to understand that after the war a difficult task is incumbent upon them, one that will be relatively long term, that of preparations with a view to the creation of the conditions necessary for the communisation of the country. … because of the international accords, it will be necessary to give up the formula dictatorship of the proletariat."

The Muscovite group has its own plan. Romania had to be 'militarily liberated' by the Soviets. A pro-communist regime was to be instated. The King and the bourgeois parties were to be eliminated together with Antonescu, on the very day the Red Army entered Bucharest. These are three versions of the same scenario of a 'world revolution' led by the Kremlin. The conspirators have betted on the external factor, on a war won by the USSR, followed by a military invasion. They counted very little or not at all on their own powers, on a rising up "of the popular masses under the leadership of the vanguard of the proletariat." The calculation was, in its cynicism, correct. The Romanian communists, wholly isolated, saw the regime they led not as one brought to power by internal forces, but as one of foreign occupation. It was an admission of the real nature of this 'Party'.

XIV
The Keys of Comrade X

The ghost of Catzavencu still hovered above us, wearing the cloak of
Stalin.
Belu Zilber

The disease of power is a very dangerous disease
Gheorghe Gheorghiu-Dej

In the 1960s, the stories Dej used to tell, frequently lingered on the period
he spent in gaol. It was there that, with rare exceptions, his acolytes had
first met him. They had the same mentality, experiences and memories,
gained at Jilava, Văcăreşti, Aiud, Ocnele Mari, Doftana, Galatzi, Rîmnicu
Sărat, Caransebeş, Lugoj, Mislea and Dumbrăveni, and in the prison camps
at Miercurea Ciuc, Caracal and Tîrgu Jiu. To have passed through these
places was the criterion for selection. What was this world of those who had
emerged from the underground? The 'myth of Doftana' and the 'prisons
myth' dominated the post-war period, and were one of the most resonant
and constant subjects of official propaganda. School textbooks, newspapers,
thousands of books with print runs of millions of copies and the radio
contributed to the presentation of the founding myth of the communist
regime. Inter-war travails justified a presence in the post-war leadership.
It was the social revenge of 'the most beloved and devoted fighters of the
proletariat'. It was obligatory for those chosen by historical destiny to have
passed through purgatory, a period of incarceration, as presumptive heroes
of the working class and, later, all-powerful chiefs. They had to have been
confirmed, legitimised as the chosen ones of Leninist providence, the elite
of the 'luminous future'. Passage through the cells of Doftana, Aiud and
Caransebeş was obligatory on the path of historic initiation into the secrets
of the party of professional revolutionaries. Everything is explainable in
terms of Marxism-Leninism-Stalinism with religious overtones. The exact
imitation of the Bolshevik political formats applied by Lenin and then
Stalin provided the content of this political myth imported by the native
Romanian communists.

The chapters in the history of inter-war clandestine misery became, after the seizure of power, the 'Acts of the Apostles'.

> "Comrade Gheorghiu-Dej ... transformed that cruel fortress of death and horror, which the bourgeoisie wanted to turn into a grave for the best sons of the working class, into a school for gaoled revolutionary fighters. Starving, cold, ill, tortured, hurled for months at a time into the terrifying cells of Section 'H', where they languished in darkness and damp, the communists never knew what it meant to submit to the enemy. At Doftana, in those cruel years, there was created a school of life and struggle, the school in which, under the leadership of the Party organisation, headed by Comrade Gheorghe Gheorghiu-Dej, communists were reared and tempered, leaders taught not to believe that hardships cannot be overcome..."[1]

A look at Dej's prison experiences will provide us with information to enable a better understanding of the man and his accomplices. Dej was to have remained in prison until 1946. His first place of incarceration was Craiova in 1934. At least in the early years, he finds it hard to cope with imprisonment. On 21 August 1934, Dej writes:

> "I cannot say that if I am in prison everyone has forgotten me. No! A proof in this sense is the fact that the entire working class of Romania and all over the world are not only thinking of us but also organising the struggle for our liberation ... I'm proud that I has fought for a great work, the work for the liberation of the working class, for the good and the interests of the poor. My thoughts will eternally be with the working class," he writes with pathos.

> "I will struggle to the end ... Life without the struggle has no meaning, you go through life like a mere news item. That's why I don't regret the fact I'm locked up because freedom for me and for any conscious worker is useful only through the struggle. If they let me out tomorrow, I would do the same thing. But if I complained about them not writing to me, about them not even answering the letters I sent them, I do it because I had the sentimental bond that I had, because I haven't ever

---

[1] *Gheorghe Gheorghiu-Dej*, Editura Partidului Muncitoresc Român, 1951, pp. 35-36.

been insincere in me life and that's why I think that everything should be like this ... But like I showed above, apart from you, dear Maursia ... nobody has replied to me."[2]

He also had problems in his private life. In 1933, Gheorghiu-Dej was already the father of two girls, Vasilica (born 1928) and Constanța (born 1931), from his marriage to Maria Stere Alexe, the daughter of a soda water vendor, imprisoned at Galatzi in 1926. Relations between husband and wife were not the best. When, in 1931, Gheorghe Gheorghiu was moved, as a disciplinary measure for communist agitation, from the CFR Workshops at Galatzi, where he was working, to the town of Dej, she refused to accompany him. This was when the couple broke up. In the very year of the strike and his first trial, in 1933, she divorces him and remarries. By letter, Dej asks friends in Galatzi to go and see his children, then to visit him in prison, to tell him about how they are. Likewise, he asks for photographs of his children. To the end of his life, he will be marked by the same excessive sentimentality, especially for his first-born, Vasilica. Here is another excerpt from the above letter:

> "This love I has not felt even for my wife, for you know what she did to me, and I kept asking her to give me photographs of the children at least for me to have in prison, but she refused, saying to the children that they don't have a father! Think what pain I am in, but it's nothing, maybe later, when the children will be growed up and will be able to judge, with all the education their mother gives them against me, they might give me justice someday. ... Maybe they will reward me with a hug if I reach old age and don't die in prison."[3]

Gh. Apostol, a long-standing, faithful friend, records in his journal: "Gh. Gheorghiu never re-married. He loved his wife very much. She was a very beautiful woman. She was conscious of her charms. This is what made it easier for the Siguranță in their wish to approach her and persuade her to become an informer."[4]

In January 1935, the PCdR organises the escape of three members of

---

[2] *Apud* Lavinia Betea, in *Magazin istoric*, no. 7 (436), July 2003, p. 18.

[3] *Idem*, p. 20.

[4] Gh. Apostol, *Eu și Gheorghiu-Dej*, Bucharest, 1988, pp. 6-7.

the Grivitza group: Constantin Doncea, Dumitru Petrescu and Gheorghe Vasilichi. Dumitru Petrescu and Gh. Vasilichi were Comintern agents, trained at the Moscow School for Party Cadres, and Doncea was the central figure among the accused at the trials. Dej was merely a background figure. "Dej remained in prison, accumulating, it seems, a huge dose of resentment against his more fortunate and, probably, more favourably viewed (by the Comintern) colleagues. Dej was not a product of the Muscovite apparatus, he had not been directly and immediately tested as to his unconditional loyalty to Stalin."[5]

Two months after the gaolbreak of the Craiova Three, he is moved to Ocnele Mari. In March 1936, when he is taken to Galatzi, he is still at Ocnele Mari. In December 1935, he had sent a certain Petre Isăcescu a crate with 15 kg of objects made in the workshops at Ocnele Mari, to be sold and for him to be sent the money. It was a typical МОПР (International Red Aid) operation. The police conduct an inquiry. He had asked Petre Isăcescu to go and see his daughters and then to come back to the prison and tell him about what he had discovered. In June 1936, Gheorghiu-Dej is transferred to Aiud. A request sent from Ocnele Mari to the administration of Aiud prison demands the "return of the 4 (four) leg irons and 4 (four) pairs of handcuffs with which prisoners Coman Ion, Gheorghe Gheorghiu-Dej and Marin Ion were transferred to that penitentiary."[6] On 3 December 1936, he is at Văcărești, for medical treatment, and is then to be sent back to Aiud. The management of Văcărești Prison report an incident in the hospital canteen. Communist detainee Gheorghiu-Dej has a heated exchange of words with Ioan Bozînțan, the head of the Iron Guardists. The Guardists swarm into the courtyard of the hospital in pursuit of Dej, who takes refuge in hall no. 3. There is a beating, beneath the gaze of the wardens, who are unable to intervene. Iosif Bugoslavski, Carol Wexler and Avram Avramovici come off with lesions to the head and body; Dej is wounded in the leg. Bozînțan is wounded in the arm.[7] Șerban Milcoveanu, a former captain in the Iron Guard, relates that the incident was provoked by Gheorghiu-Dej propositioning Ștefan Curcă, an Iron Guard prisoner, to have homosexual

[5] Vladimir Tismăneanu, *Fantoma lui Dej*, Editura Univers, 1995, p. 107.
[6] MAN Archive, MStM Fund, Dossier 60, p. 1.
[7] MAN Archive, MStM Fund, Dossier 25, p. 7.

relations.[8] Another homosexual episode was related by Al. Bîrlădeanu.[9] It occurred at Doftana, in 1938, with Gheorghiu-Dej and three other inmates involved, including Nicolae Ceaușescu.

The PCdR attempts on a number of occasions to free Gheorghiu-Dej. All the attempts fail. His depression and anger at having being left in prison is referred to in a police report of 1937: "He is very dissatisfied with the silence of the communists on the outside and might be inclined to make declarations against the Communist Party."[10] Preparations for gaolbreaks were made both for Gheorghiu-Dej and for Ana Pauker. On 12 April 1937, the Siguranța is alerted that MOPR is preparing to break Dej out of Aiud. It followed that one of the wardens was corrupt. When Dej is transferred from Doftana to Văcărești, for a short interval (he was due to appear in court), the director of the prison, Svinescu, asks for special guard measures. In 1938, Béla Breiner tries to organise his escape from Doftana.[11] An address from the Department for Penitentiaries to the management of the Văcărești Prison urges that "measures be taken so that all the communist prisoners due to be transferred and interned in hospital do not come into contact with communist detainee Gheorghiu-Dej. The latter has the mission of maintaining contact with those on the outside and reporting to MOPR everything that goes on inside the prison."[12] At Aiud there are imprisoned some of the Soviet spies captured in Romania. Here he meets Emil Bodnăraș. The group of those tried for spying in 1931 – Paul Solomon, Fritz Klauda etc. – are also at Aiud. In May 1937, Gheorghiu-Dej is sent to Doftana. In the summer of 1937, a conflict occurs between the prison administration and the inmates. The latter wage a campaign for an amelioration in conditions (letters, visits, food parcel, workshops). There are also echoes in the left-wing press. Gheorghiu-Dej and the railway workers take part in protests and negotiations with the administration. In August 1937, Dej is in transit through the Galatzi penitentiary, in order to give evidence in a trial. Here, he continues the dental treatment begun in spring at Văcărești, "being in urgent need of incisions and to suppress the existing focuses of infection,

---

[8] Interview with the author, 13 February 2004.

[9] Lavinia Betea, *Alexandru Bâlădeanu despre Dej, Ceaușescu și Iliescu*, Editura Evenimentul Românesc, 1997, p. 185.

[10] MAN Archive, MStM Fund, Dossier 34, p. 59.

[11] MAN Archive, MStM Fund, Dossier 34, p 59.

[12] *Idem*, p. 27.

which make it impossible for him to eat."[13] In November 1937, at Doftana, he is witness to a savage murder. Pavel Sporiş from Tighina, sentenced to 10 years for subversive activities, murders Nicolae Mandalog, with the same sentence, with six blows of an axe. The motive: the former had been replaced by the latter as head of the prison bakery. They were both members of the communist cell from Doftana. The episode reveals the gravity of a loss of hierarchical position in the world of the prisons. The event leaves its scars on Gheorghiu-Dej. On 24 November 1937, he is in Braşov, where he gives evidence in the trial of Vasile Luca.

A curious episode occurs at the end of 1938, when Dej takes steps to marry Elena Sîrbu, a communist activist. A telegram of engagement to Gheorghiu-Dej, on 10 November 1938, announces: "I agree. Stop. Send request to general department for our engagement. Stop. I shall do likewise. Stop."[14] Three days later, Dej registers the request at the Doftana penitentiary.[15] Elena Sîrbu (born 1915, at Soroca) had been a student of medicine, then agronomy, in Jassy. She had been in prison since 1935, having been handed a three-year sentence for communist agitation. She is imprisoned at Dumbrăveni. The head of the PCdR cell is Ana Pauker, who is acquainted with the planned marriage. At the date of this request, Elena Sîrbu was near to release. The meeting between the two took place in the Văcăreşti Prison hospital, in 1937, where both were being treated. It is possible that the plan was strictly formal. The aim would have been to facilitate contact with Gheorghiu-Dej. The law allowed contact (visits, parcels, money) only on the part of relatives. A Siguranţă document dated 2 October 1937 reports that "the dentist Dimăcescu ... retains detainees who have nothing serious wrong with them at Văcăreşti for six to seven months, the majority of those kept there consisting of political detainees. For a sum of 400 lei she intervened for the communist Gheorghiu-Dej to be brought to the prison ... only to have his teeth polished." The doctor also did the same with female communist prisoners. Among them were Ana Pauker and Elena Sîrbu (the latter kept in hospital for a year, from October 1936). The same report notes, "the common law prisoner Gheorghiu Constantin, cousin of the communist Gheorghiu-Dej, being a mechanic, is often sent into town on various jobs, which makes it easier for him to deliver correspondence

---

[13] *Idem*, p. 29.

[14] MAN Archive, MStM Fund, Dossier 21, p. 150.

[15] *Idem*, p. 158.

from the communists in prison to those in town."[16] The marriage was never finalised, for reasons unknown to us.

In August 1939, a note by the Siguranţă reveals that Elena Sîrbu continues to write to him, and that "it is certain that the above named is operating within a centre for the assistance of communist detainees [Red Aid – *author's note*]" and has connections with "Luca László, lately released" from Doftana.[17] The two continue to correspond until 1939, when Elena Sîrbu marries another communist, also a railway worker, Ștefan Pavel. It is interesting that in 1939, the Siguranţă report that Ștefan Pavel sent parcels to Gheorghiu-Dej at Doftana, which were rejected by the administration, because Pavel and Dej were not relatives. In 1942, Elena Sîrbu-Pavel is arrested once more, sentenced to 25 years, hard labour, and imprisoned in the gaol for women at Mislea. On 3 August 1943, when the US Air Force bombs the oil fields for the first time, she is in transit to the prison at Ploiești. An aeroplane crashes on top of the prison. Among the victims is Elena Pavel. She was the sister of Victoria Sîrbu, a technician and wife of Ștefan Foriș, arrested in 1949 and convicted in the Pătrășcanu trial of 1954. At the trial of 1935, Maria Sîrbu, another sister of Elena Pavel, had been sentenced to 10 years imprisonment. Freed in 1944, she became Gheorghiu-Dej's official mistress for a few years. Maria Sîrbu (Marusia) survived Gheorghiu-Dej (died 1965) as well as the whole regime. She died in the 1990s. Ștefan Pavel, as a former railway worker and illegal activist, made a career for himself in the 1950s, but came into conflict with Dej, who purged him at the plenary of June 1958, together with Constantin Doncea, Ovidiu Șandor, and Grigore Răceanu.[18]

Slowly but surely, Gheorghiu-Dej gained recognition in the world of the communist detainees. Why? Unlike Boris Ștefanov, Ștefan Foriș, or Dimităr Ganev, his predecessors, he was not a Comintern agent, which would have given him ascendency over the other communists. Some of these agents were also Soviet citizens. And the positions they held in the underground networks meant they were the top dogs in prison. Vasile Luca, Ilie Pintilie et al. also had privileged positions for this reason. They came to Doftana as members of the Secretariat. In 1933, Dej was still an obscure member of the PCdR, a middle-ranking activist, in the pay of the Comintern since 1932

---

[16] MAN Archive, MStM Fund, Dossier 23, p. 11.

[17] MAN Archive, MStM Fund, Dossier 24, p. 59.

[18] Alina Tudor, Dan Cătănuș, *Amurgul ilegaliștilor. Plenara din 9-13 June 1958*, Bucharest: Editura Vremea, 2000, pp. 33-34, 240.

thanks to the intervention of Moscu Cohn (Gh. Stoica). In prison, there were communists of much longer standing than him, more experienced in agitation, graduates of the Comintern schools, participants in subversive action since the 1920s, both in Romania and in the rest of Europe. His prison ascent begins in Aiud, where he forms close ties with the Soviet spies held there. This fact is indicative of his political instincts. Comintern agents and GPU spies were always the same thing, regardless of their mission: from couriers, who brought money, printing presses and printed materials from the USSR, to residents; from gatherers of military and political information to planters of explosives and terrorists preparing attacks. Not all spies were agents of the Comintern. They were treated with circumspection by the administration due to their foreign connections. They could be exchanged for captured spies working for Romania at any time. They were privileged, the cream of the prisons, a group apart, who refused to mix with the other inmates. They were experienced in conspiracy. They did not hesitate to use any means to achieve their goal. They had great clout among the 'native' communists, who viewed them as emissaries of the Bolshevik Revolution. For, the main duty of a communist was subordination to the interests of the USSR. The most important connection Gheorghiu-Dej makes at Aiud is Emil Bodnăraş. Spies had ascendancy over the Romanian communists, whom they viewed as poor relatives. "In prison, the former Soviet officers, instructed at special schools and sent to Romania with confidential missions, would have regarded with great reserve the idea of taking into subordination the obscure militants of an even obscurer party."[19]

In May 1937, when Dej arrives at Doftana, he meets Şmil Marcovici, Vasile Luca, Constantin Pîrvulescu et al., as well as numerous Soviet spies and Comintern agents. Dimităr Ganev is the head of the Party cell. He had taken over the function from Ştefan Foriş. Foriş from Boris Ştefanov. In 1939, Luca and Pîrvulescu are released from prison. In 1940, Ganev goes to the USSR. Dej is already a pre-eminent figure among the detainees. He has the advantage of being surrounded by a number of railway workers. Moreover, his long sentence assures him of prestige. According to tradition, among prison inmates, whoever has the longest sentence is the most respected. He had gained notoriety at the Grivitza trials. After the escape of Doncea, Petrescu, and Vasilichi, he became boss of the railway workers in prison.

---

[19] Pavel Câmpeanu, *Ceauşescu. Anii numărătorii inverse*, Editura Polirom, 2002, p. 55.

This assured him of leadership of an important mass for manoeuvre in the prisons through which he passed. However, he does not have supremacy. The Bassarabians and Soviet spies were more numerous. Some of them had even longer sentences, 15-25 years, for spying and subversion. At the end of the 1930s, Dej is nevertheless a veteran of the prisons. He is called "the old man," although he was barely approaching 40. His influence has grown. In the autumn of 1940, when Dimităr Ganev goes to the USSR, he is one of the candidates for the leadership of the communist cell. On the night of 9-10 November, an earthquake demolishes part of the prison. A number of inmates perish beneath the rubble. The episode remains, to this day, one of the most enigmatic in the biography of Gheorghiu-Dej. The myth says that he heroically led the search for survivors. Among the dead were two long-standing communists. One, Şmil Marcovici, had been a member of the Romanian revolutionary battalion in Odessa in 1918. He had been involved in the clandestine Bolshevik networks led by Alecu Constantinescu in 1919-1920. He escapes from under arrest together with Constantinescu in December 1920. He is a Comintern agent, an expert in terrorism. He is finally arrested, together with Ana Pauker and Dimităr Ganev, in the summer of 1935. At the time of his arrest, he is a member of the Secretariat. The other was Ilie Pintilie, an inmate at Doftana since the summer of 1939. He was secretary of the PCdR, higher than Gheorghiu-Dej in the party hierarchy, the latter being only a member of the CC. They had known each other since they were activists in the Red trades unions. They met in Jassy, at the Nicolina Workshops, where they were arrested together, for a short time in 1932. Pintilie was a witness at the Grivitza trial. Relations between them had never been cordial. Pintilie was his rival at Doftana.

A legend that circulated among the illegals, after the earthquake, was that Gheorghiu-Dej and his team were late in arriving at the ruined wing of the prison. It was there that Ilie Pintilie was to be found. He is put in a coffin. There is a religious service. Pintilie is found face down in the coffin. Perhaps this is just a story spread by his adversaries, the former Doftana inmates, in the 1950s and 1960s. Another accusation was that he 'intentionally' delayed reaching the site of the devastation. Another victim of the earthquake was French engineer André Prott, a Soviet spy, convicted in the Solomon-Aradi trial. Gheorghiu-Dej was close to Prott, from whom he learned the rudiments of French. With the departure of Ganev and the death of Pintilie, he remains undisputed 'chief' of the communists in prison. A number of enigmas and ambiguities persist in connection with this episode. A photograph has been 'preserved' from the earthquake, which shows Gheorghiu-Dej and Emil Bodnăraş at the edge of the pit in which the victims were laid out. The photograph makes the first page in the 1950s, when Doftana and the anniversary of the earthquake of 9-10 November 1940 were marked. After 1965, it is no longer reproduced. It was, in fact, a forgery, one piece of the puzzle that was the Doftana myth.

Another enigma: why did none of the communists escape from Doftana? Instead of escaping from the 'squalid, dreadful prison conditions', they obediently remain inside the walls, in an unguarded prison. I. Gh. Maurer comes to Doftana, dispatched by the Secretariat (Iosif Chişinevschi, Gavrilă Birtaş, Teohari Georgescu) to take stock of the situation. It is an opportunity for the two to meet. According to the version disseminated until 1965, Dej discusses escape with Maurer. Dej had been in prison for more than seven years. A few days later, the director of the prison summons him to rebuke him for wanting to escape. Maurer, when asked, is supposed to have said to Dej that the only other person he had informed was Foriş. Thus, Foriş had informed the authorities. This too is a falsehood. At the date of the earthquake, Foriş was in Moscow. And at the date of his return, the inmates had been transferred to Caransebeş a month previously. The false version had the role of 'proving' the accusation Dej levelled at Foriş a year later that he was "an agent of the Siguranţă infiltrated into the ranks of the party." One myth, that of Doftana, served another myth, that of power – even if it revealed its subterranean stratum. In the 1990s, Maurer amends the story. The two had spent a day in Cîmpina, at the house of an acquaintance. "It was then that I proposed to Dej that he should escape … He could have done so … the guard had slackened and there was a lot of confusion. Dej did not want to, however … He did not want to escape because he was afraid that his escape would have been a good pretext for the Siguranţă … to kill him."[20]

After the earthquake of the night of 9-10 November 1940, Gheorghiu-Dej is transferred to the Caransebeş Prison. It is here that he meets with Ana Pauker for two hours. After the occupation of Bassarabia and northern Bukowina, Moscow made diplomatic approaches through the Foreign Ministry to have Gheorghiu-Dej and Chivu Stoica released and brought to the USSR. The General Police Department, as well as the Interior Ministry, gave a negative response.

---

[20] Lavinia Betea, *Maurer şi lumea de ieri*, Cluj: Dacia, 2001, pp. 50-51.

"As he is regarded as one of the most fanatical and intransigent of the communist front rankers in organising revolutionary communist actions, the Central Committee of the PCdR plotted for the above named to escape, on the occasion of his transfers during the years 1935-1937 to the prisons in Văcăreşti, Ocnele Mari, Aiud, and Doftana, but this was thwarted by the rigorous measures taken by the authorities. In honour of his revolutionary communist qualities, one of the batteries of the Ana Pauker artillery group, made up of Romanian communist volunteers who previously fought in the international red brigades, bore the name 'Gheorghiu-Dej battery' ... To place the above named at liberty would constitute a permanent danger for state law and order, especially in the current circumstances, as it cannot be excluded that he would eventually be sent back to Romania clandestinely by the Comintern, with a view to intensifying the revolutionary action of the Communist Party of Romania. Order of the Minister, 31 March 1941: 'We cannot allow him to go to Soviet Russia. Gheorghiu-Dej is a determined enemy of the social order in Romania and as such of this country. Passage to Soviet Russia would increase the number of Romania's enemies who are there and who are wielded against Romania. For these motives, Gheorghiu-Dej is to stay in prison and serve his sentence'."[21]

In 1942, Dej's sister, Tinca Stoica, is arrested for Red Aid activities. The Siguranţă report that, as well as sending sums of money,

"in the interval between 7 and 20 May 1942, she sent to Caransebeş Prison in the name of detainee Gheorghiu two parcels of foodstuffs and in the same interval she herself went with an appreciable quantity of foodstuffs, making expenditure disproportionate to her precarious material situation, thus proving that these foodstuffs were not intended only for her brother Gheorghiu, but rather she was nothing but an intermediary between the inmates and the clandestine aid organisations."[22]

Tinca Stoica is part of a ramified network (20 persons), run by Elisabeta, the wife of Alexandru Sencovici, also a detainee at Caransebeş, one of Gheorghiu-Dej's loyalists. He is serving 15 years, hard labour. Gheorghiu-

---

[21] MAN Archive, MStM Fund, Dossier 24, pp. 69-70.
[22] CC of the PCR Archive, Fund 95, Dossier 670, pp. 4-10.

Dej remains at Caransebeş until 1943, when his prison sentence expires. He requests to be released. A communiqué from the General Police Department, Security Department, dated 13 August, notes: "While executing his prison sentence, Gheorghiu-Dej had good behaviour – like all the communist prisoners – in order to improve his conditions in prison. ... Good behaviour ... compared with their past record cannot constitute a motive for release."[23] The authorities prefer to keep him under surveillance in the camp at Tîrgu Jiu.

He reaches the camp at Tîrgu Jiu on 26 June 1943, after a short sojourn at Siguranţă headquarters, in Bucharest. At Tîrgu Jiu, depressed by the refusal of the authorities to release him, he spends long periods in hospital: 1 July – 1 September and then 24 September – 23 October. While he is interned in hospital, Chivu Stoica, also transferred to Tîrgu Jiu, requests, in both his and Gheorghiu-Dej's name, that the personal effects left at Caransebeş in the care of Teohari Georgescu and Pantiuşa Bodnarenko should be sent to the new address, "a short fur-lined leather jacket, a pair of boots, a pair of fur-lined trousers, a blanket, a woollen vest and two pairs of woollen socks."[24] He cannot resign himself to the idea that he is going to remain locked up. He believes that if he were at liberty he could play an important political role. The dissolution of the Comintern in May 1943, about which he had learned shortly before leaving for Caransebeş, was an issue that presented many unknowns.

"On my release from prison I reckoned that at last, after so many years of hard privation, I would be able to look after myself, I saw myself still interned in the camp, where I've stayed for more than half a year ... The state of my health keeps getting worse. I have a duodenal ulcer which needs urgent surgery, and after that – the main thing – a long-term dietary regime ... In the hospital at Tîrgu Jiu I recently had a haemorrhoids operation ... I have been tortured insufferably lately by chronic rheumatism, and my nerves have also been suffering, naturally."

On these grounds, Dej asks to be set free; he has served the term of his sentence. If this is not approved, he asks to be kept under house arrest in Bucharest, "where I have a sister and where I could easily earn my living,

[23] MAN Archive, MStM Fund, Dossier 24, p. 92.
[24] MAN Archive, MStM Fund, Dossier 63, p. 106.

as I am a master electrician," he writes, on 19 December 1943, to the Minister of the Interior. He repeats the same request, also to the Minister of the Interior, on 4 January 1944. Both requests are rejected.[25] One month later, the Siguranţă discovers an escape plan. On 11 February 1944, the Craiova General Department of Police sent a note to the Siguranţă, warning that preparations were underway for the escape of Gheorghiu-Dej and Chivu Stoica. Attention is drawn to the fact that both are being held in the camp at Tîrgu Jiu "under insufficient guard." Both are "hut chiefs," and "are quiet, refraining from any kind of displays or propaganda." Supplementary supervisory measures are taken.[26] There had also been talk of escape attempts in the 1930s and during the war years. The Siguranţă had taken preventive measures from time to time. Gheorghiu-Dej had the opportunity to escape a number of times, but refused. One such occasion, in November 1940, is described by Gheorghe Maurer. There is also complicity with the administration. Apostol tells it as follows: "The first escape attempt occurred at Caransebeş. Emil Bodnăraş who was to leave the prison ... received from Gheorghiu-Dej the task of seeing to the personnel preparing for this escape. The plan was discussed with the director of the prison and the chief prosecutor of Caransebeş. They agreed to it and backed it."[27] An administration that is up to date about a prisoner planning to escape and backs it is something very curious indeed. The escape did not take place, because Foriş is supposed to have found out about the plan, and then Gheorghiu-Dej countermanded it, explains Gh. Apostol. Another attempt occurred a year later. The inmates from Tîrgu Jiu were working at the Tismana Monastery. It was Bodnăraş who was in charge of organising it, once more. The plan failed because the prisoners were moved back to the camp, as the treasury of the National Bank was due to be transferred to Tismana. Nevertheless, on the night of 13-14 August, Gheorghiu-Dej escaped accompanied by Vanya Didenko, a Soviet spy.

It is no longer Bodnăraş who is in charge of preparations, but rather Ion Gh. Maurer. Twelve years had passed since Dej had been arrested, in February 1933. His prison sentence was due to expire on 8 November 1946. The next night, Gheorghiu-Dej reaches Rîmnicu Vîlcea. He needs only another few hours in order to get to Bucharest. Nevertheless, he remains

---

[25] MAN Archive, MStM Fund, Dossier 27, pp. 6-7.

[26] *Idem*, p. 31.

[27] Gheorghe Apostol, *Eu şi Gheorghiu-Dej*, self-published, 1993, p. 56.

here for more than a week. An extremely mysterious episode, one not elucidated to the present day.

He arrives in Bucharest after 23 August. Just in time, however, to witness the Red Army occupy the city. Gheorghiu-Dej's escape, a "heroic moment in the history of the Communist movement," was one of the central themes of the Gheorghiu-Dej myth, in the years 1944-1965. After his death, silence was to shroud this episode, too.

The period he spent in prison was decisive for Gheorghiu-Dej. Not only for inuring him to the wielding of power, but also psychologically speaking. Upon the power he wielded for two decades over Romanian society, his experiences of incarceration had an immense impact. His conceptions were forged not through reading Marxist-Leninist theory or the *Short Course in the History of the Communist Party* that was taught in the school for Comintern activists. His inner world consisted of barbed wire, cells, wardens, prisons, rations, communal living, visiting hours, secrets, promiscuity. It was from here that his resentments and frustrations came. The almost 12 years he spent between Jilava and Tîrgu Jiu marked him for the rest of his life. One of the keys in which we can read this character is his resentment against all those who had not gone through prison. His experience of life up to his arrest in February 1933 (he was born in 1901) can be reduced to the proletarian world of the railway workshops at Galatzi, Dej and Bucharest. His revolt against the bourgeois world was not the reason he was sent to prison, but rather it took shape during his detention. He was not an underground agitator planning revolt. Nor was he an implacable enemy of the bourgeoisie and the democratic regime. He wanted to be a decent, respectable, socially well-adjusted person. He was not a revolutionary, an insurgent, or a plotter. The strike at CFR Grivitza was the effect of internal competition, between rival union leaders. Beyond his demands to the directors of the CFR Workshops, Dej was jockeying for recognition among the workers. The union leaders formed a proletarian elite. It was into this elite that those who wished to transcend their proletarian condition entered. Conflicts between these leaders were violent, both verbally and physically. The advantages enjoyed by the union leaders were not to be sniffed at. They would leave the filthy world of the factories. They worked in offices and had access to significant funds (insurance, pensions, dues, social contributions). Such figures specialised in anti-owner rhetoric, with which they manipulated the workers. Deploring the poverty of the proletariat, they made themselves a fortune. They became influential. And they used this influence as a means to negotiate their various positions with the administration, the political parties, and economic circles. Many of them wanted to change their lot. They became small or large business owners, merchants, and politicians. They enjoyed good salaries in various institutions. The protests at the factories often displayed this aspect of conflict between union leaders. In such conflicts, the workers were merely pawns. Dej learned the alphabet of politics, the spirit of organisation, how to manipulate public meetings, the pleasure of popularity, election campaigns, and how to win supporters in this environment, where the most active elements of the working class vied with each other for supremacy. The 12 year prison sentence was not part of his plans. Dej was not a fanatic, an agitator or a conspirator. He was not a 'professional revolutionary'. Ideological questions, which were of overriding importance for the other members in the underground communist sect, were of zero importance for Dej. He wanted only to be a front-ranker, a recognised leader of the working class. He was seeking a position as an influential union leader; he was seeking power in his own element. From the outset, it was evident that he was very eager to have it. He liked to lead, to play a role, to make decisions. He liked to take precedence. He had a complex about his status, and wanted to be respected. He used to go around smartly dressed, 'like a gentleman', in good clothes. He spoke carefully, seeking to make an impression. He made a show of bonhomie, of cordiality. His conviction at the Craiova trial came as a real punishment. It was the opposite of what he had been seeking: respectability, prestige, career, social status. The feeling that he was being excluded and punished obsessed him. More than a decade of prison experience was to deposit its layer upon the experience he had gained in the CFR Workshops and the grimy union clubs.

What was this world of prisons in which Dej spends 12 years? A look at these prisons will help us to decipher the character. The prisons housed not only communists, but, between the political detainees and the rest, there existed a 'wall'. Party members and non-Party members formed two completely separate worlds. The communists had their own organisation among the inmates; they formed a separate world, with its own rules. What separated them was their ideology, fanaticism and subservience to Moscow. They were a quasi-religious sect. They formed compact groups, with the same attitudes; they were disciplined, identical to one another. Within this sect, there was a strict hierarchy. In spite of their egalitarian ideology, the communist groups were highly stratified. Their subordination to what were called "superior party ties" was law. Anyone who broke the rules was isolated and often expelled. Those expelled became prison pariahs; the other communists were not even allowed to speak to them. The fact had consequences that could prove fatal. The person in question, once removed from the ranks, lost access to food, to information – a monopoly of the Party leadership – and other benefits which membership of the organisation brought. The mechanism of the Party cells bears a strong resemblance to the Mafia model. At the summit of the hierarchy was a supreme chief, a 'godfather', who controlled all the resources. Around him swarmed a handful of seconds, with strictly defined attributes. He gave them his trust, under condition of fealty. The model functioned identically at Doftana and Caransebeş. His authority was uncontested; his decisions were regarded as infallible. Upon this rested the entire system. To doubt Dej would have led to internal disputes and the collapse of the system. Particularly in the circumstances that arose after June 1941, any defection would have had fatal consequences. The danger of extermination – in the situation in which the communists were a "fifth column" – was very real. This fear consolidated Dej's power and meant his calls for discipline were followed unconditionally.

The number one source of power for the Party cell and for Gheorghiu-Dej personally was control of resources.[28] Prison jobs were allocated by the head of the organisation, without any interference from the administration. Dej and his men – Bodnăraş, Bodnarenko, Chivu Stoica et al. – decided on who would be the librarian (at Caransebeş there were around 3,000 books), cooks, canteen workers, store workers, and heads of workshop. Dej decided who was to be allocated for work outside the prison, and who did fatigues. Another resource was parcels of foodstuffs, medicaments, clothing and money, which came by post, sent by relatives and specialised organisations, such as International Red Aid. One communist detainee from Doftana writes in a report to the Comintern, after he is released: "All the subventions, money and goods surrendered, as well as money from sale of goods, are to be found in possession of the administrative management. 18 July 1940."[29] The Party cell tithed all the parcels, all the money. It gave a small share to the addressee of the parcel, while the rest entered into the 'possession of

---

[28] Pavel Câmpeanu, *Ceauşescu. Anii numărătorii inverse*, Editura Polirom, 2002, p. 60.

[29] ANIC, *PCdR în timpul celui de al doilea război mondial*, 2003, p. 108.

the collective'. This 'property' was managed by the chief, via his henchmen. At Caransebeş, the task was carried out by Pantiuşa Bodnarenko, head of stores, and Emil Bodnăraş, the accountant, both loyal to Gheorghiu-Dej. They decided who was to be allocated the goods. The quantity, quality and frequency of rations depended on position within the internal hierarchy.

To oppose this arrangement brought drastic sanctions. A former inmate at Caransebeş in the years 1941-1942, Matei Gall, recalls:

"I had a friend – the lawyer Halpern. He was an intellectual type. We got talking in a critical way. We began to criticise the leadership – not only the pyramidal construction of the Party organisation in the Caransebeş Prison, but the whole atmosphere: they were better fed; we were not so well fed. ... They realised immediately that something was out of order, that every day I was meeting the lawyer Halpern and we were talking together. And so they examined us. My friend admitted very quickly that we had been criticising the leadership of the Party organisation in prison: that they didn't go to work, that only we worked, that they ate better, that they had a different sort of meat bought for them. And then he was told: 'Yes, you are not obliged to be a member of this economic collective. We accept you. But, either you accept the way we are organised, or you can join the Japanese' [the Japanese, in Caransebeş Prison slang, were inmates driven out of the Party cell for various offences – *author's note*] ... A worker from Hunedoara was also arrested, Iordan Iordan. ... We all arrived at the prison, and Iordan Iordan, after he saw how the life of the collective was organised – that there was a superimposed stratum made up of Gheorghiu-Dej, Chivu Stoica, Bodnăraş, Drăghici, Ceauşescu, Bodnarenko, Rudenko and another few, who stayed three to a cell – that's why we called them triumvirates (a triumvirate made up of Gheorghiu-Dej, Chivu Stoica and Bodnăraş were the summit of this pyramid), then there was an intermediate stratum and after that there were us, the others – he started to show his discontent, to criticise. I have to say that Iordan Iordan, the worker from Hunedoara convicted in the same group as us, died of hunger in the end. Because he continued to criticise, he was told the same thing as I was: 'You're not obliged to be part of the organisation. If you don't like it, join the Japanese'. He was told once, he was told twice, and the third time he was removed from the organisation and went from the third floor to the first floor, to the Japanese. In two weeks, Iordan Iordan was dead. ... I visited him there ... I used to clean the corridors and I would go in to him. He smoked and he would ask me to give him some of my cigarette ration. In the first week, he had everything stolen from him, because there were common criminals there too. He was left without britches. He had only a blanket. He didn't have anything to eat; he got nothing except that wretched gruel. Then he got covered in mange. In two weeks, they took him out on a stretcher, as they say. That was Caransebeş."[30] Matei Gall is transferred to the Vapnyarka camp in Transnistria. Here, too, the system is organised according to the same rules as at Caransebeş. At the top of the pyramid is Lazăr Grümberg, seconded by Bernat Andrei, both convicted in the trial of the 19, along with Ana Pauker. They control the lives of the other inmates. Other figures in this exclusive circle are Aurel Rotemberg (under the name Ştefan Voicu, a long-standing propagandist of the Communist regime), Simon Bughici, the Foreign Minister who succeeds Ana Pauker in 1952.[31]

Prison was a closed, barracks world. The atmosphere was one of claustrophobia, fear and suspicion. Interestingly, it is not the administration that inspires all this, but rather the inmates. The communists maintained good relations with the directors of the prisons and with the wardens. They obtained this by ensuring peace and order, but also by means of corruption. Doftana, Caransebeş, Dumbrăveni, Mislea, Văcăreşti etc. constituted a carceral world, an underground, an Orwellian dystopia in the laboratory stage. A life with fixed hours, with the same activities repeated over and over again, routine, order. There were, however, realities that were hidden at any first glance. Prison was, in reality, far from being amorphous. On the contrary, it was a hierarchical world, with multiple strata. A sophisticated surveillance operated, in which all the inmates were involved. The newcomer was isolated. He was allocated – not by the administration, but by the 'organisation' – a cell and an interrogator, a longer-standing prisoner. In the first few weeks, he would be questioned regarding his outside connetions and, in particular, the circumstances of his arrest, his Siguranţă

[30] Dialogue between Matei Gall and Andrei Goldner, in *Dialog*, Dietzenbach, December, 1999.
[31] Similar accounts in Adalbert Rosenberg (former prisoner in Vapnyarka), *Minimum*, Tel Aviv, December, 1987.

interrogation, and his attitude at trial. Finally, after about two months, the new inmate was integrated into a group, his 'Party connection' was allocated, from whom he received orders and to whom he owed absolute allegiance. Strict discipline and respect for the hierarchy were at the core of relations between inmates.

> "After a while, then, the inquiry would begin: why we were arrested, how were we arrested? The Party organisation would appoint an investigating committee ... [who] asked each of us how and what. We would assemble night after night, our group, in two large rooms in which the inquiry was held. After a few weeks, when this material was drawn up, sifted, analysed, we would be called again to be informed of the results. ... Thus, you were judged by the official authorities, after which you had a second trial. Like in Kafka, you were given another trial in prison, by the Communist party? – Exactly ..."[32] "Counter-investigations represented a political component of the utmost importance for the hidden Caransebeş."[33]

Besides hunting out informers and traitors, the 'counter-investigation' also had another purpose, intended to conserve the power of the Party cell: intelligence gathering. The autobiography, the nocturnal conduct of investigations, the ritual of confessions, insistence on details, the presence/absence of the comrades transformed the prisoner into an object, a man with no private life, with no psychology. The newcomers thereby entered a system, in which they were completely controlled. The bosses of the cell in prison knew everything about each inmate. Between themselves, the inmates were not allowed to communicate any kind of information about their past. This was done in the name of maintaining secrecy. It is herein that one of sources of the power of the communist leaders in prison resided. Infringement of these internal rules led to the isolation of the one guilty of the indiscretion, or even his exclusion from the party, which meant non-participation in the distribution of the benefits conferred by the organisation. The climate was one of intense suspicion. Together with his men, Dej held a monopoly on information. It was a world of secrets: each level of this structure was in possession of a limited set of information,

[32] See Matei Gall and Andrei Goldner, *op. cit.*

[33] Pavel Câmpeanu, *Ceauşescu. Anii numărătorii inverse*, Editura Polirom, 2002, pp. 79-80.

as well as goods. The inmates were arranged in a number of circles. The zone furthest from the summit of power was made up of those who were not communists: the Iron Guard, sectarians, common criminals etc. They suffered because of the communists because it was the latter who controlled the resources and strategic positions in the prisons. You could not work in the canteen, the stores, the library, as head of a workshop etc. if you were not part of the communist hierarchy, which formed a clique in control of all these positions. The prisons administration preferred to leave things as they were, because the communist inmates made up the most powerful group. The administration negotiated various matters that might arise with the communist leaders: Dej, Bodnăraş etc. The communists quite simply set out to improve living conditions and to survive their period of detention. The reports of the prison's administration and the Siguranţă emphasise "their good behaviour," order and discipline, their orderly conduct. In the 1940s, there were no cases of revolts, dissemination of manifestos, or hunger strikes. In other circumstances, it would have been regarded as 'capitulating to the bourgeoisie, making a pact with the class enemy'. Dej himself accused Foriş of these grave sins. However, both conducted the same policy, of 'conserving the Party cadres'. Collaboration with the prison's administration, the ability of the Party cell to ensure internal order, was essential. The second circle was made up of 'sympathisers'. They had participated in anti-fascist actions, collected funds for Red Aid, but they had not been admitted to the Party as such. They had been convicted for belonging to the PCdR or other organisations controlled by the Comintern, to Red Aid, the Democratic Bloc, the revolutionary unions, the UTC. The flow was in both directions. Some were expelled from the PCdR in prison, others, on the contrary, were admitted. In general, Gheorghiu-Dej preferred to enlarge his organisation, and did not use expulsion to excess. He was interested in having control over as large a number of inmates as possible. Recruiting for new members was done among the common criminals, but also among other groups, sectarians, the Iron Guard or Soviet spies. Some were mere opportunist adherents, attracted by the benefits – jobs which made living conditions easier, parcels, workshops etc. Others had been arrested by the Siguranţă for various public order offences, in conformity with the Mîrzescu-Mironescu Law of 1924/1931. Others, fewer in number, changed their convictions and adhered to communism. Another circle of this hierarchy was the 'apparatus', the intermediary leaders. They had been through the prison system before.

Moreover, they had been verified during internal counter-investigations and found to be in order. They were necessarily adherents of the group led by Dej. They had the role of supervising the members of the organisation. Above the apparatus, we find the leadership, a handful of men who took all the decisions. At the summit of the hierarchy, there was Gheorghiu-Dej, the infallible boss. It was here that it was decided who would occupy what position, what attitude had to be taken towards the administration or in political matters. It was Dej who adjudicated and settled conflicts between inmates, granted benefits, made sanctions, expelled members from the Party. He is appointed from outside prison by the Central Committee of the PCdR. He is the brains and the willpower of all the communists in prison. "He dictates, takes the measures he sees fit, and nobody from those beneath him can oppose him. He does everything in the name of the Central Committee of the Party, and then in the name of discipline everyone has to obey him."[34] His dominant position was visible. Matei Gall was arrested in 1940, for communist activities, being tried and convicted in 1941. "At the gates to the Caransebeş Prison, someone was waiting for us: a brown-haired man, with black, expressive eyes, dressed in a prisoner's uniform, but tailored, it seems, to fit. He shook both our hands, and introduced himself: Gheorghiu-Dej. He said a few words to us, asked us a few things."[35] The same thing is narrated by one of Dej's cronies, Gheorghe Apostol, who, when he is incarcerated at Văcăreşti in 1937, was greeted by the prison director and by Gheorghiu-Dej.[36]

Disputes did not erupt between inmates over doctrinal or political matters. They broke out because of food, jobs, workshops and fatigues, because of food parcel rations. Factions and groups formed, depending on the benefits conferred by one position or another. Factional conflicts were, in fact, conflicts over privileges. Whoever controlled resources and their distribution, controlled the inmates. This has nothing to do with Marxism or non-Marxism. It was a struggle between clans for survival. The conflicts between them, the so-called factional struggles, were not waged between 'Stalinists' and 'Trotskyites'. Those who lost were styled Trotskyites, Right or Left deviationists, opportunists, liquidationists. When he took over

---

[34] ANCR, CC of the PCR Archive, Collection 50, Dossier 30, p. 253.

[35] *Idem*, Matei Gall and Andrei Goldberg.

[36] Gheorghe Apostol, *Eu și Gheorghiu-Dej*, self-published, Bucharest, 1998, p. 17.

power, Gheorghiu-Dej arrived directly from the world of the cells, of the darkened corridors, of plots hatched in whispers. Gheorghiu-Dej was a man of a closed universe, bounded by the walls of the prison and the cell. He was the patron of a closed, secret organisation, of which the administration was not cognisant. Its activity was not discernable. It was consumed above all by domestic matters: the distribution of resources was a constant bone of contention. However, the outer shell consisted of ideologically tinted political disputes. There were quarrels over the pecking order, bigger rations, a better job or place in the prison camp hut, at the infirmary, in a workshop. Gheorghiu-Dej presided over all of this. Caransebeş was characterised by cleanliness and tranquillity. The Party cell was a restricted group, which was formed by invitation only. From the cell, tentacles spread to all the inmates. Maximum vigilance was focussed on potential rivals, on those who might have intended to take their place. And on the eventual formation of a group that might rival them. For Dej, as a boss among the inmates, any loss of face would have had very grave consequences. Firstly, the loss of the privileges that ensured survival, his descent to among the other inmates. He was therefore careful that no one should infringe upon his privilege to decide. He was very determined to punish whenever this happened. Later, he did not hesitate to kill: Foriş, in 1946, Pătrăşcanu and Koffler in 1954, Luca between 1952 and 1963. He would undoubtedly have killed Ana Pauker too, had circumstances allowed. He also ordered others to be killed, because they were in possession of inconvenient information about him. He had no mercy, no scruples, when he felt threatened he did not hesitate. He was hungry for power, the secret pleasure of his life. He worked through middlemen, out of a prudence learned in prison. He was a master of the shrug of the shoulders and of dissimulation. It was impossible to know what he was really thinking. The instrument of his power was the Party organisation, a world apart, of 'initiates', a secret, subterranean world, with rigours apart. The world of the prisons, of the proscribed. Gheorghiu-Dej was created by this environment. He was 'carceral man' par excellence. He formed his own gang, relatively numerous if we bear in mind the small number of communists. They were disciplined and devoted to him. Outside prison, at liberty, there could be found around 50 communist illegals in Romania in 1944. In the USSR there were around 100. And there were 650-750 in the camps and prisons. Almost all of them were subordinate to Gheorghiu-Dej. It is in these figures that the real influence of Gheorghiu-

Dej lies concealed, when the problem of power in the Party arises after the occupation of Romania by the Red Army. The strict hierarchy, plus the ideological binding material, the indoctrination of newcomers, and the common past conferred by the underground environment gave the 'apparatus' a coherence that meant it would prevail over other claimants.

"The correspondence exchanged between the Communist Party and the camps shows that the latter, far from constituting an isolating medium for the communists, were veritable schools and breeding grounds, in which the elements of trust were verified, new adherents were won and bonds were cemented between activists ... in the camps and prisons 'collectives' of experienced communists are formed. In their turn, the latter create new cells and hold courses, collect dues; patriotic cells are formed to which Iron Guardists and soldiers etc. are recruited ... these institutions for the isolation and correction of elements dangerous to society and national security become communist academies from which emerge, after they have completed their sentences, the elite elements of the movement. ... The camps and the prisons constitute for the communists propitious terrain for the recruit of new adherents," notes a Siguranță report dated 31 December 1943.[37]

The way in which the communist inmates were organised was rigorous, and always according to the same template, whether at Dumbrăveni, Mislea, Aiud, Văcărești, Galatzi, Doftana and Caransebeș or in the camps at Miercurea Ciuc, Caracal and Tîrgu Jiu. Inside the prisons, they were a segment apart, with a secret structure, which was concealed from the administration. When discovered, they deny everything. Inside the structure, there operated rules, norms and specific hierarchies. There were a number of sections. One was propaganda and education, which held lessons on Stalinism-Leninism, the history of the CPSU, foreign languages and law, the rules of conspiracy, etc. Another was the economic section, which distributed goods and money, and administered the products made in the workshops. The workshops were fitted out (with work benches, tools) and administered by the communists out of their own pockets and entirely belonged to them. The prisons merely provided them with the space.

---

[37] ANCR, CC of the PCR Archive, Fund 1, Dossier 276/1943, pp. 379-380.

The money came from relatives, from the sale of the goods made in the workshops, from various jobs carried out in the surrounding area, but most of all from MOPR. Then there was the GPU, the security section. This handled the protection of the leaders of the communist cell. It gathered intelligence about everything that was happening inside and outside the prison, but especially about the inmates, upon whom it continuously spied. It interrogated new arrivals; it had informers among the inmates. It obtained information from the wardens, from the other prisoners, from deserters, from spies, from common criminals, from the Iron Guard etc. It censored all letters. The GPU section was the most efficient means of controlling the inmates and maintaining discipline. Each section had its place established by the leadership and was staffed by 'comrades' who were trustworthy. Inside the prison, says the administration document, consisting of observations made by the communists at Doftana at the end of the 1930s, "there was a Communist republic in miniature."[38]

The question nevertheless remains. How did Gheorghiu-Dej manage to become the dictator of a European country in the middle of the twentieth century? The end of the war explains much. Gheorghiu-Dej was the quisling designated by Stalin to lead Romania. The regime he led was one of occupation. When he began to distance himself, at the close of his reign, he did so precisely because the Kremlin was planning to oust him. Without the occupying Red Army, he would have remained a mere proletarian; given the opportunity, he could have been a union leader, or opened a small business near the main railway station in Bucharest (as he once dreamed of doing) with other artisans: a small shop or a workshop for repairing lamps or installing electricity in the houses of the 1940s rich. History had a different fate in store for him. Why did Moscow choose to instate him as their man of trust? Ana Pauker's argument comes closest to the truth, when she proposed him as leader of the PCdR, saying, "We don't have anybody else." For Stalin, he was the native element, in a group that consisted mainly of Jews, Hungarians, Ukrainians and Bulgarians. He chose Gheorghiu-Dej for the simple fact that he was a worker, ethnically Romanian, and unknown. The Kremlin files did not contain any compromising items or grave sins in Stalin's eyes, such as factionalism, Trotskyism, liquidationism. He had toed the line in prison, subscribing to

---

[38] ANCR, CC of the PCR Archive, Collection 50, Dossier 30, p. 253 verso.

all the orders and ideological about-turns that came from Moscow. His file records that he had been in the 1933-1934 trials, which conferred on him legitimacy, at least among the railway workers, if not in wider circles. The same file also records that in prison he had gained supremacy over a few hundred inmates, in fact, the majority of the communists in Romania in the 1940s. This information, although crucial in a Party member's file, does not tell the whole story.

"How could a man endowed with no exceptional gifts by nature, with no culture, with no past other than having been part of a strike committee and a trial, achieve the absolute power he did? ... How did he manage to gain the trust of Stalin, Molotov, and Beria, how did he manage to defeat the Ana Pauker group, how did he manage to become an international political figure, sincerely mourned when he died? Without being stupid, he was a banal man, without organisational talents, without personal ideas. His mind was capable only of the minor adjustments of a minor provincial politician ... He was co-opted into the Ana Pauker/Vasile Luca leadership because he had held not one single opinion of his own before the arrival of the two emissaries from Moscow. ... There was no murder, crime or knavish act of which he was not the instigator. He had the gift of appearing the wisest, the most just, the best ... By what gifts did he manage to ensure this supremacy?" wonders Belu Zilber.[39] The answer is that it was precisely the banality of the man that ensured his supremacy.

"There is something that might be named the genius of banality," which means "instant adaptation to any environment, the ability to mime, to satisfy the most gregarious vanities and wishes, without the interference of reason, to be born with these qualities, not to learn them. Whoever has them succeeds ... Gheorghiu-Dej did not hold even one personal idea, but he triumphed ... Gheorghiu-Dej was made first of all by Ana Pauker, then by Stalin ... Power [for Dej – *author's note*] was a windfall ... He did not know anything, he had no ideas. Apart from power, he did not know what he wanted."[40]

---

[39] Belu Zilber, *Actor în procesul Pătrășcanu*, Editura Humanitas, 1997, pp. 206-207.
[40] *Idem*, pp. 209-210.

Gheorghiu-Dej was thus a 'man without qualities'. But if so, then, as Zilber reads the character, he came not so much from Musil as much as from Gogol. He emerges from the underground, in order to become dictator. He belongs to an interminable periphery. He is a nobody, a pariah. His humble background allows him to pass unobserved. This helps him. The public and the players have their eyes on favourites. He is not among them. His inferiority complexes impel him to seek acceptance, to be liked. He is affable and cordial, out of fear. He becomes a seducer. He succeeds in this exercise with extremely varied people, for example the 'lifers', the perpetrators of serious murders, with whom he firstly strikes up very good relations in prison. He cultivates the Soviet spies and Comintern agents, and wins their loyalty. Likewise, he wins the sympathy of intellectuals…. His entire career is doubled with this endeavour to win goodwill. He is friendly, humorous. He is the consummate dual personality. Behind the mask of the jovial, amiable, humorous man, behind the all too deferent servant, there is a hard, merciless, unscrupulous master, ready at any moment to annihilate those who threaten his interests. He first demonstrates his capacity to impose his will in the prisons, where he encounters individuals apparently more experienced than he was in survival. But after August 1944, he also encounters others, in the fierce, mortal struggle for absolute power. On each occasion, he is victorious. He kills Ştefan Foriş, Lucreţiu Pătrăşcanu and Remus Koffler. These are merely his best-known victims. He deposes Ana Pauker, Teohari Georgescu and Vasile Luca. Then Dumitru Petrescu, Iosif Chişinevschi and Miron Constantinescu. What distinguished him from the other pretenders was precisely his determination never to stop. The others hesitated, not knowing what to do, whether to eliminate their rivals or not, and in what form. Dej did not give the impression of being dangerous, of being someone capable of murder. Perhaps because some last remnant of humanity, the others wavered when it came to dealing the deathblow. Such hesitations sealed their fate. Gheorghiu-Dej, 'carceral man', inured since prison to the savage struggle for survival, always struck without mercy. He was also patient. He never struck from a position of inferiority. He would bide his time, seek out accomplices, and pose as the voice of reason, as the victim of aggression. He struck only when the opportunity was to hand and when the outcome was certain. He would never forget an affront and kept a close watch on those he regarded as adversaries. He was always ready to pounce, always smiling, amenable. All of these were skills he had learned and exercised in prison. It was also there that his resentments took shape. When he comes to power, Dej is a man of resentment. He often makes use of power for his own pleasure, in order to alleviate his frustrations, his rancour towards one person or another. When he deals the deathblow to Foriş, it is clearly a political calculation, an episode in the struggle for supremacy. But it is also a settling of accounts, an act of revenge. It is the payback for humiliations and frustrations, the belated resolution of an episode in Văcăreşti Prison and the conflict with Foriş. He had lost on that occasion; his inferiority had been made manifest. He had emerged humiliated from that clash. Foriş had much greater prestige than he did. He was educated, a gentleman, a bourgeois. He was everything Dej wanted to be. In the summer of 1946, Dej orders that he be killed. He had not forgotten. Now he had recompense for the envy he had felt in the company of this communist from a very different background to his. Gheorghiu-Dej uses his abilities not only to quench his thirst for power, but also the frustration accumulated during his 11 years in confinement. His conviction and the escape of the three strike leaders, Doncea, Vasilichi and Petrescu, but not his, organised on the orders of the Comintern, makes him feel excluded.

The Pătrăşcanu case repeats that of Foriş. The difference of class between them kindles in Dej the same burning frustration. This goes beyond the contest for power. Ana Pauker also ascertains this character trait of his. In any case, she too was to fall victim, in 1952. In 1945, at the end of October, after Gheorghiu-Dej had been designated leader of the RCP, at the first meeting of the Central Committee, she says, "Among the weaknesses of Comrade Gheorghiu-Dej, I reckon that, although Comrade Gheorghiu has the possibility of seeing the wider picture, unencumbered by resentment or prejudices, he is not always capable of disencumbering himself of them." Ana Pauker draws the attention of the Political Bureau to the fact that he displays "a commandeering spirit ... A Secretary General of the party needs to possess a certain calm, to be able to weigh matters. The weaknesses displayed by Comrade Gheorghiu-Dej will be rectified by collective labour."[41] Ana Pauker has no illusions, I think, but she hoped that she would manage to dominate him by means of the influence exerted by Moscow, or at least to share power with him. His thirst for power, however, proved unquenchable. No one in the Political Bureau, the Secretariat, the CC or his entourage succeeded. He died in March 1965, as absolute master of a subjugated country. But his

---

[41] CC of the PCR Archive, Political Bureau, Dossier 1, pp. 4-5.

power stemmed in essence from his hegemony at the top of the RCP. An elite – made up of the old guard and newcomers – which had accepted, at one moment or another, and for various reasons, to be his vassal. His ability was to present himself in any circumstances as the man on whom the fate of the political gang he led depended.

It is not only adversaries in the PCdR who fall victim to his frustrations and resentments. The entire elite (political, administrative, military, cultural) pays the price. Dej detested the bourgeoisie and all those who, in one way or another (wealth, education etc.), were superior to him. His inferiority complexes, based on deficient education, his humble origins etc., combine with the incriminations he was to direct at those 'responsible' for his 12 years in prison. In 1940, the USSR requested an exchange of prisoners. The Romanian authorities agreed to hand over only Ana Pauker. They refuse to exchange Gheorghiu-Dej and Chivu Stoica. In the summer of 1943, Gheorghiu-Dej was due for release from Caransebeş Prison. The authorities prefer to send him to the Tîrgu Jiu prison camp. As a 'proletarian', Dej might, in 1945, have poured out his hatred, accumulated in time, on a class in any case condemned by history. His class-consciousness was in fact merely resentment. Dej had nothing of the indoctrinated agitator about him. The Marxist thesis that "the proletariat is the gravedigger of the bourgeoisie" was taken by Gheorghiu-Dej literally. As 'leader of the Romanian proletariat', he had to bury each member of that class physically. The RCP was the leader of the working class, and he was the head of the RCP. In accordance with this 'historic mission', he practised repression on a huge scale. Terror made up part of the usual Bolshevik modus operandi. Those who punished him in 1933 were guilty not only for his political drama, but also for his family and personal drama. His wife left him, a blow he found hard to bear. The guilt of the bourgeoisie was that he had wasted his youth in prison. The ideology of the proletarian revolution, of the class struggle, wonderfully served him in order to unleash his passions against the bourgeoisie and its elite. He governed with resentment against the whole of Romanian society. The peasants paid with hundreds of thousands of expropriations and deportations, with arrests and internment in prisons and camps. They accounted for the largest share of the victims of repression; they paid en masse. The pretext was the massive peasant opposition to collectivisation and communisation. Dej knew from Stalin that the peasantry was reactionary and had to be annihilated. An urbanite, Dej saw things the same way. The workers were just as repressed. As a former prison inmate, he took his revenge. He had passed through the prisons. He demanded retribution. He surrounded himself with former prisoners. His entourage shared the same mindset and thirst for revenge. Dej felt in his element only among the former inmates from Doftana, Caransebeș and Tîrgu Jiu. It was a criterion for inclusion. Romania was ruled until much later, until the end of the 1960s, by former prisoners, who transformed the whole country into a prison. As the model for any utopia – including the Communist one – is identical to that of a prison, such a comparison can easily be made. A society controlled by inmates and wardens, a hierarchical society ruled by a single man, was nothing else than a prison. Between the carceral world and the 'luminous future' of Marx and Lenin there was a perfect similitude. The evil comes from the more distant past, however, from Thomas More and Campanella. They saw the perfect world, heaven on earth, as a closed city, surrounded by walls that separated it from the imperfect surrounding world. Within utopia, everything is shared; human needs are identified, quantified. Everything is measured: air, food, clothing, sex, money. Goods and services are distributed by infallible bosses. This model of the happy world of tomorrow is identical with a prison. Here, the warden allocates your cell, you have fixed hours for sleep, clothes, food, water, hours for recreation and work. Someone supervises the timetable. The rations, the calendar – everything is precisely determined.

It was Orwell who understood most accurately the malefic dimension of utopia. The difference between the two worlds – the carceral and the utopian – would be that in prison, penury and suffering constitute the normal conditions, because it is a question of punishing someone, whereas in utopia it is happiness that is pursued. When they are released, the communists have the reflexes of inmates who can no longer understand the free world except as chaos. On coming to power, they apply the lesson of prison. They are unable to conceive of society in any other way. They have forgotten anything else. A simplified world – the world as a prisoner sees it. Someone has to distribute the water, the food, the cells… The entire populace is prisoner; each person is an inmate like the others. The former prisoners become prison wardens and commandants. There is a storeroom from which they distribute the rations, a budget, a canteen, a washroom, toilets, incriminations, punishments, rewards. A perfect world: utopian, simple. Borders, the forbidden passport and censorship are the walls between the prisoners and the outside world. The populace is not to be governed, but rather punished, kept under control. The communists know they are hated; they see themselves surrounded by enemies. The populace does not understand their 'historic mission', the 'bright future'. People want to live well here and now, not to make sacrifices for an illusory future. And then the ex-inmates transform society into a prison, and the populace into prisoners. The Gulag was the perfect society according to Stalin. A prison camp with hundreds of millions of people.

Dej and his men knew very well how the carceral universe functioned. They transposed this model on the scale of society as a whole. It was the only model they understood. Communism, the ideology to which they had devoted themselves, contributed to this, but also their own experience. Society had to exist only within limits predetermined by the supreme authority. Everything had to proceed according to a programme that included everybody. The citizens were in fact prisoners. They were guilty, and had to contribute – in order to redeem themselves – to the achievement of certain objectives chosen and imposed by authority. A prison inmate unloads gravel from a railway truck; the workers and peasants had to construct the steel industry or the Danube-Black Sea Canal. The differences between inmates proper and these proletarians were minimal or insignificant. The state shops were nothing more than the prison kiosk, where inmates could buy trifles with money received for work in the prison workshop. Under Dej, Romania became a carceral society. The regime to which the members of the communist gang at Doftana, Caransebeș and Tîrgu Jiu were subjected was not one of extermination, unlike the one applied in the prisons after 1948, after the communist cell came to power, when the elimination of the bourgeois as a class was aimed at. Ideology became the substitute for the Lyubyanka. It was the extension of the carceral and clandestine mentality, in circumstances in which the communists no longer lived in the underground, but held power. They infect Romanian society with this virus picked up during the period of 'illegality'. The obsessions of this world are informers, traitors, agents provocateurs, the police lying in wait. They do not manage to rid themselves of these obsessions. They regard themselves as still living clandestinely and act accordingly. Society is for them a hostile and alien environment. They govern society using secret police methods, they infiltrate it, they control it, they spy on it. The carceral model, the model of the clandestine cell, proliferated at the scale of an entire country.

XV
The Anatomy of an Assassination

Make him disappear!

Gheorghiu-Dej to Pantiușa Bodnarenko, concerning Ștefan Foriș

4 April 1944. At 2 p.m., American B25 bombers from Libya and Egypt fill the skies over Bucharest. In a matter of minutes, the bombing destroys the Northern Station district, Calea Griviței and the surrounding area. That evening, as the army and civilians are starting to gather up the dead bodies and repair the damage, Emil Bodnăraș pays a visit to Ștefan Foriș in a safe house on Carol Knappe Street, in the Domenii district, at the edge of the area devastated by the American bombs. A few days earlier, on 30 March, the two had attended a meeting together. It was on that occasion that Foriș had asked Bodnăraș to visit him. The Siguranța, which had quite a good knowledge of what was happening inside the PCdR, had never found out what position Ștefan Foriș held in the Party or whether he was in the USSR or Bucharest. The fact that he was not in prison, when almost all his fellow communists had been captured, fuelled rumours that Foriș was working for the Siguranța. Was he or wasn't he? The visit is closely bound up with this question. Bodnăraș's mission was to fire him, and if he put up any resistance, to liquidate him. He was armed with a pistol and a hammer. It was a method of the NKVD, which had trained Bodnăraș 10 years previously, in Astrakhan and Moscow. Bodnăraș was using the story that he was a messenger from Moscow as a smokescreen. This was also a technique he had picked up in the special schools for espionage and subversion. He was in his element in this affair. It fitted him like a glove. He had appeared out of nowhere and only very recently in the closed world at the top of the PCdR.[1] No one was familiar with him. He had not operated in the underground before his imprisonment. He had not held any political positions and had no links with the cadres, with the apparatus. Nor was he even a member of the PCdR. He was a marginal figure, a stranger. This also gave him his strength. No one knew what to make of him. None of the cadres at the top of the PCdR who were at liberty in 1943-1944 had had any dealings with him. Very little was known about him, in a world where memories were extremely long.

---

[1] Cf. Romeo Runcan, interview with Stelian Tănase, April 2000.

Emil Bodnăraş played the role of the mysterious messenger from Moscow. It was known that he had had a career as an officer and been sentenced to 10 years imprisonment for desertion and espionage. Now, having appeared before Foriş, he seemed to possess secrets and be on an important mission. He was a man in love with secrecy, the shadows, conspiracy. In the world of the underground, of plots and intrigues, Bodnăraş felt at home. As his *nom de guerre* he chose 'Felix', after Felix Dzerzhinsky, the founder of the Cheka, the Bolshevik political police. Although they had met only five days previously, on 30 March, Foriş insisted on summoning him once more. The reason? A trick, a diversion, a lie. Foriş falls into the trap laid by Bodnăraş. The Secretary General of the PCdR had found out that an important courier had come to Bucharest with a message and that he was going to meet Bodnăraş on 3 April. Foriş knew very well that Bodnăraş was a GRU agent, a Soviet citizen. He was thus able to credit that Moscow had sent a messenger with orders to Bodnăraş. Between 1941 and 1944, communications to the Kremlin were interrupted. They had been lost in May 1941. Then war broke out and it had been impossible to re-establish them. Bodnăraş had been released from Caransebeş Prison on 8 November 1942. He put it about that he had managed to re-establish contact with Moscow. It was an invention. After four years of silence, Foriş was curious to learn what directives had been sent from the Kremlin. The front line had reached Jassy; the Red Army was approaching. The course of events would soon accelerate.

The trap Bodnăraş laid for Foriş worked. The story about the arrival of a messenger was a bluff. It is the same situation as in Gogol's *Revizor* (*The Government Inspector*). A man arrives from the centre of power, a man who might inspect the ledgers, investigate what you have been up to during the war. This time, however, it is not a case of mistaken identity. The inspector did not exist. Emil Bodnăraş was playing the part, hamming it up. Foriş believed that he could be fired only on an order from Moscow. He did not suspect that he was in danger. He did not think that anything bad could happen to him before the arrival of the Red Army. The only danger was that of arrest. He had taken precautions against that. He was prudent and maintained the strictest secrecy. Although he thought himself safe, the danger that did exist came not from the authorities but from within his own party. Gheorghiu-Dej, the leader of the prison communists, had managed to convince a number of militants at the top that Foriş was a traitor. They included Teohari Georgescu, Iosif Chişinevschi, Emil Bodnăraş, Iosif Ranghet, and Constantin Pîrvulescu. They believed, or liked to believe, that Foriş was a Siguranţă agent. Numerous arrests since 1941 had been blamed on him. In addition, he was accused of having committed grave political errors. Bodnăraş was acting on behalf of this group. 'Collaboration with the Siguranţă' and 'Foriş the traitor' formed an alibi, a pretext. At stake were the personal grudges and rivalries of the underground. To these must be added the time factor, always vital during a political crisis.

Time forces the Romanian communists, be they in prison or not, to take action. Two factors influence this haste: the military situation in northern Moldavia and events in Moscow. The Romanian communists in Moscow were getting ready to assume power. The offensive launched by Marshal Konev would reach Bucharest in a matter of weeks. Antonescu would be replaced by a government in which the 'Muscovites' were guaranteed supremacy. Of course, in Caransebeş, Tîrgu Jiu and Bucharest, the precise details were not known, but it was obvious that the 'Muscovites' would arrive at the same time as the Red Army. The countdown had begun. Whoever lost the race could count himself a dead man. The instinct for self-preservation is strong among Dej's cronies. The ousting of Foriş was an attack designed to alter the balance of power at the top of the Party in advance of the collapse of the Antonescu regime. Once transformed into a scapegoat, Foriş could be blamed for all the sins of the communists during the period 1940-1944. The gravest sin was the total lack of any resistance against the German war machine and the Antonescu regime. The rush to act after years of passivity derived from this calculation. The anti-Foriş plot and participation in the coup against Antonescu were aimed at creating a strong position for negotiation with the Muscovite group. As long as Dej, Pătrăşcanu, Bodnăraş, Pîrvulescu, Ranghet and Maurer had taken part in the overthrow of the military dictatorship and the changing of sides against the Axis, they could in no way be ignored in the political game. In the power play within the small Communist Party, this was the decisive gambit. The plotters could not be overlooked when it came to power being handed out. This was exactly the way the 'Muscovites' viewed the situation, too. The reversal of 23 August messed up their plans. Gh. Apostol, one of those closest to Dej, notes, "A contentious issue discussed on this occasion was their opinion [that of Ana Pauker and Vasile Luca, who arrived in Bucharest in September 1944 – *author's note*] that Foriş's removal from the function of Secretary General of the Party was illegal and that this measure had not been passed by the Comintern. It would probably have agreed to a troika made up of Ana Pauker, Vasile Luca and Foriş."[2] The troika was established in any case, but with Gheorghiu-Dej taking the place of Foriş alongside Ana Pauker and Vasile Luca. This substitution of Gheorghiu-Dej for Foriş was also the aim of the strike carried out on 4 April. Bodnăraş had not re-established contact with Moscow. On this matter we have the testimony of Constantin Pîrvulescu before the CC investigative commission in 1968: "The Soviets had no idea what was happening here. When they came to Aleea Alexandru [where the headquarters of the CC of the PCR was located after 23 August – *author's note*], they looked for Foriş."[3] Bodnăraş was bluffing. He was not an emissary of the Comintern. He had not made contact with Moscow. It was a lie that enabled him to penetrate to the head of the Party and then depose him.

Foriş had been living clandestinely since December 1940, on his return to Romania. He had crossed the Danube by rowing boat near Tulcea. The crossing was arranged by Dumitru Coliu. The Siguranţă – usually well informed – knew very little about him. They thought he was in the USSR, or even dead. Their information was that he had gone to the USSR in the summer of 1940, together with Teohari Georgescu, and had not come back.

Ştefan Foriş returned to Bucharest alone, on 31 December 1940. Perhaps this is why the Siguranţă possessed such scanty information as to his whereabouts. On his departure to Moscow, Foriş was one of the top militants in the PCdR; on his return, he held the position of Secretary General. A conjuncture of circumstances led to almost the entire Secretariat of the PCdR being arresting in a safe house in the Obor district of Bucharest in April 1941. The only member of the Secretariat who escaped was Ştefan Foriş. Ending up in Caransebeş Prison, Teohari Georgescu and Iosif Chişinevschi shared their suspicion that Foriş was a Siguranţă agent, given that he was the only one not to have been arrested. Gheorghiu-Dej, proceeding from this suspicion, in time weaves a dense web around Foriş, aiming to topple him and take his place as Party boss. The events of 4 April 1944 were the culmination of this plot. The denouement will not come until two years later, however, in 1946.

---

[2] Gheorghe Apostol, *op. cit.*, p. 87.

[3] Dan Cătănuş, Ioan Chiper, *Cazul Foriş. Lupta pentru putere în PCR. De la Gheorghiu-Dej la Ceauşescu*, Editura Vremea: Bucharest, 1999, p. 327.

Let us go back to the scene of Ştefan Foriş's sacking, as recounted by Emil Bodnăraş six years later, in 1952. His interlocutor is Constantin Pîrvulescu, who had become General Secretary of the Party after 4 April 1944.

"Foriş was a highly cautious man. He was in the habit of not staying in any safe house longer than two, three, four days. He would immediately move to another house, and he had at his personal disposal four houses, one in Floreasca, one on Filantropia, which is where I found him, and another two besides. It was clear that Foriş had to be taken from one of his houses. We didn't have the opportunity to bring him to one of our houses, because he wouldn't have come. He was the Secretary General. One of us would have to go to him, either Rangheţ or myself ... I established which were the houses where he could be found. ... Secondly, I set up the group that would assist in the coup, headed by Filipescu[4] who was the most determined element. There were Filipescu, Mutulescu, Rangheţ and myself. Four in total. All of us armed. I prepared the tools for a noiseless liquidation: hammers. I arranged a car with Matei driving, and Rangheţ another car, with Rabcea. ... I decided that the action had to be carried out by myself ... On 4 April, the American bombing came ... I thought that it would throw our plans into disarray. He was in a panic. There weren't any cars circulating. It was our luck that his technical man, Romeo [Runcan] wasn't able to fetch me in his car, and he had to use my car, Matei's. He took me to him and there to my surprise I found Koffler. I asked him what he was doing there and he said that he had been caught there by the bombing. Foriş left Koffler with Mira[5]

[4] Gh. Filipescu and Ion Mutulescu were parachuted into Romania in 1943. Gh. Filipescu died in 1968 in a suspicious road accident, in the period when he was testifying to the commission investigating the Pătrăşcanu and Foriş cases. During the war he was a protégé of Emil Bodnăraş. He was the chief investigator for the SSI until the establishment of the Securitate. He married the divorced first wife of Corneliu Mănescu, Tasia. Ion Mutulescu had taken part in the Spanish Civil War as a driver. He was a volunteer with the International Brigades. He died in 1968.
[5] Mira, pseudonym of Victoria Sîrbu, a member of the PCdR Secretariat. She was Foriş's third wife. His first wife, Lotti, had a child with lawyer Iosif Şraier in 1935, while Foriş was in prison. His second wife, Tatiana Petrovici, fled to the USSR after the Red Army invaded (cont. p. 455.)

in another room. The plan of action could not be executed for a few minutes ... To get a grip on himself ... he wanted to give the impression that he was calm ... but I could see he was anxious, he was still in a panic after the bombing. At that moment a car pulls up with Ranghet inside. He had identified the house where I was and had arrived with the group, as planned. But I had still not told Foriş what it was all about. I knew he was armed, he had a pistol, and there was also Romeo, a dog very loyal to him, very vigilant, he was always guarding him, and it was very hard for me to get him to let me out of his sight so that I could let him [Ranghet] in, because he would be coming in 20 minutes, after I had liquidated him, and I might need help, after stating the problem. The host became alarmed when he saw a car parked outside. Mira went outside. He pricked up his ears; he didn't react yet, but only after the car returned three minutes later. Then he said, 'What's all this? What's with that car?' And then I saw I had to act. I asked that Mira and Romeo leave the room and I told him it was our car ... 'It's our man Marius's, comrade, and here is the decision I have to convey to you for execution'. I was sitting with one hand on the pistol, the other on the hammer, and when I opened my coat to take out the document, the sheet of paper we'd typed, he turned as white as chalk, beads of sweat appeared, he saw the pistol in my hand, I laid it on the corner of the table and I was holding the butt, and then he said, 'I submit'. ... All of a sudden he was porridge. He looked at me. He couldn't understand a thing. I took him and I said, 'Have you heard of the GRU?' He said, 'Yes'. I say, 'That's who you're dealing with. You'll hand over to me immediately all your contacts and everything, and if you say a word or step out of line, you'll answer with your head'. I let them into the house. I took their pistol and told them if they went outside ... they would be leaving at their own risk. And I

Bassarabia in 1940. During the war, she married a Soviet officer and agent, Yakov Bulan, who in the 1950s became the Commander of the Romanian Air force and Rector of the Military Academy. She was parachuted into Romania in 1944 with the mission of creating a detachment of partisans. In the 1950s, Tatiana Bulan was head of the Zhdanov Party School. Victoria Sîrbu, a teacher, gave birth to a daughter in 1945, who took her surname rather than Foriş's. She was arrested in 1949 and sentenced to 14 years imprisonment at the Pătrăşcanu trial of April 1954. She was amnestied in 1955. She worked at the State Central Library until her retirement.

went with the briefcase to Filipescu, who was not far away. I brought
Filipescu, armed with an automatic and a grenade, and installed him in
Foriș's house."[6]

It is more like a scene from a gangster film than the resolution of a political
dispute.

Ștefan Foriș is later transported to a house in the Floreasca district, then
another in the Vatra Luminoasă quarter, where, on 24 August 1944, Ion and
Mihai Antonescu will be sequestered. He was not under arrest, but under
'confinement'. This had been the punishment meted out to Constantin
Pîrvulescu, at Foriș's orders, when he was held for a number of months
in a safe house for having forgotten a briefcase containing important
documents on the back seat of a taxi. Foriș remains under guard until June,
when Bodnăraș releases him. He is assigned to Agitprop, the agitation and
propaganda section of the Party, where he works on the first issues of the
România liberă (*Free Romania*) newspaper. He is kept under surveillance
by Bodnăraș's shock troops. He is docile. He puts up no resistance. He
attempts to clarify his situation in a memorandum addressed to the new
leadership.

In Bucharest, political groups had been reactivating since the autumn of
1943, after Mussolini had been deposed and the illusion arose in Bucharest
that Romania might repeat the same course of events as in Italy. To this
end, Romanian diplomats were busy negotiating in Cairo, Ankara, Lisbon
and Stockholm, trying to salvage something from the situation. However,
the Casablanca Conference had declared that the only formula for any exit
from the war would be unconditional surrender. Romania was trying her
luck. The Red Army was preparing a new offensive, careful not to allow
its prey to escape. It was clear that the minuscule PCdR would have an
important role to play in the new situation, one disproportionate to its
size. The ousting of Foriș was one of the manoeuvres whereby the PCdR
apparatus was preparing for the day when the Soviets would be the masters
in Romania.

***

---

[6] Dan Cătănuș, Ioan Chiper, *Cazul Ștefan Foriș. Lupta pentru putere în PCR.
De la Gheorghiu-Dej la Ceaușescu*, Editura Vremea: Bucharest, 1999,
pp. 150-151.

Who was Ştefan Foriş? Naturally, like all the clandestines, he had gone by many aliases: Illin, most often, but also Valer, Lotian, Arin, Lungu, Siegfried, and Bătrînul (the Old Man). The list is incomplete. Each false name corresponded to a step up the hierarchical ladder of the communist apparatus. He was born in 1892, into a petit bourgeois family. His parents owned a brick works. He studied Physics and Mathematics at Budapest University. He was a polyglot. In 1919, he fought on the side of Béla Kuhn. He was already a communist and member of the Hungarian Communist Party. He fled to Braşov, in Romania, to escape arrest, but also for family reasons. He was a member of the Romanian Communist Party from its inception. He quickly made a career for himself in the small world of Romanian Bolshevism. He was a militant in MOPR (International Red Aid), as well as being one of its leaders. He published materials funded by MOPR. He made a name for himself as a propagandist and journalist. In the autumn of 1928, he is implicated in a trial of communists in Cluj. He is sentenced *in absentia* to 10 years imprisonment. He flees to the USSR, where he studies at Lenin's School for Cadres. He is sent to Berlin as a Comintern agent. His cover is as a TASS press correspondent. In Berlin he carries out missions for the Comintern's Western Europe Bureau. He has connections with Georgi Dimitrov, the Comintern's Berlin representative, but he is closer to Willy Münzenberg. Perhaps this was because they were the same blend of propagandist and secret agent. Both of them combined secret operations with visible agitation. Returning to Romania, he proves his skill in mounting such operations, which, behind a thick smokescreen, conceal underground networks and subversive activities, from money delivered by couriers from Moscow via Berlin and Prague to press campaigns. During the 'splittist struggles' of 1929-1930, he backs Vitali Holostenco-Barbu against Marcel Pauker-['Luximin']. One of his missions in Romania is to douse the flames of conflict. He does not succeed. In August 1931 he is arrested in Bucharest. On 12 January 1932, his trial commences at the Ilfov Tribunal, Section 1. Together with his wife, Lotti, arrested at the same time, he is charged with offences under the Mîrzescu Law of 1924. He already had a conviction dating from 1928, but he had been amnestied, together with all the other communists, in 1929. His lawyers are Paul Moscovici (who also defended Ceauşescu in Braşov in 1936) and Petre Zissu, later indicted in an espionage case. Iosif Şraier, the head of the PCdR legal office defends Lotti Foriş, who is being tried at liberty. During the trial Foriş does not deny that he is a member of the Communist Party. In a search of his house, manifestos, leaflets, and documents proving his membership of and 'intelligence' links to the Comintern had been found. His cover as 'TASS correspondent to Romania' makes him even more suspect. In court, he says, "My trial amounts to nothing less than persecution of the Communist movement." He is sentenced to five years imprisonment and a fine of 10,000 lei. Court of Appeal ruling no. 1203/1933 reduces his sentence by four years. His wife, Lotti, is sentenced to two years.

Dej and Foriş meet in Văcăreşti Prison. The conflict between them may have been sparked in this period. Foriş was gaoled in 1932 and due for release in 1937. Dej was gaoled in 1933, part of a group of more than 100, in which he was not the dominant figure. At the appeal heard in Craiova in 1934 we find Ştefan Foriş among the witnesses brought from Văcăreşti to testify. Foriş had been part of the PCdR apparatus since 1921. When Dej entered prison he was an ordinary party member, having joined in 1932. Foriş, after a sojourn in Văcăreşti, is transferred to Doftana in the same year. Dej will be sent there in May 1937. Foriş is an intellectual, an expert in Marxism-Leninism, which gives him a higher political status than the CFR electrician. Foriş taught the detainees Marxism and Bolshevism and explained Moscow policy. Foriş has great authority in Doftana. A long-standing communist, he is leader of the Party cell. It is a position that Dej will hold in 1940. Foriş outclassed Dej. What could an intellectual – a well-read polyglot who had travelled in Europe and the USSR, which at the time represented a journey of initiation – have in common with a provincial trades unionist who had only recently joined the Party? Their attitudes, too, were different. In the first part of 1935, a conflict with the administration of Doftana Prison split the communist inmates. A part of them, those with the longest sentences, wanted to adapt to the penitentiary regime. They requested to do various jobs, which the others refused on ideological grounds. Those who refused, 18 in number, including Foriş, were isolated. The conflict came to an end in August 1935, when Foriş was released. Later, the official history of the PCdR will claim that Foriş's attitude led to "the extermination of the Party ranks, the most precious detachment of the working class." His release also stirred other controversies. Gheorghiu-Dej later used the episode to denigrate him. Dej was supposed to be a defender of the communist inmates, Foriş a conciliator, even a collaborator, a 'capitulator'. The controversy arose from the fact that, on his release from Doftana, Foriş had signed an agreement whereby he undertook not to get involved in clandestine communist activities. However,

Foriş was only obeying orders. His mission was to 'legalise' himself and to look after the left-wing press, as part of the new popular front strategy being implemented by the Comintern everywhere at that time. As soon as he is released from gaol he is given the task of organising agitation and propaganda and the legal and clandestine Party press. If he had been cowardly or acted independently of orders from Moscow, he would have been isolated and even expelled. After his release from Doftana, Foriş, wearing the halo of his years of imprisonment, becomes one of the most influential communist leaders.

His 'firm' behaviour in prison earns him a reputation. Foriş runs the protest campaigns during the trials of Petre Constantinescu-Iaşi in Chişinău and the Ana Pauker group. In September 1936, he attends the Peace Congress in Brussels with Valter Roman and Athanasie Joja. In Paris he meets Dr Nicolae Lupu, vice-president of the PNȚ, to discuss the establishment of a Popular Front. Foriş leads a non-clandestine existence. He can be seen in restaurants and public places, where his presence is recorded in the memoirs of various writers. He is behind the publications of various crypto-communist organisations, as well as ephemeral, legal magazines of the left, including *Şantier* (*Building Site*) and *Reporter*. He leads a double life, according to the Leninist rulebook. In the winter of 1937 he becomes the secretary of the CC of the PCdR. He also runs the clandestine networks, channels Comintern money into protest meetings and communist publications, and provides the fees for lawyers in 'anti-fascist' trials. Foriş is head of Agitprop. He is in charge of everything to do with propaganda and agitation. The police keep him under close surveillance, as can be seen from reports dating from this period. The Popular Front fails to materialise in Romania, in spite of the precedents created in Spain and France. In the autumn of 1937, Foriş is involved in the campaign leading up to the December elections. He writes numerous dogmatic articles in the press, repeating the official line of the USSR, Comintern and PCdR. One example, in the *Reporter* weekly, defends the accord between the PCdR and PNȚ. The presence of the Legionaries had caused protests on the Left, among the radicals, in particular the Social Democrats, and among independent anti-fascist intellectuals. Foriş responds, defending the PCdR line, in *Reporter* (25 December 1937), protesting "against the terrorism of the Tătărescu government." The royal dictatorship, the suspension of the Constitution, the formation of a single party – the Front for National Rebirth – the formation of guilds to replace the unions, and the Munich accord radically change the political context. Ravaged by contradictory indications from the Comintern and the demands of the tense domestic situation, the PCdR reacts equivocally and hesitantly. In addition, the expulsions dictated by the Comintern, an extension of the Great Terror, in effect annihilate the Party. In 1937-40, following the arrests in the USSR, the Political Bureau ceases to exist. Ilie Pintilie, Béla Breiner, and Ștefan Foriş take charge of the internal leadership, the Secretariat, in 1938. In Spain, the volunteers, infiltrated by the NKVD, carry out purges, eliminating anarchists, deviationists, opportunists, liquidationists, etc. Those most hunted are the so-called Trotskyites. They are expelled, or else murdered (the case of Vasil Ghica, a Romanian volunteer, executed for Trotskyism). In Bucharest the atmosphere is the same: expulsions, sackings, sanctions. It is all an effect of the Kremlin's change in direction and the Great Terror. The context alters quickly and the well-disciplined PCdR Secretariat awaits orders from Moscow. With every change, the executants of the old policy are eliminated: Alexandru Sahia, Solomon Schein, Eugen Iacobovici, Popescu-Puțuri, et al. In Bucharest, Béla Breiner, Ștefan Foriş and Ilie Pintilie pursue ideological purity and rigid adherence to the Comintern line. However, this line is ambiguous and contradictory, and no one knows how to define it precisely, for example, in the matter of the Front for National Rebirth. The order from Moscow is that Party members should join the front and fight it from the inside. This order is later rescinded, and the adepts of the policy are punished as 'capitulators'. The same in the case of the guilds, after the dissolution of the unions. The Comintern decision is that the communists should join the guilds and take over the leadership. Nor in relation to the extreme Right are the orders any clearer. It is demanded that the communists should work with the Legionaries, as 'adversaries' of the royal dictatorship; others continue to identify them as the communists' principal adversaries. These differing, sometimes contradictory positions split the small group of communists still at liberty in Bucharest, as well as those in the prisons. In the period 1937-1941, subordination to Moscow frequently gives rise to such 'turnabouts'. In that period it was unimaginable for the Romanian communists to have their own line or take their own decisions. Few leaders were able to cope with the continual zigzagging. Some retired, others were marginalised or eliminated by their own Party cells. Only the most subordinate, the most dogmatic, and the most capable of surviving in differing situations and displaying their loyalty to Moscow made it through this extremely turbulent period. One of the survivors was Ștefan Foriş, whom we find in all the line-ups of the Secretariat.

Gheorghe Stoica (Moscu Cohn), like Foriș one of the founders of the PCdR, writes in a report to the Cominern in 1940 that Foriș is "a functionary devoted to the Party, the Comintern, the USSR. Foriș has spent his entire life within the Party. Comrade Foriș is a journalist ... a Party pedagogue. It should be mentioned that many of the younger comrades gained their knowledge of Marxism-Leninism from him and left prison with an education ... But Comrade Foriș, and I think this is his most vulnerable side, thinks ploddingly, he reacts tardily and acts even more slowly. In practice, organisational work ... in the ranks of the masses is another of his weak points. It is difficult for him to lead independently – within a collective he is able to work better."[7] The author of a report for the General Department of Police writes in 1938, "Foriș is an intransigent communist and refuses under interrogation to make any kind of statement about his activity, abiding by the conspiratorial rules of the Communist Party."[8] Foriș was always an individual who submitted to the iron rules of the underworld. He acted only under orders. He was a man of secrecy, of conspiracies, completely in the service of the shadowy networks directed from Moscow. He was a highly disciplined man, without any inclinations toward independence. The Ribbentrop-Molotov Pact does not alter his attitude. Even though he had conducted numerous campaigns against fascism, and organised and taken part in the effort to form a popular front, the turnabout of 23 August 1939 does not trouble him. For him, loyalty to Moscow was the supreme law. He does not follow Willy Münzenberg, who, after the signing of the pact, broke with the Comintern and was later killed by Soviet secret agents, in 1940, for treason. Foriș, too, would share the same fate, in 1946, under similar circumstances, slain by his own comrades for 'treason'. The difference is that Foriș remained loyal to Moscow until his very last breath. Not a shadow of doubt, not a heretical thought, ever disturbed him.

His blind obedience to orders marked him out for the position of Secretary General when it became vacant. In relation to Breiner and Luca, Foriș had the disadvantage of being an intellectual, a quality of which Stalin was extremely suspicious. On the other hand, he was, like the other two, an ethnic Hungarian, which corresponded to the tactic of not choosing someone from the ethnic majority: such a leader might put down roots,

[7] ANR, *Partidul Comunist din România în anii celui de-al doilea război mondial*, 2003, p. 140.
[8] ANR, DGP Fund, Dossier 34/1938, p. 36.

even become popular and develop pretensions to independence. In any case, the Comintern had no other solutions in the autumn of 1940. The Romanian communists had either been massacred in Moscow in 1936-1938, were in prison, or were refugees in the USSR. Foriș and Georgescu were staying at the Hotel Lux in Moscow. They have talks with Georgi Dimitrov, Dmitri Manuilski, Palmiro Togliatti and Wilhelm Pieck. They meet Boris Ștefanov and Vasile Luca. Likewise they hold talks with the members of the international brigades back from Spain. The talks do not go very smoothly. The PCdR was absent from the political scene and had a tiny number of members. There are also criticisms of the mistakes made in the previous two years: the Romanian communists' position towards the royal dictatorship, when it had demanded its members join the Front for National Rebirth; its position towards the guilds, when it had adopted the same policy of 'entryism'; the position towards the Legionaries, with whom the communists had maintained ambiguous relations, as an effect of the Molotov-Ribbentrop Pact. It was not the fascists of Nazi Germany that were the communists' enemies, but the 'Western plutocracies, Britain and France'. The fascists and the communists had a common enemy. In Romania it was King Carol and the royal dictatorship. Their shared aims and collaboration are a historical fact.

While Ștefan Foriș and Teohari Georgescu are in Moscow, France surrenders. The USSR occupies Bassarabia and northern Bukowina. The Quadrilateral and northern Transylvania are ceded. King Carol leaves the country. In Bucharest, the regime of Ion Antonescu and Horia Sima seizes power. Foriș wanted to remain in the USSR, as a political refugee. He asks the Comintern's permission to stay, but he is turned down. He was more useful to them in Bucharest than Moscow. Teohari Georgescu returns to Romania in October. Iosif Chișinevschi and Gavrilă Birtaș, the two members of the Secretariat not in the USSR or prison, were isolated and overtaken by the situation. Foriș remains in Moscow another two months for talks. He is trained in sabotage, the use of ciphers, subversion, and espionage techniques. He reaches the Romanian border at the end of the year. He lingers for a few days, waiting for a favourable opportunity to cross the Danube. Deferently, he sends a letter to the Comintern, addressed to Boris Ștefanov, dated 28 December. "The class enemy has been unable to destroy our Party," he writes, but it has managed to "deal heavy blows." The PCdR "has lost half its members." The problems confronting the Party are the same as those faced by any sect weighed down by intrigues, expulsions, ambitions, disagreements and conflicts. Foriș does not seem to be intimidated by this. On the contrary, he is in his element. He knows the plot and all the players. In order to make himself understood, he uses the ritual phraseology of the Comintern:

"The latest indications from Comrades Dimitrov and Pieck have provided a complete response to the above-mentioned problems. I shall strive with all my might to apply them and achieve them in Romania. Naturally, I shall not forget the words of Comrade Dimitrov: 'Not even the best resolution can replace the head of the comrades.'"[9]

On 31 December, Foriș crosses the Danube and lands in Tulcea, and thence to Bucharest. He discovers a reality different to the one he had left behind on 22 May 1940. In the meantime, Romania had lost a third of its territory and population. The German Army was already installed in strategic regions, along the Prahova Valley and around the capital. The PCdR was in a highly ambiguous position, with very few members and no clear line. Moscow, itself ambiguous, was cultivating special relations with Hitler's Germany and was in the midst of a war with Finland. On 1 January, the Secretariat of the PCdR, consisting of Teohari Georgescu, Gavrilă Birtaș and Iosif Chișinevschi, gathered in a safe house in the Obor district in order to receive directives from the Comintern.[10]

Foriș was obsessed with clandestinity. He was an agitator imbued with the doctrine and practical canons exposited in Lenin's *What is to be Done?* In 1935, on his release from Doftana, it is hard for him to accept operating legally, but he obeys. He would have preferred to operate clandestinely. He believed that it was more effective and represented the true spirit of Bolshevism. Lucrețiu Pătrășcanu, when forced to 'legalise' in order to conduct the defence in the 'trials of the anti-fascists' in 1936, showed the same reluctance. The two belonged to the same generation and the same school of 'professional revolutionaries'. Whereas Pătrășcanu understood why the communist sect had to open up to other political forces and the tactic of the Popular Front, Foriș did not. Nor did he understand the spirit of genuine, normal politics conducted in contact with society. The masses

---

[9] Dan Cătănuș, Ioan Chiper, *Cazul Foriș. Lupta pentru putere în PCR. De la Gheorghiu-Dej la Ceaușescu*, Editura Vremea: Bucharest, 1999, p. 19.
[10] Interview with Romeo Runcan, Ștefan Foriș's host between 1940 and 1944 (April 2000).

intimidated him, even if he often spoke in their name. He was a loner. He would have preferred to go on living clandestinely. He obeys for reasons of discipline, always the essential thing for him. Foriş felt more comfortable in the underground, surrounded by secrets, plotting, hiding, going by false names, using forged papers, living in safe houses, threatened with betrayal and capture by the police. He lived dangerously, without an identity. He was not necessarily a harried man, a pariah. Clandestinity was a way of life, not just an unfavourable circumstance. To be proscribed was an honour, a post-romantic pose. To live dangerously, risking gaol and even the firing squad in the name of the 'proletarian revolution' and Stalin, was the only thing that gave his life meaning. The circumstances in which he takes over the leadership of the Party are critical, but allow him to give free rein to his proclivity for clandestine living. For Foriş, the loss of contact with Moscow, which happens in May 1941, is extremely grave. First of all because the Party he had been running for six months had since its inception operated only in accordance with orders from the Comintern, and now those orders could not get through. Secondly because Foriş was nothing but an executant, dependent upon his hierarchical superior. Left to his own devices in the extremely complicated circumstances of 1941-1944, he is lost. He possesses neither the political imagination, will, intelligence, nor courage demanded by the times. Foriş is not a leader, but rather an ideologue, a patient teacher, a journalist, a dogmatic intellectual. Unlike Tito, for example. In charge of a PCdR that is on the verge of extinction, the only thing that he knows how to do is to give the order for 'profound clandestinity'. The PCdR is a shadow. He decides to pass unobserved. The cadres are few, in the dozens, concentrated mainly in Bucharest. The majority are in the prisons and camps. The Siguranţă must in no way be provoked, in order to avoid raids, searches and arrests. "Reckoning that at present heightened activity would mean 'the complete collapse of the movement', the instructions given recommend strictly clandestine activity, so that the general impression will be that the Communist Party's lack of contact with the Comintern has led to a complete paralysis of communist action."[11]

The PCdR does not escape either Siguranţă repression or upheaval within its own ranks. The communist sect, hiding in the underground,

---

[11] SSI note, "Dispoziţiuni de activitate date de conducere Partidului Comunist," 2 May 1942, CC of the PCR Archive, Fund 1, Dossier 274, p. 312.

is prey to violent, venomous conflicts. Each member detests the other. Resentment and suspicion dissolve even the smattering of solidarity that might have been expected from individuals who share the same cause and destiny. Arrests merely fuel the mutual accusations. The only solution Foriș can glimpse from his hiding place is to accuse the others of breaking the rules of conspiracy, to formulate new regulations, to impose sanctions. He expels, suspends and isolates various militants. He then demands that each deliver a self-criticism in order to be accepted back. It is a ritual determined by conditioned reflexes. Foriș is severed from reality. For him everything comes down to the clandestine life. His is an incognito life of hiding places and secret orders. Foriș surrounds himself with paperwork, like a bureaucrat. He constantly drafts documents to send out to the few dozen communist militants. In spite of the danger of interception, he keeps up an extensive correspondence. His missives contain criticisms, attacks, justifications, and threats. Besides such vacillations, Foriș continually "lectures" on the rules of conspiracy: "The leadership of the Communist movement upholds that these arrests are the result of a failure to abide by conspiratorial rules and the introduction into the movement of unverified elements. This is why it has been decided that all those elements of the movement that have had contacts with those arrested should be relieved of responsibilities for reasons of security and at the same time the situation of each of them should be checked. In order to avoid future arrests that will place the movement in difficult situations, the central leadership has ruled on the following with regard to conspiratorial rules: (1) conspiratorial meetings shall be scheduled in advance and at short notice, a maximum of two days; (2) the streets on which conspiratorial meetings are to take place shall be little frequented in order for those due to come to the meeting to be able to make a thorough reconnoitre and verification a quarter of an hour in advance; (3) meetings shall be held mostly in the daytime; (4) test meetings shall take place on the same day, not at intervals of 2-3 days as previously; (5) the use of public transport to get to conspiratorial meetings shall be made as follows: buses shall be taken only when there is a single bus at the stop and if passengers have alighted at that stop; (6) safe houses shall only be camouflaged by trusted members of the movement; (7) each Party member responsible for raising funds for the movement shall continue to collect membership dues and hold them until the movement leadership designates a new method."[12]

---

[12] *Culegere de documente. Prefectura Poliției Capitalei*, vol. 3 (cont. 466.)

This is the type of literature that was circulating among the communists. In the 1940s the entire existence of the PCdR boils down to this. The sole preoccupation is how to hide from the Siguranţă, how to run a safe house, how to obtain forged papers. Suspicion is rife. The Siguranţă makes a number of captures, thanks to recruits from inside the PCdR. It keeps track of the numerous conflicts and does not intervene except when the communists go into action, pasting up manifestos, establishing cells in the factories, raising funds or corresponding with those in prison. In such situations, an informant activates and arrests are made. A trial and heavy sentences follow. Arriving in prison, the communists investigate the new inmates to discover the circumstances of their arrest and whether they have talked under interrogation or betrayed the names of other comrades. The detection of informants – the major obsession of the underground – is vital. The rule is that whoever has not been arrested is the one who has given the network away. Foriş becomes the target of these suspicions. The raids on the printing presses in 1940, the arrest of the members of the Secretariat at Easter 1941, the capture of the terrorist group led by Francisc Paneth and A. Kornhauser in November 1941, the capture of the groups led by Ion Vincze and Constanţa Crăciun, the arrest and execution of Petre Gheorghe in the summer of 1942, the discovery of the printing press in 1943 and the Malaxa communist cell, and the capture of the leadership of the Union of Patriots in December 1943[13] heighten the suspicions, creating paranoia in this underground world. There are hundreds of arrests, investigations and trials, with heavy sentences, sometimes even executions by firing squad. Ştefan Foriş, the survivor, is held to blame. On the other hand, from the viewpoint of the Comintern, to be arrested was also a crime, almost treason. You would become suspect. Above you hovered the suspicion of having become an enemy of the Party, be it out of negligence in applying the rules of conspiracy, be it because you were in the pay of the Siguranţă. If you happened to give away the names of other communists under interrogation,

---

(16 November 1943), pp. 624-626.

[13] On 28 February 1944 the Union of Patriots trial was held. Etty and Paul Wexler, Mircea Biji and Mihai Levente (*in absentia*) were sentenced to 25 years, hard labour; Mihai Magheru, Vlădescu-Răcoasa and Ion Petre to 15 years; Ana Solomon and Ernestina and Anca Magheru to 10 years; Gheorghe Simion to three years; others, including Manea Mănescu, a future communist Prime Minister, were acquitted.

you were expelled. The only escape for a communist who 'fell into the claws of the Siguranţă' was to accuse someone else who was at liberty of treason. Thus, the more communists the Siguranţă threw into gaol, the more insistently was Foriş, now virtually alone in his hiding place, accused of treason. He thereby became the prime suspect for the arrests that had occurred since he took over the PCdR leadership.

Foriş is incapable of leading a normal existence. The underground seemed to be his natural environment. He was too lacking in imagination and determination to be a combatant, a Party leader. He was waiting for orders. He was dogmatic, seeking in the resolutions of the Comintern and the works of Lenin and above all Stalin solutions to the problems of the everyday. He was perplexed when these did not correspond to reality. He was in the habit of thinking that the texts were real, not what was happening around him. He hastened to punish heretics, insubordinates. He demanded self-criticisms and recognitions of guilt for imaginary or real trespasses. As a matter of reflex he saw 'splittist' and enemies everywhere, enemies of himself and the Party he embodied. He had a 'consciousness of his historic mission' as head of the PCdR, the vanguard of the working class. All these traits isolate him even from the political sect he leads. For as long as he is Secretary General he quarrels with everyone. The conflicts were often not so much political as much as personal in nature. He is vehemently opposed by Petre Gheorghe, Ronea Peisacovici-Gheorghiu, and Ivanka Slarski (Rudenko), the wife and sister of the former and latter respectively. Likewise, he is opposed by Elena and Ştefan Pavel (husband and wife), Ilona Popp and Grigore Rangheţ (also husband and wife), the Moisescu couple, Rangheţ and others. The communists form veritable clans. Ştefan Pavel and Ştefan Foriş were brothers-in-law. Elena and Victoria Sîrbu were sisters. Pavel was one of Foriş's most obdurate opponents. Intimate relations within the movement are common and further complicate the disputes. A list of just some of the couples that combined clandestinity and romance would include Constantin Pîrvulescu and Ana Toma, Remus Koffler and Lili Weigl, Ion Vincze and Constanţa Crăciun, A. Kornhauser and Lilli Paneth.

Foriş comes up against resistance on the part of the communists in prison (grouped around Gheorghiu-Dej) and those at liberty. One of his adversaries is Petre Gheorghe, the head of the Bucharest organisation. Gheorghe is a typical 'splittist'. He sees himself as head of the Party after the marginalisation of Boris Ştefanov and the death of Béla Breiner. The

Comintern has another option. In December 1940, in a report to Boris Ştefanov, Foriş, recently appointed head of the Party, with the powers conferred by the position of Secretary General, writes, "In his attitude [i.e. that of Petre Gheorghe] I can see immense dissatisfaction and a sickly vanity of which the comrade needs to be cured. Otherwise, he is on a slippery slope."[14] The conflict paralysed the PCdR. A year later, Foriş writes in a circular, "This muddle-headed and incorrigible 'splittist' also tried last year to wage a 'splittist war' against the CC. Iancu [pseudonym of Petre Gheorghe] is the pupil of [Marcel] Pauker, the criminal enemy of the people, who prepared and began the 'splittist struggle' within our Party in 1930. Iancu has learned from him the vile habits and methods of an adventurer. Since the end of 1936, he has been in permanent conflict with the Party leadership."[15] In fact, during those years, the PCdR was suffering from the same phenomenon as in 1929-1931 – 'splittist battles'. Rival groups vied for supremacy and accused each other of treachery and collaboration with the Siguranţă, of disobeying the orders of the Comintern and the Central Committee. The Party is, like so often before, on the brink of extinction.

Another conflict is between Foriş and Constantin Pîrvulescu. Grigore Răceanu ("a member of the gang of Hitlerist traitors, Petre Gheorghe, Ştefan Pavel, Ioan Meţiu"), long at odds with the head of the PCdR, marries Ilona Popp, the head of the UTC, up until then a Foriş supporter. Comrade Răceanu joins forces with her husband and persuades Constantin Pîrvulescu to join the group opposing Foriş. Foriş promptly labels the situation 'splittism'. Ilona Popp-Răceanu, Petre Gheorghe and Ştefan Pavel are expelled. Pîrvulescu is let off with a minor reprimand, on account of his long-standing in the PCdR, but also because of his special status. He was a Soviet citizen, connected to the Soviet secret services. Foriş errs on the side of caution. Not even when Pîrvulescu makes serious mistakes does he expel him. For example, when Pîrvulescu leaves top-secret documents behind on the back seat of a taxi, which results in the arrests of dozens of communists and trials with sentences totalling more than 100 years imprisonment, Foriş merely suspends him and confines him to a safe house. Pîrvulescu takes his revenge by participating in the plot hatched against Foriş by Bodnăraş and Ranghet. How such a leader, laden with such guilt, for which so many comrades paid dearly, a leader lacking in credibility and viewed with reproach

---

[14] Dan Cătănuş, Ion Chiper, *op. cit.*, p. 20.

[15] ANR, *PCdR în anii celui de al doilea război mondial*, 2003, p. 191.

could become head of the PCdR is a mystery perhaps explained by the Party's innate "Byzantinism," to use Vladimir Tismăneanu's word. Rangheţ, too, the other member of the triumvirate of plotters, was in conflict with Foriş. In contrast to Pîrvulescu, he had once been Foriş's protégé. In the autumn of 1940, when the Comintern asked him to work with Pîrvulescu, Foriş refused. It was Foriş who brought Rangheţ to Bucharest and instead of punishing him for blowing the cover of the network in southern Transylvania, he promoted him as head of the military commission. One actor in the 'splittist' drama (Ioan Meţiu, an adversary of Foriş, close to Petre Gheorghe) writes in a report of 1941, "Rangheţ, a Hungarian Soviet worker ... is an impertinent type, gullible and full of himself. He is a parvenu in the gang of his old friend, Foriş ... they are our deadly enemies, more dangerous than Hitler and Antonescu, because they are in our midst ... and they stab us treacherously in the back." Rangheţ, devoted to Foriş, is ousted by Emil Bodnăraş as head of the military commission. He then joins the anti-Foriş plot, recruited by Bodnăraş himself.

The inmates in Caransebeş Prison also vehemently contest Foriş. There are numerous charges against him. The most serious is that he is a Siguranţă agent. The Caransebeş prisoners spread the accusation to other gaols and manage to form a coalition against Foriş. It is a typical 'splittist' move. This is how it would have been categorised if Foriş had won the game. It was not the only accusation he came up against and nor was it the only conflict he had to smooth over. In the camp at Tîrgu Jiu the Divisions are equally strong. There are a number of groups and leaders vying for supremacy. In time, all the communist prisoners are sucked in. The main figures in the dispute are Ovidiu Şandor, Alexandru Iliescu, Lucreţiu Pătrăşcanu, Athanasie Joja, Grigore Preoteasa, Gh. Apostol, Gheorghe Gheorghiu-Dej, I. Gh. Maurer, and Chivu Stoica. Disputes also occur among the communists imprisoned in Jilava, Lugoj, Mislea and Văcăreşti. The mutual accusations and terms in which they are framed are inversely proportional to the political and military passivity. All these agents of the USSR, Comintern and GRU exhaust their resources in writing letters filled with imprecations, in meetings of criticism and self-criticism, in stigmatising the enemy within. The following is from a document that circulated among the communists:

"Foriş the Hungarian intellectual, the chauvinist, without any devotion to the proletariat or the Romanian people, without any past in our organisations, in the struggles of the working class ... this bandit is no stranger to the fall of the CC ... we have ascertained that he holds meetings with the window open, ranting like a madman ... The so-called CC of the [Foriş] gang is a Hitlerist bandit agency infiltrated into the leadership of our Party ... The day of reckoning is nigh and the F. gang will answer for their crimes. Out with the Hitlerist filth F. and C. [Conrad, i.e. Koffler] from our ranks, out with them if we do not wish to perish as a Party and comrades. Drive out these communist killers from our ranks. The facts have proven that unity with them is a crime against the proletariat and the people and against the Soviet Union."[16]

"Little by little, he [Foriş] became the imaginary leader of a Party which in its turn existed most of all in his imagination ... the Secretary General was arrested not by the Siguranţă but by the real Party, which thereby displayed its refusal to be led by him. Gradually Foriş came to devote his main energies not to his natural conflict with the military dictatorship, but to the conflict with the Party that did not accept his leadership. The price for his not being arrested by the Siguranţă was his arrest by the Party ... There remains his striking inability to lead the Communist Party during such a complex historical period."[17]

***

According to the appeal to 'patriotic forces' launched on 24 August, Foriş presents himself at PCdR headquarters. A few days later he is deposed. He had spent the last two months working on the first issues of the *România liberă* daily. It seems that his situation had been clarified. In June, the man who had conducted the operation to remove him, Emil Bodnăraş, lifted the guard on the house where he was confined. He is allowed to circulate through the city only if accompanied. After the change in his status, he writes a memorandum to the new leadership. He reports on the previous four years and asks to be reintegrated. The mores of clandestinity dictated that once you had lost your position you were treated like a pariah. To sin before the Party meant that you were an 'objective' enemy; that you had played the

---

[16] Dan Cătănuş, Ioan Chiper, *op.*, *cit.* p. 25.

[17] Pavel Cîmpeanu, *Ceauşescu. Anii numărătorii inverse*, Editura Polirom: Jassy, 2002, p. 111.

enemy's game; that you had betrayed. This was the logic within the PCdR. But the reality of the underground was the only one Foriș knew. He had lived for many years in clandestinity; he had no other identity. His reflexes were strictly connected to this way of life: secrecy, safe houses, hiding from the police. It was complicated to adapt to normal life. The alternatives for Foriș, in his situation as a pariah inside the PCdR, were to emerge on the surface and surrender to the police, or to accept complete isolation, to wait for an investigation conducted by those who had deposed him, or a bullet from the same people. Foriș, who knew very well how the Comintern and GRU worked, did not harbour any illusions. He knew exactly what the procedure was once you had fallen into disgrace, once you were accused of treachery. There was no mercy. It did not matter where you were in USSR-controlled territory, the 'long arm of the Revolution' would reach you wherever you were hiding. Foriș's belief in the omnipotence of the Soviet secret services caused him to concede when, on 4 April, Bodnăraş told him he had been sent by them. There are numerous examples. Willy Münzenberg, a Comintern representative of the highest rank, had been found dead in France. Walter Krivitsky likewise. Foriș would not have been the first case and nor the last. The most famous example, of course, is that of Leon Trotsky, assassinated by Ramon Mercader on Stalin's order in Mexico in August 1940. While Foriș may not have known about the first case, even though he had known Münzenberg well in Berlin in the 1920s, he certainly knew about the third.

All Foriș can do is wait and try to elucidate the situation. He docilely accepts the treatment meted out to him. He is allowed to work for Agitprop, however. He had been head of the section before 1940. His abilities in the field were acknowledged. *România liberă* needed such organisational skills when it was launched immediately after the fall of the Antonescu regime. PCdR cadres were scarce, 90 per cent of them being in prison. The fact that printers could not be found to operate the clandestine presses says much. The Bodnăraş-Pîrvulescu-Rangheţ triumvirate do not accuse him of having been a Siguranţă agent. For the three the reason for deposing him is purely political, and is to do with the situation of the PCdR after the imminent arrival of the Red Army. However, to remove Foriș required serious accusations. How else could the removal of a Party chief appointed by Moscow be justified? To usurp this exclusive Comintern privilege was an extremely serious act. It was not until 1956 that a local Communist Party dared to appoint its own leader – Wladislaw Gomulka.

For Dej and his accomplices the handiest accusation was treachery. Hard to prove, but grave. Dej was not long in employing it. Bodnăraș took care of the business, along with Vanya Didenko and Pantiușa Bodnarenko. All three are proven Soviet spies, tried and convicted in the 1930s, imprisoned in Doftana and Caransebeș. Gheorghiu-Dej denies Foriș access to the headquarters of the CC of the PCdR. His status becomes extremely unclear. He had not been expelled from the Party, he had not been sanctioned, he had not been tried. Henceforth he becomes a non-person, a man without identity, a living corpse. No one will go near him. He is a pariah. Dej's circle knew very well the dislike he harboured against the former head of the PCdR and no one dared to go to Foriș's aid. Outside the narrow world of the communists, Foriș was also a man to be avoided like the plague. He was detested not only because he was a communist but also because he was complicit with the occupier, and feared because he was an instrument of the Kremlin oppressor. As Romania had been subjected to large reparations and systematically looted, as violence by Red Army soldiers was the order of the day, the isolation of the PCdR and the feelings of the general public and democratic politicians were inevitable. Foriș was thus doubly a prisoner. In any case, it did not even occur to him to leave the PCdR, to renounce communism. In spite of the treatment to which he is subjected, he remains loyal to the cause and in May writes a number of letters to the PCdR leaders, Ana Pauker and Gheorghiu-Dej. It would have meant negating his entire life, all that he had up until then done in the service of the Comintern and the 'proletarian revolution'. He still nurtured the Bolshevik illusions of 1917. He had remained a Leninist, drunk with the enthusiasm and utopias of the time. As an old Bolshevik, he was one of Stalin's favoured quarries. We do not know whether Stalin found out about Foriș's incarceration from the reports of the Soviet advisers that thronged the PCdR. Naturally, Ana Pauker and the others knew of the Kremlin boss's dislike of the old guard, and his distrust of intellectuals, whom he saw as unreliable, hesitant and petit bourgeois. Thus, they had nothing to fear on his part. Of course, a show trial was the prerogative of Moscow. But as long as Foriș was kept out of the way, now under arrest and investigation, now at liberty and under surveillance, things appeared normal. Keeping up appearances was the priority at this time, now that the PCdR had begun to operate legally. Foriș was spared in the autumn of 1944 because of internecine battles for supremacy. Ana Pauker's return to Bucharest on 16 September complicated the situation within the Party. Pîrvulescu, who in the first issue of *Scînteia* appears as Party chief, is relegated to second place. Ana Pauker had the greater influence. Gheorghiu-Dej was also asserting his claim to supremacy. The new, extremely dynamic political situation delayed resolution of the Foriş case. Moreover, his fate was far from having been decided. Dej and those grouped around him would have killed him on the spot, gangster-style. But they did not have complete decision-making power. Ana Pauker, Pătrăşcanu and the other leaders who had worked with Foriş would not have agreed to the killing of one of their own. It would have opened the way to a series of other assassinations. Only if Moscow had ordered it would they have submitted. But no such order came.

A battle for power at the top of the Party erupts in September 1944. The successive governments, the Red Army moving into Bucharest lock stock and barrel, and organisational matters keep all the communist leaders and their small Party busy. Who had any use for a legitimate candidate for the leadership, appointed by Moscow in 1940 and never dismissed by the Comintern? Should he have been reinstated as Party chief or reintegrated into the ranks of the Political Bureau or the Secretariat of which he had been a member for 10 years? No one wanted to have him as a rival. The punitive measures against him are not long in coming. The logic of the underground is all-consuming. Foriş is arrested by Bodnăraş on 15 September, a day before the Pauker group arrives in Bucharest. Dej wanted matters to be already irreversible on the arrival of the Muscovites. Foriş is sequestered with Victoria Sîrbu in a safe house. He is forced to write countless declarations. He is interrogated by Vanya Didenko (Dej's right-hand man, with whom he had escaped from the Tîrgu Jiu camp in August) and Pantiuşa Bodnarenko. He is not put on trial or handed over to the police. He is sequestered. There was not a court in Romania that would have convicted Foriş. He had committed no crime, broken no law. For his communist activities an amnesty had been declared by the King in the communiqué read out on the evening of 23 August. Dej and the others, with their contempt for justice, saw things differently, however. For them crimes against the Party were the most dangerous. They were not content merely to expel him from the Party. It would have been too little according to the morals of the 'professional revolutionary'. He had to be punished, killed, to set an example and cement the movement's unity with his blood. We find a detailed description of such a murder in Dostoevsky's *The Demons*. To err was more serious if you served 'the cause' than if you had never served it. In the second case you were an objective enemy; you belonged to the bourgeoisie, the exploiters. If you had been an insider and you were seen as a traitor, there was no escape. You had to be killed. To place yourself outside the Party after having been a member was a crime that the Leninist catechism, inspired by Nechayev, punished with death. The Party constituted a para-reality, with its own rules, its own justice, its own judges and executioners. Like the Mafia. In this case, a political mafia. Even if the PCdR had become a legal Party after 23 August, they still behaved like outlaws. Nothing gave the PCdR bosses the right to sequester a man, to try and execute him. Dej and co. were acting like gangsters. They cloaked themselves in an ideology which, founded on a revolutionary utopia, 'permitted' them to kill anyone at all. A revolution means exceptional times, in which laws and justice are suspended, and which demand measures outside the rules of democracy. Respect for human life crumbles during such times. Using this logic, Dej and co. disposed of the lives and goods of whomever they wished. In the autumn of 1944 the communists had not shed the habits of clandestinity. And nor would they manage to do so until December 1989. They lived on two levels: one legal, official and at the surface of public life, the other subterranean, secret, conspiring to seize power. Once in power, they would conspire against society as a whole.

Foriş's fate was sealed. It was only a question of time, until his enemies in the Party gained a respite to deal with him. His fate depended on that of the faction led by Dej, his archenemy. The news from this direction was extremely bad. Dej was gaining ground. His visit to Stalin in January 1945 consecrated him as leader of the PCdR, with an influence equal to that of Ana Pauker. With Ana Pauker as Secretary General of the PCdR perhaps Foriş would have escaped with his life. She, at least, did not harbour a dislike for him or see him as an implacable enemy. On 6 January, Ştefan Foriş and Victoria Sîrbu-Foriş are released without any accusation being brought against them. The influence of Moscow?

We discover what happened in a note written by Victoria Sîrbu in 1945, immediately after her husband's second arrest:

> "After the changes of April 1944 there was a series of contradictions as to the nature of Foriş's situation about which not even Comrade Luca was able to give me any answer. Thus, when I was read the declaration

of Comrade Teohari in connection with the change of 4 April in which Comrade Foriș was called a Siguranță agent, Comrade Bodnăraș declared that the Central Committee did not share the same opinion. In September 1944, Comrade Didenko declared that there was evidence against Comrade Foriș. On 6 January, Comrade Didenko together with Comrade Bodnăraș declared on setting us free that we were not guilty and offered us work in the Party. In February 1945, Comrade Foriș was to receive Party work. In March he was arrested by the Siguranță and detained at the Party's pleasure and at the same time it was communicated to me from the Central Committee that I should separate from Comrade Foriș ... but Comrade Foriș was immediately released, only for us now to be told that there is proof he is a traitor."[18]

The note was written at the end of March, when, after a search of his house, Foriș was once again arrested, as revealed in the police written statement.[19] The author of the document notes that the search was made "on the basis of the instruction to carry out investigations in connection with the manifesto entitled *The Independent Communist Party*, which is subversive by nature of its contents and dissemination." It is hard to understand today why the formation of another Party, even a Communist Party, was so subversive. At the time it was a cardinal sin, an act against the unwritten Bolshevik law. On the other hand, it was a provocation. There is no other document to confirm that Foriș was caught up in the creation of another Party. A pretext was needed in order to arrest him. Three policemen rummage through flat No. 130 Pasajul Victoria, entrance B, 1st floor, inhabited by four persons: Ștefan and Victoria Foriș, his mother, and their newborn child. The same as during the clandestine period, the detectives confiscate all the documents they find in the personal archive of the former head of the PCdR. What must Foriș have thought, having been arrested and searched so many times? Instead of experiencing elation that his Party was legal and had won the race for power, he was once again a pariah, arrested, searched and demoted, this time at the orders of his own comrades. Among the documents confiscated could be found everything that would have been of interest to the Siguranță before August 1944. The items included:

[18] CC of the PCR Archive, Fund 95, Dossier 56, vol. 2, p. 21.
[19] CC of the PCR Archive, Fund 95, Dossier 56, vol. 1, p. 90.

"A notebook with the title *The Party Line*, with nine pages written in ink, a note with the names of various persons, excerpts from the CC decision of June 1943 with the title *Dissolution of the Communist International, with the duties of the PCdR*, consisting of 12 pages written in ink, with the following titles: *The fall of the UTC organisation in Ilfov county, Resolution of the Ilfov county committee regarding the arrests of November-December 1943, România liberă*, the circular of 8 June 1941, *The CC platform of 6 September*, the Resolution of the Central Committee of the PCR, dated January 1942, *The struggle for the Party line and unity*, etc."

The report is not drawn up for the use of Antonescu's Siguranță, it does not go to the SSI, but rather to the Secretariat of the CC of the PCdR. Foriș was just as prone to arrest as if there had been no change of regime at all.

What were the police looking for? Archive documents. The history of the PCdR was beginning to be rewritten, falsified, mystified. No scrap of evidence could be left behind. Dej was obsessed with archives and documents. He wished to hide invaluable documents, to conceal the past, to erase his tracks. In 1960, he burns the compromising documents in the CC of the PMR/PCR archive. For the same reason he will give orders that persons, witnesses and participants in events involving him be murdered. Other unfortunates will be tossed into the same grave as Foriș, those who claimed to know certain things about Dej, murdered at his orders by Bodnarenko. In their preparations for the assassination, Dej's accomplices and vassals rummaged through the archives of the Siguranță. They interrogated former commissars, who had in the meantime been arrested. They gathered statements from those who had collaborated with Foriș. The mystification of the past, necessary for every totalitarian regime, had begun.

The successive arrests and releases depend upon the shifting fortunes of the battle at the top of the PCdR. Foriș is a pawn in a struggle for power and he is employed as such by all those involved. He is now 'a reckless mistake on the part of Dej and Bodnăraș', now 'a necessary action' undertaken by the same two. The way in which the PCdR part in the 23 August coup was read is closely tied up with Foriș's fate. For Dej and Bodnăraș it was an act of salvation. Therefore Foriș had to be liquidated. For Pauker and Luca, contrariwise, Foriș had not to be removed. The installation of the Dr Petru Groza government and preparations for the PCR national conference, which had been postponed from summer until autumn, meant that the Foriș case had to be solved quickly. The Dej faction had the upper hand. Emil Bodnăraş was head of the Government's Special Intelligence Service. He orders an investigation of Foriş and keeps him under strict surveillance. A number of informants are planted in his entourage. Teohari Georgescu was Minister of the Interior. Both Bodnăraş and Teohari Georgescu were Dej henchmen. But Dej did not take action via either the Special Intelligence Service or the Minister of the Interior, both of which he regarded as still insecure. Foriş is arrested by a team of former Soviet spies led by Pantiuşa Bodnarenko, the head of the Administrative Department of the CC of the PCdR at that time, Dej's right-hand man. Foriş was kidnapped in broad daylight in the centre of Bucharest. The scene is reminiscent of a gangster feud. At noon of 9 June, Foriş disappears in the area near the university. His family raise the alarm. The next day, Ana Foriş, his mother, and Victoria Foriş, his wife, go to the police. "On 9 June Ştefan Foriş who lives with us in the same domicile in Bucharest, Pasagiul Victoria ... left home in the morning and did not return. He parted from our friend Mr Remus Koffler at 11 a.m. in Brătianu Square, saying he was going home. Since that time there has been no trace of him." The two worried women believe that because Foriş "was for a long time a member of the Communist Party for Romanian leadership he might have enemies in reactionary-fascist circles." We do not know whether they really believed that the Legionaries, Peasant Party members or Liberals were responsible for the kidnapping, or whether they were merely words to lower the guard of those who had in fact ordered the abduction. Were they deceiving themselves? Ultimately, Foriş could have been summoned by the police or the Party. He would not have hesitated to go. Why then did they prefer this risky and unusual way of going about things? The answer was so that they would leave no traces. Victoria Sîrbu did not discover the real fate of her husband until many years later, not until after the investigation and trial in which she was implicated alongside Pătrăşcanu, Koffler, Belu Zilber, Calmanovici et al., not until after she was released from prison in 1956. The PCR, like any body with clandestine reflexes, spread all kinds of stories about Foriş's fate: that he had been killed by reactionaries, a fascist gang or bandits; that he had been taken to the USSR; that he had run away from home because he was having an affair, etc. Not having been able to find out anything from the police, the two women look for him at Party headquarters. Here they come up against the same labyrinth of rumours, false explanations, shrugged shoulders, and doors slammed in their faces. No one knows anything, apart from that Foriş was not in the building. The following is from another memorandum they send to PCR leaders:

> "Comrades, in a discussion with Comrade Luca it has been brought to my attention (1) that Comrade Foriş is a traitor and there are proofs of this; (2) that the Party does not know where Comrade Foriş is and is not interested in his fate ... On my asking him about the proofs of his guilt, Comrade Luca told me that they do not concern me given that the Party established that he was a traitor as long ago as the arrests of 1939 ... The Central Committee tells me that it does not know where Comrade Foriş is and that he has fled from responsibility, and from the Soviet side it has been communicated to me that he was taken away for further investigations."[20]

The letter was drafted shortly before the PCR conference due to take place in October. Victoria Sîrbu-Foriş demands the organisation of an investigative commission. The members of the commission should be "comrades without connections to the conflicts in the old CC or from the Party during the period of the anti-Soviet war. ... Before this commission," Victoria Sîrbu-Foriş naïvely writes, "I shall disprove the accusations relating to falsification of the Party's history."

Herein lies the key to the whole affair. It is exactly what the leaders at the top of the PCdR do not want. They are all busy re-writing the past. Mystifications, lies and fictions form a layer over the recent past. It had only been a year since the Party was legalised. The eyewitnesses and participants were still living. Whoever managed to impose his own version of the Party's history would win power. Here, history is not an academic matter, for the university lecture hall, but one of life and death. It is an Orwellian situation. Whoever controls the past controls the future. Khrushchev will say the same thing in the 1950s. The hardest thing to foresee is the past. Writing what she did in her memorandum, Victoria Foriş condemned not only herself, but also, above all, Ştefan Foriş. Might she not have grasped what was at stake? Foriş had been sequestered precisely so that they could erase their tracks. He knew too much about the 'gang of conspirators'. He had to disappear so that he would not confess. Of course, it is unlikely that

---

[20] CC of the PCR Archive, Fund 95, Dossier 56, vol. 1, p. 22.

he would have written his memoirs or that in a Stalinist show trial he would have denounced his former comrades. Nevertheless, while still alive, he was a permanent danger, a witness who might talk. He might also have been politically rehabilitated by Moscow. In the period that followed the political situation was continually shifting. The Stalin-Tito conflict, the László Rajk and Traycho Kostov trials, the death of Stalin, Khrushchev's report of February 1956, and the Hungarian Revolution were all turning points at which a figure like Foriş could have caused a lot of unpleasantness for those in power. Of course, no one had any calendar of future events, but the rules of the game were no secret at the top of the PCdR. An inconvenient witness is better in the coffin than alive. And who could have been more inconvenient than the former Party boss? For the pretenders to power, Foriş was an enemy more despised, more dangerous than even the King or the leaders of the historical parties. The Kremlin, Red Army and KGB took care of 'that lot', those too big for the Party to swallow. Whatever was to be dealt with in-Party would be decided by a typical settling of scores. Foriş was not only an inconvenient witness but also a legitimate claimant to power. He was living proof that things had happened differently than in the official version. By his mere presence he proved that far from being an episode in the 'heroic struggle of the working class', his ousting had been one more episode in the Party's habitual and never-ending factional fighting. Alive, Foriş would have defended himself against the accusation of betrayal or being a Siguranţă informant. These were the self-seeking fabrications that provided the pretext for him being ousted. The sacking of Foriş was the result of a plot rather than a statutory decision taken by the Party or imposed by the Kremlin. Dej was a usurper. This is why he was the one most interested in Foriş's liquidation. As long as Foriş was alive, Dej was in an insecure position. What is in action here is the well-known mechanism of clandestine political sects, professional terrorists and gangsters. Only once Foriş had been silenced for good could history begin to be rewritten. Only then could the booty be shared out, meaning absolute power in Romania.

Foriş knew very well in what he was enmeshed. For him, the fatal game had commenced. He was initiated in the ways of the Comintern. He had long experience of clandestinity. He was no stranger to the secrets of the Moscow trials. A generation of communist leaders, some of them close acquaintances of Foriş, had been killed in the USSR. If fact, he had even benefitted from the empty space that had thus been created among the cadres. He knew that once you had lost power and fallen into disgrace, the countdown began. There was no need for a show trial like the ones held in Moscow in 1936-1938 in order for you to be liquidated.

On 7 April 1945, after a 10-day hunger strike, he draws up his will. He had been taken on 22 March, after the search of his house, described earlier. In the preamble, he writes, "because of my advancing years and the very harsh conditions of five years of clandestine life, I feel very frail. In the event of my death. ..." He was 45, but he knew what he knew. He did not believe that his ruined health would kill him. Anything could happen to him, at any moment. His intuition was precise, as destiny was to prove. He leaves his mother a gold pocket watch, "a memento of father," and some personal items. To an aunt he leaves the chain of the same watch. To Victoria Sîrbu he leaves his Romanian-language books, another watch, of no value, and a few photographs. To a cousin he leaves "clothes and items that can be used by her son Ştefan, who is ill." Remus Koffler was to receive all his German-language books, his alpaca cigarette holder and a photograph. There follows the political part of his testament:

"To the Party, I leave all the fundamental documents of the Central Committee that I drew up and those seized in December 1943. I leave behind me the honest toil and devotion of a quarter of a century, acknowledging the mistakes and weaknesses I committed during my work. To the Party, headed by the CC, I leave my unflinching faith that it will establish the Party-minded truth with regard to my labour as the head of the former Central Committee, that I preserved the Party organisation and held the Party flag high during the hardest conditions of the war and bloodthirsty Hitlerist terror. I die with the unflinching faith that our Party, headed by the CC, will, following the first great victories, such as the reintegration of northern Transylvania, the formation of a people's democratic government, and agricultural reform, lead in the vanguard of the free and democratic Romanian people. And after the final victory over the Hitlerist beast, it will be in the vanguard of the victorious struggle to liberate the working class and abolish the exploitation of man by his fellow man, creating a socialist Romania, advancing victoriously towards a communist society. Long live the Party with the Central Committee at its head. Long live the Union of Soviet

Socialist Republics. Long live Stalin. This is my last wish and my last desire. Bucharest, 7 April 1945. Ştefan Foriş."[21]

The text is dramatic and moving. The man was living a lie, a mystification. He had sold his soul to a cause devoid of all meaning. He did not want to relinquish the illusion. He was unable to do so. The hour of truth had not yet arrived for him. What meaning would his detention have had if everything had been nothing more than a wretched, blind struggle for survival between puppets that desired only to liquidate him? He was to be killed like a dog, and not even by the bourgeoisie or the police. He was to perish in a cellar. There was nothing grandiose about it, nothing of the revolutionary death he had imagined in 1917-1921 when he became a Bolshevik. It was sooner the finale of a feud between rival gangsters. For Foriş, those who wanted him dead represented the Party. And the Party was never wrong. He knows he is sentenced to death. He is certain of his own death. All that remains for him is that the truth will ultimately be reinstated.

He accepts his death docilely, the same as he had accepted his overthrow on 4 April. He submits with discipline to the Party's order that he must die. He does not resist in any way. He awaits his death as if it were his final duty to the Party. Not for one moment does he break out of the narrow circle of ideology, of blind obedience to Stalin and Bolshevism. He remains prisoner to a belief that he will not abandon even when it murders him. Foriş dies a steadfast believer in the cause. There is nothing of the heretic about him. He belonged to the same tradition as the Bolsheviks who died in front of the firing squads in the 1930s shouting, "Long live Stalin! Long live Lenin!" convinced that a mistake was being committed which the Party would later rectify. Or maybe they did not want to believe it, so that their whole life would not seem a meaningless waste to them. They refused to look the truth in the face. The truth was that they did not belong to a movement for world emancipation. The ideal of communism was a bluff. Everything was nothing more than blood, violence and suffering. They were prisoners of the utopia of proletarian revolution. For them the essential thing was to be in the Party, the vehicle of this utopia. Cast out of the Party, they would have been on the side of evil in history. They would have been déclassé. Even in death, with their eyes closed, they believed that they would be part

---

[21] CC of the PCR Archive, Fund 95, Dossier 56, vol. 2, pp. 29-31.

of the paradise they dreamed of, albeit only in the history books, because they did not believe in any other life after death. History had reserved for the Bolsheviks an unusual destiny, that of the founders of a 'classless society', where all men were equal. To achieve it they had the right to kill anyone that opposed them. They ended up killing each other. Foriș is no more than one case among all those enmeshed in this infernal machinery. His resignation and docility can be explained by his final hope that in the future, after his death, his name would be rehabilitated. That the Party would eventually analyse his situation and discover that he had not been an informer, that he had not betrayed the Party. Nothing inside him rebelled. He did not question in any way the right of someone to kill him because he had supposedly betrayed the Party or disagreed with it. He did not ask whether he ought to have first been put on trial. For that he would have had to have faith in 'bourgeois justice', in democracy, in the values of humanism. If he had believed in these, he would never have become a Bolshevik, a declared foe of the bourgeoisie. A propagator of hatred, he himself fell beneath the hatred of one more powerful, crueller, and more cunning. Foriș knew Dej hated him. But the Party was higher than his own destiny now that the end drew near. Not a heroic end, but one that was wretched, in the filthy underground. Destiny strides down the Kafkaesque corridor of the building where Foriș is a prisoner in a makeshift cell. At the door is an executioner, armed with a crowbar. He has come to kill him.

***

Between the arrest and the slaying of Ștefan Foriș a year elapses. The prisoner's situation remains unclear. He is a hostage whose fate has not yet been decided. From time to time various persons interrogate him: Teohari Georgescu, the Minister of the Interior and a member of the Secretariat of the PCR; Iosif Chișinevschi, a member of the Political Bureau; Emil Bodnăraș, the head of the Government's Intelligence Service; and Ana Pauker. But his main interrogator is Gheorghiu-Dej himself. None of the other communist leaders has access to Foriș unless accompanied by Gheorghiu-Dej. Foriș is kept for most of the time in the headquarters of the CC of the PCdR. The room in which he is held is near Gheorghiu-Dej's office. How strong Dej's fear of and obsession with his victim must have been! Dej obstinately insists on knowing that Foriș is close by, that he is under guard, and that no one else has access to him. It is in this building that he will be assassinated, after being held a prisoner for a year, in a room adjacent to Dej's office. Dej wanted to know his every move, to know above all that he was under lock and key. This was a mixture of care not to let a rival to his supremacy out of his sight and much resentment. Foriş's imprisonment in the headquarters of the PCR was a well-kept secret. Not all of the members of the Political Bureau knew of the presence of the prisoner in the building. The most they knew was that he had disappeared from home. Victoria Sîrbu and above all Foriş's mother could often be seen on the stairs of the building in Aleea Alexandru, demanding the release of the vanished husband, respectively son. No one knew where he was. There were only rumours and suspicions. It never entered any of their heads that he was right there, in the Party's headquarters, guarded by Pantiuşa Bodnarenko. He was not allowed to look out of the window, to speak, or to make a sound. He was not to let anyone sense his presence. Gheorghiu-Dej was deceiving all the others. Foriş was a vital capture in the struggle for supremacy. Moreover, his isolation was equivalent to his silence. Only Dej and his trusty henchmen would hear whatever he might say. Gheorghiu-Dej wanted what Foriş knew to remain buried. He would bury the secrets of the past together with the man who held them.

A year later, in a meeting of the Secretariat which, as usual, took place in the office of Ana Pauker, Gheorghiu-Dej broaches the question of the liquidation of Foriş. The others present – Teohari Georgescu, Vasil Luca, and Iosif Chişinevschi (who was not a member of the Secretariat) – are in agreement. There is one objection, on the part of Ana Pauker, who demands that Moscow should be consulted. Dej says this is not necessary. He is supported by Chişinevschi and Teohari Georgescu, who are convinced that their arrest in April 1940 was the result of betrayal by Foriş. Or else this is what they wanted to believe. Pauker and Luca finally concede. Dej personally gives Pantiuşa Bodnarenko the order to liquidate Foriş. The scene perfectly recalls the one described by Dostoevsky in *The Demons*. Since the days at Doftana, Bodnarenko had been the man to do all the dirty work.

"Gh. Stoica: Who assigned you the task to liquidate him in the first place? Comrade Gh. Pintilie [Pantiuşa Bodnarenko]: Firstly Ghiţă then Teohari. Mostly I was scared because there was no way I could do it.

After a while he asked me: Are you done? I told him no. Two to three weeks after he told me, he asked me again if I was done ... I told Ghiță and he says: Why are you so stupid? I asked his advice. He told me: Let me give you some advice. What, haven't you got a brain? And so I found the solution and I told Ghiță I was done. And he congratulated me. He told me: Bravo, a good job it's done. Fuck him! ... He asked me once again: Hey, are you done? ... A good job that you and we are done [with him]. That's what Ana [Pauker] told me. I tell you honestly that I did it out of conviction."[22]

No minutes of the sessions of the Secretariat were kept. Accomplices to murder, they were careful not to leave any traces. We do not even know the date of the execution. What we do know is that Dej impatiently pressed Bodnarenko to carry out the order. The summer of 1946 was a complicated time. A drought scorched the Romanian plains. On 1 June, the Antonescu group were executed at Jilava Prison following a trial with a great many complications. There were complications in Transylvania. After northern Transylvania was returned to Romania, there were clashes between ethnic Hungarians and Romanians in Cluj. Lucrețiu Pătrășcanu tours a number of cities, trying to calm spirits. He gives a speech in Cluj against revisionism and chauvinism. He is accused of being a nationalist by Gheorghiu-Dej and Ana Pauker. It is demanded that he deliver a self-criticism in public, after a stormy session of the Political Bureau. Pătrășcanu refuses. In August, a delegation travels to Paris for the Peace Conference. Among the delegates are Gheorghiu-Dej and Pătrășcanu. When was Foriș murdered? Probably just before the departure of the delegation from Bucharest and after Pătrășcanu's speech in Cluj. Dej could not predict how the Paris Peace Conference would turn out. He was fearful that the Allies might reach an agreement over his head and impose a different political solution, one unfavourable to him. When a change of political situation is in the offing, it is best to kill your political adversaries. Such was Gheorghiu-Dej's rudimentary philosophy. He applied the rule a number of times. In 1954 he did the same to Pătrășcanu. It was in this way that he parried the eventuality of his replacement when the situation in Moscow was uncertain and his

---

[22] In Dan Cătănuș, Ioan Chiper, *Cazul Foriș. Lupta pentru putere în PCR de la Gheorghiu-Dej la Ceaușescu*, Editura Vremea: Bucharest, 1999, pp. 265-266.

throne was teetering. It was the same reflex that led Dej to order Foriş's liquidation before his departure to Paris. The pretext Dej uses in order to press Bodnarenko to carry out the death sentence is an imminent inspection of Party headquarters by the Allied Control Commission. It was rumoured that they would be checking for hidden caches of weapons and prisoners. The headquarters had to be 'clean' before the arrival of the commission. Weapons were moved to another building. Because a pistol would make too much noise, Pantiuşa Bodnarenko decided to kill Foriş using a crowbar. On 4 April 1944 he had been carrying a hammer under his coat, in the event that Foriş put up resistance. In 1968, Bodnarenko, now calling himself General Gheorghe Pintilie, is interviewed by the commission set up to investigate the disappearance of Foriş. Moscu Cohn (now calling himself Gheorghe Stoica, a Party member since 1921, knowledgeable about the underbelly of communist history) asks him,

"Who executed him? Comrade Gh. Pintilie: My driver hit him over the head once. Comrade Gh. Stoica: Did he cry out? Comrade Gh. Pintilie: No. Comrade Gr. Răduică: The driver climbed onto a chair because Foriş was tall and he couldn't reach. That's how he killed him. Comrade Gh. Stoica: Where was the driver from? Comrade Gh. Pintilie: From the Soviet Union. Let me tell you how it was: I dug the grave. I took care of everything personally. I didn't want anyone else getting mixed up in it. I was afraid in case Foriş's name got out. ... Comrade Gh. Stoica: After you killed him, did you place a layer of concrete? Comrade Gh. Pintilie: We laid earth, water, left it two to three days until it settled and poured in more water and the *only concern* [emphasis in the original] was for the earth to settle. The floor was made of unpainted planks and we wanted to paint them, but paint was not to be had, so we left them as they were. We fetched the water from the sink. ... Comrade Gr. Răduică: Once he was struck did he fall into the grave? Comrade Gh. Pintilie: The grave was made a week earlier. Another two individuals were placed in the grave. ... When Comrade Răduică asked Bulgaru [Foriş's 'gaoler' – *author's note*]: Tell me, when you opened the door didn't you see the bare earth? Bulgaru said no, it was dark. He came to the door. I wouldn't let him enter because there were another three corpses that had been executed in the same way. Comrade V. Patilineţ: Over how long a time were they killed? Comrade: Gh. Pintilie: Over a week. The first was

Foriş, then Pîrgaru [Ion Pîrgaru, a former member of the CC of the PCdR in the mid-1930s, a Siguranţă informer – *author's note*] and then the German [?]. The two of us killed all three. They were laid one on top of another in the grave. We worked on digging the grave only at night ... Comrade Guină: A year later they were not putrefying, because it would have stunk. Comrade V. Pintilineţ: If the soil is wet, the putrefaction is faster. Comrade Gh. Pintilie: We put earth in the hole and let it settle. It didn't smell from one day to the next. It was less than four metres deep. Comrade V. Pintilineţ: What do you think: might the driver [Dumitru Neciu] have said anything? Comrade Gh. Pintilie: Even if I go to the gallows this very day, let him live. But he couldn't say anything ... He was a Soviet citizen and he was a Soviet prisoner here. He left the country... He stayed another week and then he left ... He's living there now. He's probably still a driver. He must be 40 or 45. He left here a trustworthy man, decorated with a medal ... He was a good lad."[23]

Hélène Carrère d'Encausse differentiates between four types of murder in the 'tenebrous history of Bolshevism.[24] 1) The fratricidal murder, aimed at eliminating anyone who stood in the way of Stalin's absolute power; 2) the show murder, the rationalisation of Soviet mass extermination, judicial murder following show trials; 3) social murder, the killing of social categories under the pretext of social engineering – the peasants, Jews, the bourgeoisie, intellectuals, etc.; 4) the export murder, the killing of foreigners implicated in Kremlin activities. The killing of Foriş falls under the first category. Foriş was a militant communist, a legitimate leader, a member of the Party since 1921, with long experience in the clandestine movement, appointed General Secretary by the Comintern in 1940. He was not killed because he was an intellectual or ethnic Hungarian (category 3). He was not killed as part of a 'show trial' – unlike László Rajk, Traycho Kostov and Rudolf Slansky – mounted for propaganda purposes (category 2). Export murder (category 4) was the strict monopoly of Moscow. Bucharest was nothing more than a peripheral branch of the Bolshevik Revolution. With the death of Foriş, many tracks could be erased. History could be rewritten. Dej already harboured a significant dose of hatred and resentment. He kills

---

[23] Dan Cătănuş, Ioan Chiper, *op. cit.*, pp. 336-338.
[24] Hélène Carrère d'Encausse, *Blestemul ruşilor. Eseu despre asasinatul politic.* Editura Polirom: Jassy, 2000, pp. 203-209.

Foriş above all so that he can dispose of a rival who stands in his way, so that he can move closer to the absolute power he is dreaming of. The murder of Foriş, hit over the head with a crowbar, is reminiscent of a killing carried out inside a prison, in the showers, a settling of accounts between convicts. Gheorghiu-Dej had witnessed such killings in the prisons through which he passed, and perhaps he even ordered some of them himself. With Foriş he repeated the example.

XVI
Koffler, with a 'K' as in Kafka

Remus Koffler is arrested on 15 December 1949 in the house where he has been hiding, located at No. 88 Clucerului Street in Bucharest, near the Triumphal Arch. After an investigation lasting 52 months, he is shot. Who is he? History has not recorded much about him, apart from that he was implicated in a political trial. No one really understood why. What was the crime he had to atone for? Why was he sentenced to death and executed? Koffler had not vied with Gheorghiu-Dej for leadership of the PCdR, unlike Foriş and Pătrăşcanu. He had not been in conflict with Dej, unlike Vasile Luca. He did not have the notoriety of Ana Pauker, whom Dej had likewise wished dead, but who had been saved by the efforts of Molotov. Koffler was a technocrat, an administrator, not a political leader. He had never had the ambition to lead or to occupy a higher position. Nevertheless, Dej decided that he should be sentenced to death. Why? Let us essay a few explanations for this murderous impulse against such an obscure figure in the apparatus.

Firstly, Koffler was Foriş's closest collaborator. After he ordered that the former General Secretary of the PCdR be killed, in the summer of 1946, Gheorghiu-Dej needed to legitimise his crime urgently. He demanded that evidence of Foriş's betrayal should be sought in the archives of the Siguranţă. Former commissars and participants in clandestine communist life were interrogated – anyone who might be able to provide information. Nothing to compromise Foriş was found. The accusation that he had been a Siguranţă agent had been a cover. Dej needed to justify himself, to prove he had been right to order the killing of the former head of the PCdR. Dej had in fact usurped Foriş. Even among members of a fraternity of this kind, the murder had to be covered up. A trial in which the accused confess to betrayal, collaboration with the Siguranţă, seemed a safe bet, an alibi for the murder committed. And so it was that Remus Koffler, a nondescript, anonymous figure, was arrested and indicted in a case that had been prepared against another of Dej's rivals, Lucreţiu Pătrăşcanu. His offence: he had been among Foriş's immediate circle and was thus his accomplice. Koffler's murder would also incriminate Foriş. The accusations therefore had to be similar: betrayal and collaboration with the Siguranţă. Petru Groza was arrested in December 1943. The report of the General

Department of Police notes that he had met a certain 'Sergiu' in a safe house, an important person, the operative observes, who was responsible for the financial commission of the PCdR. 'Sergiu' was Koffler's code name. Groza declared under interrogation that he had refused to take part in any important discussion because he was suspicious of his interlocutor (i.e. a communist chief) and above all because he had an unpleasant impression of the attitude of 'Sergiu', who "imperiously demanded, and with a superior tone of voice, that he commence activity within the Patriotic Union."[1]

Two years later, the same Petru Groza, now head of the Soviet-controlled government, writes in his memoirs[2] that he realised that the "file was a stitch up. It smelled like a provocation from a mile off. And, as I have said before, my sense of smell as a politician never fails." Groza, who was close to the communists, was echoing the suspicions regarding Foriş and Koffler that were harboured at the highest level of the PCdR. Koffler was an initiate in the secrets of the 'factional fighting' of 1940-1944. Gheorghiu-Dej wanted to impose his own version of this conflict that had eaten away at the PCdR. Koffler was an extremely inconvenient witness. History is written by the victors, as is well-known. The dead write no memoirs. They tell no tales. They do not contest the official version of events. Koffler had to die because he knew far too much about who had done what, about where each communist agitator had been at the time, about when one event or another had taken place. The haste with which the beneficiaries of the fall of the Antonescu regime doctored their autobiographies was connected to the decisive problem of power and the role each was about to play. The conclusion: Koffler had to be killed. After Foriş, Koffler was the most knowledgeable of the secrets of the underground in the 1940s: the connections with those in the prisons and camps, Siguranţă informers, behind the scenes manoeuvres, the 'heroism' of each individual communist, factional struggles.

In the third place, in his capacity as Head of the CCF (Central Financial Commission), Koffler knew where the Party's funds came from, by which channels, how much had been donated, and by whom money had been spent. On his list were the names of not only Ştefan Foriş, but also Gheorghiu-Dej himself, Emil Bodnăraş, Teohari Georgescu, Iosif Chişinevschi, Pantiuşa

---

[1] CC Archive of the PCR, Fund 1, Dossier 340, p. 81.

[2] Dr Petru Groza, *În umbra celulei. Malmaison 1943-1944 Iarna*, Editura Cartea rusă: Bucharest, 1945, p. 225.

Bodnarenko, Miron Constantinescu, Ion Vincze, Alexandru Sencovici, from the prisons, and Iosif Rangheț, Ion Gheorghe Maurer, Constantin Pîrvulescu et al. from outside prison. All of them received money and assistance of various kinds from Koffler between 1940 and 1944. With so many powerful men desirous to see him dead, disappeared, Koffler was a condemned man. Nor was his profile as a communist typical. An attack against Foriș coming from the faction led by Petre Gheorghe describes Koffler as follows:

"Conrad [one of Koffler's pseudonyms – *author's note*] a capitalist Jew who came from Germany after Hitler was enthroned and who joined our party through no one knows whom. Foriș set him to work on a series of tasks close to himself. Together with Foriș he wrote almost all the CC documents. Although he did not engage in lowly work in any of our organisations, he knows through Foriș very many activists in Ilfov. He gives Foriș larges sums of money of dubious origin (not even he knows where it is from). Although a Jew, he nevertheless has brothers in the Siguranță. He lives with a relative (probably a Gestapo agent)."[3]

This figure in the immediate vicinity of the gang leader arouses even stronger resentments than this. The General Secretary, it is to be supposed, (still) emanates the aura of the magical powers conferred upon him by the gods (read the Comintern) at his investiture. Koffler, the adviser from the shadows, the favourite, is despised. In the fourth place, Gheorghiu-Dej was also looking for revenge. He has read all the written statements from the interrogation. He scribbles notes in the margins; he orders what questions should be asked and what methods applied. Moreover, on a weekly basis he summons Iosif Chișinevschi, Teohari Georgescu (up until 1952), Alexandru Drăghici, and Pantiușa Bodnarenko, in order to analyse the progress of the investigation. The harsh treatment to which Koffler was subjected was the result of a decision taken by Gheorghiu-Dej personally. One investigator, Mircea Anghel, interviewed in 1967 by a commission of inquiry, says in his declaration: "Likewise, I saw when Micle [a Securitate interrogator – *author's note*] ripped out more than a third of Koffler's white hair, starting from above his ear."[4] Under arrest, Koffler is subjected to torture, moral

---

[3] Dan Cătănuș, Ioan Chiper, *op. cit.*, p. 227.
[4] SRI Archive, Dossier 40002, vol. 203, p. 1.

pressure and blackmail. He has a heart attack and is taken to the Victor Babeş Hospital for treatment. Back under arrest, he is beaten severely at the orders of Interior Minister Alexandru Drăghici. The interrogator requests the minister's permission, after receiving indications from Soviet advisers, to apply harsh methods. The orders for Koffler's torture come directly from the minister, who reports to, and receives instructions from, Dej. Koffler is suspected of losing his mind and is diagnosed with extreme schizophrenia. Some physicians believe he is faking. If so, then it means he is fighting to get out of interrogation. He is trying not to incriminate others by giving declarations under torture. Pătrăşcanu, too, attempted to commit suicide, with the same intention. To other doctors, Koffler really is ill, which means that he has lost his mind under torture. He did not accept any of the prosecutors' accusations. The lengthy interrogation to which he was subjected by the president of the court paints the picture of a tenacious struggle. Koffler did not give in and continued to declare himself innocent. This stubbornness determined Dej to lump him together with another death already decided, that of Pătrăşcanu. Belu Zilber won his life by services to his accusers. The crimes of which Koffler was accused did not mean an automatic death sentence, even by the standards of the show trials of post-war Eastern Europe. His killing was an act of cruelty. It was thus that he paid for the fact that he had been Foriş's second-in-command, and he had to provide indirect proof of the latter's guilt. Likewise, he died because he knew too much. Behind this sentence and the execution stand the fear of those in power towards one of their own, a witness of the turpitude, intrigues and promiscuity of the underground world.

> "I was born in Bucharest in 1902. My father was a merchant, then a manufacturer and landlord, who lost his fortune in 1926. His father had been a merchant in Galatzi. Father died in 1941. My mother, née Blatt, was the daughter of a merchant. My social origins are therefore bourgeois."[5]

Like Kafka, Koffler is obsessed with the father figure, "an authoritarian, tyrannical man. The quarrels between my parents left tragic scars. My father was a spender. He had made a fortune during the German occupation, selling liquor *en gros* to the occupier. Mother died in 1920." Remus Koffler

---

[5] SRI Archive, Dossier 40002, vol. 45, p. 34.

was a Christianised Jew. He studied at the local Catholic school, then at the Evangelical school. He took courses at the Matei Bassarab Lycée. He passed his Baccalaureat in Zurich in 1920, as we discover in his autobiography, written in January 1950, while under arrest by the Securitate. He confesses that even in primary school he had a strong interest in politics. During the First World War he was on the side of Germany, "influenced," writes Koffler, "by my father. Towards the end of the German occupation I became a Zionist. In 1919, I read Marx, the *Communist Manifesto*, and in Paris I read *The Victory of Bolshevism* by Trotsky. When I arrived in Zurich, in 1919, I declared myself a communist."

In 1920, he enrolled in the Socialist Party in Bucharest. He then goes to Berlin to study.

> "I began to attend communist meetings and to take part in demonstrations. In this way, I was at the demonstration of 7 November ... I was with student groups in the Lustgarten, on the way to the Friedrichsfelde Cemetery, to the graves of Karl Liebknecht and Rosa Luxemburg ... I demonstrated for communism and for the USSR."

He marries and has a daughter, born in 1925. Also in 1925, he returns to Romania, at the summons of his father, without having completed his studies. His father is in financial difficulties and goes bankrupt. In Bucharest, Koffler meets Timotei Marin, whom he conceals after his escape from the trap set by the Siguranţă for him, Pavel Tkachenko, Boris Ştefanov and Elek Köblős on 15 August 1926. He also meets Lucreţiu Pătrăşcanu. Koffler *fils* runs a company until 1927, when he again goes to Germany. He is active in the communist movement, adopting the name Conrad, by which he is known in the clandestine networks. Berlin is a major and turbulent communist centre. It is also a nexus for all the Comintern networks throughout Europe. Moreover, the political crisis of the Weimar Republic, combined with the economic crisis, creates a very fluid medium. Koffler is mixed up in demonstrations, street protests and campaigns. In 1930, he joins the German Communist Party. In 1932, again summoned home by his father, he returns to Bucharest, without completing his studies. He works in his father's firm, then leaves, when father and son fall out. For a time he supports himself by giving private German lessons. Then he takes a job as a functionary. "Between 1932 and 1935, we lived in cramped conditions in a single room with the child, and we took our meals with my parents-in-law and brothers-in-law." In the bedsit he rented on Burghele Street, communist meetings organised by Lucrețiu Pătrășcanu are held. He occasionally acts as a courier to Prague, where the PCdR has its Political Office. He works with Ana Pauker, Nicolae Goldberger and Șmil Marcovici, members of the PCdR Secretariat. He is part of the Agitprop section run at the time by Marcel Pauker. He works in the editorial offices of the clandestine communist gazette *Scînteia*, for which he frequently writes articles. He works with Solomon Schein, Ion Popescu-Puțuri, Aurel Rotemberg (Ștefan Voicu). The central event of this period is the arrest in June 1935 of three members of the Secretariat – Ana Pauker, Șmil Marcovici and Dimităr Ganev – denounced by a fourth member, Ion Zelea Pîrgaru, with whom Koffler was in contact. In 1936, Nicolae Goldberger and Constantin Pîrvulescu are arrested. Again, they are in contact with Koffler. From the autumn of 1936, he organises the CCF, the central financial commission of the PCdR. His role was to raise funds. He holds this position until September 1944. From 1941, he is a Ștefan Foriș's closest aide. From December 1942, he is responsible for the establishment of the Patriots Union, a communist organisation camouflaged by the presence of a few left-wing intellectuals. From 1943, he is responsible for the publication of the *România liberă* (*Free Romania*) newspaper. In September 1944, he is dismissed from the position of head of the CCF. In 1949, he is arrested. In brief, these are the data that make up the biography of Remus Koffler. He is made to write them all down after his arrest on 15 September 1949. The aim of the investigator is to obtain a complete confession. A man of the underground, Koffler assumes that they know everything about him; that even the most intimate of details are already on file. Koffler's autobiography is a mixture of psychoanalysis and Marxism. It is a testament of cadre rigours, a confession of libido and class struggle. In 47 typewritten pages we discover, among other things: "From the age of 14 I practised onanism." Koffler's first sexual encounter took place in a Viennese brothel, "with a negative result," he adds. In Berlin, in September 1920,

> "I made the acquaintance of a girl whom I took home, but with whom I was impotent, which greatly discouraged me. Nevertheless, I contracted syphilis from this girl. ... Eight years later the illness flared up again and I took a fresh course of treatment until 1931, but afterwards I did not go

back to the hospital for a check-up, as I was preoccupied once more with another woman. Because of my burdened conscience as a result of my youthful negligence, I took a massive dose of penicillin in 1948."

Koffler descends into the underworld. He debases himself. He presents himself as a sinner. If the Party has expelled him, then he is no longer a human being. He depicts himself as a vile creature. This is a way of showing the interrogators he is being honest. The more loathsome is the deed under discussion, the greater the sincerity of the man under interrogation appears to be. If he had claimed to have led an unblemished life, he would be accused of lying. The description of his own debasement is the central theme of his autobiography. He confesses,

"In 1926 ... my former wife was ill, having had an operation on her leg. We were sleeping in the same bed with my sister-in-law and I attempted intimate relations with her, without any result, as she wanted to preserve her virginity. My sister-in-law was at the time engaged to her present husband, engineer Alfred Löbel ... I had no scruples or remorse for this relationship."

And that was nothing:

"My ex-wife told me that in Germany she had had an intimate relationship with the husband of the girlfriend with whom she was staying. Rather than jealousy, it aroused in me sexual satisfaction and I was constantly pursued by the thought of enacting in reality the scene I dreamed of while practising onanism, i.e. to witness a sexual act between my former wife and another man ... My wife, probably happy that the sexual bond between us was strengthened, accepted to play this game and tried to bring it about. This happened in 1933-1934, four times, with a barber. I watched without the man's knowledge from behind the door or a wall hanging, practising onanism and after his departure had normal sexual relations with my wife of the time. After the barber there was a mechanic from the block of flats where my father lived, who came just once, and then engineer R. Löbel, the brother of her sister's husband, once, in total six or seven times. I realise that this bestial behaviour of mine proved a total lack of conscience and scruples, as well as discipline.

By my behaviour I caused my former wife to follow the path of vice, I turned her away from the concerns of our child's education, and I myself, by my whole attitude, descended into the filthiest latrine imaginable."[6] Lower than this is probably not possible. The author himself is forced to admit it in his autobiography. Confessing to abjections of this kind, Koffler wanted to show the interrogators that he had nothing to hide, not even the most intimate of details. This means that in his political confession he was equally sincere. For this reason he lays it on thick. He creates for himself the image of a monster. Since he has been expelled from the PMR, it means he is no longer a human being. The Party/God cannot be deceived. Its priests are infallible; they must be served. When they demand sacrifices of you, it is an honour that they have chosen you. Is Koffler still a moral being when he writes such things? What value can we place on these confessions? His intimate life reveals a deviant.

There are, however, heroic episodes in the youth of every revolutionary: "So, when my father found out that I had joined the Party, he beat me and took away my Party card, which I found again after his death. Likewise, he beat me for reading *Socialistul* (*The Socialist*) in front of him." The father, a businessman, a merchant, is unhappy with this recalcitrant child, this failure swept up by Bolshevism. He would have liked him to take over his businesses, to have a career in commerce, to make money. To be a bourgeois. Instead, his son is an extremist. He lives clandestinely. He frequents highly dubious individuals.

With regard to money the same as to sexual relations, Koffler is a deviant. He is dishonest. He pilfers. He embezzles millions of lei from the firm he works for in the 1930s. He is a big spender, and here he takes after his father. He procures the sums he needs, without too much concern for the means. During the war he is a currency speculator. He tries various moneymaking schemes, like a small-time capitalist. Outside 'proletarian morality', he is attracted to profit, as well as to women. "I saw no contradiction between the communist principles I made a show of and level that would have made me an exploiter." And under this financial heading, too, his autobiography is a series of grave sins, which he hastens to confess. How much he was exaggerating or lying and how much truth there is in what he writes is impossible to establish today. Is he not wearing his usual masks? Is he

---

[6] *Idem*, p. 46.

not playing one of his countless roles? He knows that under arrest by the Securitate it is demanded that he show himself to be a villain, to confess to cardinal sins. And this is what he does. Why not? It is yet another role he has to play. It is part of the canon of clandestine life, of the oath of loyalty made on joining the Party. If the Party demands that you declare yourself guilty, you do so. If the Party has arrested you, it means you are guilty. You must then find in your own past the evils you have done, your betrayals, lapses, vacillations. Remus Koffler blends together in his autobiography sexual squalor with shady financial dealings. He will, of course, also add political errors. As far back as when he was in Berlin, while he was the cashier of an association that raised funds for victims of the famine in Russia in 1922, he pilfered a part of the money, then covered the shortfall, engaging in currency speculation during hyperinflation. "I committed one of the basest of deeds,"[7] he writes.

He has a special inclination for being a cashier, a bookkeeper, for having other people's money at his disposal. He inspires trust; he seems sober, loyal, correct. His career as a crook continues unhindered. He is never caught by the business owners he steals from or detected by the Siguranța as being a dangerous conspirator. His dissimulation, his skill at burying his pilfering in the paperwork, is identical with his ability to blend in anonymously in politics. He knows how to pass unobserved, as a nondescript person.

> "[T]he accountant for Apometru [a company at which Koffler worked – *author's note*] Ulrich Goldenberg suggested to me that we withdrew money from the company's funds by means of creative accounting... I had the weakness to accept not only a grave deviation from proletarian morals, but also I thereby endangered my work for the Party. Moreover, I displayed the mentality of a blackmailer, by the fact that I supposed that nothing would happen to me because I knew the company's secrets ... I spent the embezzled money on excursions, gifts and other personal expenses."[8]

Koffler, although a "communist, an austere, anti-bourgeois man," plays roulette at the casino in Sinaia. He is a regular customer there after 1937. It is another role aimed to allay Siguranța suspicions. Would "Auntie

---

[7] *Idem*, p. 39.

[8] *Idem*, p. 55.

Varvara" have suspected an ambiguous character of no definite trade, like so many in the casinos, of being in fact a communist? No. Nevertheless, it is not a disguise; it is not camouflage. Koffler was a passionate gambler and spender. He liked to test his luck. He enjoyed the thrill, the atmosphere, the excitement. He had also joined the Bolshevik movement from a spirit of adventure, as he once confessed. Revolution, conspiracy, secrecy, risk, the forbidden excited him. At the casino he gambled money he had made from currency speculation or embezzled from Apometru, as well as funds collected for the Party. A lot of money passed through his hands and he no longer knew where it all came from. He kept only a rough record of it. After 1940, because of his spendthrift nature, shortfalls in the Party treasury occur. Given the special conditions under which clandestine accounts are kept, he is not inspected. It is exactly the environment in which Koffler can operate unhindered. Koffler is not, however, an incorrigible embezzler. He often replaces the money, when he makes earnings from his businesses. He provides money from his own pocket for Party emergencies in various situations. He gives personal loans to some of the PCdR Party leaders, who do not provide him with a receipt. Often this money is not intended for Party purposes, but for private reasons. The beneficiaries are Béla Breiner, Ștefan Foriș, Teohari Georgescu, Iosif Chișinevschi, and others. The PCdR leaders live beyond their means, beyond their incomes, when they have an income. They have a pronounced taste for comfort. Koffler is called upon whenever such needs arise. Safe houses, motor cars, furniture, holidays. "In 1938, Foriș asked me to procure for him from a man in the CCF some money to rent a house where his aunt was going to move, and where he was going to stay, to the sum of 25,000 or 30,000 lei. I gave him the sum from my own money, without telling him where it was from. He asked for money again in 1939 when he was on holiday with Tassia Petrovna in Bușteni ..."[9] Such requests were not few.

Koffler was a spender, and he was always mixed up in some stormy love affair or other. Let us say that he was a tall, handsome man, with grey hair even in his youth. He dressed well. He was polite, charming, a seducer. He liked to frequent places of privilege, fine restaurants and hotels. He had a dual image. He was the perfectly placed man. A successful man, even. He had the appearance of a businessman, rather provincial, mysterious, of indefinite profession. No one really knew what it was that he did. In

---

[9] *Idem*, p. 53.

the mid-1930s, his standard of living improved. He bought a house and employed a maid. Koffler was always to be seen in the company of elegant, coquettish women. Not always the same ones. He liked sophisticated women. It was hard to suppose that such a person could lead a double life, that he was a conspirator, that he dealt in something other than making money and courting women. Like K the land surveyor,[10] he seemed to be a middle-ranking functionary. He spoke little; he was taciturn, reticent in his relations with others. He did not get mixed up in arguments; he did not display his own opinions. If you were not specifically watching him, he did nothing to attract your attention in any way. He had a bourgeois air. You might perhaps guess his Jewish origins. There was nothing excessive or eccentric about him. He adapted easily to the environment in which he was living. The Siguranță had in fact never known what it was he did, or that he was a communist, let alone the position he really held. This was very strange, because Koffler had for many years been in contact with all the important leaders of the PCdR: Pătrășcanu, Foriș, Pauker, Breiner, Maurer, Birtaș, Pîrvulescu, Rangheț. All of them were under close surveillance by the Siguranță, yet Koffler never appeared suspicious to the secret police or caused them to think he was anything other than a chance acquaintance. Their reports do not mention him. Moreover, in 1943 he was even arrested by the Siguranță. Lili Weigl was arrested and in her handbag was discovered a report of the CC of the PCdR. Koffler was taken to the police station. He got away with it by claiming he was the lady's lover – which was true – and in no way mixed up in subversive activities. A search is conducted: nothing is found on his person or in his house. The next day he is released. This is the worst that ever happens to him. Koffler is a shadow; he is elusive. His talent for disguise and dissimulation, for playing different roles, was real. He was able spontaneously to become a double. He blends perfectly into the background. Koffler is a chameleon. He gives the impression of an ordinary, nondescript person. But he leads a double life. He is nonetheless one of the leaders of the PCdR. He collects millions of lei for the Party every month. He organises the sending of aid to communist prisoners via the Red Cross. The collection of these funds places him in contact with many persons, in difficult wartime conditions. Koffler works in exposed conditions, without rousing the suspicions of the Siguranță. He manages perfectly to mask his real occupation from their eyes. He is a master of conspiracy and disguise.

---

[10] I.e. the protagonist of *The Castle* by Franz Kafka. – *Translator's note.*

The politics of the underground, besides being dangerous and without horizons, is also very costly. Money has to be found to rent and furnish houses. Lawyers fees have to be paid, and not the cheapest lawyers either. Paper has to be bought and printers paid. Propaganda materials have to be distributed. Magistrates, policemen, secret service agents and functionaries have to be bribed. Papers have to be forged, usually via the criminal underworld. Food, clothing and money have to be provided to the families of activists in prison. Wages have to be paid to those strange persons willing to live incognito. Where does all this money come from? A pertinent question for any political sect. It comes from Moscow. The Comintern covers the expenses of its vast clandestine network. The financing of the communist parties, all of them, in fact, sections of the Comintern, had two phases. The first, when Lenin and Trotsky conducted a policy of exporting revolution. "Moscow squandered millions of gold roubles, dollars, pounds, marks, crowns, etc., all obtained through sale of the Tsar's gold reserves or ecclesiastical treasure ... The emissaries of the Comintern travelled throughout Europe and other parts of the world with suitcases crammed with hard currency and various valuable objects."[11] One example: Lenin writes to his emissary in Stockholm, Angelica Balabanoff:

> "Dear Comrade ... don't mind the cost. Spend millions, tens of millions if need be. We have money galore at our disposal. I understand from your letters that some of our couriers have not been delivering the papers on time. Please send me their names: these saboteurs must be shot."[12]

Balabanoff recalls how "large sums of money begin to arrive ... most of it ... to pay our agents who were creating 'Bolshevik' movements and newspapers all over the world."[13] Lenin was under the illusion that the scenario of the Petersburg Bolshevik putsch (a small but disciplined detachment, supported by massive foreign funds, German in this case) could be repeated. He believed that unless another takeover of power by the extreme Left occurred somewhere else in Europe, the regime he presided over would be destroyed. Whence his appeals of this kind – for the expenditure of huge

[11] Dmitri Volkogonov, *Lenin, o nouă biografie*, 1996, pp. 426-28.

[12] Angelica Balabanoff, *My Life as a Rebel*, Indiana UP: Bloomington and London, 1973, p. 175.

[13] *Idem*, p. 176.

sums of money, for the financing of pro-Bolshevik groups in other countries. "Russia was writhing in the claws of a civil war, of disease and hunger, but millions of gold roubles were being swallowed up by the shifting sands of the world revolution."[14] Once Stalin succeeds Lenin, the Kremlin moves to a policy of 'socialism in a single country'. The usefulness and value of the communist parties abroad is reduced, and so is the interest in exporting the Revolution. As a consequence, the financial resources allocated to these Parties decreases, without disappearing, however. "The expenditure of the Comintern was supervised somewhat more severely in Stalin's time, the ends being better defined. ... When Georgi Dimitrov ... wished to finalise the budget, he had to take it before Stalin, who entertained no great illusions with regard to the Comintern, and so he offered him only enough money to keep it afloat."[15] The communist parties were urged to support themselves from their own means.

For this reason, in 1936, the PCdR set up a Financial Commission, attached to the Central Committee and run by Remus Koffler. The other members were Emil Calmanovici and Jacques Berman. Its role was to supply the Party apparatus with funds. The Third International, the financer of Romanian communist operations, was at that time drastically reducing the sums it allocated. Stalin saw the Comintern was an unnecessary appendage, a hotbed of spies and deviationists. The PCdR was completely unimportant. An insignificant party, a handful of men who had been frittering away funds for almost two decades, without producing any results. The PCdR was not part of Moscow's plans to the same extent as the French or Spanish Communist Parties were, for example.

The PCdR continued to make repeated requests for funds, and the Comintern, within certain limits, to deliver them. Another matter supervenes: at the end of the 1930s, at the same time as Germany's expansion, the old channels of communication between Bucharest and Moscow are interrupted. In 1938, Austria and then Czechoslovakia are occupied. A number of the routes for couriers, money and correspondence pass through Prague and Vienna. In 1940, France is occupied, and the same situation occurs. The Moscow-Paris-Bucharest route is severed. Paris was a major junction for the Comintern, as well as for the PCdR. In the 1920s and 1930s, the PCdR had a representative in Paris who looked after its affairs. In the 1920s the

---

[14] Dmitri Volkogonov, *op. cit.*, p. 431.
[15] *Idem*, p. 435.

task was performed by Alecu Constantinescu. From the end of the 1930s, until his arrest by the Gestapo, the representative was Gheorghe Vasilichi. The Varna-Odessa route through Bulgaria and the Istanbul route were impracticable and dangerous. The police in Bulgaria and Turkey frequently intercepted consignments. The legislation in the two countries also handed down very severe punishments to those caught. The least practicable route, however, was that over the Dniester. The Siguranță, gendarmes, and border guard had managed to close this corridor. There were few other places from where it was possible to cross into and from the USSR. In 20 years, there had been thousands of interceptions of correspondence, couriers, agents, money, arms, explosives, and propaganda literature.

The sums sent by Moscow dwindled, especially in 1936, when the Great Terror was unleashed, and Stalin's interest in the Comintern abruptly decreased, likewise the Comintern's interest in the PCdR. The sums were at the lowermost limit required for the survival of ongoing activity. Even so, receipt of these small sums was problematic. The sums received within Romania as members' dues were tiny. In the first six months of 1939, only 50,000 lei was raised in this way.[16] In the same year, according to a Comintern report, the PCdR had only 26 paid activists. Béla Breiner in Bucharest and Gheorghe Vasilichi in Paris assailed Moscow with alarming reports in January and February 1939. "If the financial situation does not improve, then neither will the Party's work improve," Breiner writes to Boris Ștefanov, who in his turn writes to Georgi Dimitrov. On 4 February, Dimitrov authorises 1,000 U.S. dollars for Vasilichi.[17] Remus Koffler goes to Paris to make contact with Vasilichi.

> "In June and July 1939, I established contact with Comrade Béla Breiner, who gave me instructions to obtain a passport and go on a mission to Paris. I left at the end of July with material and verbal instructions for our representative in Paris, Comrade Vasilichi ... I stayed a total of two weeks, as long as Comrade Vasilichi detained me, until I received the material I was to bring back to Romania. On my arrival, I reported to Comrade Breiner."[18]

---

[16] T. A. Pokivailova, *Magazin istoric*, March 1997.

[17] *Idem*.

[18] SRI Archive, Dossier 40002, vol. 45, p. 53.

In the summer of 1940, when Foriş and Teohari Georgescu cross the Dniester into the USSR and meet with the leaders of the Comintern, Foriş complains that the PCdR is in financial crisis and requests more consistent subsidies. Strangely, Teohari Georgescu does not back Foriş up in this endeavour.[19] In 1967, he recalls:

"Following the entry of [Soviet] troops into Bassarabia, many citizens donated money so as to get in with the Party, so that it would arrange their situation for them, and the financial state of the Party was good. All the same, it requested funds for Romania and it was a question of hard currency – dollars. They discussed this issue, but when they asked me about the subject I told them the truth ... It was a question of 10-15 million lei."

Teohari Georgescu was lying. Gheorghe Stoica (Moscu Cohn) took part in the discussions in Moscow in 1940, as well as those in 1967, when Teohari Georgescu was questioned to clarify the circumstances of Foriş's assassination. He recalls: "It was during the time of Béla [Breiner] when the party had been surviving for almost two years without funds from abroad."[20] At the beginning of the 1930s, Moscu Cohn, an old Comintern agent, had been one of those who had handled funds 'from abroad'. It was via Moscu Cohn that lawyers were hired for the Grivitza trials, for Petre Constantinescu-Iaşi, Ana Pauker et al. On his list were V. V. Stanciu, Alfons Nachtigal, Stelian Niţulescu, C. Paraschivescu-Bălăceanu and others. The Comintern, in the midst of its anti-fascist campaign, used these trials for purposes of agitation and propaganda, as political spectacles, which brought benefits in terms of image. And so large funds were allocated to them. It was through Moscu Cohn that all the money required for the illegal and legal printed matter produced by the PCdR passed. Moscu Cohn, along with Lucreţiu Pătrăşcanu and Ştefan Foriş, managed these funds. From 1936 onward, the Comintern entered a phase of Stalinist purges and was no longer interested in financing anti-fascist campaigns or trials in Bucharest. Stalin had reduced its budget by a quarter. It was the moment when the Central Financial Commission (CCF) of the PCdR was set up, with the aim of replacing the missing funds.

---

[19] Dan Cătănuş, Ioan Chiper, *Cazul Ştefan Foriş. Lupta pentru putere în PCR. De la Gheorghiu-Dej la Ceauşescu.* Bucharest: Editura Vremea, 1999, p. 272.
[20] *Idem*, p. 274.

The commission was unexpectedly – for the communist medium – stable, keeping the same format until 1944. The head of the commission was Remus Koffler. Its members were Emil Calmanovici, Jacques Berman, Emil Herstein and Egon Weigl, all Western-educated Jews of 'bourgeois origin'. In 1937, "CCF-created revenues increased ... to 30-40,000 per month, which we handed directly over to the contact in the Secretariat." The CCF also ran businesses. One of them was set up by Calmanovici and Berman. It involved the construction of a block of flats, which brought in a profit of two million lei. When Foriş reached Moscow, he was criticised for this kind of venture, one unheard-of for communists. Wilhelm Pieck, one of Dimitrov's lieutenants, drew attention to the fact that bourgeois money might be influencing Party policy. Moreover, the Comintern attributed the mistakes of the 1938-1940 period precisely to the bourgeois elements at the top of the PCdR. The target of these criticisms was in fact the CCF run by Koffler. Without Koffler, however, and the group around him – Calmanovici, Herstein, Berman – the PCdR would have ceased to have any presence. With the money they raised, the costs of safe houses (some for living quarters, some for meetings) were covered, wages were paid, and maintenance expenses were covered. Aid for a few hundred communist prisoners was paid for (parcels, money, clothing, food) and their families were supported. Lawyers were paid. Judges, policemen, prison directors and guards were bribed.

"The work of the Central Financial Commission developed satisfactorily in the years from 1939-1941, widening the circle of fee-paying members and donors through regulated policy. At the beginning of 1941, the monthly income exceeded 50,000 lei and covered expenses. Throughout the period after 1939 there was no demand to the Secretariat that could not be immediately satisfied. Beginning in 1942, the monthly revenues remained at 2,000,000 per month ... growing to around 3,000,000 in 1943, and in 1944, after the replacement [of Ştefan Foriş, on 4 April 1944] I was given the responsibility of increasing the monthly income to 5 million and to create a reserve of 20 million, which was achieved in six weeks. The main drawback of the CCF was that the donors were in their great majority Jews."[21]

---

[21] SRI Archive, Dossier 40002, vol. 45, p. 55.

Under interrogation, Koffler recalls the following receipts of cash and fee-paying members: in 1943, "Calmanovici, 8.4 million, Jac. Berman, 7 million, engineer Ștefănescu, 2 million, engineer Șandor, 700,000 lei, engineer Ilovici, 700,000 lei, Mayer, 800,000, Ad. 400,000, Vexler, 450,000, Renharz, 500,000, engineer Popp, 400,000, Textila, 3.6 million, in 1944, up until 23 August, engineer Calmanovici 12 million, engineer Berman, 3.3. million, engineer Ștefanescu, 6.1 million, engineer Șandor, 1,050 million, engineer Prager, 3.3 million, Auschnit, 7.5 million, Textila, 7.4 million, Ad. 800,000, engineer Popp, 500,000, Mayer, 600,000, engineer Ilovici, 600,000."[22] Among the donors we find a number of industrialists. The best known were Max Auschnit, Dragoș Popp, and Alexandru Ștefănescu. There were also builders/entrepreneurs such as Emil Prager, Emil Calmanovici, and others. A simple calculation shows us that in 1943 the CCF received almost 30 million lei. And in 1944 (up until 23 August), 46 million lei. These were considerable sums. Three times larger than in 1942. In 1942, the PCdR budget had been around 1.5 million lei per month, i.e. 17.4 million lei. In 1943, one single sector of the Party swallowed up 1.5 million lei a month, as revealed in a MAI memo of 31 December 1943.[23] The money came mainly from Jewish circles, but also from Anglophile circles, from businessmen who foresaw an Allied victory. On 5 August 1943, the Siguranța noted the clandestine activities of Koffler, without identifying him:

> "In connection with the instructions given by the communist leadership to the subordinate organisations to intensify fund-raising (previously signalled) the MOPR section reported to the Central Committee that the movement's members and in particular the Jews 'have understood the party's financial difficulties and are coping with the new requirements laid down'."[24]

The Siguranța noticed towards the end of the 1943 that the PCdR had at its disposal considerable funds. When the Red Aid network in Bucharest was annihilated, the report mentions the following:

---

[22] Quoted by Lavinia Betea, *Recunoștința partidului pentru cei care l-au subvenționat*, in *Magazin istoric*, no. 3-4, 1997.

[23] CC of the PCR Archive, Fund 1, Dossier 276, p. 376.

[24] CC of the PCR Archive, Fund 1, Dossier 276, p. 144.

"Four safe houses were discovered, one equipped with two radio receivers. The organisation was channelling around 1 million lei for payment of rent on safe houses, plus funds to pay wages and separate sums to make bribes in the case of arrests ... To be remarked are the large sums of money at the disposal of the Party and the tendency to accumulate guns and ammunition."[25]

The arrest of the members of another network confronts the Siguranţa with the same reality:

"Eight safe houses were discovered on which an annual rent of 1,000,000 lei was being paid ... this discovery has led us to conclude that at the present time Communist Central has extraordinarily large sums of money at its disposal ... All the leading members of the communist movement, in order to be able to devote their entire activity only to the interests of the movement, are paid wages between 12,000 and 50,000 lei monthly, plus travelling expenses. The cost of clothes, food and medicaments sent monthly from Communist Central to prisons and camps amounts to a few million lei. Communist Central also looks after the families of those in prison from the material point of view and pays their rent, clothing, food, and even school fees for the children. If we add to these extraordinary expenses the sums that are paid to lawyers in trials involving communists, we have a picture that leads us to the definite conclusion that all this money is raised not only inside Romania, but also the treasury of the Central Committee is abundantly supplied with funds from abroad."[26]

The conclusion of the Siguranţa is inexact. Links between the PCdR and Moscow were broken off in 1941. Ana Pauker, Petre Borilă, and Vasile Luca try unsuccessfully to re-establish contact with Ştefan Foriş. In 1942, the Comintern is preparing a large-scale operation. Forty-five agents will be sent to almost every country in Europe. Five of them are supposed to arrive in Romania. Georgi Dimitrov requests 335,000 dollars, which are required for the closing months of the year. The Kremlin authorises less than a tenth of

[25] SSI memo, 10 November 1943, CC of the PCR Archive, Fund 1, Dossier 346, p. 378.
[26] CC of the PCR Archive, Fund 1 Dossier 377, pp. 19, 22.

this sum, i.e. 30,000. On Dimitrov's list, the PCdR is allocated 5,000 dollars, likewise the parties in Finland and Hungary. The money is to be delivered by five agents parachuted into the country. The mission is postponed, and later fails.[27] Links between Moscow and Bucharest will not be re-established until after 23 August 1944. The truth is that the sums required by the Party were collected only from within Romania. Remus Koffler, arrested in 1949, answers his interrogators in March 1950 as follows:

> "In the initial period there were no reserves, with money collected failing to cover Party expenses ... The sums collected by the CCF were at first, in the first few years, less than a few thousand per month, besides those from Comrades Calmanovici and Berman ... Later, they gradually increased to ... hundreds of thousands a month, after the start of the war. ... In the last year of the war, they were in the millions. No sum of money was ever received that was bound to political conditions."[28]

Those who had access to this money over time were Béla Breiner, Ștefan Foriș, Ion Popescu-Puțuri, Gavrilă Birtaș, Ana Ruski, Victoria Sîrbu, et al. After the war, the most active members of the CCF were arrested, investigated and tried in April 1954 for 'crimes against peace' and 'high treason'.

> "Alexandru Ștefanescu, 66, born in Ploiești, son of Alexandru and Maria, industrialist by profession: life, hard labour; Remus Koffler, 52, son of Isaac and Ernestina, functionary by profession: death; Jac [sic.] Berman, 54, born in Bucharest, son of Moriț and Ernestina, engineer by profession: 10 years, hard labour; Emil Calmanovici, 58, born in Piatra Neamț, son of Mendel and Ana, engineer by profession: life, hard labour."

All the property of those convicted is confiscated by the state. Alexandru Ștefanescu died in Aiud Prison in 1955, and Emil Calmanovici on 12 March 1956, after a hunger strike of 42 days. Remus Koffler was executed on the same night as Lucrețiu Pătrășcanu, on 17 April 1954, at three o'clock in the morning, with a bullet to the back of the neck.

---

[27] Tatiana Pkivailova, Ioan Chiper, *Studii și materiale de istorie contemporană*, new series, vol. 2, Romanian Academy, Nicolae Iorga Institute of History, 2003, pp. 68-69.

[28] *Sfera Politicii*, no. 63, October 1998, pp. 28-29.

XVII
The Conspirator

Pătrășcanu is a foreign body in our Party.
Ana Pauker

The body of Lucrețiu Pătrășcanu was buried in April 1954, a short distance from the cemetery of Jilava Prison. With no cross or other sign to indicate that he was there. The spot was identified 14 years later, in 1968. He was exhumed, cremated, and his ashes were placed in the Monument to the Heroes of the Homeland in Liberty Park, Bucharest. Here too could be found the earthly remains of other 'illegals', including those of Gheorghiu-Dej, the man behind the warrant for Pătrășcanu's death. In 1991, after the fall of the Communist regime, Elena Pătrășcanu-Veakis, the widow of Lucrețiu Pătrășcanu, took the urn to Snagov, where the couple had had a house; she cast the ashes into the waters of the lake. The restlessness of the former communist leader's mortal remains mirrors his restless life.

> "In connection with the discovery of the bones of Lucrețiu Pătrășcanu we can specify the following: the place where he was buried has been identified. This was established on the basis of the declarations made by the two sub-officers who dug the grave and threw the bodies of Lucrețiu Pătrășcanu and Remus Koffler therein, after their execution. The sub-officer declared that in the grave they dug there were the bones of three to four corpses buried previously, that they threw the corpses of Pătrășcanu and Koffler on top of these, together with the stretcher on which they had been transported. All this has been confirmed inasmuch as in the place they indicate there have been found the bones of six corpses, including two complete skeletons."[1]

The slaying of Pătrășcanu was ritualistic – an extension of the factional fighting of the past, but also of the Moscow trials of the 1930s. The illegals, the clandestines, committed murder amongst themselves. In the underground, the only solidarity is meted out in corpses. The acolytes

---

[1] Handwritten, unsigned, undated document, SRI Archive Fund 9604, p. 30.

disappear, they betray, if they are not held in check by grave complicity. They are involved in the assassination of Foriş, but also other political murders from the enigmatic years 1944-1948. The assassination of Lucreţiu Pătrăşcanu and Remus Koffler, one night in April 1954, gives rise to myths, rumours, veracious but truncated information, and much information wholly false. In Bucharest, mystification and lies are generated spontaneously, or else launched by the secret services. Ultimately, the Pătrăşcanu myth was created and nurtured by the circumstances of his trial. Without his 'tragic demise', he would have remained in memory as a nondescript communist, a member of the Political Bureau, listed in the biographical dictionaries, with five lines under the letter P and no more. Of course, the tragedy in which he was to become embroiled was of his own making. He was singled out by the 'comrades' as a victim, ripe for sacrifice in the rituals of death demanded by Stalin in his zeal to consolidate his power in occupied Europe. The death of Pătrăşcanu did not pass unnoticed. The excitement was fuelled by the authorities, because they needed to set an example, to intimidate people. If Pătrăşcanu – who was part of the inner circle of this exclusive sect, one of the hard core, one of the initiates – could be liquidated, it meant that no one was safe, regardless of his past. One's past became more threatening the more glorious it was. Some even refused to believe that the communists' most popular man, who had plotted with the King, Maniu and Brătianu, who had signed the armistice, had really been liquidated by his own. It was subsequently rumoured that Pătrăşcanu was alive, that he had not been killed, that he was in the USSR, in the Crimea, that he was writing a book. Or that he was living in his house at Snagov. Some were convinced that he had been spirited out of Jilava Prison and delivered for a price to the British spy network he had served, or that he had been exchanged for a big Soviet spy captured in London. He was to live under Western protection, with a changed identity. Some heard that he had had an interview with Dej, in his cell, and that they had made their peace. After the masquerade of the trial, he could no longer be released officially, but rather he had been offered his life after agreeing to live incognito. Another version: he had not been executed because he had gone insane when his sentence was read out. Others believed that he had lost his mind earlier, in March 1953, on the death of Stalin, news which had severed him from reality. The communiqué in *Scînteia* published in April 1954, which announced the trial and the execution, was supposed false, because Pătrăşcanu would already have been dead by that date. He was supposed to have died under torture during interrogation. Others believed that he had committed suicide by taking cyanide, or that he had hanged himself from the door of his cell. Even those who knew that he had been executed nevertheless imparted different versions. For example, that he had refused to be blindfolded and had sung the *International* in front of the firing squad. Or that he had fallen to his knees and begged forgiveness, sobbing loudly, so that the Sergeant Major in charge of the firing squad had been forced to shoot him like a mad dog, as someone put it. Others knew that, on the contrary, he had burst out laughing and that it had spread to the officials in attendance. The parting had been extremely merry, with tears in the eyes. Then, it was believed that those who had taken part in the trial had been touched by a curse. All of them – magistrates, prosecutors, investigators, witnesses – had died in the following period from various causes: motor car accidents, incurable diseases, or, more frequently, suicide, such as in the case of the supposed assassin, a lieutenant. Some suspected that Gheorghiu-Dej had sent him to his death in order to cover his tracks, others that the executioners and accomplices were remorseful and resorted to suicide in order to free themselves of the burden.

There is, nevertheless, an official statement, which reads:

"We, Colonel of Justice Rîpeanu Grigore, having been given orders by the Supreme Court, Military College, proceeded to Jilava penitentiary, together with the comrade assistant judge, captain of the judiciary Vasile Varga, delegated by the president of the Supreme Court in order to assist in the implementation of sentence no. 49 of 14 April 1954 of the Supreme Court, Military College, the sentence having been declared final, whereby Lucreţiu Pătrăşcanu … by profession a lawyer and university teacher, was sentenced to death, having declared on 14 April 1954, on the occasion of his sentence being communicated to him, that he would not be making any appeal for a pardon. At 1.30 hours we arrived at Jilava penitentiary [accompanied by – *author's note*] Lt. Bădica Ilie, commandant of penitentiaries, Major Savenco Ilarion on the part of the administrative authorities, Major Cahana Moise the MAI coroner and Capt. Andronache Nicolae commandant of the firing squad. At 02.00 hours, i.e. one hour before the hour set for the execution, we went to the cell of the condemned man, informing him that the time had come to atone for his deeds and when asked whether he had anything to confess or any last wish, his answer was in the negative. As the implementation of the sentence was set for today, 17 April 1954, at 03.00 hours, the condemned man Lucrețiu Pătrășcanu was led under escort to the place of execution, where he was formally identified. After the commandant of the firing squad had reported for duty, the Assistant Judge of the Supreme Court, Military College, read out the sentence, which had remained final, to the men in the firing squad. Lucrețiu Pătrășcanu was led to the execution pole and blindfolded, after which the death sentence was carried out by firing squad, today 17 April 1954, 03.00 hours. After the condemned was executed, coroner Major Cahana Moise ascertained the death of the condemned by gunshot, which was verified by the military prosecutor. Subsequently, at 04.00 hours, i.e. an hour after the execution, the corpse of the condemned was surrendered to the commandant of the penitentiary in order that burial could be arranged according to law. This written statement of the implmentation of sentence no. 49 of 14 April hereby concludes ... in five copies, of which one has been surrendered to the administration of Jilava penitentiary, who are required to inform the officer of the civil list in the commune of Jilava, Bucharest Region, communicating the necessary data for recording of the death of the above-named in the registry office."[2]

The document, although it bears the signatures of those mentioned as having been present, is a forgery, and does not render the execution as it happened. Pătrășcanu did not have the honour of 'benefitting' from a firing squad; he was not read his sentence. The solemn ceremonials to which any man condemned to death is entitled were not respected.

"In reality, the execution occurred in the following manner: those who were to take part in the execution went to the cell of those condemned to death, where Pătrășcanu and Koffler were held, and asked Pătrășcanu if he had any wish to express. At which Pătrășcanu replied, quietly and dignified: 'You started it, now get it over with!' After which, they put the spectacles on him [blinkers which did not allow the wearer to see where he was being taken – *author's note*], then they left the cell and went down the corridor, at the end of which they entered a closed space – a kind of inner courtyard, where the sand store was kept – and where, while

---

[2] SRI Archive, Fund P, Dossier 40002, vol. 12, pp. 954-55.

Pătrășcanu was being pushed to keep him walking ahead, a pistol was put to the back of his neck and he was shot. After he fell, because he was still moving, he was shot a number of times more. The same procedure was carried out for Koffler, with the difference that, when he had been taken from the cell, he had almost lost consciousness and needed to be dragged to the place by two men, and after they had arrived in the space with the sand, he was shot in the back of the neck, while being held by the armpits by one of the ones who had dragged him there. For him, a single bullet was sufficient for him to die instantly."[3]

The execution at Jilava was a ceremony nevertheless. A ritual of contempt. Whoever gave the order for them to be executed from behind, with a bullet in the back of the neck, was contemptuous of them. He dealt them death, but also humiliation. Of course, Pătrășcanu wished to die a dignified death, because he was concerned with what history would say about him. He would probably have assumed a defiant, calm posture. Perhaps he would have prepared his last words … This is precisely what the man who ordered his killing – on 17 April, in the dark, at three in the morning – wanted to take away from him: the chance to leave a heroic impression, as he would have wished. For, it was Gheorghiu-Dej who was behind this undignified, ritual slaying.

***

There are many reasons that can lead you to become an enemy of the world in which you live, as one ill adapted. They were the same reasons which led some to join extremist political movements in the nineteenth century. Lucrețiu Pătrășcanu takes a separate path in the world when he chooses Bolshevism. At the end of the First World War, the Petrograd Revolution won over the lycée college pupil. Was it the reaction of a politicised temperament? Was it the natural reaction of an adolescent rebelling against family and social environment? No. It was rather a reaction of fidelity, a gesture of protectiveness towards his family, albeit in a paradoxical form. His father, D. D. Pătrășcanu, was a well-known author of textbooks and a

---

[3] Grigore Răduică, *Crime în lupta pentru putere. 1966-1968. Ancheta cazului Pătrășcanu* [*Murders in the Struggle for Power. 1966-1968. The Inquiry into the Pătrășcanu Case*â. Evenimentul Românesc, 1999, p. 168.

satirist. Together with Garabet Ibrăileanu and Constantin Stere, he founded the *Viaţa Românească* review in Jassy. In the autobiography he writes for the Comintern on 26 October 1933, while a refugee in Moscow, Lucreţiu Pătrăşcanu declared, "I was born … into a well-off Romanian family. My father was a teacher by profession and was the descendent of a boyar family. My mother is from a noble family."[4] In spite of its anti-aristocracy and anti-bourgeois ideology, Bolshevism had, among its front-rankers, militants of aristocratic and bourgeois origins. Lenin himself was a noble. As inspector general of education for his *guberniya*, his father had been ennobled. And he was not the only non-proletarian in the Bolshevik movement. There were also Chicherin, Lunecharsky, Dzerzhinsky, and Alexandra Kolontai. Others came from bourgeois families, such as Vyacheslav Molotov, or themselves had become 'bourgeois': Leon Trotsky, Alexander Helphant-Parvus. Nor was Romanian communism lacking in such figures: Cristian Racovski, Scarlat Callimachi, N. D. Cocea, Anca and Mihai Magheru, Athanasie Joja, and Mihai Macavei had boyar roots. Alexandru Dobrogeanu-Gherea, Marcel Pauker, Jacques Berman, Eugen Rozvany, Emil Calmanovici, Remus Koffler, Ion Gheorghe Maurer and Constanţa Crăciun were of bourgeois extraction. Some of them even had considerable material wealth. Then there was a gallery of intellectuals: Ştefan Foriş, Belu Zilber, Egon Weigl, Petre Constantinescu-Iaşi, Tudor Bugnariu.

Lucreţiu Pătrăşcanu was part of the generation that emerged around the year 1900, and who, in the period 1917-1920, adhered to Bolshevism. His birth certificate states that he was born in the "city of Bacău, on 4 November, at eight in the morning, in the parental home No. 5 Cuza Vodă Street, the parents being Dimitrie Pătrăşcanu and Lucreţiu Pătrăşcanu née Dimitrie Stoica, aged 26 years."[5] He spent a happy childhood. His father, during the years of German occupation, 1916-1918, collaborated with the gazettes published by the occupier. Petre Pandrea notes succinctly: "Lucreţiu Pătrăşcanu – son of a politically bankrupt teacher, a Germanophile, accused of treachery and making a pact with the enemy …"[6] Prominent writers Tudor Arghezi, Ion Slavici, and Gala Galaction did the same thing.

---

[4] Gh. Buzatu, *Românii în arhivele Kremlinului* [*Romanians in the Kremlin Archives*], Bucharest: Univers Enciclopedic, 1996, p. 344.

[5] ANCR, Archive of the CC of the RCP, Fund 95, Dossier 122218, p. 10.

[6] Petre Pandrea, *Memoriile mandarinului valah* [*Memoirs of the Walachian Mandarin*], Bucharest: Albatros, 2000, p. 150.

They were arrested in 1919 and taken to Văcărești Prison in order to be brought to trial. Immediately after the war, the question of collaboration intensely agitated public opinion. The 'collaborators' were ostracised from society. The most notorious cases of public figures hounded until the end of their lives for collaborating with the occupier were Constantin Stere and Alexandru Marghiloman. D. D. Pătrășcanu suffered the same treatment: he was tried, imprisoned at Văcărești, dismissed from the education system. His son's adherence to Bolshevism was a reaction against a world from which his father had been excluded. The young Pătrășcanu set himself up as radical critic of the bourgeoisie and democracy. He opted for a marginal, pariah position in inter-war Romanian society. He remained outside the mainstream created after the formation of Greater Romania, a country very proud of its new status after the Union of 1918. In this jubilant Romania, Pătrășcanu might have forged a career for himself, had he not borne the stigma of collaboration that darkened his family name. He rejected the 'mediocre destiny' reserved for him. His Bolshevism was that of a man frustrated in his ambitions. It was an opportunist, circumstantial Bolshevism. The grapes are bitter for an ambitious man who knows he can no longer attain the position on the social ladder he craves. You become a marginal, a critic of the system. You become a 'revolutionary' who dreams of overthrowing the system, in order to play the role you 'merit' in the 'new world'. This is also the case of Pătrășcanu, who built his destiny on top of this frustration. It was the frustration of a man denied a career at the top, because of his sullied family name. The plots he hatched against the democratic regime and the bourgeoisie, the underground into which he withdrew, from whence he dreamed of and plotted world revolution, were alibis for his revolt of 1918-1920, when his father was no longer received in any of the houses of good society in Bucharest. Of bourgeois and boyar extraction, those who turned their backs became the enemies of the adolescent Pătrășcanu.

Those who knew him observed that he was an atypical communist. He had bourgeois hang-ups; he was a 'salon communist'. He was bourgeois in his style of life, his manners, and his culture. As a well-read man, with a Doctorate in Philosophy from Germany, he could have been a professor, a lawyer, or a political leader in a bourgeois party. Pătrășcanu had a good education and was highly cultured. He was unable to derive any benefit from these in the 1920s and 1930s, because of his adhesion to the Comintern. In life, as in death, he was a man without any place. Communism was a refuge for him. He clung to Bolshevik ideology as the grounds for his rejection of society. He was an alien among the communists, just as he was an alien in the world he inherently frequented and to which he belonged by extraction. Little inclined to creation, a loner's path or innovation, he was always disciplined. It suited him to be part of a collective, of a structure, to belong. The extremely ramified network of the Comintern gave him the sensation of power, a sensation he needed in order to counterbalance his complexes as one rejected, excluded. He was very close to his father, the 'victim of the Romanian oligarchy', and hoped one day to avenge him. By belonging to the secret society of the Bolsheviks he was able to think of himself as an initiate, a bearer of a messianic message. It was as if he harboured an absolute secret: that he was a 'chosen' one. He was chosen, in spite of being rejected by the wretched Romanian bourgeois-landowner class he detested, although there was nothing more he wanted than to be acknowledged, esteemed, feared and respected by that very class. To that end, he prepared clandestinely. He plotted, moving between Bucharest and Moscow, via Berlin and Prague, the coming of the world of tomorrow. This world would destroy the one that had humiliated his father. He imagined himself as a member of a vast brotherhood. He was proud. He made a show of the superiority of his social background, education and culture in the squalid peripheries, among the illiterate and semi-literate, the disaffected, the lumpenproletariat fanatics who made up the sect of professional revolutionaries. In fact, he despised these promiscuous figures of the underground. It seemed evident to him that he should have precedence over them. He was a polyglot, a Doctor of the University of Leipzig, a participant in Comintern meetings, a founder member of the PCdR, and often one of the leaders of the Party. He was ambitious, and wanted to be the leader of the unworthy ones with whom he had dealings as part of the universal conspiracy in which he was enmeshed. He did not possess the qualities demanded of a leader and was as alienated from the masses as he was from the elite of his day.

He was viewed as a foreign body by the communists. An aloof man, he soon stirred their resentments and suspicions. He remained an intellectual, a bourgeois in search of a place for himself. He had strayed into the extremist politics of the Left. He did not practise a traditional form of politics that might eventually have taken him to the top of the social pyramid, the position for which, as it seemed to him, he was destined. He practised a form of politics that was trying to overthrow society and its established elite. Pătrăşcanu had a double, contradictory position regarding the establishment. He belonged to the bourgeoisie and had aristocratic roots. At the same time, he had adhered to communism, which was bent on their destruction. It was an ideological but not an organic affiliation. In order to take this step, he broke away from his world. However, he did not break away completely; he always looked back. He was a prodigal son and not a renegade. He is split between two worlds. Whereas, at the end of the 1930s, against the backdrop of the Moscow trials, he seems to renounce absolute fealty to Stalin, by the middle of the 1940s, in the circumstances of the great military victories of the Red Army, he returns to the fold.

"I had thought that his philobourgeoisism was the fruit of snobbery, of boyarism, which he got from his father. Now I think that it is something more serious, that it is an involuntary sympathy for the bourgeois class. … Pătrăşcanu nevertheless remains far more tied to the communist than to the bourgeois mentality. If he was, in the years after 1944, capable of showing a brazen face, it is because of the services he did for the Party and the communist aureole he wore in public gave him the idea that no one would contest his communist soul. To this might also be added the intoxication with political power to which a non-serious man is liable. And Pătrăşcanu was a man who was frivolous in great part, like any impulsive, hot-headed, vain, snobbish man. But such a lack of seriousness is not indelible. I am sure that today, when he is named an 'enemy' by his comrades, today his yearning for communism, his need to be seen once more as one of the faithful, this need must, I believe, be overwhelming for him. His communist background is much stronger than the rest, however deplorable this rest might be – or might have been. Often, you don't appreciate what you have until you lose it."[7]

The author of this declaration, under interrogation, was trying to defend Pătrăşcanu, whom he knew had been arrested, and give a verdict that might help him

Lucreţiu Pătrăşcanu adheres to the Communist movement as early as his time at lycée college. He rapidly finds a niche for himself in the hierarchy, as a militant radical. In December 1922, Marcel Pauker and others reorganise

---

[7] From the declaration given by D. I. Suchianu to the Securitate on 10 May, in *Adevărul literar şi artistic*, 3 February 2004.

the PCdR. Pătrășcanu, close to Pauker, is one of the heads of the legal and illegal press operated by the Party. He had been to Russia with the Paukers that year, when he took part in the Fourth Congress of the Comintern. He becomes a 'professional revolutionary', preparing and dreaming of the 'great struggle' destined to overthrow the detested bourgeoisie. In Russia, he has occasion to meet Lenin and immerses himself in the illusion-nurturing atmosphere of Moscow after the end of the civil war. It is now that he talks with Cristian Racovski, whom he knew from Bucharest. In 1923, he goes to Germany to study, but also to research doctrine, in the homeland of Marx and Engels. In 1927, he gains a Doctorate, with a thesis on agrarian reform in Romania. He is already an agent of the Comintern, inured to clandestine life, operating within the German Communist Party. He returns to Romania. Meanwhile, in 1924, the PCdR had been outlawed. The communist youth of the beginning of the 1920s, Pauker, Gherea, Finkelstein, Köblős etc., led a small network that was now unravelling, the dream of a party for the masses lay in ruins. Surveillance by the Siguranţă, searches, raids, arrests, trials, and censorship of the Bolshevik-inspired press had turned the communists into pariahs, eccentric, isolated figures, who, when not living abroad, were to be found in prison or under police arrest. Having returned to Bucharest, Pătrășcanu is co-opted into the leadership of the Peasant Workers Bloc, a legal organisation of the PCdR. He joins the Ilfov Bar and, as a lawyer, he defends radical union leaders, strikers, and communist leaders at various trials. He cuts a public figure as a 'man of the Left', as an intellectual. He contributes articles to newspapers that oppose the bourgeois government from the stance of the class struggle.

This is the visible part of his life. Like any disciple of Lenin, however, he leads an existence on two levels; one at the surface of things and the other in the secret underground of the Bolshevik networks. He has a talent for this double life. He has a complex regarding secret initiation and mysteries. He sees himself as the bearer of a universal truth imparted to but few. He prides himself in being one of the chosen. He is prudent, reticent; he thrives on secrets and conspiracy. His favourite book in adolescence and in later life, a book which inculcated his taste for clandestinity, political sects and secret societies, was *Underground Russia* (1885) by Serghey Kravchinsky (Stepnyak). Through the contacts he makes in Germany and Russia, Pătrășcanu has good connections with the Comintern, which he will represent in Bucharest for a time. From the shadows, he organises the routes for the couriers and the distribution and use of the funds sent from Moscow. Not much time passes before he finds himself in the sights of the Siguranţă. He had already been arrested in 1924, for 21 days. He goes on hunger strike, as demanded by the Bolshevik rulebook in such situations. The press takes up his case. This is what he has been after: agitation and an opportunity for propaganda. As usual, Gh. Costa-Foru mobilises public opinion, according to the time-honoured script. He is arrested again in 1928, caught red-handed at a rendezvous with a representative of the KIM, the Communist youth movement affiliated to the Comintern. It is a cloak-and-dagger episode. Pătrăşcanu holds a meeting in the Bellu Cemetery. Someone denounces him. The next day, Pătrăşcanu and Léon Mauvais are captured on the shore of Lake Herăstrău. Pătrăşcanu escapes from the headquarters of the Siguranţă on Pache Boulevard and alerts the press. The *Dimineaţa* newspaper publishes a protest; the Frenchman is released and then deported. The Siguranţă reports signal his attendance at various meetings and trials, and his frequent international comings and goings along the Berlin-Moscow route.

In 1932, Pătrăşcanu is arrested once more, during the electoral campaign: he was standing for the Peasant Workers Bloc. But this was not the reason for his arrest – as he was to claim – but rather the Siguranţă had uncovered the clandestine network of which he was part. Held for two months at Văcăreşti, he is subsequently investigated at liberty, along with the other accused. He is implicated in a trial with 29 other accomplices. Among them was Gustav Arnold, a Comintern agent and member of the German Communist Party, who had come to Romania to revive the clandestine networks with an injection of substantial funds. In the group there were also Moscu Cohn (Gheorghe Stoica), Béla Breiner (future head of the PCdR, in the years 1938-1940), Lazăr Grümberg (convicted in the Ana Pauker trial of 1936, dead in Vapnyarka in 1944), Ştrul Zigelboim (a member of the Secretariat in 1940; he later tried to cross the border into the USSR with Vasile Luca, but they were both caught), Paul Hollinger (who changed the money brought by Gustav Arnold – around 1.2 million lei). Pătrăşcanu defends himself, saying, "This is not a juridical but a political trial, intended to prevent me from standing in the elections." He was head of the electoral list for the Peasant Workers Bloc, which was based at No. 4 Smîrdan Street. The lawyers for the defence were C. Vicol, Paul Moscovici, V. V. Stanciu, I. Ştraie and Stelian Niţulescu, whom we also find at other trials. All of them are members of the PCdR Legal Bureau. Pătrăşcanu and some of the other accused are acquitted. Among them are Moscu Cohn, Lazăr Grümberg, Paul Hollinger and Ştrul Zigelboim. Gustav Arnold and Béla Breiner are convicted. Lazăr Grümberg was the distributor of substantial МОПР funds. He escapes a few weeks later, in the meantime having posed as a prisoner of conscience, an intellectual persecuted for his opinions. In fact, it was quite simply a case of money supplied by the Comintern to pay for a clandestine printing press and agents' salaries. Three of the accused were members of the PCdR Secretariat: Béla Breiner, Moscu Cohn and Lucreţiu Pătrăşcanu. And the other two, Lazăr Grümberg and Ştrul Zigelboim, were part of the PCdR leadership.

A year later, he was arrested once more, on suspicion of being one of the organisers of the strike at the CFR Workshops in Grivitza. Which was true. He was released two months later, together with 200 strikers, and was due to stand trial among the second batch of the accused. The trial is finally held, after numerous postponements, in 1939, and he is acquitted together with the others. He flees to the USSR. He is arrested for the fifth time in 1940. On 31 July 1940, after spending two months as a conscripted officer, he is arrested and interned in the camp at Miercurea Ciuc. On 1 September, he is transported to the military hospital in Braşov. He is released in October, at the same time as Scarlat Callimachi, the 'Red Prince', with both of them signing undertakings to refrain from any further political activity. In February 1941, after the Iron Guard rebellion, he is arrested yet again. He is taken to Poiana Ţapului and held under house arrest. Here, he writes his books, until January 1943, when he is imprisoned at the camp in Tîrgu Jiu. He is released at the beginning of August of the same year and sent back to Poiana Ţapului. On 28 April 1948, he is imprisoned once more, this time by the communists, and investigated over a period of six years. In April 1954, he is tried, convicted, sentenced to death and executed.

It is between these periods of detention that Pătrăşcanu's career as a communist unfolds. Like any Bolshevik, he had a series of pseudonyms. Firstly, Andrei Moldoveanu, or simply Andrei, the alias he adopted as early as 1922. Then, Ion C. Ion, as he signed his articles in *Viaţa Românească*. He also had other false names: Bercu, Coca, V. Malin, Mihalcea, Titu, Grigorescu, Măcin, Radu Boldur, and the list goes on. He likes to change his address frequently. This is also specifically stated in a report by the General Department of Police: "The above-named, knowing he is being followed, is in the habit of changing his domicile very often in order to lead the surveillance organisations astray." As a Leninist, a 'professional revolutionary', he was above all a conspirator, a man of the underground. This pleasure in clandestinity, secrecy and anonymity is surprising in someone accused in 1994-1948 of craving popularity. It will even be proven that he does crave popularity. "He likes to conspire, not to administer."[8] From 1919, he is mixed up in most of the affairs of the clandestine groups controlled by the Comintern. He is always present in the PCdR leadership, be it in the Political Bureau, be it in the Secretariat, be it in the Central Committee; he runs various sections. We find him among the leaders of МОПР, distributing funds sent by the Comintern. Clandestinity was, for him, a way of life. When, in the winter of 1936, he is asked to go legal, he refuses. He prefers to live illegally, in the underground, under a false name, away from his family, in a place where no one knows his identity. He is never absent from the conclaves of the communists from the Comintern network, at congresses and meetings of the PCdR. But we also find him in obscure Party cells in the provinces, menaced with discovery and arrest. He is won over by clandestinity, even if he also has a public existence: trials, appearances at various political and union events. However, he regards such public visibility as merely camouflage for the plot he is hatching 'against the oligarchy'. He regards himself as 'a soldier of the great socialist revolution of October 1917', in accordance with the teachings of Lenin. He belongs to a vast organisation, which gives him a feeling of power. He needs this feeling in order to counteract another: that of isolation, rejection, pariah status, failure.

In the summer of 1921, he is part of the provisional leadership of the PCdR, in the absence of those arrested at the May congress. In 1923, he goes to Germany to study for his Doctorate and no longer frequents the upper echelons of the PCdR. He reappears in 1928, when he takes part in the Fourth Congress of the PCdR, held between 28 June and 7 July at Chugevo, near Kharkov, in the USSR, together with Al. Dobrogeanu-Gherea, Imre Aladár, Ștefan Foriș, Dori Goldstein, Vasile Luca, Elek Köblős, Solomon, Schein, Vitali Holostenko, and Berger Aladár. He is a member of the PCdR Legal Bureau. He appears as a lawyer for the defence in the trials of communists. He pleads for the defence in Cluj, during September-November 1928, when his clients are Victor Aradi, Ștefan Foriș, Eugen

---

[8] Belu Zilber, *Actor în procesul Pătrășcanu*, op. cit., p. 192.

Rozvany, David Avramescu, Haia Lifşiţ, Imre Aladár et al. In September 1929, he conducts the defence at the trial in Timişoara. It is here that he meets Panait Istrati. The trial, widely reported in the press, besides causing his name to circulate, also brings him serious harassment. In Cernăuţi/ Czernowitz, he is attacked by an Iron Guard gang. It was a reaction to the attempt to assassinate Interior Minister Alexandru Vaida-Voievod, on 5 October. The attack was carried out by Avram Goldenberg, a 19 year old communist from Jassy, and was motivated by the Lupeni episode and the death in prison of Haia Lifşiţ, whom Pătrăşcanu had defended in the Cluj trial a year earlier. After the press publish the story on 7 October, Iron Guard gangs attack the Jewish quarters of Jassy and persons known as communists. In Cernăuţi/Czernowitz for the trial, Pătrăşcanu is identified and beaten up. He will not omit to mention the incident in the autobiography he writes for the Comintern in 1933. The years 1928-1930 were a period of splits and serious internal conflicts in the PCdR. Life in the political sects is one of ruptures, quarrels, betrayals, 'factional fighting'. The so-called Communist Party reaches the verge of extinction. Pătrăşcanu prefers to play a waiting game, not rallying to any camp. "Pătrăşcanu (Grigorescu) was also neutral, but for his own, individual advantage," recalls Marcel Pauker in November 1937, while under investigation in Moscow.[9] Pătrăşcanu is fearful lest he be expelled from the Party. In the context of the struggle for power between Stalin and Trotsky, many Bolsheviks in the USSR had been expelled, accused of factionalism. The years 1928-1930 see massive purges. In the summer of 1930, the Comintern sacks the leadership of the PCdR. All those implicated are suspended, purged, unmasked, obliged to provide a self-denunciation, assigned to do 'lowly work'. The Siguranţă arrests whomever remains, because the professional revolutionaries, the missionaries of utopia who are out to save the world, do not hesitate to denounce their rivals. The Party is infiltrated by Siguranţă agents, all the way to the top. Like any underground, the PCdR is infernal. Pătrăşcanu observes the intrigues, the scandals, the denunciations. The struggle for power – albeit infinitesimal power – is fuelled by ambitions disproportionate in relation to the stakes: control over a small group. He did not lose faith. This would later happen, paradoxically, after he came to power, as a minister. His waiting game can be explained not

---

[9] *O ancetă stalinistă. Lichidarea lui Marcel Pauker* [*A Stalinist Investigation. The liquidation of Marcel Pauker*], Bucharest: Univers Enciclopedic, 1995, p. 98.

only by his fear of being branded a factionalist, but also by his education. He could not descend to the level of such bickering. Moreover, his condition made him less dependent on funds transferred from Moscow, on a position in the hierarchy of the Party. For him, the vision of human liberation he had in 1917-1918 still counts, even if its avatars had embroiled him in a world of sordid clandestinity, a mixture of the déclassé, the proletariat, adventurers, the semiliterate, spies, terrorists, agents, and the criminal underworld. He is constantly reproached for his arrogance and pretensions to superiority, to being a guru, a Lenin of the Romanian underground. He really does have such pretensions and makes no effort to conceal them. He displays them on many occasions, there is something seignorial and aloof about him, which irritates the 'comrades'. He acts out the comedy of fraternity with the proletarian and humble. This was a result of German influence. He had lived there and had seen this kind of behaviour. In the manner of Brecht, he mixes with sordid milieux in order to show himself to be an anti-bourgeois, an intellectual radical who disdains his social background. He played the role of the lumpenproletariat-intellectual, although he was not one. His attempts at travesty, the masks he wears, are not convincing. He is an alien, and therefore suspect. His relations with the successive leaders of the Party are always tense. But the distinctions are not yet clear. They will be observable 10 years later, in the years of the Moscow trials. For the moment, the differences seem a negligible detail.

In 1931, he is involved in the electoral campaign. He stands as a candidate in the parliamentary elections. He is elected member for the county of Timiș on the list of the Peasant Workers Bloc. His election and that of four other communists (Imre Aladár representing Satu Mare, Eugen Rozovany representing Bihor, Ștefan Dan representing Mureș, Vasile Cașul representing Cernăuți/Czernowitz) is invalidated by Parliament. After emerging from clandestine life, in 1944-1948, he was fond of reminiscing about this period: the electoral campaign, the polemics in the press, the few sessions of Parliament he attended, when he was defended in a speech by Corneliu Zelea Codreanu,[10] newly elected as a Member of Parliament, and who opposed the invalidation of the five communists. During the interval 3-24 December 1931, he takes part in the Fifth Congress of the PCdR, at

---

[10] Corneliu Zelea Codreanu (1899-1938), known as 'the Captain," founder of the fascist Iron Guard or 'Legion of the Archangel Michael' – *Translator's note.*

Gorkovo, near Moscow. He attends together with another 38 people. On the part of the Comintern, there were, in attendance, Béla Kuhn, Georgi Dimitrov, Dmitri Manuilsky, and Mátyás Rákosi. Pătrășcanu is elected to the Secretariat, as a deputy, along with Béla Breiner and Alexandru Nikolski. This does not spare him from the attacks of Béla Kuhn, who is in disagreement with the report presented by Pătrășcanu, and nor from those of his erstwhile lover from the time of their common beginnings in the communist networks, Elena Filipovici. She characterises Pătrășcanu as follows: "He represents yet another conduit of the petit bourgeois intellectual, coming from the ranks of those bourgeois intellectuals who, during the past of the workers' movement, did much harm to the working class."[11] Ana Pauker, with whom Elena Filipovici had, at the beginning of the 1920s, opened a tailor's workshop on Calea Victoriei,[12] as a front for communist activities, says more or less the same thing: "Pătrășcanu is a foreign body in our Party." It is to be observed that these Secretariats, political bureaux, and central committees were ephemeral. In effect, they changed their composition every six months. This fluidity in the leadership of the PCdR perfectly reflected the state of affairs in the Party, its vulnerability, its perpetual crises, the dissent between the leadership structures, situated in Moscow, Prague, and Bucharest, and above all the uninterrupted immixture of the Comintern. The names of functionaries come and go in the documents. To reconstruct the career paths of the communist leaders is well nigh impossible, because of their parallel posts and above all the organisational chaos.

Pătrășcanu oversees the railway workers' strike, as the only member of the PCdR Political Bureau in Bucharest. The Siguranța is not aware of the real role he plays in the situation at the Grivitza Workshops. Here, we discover his abilities to manoeuvre from the shadows, his talent as a conspirator, his double life, his experience as a long-standing Comintern agent initiated in the rules of subversion and conspiracy. At 32, he was not only a Marxist intellectual, but also a professional revolutionary. He is always behind events, without making his presence felt. Nevertheless, he is arrested on 24 February, and imprisoned along with the other strikers. Interrogated

---

[11] Archive of the CC of the RCP Fund 1, D 33, p. 647, *apud* M. C. Stănescu, *Stînga politică din România în anii crizei, 1929-1933* [The Political Left in Romania during the crisis years], Mica Valahie, 2004, p. 86.

[12] The main thoroughfare in inter-war Bucharest – *Translator's note*.

a number of times, he is released two months later and scheduled to be tried at liberty in the second batch of 200 accused. A few weeks later, in May, he flees clandestinely to the USSR. The danger that the Siguranţă might discover his true activities and his share in a drama that culminated in dead, wounded, more than 1,500 arrests, and harsh trials, was very real. Wearing the aureole of his merits in the class struggle and in mobilising the masses, he is named a PCdR delegate by the Comintern.

His sojourn in the capital of the proletarian revolution was less glorious. He frequents Cristian Racovski. At the Fifth Congress of the PCdR, Béla Kuhn had accused Pătrăşcanu of not criticising Racovski. Meanwhile, Racovski had been rehabilitated and was living in Moscow as Deputy Minister of Health. Pătrăşcanu visits him together with Al. Dobrogeanu-Gherea. Other Romanian Bolsheviks of the old guard come to meet him. The visits do not go unobserved. Pătrăşcanu does not adapt to life in Moscow. He stays in the USSR from May 1933 to January 1935: a year and a half. For him, it is an opportunity to compare the illusions with the realities of the communist world. His impressions are not overly positive. He circulates, talks with all kinds of people, collects information for himself, and lives like a local. He relates everything to the official propaganda; he compares. Nor is he charmed by the atmosphere at the Hotel Lux, where he is staying along with other characters in the cosmopolitan apparatus of the Comintern. "Once they arrived in Moscow on 'business', the foreign communists entered a terrifying atmosphere of denunciation, delation, intrigue…"[13] He is present at the funeral of Clara Zetkin, deceased on 20 June 1933. His sojourn in Moscow coincides with the Leipzig trial of the 'Reichstag incendiaries', during September-December 1933, in which Georgi Dimitrov cuts a figure. Dimitrov arrives in Moscow at the end of February and is given a triumphal, hero's welcome. The Comintern apparatus is present, therefore so is Pătrăşcanu. In a short time, Dimitrov becomes leader of the Comintern. The second trial of the Grivitza railway workers, in the summer of 1934, copies the 'Leipzig model', following the indications of the Comintern, processed and sent by Pătrăşcanu. The period 1933-1934 is one of great tensions in the PCdR, provoked mainly by the differing analysis of the events in January-February 1933, by the reciprocal accusations that different leaders aim at each other. Moreover,

---

[13] Arkadi Vaksberg, *Hotel Lux. Partidele frăţeşti înslujba Internaţionalei Comuniste*, Bucharest: Humanitas, 1998, pp. 56.

after Hitler takes power, on 30 January 1933, Stalin makes an about-turn, orienting the Comintern along other lines. The Social Democrats are no longer regarded as 'social fascists', irreducible enemies. An alliance has to be made with them; a 'united front of workers' has to be constructed, as a tool to combat National Socialism. Moreover, the boundaries of the proletariat have to be crossed, and there has to be collaboration with the bourgeois parties, with the 'democrats, the intellectual sympathisers', on the platform of anti-fascism. In such situations, those who executed Comintern orders up until that point are blamed for the old policy and purged. The members of the Political Bureau and the Secretariat of the PCdR are replaced – they are regarded by the Comintern as too sectarian, incapable of opening to other forces. Alexander Stepanski-Gorn is replaced by Boris Ştefanov as head of the Party. During all this time, Pătrăşcanu is in Moscow. We do not know whether he was consulted, or whether he plotted to become head of the Party, the thing he wished for. He had entered into conflict with the old leadership following an article published in the *Communist International* review. The Political Bureau – Elena Filipovici, Alexander Stepanski-Gorn, Nicolae Goldberger – who are in Prague, repudiate him in a resolution of 25 May 1934. He also has conflicts with leaders of the Comintern. He is dismissed. He asks to be sent back to Romania. He manages to return, in spite of the intention of his hosts at the Hotel Lux to detain him in Moscow. On 1 December 1934, Kirov is murdered in Leningrad, on Stalin's orders. The Terror is being prepared in the Kremlin and in the Lubyanka. It is in this atmosphere that Pătrăşcanu departs from the USSR. His thoughts about the homeland of socialism have partly changed. He has undergone an experience similar to that of Istrati, albeit one less intense, due to the differences in their temperaments. The communism practised in Russia, due to its backwardness, is not suitable for European countries: this is his conclusion. Nevertheless, he decides to remain in the Party and to live in the underground, as a disciplined soldier. Life outside the Party had no meaning for him, as for so many 'professional revolutionaries' of the Bolshevik old guard. He continues to militate within the Comintern and the PCdR for proletarian revolution. His revenge against the bourgeoisie is a personal revenge, which he will not give up. At the beginning of January 1935, he receives a passport and, via Warsaw and Berlin, he arrives in Prague, and thence crosses the border clandestinely, at Sighet. He arrives in Bucharest, after many adventures.

In 1935, he faces a difficult situation in the Party. The internal leadership is up to date with his 'errors' in Moscow. Marcel Pauker, Moscu Cohn, Vanda Nicolski, Ana Pauker, Şmil Marcovici and Dimităr Ganev hear his report. Pătrăşcanu accepts a secondary role in the PCdR, he is reprimanded and sent to Jassy. He submits to Party discipline. What if he had withdrawn, if he had resigned? What would a book signed by Pătrăşcanu, in which the author, like Istrati, repudiated communism, have meant? He wrote no such thing; he did not renege communism. Can this have been a question of his mentality as disciplined soldier? His incapacity to remain alone, to follow his own road? He had lived through the experience of exclusion, of being a pariah, in 1919-1921. He did not want to abandon the borrowed "family" to which he belonged. Then again, he did not wish to return to the bourgeois world, defeated by his experience as professional revolutionary. He would have had to recognise that the bourgeoisie, that the democratic regime, was superior. Had he deceived himself? He stubbornly persisted, although he no longer harboured any illusions, and remained among the Bolsheviks. Moreover, Pătrăşcanu could not conceive of emerging from the underground. 'Underground Russia'[14] still obsessed him. The secret man in him forbade him to lead a normal life. He remained a conspirator, fascinated by plots and the clandestine. He was a wanderer, the prisoner of a decision taken in youth. Instead of parting from the PCdR, he provides a self-denunciation of his attitude in Moscow. In Jassy, he lives clandestinely in the house of Garabet Ibrăileanu's daughter, having been consigned to the reserve of activists, engaging in insipid PCdR propaganda in Moldova. A year later, at the beginning of 1936, on the orders of his chiefs, he emerges from the underground. The Sixth Congress of the Comintern has made an about-turn and his services were required. He is summoned to Bucharest by Marcel Pauker and Ştefan Foriş. He re-emerges on the surface, claiming that he had been living abroad in order to avoid the trial prepared by the courts in 1933. He is 'legalised', removed from clandestine life. He is given the mission of handling the scheduled trials of Petre Constaninescu-Iaşi and Ana Pauker. During the Craiova trial, Pătrăşcanu is suspended from the Ilfov bar, because of the proceedings against him in the Grivitza case. A letter he sends on 15 October 1936 to the Political Bureau of the PCdR Secretariat

---

[14] *Underground Russia* (1882), the book mentioned above, by Serghey Kravchinsky (Stepanyak) (1852-1895), a Russian writer and revolutionary, containing memoirs of the clandestine life of the author up to 1878, when he left Russia.

reveals him as quite critical. He was unhappy with the way in which the trial had gone. The PCdR had not ensured a sound defence; it had not sufficiently mobilised public opinion. The trial – through the transformation of the dock into a political tribunal – had not served the cause as much as Pătrăşcanu would have wished.[15] Another mission he has is to negotiate the creation of the Popular Front. The attempt does not succeed.

In the 1940s, thanks to his public exposure, Pătrăşcanu becomes a well-known figure. He appears at trials covered by the press, he writes theoretical articles for various newspapers, under a pseudonym. His reputation as a communist leader of high standing takes shape. The Moscow trials of 1936-1938 find, in Pătrăşcanu, a well-informed observer. All those who have had connections with Racovski are executed. Had he remained in Moscow, Pătrăşcanu would have shared the same fate. He does not repudiate communism, although he is profoundly upset by what he discovers. He remains disciplined, faithful to the cause. He deals with the recruitment of volunteers for the International Brigades in Spain. In December 1937, there are general elections in Romania. Pătrăşcanu is involved in the negotiation of a common platform with other left-wing parties, alongside Ştefan Foriş and Mihai Gheorghiu Bujor. Pătrăşcanu and Mihai Gheorghiu Bujor were relatives. "My mother-in-law was … a Habsburg baroness, her father being Demetrius Stoika, Graf von Wenezel und Salla, doctor in philosophy at Vienna, brought by Simion Bărnuţiu to teach Latin at Jassy University, married to a Moldavian woman named Drăghici, who died young, then married to another Moldavian woman, from whom Mihai Gheorghiu Bujor was descended …" writes Petre Pandrea, Lucreţiu Pătrăşcanu brother-in-law.[16] The negotiations are unsuccessful. On an order from Moscow – to create an anti-PNL coalition around the PNŢ, a simulacrum of the Popular Front – the PCdR, via Lucreţiu Pătrăşcanu, signs a pact with the PNŢ, which had a non-aggression pact with the far Right. The communists thereby ally themselves with the Iron Guard.

In February 1938, Carol II imposes a royal dictatorship. The PCdR position is hesitant; the orders from the Comintern are contradictory. Pătrăşcanu visibly reduces his activity within the Party. He is at odds with the

---

[15] ANR, *Copilăria Comunismului românesc în arhiva Cominternului* [*The Childhood of Romanian Communism in the Comintern Archives*], 2001, p. 383.
[16] Petre Pandrea, *Memoriile mandarinului valah* [*Memoirs of the Wallachian Mandarin*], Bucharest: Albatros, 2000, p. 321.

PCdR leadership on a number of points (the participation of the communists in the Front for National Rebirth, their entry into the guilds etc.). He refuses to make a self-denunciation, although it is insistently demanded that he should do so. He holds his ground. He is isolated. Here we also find his disquiet, his frustration as regards the Moscow trials. An entire generation of communists, whom Pătrăşcanu had known well, perished under the accusation of Trotskyism and spying for Romania. It was true: they were indeed occupied with spying and conspiracy – but for the USSR and against Romania. Among the victims of the Great Terror, are his old acquaintances Marcel Pauker, Al. Dobrogeanu-Gherea, Elena Filipovici and their mentor Cristian Racovski. Pătrăşcanu no longer has a 'Party connection', the only lifeline in the clandestine world. He does not criticise the Party leaders, he is prudent, so as not to be accused of factionalism. He views what is happening in the USSR quite critically. He does not leave the PCdR, and nor does he denounce the crimes of Stalin. Disciplined, he continues to be a communist devoted to the cause of 'world-wide proletarian revolution'. Nonetheless, he writes a letter to the CC of the PCdR. The latter sends the text with comments to Vasil Kolarov at the Comintern.

> "The attitude of our p. [Party – *author's note*] towards the Front for National Rebirth and towards the other parties, with which I do not agree. The other Parties have boycotted the elections. Our Party has decided to take part in the elections. … Consequently, says Andrei, we have isolated ourselves from the other Parties, and on the other hand, we have helped the Party of government to strengthen itself at the expense of the other Parties."[17]

Vasil Kolarov makes no reaction. The PCdR is too insignificant on the Comintern map. Pătrăşcanu divergences with Ştefanov, Foriş, Ilie Pintilie and Béla Breiner (left to be head of the Party in Romania, after the departure of Ştefanov to Moscow in 1938) are multiple. Although he was a member of the Secretariat in 1938, he is no longer a part of it in 1939. Without leaving the Party, he is no longer active and no longer holds any functions. On 23 August 1939, the Ribbentrop-Molotov pact supervenes, which places the communists

---

[17] Archive of the CC of the PCdR, Fund 1, Dossier 35/1939, letter of the CC of the PCdR dated 29 May 1939 and addressed to Vasil Kolarov, Comintern.

and the Nazis (Iron Guard) in the same camp. The episode further fuels Pătrășcanu's suspicions as regards Stalin and the Bolshevik regime. He maintains the same attitude. He says nothing, without repudiating the Party or demonstratively handing in his resignation, as happened in a number of the Communist Parties in the West. Willy Münzenberg, one of the key figures in the European Comintern networks, whom Pătrășcanu had known well since the 1920s, in Germany, proceeded in this way. He was assassinated in France, in 1940. Being closer to the Soviet border, Pătrășcanu would have shared the same fate. By not withdrawing from the PCdR and the Comintern, he postponed, for another 14 years, his appointment with death – arranged, as in the case of Münzenberg, by his own comrades. He prefers a stopgap solution. He remains in the ranks of the PCdR, but his activity is all but non-existent. He is viewed with increasing mistrust; he is under suspicion. His opinions about the Moscow trials and the Ribbentrop-Molotov pact have not been recorded. It was of no importance that the Comintern frequently changed its directives and slogans. Exclusive discipline and unconditional obedience were demanded. Pătrășcanu sinned in that he had his own opinions and did not hesitate to reveal them, even if he was a man who was circumspect and secretive by nature, a man of the shadows. He had been initiated into the Bolshevik catechism, he knew what awaited traitors to the cause. In essence, I think, he saw himself as a 'Leninist' who detested Stalin's methods. It was a kind of refuge, an alibi. He had remained the prisoner of his adolescent 'revolutionary' vision, but had in the meantime become alienated from the practices of Stalinism. He had the illusion that a different kind of communist regime to that practised in the USSR in the 1930s was possible.

Taken from under house arrest at Poiana Țapului, where he had a residence, Pătrășcanu arrived in the camp at Tîrgu Jiu on 3 January 1943. He had been forced to withdraw to Poiana Țapului in October 1940, after being interned at the camp in Miercurea Ciuc, where the communists still at large had been imprisoned after being rounded up by the Siguranța.

"We had a ferocious commandant, a professional military man with the rank of colonel, who had decided to subject us to a harsh regime of military drill … in August 1940, the formation of a delegation was decided upon … which included Alexandru Iliescu, C. Trandafirescu and had Lucrețiu Pătrășcanu at its head. … In discussions with the commandant of the camp, instead of employing a moderate and calm tone in his presentation of the harsh conditions we were living under in the camp … he employed on the contrary a provocative tone, declaring that we would not execute the orders for military drill. … The commandant gave the order for the delegation to leave his office and took measures to isolate some 40 internees, regarded as dangerous communists, in one wing of the building," recalls Gh. Apostol[18] – an adversary, close to Gheorghiu-Dej – desribing the attitude of Pătrășcanu at Miercurea Ciuc.

It could not be said that he was lacking in courage. After the outbreak of military hostilities in Europe, in the summer of 1940, and the subsequent loss of Romanian territory, the Government took measures against Soviet spies. In September, King Carol abdicates and the army, through General Ion Antonescu, takes power, together with the Iron Guard movement, led by Horia Sima. After the Vienna Diktat, the detainees at Miercurea Ciuc are moved to the camp at Caracal. Pătrășcanu, ill in a hospital in Brașov, manages to escape. His relatives pay 50,000 lei to a magistrate, Vasile Gelep, to have him brought to Bucharest. Here, together with Scarlat Callimachi, he is released. The pair are freed by Deputy Interior Minister Al. Ghika, an Iron Guard member and a relative of Callimachi, not, however, before demanding that the two boyars, who chance to be among the communists, give up politics. His goodwill is not only due to the fact that he is a relative, but also to the collaboration between the extreme Right and the extreme Left that had been established at the same time as the Ribbentrop-Molotov Pact. Pătrășcanu and Callimachi sign declarations whereby they undertake to refrain from political activities. Pătrășcanu is alarmed by this turn of events. The military/Iron Guard dictatorship might begin to execute communists. And as the best known amongst them he was therefore the most at risk. A few days after the assassinations at Jilava, he meets with Teohari Georgescu, at that time Secretary of the CC of the PCdR, only just returned from Moscow and, until the return of Ștefan Foriș, the head of the Party. He asks "to be sent to Moscow, because his life was in danger. I answered him, 'if you go, we all go. What will the ones in prison do?'"[19] At this meeting, he gives Teohari Georgescu a list of informers in the communist network, some of them infiltrated at the top. The one who had given it to Pătrășcanu

---

[18] Gheorghe Apostol, *Eu și Gheorghiu-Dej*, self-published, 1993, pp. 108-9.
[19] Archive of the SRI, Fund P, Dossier 40009, vol. p. 458.

demanded that, in exchange for the list, he should be taken to the USSR. The list of informers caused a commotion; it was checked by Ștefan Foriș, Petre Gheorghe and the others. It is mentioned in the correspondence between Foriș and the detainees in prison, Gheorghiu-Dej etc.

In 1941, Pătrășcanu tries to enter into contact with the PCdR, through Ion Gh. Maurer. Teohari Georgescu and the entire Secretariat – sans Foriș – had been arrested in a safe house at No. 15A Lirei Street, between Foriș and Obor.[20] Pătrășcanu wanted to find out what the situation in the Party was after these arrests and, eventually, to be co-opted into the new leadership. The connection he requests is turned down, probably by Foriș personally, but also by I. Gh. Maurer. It is possible that the latter was not in agreement with reactivating his rival, Pătrășcanu.

Having withdrawn to Poiana Țapului in March 1941, isolated, severed from the party, Pătrășcanu writes *Under Three Dictatorships*; *A Century of Social Upheavals*; *The Fundamental Problems of Romania*; and *Movements and Trends in Romanian Philosophy*. On 24 February 1942, the Bucharest Prefecture of Police reports,

"He has finished writing a work in which he deals with the Communist Party subjects, on the agrarian problem in Romania. He intends that this work should be published by the clandestine press of the PCdR shortly. The work will be circulated among the members and sympathisers of the movement. The information was gathered from communist elements who maintain links with Pătrășcanu, via his wife."[21]

He is kept under close surveillance by the Siguranța. In March of the same year, 1942, the Bucharest Prefecture reports,

"He is maintaining close contacts with the central leadership of the PCdR. These links are maintained via his wife, with whom he lives at his villa in Poiana Țapului. He receives information and instructions and sends typed manuscripts for the Party's clandestine press. ... Meetings between Pătrășcanu's wife and the Party delegate, who makes contact, take place in the context of ski races in order to confuse and distract the attention of the surveillance organs in the locality. The communist

[20] Areas of Bucharest – *Translator's note*.
[21] Archive of the CC of the RCP, Fund 95, Dossier 1565, p. 50.

leadership circles are satisfied by the way in which they maintain contact with Pătrășcanu."[22]

The report is fantastical, the product of a detective-story imagination. Pătrășcanu had no connection to the PCdR in 1942. His contacts were strictly limited to the few persons who supplied him with books. Of course, these persons were suspected of communism. The people who supply him with books, via his wife, are Belu Zilber, his brother-in-law Petre Pandrea, Sabin Manuilă, D. I. Suchianu et al. His political contacts are sporadic. He is visited on rare occasions by Mihai Ralea, Ștefan Voitec or Petre Constantinescu-Iași. In December 1942 – immediately after the catastrophe at Stalingrad – the Interior Minister orders his internment at the camp in Tîrgu Jiu. He arrives in the camp in January 1943. Asked where he wants to be barracked, he prefers to stay among the communists, in Group Two. Another 'conditional' communist, I. Gh. Maurer, imprisoned at the same time as him, preferred Group One, where the non-communists were held, the superior officers, businessmen, intellectuals, and bourgeois. Group Two is in the midst of a 'factional struggle'. The splits, the conflicts were poisoning the lives of the detainees. The incriminations, the criticism combined with self-criticism and the mutual exclusions were endless. Ovidiu Șandor is the PCdR delegate recognised by Ștefan Foriș as head of the Party cell. His authority is not, however, recognised except by part of the camp inmates. Pătrășcanu – the best known of the communists – is elected chief, with the task of settling the conflicts. The crisis is not resolved; the different camps remain just as determined to eliminate each other. One ally of Pătrășcanu is Alexandru Iliescu,[23] whom he had met at the Fifth Congress of the PCdR and in the camp at Miercurea Ciuc.

---

[22] Archive of the CC of the RCP, Fund 1/1942, Dossier 274, p. 83.

[23] Born in 1901, in Oltenia, Alexandru Iliescu, a mechanic by trade, had had two convictions. The first, for three months, in January 1926, for forgery of public documents, served at Văcărești; the second, for six months, in September 1939, for communist activities, served at Jilava. A refugee in the USSR from 1931 to 1935. From July 1940 to August 1944, interned in the camps at Miercurea Ciuc, Caracal and Tîrgu Jiu, "for agitating the masses of railway workers, urging them to strike. (ANCR, Archive of the CC of the PCR, Fund 50, Dossier 19, pp. 182-3). At Tîrgu Jiu, he is expelled from the PCdR, on the demand of Gheorghiu-Dej. He dies in 1945.

Another ally of Pătrășcanu was Athanasie Joja. Șandor accuses Pătrășcanu of being a Siguranță agent. He is backed up by I. Gh. Maurer. At the trial of Pătrășcanu in 1954, Ovidiu Șandor appears as a witness for the prosecution, upholding the same accusation. In July 1943, Gheorghiu-Dej and Chivu Stoica arrive at the camp from Caransebeș. It is a crucial moment for what is to follow in the life and career of Pătrășcanu. Gheorghiu-Dej distances Lucrețiu Pătrășcanu and replaces him as head of the Party cell with Ovidiu Șandor. He demands that Pătrășcanu, elected on 6 June, should withdraw. Pătrășcanu hesitates. The atmosphere between the two is tense. Gheorghiu-Dej is not used to having his supremacy contested. He has been head of the communists in prison for a number of years. He does not look kindly on the other's prestige among the inmates. Șandor was also a railway worker, tried and acquitted in the Grivitza trial. He was thus from the same background as Dej. Moreover, he does not question his supremacy. The fact that he was also a worker and that he was not well-known, that he did not pose any threat to his position, makes him preferable in Gheorghiu-Dej's eyes, compared to the all too famous lawyer who eluded his authority. Gheorghiu-Dej and Pătrășcanu had met for the first time in February 1933, at Jilava Prison. Pătrășcanu was already a leader; Gheorghiu-Dej was an obscure trades union agitator, active in the communist networks for at most a year. They meet again 10 years later, in the camp at Tîrgu Jiu. They rapidly enter into conflict. The motives? The competition for supremacy and the fact that Pătrășcanu does not side with Dej in the anti-Foriș plot. Each has a low opinion of the other. Each is ambitious to be head of the Romanian communists. Pătrășcanu seemed to have many chances. Educated, a member of the Party since 1921, a continual presence in the leadership, knowledgeable of Marxist doctrine, he had represented the PCdR in the Comintern. Gheorghiu-Dej was a worker, with a nebulous past in the communist networks. Nevertheless, he had served 10 years in prison – the only thing that recommended him, besides the fact that he had risen to be leader of the incarcerated communists. This ought to have put Pătrășcanu on his guard as regards Dej's abilities. Gheorghiu-Dej's visiting card did not say very much. Dej was a leader from the secondary echelon of the railway workers. Pătrășcanu – together with Marcel Pauker, Moscu Cohn and Vasile Luca – had been among the instigators and shadowy organisers of the strike at the Grivitza Workshops. Gheorghiu-Dej had been nothing more than an activist on the ground, an executor. One without merit, because his arrest had supervened a few days before the strike. Pătrășcanu, himself a proud man, did not accept Dej's supremacy. For him, Ştefan Foriş was the legitimate head of the Party. In contrast to Gheorghiu-Dej, who detested anyone who stood in his way, Pătrășcanu was more tolerant as regards Foriş, although he did not have a very high opinion of him. The bourgeois, intellectual Pătrășcanu felt closer to Foriş, who had also studied in Germany and was well-read, as he is described by those who knew him. Although a communist, Pătrășcanu remains a man of his own class.

But the removal of Pătrășcanu came about not only as a result of Gheorghiu-Dej's complexes, but also for reasons of power. In discussions with Pătrășcanu in the camp, Gheorghiu-Dej raises the question of Foriş. Dej wanted him out of the PCdR leadership. He was working towards this in the summer and autumn of 1942. The discussion between the two was aimed at drawing Pătrășcanu into the plot. Gheorghiu-Dej accuses Foriş of being a Siguranţă man and betraying a number of arrested and convicted comrades. Given his duplicity, his talent for intrigue, and his expert way of manipulating people and using them, it is hard to say what he believed in reality. He needed these grave accusations in order to eliminate Foriş. At his urging, the group of communists in prison breaks off ties with the CC of the PCdR run by Foriş. From the time when Foriş became head of the PCdR, they had not met. Pătrășcanu was no longer active in the party. He had no connection, and when he had requested this, in 1941, he had been refused on the orders of Foriş, who no longer had any faith in him after the quarrels of 1937-1939, arguments that had caused a rift between them. For his prestige in the Party, Gheorghiu-Dej needed a figure of Pătrășcanu's stature. He wanted to draw him into the plot. Pătrășcanu was not to be persuaded, saying, "Don't cause faction!" For him, even if he did not hold Foriş in high esteem, the latter was the head of the PCdR and only Moscow had the right to replace him. Throughout the factional struggles that permanently convulsed the PCdR, Pătrășcanu never took any side. Factionalism was a cardinal, unforgivable sin in the eyes of the Bolsheviks. In 1936-1938, Stalin had executed many of his victims under this accusation. The 'professional revolutionary' has the overriding obligation to submit to orders and to accept the chiefs chosen by his hierarchical superiors. For him, Foriş had been appointed by the Comintern, and could not be replaced by an obscure activist. When he declined to do Gheorghiu-Dej's bidding, he made himself a mortal enemy. Gheorghiu-Dej could not accept any infringement of his authority. His first decision is to remove Pătrăşcanu from the leadership of the communist group.

Gheorghiu-Dej and Pătrăşcanu bore no resemblance to each other. Everything separated them. During the days they spent together in the camp, in June 1943, they ended up hating each other. Gheorghiu-Dej, with his sectarian fanaticism, reduced everything to 'whoever has power', to the struggle for supremacy. Pătrăşcanu is more sophisticated. He is learned. He has weaker political instincts. Gheorghiu-Dej is a political animal. He has instincts. He has honed the skills necessary for political intrigue in the cells of Doftana and Caransebeş, where survival was not the easiest thing. Pătrăşcanu is less attentive to such questions, which relate to survival and power. He comes from a background that is open and tolerant, unlike the closed world of the prisons. He looks down on this electrician, who puts on airs of being the boss. This will cost him his life.

In August 1943, the episode is closed. Thanks to the interventions of his family, Pătrăşcanu is released and placed under house arrest in Poiana Ţapului, at his parents' house. One more motive for Gheorghiu-Dej to suspect and hate him. He had requested to be released on the expiry of his prison sentence. The Interior Minister preferred to intern him in camp.

> "Andrei [i.e. Pătrăşcanu] gave me to understand that when he was in the camp he had enjoyed a certain degree of trust among the comrades, until the arrival of Gheorghiu-Dej at Tg. Jiu … he said … that he felt he had to step aside, but he could not step aside in a servile manner. He felt that it was from this that everything started. Perhaps I made a mistake, I should have been more servile towards Gheorghiu-Dej, but I could not do such a thing. … They were personal matters – about who had the greatest say."[24]

Returning to Poiana Ţapului, Pătrăşcanu prepares to re-enter politics. The disputes in the camp had reinvigorated him. Moreover, the approach of the Red Army spoke loudly and clearly: the communists would play an important role. In the new context, men with a past such as his were destined to a great career. He resumes his connection with the Party, via Emil Bodnăraş, who had been assigned to him in Tîrgu Jiu by Gheorghiu-Dej himself. He also meets with Constantin Pîrvulescu, Petre Constantinescu-Iaşi and

---

[24] ASRI, Fund P, Dossier 40002, vol. 202, p. 207.

Constantin Agiu, a long-standing activist, a participant in the bomb attack on the Senate in December 1920. In the winter of 1943-1944, when the two see each other again, he was leader of the Union of Patriots, a phantom organisation of the PCdR.

The happiest year of Pătrășcanu's life is 1944. It seems that everything he had done up until then had been nothing but an extended rehearsal for the role he was now to play. He is enmeshed in a conspiracy of vast proportions: the overthrow of the Antonescu regime. He is not plotting a revolution, arming the workers. He is not conspiring with the lumpenproletariat and the déclassé in whose world he had been lingering for 25 years. He frequents the established political leaders of the detested 'Romanian oligarchy': Iuliu Maniu, Ion Mihalache, C. I. C. Brătianu, Gh. Tătărescu et al. Moreover, the chief conspirator is none other than King Mihai I himself. It is a paradoxical, even absurd, situation. Far from the class sentiments that a Bolshevik ought to have nurtured, Pătrășcanu feels honoured. In fact, he belongs to this world, in which he rediscovers himself. He has connections at the palace, in the ranks of the bourgeoisie; he is linked to businessmen, to important politicians, and to the intellectuals of the elite. When the King seeks out a communist to join his plot to overthrow Antonescu – as had been demanded by the Allies in Cairo – he is handed the name of Lucrețiu Pătrășcanu. The latter fulfilled two conditions: he was a communist and he came from a 'good family'. He is invited to take part in the plot. Pătrășcanu accepts, honoured.

> "In the evening, I had a meeting with Pătrășcanu – the head of the Communist Party – who communicated to me that he is on the point of achieving an opposition bloc. In any case, the King was the one who desired this union of the entire opposition. Pătrășcanu also realises the difficulty of our leaving the Axis and, if need be, has offered to go to Moscow in order to arrange the clauses of the armistice. Pătrășcanu is putting his heart into it, and he is dynamic, so that I have every confidence that he will be of use to us," notes General Sănătescu, the head of the royal household, on 8 May 1944.[25] As a conspirator, Pătrășcanu is in his element. This is what he has been doing all his life. His skills, honed for more than 20 years in the underground, when

---

[25] Constantin Sănătescu, *Jurnalul generalului Sănătescu*, Bucharest: Humanitas, 1993, p. 153.

he operated as a Comintern agent, are functioning perfectly. He has experience – in contrast to the other participants. He enjoys it; he has abilities. He knows what is to be done. The rules of conspiracy were part of the professional revolutionary's alphabet. He looks for safe houses in which to hide and meet with other communists and participants in the plot: generals, colonels, envoys of the King, political leaders.

How secret does this plot remain? Dozens of people are in on it: at the palace, high up in the political parties, in the army, at newspaper offices, in various entourages. This is a world in which indiscretion is the custom. There are no secrets here. An operation of such proportions could not pass unobserved. Let us take the PCdR as just one example. "More than half of them (the communists) were our informers," admits Eugen Cristescu, head of the SSI.[26] Pătrășcanu is under close surveillance. Around him, informers observe and report what he does, what he says. He is shadowed 24 hours a day. His multiple meetings – with people at the palace, with Iuliu Maniu, C. I. C. Brătianu and Constantin Titel-Petrescu, with communist leaders – are known. It is not until June that he succeeds in shaking off the Siguranța men and disappearing. On 26 June, the General Department of Police reports that lawyer Lucrețiu Pătrășcanu, under house arrest in Poiana Țapului until 28 December 1943, "on 3 June this year managed to vanish from under the surveillance of the police organs that were following him, in a new motor car, a Buick, in a direction unknown. … in case of identification, he will be kept under surveillance in order not for him to disappear again."[27] Thus, he was not to be arrested, sent to the camp or back to Poiana Țapului, but only watched in continuation. The threads of the plot led to him and information could be obtained by following him. Moreover, it is to be supposed that there were accomplices at a high level, who protected the plot or were concerned with using it to their own ends. The conspiracy, far from passing unobserved, was closely watched by the SSI, by military counter intelligence. As early as 3 June, all Pătrășcanu's meetings were under surveillance. Informers were to be found at the palace too, as well as around Maniu and Brătianu, and among the generals. Having escaped

---

[26] Cristian Troncotă, *Eugen Cristescu, asul serviciilor secrete românești. Memorii, mărturii, documente* [*E.C., Ace of the Romanian Secret Services. Memoirs, Testimonies, Documents*], Roza Vânturilor, 1994, p. 11.
[27] ANIC Archive, Fund 95, Dossier 31/1789, p. 22.

from his shadows, Pătrășcanu hides in one of the houses arranged by his brother-in-law, Petre Pandrea, in Labirint Street. Pătrășcanu takes little care to conceal his movements. He walks around Bucharest, on Armenească Street, close to his address at No. 100 Vasile Lascăr Street. He appears on Calea Victoriei, where he has two addresses. He is active, tireless, excited by the idea of the conspiracy and his important role. He comes and goes from meetings, conspires frantically, in a deluxe underground, with high-up accomplices.

The story of the conspiracy begins in November 1943, when Pătrășcanu is sought out by palace circles, via Octav Ulea, a cousin who puts him up at his farm in Pantelimon[28] after New Year 1944. Discussions take place – without the knowledge of Foriș, the head of the Party. He meets Iuliu Maniu on a number of occasions and discusses the political situation in detail. They agree that Romania should leave the Axis, and that the Anonescu regime should be overthrown. The talks in Cairo and the example of Italy encouraged such preparations. The Red Army offensive on the Eastern front hastened them. The other camp also wanted to collaborate with the communists. In April, Mihai Antonescu sent envoys to Pătrășcanu with an offer to join the delegation that was to go to Soviet territories for peace talks, with Mihai Antonescu showing himself inclined to sign an armistice, after the deposal of Ion Antonescu. The offer is rejected by the PCdR leadership. Separately, Ion Antonescu also wants to meet Pătrășcanu. The meeting is set up through Piki Vasiliu, the Interior Minister. The new PCdR leadership – Bodnăraș, Rangheț, Pîrvulescu – agrees to the meeting. The topic of the discussion was to be the Marshal's intention to sign a separate peace with the Allies. Pătrășcanu presents himself at the meeting place, Romană Square, whence he was to be taken by motor car. General Piki Vasiliu arrives, but informs him that the Marshal has changed his mind. It is hard to say why he changed his mind. One reason, expressed during his trial in 1946, was that Pătrășcanu had confirmed, in discussions with Piki Vasiliu, that he had no contacts with the PCdR leadership and did not speak for the latter. In fact, we should wonder whether, during this interval – from November 1943, when the first steps were taken in the conspiracy, until 4 April, when Foriș was deposed – Pătrășcanu really represented the PCdR at all, whether he acted under orders or not. Was it his idea to implicate the PCdR in a Royal Coup? Did he act alone? In the investigation he will answer the question

---

[28] An outlying district of Bucharest – *Translator's note*.

as follows: "On whose authority and with what aim did you make contact with Maniu in 1943?" Pătrășcanu: "On the authority of no one, but on my own initiative."[29]

A joint operation between King, Army, bourgeois parties and communists was something without precedent. It broke the mould imposed by the Kremlin. In any case, the USSR would not have recognised any formula that did not include the communists. Pătrășcanu made his calculations correctly. From pariahs, harried as agents and terrorists, the handful of communists now become important players in the political game. Pătrășcanu is an imposter. Yes, he is a communist, he answers the messengers from the palace. Yes, he is interested in a scheme to snatch the country from the jaws of disaster. After sounding him out, the same messengers raise the question of whether he represents the PCdR. Pătrășcanu was not in contact with Foriș and was not part of the leadership. He had given up underground activities a few years ago. It was not until January 1944 that Foriș and Pătrășcanu met for the first time since the appointment of the former as head of the PCdR. As Belu Zilber says, in 1968,

"For as long as Pătrășcanu was at Poiana Țapului, he had no links with anybody. He came to Bucharest, he made contact with the palace through Ulea and Safian. When the people at the palace put him on the spot … 'What proof do we have that you represent the Communist Party?' Pătrășcanu broke off ties with the palace until Foriș and Koffler were liquidated. … I deduce from this matter that he did not have any mandate from anybody and that what he did was a hoax. He played it very well, however, it was to his advantage. … Pătrășcanu pulled off a hoax, which might or might not have succeeded… He played it on his own behalf and the second man in the Party, Bodnăraș, intervened only after the new Political Bureau had already been formed. Before that it was only he who was playing, who was in discussion, and when the new Central Committee was formed, he presented himself before it with the entire matter already a done deed."[30]

---

[29] Archive of the SRI, Fund P, Dossier 40002, vol. 2., p. 361.

[30] *23 August 1944 în arhivele comuniste* [*23 August 1944 in the communist archives*], Majadahonda, 2000, p. 131.

Besides the plot against Antonescu, there was another in which Pătrăşcanu refused to take part. That organised within the PCdR against the head of the Party, Ştefan Foriş. Fearing the accusation of factionalism, Pătrăşcanu preferred the waiting game. Nor had he been involved in any of the intrigues at the top of the PCdR for many years. He did not get involved, but nor did he denounce the perpetrators to Foriş. Questioned once more, this time by Bodnăraş, he replies the same as to Gheorghiu-Dej in the camp: "I don't take part in factionalism." The conspirators do not waste time and leave him on the sidelines. "When I saw Pătrăşcanu's position, that he was dithering on the Foriş question, I didn't bring him into it after that. He didn't know about the plan, or the date, nothing, we informed him only afterwards," declares Bodnăraş in 1953, when Pătrăşcanu was already imprisoned and had been under investigation for four years.[31] Faith in him is also undermined by this attitude. This was in addition to his poor relationship with Gheorghiu-Dej, which makes him thoroughly suspect to the 'comrades'. He continues to present himself at negotiations, because the PCdR did not have any other man for relations with the palace, army and historical parties. Moreover, some of these relations were strictly personal. The effect of his non-involvement in the elimination of Foriş was discovered on 5 April. A day earlier, Foriş had been sequestered and a troika had taken his place: Bodnăraş, Pîrvulescu, Rangheţ. Behind them was Gheorghiu-Dej, the one who demanded this solution "without Pătrăşcanu." On the evening of 5 April, when he meets with the troika, he finds out that he is not part of the new leadership, in spite of the role he had played in the other plot, against Antonescu.

"Constantin Pîrvulescu: When I called Pătrăşcanu in the evening … I informed him. He raised the issue of being brought into the leadership. … I said that this leadership had been appointed on the basis of consultation with active Party members, on the basis of the indications of Comrade Gheorghiu-Dej. … He came and said 'I have to be in the leadership'. – Comrade Bodnăraş: He said, 'I consider it necessary for me to be in the leadership, it is a political mistake if I am not and I request that you take into account the letter I want to send to Comrade Gheorghiu'. – Constantin Pîrvulescu: I too reproached him that the

[31] Dan Cătănuş, Ioan Chiper, *Cazul Ştefan Foriş. Lupta pentru putere în PCR de la Gheorghiu-Dej la Ceauşescu*, Bucharest: Vremea, 1999, p. 48.

situation is very grave, not to mention the issues that we also had when [he was] … in the Comintern and that he had to adapt to the job, that he would be given a job with responsibility, he was being demoted. But he nevertheless wrote the letter. – Comrade Bodnăraş: I refused him too, I said that we are the leadership and we cannot but prevail. We communicated the same thing to Comrade Gheorghiu, he agreed, and Pătrăşcanu was brought down a notch."[32]

One month later, Pătrăşcanu hands over the letter for Gheorghiu-Dej and Teohari Georgescu (the head of the Party cell at Caransebeş), via the troika.[33] The reaction of those concerned is to send Emil Bodnăraş, Petre Constantinescu-Iaşi and Constantin Agiu to accompany him at negotiations. Pătrăşcanu is not sufficiently trustworthy. Previously, he had been doubted in palace circles. Now he is also doubted by his Party accomplices. His ambiguous status arouses suspicions everywhere. He is always an elusive figure, because he does not entirely belong to either world. He is neither a bourgeois politician, nor a true professional revolutionary. Pătrăşcanu overplays both roles. Nonetheless, in contrast to Foriş, the new leaders agree to continue conspiring with the King, the generals and the leaders of the bourgeois parties. In a way, his imposture towards them comes to a close. Now he has a mandate, he no longer represents only himself. He becomes the executor of precise orders. The plot enters a precise stage, in which decisions are taken, and responsibilities and deadlines are set. Elements of farce and bluff are not lacking. One example is when Bodnăraş claims in front of the generals that he has 12,000 armed men in Bucharest.

"Almost every night we gather discreetly in various houses to work out in detail internal action in the event that the plan to break from the Germans is put into action. Never absent from these meetings are generals Mihail and Vasiliu-Răşcanu, Col. Dămăceanu, Buzeşti, Stîrcea, Pătrăşcanu and Bodnăraş. I have great need of the latter two in order to organise the workers in the factories on whom I am counting to make up for a lack of troops,"

---

[32] *Idem*, p. 154.

[33] Letter published by Florin Constantiniu in *Dosarele istoriei* no. 8/2004.

General Sănătescu notes in his diary on 22 June 1944,[34] he himself a victim of communist mystification. It is probable that the manpower controlled by Bodnăraş did not exceed 12 men. Everything takes on an aspect of vaudeville. The plotters are in a hurry, with their eyes on the map of the Eastern front. In any case, everyone else in Bucharest is also conspiring. The city is full of rumours and truncated information. Everyone is in on it. Only Antonescu, the one targeted, seems not to be. What is certain is that he does nothing to annihilate the conspirators. Did he know what was afoot or not? There is now no way of knowing. In any case, in this atmosphere of complicity, of secret games and scheming, of Bucharest chiaroscuro, Pătrăşcanu is one of the protagonists.

On 23 August, the Antonescus are arrested. Pătrăşcanu goes to the palace in the evening. He is the only one of the plotters to meet the King under the circumstances. The other leaders, such as Maniu and Brătianu, prefer to stay away from the palace, or else arrive after the King has left, the case of Titel Petrescu. Pătrăşcanu deals with recording and broadcasting the declaration of King Mihai I, who puts an end to the military dictatorship. He was the author of the declaration together with Belu Zilber. Between him and the King, there is a strange relationship, if we consider that one was a king and the other a communist. The King esteems him from their very first meeting. It seems to him, without him suspecting that Pătrăşcanu is not a typical communist, that it is possible to do politics with them. Pătrăşcanu also shares the close feelings. The young King, who is 22, convinces him. Pătrăşcanu also feels honoured by the company. His social snobbery manifests itself in these circumstances. He had come from the periphery of Romanian society to its very heart. Pătrăşcanu is a proud man. This unusual conspirator must have felt very special that evening. His game of conspiracy, begun in November 1943, had succeeded. Before the King leaves the palace to reach safety, he asks him to designate him Minister of Justice, thereby breaking the agreement between political leaders, which demanded that they remain outside, as ministers without portfolio. The King agrees. Pătrăşcanu thus becomes interim Minister of Justice. He is the only civilian minister. It is not the first time that he forces the hand of fate. Nor the first time he offers himself. His entire participation in the conspiracy had been the result of an attitude at the very limit of imposture. Nor will it be the last time. In February 1945, he offers to serve the King as

---

[34] Constantin Sănătescu, *idem*, p. 155.

his Prime Minister. This time he does not succeed. The Kremlin has other plans, another name: Dr Petre Groza.

A few days later, Pătrășcanu leaves for Moscow. He is head of the delegation.[35] He had offered to go to Moscow, demanding that not only military personnel be sent. As he was the only civilian in the government, it was obvious he was referring to himself. He proposes himself as a member of the delegation in the meeting that takes place in the basement of the National Bank on 25 August. As he is the only minister in the delegation, it devolves upon him to be its leader. It is exactly what he was pursuing. He wanted to be the first Romanian official to arrive in Moscow to conduct peace talks with the Soviets. He makes the journey, squeezed into a small aeroplane. He arrives in Odessa after a low altitude flight over the Black Sea, in order not to be detected. He waits there for a few hours – the Russians are taken unprepared – before getting approvals from the Kremlin. Then, in a Douglas aeroplane, he arrives in Moscow. Besides Pătrășcanu, the official delegation from Bucharest includes Colonel Dumitru Dămăceanu, and Ghiță Pop. Barbu Știrbey and Constantin Vișoianu arrive from Cairo. They are greeted at Vnukovo Airport by an official from the Foreign Ministry. They are accommodated in a comfortable villa in the suburbs, which is where Churchill also used to stay when he came to Moscow. Once more, they are left to wait for a number of days. The arrival of Pătrășcanu, accompanied by an elegant wife (he is the only one who has brought his wife with him), both of them with an entirely non-proletarian air, makes a bad impression on the Soviet officials. As we know, he comports himself on two levels. He is a veteran communist, he has been to Moscow a number of times before, for the first time in 1922. He is known at the Kremlin. On this occasion, his Comintern file is closely examined. Another is the official level. He is head of the delegation; he represents the Government of Romania. The interests of the two positions are contradictory. As a communist, he had to defend the interests of the USSR, as laid down in the Comintern statutes to which he had subscribed in 1921. He had worked for the Comintern and, here, employment was for life. The interests of the USSR were to occupy Romania and install a pro-Soviet government in Bucharest. As head of the delegation from the Romanian Government, he had come to sign the armistice and had to act in the contrary sense. To salvage what could still be salvaged: democratic institutions, the monarchy, the parliamentary system,

---

[35] Archive of the SRI, Fund P, Dossier 40002, vol. 14, p. 346.

and the existing structure of Romanian society. He had to protect Romania from the occupying Red Army, to obtain the status of Allied nation.

His behaviour reflects this internal rupture and the contradictions of his position. In Bucharest, by the very fact that he was a communist, a former Comintern agent, it was hoped that lenient conditions would be obtained from the Allies. It was also the reason for which he had been brought into the plot. What does Pătrășcanu do? He sends a personal letter to Molotov,[36] "I shall remain grateful to you if you could facilitate a meeting for me with one of the members of the Romanian group in Moscow, Ana Pauker or Luca Laszlo." He likewise asks Molotov to assign an agent to him, "to establish direct and unofficial contacts" with the Kremlin. The agent was to be a "personal acquaintance." It was inappropriate, if not treacherous behaviour.

He meets Ana Pauker again. They have known each other since 1921. He had conducted her defence, in the trial of 1936. In September 1944, Pătrășcanu hears nothing but incriminations. That he, a communist, Pătrășcanu could not have conspired with the King against Antonescu. It would have been better for them 'to have been liberated by the Red Army'. This would have led to the immediate installation of a government of 'dictatorship of the proletariat', In the present situation, with a popular king, and a working coalition government, the installation of a Soviet regime will have to be put on hold. Instead of praise, Pătrășcanu finds himself buffeted by furious criticism. As Elena Pătrășcanu recalls, in 1967,

"When we went into Ana Pauker's house, there was a large map on the wall with little flags that marked the front and Comrade Ana told Andrei: 'Look, here are our troops [the Soviet Army – *author's note*], they have managed to encircle the enemy [the Romanian Army – *author's note*] … in Moldova'. Comrade Ana held the view that Soviet troops had conquered Bucharest and Andrei said that we had done the deed on 23 August, and that things did not stand the same as they did in … other countries…" Gheorghe Stoica (Moscu Cohn), the veteran communist, asks her: "How did Ana receive him?"

---

[36] INST, *Misiunea lui A.I. Vîşinski în România. Doasare secrete* [*The Mission of A.I. Vyshinsky in Romania. Secret Files*], 1997, p. 63.

Elena Pătrășcanu answers:

> "They embraced and she looked at me penetratingly, telling me that we
> didn't have it bad in Bucharest, that we were well dressed (she was badly
> dressed). She said it with a kind of subtext, that we didn't have it bad, with
> a bit of malice, and when we left to go home, Andrei told me that Ana
> did not like the fact that 23 August had happened, that she would have
> preferred to come herself, not for us to do the 23 August deed. They
> discussed the front a lot. She made Andrei relate to her what the arrest of
> Antonescu had been like. She couldn't believe something like that could
> have happened...."[37]

For days on end, the Soviets refused to negotiate. "Andrei thought that he
would be received by Stalin, but he was received only by Molotov."[38] After
two weeks, during which there were no negotiations, the delegation is
invited to the Kremlin. At a given moment, there are fireworks. As Molotov
informs them, "They are in celebration of the liberation of Bucharest by the
glorious Soviet Army." They had left Bucharest emptied of Germans and
with a Romanian Government in control of the situation. The Red Army was
hundreds of miles away. Molotov did not hesitate to tell Pătrășcanu, "The
Red Army had been greeted with flowers in Bucharest." Arriving home,
on relating the scene to his wife, he remarks: "This is going to cost me my
head."[39] It was a premonition. He knew with whom he was dealing.

Pătrășcanu is kept under close surveillance by Soviet agents. They want to
see whether he is the right man to take over the leadership of the tiny PCdR.
Can they trust him or not? The attitude he takes at the negotiations, where he
upholds some Romanian positions against Soviet demands, enlightens them.
For them, Pătrășcanu remains a bourgeois, because he does not situate himself
along class lines. He does not behave in a Party-minded way, i.e. he does not
defend the interests of the USSR, the 'homeland of the proletarian revolution',
against the 'Romanian oligarchy'. It is a position that is unintelligible on the
part of someone who had worked for the Comintern. They were expecting
him to give priority to the interests of the Kremlin. He showed himself to
be a 'chauvinist patriot' etc., etc. Their lack of trust in Pătrășcanu was long-

---

[37] SRI, Fund P, Dossier 40002, vol. 202, p. 206.

[38] *Idem*, p. 206.

[39] *Idem*, p. 205.

standing. He had turned up in the 1930s, when he was a representative of the PCdR in Moscow. He had escaped the Lubyanka, because he had had the good fortune to return to Romania in time. As a Bolshevik of the old guard, he would not have escaped the firing squad. His role as negotiator for the King and the historical parties was also blameworthy. Pătrăşcanu was not the man they needed. Edified, Dimitrov, on Stalin's orders, entrusts the leadership of the PCdR to Ana Pauker. Pătrăşcanu returns to Bucharest on 13 September. Ana Pauker arrives three days later, on 16 September, at Băneasa,[40] with a mandate to take over the leadership.

Pătrăşcanu returns to Bucharest to an atmosphere of great expectations. Everyone believed that the war was almost over and that things would get back to normal. They believed that Romania was on the side of the victors. There was also the illusion that the British and Americans would not allow the USSR to occupy South Eastern Europe militarily or dominate it politically. The 1922 Constitution is once more in vigour, at Pătrăşcanu's suggestion. Molotov's declaration of 12 April gave assurances that Moscow would not change the political system, and in Bucharest – prey to a kind of historical amnesia – the declaration is believed. No reasons for concern can be seen. In the autumn of 1944, Pătrăşcanu is living out his hour of glory. A protagonist of the 23 August coup, a signatory of the armistice, a minister... It is much more than he had hoped. He is not just a successful politician. He is a historic figure. While he was operating in the underground with the hope of one day rising to the surface, he had a complex about failure. Things had changed radically. A few months previously, he was a pariah, he was still in hiding from the Siguranţă, he was a man with no face, no name. On reaching the heights, he discovers history. He is preoccupied with his place in history. Now he has one. His name can no longer be erased from the history books. It was not quite the revolution he had dreamed of in his youth, but it was still something. He has in mind the drama of his father, which had obsessed him. He had dreamed of a revolutionary conflagration which would burn everything to the ground, destroy society, the bourgeoisie, with King Ferdinand at its head, whom he saw as the symbol of the world that had ostracised his father. Here he is now alongside the King, his accomplice, and alongside the leaders of the Romanian bourgeoisie. And he does not feel at all bad in this company. He belongs to this world, in fact. It is the homecoming of the prodigal son.

---

[40] The airport outside Bucharest – *Translator's note*.

Had he ever been an 'authentic' revolutionary? Or had the idea of revolution, of 'razing the old world' been merely a mental refuge, an expression of frustration? He wanted to be part of that world and not its destroyer. He wanted recognition from the background from whence he came. He wished it ill in order to punish it for having made his family suffer. In August-September 1944, he has his revenge for the opprobrium he lived through in 1919-1921. And not just anyhow. Communism, of which he regarded himself as the flag bearer, was a mortal threat to the Romanian establishment. Pătrăşcanu is the man of the hour. He is sought after, flattered, feared. He gathers a clique of admirers who accompany him everywhere. Many of them are to be found in the investigation and trials of 1954. In the autumn of 1944, however, his career seems to be a success story. He is popular; many put their hopes in him. He is perceived as a civilised, educated communist, with honourable social origins. He is a kind of hybrid, always a double figure. Part of his existence has been spent in full view, in public, another part in the underground. He has the appearance of a typical politician, or rather of a bourgeois lawyer/professor. The King too had been taken in by the way Pătrăşcanu presented himself. But appearances proved deceptive. Underneath, we find his conspiratorial nature, the secret personage, gnawed away by complexes and unhealed ambitions. In a discussion, he is asked by Belu Zilber, at the time when he was beginning to have difficulties with the Political Bureau, why he did not resign from the CC. "As if illumined by a beatific vision, he answered: 'Not that! Power is so pleasant'."[41] Here is the whole character, a 'Leninist', absolutely obsessed with power. And after 23 August 1994, he possesses it. He is a minister. His books are published one after the other. He finds himself – a man who was formerly anonymous, with an uncertain social status – at the centre of attention. He gives interviews; his photograph appears almost daily in the papers. He is often the subject of news stories and articles. He frequents high society events, the theatre, attends the *vernissages* of exhibitions and diplomatic receptions. Moreover, his name is chanted by crowds at meetings and demonstrations. He is the most visible, most popular figure in the RCP. He is the preferred negotiating partner for the other parties and the Royal palace. Does he feel that he is taking revenge for the drama of his father? If so, it is a sorry revenge. From pride, from ideological blindness, he makes himself a tool of the Soviet occupier, just as his father had been the tool of

---

[41] Belu Zilber, *op. cit.*, p. 198.

the German occupier. He will understand this bitter irony of fate when he says: "We are nothing but Quislings." The power he possesses is factitious, a surrogate. It is the Soviets who dictate. He is not even a minister, but rather he plays the role of minister in an occupied country. It is the occupier who possesses all the power. He is a collaborator, in a form more grave than his father had been.

***

At the beginning of October 1944, not even two months after the Royal Coup, there is a demonstration in Bucharest, under the patronage of the RCP. Passing in front of the podium where the Party leaders are assembled, the column of workers chants "Pătrăşcanu Prime Minister." The next day, Emil Bodnăraş gives the order to some former inmates from Doftana and Caransebeş, Soviet spies the same as him (Vanya Didenko, Serghei Nikonov, Mişa Postanski, Petea Goncharuk), to keep Pătrăşcanu under surveillance. The motive was not treachery, but Pătrăşcanu's popularity. He was popular, liked by the King, accepted by the leaders of the bourgeois parties. In his own Party, on the other hand, he was viewed with mistrust, disliked. This was particularly apparent at the top, where he was seen as a dangerous counter-candidate for the leadership. The PCR, only just having emerged from clandestinity, was a conjuncture of clans, of small groups, bound by invisible networks. The conflicts that had continually convulsed the Party were not forgotten and nor were they over. They were now prolonged at a new stage: that of the conquest of power. Two groups dominated. One led by Ana Pauker, the other by Gheorghiu-Dej. The first was made up of refugees from the USSR: Vasile Luca, Gh. Stoica (Moscu Cohn), Constantin Doncea, Dumitru Petrescu, Leonte Răutu, Valter Roman, Manole H. Manole, Leonte Tismăneanu etc. The second united the prison inmates: Teohari Georgescu, Miron Constantinescu, Iosif Chişinevshi, Chivu Stoica, Grigore Preoteasa et al. There were also other communists, few in number – who did not constitute any group per se, because they had no cohesion – those who had been at liberty: Lucreţiu Pătrăşcanu, Constantin Pîrvulescu, Emil Bodnăraş, I. Gh. Maurer, Iosif Rangheţ, Constantin Aghiu, Petre Constantinescu-Iaşi. Loyalties and sides later switched, but, in the autumn of 1944, these were the policy makers in the RCP. They vied for power under the watchful eyes of the Soviet emissaries. This does not mean that there were differences of opinion among them. They were all convinced internationalists, subordinate to the will of Stalin, regardless of where they came from. The fact that they had spent the war as refugees in the USSR or in prisons in Romania was a circumstance of no influence on their stance. The 'Moscovites' and the 'prisoners' rapidly agree on the isolation of Pătrășcanu. A plot – the house speciality – begins to be woven.

In October 1945, a year after the demonstration following which Bodnăraș gave the order for him to be watched, a RCP conference takes place, an opportunity for the first shots to be fired by the tacit coalition that was forming against Pătrășcanu. Gheorghe Apostol recommends to the auditorium that they elect Pătrășcanu to the CC of the RCP, characterising him as "a lawyer who has defended communists at trial." Gheorghiu-Dej interposes, saying that he will support the candidature even if Pătrășcanu is an individualist who displays bourgeois hang-ups and causes 'theoretical tangles'. Pătrășcanu feels slighted. He was not only a lawyer, but one of the founding members of the RCP, a leader during almost the whole of the clandestine period, one of the architects of the 23 August coup, a signatory of the armistice, the best known of the communists. His pride having been wounded, he has the impression that he is being given less than he deserves, that he is not being held in sufficiently high esteem, that he is being sidelined. But it is not only pride and frustrated ambition. He glimpses here the warp of the plot that is being woven against him. The criticisms to which he is subject might, as indeed happened, be the prelude to his political liquidation. The next day, at the first meeting of the members of the CC, he reads the letter of resignation from the post of Minister of Justice that he intends to present to Petre Groza. In addition, he asks his election to the CC not to be validated, and "to be sent to do lowly work," something which had already happened to him, he recalls, during the time of the Foriș Secretariat, i.e. in 1935, after he returned from Moscow. His attitude provokes a storm. He finds himself assailed by invectives and threats. Vasile Luca: "It's petit bourgeois ambition, I raise the matter of petit bourgeois residues, he is a petit bourgeois intellectual. … The attitude of Comrade Pătrășcanu is the greatest demonstration of his petty bourgeois intellectual residues, in which he places the 'Me' above the Party."[42] Nor does Ana Pauker spare him: "For you to do such a thing, it must be because your ambition and your individualism have completely clouded your mind

[42] *Sfera politicii*, no. 37, April 1996, p. 36.

… in this way you are going against the Party." Miron Constantinescu: "By this attitude Comrade Pătrășcanu serves the enemies of our Party."[43] Iosif Rangheț: "Comrade Pătrășcanu is a very learned comrade, more learned than all of us, but he hangs around in bourgeois circles and suffers from that influence. … This is why it should be made sure that this environment should no longer influence you, but rather the environment you are in now should influence you."[44] C. Pîrvulescu: "Is such a thing permissible? This is without precedent in our Party, to come and threaten us with resignation from the Government … It would mean not only a blow to the Party, but it would also mean assisting our enemies." C. Vasilichi: "I think that Pătrășcanu is pursued by the idea that he is persecuted as an intellectual. And I remember what Lenin wrote about intellectuals, about these intellectuals who move with all their baggage to the working class, and makes a distinction between these and those who, being intellectuals, want to lead the Party rather than have the Party to lead them. … He raises the issue of resignation, I consider it a dereliction of duty for a communist today." Gh. Apostol: "And not only a dereliction. It has a more serious character. I find in Comrade Pătrășcanu a kind of factionalist mentality. Because he … places his pride above the interests of the Party … I find that he ought to examine his conscience and to come before the CC with a profound self-denunciation." Al. Moghioroș: "It is not a desertion … It is a crime, comrades!" Iosif Chișinevschi: "The matter of resignation is unheard of in the Party." Gheorghiu-Dej:[45]

Comrades, personally, I have nothing against Comrade Pătrășcanu, I have no quarrel with him. We were in the camps together and we know each other well. … On Radio London, they are commenting on the divergence that exists between Comrade Pătrășcanu's political line and that of the rest of the members of the CC … When the question of the unity of the entire Party is raised before reactionaries, and thus demands iron unity in our Party, Comrade Pătrășcanu comes along with this resignation … The Pătrășcanu case is one that is very thorny. I draw to the attention of the members of the CC, that this is a closed session of our plenary, under the sanction of taking the severest measures against those who do not hold their tongues … I don't want to scratch Comrade Pătrășcanu's sensibilities … Let Comrade Pătrășcanu take back his words against us and revise his entire attitude.

---

[43] *Idem*, no. 38, May 1996, pp. 31-2.

[44] *Idem*, p. 33.

[45] *Idem*, no. 39, June 1996, pp. 33-4.

To this assault, in which he finds himself entirely alone, Pătrăşcanu responds: "There ought to be no Pătrăşcanu case ... The declaration I made as regards Party unity is strengthened by my entire past ... Anything, except factionalism. I have never and shall never practise factionalism. But I ask that this case be liquidated ... according to the proposal I have made."[46] Vasile Luca: "Comrade Pătrăşcanu says that the CC has had suspicions regarding him, let him explain for what reason the CC had suspicions regarding him. – Comrade Pătrăşcanu: comrade, you should ask yourself that, and Comrade Ana and Comrade Teohari and Comrade Gheorghiu-Dej, too."[47] Gh. Vasilichi: "I don't think it is the task of Comrade Pătrăşcanu to discuss what should or shouldn't be done. He is a chapter of the Party and the Party should place this chapter where it deserves."[48] Gheorghiu-Dej: "Have you anything else to say? – Comrade Pătrăşcanu: "I have nothing else to say."[49] The discussion is closed; Pătrăşcanu withdraws his resignation. I have reproduced long passages from the shorthand record of this plenary because it is here that we find the protagonists of the drama, it is here that we are able to anticipate the denouement. It is but one act. Others will follow. Here we see at work the coalition that has formed against him. No one comes to his defence. We can see the methods of those experienced veterans of the underground. We witness an execution. Although they have emerged from 'illegality', their behaviour remains that of the underground.

The coalition proceeds to isolate Pătrăşcanu. Its members use the same techniques acquired in clandestinity. They prepare to unmask him, excommunicate him; they prepare his downfall. He will be transformed into a non-person and, after a long ritual, prosecuted. There follows a ceremony of degradation – he is declared a 'spy', 'renegade', 'traitor', 'Titoist', 'nationalist', 'bourgeois', by Gheorghiu-Dej, Teohari Georgescu, Vasile Luca, Miron Constantinescu, Iosif Chişinevschi – one that is repeated many times during the period 1948-1954. He is humiliated, spurned, slandered in every way possible – the same as Lenin used to label his adversaries 'insects' before they were murdered, sent to Siberia or deported – in order to counterbalance his popularity, the respect he enjoyed. Firstly, an image of Pătrăşcanu as a degenerate human being, as a monster had to be

---

[46] *Idem*, p. 34.

[47] *Idem*, p. 34.

[48] *Idem*, p. 34.

[49] *Idem*, p. 35.

spread. Only after this ceremonial could he be tried and assassinated. The demolition of his popularity will take the 'conspirators' quite a while – six years from the moment of his arrest in 1948. An anonymous militant could disappear overnight without any prior preparations, as in the case of Foriş. The procedures of those who had emerged from the underground had not changed. They are repeated in the new circumstances of a country under foreign occupation, in which the masters are themselves denizens of the underground.

This is the ambiguous post-war world; a world that does not yet know in which direction it will move. The habits of clandestine life were acquired in prison and in emigration. It seems that nothing has changed in this sect. The communists now live as a veritable Bolshevik Party, according to the canons of Lenin. Part of their existence is led at the surface, another in the underground, in the cellars of Romanian society. As if they were still creatures of the cellars. Even if the RCP has in the meantime come to govern Romania. The murder of Foriş is typical of this hidden face. They are a political gang that murders, outside any law, any acolyte who has fallen into disgrace. Finding out about the assassination – this is in the summer of 1946 – Pătrăşcanu is fearful that he will supply his comrades with the next corpse. He knows the rules; he himself is a conspirator. He knows with whom he is dealing. For him, however, Gheorghiu-Dej has decided upon different procedures for liquidation. Firstly, because he has to delay the settling of accounts. Pătrăşcanu is too popular for him to be 'disappeared' like Foriş. But attempts to assassinate him are not lacking. As on 24 February 1945, when Pătrăşcanu is shot at in Palace Square, just as he is giving an anti-government speech, perched, in a heroic attitude, on the statue of Carol I. The Party needed a few ad hoc martyrs to gain additional legitimacy and an aura of historical necessity. The communist mythology was still impoverished at the time. Had a hero slain by the bullets of reaction been forthcoming, the popular imagination would have done the rest. Had not Lenin been wounded before becoming a god for the Russian *muzhik*? The assassination attempt had been organised by the Cheka, the Bolshevik political police, in order to unleash the Red Terror.

In February 1945, Stalin had decided to install a government loyal to him in Bucharest. The corpse of Pătrăşcanu, the most famous Romanian communist, would have come in extremely handy. It would also have solved the problem of the man himself, too incommodious and too disliked by the others. The bullets of "reaction," fired by weapons handled by its own provocateurs, would have been the perfect opportunity for the Red Army to intervene, to commence reprisals and to install the desired government, in place of General Rădescu, who had declared in the Aro Auditorium: "Those without God or country, led by two aliens, Ana Pauker and the Hungarian Luca, have decided to drown this country in blood. ... We cannot wait for God to punish them. The army and I have done our duty, let you too be at your posts." But the bullet with Pătrășcanu's name on it misses its target. Pătrășcanu protests vehemently to his comrades. Apparently because he had been left unguarded, exposed to bullets. No one seems to know anything. He has no illusions; he suspects who is behind the incident. Elena Pătrășcanu will not forget to bring up the circumstance in 1967-1968, when the affair is uncovered.

As early as November 1945, *Scînteia* and *România Liberă* receive orders not to write about him. He is already being watched, his telephone conversations are intercepted and microphone bugs are planted in his home.[50] Informers are recruited from among his entourage, other informers from outside set to spy on him. Provocations are set up for him. He is stalked; his mistakes are hunted. The pieces were being gathered for an indictment. There would follow his political and physical liquidation. Gheorghiu-Dej's killer instincts had been proven. The others were less accustomed to murder. The Revolution required such ritual gestures, the liquidation of the inconvenient. Pătrășcanu is thrust into controversial situations, often to the very limit. The period up to 30 December 1947 is a kind of prelude to the investigation. The antechamber of death. The preparations are meticulous and made in advance. All that remains is to wait for the opportune moment in order to deal the deathblow. Everything he says and does is interpreted negatively. He is not invited to many of the meetings of the RCP leadership, although he is a Communist minister. It is unclear whether he is a member of the Political Bureau or not. In order to clarify the situation, Gheorghiu-Dej and Ana Pauker pay a visit to Stalin. This is without result, although Stalin says that he ought to be in the Political Bureau, bearing in mind his popularity. Everything seems unreal. At the top of the RCP, the situation fluctuates. Characters come and go; the ephemeral is the principle of the

---

[50] Grigore Răduică, *Crime în lupta pentru putere, 1966-1968: Ancheta cazului Pătrășcanu* [*Crimes in the Struggle for Power, 1966-1968*], Evenimentul Românesc, 1999, p. 76.

period. Characters with a dubious past appear, with physiognomies that are reminiscent of the darkness of the underground. Secret agents, adventurers, spooks, gamblers, gangsters, members or otherwise of the sect that has only just emerged into the light, all attracted by the mirage of the benefits of power in the murky post-war world.

In a political sect, what is essential is who holds power. Especially in a strict hierarchy, as in the Communist Parties. Pătrășcanu, on the one hand, and Gheorghiu-Dej and Ana Pauker, on the other, were separated by many things. Ana Pauker and Gheorghiu-Dej, the leaders of the most powerful faction, were vying for supremacy. Both commenced a dangerous dance, whose aim was the liquidation of the other. What was decisive was who had the backing of Stalin, the only one to decide. The first obstacle was Pătrășcanu: as long as he passed as a pre-eminent figure for the Romanian communists, there was no chance of them imposing themselves. Hence the haste to undermine his position and the complicity of the two, otherwise incompatible, rivals in this operation. Not only reasons of power separated them, but also their political views. Pătrășcanu believed that Stalinism was inapplicable in Romania, a country whose traditions, history and problems were different to those of the USSR. In addition, the RCP was a party too small to take over government. He envisaged the period that followed as a slow transition from capitalism to communism. Only after the formation of an industrial proletariat could the question of the communisation of Romania be raised. Pătrășcanu had nonetheless remained a communist, even if he was experimenting with a different formula. He had been in the USSR in 1933-1934 and disapproved of the Great Terror. Moreover, he was of the opinion that Romania's entry into Moscow's sphere of influence would lead to disaster. The RCP had – at least for a while – to find allies. He was an adept of 'popular democracy' – a concept that meant a communist regime to a recipe other than that applied in the USSR.

The old parties and remnants of democracy still had their place. It was a product for export, made in the Kremlin, good for occupied Europe. The Soviets were interested in preserving an appearance of normality in these countries. They weren't happy with the supposed image of them being countries occupied by the Red Army, with puppet governments. The entire ideology of worldwide proletarian revolution, behind which Stalin lurked, would have been emptied of meaning. Many believed in the scenario of European Bolshevism, different to the Soviet version. According to this,

Moscow would leave these countries free to set up whatever political regime they wanted. They all believed that there would be significant Soviet influence, of course, but not rule by diktat, not regimes of occupation. Pătrăşcanu was one of the adepts of a regime of 'popular democracy'. He harboured illusions as to the intentions of the Kremlin, as did Georgi Dimitrov, who had led the Comintern since 1934 and whom he had known since the 1920s, from Berlin. So too did Tito, Klement Gottwald etc. The dissolution of the Comintern in May 1943 and Molotov's declaration of 12 April 1944 encouraged them to believe that democracy would, at least partially, exist in Eastern Europe. His experiences in Moscow during the 1930s had alerted him to the fact that the Soviet regime was undesirable. He had also inherited a poor opinion of the Russians from his father. He hoped that evil, a Stalinist dictatorship, would not prevail. If the RCP took power, it meant the dictatorship of a tiny minority, imposed by the Red Army. This is why he wanted the Party to move towards power more gradually: first of all, it should create a mass following, make temporary alliances with the petit bourgeoisie, and co-operate with other political forces. He was rejected, viewed as an alien and, ultimately, as a traitor. Moscow had other plans, and the small group of Bucharest Bolsheviks were aiming at power, at any price. His gloomiest visions were fulfilled.

When Stalin decides in the summer of 1947 to install a 'dictatorship of the proletariat' in the occupied countries, renouncing 'popular democracy', Lucreţiu Pătrăşcanu realises that he is lost. He saw the Romania of the 1940s and 1950s as a left-wing majority democracy, a regime of a popular front type, as in Léon Blum's France. He understood that the Stalinisation of Romania was equivalent to repression, dictatorship and terror. The only hope he glimpsed of Romania not falling under a Stalinist regime was that the USA and Britain would preserve their influence here. The Romanians were not inclined to communism. He knew this from the books he had written in the 1940s, years of tenacious reading, of statistics and analysis. He was the only one among the communists who had a vision and a well-grounded knowledge of the realities, even if he interpreted them in a communist key. He believed in traditional bourgeois politics. The proof: he counted on popularity, essential for any politician in a democracy. Gheorghiu-Dej counted on the Party apparatus. The apparatus did not allow any game other than the one played by its own rules. The apparatus had its own hierarchy, its own internal power relations. The pre-eminence of the apparatus over any other considerations came from Lenin. It dated from 1903, and was the fundamental rule. Pătrășcanu's popularity got in the way of the apparatus because it upturned the Party's internal hierarchy. His popularity was not only an obstacle in the path of Gheorghiu-Dej imposing his absolute power over the Party, but was also incomprehensible. It was not only a personal matter between two rivals, but also between two different rules, two different norms, two different standards. Dej was exclusively a man of the apparatus. He was an excrescence of the apparatus. Pătrășcanu was the product of traditional politics, where events create the leaders. Pătrășcanu had taken part in the armistice of 23 August, at the Peace Conference. He was esteemed, popular. This is of no help to him. On the contrary, it marks him out as a sure victim, as a wanted man at the top of the PCR. In spite of their obsession with the masses, Gheorghiu-Dej, Pauker and co. ignore the working class, manipulate them. The masses were their tool for manipulation and egalitarian demagogy. Pătrășcanu too is concerned with the masses. He seeks popularity, which he sees as the condition for a political career. But also as a guarantee in relation to those who seek his destruction. The speech he gives at Cluj is an attempt to repair the position he had had in the autumn of 1944. He is in search of the support of the masses. Once more, Gheorghiu-Dej, Ana Pauker and their clique censure him. *Scînteia* attacks him, the members of the Political Bureau meet to demand he makes a public self-denunciation. However, this would have annulled everything he had done. Pătrășcanu refuses. He set more store on popularity than on the appreciation of Dej, Pauker, Chișinevschi, Teohari Georgescu, Luca and Bodnăraș.

He was relying on the masses when he claimed to be the leader of the RCP, because he was the only well-known communist. For the apparatus, however, this was a counter-argument. A hold on the masses was a threat. Stalin liquidated anyone who became popular, who was well liked. Kirov was murdered for this. Lenin too saw the masses only as something to be manipulated, good enough only as assault battalions led by his Party apparatus.

"Gheorghiu-Dej was more intelligent than Pătrășcanu. But lacking in the latter's culture and past, he hated him ... Strong in his past, Pătrășcanu scorned him ... While all the others were setting themselves up in palaces, in the Party and at the Kremlin, he was living in three small rooms inherited from his father, happy to have had his first book published, that he had entered history through the coup on 23 August and the signing of the armistice. He wrote. He went to shows and receptions. He played sport. He was incapable of forming a clique; he wasn't even interested. He was aware that he was handicapped by the organisational mania of the others, but he had an aversion to Party coteries. He liked to conspire, not to administer. He counted on no one but himself for his political situation. Once, observing that he had called the reporters to his house to ask them to print a speech, I asked him why he had done it. His answer was: 'What else can I do, they have the apparatus, I am on my own'."[51]

The apparatus will be what identifies him as a foreign body. It will reject him, then it will morally destroy him, and finally it will physically liquidate him.

Pătrășcanu's position should not be understood only from one angle. He is not just the quarry harried by his comrades. He is party to the whole process of installing the dictatorship, as a RCP leader and Minister of Justice, as an ideologue. He is a man of contradictions and of situations to match. In all the Communist Party's machinations, from 1944 until 28 April 1948, when he is arrested, we also find Pătrășcanu: the fall of a number of governments in the autumn of 1944, the installation of the Petre Groza Government, the Royal Coup, the rigging of the elections in November 1946, his position at the Paris Peace Conference, and laws that changed the face of the Romanian judicial and political system. He was complicit in the given situation, and even when he knew he was threatened, he remained a prisoner of the Party. He refuses to emigrate, an act that would have saved his life. He remains hypnotised, a prisoner of the prejudices of his youth. He cannot break away from the Party, from his imagined revolution. In addition, he loves power. He is incurably proud. "Pătrășcanu, like so many others, had lost faith as soon as he gained power. Besides power, which ensured his place in history, he had nothing else to fight for. Immediately after 23 August, he thought only of publishing the books he had written during the war, of the speeches that ensured his popularity and of keeping in with the Russians he detested."[52]

---

[51] Belu Zilber, *op. cit.*, p. 192.
[52] Belu Zilber, *idem*, p. 205.

But if he lost faith in Bolshevism, it meant that he remained a cynic of power, a servile technocrat. Moreover, he does not wish to lead a civilian life outside power. He wants to be somebody; he hates the anonymity of his background. The underground has left him with nasty memories. For all his secretive, conspiratorial nature, which will never abandon him, he likes the notoriety he enjoys. High-level politics is his very life. In exile, he would have been a nobody, so he rejects the proposals to defect to the West.

"He never had partisans, in the strict sense. ... He was a loner, working in the abstract, at the theoretical level, along the lines of the Party, of the Comintern, of Stalinist Marxism-Leninism, fascinated by underground Russia. ... He was an impassioned politician. He used to say in jest to his sister: 'I like women. How could I not like them? But my number one mistress remains politics'. I said to him in a moment of anger: 'You're a political beast, a true native Wallachian politician!' He made the epithet 'political beast' quite simply a title of glory. He communicated it to his entourage. He used to brag about it in the conclave of his comrades when he had to take a more ferocious decision in his glory years of 1944-1948."[53]

Even by staying in the country, outside the RCP he would have been cast to the periphery of political life. This is also the reason for which, although disliked, 'worked' by his own accomplices, he does not retract. Without having any more faith in Bolshevism – not even in a remedied, more tolerant form – he remains in the Party. It was the only way of surviving politically at the top. In fact, he was in a trap, entangled in his own contradictions.

On the morning of 28 April 1948, he sets off to the Ministry of Justice, summoned there by telephone. He is arrested. He returns to the underground. He will never emerge again.

---

[53] Petre Pandrea, *Crugul mandarinului. Jurnal intim, 1952-1958*, Bucharest: Vremea, 2002, p. 364.

XVIII
Far Too Long an Epilogue 1944-1989

> *Comrade Pătrășcanu:* "That's the problem:
> the entire appearance was that it is."
> *Comrade Ana Pauker:* "… We are not
> interested in appearances."

Plenary Central Committee of the Romanian Communist Party, 22 October
1945

In his address to the nation on the evening of 23 August 1944, King Mihai announces the release of all political prisoners. The ban on the PCdR is lifted. The prisons and camps are emptied. On leaving prison or returning from the USSR, the few militants discover that their Party is all but non-existent, and not at all a 'Party of the masses' poised to launch a revolutionary assault against the bourgeoisie. They were a small group in a network conducted from Moscow. Their political praxis was limited to conspiracy. Their aim was to seize power, an operation conceived of in terms of large-scale subversion. It was no longer a question of organising phantom Party cells and holding secret meetings in the cellars of the slum quarters, or of playing a treacherous double game with 'Auntie Varvara', or of printing manifestos on makeshift presses and pasting them in the vicinity of factories and barracks, or of gathering military intelligence, or of infiltrating favourable articles into the left-wing press. Power was now at stake. The Kremlin was conspiring on their behalf. On 23-24 September 1944, the RCP leadership meets legally for the first time. Many of them did not even know each other. Ana Pauker observes, "We are few in number." She goes on: "We, the illegals of yesterday, who did not even know how best to hide ourselves, so that they [the Siguranța – *author's note*] would not see us, we, the erstwhile prison convicts, each one of us must today go into politics."[1] The instincts the communists hone between 1918 and the middle of the 1940s belong solely to the underground. They operate in a hostile environment. They are aliens, interlopers. Having a complex

---

[1] ANCR, *PCdR în anii celui de-al doilea război mondial, 1939-1944*, 2003, pp. 372-73.

of alienation, of belonging to another reality, another space, another tradition, is dominant. Their behaviour is a mixture of arrogance, which is an effect of their complicity with the foreign occupier, and humility, which is an inferiority complex produced by their status as tools of Moscow. Their marginality in relation to society is a given. Imposture is the main trait of this 'revolutionary elite'. Society is taken by storm by this 'detachment of the great army of the world-wide proletarian revolution'. Victory for the local communists in Romania was provided by the Soviet occupation. Thus, it was not a revolution, but a military occupation. As Pătrășcanu himself said, the Romanian communists were nothing but 'quislings'. Likewise, Ana Pauker says, at a meeting of propaganda activists on 30 January 1945, "After years of illegality, we emerge into legality to be met with an unusual situation, a political situation to which we were not accustomed during our illegality. … We are confronted with a new domestic and foreign enemy, in that the enemy's aggressiveness is greater and in that we now have the chance to strike at his head … We are lucky that the Red Army will be staying here for a good while."[2] The new, public period in the existence of the RCP commences under the sign of imposture and violence, an expression of the underground world from whence they originated. The communists 'agitate' the masses, provoke disorder, apply the Leninist method for seizing power. This meant deliberately fomenting a state of chaos, a state of civil war. It was the climate in which their plans could succeed. Lenin and Trotsky had proceeded like this in Russia between 1917 and 1921. Without chaos, the dictatorship would not be able to establish itself or survive. Romania becomes a laboratory where this method is tested. The periphery of Romanian society is mobilised by means of propaganda, administrative measures, and the imposition of a harsh occupation. Those who answer the calls of the RCP are also attracted by the rigorously formalised agitation: the red flags, the placards, the chanting of radically populist, extremist and anarchist slogans. The rituals of social and economic revenge also play their part. The demonisation of the 'class enemy' replaces the previous demonisation of the Jews.

The illusion of a world emerging from war exerted a powerful pull. The world was divided between the victors and the vanquished. Scapegoats were sought. The communists – arriving in Red Army trucks – were in the winning camp. It was part of the script that the Kremlin fictionalised the

---

[2] INST-ANCR, *Stenogramele ședințelor conducerii PCR, 23 septembrie 1994-26 martie 1945*, 2003, pp. 315-16.

reality they were preparing to control. They were the incarnation of anti-capitalist political myths: 1) 'a world of equality' and 2) 'the dictatorship of the proletariat', rule by the majority to the detriment of the rich minority, the 'bourgeois-landowner class'. Disorder and the incitement of the lumpenproletariat, the socially marginal and the underworld were aimed at splitting Romanian society, antagonising it and drawing it into the logic of 'class struggle'. Moscow's band of Romanian agents required chaos to bring them closer to power. A wholly unrepresentative party cannot come to power or govern through democratic means. Only the use of violence was efficient. Collaboration with society was impossible for such a party, because it did not belong to society. For the RCP, nothing had changed since its clandestine period. The Party was still an interloper, operating within a foreign medium. The communists confer imaginary legitimacy upon themselves, in the absence of any real legitimacy. Barely have they emerged from clandestinity then they present themselves as the sole wearer of the halo of anti-fascist resistance. The RCP leaders accuse the other parties of complicity with the Antonescu regime. Whoever was not a communist or a 'fellow traveller' was labelled a fascist. The totalitarian principle of 'whoever is not with us is ostracised', 'whoever is not with us, with the communists and the Soviet occupier, is against us', holds full sway. And whoever is against us must be destroyed. This logic leads directly to the prison camp system. The communist sect declares war on Romanian society, because that society is 'impure', 'uninitiated' into the utopia of the classless society. Its sins were civil liberties and private property.

Two institutions are characteristic of any political sect: propaganda and the political police. With massive Soviet support, the RCP maintains a continuous state of agitation and mobilisation of society. The campaigns follow one another relentlessly. 'Enemies of the people' are identified and then stigmatised at public rallies: demonstrations, press campaigns, purges and trials. The communists furiously attack the 'bourgeois' political class, in the 'name of the proletariat' they claim to represent. The men of the Antonescu regime and the leaders of the democratic political parties are all lumped together as fascists. Within a short space of time, newspapers, magazines, posters, manifestos and leaflets are published – millions of copies. An army of activists trained to 'agitate the masses' is raised, using Soviet money and instructors. Strict censorship begins to be enforced. Petre Constantinescu-Iași, Iosif Chișinevschi, Leonte Răutu, Miron Constantinescu, Grigore

Preoteasa and a handful of the other 'illegals' are the lynchpins. The propaganda apparatus launches a huge operation to extirpate collective memory, to confiscate and falsify the past, to mystify the present. The fiction of a communist utopia is imposed through every means, especially in the press and in schools. Whoever does not submit is censored, ostracised or imprisoned. Where propaganda and censorship are not effective, repression is employed. The political police are set up, an extension of the internal police of the PCdR during the clandestine period. The lynchpin of this political police is Emil Bodnăraș. He has two advantages for the job: he is both an NKVD agent and one of Gheorghiu-Dej's henchmen. The other key figures are Pantiuşa Bodnarenko, Serghei Nikonov, Petea Goncharuk, Sergei Babenko, and Alexandru Nikolski. All of them were Soviet agents, terrorists, spies, who had been captured and imprisoned in the 1930s. In the prisons, they teamed up with the local communists. After August 1944, they continued to work for Moscow as agents. In any case, the leaders of the RCP were themselves no different. They were either citizens of the USSR, agents of the former Comintern, Soviet spies, Red Army officers, or members of the CPSU. Some of them were all these simultaneously, such as Ana Pauker, Lucreţiu Pătrăşcanu, Gheorghiu-Dej, Vasile Luca, Iosif Chişinevschi, Petre Borilă, Emil Bodnăraş, Constantin Pîrvulescu, Teohari Georgescu, Gheorghe Stoica, Gheorghe Vasilichi, Dumitru Petrescu, Constantin Doncea, Leonte Răutu, Valter Roman, Petre Constantinescu-Iaşi. None of the communist leaders was a 'free Romanian citizen'.

The political police, under Soviet control, set about placing Romanian society under surveillance. The communists' obsession with control, espionage and delation was inversely proportional to their lack of any political mandate or any real influence. The political police were, in fact, the core of 'revolutionary' power during the entire post-war period. Society was encircled by agents, infested with informers. First of all, open adversaries are targeted: the politicians of the traditional parties, then the press, military and business circles, and intellectuals. Gradually, the network extends like a net over the whole of society. The communists' own networks had been made up of double agents, many of them informers in the pay of the Siguranţa. After 1945, they externalise the reality of the clandestine networks to encompass all of society. Romania as a whole gradually began to resemble the inter-war underground in which the communists had lived clandestinely. Over every person in the country there hovers the suspicion of guilt, of betrayal, of siding with the enemy. The populace was made up of the 'arrested and the arrestable', as Belu Zilber correctly noted. The trials of the years 1948-1952 and those of 1958-1962 were dominated by an obsession with plots and 'anti-revolutionary conspiracies'. These would be a mirror image of the trials brought against the communists in the inter-war period. The communists had lived on two levels, legally and illegally and now they transferred this modus vivendi onto those outside the underground. The difference was that in the 1920s, 1930s and 1940s it really was a question of enemy agents: Soviet spies trained in subversion by the Comintern and GPU. In the post-war trials, too, there is talk of agents – American, British etc. – but this time they are fictive. The communists were taking their revenge. They drag the 'class enemies' through the courts. They throw them into gaol. They send them to their deaths. It is a settling of accounts in the style of the clandestine cells. It is also a gross political caricature: it understands the 'disappearance of the bourgeoisie as a class' as the extermination of the individuals who were part of the bourgeoisie up to 1944. They believed that this was how they would achieve the Marxist utopia of a classless society. In fact, the old elite is merely replaced by a new governing elite drawn from the erstwhile 'illegals' of the communist sect. The classless society proves to be illusory.

The factional struggles, betrayals, unmaskings, purges and murders had been relentless. But once the communists come to power, the old diseases blight not only the underground, but also the whole of society. The essential thing is that the militant communists are not, as they imagine themselves to be, genuine revolutionaries, but rather puppets who govern an occupied country. The puppet-masters see to the casting and script. The struggles for supremacy in the upper echelons of the RCP are fomented by the Kremlin as a means of controlling the Party. The model, which would evolve over the decades to encompass the whole of society, was the clandestine cell: a closed, strictly hierarchical group, in which the members rarely know each other's real identity. It is a masked performance. Admittance to the sect was preceded by a complicated rite of initiation. Life in the underground was obsessed with secrecy and betrayal. The main protagonist in this drama was the Siguranță, which the 'professional revolutionaries' equated with the real world and, in particular, its political institutions. It is true that the illegals were ideological fanatics. But their political methods were imposed by the Soviet secret services, whether they belonged to the Comintern or not. The majority of them were, at the same time, agents of the Siguranță. This is the baggage of experience the illegal communists carry as they advance towards power. Rather than governing, they will practise subversion at the level of government for decades. Romanian society would never have accepted to be ruled by this insignificant party, made up of conspirators, terrorists and foreign agents. The policy of the RCP was aimed at dismembering Romanian society, destroying its classes, its democratic parties and institutions, its elite, private property, and civil liberties. Without this subversive operation, the domination of the sect that was the RCP would have been impossible. The RCP unleashed a war against this society, which it could not govern, but which it could destroy. The illegals form the vanguard of an imagined 'revolutionary elite'. They regard themselves as the axis of the Romanian world, as the messianic agents of a new world centred in Moscow, where the tutelary god is to be found: Stalin. The RCP mechanism reproduces the Kremlin model on the scale of the whole of Romania. It is a mechanism constructed from concentric layers.

1. The hard core: Pătrășcanu, Pauker, Gheorghiu-Dej, Pîrvulescu, Luca, Teohari Georgescu, Bodnăraș, Chișinevschi, Maurer, Rangheț, Doncea, Șraier, Gh. Apostol et al.

2. The second circle: the activists and the militants around them, those who 'struggled during the illegal period'. passed through the prisons, were trained in the USSR, and dedicated themselves to 'world-wide proletarian revolution' and the 'liberation of man from exploitation'. They have undergone the rituals of initiation into the clandestine cells; they have passed through successive purges and repeated factional struggles and schisms, through denunciations and self-denunciations. They are the survivors of the murderous Stalinist trials in the USSR, during the years 1936-1938, but also of civilian trials in Romania brought by the 'class enemies', the bourgeoisie, without receiving capital punishment and even being granted numerous amnesties. They had spent years in the Romanian prisons, which became places of initiation, Party schools. They have grown used to practising absolute obedience to the Kremlin. Whoever has not undergone these experiences is an 'alien'. Participation in the 'clandestine movement' formed their political capital. Because of their past they were separate from the rest of Romanian society. Whoever had not undergone the ceremonies of initiation into the communist

underground, had not learned the catechism of the works of Lenin and Stalin and the resolutions of the Comintern, had not paid dues to Red Aid, or had not been arrested, interrogated and imprisoned for plotting against State Security, was part of the profane world, doomed to perish.

3. The third circle: consisting of those recruited after August 1944 and those returning from exile in the USSR. The limited number of RCP members in Romania leads – in an extremely politicised climate – to the launch of a campaign to 'swell the ranks'. The new recruits were unemployed agricultural workers from the country and, in large numbers, members of the national minorities.

"There were likewise numerous contingents of former prisoners of war, returning from Russia … to these could be added, ultimately, other organisations, groups of the Iron Guard and other fascist parties. … The communists were also involved in more specialist recruitment. They very soon attracted some members of the upper echelons of Bucharest society. These included generals and commanding officers, who bore heavy responsibilities for war actions undertaken in Bassarabia, Transnistria and Ukraine; some Orthodox metropolitans; the heads of Antonescu's police and, in particular, secret police and secret services; writers, journalists and university professors, who had been on the lists of correspondents, if not in close relations with the German embassy; businessmen, bankers and industrialists were also drawn in, believing that they could buy their place in the future dictatorship just as they had done in the previous ones. Finally, there were also those politicians who, after they had served in various high positions in the previous dictatorships, now offered their services to yet another one. At the lower levels, and in the provinces, the same pattern was repeated, with the same categories of people, who, probably inspired by the example or advice of their counterparts in the capital, emerged reinvigorated from the recruiting offices of the communists and the NKVD."[3]

4. The fourth circle: the 'sympathisers', the 'fellow travellers'. It was an intermediate zone between traditional Romanian society and the communist sect. The 'fellow travellers' acted out of various interests: some out of fear of persecution because of their pasts; some from

---

[3] Ghiță Ionescu, *Communism in România*, Kishinev: Litera, 1994, p. 129.

opportunism; some from the desire to save their careers, lives, fortunes. Others, however, did so from conviction: those who came from the margins of society, who now hoped to rise above their lot, Jews persecuted by the Antonescu regime etc. The communists recruit the 'fellow travellers' above all from among public figures, the professional elite. On their lists we find Mihai Ralea and Gh. Tătărescu, Mihail Sadoveanu and G. Călinescu, C. I. Perhon, Dumitru Bagdasar, Simion Stoilov et al. Likewise, we find members of the administration, officers, diplomats, second-echelon politicians. Ever in search of a mask, the communists wished, by constantly appearing with such people, to camouflage their true intentions: the communisation of Romania. This scenario remains the secret of the initiates. The role of the 'fellow travellers' was to dissimulate the assault on Romanian society. Their presence conferred credibility on the communists. It lessened suspicions regarding the Soviets' plans. It lent a veneer of normality to political life and the crisis maintained by Moscow via its tools in Romania.

Beyond the trenches populated with the 'fellow travellers' stretched the world that was to be destroyed and replaced with the utopia of a classless society. The communists emerged from the underworld with a single obsession: power. It now replaced their other obsessions: survival, betrayal and delation. The thirst for social revenge torments them. Resentments connected to their precarious condition are intense, likewise frustrations. They are the periphery of Romanian society, the underworld, the déclassé. Persecutions, periods in prison or as refugees in the USSR confer upon them an imaginary aura as ones greatly wronged by mankind, ones sacrificed for a just cause, heroes. This phenomenon, fuelled by propaganda, attains quasi-religious dimensions. The moral of suffering and revenge is at the front of their minds. Having been marginal, pariahs, now they play the role of an elite on the road to power. It does not matter that this road has been opened up to them by the Red Army and the diplomatic games of the Great Powers. Hugh Seton-Watson outlined three stages for the takeover of power by the Communist Parties in Eastern Europe: 1) genuine coalition; 2) bogus coalition; and 3) monopoly of power.[4]

---

[4] Hugh Seton-Watson, *The East European Revolution*, New York: Frederick A. Praeger Publishers, 1951, pp. 167-171.

1. Dissimulation and camouflage are the techniques practised by the veterans of 'illegality'. Having emerged from the underground, the approach route to power is one of zigzags of ever changing measures and attitudes. In order for these measures, typical of the underground, to be successful, the RCP hides behind apparently traditional, non-communist organisations. Behind the scenes, however, we find the same persons whom we know from the inter-war period. Acting according to long-acquired instincts, the communists present an anonymous, grey face to the world. They adopt various guises, frequently changing them depending on circumstances, obsessed with blending into the background in order not to be observed. Such techniques of dissimulation were also employed – via the Comintern – in the 1930s: organisations for mutual aid and defence of various specific interests, popular fronts, trades unions and various civic groups masked the existence of communist activities. They return in 1944, when the ban on the RCP is lifted. Behind the façades of these para-institutions, there lurk the preparations for the destruction of democratic society. Surrounding the RCP, various front organisations camouflage multiple subversive operations.

2. Prisoner to the old habits of conspiracy, the RCP attacks the government of which it is part. Orders from the Kremlin outline the RCP tactic. As is its wont, it operates via other groups, factions of the historical parties, and politicians past their sell-by date: Mihai Ralea, Anton Alexandrescu, Gh. Tătărescu, Lothar Rădăceanu, Ștefan Voitec. The PNL and the PNȚ move into opposition. The RCP, surrounded by various phantom groups, remains in government. The non-communist members of government are there by the grace of the RCP and execute the latter's orders docilely.

3. The last act of the drama is played out in the summer and autumn of 1947, and the denouement comes on 30 December 1947,[5] when the communists' monopoly on power becomes final. The 'fellow travellers' are driven out. In many cases they are taken from the benches of Parliament and from the ministries directly to prison.

---

[5] When the King is forced to abdicate – *Translator's note*.

At each moment of this prolonged campaign, the illegals take on a different guise. In the initial phases, they mimic bourgeois politicians and manners. They try to appear respectable. They mix with people. They dissimulate according to techniques long since perfected in the underground. They want to cause the radical differences that separate them from the Romanian world to be forgotten. They want to be accepted. They refrain from frightening people, from looking like revolutionaries bent on overthrowing the social order. They wear countless masks. They display the most insipid banality. They do not refuse to attend receptions. Indeed, they themselves often hold receptions, in particular when Soviet envoys arrive in Bucharest. They give interviews to the foreign press. They dress conventionally, even luxuriously. They are quick to move into villas in plush residential quarters. Apparently, there is nothing revolutionary, terrorist or violent in this behaviour. The underground has induced a chameleon-like behaviour in these improvised messiahs. At society events and in their ministerial offices they give up drab, Soviet-inspired proletarian garb. We find them in the company of the royal household and bourgeois politicians, in particular among those who are compromised or marginalised, whom they hope to use. Around them, there swarm profiteers and opportunists, those who have got rich from the war, businessmen. It is said, 'you can do good business with the communists'. It is true. They acquire a taste for money, for good living. They rapidly grew accustomed to the opposite of the kind of life they had led up until then. Some did not believe that this lie would last and thought that the Americans would prevail over Stalin. Prudently, they deposited their money in foreign banks. They hastily hoarded hard currency, gold coins and other valuables. Many interpret the expropriation of the bourgeois-landowner class as an opportunity to enrich themselves (with houses, motor cars, furniture, jewels, artworks, properties). 'Dodgy' dealings presided over by the communists were a feature of the period. Among those who, uncertain of the regime's future, accumulated wealth we find Emil Bodnăraş, Teohari Georgescu, Ana Pauker, Gheorghe Gheorghiu-Dej, Vasile Luca, Constantin Doncea, Lucreţiu Pătrăşcanu, Iosif Şraier et al. Corruption rapidly ensconces itself in the communist apparatus.

The more power they swallow up, the more they shed their masks and give up their charades. We see one such change, for example, after 6 March 1945. Their authoritarianism becomes more pronounced. They imitate the 'humble worker', the poor peasant, the proletarian intellectual: overalls, flat caps, coarse language. Socially, they mimic the habits of the proletariat they politically ignore. They ape the attitudes, bearing and speech of the occupier. Within the RCP, strict hierarcy, party discipline and the pose of austerity go down well. A further change can be detected after the elections of 1946. The erstwhile illegals no longer have to simulate being ordinary politicians, democrats, pastiche a 'historic compromise' with the other parties, or justify themselves to foreign observers. They violently seize control of Romania. Faint after-effects of the traditional political style still linger. In 1946, the myth of the 'people's democracies', in which a few remnants of the old bourgeois regimes were still to be found, was still functional. The King was still in the country. The 'professional revolutionaries' take care to keep up appearances. In the summer of 1947, the democratic parties cease to be active in a now moribund Romania. Once the Iron Curtain comes down, the communists show their true face: as despots, Stalinists, irreconcilable adversaries of the free world. The abdication of King Mihai marks this radical break with the past. The communists retain their taste for good living and luxury, and displaying it unabashed before an ever more impoverished nation. They no longer conceal their power. They show it off in full view. The privileges they accumulate for themselves separate them radically from the world around them. The veracity of the egalitarian utopia is put to the test. The real elite is replaced with another, factitious elite, a product of foreign occupation and with no connection (legitimacy, roots, common values) with society. It is, to put it in the terms used by Max Weber, a reversion from a 'class society' to one of 'status'. These anti-modern masters claim to govern not in their own name – like the profiteers of historical circumstance that they were – but in the name of others, in the name of the proletariat, with a view to the construction of a post-capitalist utopia. They hide (a reflex of clandestinity) behind the ideological fiction of a 'classless society', the same as they had once hidden behind phantom organisations. They destroy the old elite, but not merely because Marxist dogma demands the liquidation of the superposed classes: the aim is to establish a hegemony of 'illegals', of the so-called 'professional revolutionaries'. In parallel with this operation to replace the real elite with a false elite, they destroy society's connection with its past. Fiction and utopia, accompanied by repression and terror, usurp the public space and destroy it.

***

The 'war against society' provides no liberation from the ghosts of the past. The illegals devour each other. The factional struggles are not merely a memory of the underground past, but an all-consuming present. It is the natural state of a political sect. The conflicts flare up once more after their emergence on the surface, with much greater virulence than in the past. Power is at stake. The 'Muscovites' and the 'prisoners' are the most influential groups. In September 1944, the rivals are Lucrețiu Pătrășcanu, the most popular of the communists, and Gheorghiu-Dej, the leader of the prison communists. Gheorghiu-Dej and Pătrășcanu had met on two previous occasions. The first time was in Jilava Prison, in February 1933, after their arrest during strikes at the CFR Grivitza Workshops. Ten years later they met again in the camp at Tîrgu Jiu. Gheorghiu-Dej and Ana Pauker had met only once previously, at Caransebeș Prison, at the end of November 1940. However, Pătrășcanu and Ana Pauker had known each other since 1921. In 1922, they travelled to Moscow together, to the Comintern. Over the course of the years that followed they would meet in Berlin, Paris, Prague and Moscow. Pătrășcanu acted as her defence lawyer in the trial of 1936. In September 1944, they meet again in Moscow. The Kremlin decides that not Pătrășcanu but Pauker will be the leader of the minuscule Bolshevik Party in Bucharest. Stalin's line when appointing gauleiters in the occupied countries was to choose those who had sat out the war in the USSR: Boruslaw Bierut in Poland, Wilhelm Pieck and Walter Ulbricht in East Germany, Klement Gottwald and Rudolf Slanski in Czechoslovakia, Mátyás Rákosi and Ernö Gerö in Hungary, Georgi Dimitrov, Traicho Kostov and Vasil Kolarov in Bulgaria. In the West, it was the same procedure: Palmiro Togliatti in Italy, Maurice Thorez in France. All had close links to the GPU/NKVD. Pauker fulfilled both conditions. In 1956, when investigated, she recalls,

> "I was in Moscow. I was summoned by Comrade Dimitrov, who told me: 'Go back to your country'. Then he gave me two female radio operators and told me: 'Take over the leadership in Romania and find out what is going on there, because we have no idea'. Comrade Borilă who was also there knew that there was no link to Romania and that nothing was known. And then, straight away, I said, 'Comrade Dimitrov, I am a woman. I wasn't in Romania during the war. I was in prison and I have no idea how things stand. Ten years have passed and it is hard to do this thing. I am a woman, a Jew, an intellectual'. 'But who is there to take

over the leadership there?' I said that there was a popular comrade, a worker, Comrade Gheorghiu. I didn't know him very well. I had met with him for two hours at Caransebeş, but I knew that he was a very popular comrade, a railway worker, an experienced man. 'Look, he could be the leader of the Party', I said. Dimitrov said, 'For four or five years we haven't had any information from Romania. We don't know anybody. It is you we know'. Comrade Borilă knows that he also said to the group, 'See what is happening there and take over the leadership', because he didn't know what was going on in Romania. Go with two radio operators, inform me as to how things are. You can communicate a number of times a day on how things stand. I'm also sending Luca to be of assistance and mind how you go'. With that, I left."[6]

In the Kremlin, very few things were known about Gheorghiu-Dej. He passed as an obscure activist with an unremarkable past, one who had been cut off in prison. In September 1944, he nevertheless had advantages. Firstly, he had the manpower. In prison, he had managed to win loyalties and, by 1940, he had become leader of the communist cell at Doftana, where most of the activists were massed. His authority was confirmed in Caransebeş and Tîrgu Jiu. He benefited from the 'Grivitza myth' but also imposed his will through patience and his exceptional skill at doing politics and dominating others. The closed environment of the prisons honed his reflexes, instilled in him suspicion and prudence. It familiarised him with plots and intrigue. It was a medium obsessed with betrayal, denunciations, and internecine struggle. On the road to power, he makes use of the lesson of the prisons. What other advantage did Dej have in order to gain supremacy over the RCP? His working-class origins and the fact that he was a Romanian in a party dominated by foreign elements. The Soviets needed someone who could make an impression upon a populace with powerful national sentiments. His Comintern Party member's file – in its scantiness – also helped him. The fact that he had been in prison in the 1930s shielded him from the internal conflicts in the PCdR, be they waged in Romania or Moscow. Stalin had such an aversion for those mixed up in 'factional struggles' that it was from among the factionalists that he most often picked victims to put in front of the firing squad. When the question of Gheorghiu-Dej was raised, Stalin could not remember him as having participated in any factional struggle, in

---

[6] See the shorthand record in *Sfera politicii*, no. 60, 1998.

any about-turn of the Popular Front, in the Ribbentrop-Molotov pact, in any of the Moscow trials, or in left- or right-wing deviationism. Precisely the fact that he had no past was an advantage in Stalin's eyes. Between Antonescu and Sima,[7] Hitler had chosen Antonescu because he was best able to ensure a working government. Stalin chooses Gheorghiu-Dej over Ana Pauker for the same reasons. Among the RCP leaders, Gheorghiu-Dej was acknowledged as leader by most of the erstwhile illegals. Ana Pauker was not. She could not have ensured order in the RCP. Since 1940, Gheorghiu-Dej – as leader of the prison communists – had laid claim to the Party leadership. Nevertheless, it was Foriş who had been appointed by Moscow. During the period 1940-1944, contact between the PCdR and the Comintern had been severed. In this way, Stalin could not accuse Dej of not having toed the line. Another circumstance that favoured Dej was the fact that in the years 1936-1938 many Romanian communist refugees in the USSR had been executed during the Great Terror. The first generation of the communist elite, the militant Bolsheviks and professional revolutionaries, had perished. Given the vacuum in the ranks, Gheorghiu-Dej became of interest to Moscow. In 1940, on the list of exchange prisoners requested by the Kremlin, his name was alongside those of Ana Pauker and Chivu Stoica. The Romanian Government refused, because it considered that there were already too many dangerous Romanian communists in Moscow. According to another version, Gheorghiu-Dej – on an understanding with the authorities – refused, having been informed of the massacre of the old guard during the Great Terror. In the 1940s, Gheorghiu-Dej was, as far as Stalin was concerned, a middle-ranking activist, cut off in a Romanian prison. During all this time, Dej did not do anything to make himself stand out. His sole concern, after that of physical survival, was to oust Ştefan Foriş. The 'German war machine', the 'Struggle against the occupier', the 'military dictatorship of Marshal Antonescu', and the 'anti-fascist resistance' were all so many slogans, which had no meaning for him.

The arrival of Ana Pauker in Bucharest on 16 September marks the start

---

[7] Horia Sima (1907-1993): after 1938, the leader of the fascist, paramilitary Iron Guard, or 'Legionaries'. He was the instigator of a series of pogroms, whose brutality appalled even the Germans (in the Bucharest Pogrom of January 1941, for example, Jews were hung from meat hooks in an abattoir and hacked to death with cleavers, among other atrocities). He died in exile in Madrid. – *Translator's note*.

of the struggle for power. In autumn 1944, Pauker and Luca are in search of an ally in Bucharest. They were in urgent need of legitimacy. What they needed was a working-class figurehead with a Romanian surname, who had lived in the country for the duration of the war, preferably in prison. Pauker and Luca were synonymous with the Red Army and the occupation. Whereas, within the Party, this circumstance was a source of legitimacy, for the populace it was exactly the opposite. It was hard to impose a RCP run by Romanian leaders who had arrived from Moscow in the trucks of the Red Army. What was needed was cosmetic surgery to make the minuscule RCP more attractive. The populace nurtured strong anti-Russian sentiments and the fear that Stalin would impose a Bolshevik regime. Gheorghiu-Dej – a worker, former political prisoner, and Romanian – suited Stalin's intentions. Pauker had been notorious in Romania as a fanatical communist since the time of her trial, in 1936. In addition, she was a woman in a country that still remembered Elena Lupescu,[8] and where women held a socially and politically subordinate position. She was also Jewish, in a country where anti-Semitic prejudice was rife. Ana Pauker needed someone who could occupy the place of honour in the presidium. She was looking for someone who had not taken any direct part in the Royal Coup of 23 August 1944, of which she disapproved, because, as she said, it had delayed the "installation of the dictatorship of the proletariat." Pătrăşcanu was too popular and too conceited, too conscious of his own worth. For this reason, Ana Pauker, although she had known him for two decades and had worked with him, refused to make him an ally. Moreover, the Soviets disapproved of him because of his attitude during the negotiations for an armistice when, in their opinion, he had defended the interests of Romania rather than those of the 'homeland of communism'. This was heresy for the Kremlin – given that Pătrăşcanu was a longstanding Comintern agent. Another pretender, Ştefan Foriş, now in disgrace, was accused of having been a Siguranţă agent. How much this story was believed we do not know, but it is certain that he was unpopular in the Party, especially among those who had been in prison. Besides anything else, he was Hungarian. There remained few other names that might have joined the fray in the struggle for supremacy. Most of the militants had been purged and murdered in the USSR, on the orders of

---

[8] Elena Lupescu (1896-1976): the mistress of King Carol before and during the latter's royal dictatorship; she was widely disliked by the Romanian people – *Translator's note*.

Stalin himself. Of those who were left, Stalin did not have much choice.

One candidate might have been Constantin Pîrvulescu, also known as George Popov, Andreescu Mihail etc. In September 1944, he had been acting head of the Party for a few months. Born in 1895, in Olănești, Vîlcea (died 1992). During the First World War, he works as a repair man in the Bucharest Communal Workshops. Joining the exodus from German occupation into Moldova, he arrives in Jassy. The events of 1917 find him in Russia where he joins the Bolsheviks. In the period 1925-1926, he studies at the V. I. Lenin School for Comintern activists. Subsequently, he teaches there. He receives Soviet citizenship. At the end of the 1920s, he is sent to Romania as a Comintern agent, with the mission of settling the conflicts in the PCdR. He does not succeed. In the summer of 1930, the Comintern dissolves the parallel leaderships of the PCdR. Pîrvulescu is appointed to the Secretariat, a step that reveals his high standing in the communist hierarchy. He plays a dominant role in the Secretariat, surviving in the job for two years, until 1932, when it looks like he will go on to be the next General Secretary of the PCdR. He is the head of the group that organises the Fifth Congress of the PCdR. He does not rise to become General Secretary, but he is appointed to the Central Committee *in absentia*. The event will leave its mark on his ambitions. On the way to the congress, he has the misfortune to be arrested in Kosice. He is expelled and banned from returning to Czechoslovak soil. He is considered a dangerous Soviet agent. Many secret Comintern routes passed through Czechoslovakia. As a rule, the Romanians operated along this route when they were coming and going between Bucharest and Moscow. In 1935, he is arrested again, in Prague, this time along with Solomon Schein, former head of the PCdR, during the period 1928-1929, a Comintern agent, like him (expelled from the Party in August 1937 and executed in Moscow). Pîrvulescu is extradited to Romania, where there is a general warrant for his arrest. In June 1934, he had been arrested in Bucharest, in a group of eight communists (including Teohari Georgescu). The Siguranță had uncovered a huge quantity of printed matter, documents, money and an illegal printing press. Pîrvulescu was running the operation. The investigators did not realise his importance in the underground and let him go, leaving him to be tried at liberty. Pîrvulescu slipped across the border. Tried *in absentia*, he was sentenced to 10 years in prison. Brought to Bucharest, after his capture in Prague, he is tried once more, after the expiry of the previous conviction, in 1936, and he is sentenced to three and a half years in prison. He is taken to Doftana, where he meets other communist activists and Soviet spies: Petre Constantinescu-Iaşi, Dimităr Ganev, Gheorghiu-Dej, Vasile Luca, Emil Bodnăraş, Pantiuşa Bodnarenko, Chivu Stoica, Gh. Apostol, Alexandru Drăghici, Alexandru Moghioroş, Bernat Andrei, Nicolae Ceauşescu et al. He is released from prison in the autumn of 1939 and summoned for military service. He had been named as a deserter since 1932. He vanishes into the underground labyrinth. There must be something not quite right about him, because he is not co-opted into the Secretariat (the case with Luca, also released from Doftana). Instead, he is sent to Constanţa, as head of the Dobrudja regional network. The Secretariat is made up of men who emerged later: Iosif Chişinevschi, Béla Breiner, Teohari Georgescu, Nicu Tudor (a Siguranţă informer, deceased in July 1940), Ştrul Zigelboim (remaining in the USSR after 1940), Gavrilă Birtaş. His relationship with Ştefan Foriş is poor. In the autumn of 1940, while in Moscow, Foriş was asked to appoint Pîrvulescu to the Political Bureau, but refuses.

In the summer of 1941, Pîrvulescu is reprimanded for the arrest of the Dobrudja network by the Siguranţă. The collapse of the network had serious repercussions, because, led by Dumitru Coliu, it ensured links with Moscow. Among those arrested was Filimon Sîrbu, a future myth of the working class in the 1950s. He was executed on 26 June 1941, after being caught transmitting Romanian and German positions in Constanţa to the enemy. Pîrvulescu, frightened by the conjuncture (the attack against the USSR), and by the measures the authorities took to annihilate the communist fifth column, abandoned his comrades in Dobrudja and fled to Bucharest. The episode was not forgotten, even much later, and left the impression of a weak man, of a deserter. The arrest in April 1941 of four of the five members of the Secretariat, and given the lack of any other experienced personnel, led Ştefan Foriş to reinstate him. In September 1941, he is part of the Secretariat once more. He has the mission of maintaining links with the Bucharest organisation, run by the recalcitrant Petre Gheorghe. His diplomatic abilities are non-existent, and in any case the conflict is all but irreconcilable. His vacillating attitude causes Foriş to suspect him. After 1942, he is no longer part of the Secretariat. Foriş keeps him to hand in order to keep an eye on him, entrusting him only with formal tasks. In May 1943, Pîrvulescu leaves a briefcase full of documents behind in a taxi. As a result there were dozens of arrests and a number of trials in the winter and spring of 1944, with heavy prison sentences. Foriş quarantines him at a safe house. He receives no more missions. When Gheorghiu-Dej made him part of the triumvirate to replace Foriş, Pîrvulescu was in disgrace, guilty of the arrest of dozens of communists. Paradoxically, in Gheorghiu-Dej's eyes this made him appear as a providential figure. As he was vulnerable, he could be replaced at any time. Pîrvulescu is willing to take part in the plot, all the more so given that he is thereby given a place within the Party leadership. It was his chance to rehabilitate himself and avoid liquidation, in accordance with the customs of the underground, for his gaffe of May 1943. Pîrvulescu, the oldest of the triumvirate, and with the longest service in the underground networks, replaces his 'persecutor', Foriş, on 4 April 1944. He does not take part in the sequestering of Foriş, unlike Bodnăraş and Ranghet, preferring to stay out of harm's way in a safe house. In September 1944, the episode of mislaying the PCdR archive was still too recent for him to be a credible chief in the eyes of the illegals. Many of the victims of the incident, having been released from prison, were already playing influential roles. Pîrvulescu lacked prestige and authority, exactly when he needed them the most. Although he had been General Secretary for a few months, Ana Pauker – also with a mandate from Moscow – replaced him with ease. In the second legally printed issue of *Scînteia* (*The Spark*), Pîrvulescu features in a photograph and where he is identified as General Secretary of the PCdR. In less than a week, he loses the position. Emil Bodnăraş had made use of him in order to do away with Foriş, because he had been in the PCdR leadership from as early as 1930, and he needed continuity and legitimacy in the eyes of the communists. No one saw in Pîrvulescu a real leader or a dangerous rival. The replacement of Constantin Pîrvulescu with Ana Pauker in September was not even a problem. He is summoned to Moscow and detained there for two months, questioned by the NKVD and a CPSU commission about PCdR activity during the war and, in particular, about the elimination of Foriş and his participation in the Royal Coup. Pîrvulescu will, on his return, be head of the Control Commission for many years. He will conduct the investigations and purges in the PMR between 1948 and1953. The balance sheet: 190,000 expulsions.

Another hopeful was Emil Bodnăraş. He hoped that the role he had played in 1944 would propel him to become leader of the RCP. His relations with the secret services in Moscow – better, in his view, than those of Gheorghiu-Dej – led him to hope that he would become leader of the Party after the

Red Army occupation of Romania. He saw Dej's alliance with Pîrvulescu as temporary, as being aimed at counteracting the Muscovite group. He wanted to be head of the Party. Gheorghiu-Dej sensed it, and relations between them cooled. They remained allies, but Bodnăraş was assigned secondary posts. He was not part of the executive leadership of the RCP, who were appointed by Ana Pauker. Its members were as follows: Pauker, Gheorghiu-Dej, Pîrvulescu, Vasile Luca, and Teohari Georgescu. Bodnăraş shares the same fate as Lucreţiu Pătrăşcanu, another main player in the coup of 23 August: he finds himself sidelined. Both fall victim to the reticence with which the participation of communists in the overthrow of the Antonescu regime is viewed. One legitimate claimant was Constantin Doncea. His career in the 1930s could boast more 'armed deeds' than Gheorghiu-Dej's. As leader of the railway workers' strike of 1933, he came to prominence in the two trials that followed. The Comintern arranged a spectacular escape for him, and he arrived in the USSR, where he became a 'professional revolutionary'. He was the most famous figure among the Romanian volunteers to the International Brigades. He fought in the Red Army. On 19 August 1944, he was parachuted into Romania. Stalin and Dimitrov did not have Doncea in view as a potential leader of the RCP. He was regarded as incapable, unstable. In any case, even though he was a worker and ethnic Romanian, Doncea was arriving from Moscow, like Ana Pauker, and thus he could not be the chosen one. In addition, Ana Pauker – who had a lot of say in the entourage of the leaders of the former Comintern and in the Kremlin – disliked him personally. Ana Pauker needed to rule from behind the scenes, with someone else up front. Gheorghiu-Dej seemed the suitable person. He appeared to be extremely deferent. He seemed obedient and devoid of personal opinions. In August 1944, he had not been in Bucharest. He could not claim any heroic deeds, unlike Pătrăşcanu, Bodnăraş, Doncea or even Pîrvulescu. For him, Pauker was Moscow, and Stalin and Dimitrov were the Kremlin. That is to say, power.

The 'prisoners' viewed the 'Muscovites' with mistrust. Their arrival retied the knot with Moscow and re-established its control over them. The 'Muscovites' were viewed more kindly by the Soviets and snapped up all the best jobs. Gheorghiu-Dej, their boss from prison, becomes their representative in this internecine struggle. He has a more neutral attitude; he is more servile, more patient. He receives Ana Pauker well, even courteously. He is appointed to the Secretariat, where he is flanked by

Pauker, Vasile Luca and Teohari Georgescu. Constantin Pîrvulescu, Iosif Rangheț and Emil Bodnăraș – the former PCdR leadership, the 'triumvirate' – are relegated to second place. Together with Pătrășcanu, they were 'guilty' of working with the King and the traditional democratic parties. Gheorghiu-Dej had not showed up in Bucharest until after the change of regime. He could not claim for himself any of the merit for the 23 August coup. For a whole year, until October 1945, Pauker is the uncontested leader of the PCR. Behind her lurked Gheorghiu-Dej, ready to pounce, waiting his turn. Firstly, however, he had to adapt to an environment different to that of the prisons. At liberty, his authority is contested, whereas at Caransebeș and Tîrgu Jiu no one dared to do so. Once he emerges from the underground, he has to share power with others. Another factor was the immediate and brutal presence of the Soviets. There had been no links with Moscow from 1940 until the Soviet occupation in 1944. If Gheorghiu-Dej wanted power, he first had to ingratiate himself with the masters. In 1944-1945, he did not enjoy the celebrity or the Kremlin backing that Ana Pauker did. Her name is circulating; Gheorghiu-Dej is nobody. Gheorghiu-Dej, ever the consummate hypocrite, always outwardly humble, gives the impression of being the perfect servant. It is only an appearance. The truth is that he is painstakingly preparing to seize power.

There is intense jockeying for position, alliances are forged, and behind the scenes talks held. At the PCR Conference of October 1945, Georghiu-Dej becomes official head of the Party. Ana Pauker takes a step back. She remains 'merely' a member of the Secretariat and Political Bureau, convinced that she will be able to go on running the Party *de facto*. Between the two camps, the 'Muscovites' and the 'prisoners', an armistice is agreed. A number of matters had to be resolved, before the decisive battle for absolute power could commence. The first victim of the pact is Ștefan Foriș. In the summer of 1946, he is assassinated on the orders of Gheorghiu-Dej, with the assent of Ana Pauker, Teohari Georgescu and Vasile Luca. There are no legal procedures, arrest, inquiry, trial or sentence. He is kidnapped, sequestered and hit over the head with a crowbar. It is an execution typical of the underground networks. The murder of Foriș, insistently demanded by Gheorghiu-Dej, was intended not only to eliminate a rival, but also to consolidate the cell at the top of the RCP. Then there was his overriding obsession with concealing his tracks, with keeping everything secret. The secret is not kept, but there is no reaction on the part of the others, as they themselves are exposed to being murdered in the same fashion. Pătrăşcanu, Chişinevschi, Rangheţ, Maurer, Bodnăraş, Şraier, Agiu and Doncea remain silent. They accept what has happened to their former leader. They can become victims at any time. The Mafia-style system affects them too. No one brings into question the murder, because they all accept the privilege of the Political Bureau and of the Secretariat to liquidate an 'enemy of the Party'. It was an act of will on the part of the supreme leader. The same thing had happened to the Bolshevik old guard: Trotsky, Kamenev, Zinoviev, Bukharin, Rykov, Tomski, Racovski. It is the very nature of the political gang to devour themselves. The decision to liquidate Foriş in fact establishes Gheorghiu-Dej as boss. The others, hesitant, reveal their limits, their 'bourgeois residues', their 'legalist prejudices'. Ana Pauker hints at an objection, when she asks 'whether Moscow knows about it', but that is all. The assassination assures Gheorghiu-Dej of supremacy. Stalin must have liked the lack of scruples with which Dej executed Foriş. He recognised him as a peer. They both belonged to the class of political murderers, of the 'masters'. The Foriş case is one episode in a long history of unmaskings, denunciations, purges, and political murders within the clan. Lucreţiu Pătrăşcanu, Remus Koffler, Ana Pauker, Teohari Georgescu, Vasile Luca, Dumitru Petrescu, Iosif Chişinevschi, Miron Constantinescu, Constantin Doncea et al. plus others with secondary roles – such as Belu Zilber, Ovidiu Şandor, Ileana and Grigore Răceanu, Mihai Levente, Aurel Vijoli, Ştefan Pavel et al. – are purged one by one. Death awaited some of them; others rotted in goal, were sidelined or became 'non-persons'. But all of them were, above all else, players in this dirty game, in which normal moral values did not exist. They accepted it. They were its fanatical agents, until they fell victim to their own accomplices. Gheorghiu-Dej's favourite targets in the Party were those who had a 'meritorious' past among the professional revolutionaries. Obsessed with erasing his tracks, as a man of the underground, he is essentially obsessed with rewriting the history of clandestinity. He resorted to murder, in the case of Foriş, Pătrăşcanu etc. Their biographies presented the greatest danger; it exposed them to death. Not only Pătrăşcanu, the conspirator, who had ensured his place in history, was obsessed with it, but also Gheorghiu-Dej. The difference was that Gheorghiu-Dej was above all a slave of power, and Pătrăşcanu of history. Each obtained what he most wished.

The elimination of the erstwhile illegals played the same role as the elimination of the old guard did for Stalin during the Great Terror. It went on for decades. Prior to being a settling of accounts with the other aspirants to the position of leader, it is a vast operation to rewrite the past. It was aimed at absolute control of power. The rewriting of history is politically vital in non-democratic regimes. To achieve this, the actors who had played a role in various episodes of the shadowy story of clandestinity had to disappear. Another scenario was for the illegals to agree to tell the version of the story desired by Gheorghiu-Dej. Those who did so survived. Bodnăraş, Pîrvulescu, Maurer and the others, when the circumstances change, do not hesitate to tell a different version of past events. Silence was not wholly secure – although we are in a world of secrets and shadows – because it might at any time be interpreted as disagreement with the Political Bureau, with Gheorghiu-Dej, with the Party. Silence could be broken.

The witness is a threat in closed political systems. One word might destroy the clique in power. Someone might speak at any moment, and the usurpation, the lack of legitimacy, the falsification and mystification of history might be discovered. Gheorghiu-Dej required a version of events that would glorify him. The events of the past constantly acquire a different aspect. Official memory bends to the momentary political requirements of power for Gheorghiu-Dej and his political gang. The slaying of Foriş is such an episode, whereby an entire chapter of the communist underground is erased. One of many episodes. Once Foriş has been murdered, the mystifiers can say anything they like. Foriş is 'abolished' as a memory, after first having been slain physically. His memory is blackened, falsified. He is a 'spy', a 'renegade', he 'sold out', he is 'a Siguranţa agent'. Without 'Foriş's betrayal', his deposal and assassination were unjustifiable. This is why the Political Bureau and the Secretariat are so eager to demonise him. The 'Muscovites' and the 'prisoners' are in agreement. The memory of Foriş inconvenienced them. References to him are strictly defamatory for decades afterwards, regardless of from whom they come. Foriş is a *nomen odiosum*, a typical scapegoat. His role is to 'purify' the underground by his disappearance. The Party, cleansed of those guilty for its dirty past, of the traitors infiltrated within it, can move forward. By means of his corpse, a wretched past is justified. All the leaders of the Party dedicated themselves to this inverted cult. The register is large, from the complicit silences of Pătrăşcanu, to the formal and complicit stance of Ana Pauker, and the attitude of Gheorghiu-Dej. Up to 1965, the plenary sessions of the CC of the PMR are the formal setting for Gheorghiu-Dej's recollection (the point of obsession) of the nefarious role played by Foriş. The complex of the usurper is present here in all its splendour. The other beneficiaries of Foriş's assassination do not hesitate to join Gheorghiu-Dej in this imposture.

***

The second victim of the pact between the 'Muscovites' and the 'prisoners' was Lucreţiu Pătrăşcanu. On 28 April 1948, he is sequestered in a safe house. Such houses still existed, in which the PCR leaders carried on secret operations, as in the time of clandestinity. Pătrăşcanu was expecting to be arrested, he carried poison with him. "I carried this phial on me until the summer of 1949 when, because of the heat and the damp, the poison decomposed and I threw it away," he writes on 5 April 1950.[9] He makes two suicide attempts while under arrest. The first is in June 1948, two months after his kidnap, after a confrontation with a witness/agent provocateur from the SSI, who claims that he is getting ready to flee the country. The second is in March 1949, when he slashes his veins with a razor blade. From now on, he is kept under close guard. Gheorghiu-Dej needed a trial, not just his death. Not least because a suicide would have incriminated him. Just as there was no resigning from the Party, so there was no taking of one's own life. Gheorghiu-Dej had the right of life and death over all his subjects. In the first phase of the inquiry, Pătrăşcanu is investigated by Teohari Georgescu, Iosif Rangheţ, and Alexandru Drăghici. In October 1949, he is transferred to the SSI. From December 1950, he is investigated by the MAI, by Teohari Georgescu, the Interior Minister, and by Alexandru Drăghici, his adjunct. After 1952, when Teohari Georgescu falls into disgrace, his replacement Alexandru Drăghici takes charge of the entire affair. Gheorghiu-Dej and Iosif Chişinevschi take a personal interest in the case. They read the written statements, they give indications as to who should be arrested, and how the case should be investigated.

The critical moment that led to his downfall occurred in January 1948, when Pătrăşcanu presented himself to the Soviet Ambassador, Sergey Kavtaradze, to complain about his ostracism. The blow dealt by his comrades, who had forced King Mihai to abdicate, had found him at Păltiniş. He had not been involved in the preparations, although he was a minister and one of

---

[9] Archive of the SRI, Fund P, Dossier 40002, Vol. 14, p. 159.

the heads of the Party. They had acted conspiratorially. Pătrășcanu learned of the abdication over the radio. He had completely lost faith in his former accomplices. He arrives in Bucharest by motor car. On New Year's Eve, he goes uninvited to Ana Pauker's house, where the 'comrades' are celebrating their victory. He is greeted with hostility. Gheorghiu-Dej asks: "What is this traitor doing here? If Pătrășcanu stays, I'm leaving!" Pătrășcanu presents himself to Sergey Kavtaradze at the Soviet Embassy to obtain support. The result of the audience is a summons before the Political Bureau of the Secretariat. He is informed that he will not be re-elected to the CC at the congress. After the PMR Congress and his forced resignation from the Ministry of Justice, he becomes a 'non-person'. SSI agents isolate him. Very few remain loyal to him. The courageous will pay for this with lengthy and harsh inquiries, with many years in prison. The only ones who escaped such treatment were the informers and provocateurs infiltrated among his entourage to manipulate and control him. The manner of spying on and isolating a person does not differ from that employed in clandestinity.

Pătrășcanu is the victim of a conspiracy typical in the underground. The first incriminating document regarding him emerges simultaneous to his fall. At the congress in February, Teohari Georgescu attacks him in the plenum, incriminating him for his 'bourgeois residues'. It is barely the beginning. A resolution passed by the CC of the PMR on 10-11 June 1948 brands him as 'an enemy of the Party', one who promulgates collaboration with the exploitative classes in detriment to the class struggle. He is also criticised for his published books, because he has falsified the history of the heroic class struggle waged by the Party. He is also guilty of having written about the 'lack of influence and powerlessness of the proletariat', about the weakness of the RCP. He is regarded as a 'nationalist chauvinist'. It is a menacing accusation in the context of the Kremlin's offensive to liquidate the independence of the occupied nations. The conclusion of the resolution: Pătrășcanu had become a "carrier of bourgeois ideology and interests within the ranks of our party." Before being slain, the former 'hero of the working class' must be desacralised. The myth of the 'great leader', the man of the 23 August coup, is replaced with that of the traitor. The arrest warrant does not come until 24 August and is another incriminating document. The accusations of June are replaced with criminal charges, according to which, "in his capacity as an agent of the bourgeois landowner Siguranța and agent of the British secret service, he conducted criminal activity to paralyse the actions of the Romanian Communist Party and destroy the Party from within, thereby contributing to the provocation, support and continuance of the war against the USSR."[10] He is taken to a house stuffed with listening devices. The leaders of the PMR take part in the investigation. This is a Mafia-style gang that isolates one of their own who is accused of treachery. Gheorghiu-Dej pays him a visit accompanied by Teohari Georgescu. The device is primed to kill. If the Kremlin demands the staging of a public spectacle in the form of a trial, Bucharest must be ready to mount one. The cast and script are not yet finalised. But Stalin and Molotov will not accept second-rate actors. They need a star-studded cast, with members of the Political Bureau and the Secretariat, with a 'heroic' past in clandestinity, in the 'struggle against fascism'. In the other communised countries, the victims originate from the top of the Parties. It is suggested that 'bourgeois rot', betrayal and plotting have penetrated to the uppers echelons of the Party. The spectacle demanded well-known international figures in order to give the trial glitter. Without a cast of political stars in the witness box, Soviet propaganda and foreign policy would not have been sufficiently served. The detention and arrest of Pătrășcanu was designed to indicate to Stalin, Beria and Molotov that Bucharest had understood what was demanded. Pătrășcanu would be cast in the role of the Titoist and the nationalist chauvinist. His elimination would prove to the Kremlin that vigilance was at its maximum, and that no one would escape unpunished. If Gheorghiu-Dej, Pauker, Chișinevschi, Bodnăraș, Teohari Georgescu and Pîrvulescu had not supplied victims, they themselves would have been liable to be sacrificed. Intrigues and plots, whether real or imaginary, are the order of the day. The main tool is denunciation. For Moscow, the leaders of the PMR accuse their accomplices of every evil, real or imaginary. Some are closer to Lavrenti Beria (Emil Bodnăraș, Chișinevschi), others to Molotov and Manuilsky (Ana Pauker), others to Stalin and Malenkov (Gheorghiu-Dej). The lots are changeable. Moscow often changes its humours, depending on the interests of the Soviet empire and Kremlin intrigues. One example is the difficult situation Gheorghiu-Dej finds himself in during the summer of 1948, after the meeting of the Information Bureau, Kominform. He finds himself suspected of Titoism and his enemies seem to have gained Stalin's permission to eliminate him. He is threatened by a trial in which he would have had to appear in the dock next to Pătrășcanu, with both being accused

---

[10] *Cartea albă a Securității*, SRI Press, 1994, vol. 2, pp. 156-157.

of 'nationalist chauvinism', 'right-wing deviationism' and 'spying for the British and Americans'. For a while, in the summer of 1948, Gheorghiu-Dej no longer leads the Party and is under investigation by Soviet advisers. Rumours about his fall thicken. The atmosphere is paranoid, on the verge of hysteria.

In December 1961, Gheorghiu-Dej tells the story to Party members, gathered for the plenary CC of the PMR:

> "Chișinevschi goes to the CFR ... All the railway workers are expecting Dej to come, and were concerned about the fate of Gheorghiu-Dej, and what was happening with Dej, whether he could have been arrested. ... When they see Chișinevschi there [they told themselves] you know that he's with him. They began to talk. ... The hall erupts in a shout. They were shouting Gheorghiu-Dej, but so loudly that the hall was booming and when they calmed down, after an outburst like that, Chișinevschi says ... 'Let's see whether, if we shout Stalin, Stalin, you'll shout as loud as you shouted Gheorghiu-Dej!' There was murmuring; it was clear to everybody that something had happened [to Dej]. And people began to shout Stalin, Stalin, but the crowd wasn't reacting. They started here and there, more from fear, from shame, they'd been trained ... but it was clear that they weren't shouting Stalin, Stalin as loud as they shouted Dej. ... That evening, after the meeting, a few groups of railway workers came to me, really scared, they repeated to me what that sinner [Chișinevschi] had said. ... I spoke to Kavtaradze. [I told him] The enemy is no longer satisfied with that victory [Tito's heresy]. He has managed to spread the rumour about Gheorghiu-Dej. Now Gheorghiu-Dej has become a standard, they are chanting to take to the streets, to demonstrate, to start fires, to destroy motor cars, demanding the salvation of poor Gheorghiu-Dej!"[11]

Gheorghiu-Dej understood how far his power was limited by the occupying Soviets. He becomes the most Stalinist of the communist leaders in Bucharest. In 1949, he will recite a Kominform report, written in Moscow, "The Yugoslav Communist Party in the hands of bandits and spies." It is the

---

[11] ANCR, Archive of the CC of the PCR, CC of the RCP/1961 Fund, Shorthand report of the plenary of the CC of the PMR, 30 November/6 December, pp. 122-123.

price paid for his 'forgiveness'. It is also an opportunity for Gheorghiu-Dej to attack his captive:

"The facts revealed in the Budapest trial [the trial of László Rajk – *author's note*] in the People's Republic of Bulgaria [the trial of Traicho Kostov], in the People's Republic of Romania and in the other people's democracies, have fully proved that Tito … Pătrășcanu and those who share their ideas are agents of the imperialist Anglo-American secret services. These odious spies and traitors even during the Second World War helped the Anglo-American imperialists to prepare points of support for the achievement of their plan for world domination. This gang of spies and traitors was infiltrated like a Trojan horse in to the ranks of the communist and workers' parties. Executing the orders of their masters, they pursued the criminal aim of laying their hands on the leadership of the Party and the power of the state in the countries in which the working class had come to power, to crush the revolutionary movement and to ensure the restoration of bourgeois dominance."[12]

Once classified as a spy, Pătrășcanu was as good as convicted. The investigators had the task of collecting evidence for all the accusations made by Gheorghiu-Dej. It was through him that the Party, 'the revealed truth', spoke. The investigators' conclusions could not differ from what had been claimed at the Kominform meeting. In addition, Stalin might at any time solicit the organisation of a trial in Bucharest. With his past, Pătrășcanu was the most precious 'political cadaver' for Gheorghiu-Dej. He was a security deposit, a hostage who could be delivered on demand for a sacrificial ceremony. The guarantee of Gheorghiu-Dej's supremacy in the Party during the period of the show trials was provided by the 'heads' he could offer to the Kremlin. In 1948-1951, when the fever of the hunt for 'traitors' abates and the inquiry stagnates, Pătrășcanu is the only one left. In 1952, however, Stalin shows new signs of 'revolutionary madness'. The pressure for a big trial resumes. Gheorghiu-Dej lengthens the list of available victims, adding Ana Pauker, Vasile Luca and Teohari Georgescu, in the hope of mollifying the tyrant. If he did not find persons for sacrifice, his own expiation would follow. Stalin dies on 5 March 1953. The ritual

---

[12] Gh. Gheorghiu-Dej, *Articole și cuvîntări*, 3rd edition, Editura pentru literatură politică, 1952, p. 412.

sacrifices demanded by the Kremlin cease. Nevertheless, Pătrăşcanu will not escape.

***

A paltry gallery of characters emerge from the underground. This does not make them any less dangerous. They compensate for it by the fact that they are the possessors of absolute power over Romania. A power conferred by the occupier, not won legitimately from the inside. The illegals govern, by imposture and violent means, a defenceless society. The typology of these characters is various. We find here well-known figures. The following is a short compendium of those who make their mark in this period.

Iosif Chişinevschi (born 1905, in Bălţi, died 1963), a Jew from Bassarabia; real name Roitman; he adopted the name of his wife, Liuba Chişinevschi. In 1924, he becomes a member of the UTC and, four years later, he joins a PCdR cell. He is an autodidact, which gives him ascendancy over the semi-literate and the lumpenproletariat in the Party. In 1930, he is arrested and sentenced to two years in prison. He is released in 1932. He studies at the V. I. Lenin School for Comintern activists, in Moscow, becoming a GPU agent, like many others. Collaboration with the Soviet secret services was an 'honour for a professional revolutionary'. He returns to Romania, and works clandestinely, in the secondary echelons of the Party. He operates especially in the area of propaganda and the legal and illegal communist press. He seconds Foriş, distributes Comintern funds, and engages in espionage. His mission is to inform Moscow about the situation in the Party, without the knowledge of the others. In 1938, he is a member of the CC. In 1939, he becomes a member of the Secretariat. In the absence of Ştefan Foriş and Teohari Georgescu, who are away in Moscow, he runs the Party in the summer and autumn of 1940. Arrested in April 1941, he is sentenced to 10 years, hard labour. He ends up in Caransebeş Prison, where is co-opted by Gheorghiu-Dej into his group. Chişinevschi accuses Ştefan Foriş of being a Siguranţa agent, claiming that he is guilty for his arrest. Chişinevschi's capture was due to a Siguranţa informer, not to Foriş. It was due, above all, to the 'conspiratorial negligence' of Chişinevschi himself, as emerges from the Siguranţa reports, since he was shadowed and led the Siguranţa directly to the members of the Secretariat. Foriş, who was prudent, escaped the trap set by the Siguranţa. Guilty of the arrests in April 1941 and cowardly under interrogation, Chișinevschi blames Foriș. This tells us a lot about the character of the man, but also about his abilities. When verified at Caransebeș, he comes out unblemished. The accusation against Foriș convinces Gheorghiu-Dej and gains Chișinevschi his protection. Gheorghiu-Dej will make use of him in the machinations of the plot against the head of the PCdR. Chișinevschi becomes a member of the small group that leads the prison communists. He remains at Caransebeș until 23 August 1944. After that, he becomes a member of the Political Bureau, the Head of Propaganda. He continues to work directly with the NKVD, as a resident at the top of the PCR. His contacts include Lavrenti Beria. It is for this reason that Gheorghiu-Dej keeps him close. In the game of power, each has his protector in Moscow. Moreover, most of them work directly for the Soviet secret services: Emil Bodnăraș, Vasile Luca, Constantin Pîrvulescu, Dumitru Coliu, Petre Borilă, Alexandru Moghioroș, Teohari Georgescu, Gh. Stoica, Dumitru Petrescu, Iosif Rangheț, Leonte Răuta, Valter Roman and, of course, Iosif Chișinevschi. Some also work for the USSR Embassy, others for Soviet advisers. All of them insistently cultivate relations with the Kremlin. Kavtaradze, Shutov, Susaykov, Malinovsky etc. were in direct contact with Gheorghiu-Dej, Pauker, Bodnăraș etc., not only via political but also intelligence channels. Chișinevschi was responsible for the propaganda section in the years after the war. He was the main architect of the Sovietisation of the Romanian public space. He was the Party's number one censor and principal ideologue until he was purged in 1957. Chișinevschi was a typical product of the clandestine world. After the legalisation of the Party, he suffers from the same illness that all the former denizens of the underground display. They are incapable of adapting to the new medium and behave as if they are still living clandestinely. They plot, wear masks and are chameleon-like in their behaviour. Denunciation, behind the scenes machinations, operations behind closed doors, a morbid obsession with secrecy and coups comprise the political arsenal of such a personage.

"Ignoring and detesting true intellectual problems, alien to the theoretical polemics of the Marxist Left, Chișinevschi venerated surrogates of Stalinist provenance. His fundamental reading was Stalin's *Problems of Leninism*, that shameful catechism intended to offer quick, easily digestible, solutions to some of the thorniest questions. ... His profession was revolution, and the methodology of revolutionary-subversive action had been codified in an exemplary way, in his opinion, by the coryphaeus of Kremlin science."[13]

The Comintern School for Activists

"would be the sole source of spiritual education for the man who, after 23 August, was despotically to conduct the destiny of Romanian culture. … The years spent in the Leninist school will initiate Chișinevschi into the labyrinths of intrigue and the personnel of the Red Byzantium, they will mobilise his destructive potential, they will convince him of the advantages of the most venal opportunism. Moreover, in that period, the future dictator of Romanian culture would come to understand the determining function of the political police within a totalitarian system … The Muscovite pedagogy bore fruit … in the closed space of the communist sect. Chișinevschi proves himself a master of manipulation, he excels in the art of ignoble intrigue and poisonous calumny … After 23 August … he is Stalin's man in the Romanian communist leadership, the professional plotter, outwardly Jesuitical and honeyed, always with a dagger up his sleeve. Orders sent from the Kremlin were the gospel for this character. With no restraint or hesitation he would strike whomever he was ordered to strike. Dej had understood this very well, and precisely for this reason he strove to draw Chișinevschi over to his side in the struggle against Lucrețiu Pătrășcanu."[14]

Another tool used by Gheorghiu-Dej was Alexandru Drăghici (born 1913), who became Interior Minister in 1952. He speeds up the Pătrășcanu investigation, ordering the use of violence in order to obtain the forced confessions needed for a show trial. We have met Drăghici in the dock at the Craiova trial of 1936. His lawyer, V. V. Stanciu, pleaded as follows at the time:

"A Romanian according to the strictest criteria, that is, both by ethnicity and by name. Born in a village in Buzău County. Likeable, as you can see. Intelligent, as you will have observed from the answers he has

---

[13] Vladimir Tismăneanu, *Arheologia terorii*, Allpha, 1996, p. 183.
[14] *Idem*, pp. 184-85.

given to the questions put to him. Twenty three years old, thus in the prime of youth. A locksmith by trade. A mechanic at the CFR Grivitza Workshops. From this presentation, I ask you to retain two aspects: young and worker. ... These young men ... are anarchic elements in the present state. All are extremists, whether right-wing or left-wing. ... Drăghici is young, therefore an extremist. A worker, he cannot be a right-wing extremist, which is to say, a fascist ... he has realised that fascism is a trap for the naïve. ... Drăghici is thus an anti-fascist, which is to say, he wants to build a barrier against fascism, which threatens war, hunger, dictatorship. Is the danger of fascism an invention ... or a reality? ... He has been accused, like the others, of having an anti-national attitude. A mistake. Anti-fascism not only precludes this, but implies it. ... The French Popular Front is also nationalist. What does Drăghici have in common with the other 18 accused? Nothing except two ideas: the fight against war and the fight against social inequality. Ideas are to be combatted not prosecuted [by the police – *author's note*]."

After 1952, Drăghici becomes a copy of Lavrenti Beria in Bucharest. The mere utterance of his name creates fear and panic. He was synonymous with danger, terror, summary execution. Prudently, the author of the above eulogy, lawyer V. V. Stanciu, fled to the West immediately after the war. He knew the 'clients' he had defended at trial all too well. He preferred not to wait for the gratitude of the 'illegals'. It would have meant a prison cell.

Drăghici is imprisoned (1936-1944) at Doftana and Caransebeș. He is loyal to Gheorghiu-Dej. He sleeps in the same cell as him and serves him. He will remain Dej's henchman. In 1946, he is the public prosecutor in the Ion Antonescu trial. He is head of the PCdR Bucharest organisation, but is deposed by Ana Pauker. The protection of Gheorghiu-Dej saves him. In 1949, he becomes Under Secretary of State in the Interior Ministry and in 1952 Interior Minister. Gheorghiu-Dej makes use of him to do his dirty work. Some of it is in the family, such as in 1959-1960: Drăghici orders the arrests and the fabrication of a trial against the lover of his patron's daughter, Lica, at the orders of Dej. The hapless lover dies a year later, in suspicious circumstances, in prison at Rîmnicu Sărat.[15] Drăghici is one of the key figures in Gheorghiu-Dej's entourage. His main accomplice is Nicolae Ceaușescu. In 1965, on the death of his patron, he is embroiled

---

[15] Stelian Tănase, *Anatomia mistificării*, Humanitas, 2003, pp. 332-337.

in the squabbles to settle the succession. In 1968, he is purged, in the old tradition of the underground. During his 16 years as a minister, he had accumulated too much power. Those around him, the political barons, feared him. Ceaușescu, his erstwhile ally, deposed him because he acted as a limitation on his power. Both of them were familiar with the ritual of ostracism, having learned it as apprentices in the ways of the underground at Doftana and Carasebeș. Drăghici survived Ceaușescu, whom he had, because of his deposition, ended up hating. He died in 1993, a refugee in Budapest.

Another denizen of the inter-war underground, who forged a ministerial career for himself after 23 August 1944, was Teohari Georgescu. Born in Chitila, near Bucharest, in 1908 (died 1976). His father was a grocer. Under arrest by the Securitate and in various plenary sessions of the CC of the PMR, he will be castigated for his 'petit bourgeois residues'. "Small, stocky, stout and morose … he was a type-setter by trade. For years, he typeset patriotic prose for nationalist and business newspapers, principally *The Universe* and the tedious *Official Gazette*."[16] In 1923, he takes an apprenticeship at the Cartea Românească Printing Press. A member of the Gutenberg Print Workers Trade Union. In 1927, he becomes a communist agitator. Arrested on a number of occasions, in 1933, 1934 (together with Constantin Pîrvulescu, Vasile Vîlcu, Ștefan Mladin – the latter will head the team that apprehends Ion Antonescu in the Royal palace on the night of 23-24 August 1944), 1935 (when he makes 'compromising statements' to the Siguranță), 1937, and 1938. He is sentenced to various short prison terms, and to 10 years in 1935, a sentence which is subsequently quashed. Hence, there arise suspicions regarding his collaboration with the Siguranță. Iosif Șraier, the head of the PCdR legal bureau, deals with his investigations and trials. In 1938, he is made head of the PCdR Bucharest organisation, and a year later, a member of the CC. From March 1940, he is a member of the Secretariat. In May 1940, he clandestinely crosses the border into the USSR with Foriș. He spends a few months at the Comintern, in Moscow. Here he struck up a friendship with Vasile Luca, whom he previously met in Romania. A few months after his return to Bucharest, he is arrested again, at Easter in 1941, along with Iosif Chișinevschi, Gavrilă Birtaș, and Parascheva Breiner. The five of them, plus Foriș, who was not arrested, made up the entire PCdR Secretariat. He behaves well during the investigation, in contrast to

---

[16] Petre Pandrea, *Reeducarea de la Aiud*, Vremea, 2000, p. 374.

the others. This version does not take account of the other, which reveals that Teohari Georgescu gave information to the Siguranța and was treated leniently by the investigators. He is sentenced to 10 years hard labour and sent to Caransebeş Prison. He becomes close to Gheorghiu-Dej. At this time, Teohari Georgescu, as Party Secretary, was more highly placed than Dej in the PCdR hierarchy. In 1942-1943, he is in Văcăreşti Prison, brought there as a printer to carry out various tasks. Here, he conducts anti-Foriş propaganda, having made an agreement with Gheorghiu-Dej, and heads the Party cell. When Gheorghiu-Dej leaves Carasebeş Prison, in June 1943, he designates Teohari Georgescu as head of the communist cell. It was a sign of his authority among the inmates. He was viewed as a Moscow man, because of the trip he made there in the summer of 1940. In Moscow, he had been trained in special operations and was a keeper of the Party's secret cipher. He maintained direct links with the Comintern, without the knowledge of Foriş. In Moscow, he had had meetings with the Comintern leaders, including Georgi Dimitrov,[17] who received him in his office. Petre Borilă[18] acted as translator during the interview, as Georgescu did not know

---

[17] Archive of the SRI, Dossier 40009, Vol. 1, p. 519.

[18] Petre Borilă, a graduate of the V. I. Lenin School for Comintern activists and of GPU courses, a member of the 'Bulgarian Mafia' within the PCdR, participant at the Fifth Congress of the PCdR, Comintern functionary, responsible for special operations. A member of the International Brigades in Spain, carrying out special GPU missions. During the war, he is a high functionary in the Comintern. He returns to Romania in 1944, with the Horia, Cloşca and Crişan Division, within which he is a political commissar. From 1952, he is a member of the Political Bureau, replacing his protector in Moscow, Ana Pauker, on whom he had spied for the Soviet secret services. He is present at the meetings between Ana Pauker and Dimitrov, in September 1944, and is Gheorghiu-Dej's confidant, planted by the NKVD. During all this time, he spies for Moscow. In February 1956, he accompanies Gheorghiu-Dej to Moscow, for the Twentieth Congress of the CPSU, where Khrushchev gives his famous report on the Stalin personality cult. He supports Gheorghiu-Dej in not complying with the de-Stalinisation initiated by the Kremlin. When Gheorghiu-Dej begins to emancipate himself from Moscow in the winter of 1961-1962, their relations cool. He loses his positions after 1965, and is removed from office by Ceauşescu.

any foreign languages. Dimitrov tells him that he has to memorise a cipher and keep in touch with the Comintern. This link has to be made without the knowledge of Foriş. Throughout his sojourn in Moscow, he is in contact with the secret services, which train him in the use of subversive methods. He was responsible for PCdR special operations, and Foriş for political matters. This reveals to us that Teohari Georgescu was a secret agent, and not merely a trades union agitator.

> "On the eve of my departure from Moscow (August 1940), when I went to the cabinet with Boris Ştefanov, to take my leave, the latter told me that I was regularly to keep the International and Romanian sections informed, that I was to maintain the link with the International, without saying anything over the usual channels … that no one should know about it, not even Foriş. Boris Ştefanov went on to tell me that I could write to him personally if I saw things were not going well."[19]

He returns clandestinely to Romania in October, via Ismail, in Tulcea County,[20] through a network run by Dumitru Coliu, a member of the Bulgarian branch (real name: Dimităr Kolev), a Comintern agent, a spy, later a member of the Political Bureau. Coliu is the last channel of communication with Moscow. Georgescu – and Foriş, two months later – are among the last to use this channel. The network is discovered in May 1941, Coliu flees to Moscow, and all links with the Comintern are severed until 23 August 1944.

The appointment of Teohari Georgescu as head of the Party cell at Văcăreşti and Caransebeş was nothing unusual. Since 1940, he had been Secretary of the CC of the RCP. In Moscow, in 1940, the Comintern had proposed him as head of the Romanian Party, an offer he refused – if we are to believe what Teohari Georgescu himself was to claim much later – on the grounds of his lack of experience. Loyal to Gheorghiu-Dej until his release from prison, on his arrival in Bucharest he sides with Ana Pauker, becoming her unconditional supporter. He is once more a member of the Secretariat, together with Vasile Luca, Ana Pauker and Gheorghiu-Dej. He is the only

---

[19] Archive of the SRI, Dossier 40009, vol. 1, p. 520.

[20] Ismail was part of Greater Romania (1918-1944) at that time, but is now part of Ukraine. The town is a port, lying on the Kilia branch of the Danube, 80km from the Black Sea. – *Translator's note.*

surviving member from the 1941 line-up. In November 1944, he becomes Under Secretary of State in the Interior Ministry, and on 6 March 1945, Interior Minister in the Government of Dr Petre Groza. His adjunct is the man who had defended him in court, lawyer Iosif Șraier. In 1947, Șraier was sacked after it was discovered that he had been working for the Siguranța, and defected to the West. Georgescu was a long-lived minister, controlled by the Soviet secret services, for which he worked. Nor could he have been given the portfolio of the Interior Ministry had he not enjoyed the trust of the occupiers and worked for them.

Teohari Georgescu's behaviour in power, compared with that during clandestinity, is symptomatic. He is one of the most corrupt ministers.

> "Teohari Georgescu entered the workers' movement out of hatred for his overly opulent bosses, determined to catch up with them and overtake them. His private life, once he had 'arrived', surpassed the turpitude of his patrons. He left his wife, who had taken care to bring him clean clothes in prison, adulterously conquering the wife of a subaltern, if such a thing can be named a conquest. ... Teohari never understood charity for a suffering neighbour. Teohari understood theft, embezzlement, forgery, swindling. He always trod at the fringes of the penal code. He was full of hate. He lived opulently and shamelessly. He understood and lived the dark, criminological side of man. ... Named TG ... he is not even a communist, but a money-grubbing typesetter. He printed subversive manifestos for unknowns, for a price ..."[21]

His unlimited power leads him to abuse his function copiously. The inquiry of 1953-1956 reveals the names of dozens of women whom he had forced to have sexual relations with him in exchange for services: passports, the release of relatives from under arrest etc. He deposited money in foreign banks, an action in contravention of the law at the time. He divorces – a phenomenon frequent among the illegals, who, coming from a lower social stratum, seek women to match the rung on the social ladder they have now reached – and marries a woman from the bourgeoisie. He is out to get rich. Expropriations and the requests of rich, especially Jewish, families to leave the country, bring hefty commissions for the 'communist' Interior Minister. He moves into the most select district of the capital, into a sumptuous,

---

[21] Petre Pandrea, *idem*, pp. 376-380.

confiscated villa. He wears deluxe tailored clothes. He has a lifestyle that mocks the poverty around him. In his entourage are to be found adventurers, parvenus, opportunists and many characters from the criminal world. His numerous family forms a clan over which he presides. This family, plus the Party clientele, gather around them a clique of fishy businessmen, whose 'Godfather' is Teohari Georgescu. Throughout this period (1944-1952) he remains a member of the Secretariat. He is a public figure. He speaks at demonstrations and at meetings of the CC of the PCR/PMR. He has a powerful position in the Party, thanks to his collaboration with Gheorghiu-Dej, his closeness to Ana Pauker, and, above all, the backing of the Soviet secret services. He is intelligent. He has the cunning of a provincial politician. He is a demagogue, an intriguer, always coming off the better from all kinds of schemes. He is unscrupulous, avid for pleasure and money. He is a wholly non-ideological character (like Gheorghiu-Dej), the opposite of a person like Chișinevschi. In contrast to the latter, who is detested by everybody, he is sociable, even popular within the Party. However, he is, above all, feared. The period in which he is Minister is one of intense terror.

***

Another influential figure was Ion Gheorghe Maurer. As revealed in a Siguranță report of spring 1944, he had never been imprisoned or investigated in connection with communist activities. In any case, there would have been no reason for the Siguranță to investigate him. In the 1930s, he had behaved in a strictly professional way. He was a lawyer, an 'anti-fascist democrat', a left-wing sympathiser, a non-ideological and pragmatic type. His attitude reveals him to be obliging, on the lookout for a market for his wares. He moves within an ambiguous zone, watching for opportunities, eager to seize any chance to profit. His mentors are Girgore Iunian and N. D. Cocea. From the former he learns the cunning wiles of the politician, the art of manipulating others, and courtroom skills, and from the latter, unscrupulousness, cynicism, hedonism. Such traits were, in any case, innate to him. N. D. Cocea was consummately amoral and immoral, his sources of income nebulous, his occupations hazy, financed simultaneously by the Comintern, by Moruzov, the head of the SSI, and by the King via Malaxa.[22]

---

[22] Nicolae Malaxa (1884-1965). Romanian industrialist. Malaxa's factories produced armaments, railway locomotives, rolling stock, (cont. p. 594.)

Maurer acquires the techniques of survival and a flair for scheming. He learns how to profit from people and situations. Outwardly, he does not belong to the underground; he was a bourgeois. But by his lack of faith in anything, coldness of heart, radical egoism, and indifference to others, he is a denizen of the underground. He was deaf and blind to the suffering of those years when suffering reached its apogee. Under his mask of bonhomie, affability, and seigneurial air of a man lacking in ambition, there lay concealed the opposite character. There was something seductive but at the same time repulsive, something diabolical about him. He would have served any regime with the same zeal, if it satisfied his thirst for power and luxury. His vanity was boundless. He was a jovial devil, always ready for any bargain. He resembled Ralea, Sadoveanu and the other servile fellow travellers eager to make a pact with the occupier.

Maurer was born in Bucharest, in 1902. His mother was French, his father German. He graduated from the Military Lycée in Craiova and studied at the Law Faculty in Bucharest, becoming a magistrate at Agnita and a prosecutor in Sighişoara. He gives up these posts and returns to the capital, where he works as a jurist for the *Dimineaţa* and *Adevărul Press Trust*. He is a prominent member of the small Peasant Radical Party, which was led by lawyer Grigore Iunian, who was close to Nicolae Malaxa. In any case, the Party was funded by Malaxa. Maurer looks set to enjoy a conventional bourgeois career. He goes into the law and dabbles in politics, the typical choice in inter-war Romania. Maurer is a careerist. He feverishly seeks out any profitable placement. He is always in search of clients. He tries his hand at various businesses, without much success. We find him getting mixed up in all sorts of causes. He fishes in murky waters. He frequents many different circles: the press, political parties, business. And in politics, too, where he

---

motor cars, etc. He also owned much of the Romanian steel industry. He was close to King Carol I and his detested mistress, 'Lupeasca' (Elena Lupescu). He had business links with Nazi Germany and collaborated with Goering in confiscating the assets of Jewish Romanian industrialist Max Auschnitt. In 1940, after the fall of Carol I, he was imprisoned briefly on charges of extortion. Starting in the 1930s, he financed the fascist Iron Guard, which used weapons manufactured in Malaxa's factories during the Bucharest Pogrom of January 1941. Sent to New York by King Mihai as part of an economic mission in 1945, Malaxa remained in the United States as an exile. *–Translator's note.*

will excel, he plays a double game. He cultivates relations with the Left, the Centre, and the Right, where his German background, at a time when Germany was becoming a dominant force in Europe, lend him credibility. His feelings of superiority are blatantly manifest. In 1935, he funds the Democratic Lawyers group (with Iosif Șraier, Radu Olteanu etc.) which opposes the Christian Lawyers group, led by Istrate Micescu. In February 1938, he heads the electoral list for the Peasant Radical Party in Dîmbovița County during the parliamentary elections. He is also the head of the Party's county organisation. He is not elected. He enters into contact with the communists via the 'anti-fascist' trials. He pleads in defence of Vasile Luca, in Brașov. He is among the team defending Petre Constantinescu-Iași in the Kishinev trial, along with the head of his Party, Grigore Iunian. He represents Ana Pauker at the trial in Craiova. In both trials, his spontaneous rivalry with and dislike of Pătrășcanu stands out. Also in 1936, in August, he defends 27 'anti-fascists' in the Democratic Bloc trial. These trials are widely covered by the press, which helps him to make a name for himself. They are also well paid: the Comintern finances the defence. Matters take their course. He frequents the Soviet legation. He receives fees for consulting; he is hired as a jurist in financial schemes patronised by the legation. The Siguranță take note. In 1938, the Siguranță also reports that he has links to David Segal, a reporter for *Dimineața* and a Comintern agent.[23] In 1938, he exerts pressure on Grigore Iunian to sign an accord with the PCdR and the PSD, to form a popular front. Also in 1938, he is part of the administrative board of a company that publishes the *Lumea Românească* [*Romanian World*] newspaper (director: Zaharia Stanca), a publication financed by the SSI. In the winter of 1939, he takes steps, having been entrusted to do so by the PCdR, to obtain authorisation for the publication of a magazine, *Orientarea* [*Orientation*], which was to be run by N. D. Cocea, who is also on the payroll of Mihai Moruzov. He is lawyer for the official Carlist gazette, *România*, run by Cezar Petrescu. He frequents Francophile, pro-American and British circles. The same SSI report notes that Maurer maintains contact between Constantinescu-Iași and the PCdR leadership. In the summer of 1940 he is in Tighina with the 3rd Bolgrad Hunters Regiment, having been called up as a sub-lieutenant in the reserve. He manages to beat a timely retreat from the Dniester river to the Prut river, without incurring any losses. He could have crossed over into the USSR, as a large part of the communist

---

[23] Archive of the MAN, MStM, State Security Fund, Dossier 118, p. 17.

activists did. Having been demobilised, he continues to practise law. In November 1940, after the earthquake, we find him at Doftana, where he is dealing with the situation of the communist inmates. He offers to help Gheorghiu-Dej to escape, but the latter declines. Gheorghiu-Dej is afraid of being assassinated. In 1941, he defends, at the appeal court, Friedrich Klauda, indicted in the 'Soviet spy trial' of 1931. Also in 1941, he takes care of the preparations for the trial of 15 arrested communists – among them members of the PCdR Secretariat. This indicates his important position alongside the Party. After the withdrawal of the Soviet legation, the Siguranța discover that Maurer is on their payroll. This earns him his first stretch in prison. On 1 June 1941, he is arrested, and on 28 June he is sent to the camp at Tîrgu Jiu. It is an experience that does not suit him. He signs a declaration whereby he undertakes to give up all political activity. He is released on 26 November 1941. He is mobilised by the Bucharest recruiting centre. In 1942, industrialist Ghiță Pop – with whom he has good and long-standing relations, and who, in 1943-1944 will be one of the major sponsors of the PCdR – asks him to suggest to the Soviets, via the Party, the publication in Moscow of a declaration whereby the USSR would affirm that it had no territorial claims on Romania. In return, Maurer asks Pop to make overtures to Iuliu Maniu, in order to solicit from Antonescu measures to ameliorate conditions for Soviet prisoners.

In December 1942, in the context of the battle of Stalingrad, he is arrested and interned at Tîrgu Jiu once more. He opts not for the Second Group, where the communists are to be found, but for the First Group. He remains among the bourgeois, officers, functionaries and intellectuals. The moment defines his situation exactly, the status he himself claims (as a non-communist, or one in disguise), the ambiguities of his character. He re-establishes ties with Gheorghiu-Dej, brought from Caransebeş at the end of June. He backs him in the conflict with Pătrăşcanu and agrees with the plot against Foriş. In contrast with the other communist leaders, Maurer got on with Foriş. Pătrăşcanu refused to get mixed up in such internecine Party squabbles, even though he was not at all close to Foriş. Between Maurer and Pătrăşcanu, relations are extremely poor. Their rivalry had become manifest since as long ago as the anti-fascist trials. Maurer was jealous of Pătrăşcanu's abilities, of his political past. He envies him for his popularity, for the reputation as an ideologue he had gained by publishing a number of books. He, too, had had ambitions to be a writer, but had failed, which was one more reason to despise Pătrășcanu. When, in camp, Ovidiu Șandor accuses Pătrășcanu of being a Siguranță agent, Maurer backs him up.[24] On 27 July 1943, he is released and sent to the front. He takes part in the retreat from the Crimea. Arriving in Constanța, he deserts. He goes to Bucharest, where he lives clandestinely, in the underground. Gheorghiu-Dej requests that he handle his planned escape from the prison camp. With the connivance of the authorities, which had slackened the prison camp guard on the night of 13-14 August, Gheorghiu-Dej and Maurer arrive in Rîmnicu Vîlcea, where they remain until after 23 August. Starting in September, Maurer attends meetings of the government on behalf of the PMR. In November, he becomes a member of the board of the newly established Friends of the United States association. Maurer navigates murky and unpredictable waters. On 15 November, he is appointed Secretary General in the Ministry of Communications, brought there by the then minister, Gheorghiu-Dej. He sits on the board of ARLUS[25] from its foundation in 1945. When the scales tip towards Moscow, and the other members of the Allied Control Commission voice no protest, Maurer makes a show of being a 'loyal communist'. In the PCR, which is convulsed by factions and rivalries between leaders, he is viewed as being close to Gheorghiu-Dej. In July 1946, he heads a Romanian economic mission to Moscow. In 1946, he drafts the SovRom[26] law. He takes part in the Paris Peace Conference.

Maurer was an influential figure in the entourage of Gheorghiu-Dej. Up until 1948, he held high-level positions. He took part in the summit meetings of the PCR. These were the years when his instincts, careerism, and pleasure in the game were unfettered. The epoch was ambiguous, an epoch of cynicism and brutal opportunism. Whoever allied himself with

---

[24] Mihai Novikov, *Moartea lui Grigore Preoteasa*, Evenimentul românesc, 1998, p. 123.

[25] Asociația Română pentru Legături cu Uniunea Sovietică (The Romanian Association for Ties with the Soviet Union). – *Translator's note.*

[26] The SovRoms were joint Soviet-Romanian ventures, including SovRomPetrol, SovRomTransport, SovRomGaz, SovRomLemn (timber), SovRomTractor, SovRomFilm etc. Their aim was supposedly to generate revenues for reconstruction during a period of economic isolation for Romania, but in practice they resulted in a drain of resources from Romania to the USSR. They were phased out between 1954 and 1956. – *Translator's note.*

the Soviets and their lackeys was rewarded. There was, however, a price for all this: moral compromises and adaptation to the harsh conditions of the political medium, essentially to occupation. Many tragedies and betrayals occurred. Two examples: Maurer appears as a witness for the prosecution in the trial of Colonel Zlotescu in 1946, although on his release from the camp at Tîrgu Jiu, where Zloescu had been commandant, he had thanked him for the way in which he had been treated. On the same occasion, in 1941, he also gave a declaration renouncing communist activities. A similar declaration was imputed to Pătrășcanu, in the trial of 1954, as being a "betrayal of the proletarian cause and of his Party." Industrialist Ghiță Pop (a client of Maurer's since the 1930s), a friend, a sponsor of the Party during the war, is convicted at the Maniu Trial. Maurer refuses Pop's relatives any help, including a life-saving passport, as had been the procedure in other similar situations. Maurer is among the initiates of the new power. He participates behind the scenes in all the conflicts for supremacy. He backs Gheorghiu-Dej against Ana Pauker and Vasile Luca. He hatches plots against Pătrășcanu, whom he detests. His situation is transformed as a result of the denunciation Emil Bodnăraș sends to the Kremlin, a denunciation aimed at Gheorghiu-Dej, but which directly strikes Maurer. His career, which had promised to be so brilliant, enters a cone of shadow. He is accused of Anglo-American sympathies, of exerting a malign influence upon Gheorghiu-Dej. He is watched, shadowed, his telephone calls are intercepted. A number of times he is on the verge of being arrested. A public trial is being prepared against him. He was to appear in the dock alongside Gheorghiu-Dej, in the summer of 1948, or alongside his rival Pătrășcanu, already imprisoned, then and later. Until March 1953, he is in the sights of Soviet advisers in Bucharest, as the potential centrepiece for a show trial. He fits the bill as the perfect victim for the Kremlin's paranoid fury. It is the protection of Gheorghiu-Dej that saves him. The insistence of the Soviet advisers and the intrigues of his Party rivals come to naught. He moves to the periphery of the regime. He survives. He camouflages himself in a nondescript post. As a 'bourgeois' he was a prized quarry, like Pătrășcanu, Koffler, Calmanovici and Zilber, who were incriminated for their social background and 'the nefarious influences of their background'. As a 'fellow traveller', he could, like so many others, have been enmeshed in a show trial, marked out as a class enemy and imprisoned. He enters a deluxe underground, as a protégé of Gheorghiu-Dej. He will re-emerge on the surface 10 years later, as president of the Great National Assembly, Foreign Minister, and Prime Minister, in 1961. In March 1965, on his deathbed, Gheorghiu-Dej proposes that he succeed him. Maurer refuses.

Maurer was contaminated by the underground networks he frequented as a lawyer. But to his dying day he remained a bourgeois and amoral cynic. He wanted to reach high office. Under what regime was unimportant. He held no deep-seated convictions. Had Romania not been occupied by the Soviets, he would have forged a career in one of the traditional democratic parties. If history had turned out like this, Gheorghiu-Dej would have been the tradesman who installed the wiring in Maurer's villa, or the trades union leader with whom Maurer the bourgeois minister would have had to negotiate. He was a political poker player. He guessed correctly what was going to happen after the war, and, the consummate realist, he adapted himself accordingly. Did he have an inkling of the future career of Gheorghiu-Dej? We do not know. Dej was one of the horses in the running, and Maurer, like others, laid his bet on him. He had also betted on the politically opposite extreme. He maintained contacts with the Iron Guard and had defended its members in court.[27] His handsomely paid complaisance with Comintern agents in the 1930s was a tactic. He 'adheres to communism' when the situation becomes clear from the political point of view. The Iron Curtain had fallen; the West was far away. He had performed various services in the 1930s. Over the years, he had fraternised with the criminal underworld. He had entered the underground. He had cultivated relations in this world apart, which the next day might rise to the surface and seize power. Maurer was a 'fellow traveller', a lawyer in search of wealth and status. He was the archetype of the impostor, an arriviste. He was not 'faithful to the cause of the liberation of the proletariat and of the world revolution'. Such sentiments – which made Ana Pauker, Iosif Chișinevschi, the 'true believers', as well as other sectarians, the dogmatic and the ideological fanatics, palpitate passionately – left Maurer cold. He was a denizen of the underworld, among its most malign. He served a cause in which he did not believe. He understood the vacuity of the Bolshevik utopia, he anticipated its failure and imposture, but he served it. He was too much in love with power, rank, prestige, status. He could not care less who conferred them upon him and under what conditions. He lived to see the fall of the communist regimes. He died in the last year of the twentieth century.

---

[27] Archive of the MAN, State Security Fund, Dossier 121, p. 10.

***

The Pătrășcanu investigation extended over six years, from 1948-1954. In the meantime, Moscow mounted show trials in Budapest, Sofia and Tirana, against the backdrop of the Tito conflict, in the first phase and then, in the second phase, in Prague, this time in the context of the massive anti-Semitic excesses ordered by Stalin. Bucharest is bypassed on each occasion, although preparations are begun, firstly, in 1948, with the arrest of Pătrășcanu and the arrest of Dej and then, in 1952, with the deposal and arrest of the Ana Pauker/Vasile Luca/Teohari Georgescu group. In 1952, the plan was to lump together Pătrășcanu and Ana Pauker and co., in preparation for a major show trial, set for the autumn of 1953. Whereas originally, in 1948, political calculations had led the Kremlin to postpone and then cancel the trial, this time, in 1953, it was halted by the death of Stalin, on 5 March. Arrested a month earlier, on 18 February, Ana Pauker was released by the Securitate at the end of April. It is only then that she is informed of the death of Stalin. Ana Pauker breaks down in tears. Al. Moghioroș (who had been with her in the dock in the trial of 1936 and had subsequently become close to Gheorghiu-Dej) tells her: "If Stalin were still alive, you'd be dead."[28] The trial would have resulted in capital punishment for her, Pătrășcanu, Luca, and Teohari Georgescu. Sentences were handed down depending upon position in the hierarchy – the higher the position, the greater the risk of a death sentence. Stalin had rediscovered the pleasure of liquidating Bolsheviks, and Bucharest was next on the list. The conflict for absolute power that erupted in September 1944, on Ana Pauker's arrival in Bucharest, came to an end in 1952. Relations between Gheorghiu-Dej and Ana Pauker get off to a bad start. The Pîrvulescu/Bodnăraș/Ranghet troika,which is preparing the ground for Dej himself to take over the leadership, is dissolved by Ana Pauker. The only positive thing, as far as Gheorghiu-Dej is concerned, is the fact that he hated Pătrășcanu who is not co-opted into the new leadership. In addition, among the activists from Romania, Dej is picked alongside Teohari Gerogescu. He docilely submits to Ana Pauker (October 1944-1945). He comes to double for her (1945-1948), to sideline her (1949-1951) and finally to depose her (1952). He draws his influence from the authority he wields over the communist ex-prisoners.

---

[28] Quoted by Robert Levy, *Ana Pauker: The Rise and Fall of a Jewish Communist*, University of California Press, 2001, p. 219.

Numerically, they are in the majority at every echelon. They exert a control that eludes the 'Muscovites', much fewer in number. Although the latter were placed in strategic positions, the Party, and above all the apparatus, gradually comes to be organised by those loyal to Gheorghiu-Dej (1944-1948).

The 1948-1952 campaign of purges enlarges the power base of the 'camp inmates'. In the period when she was deposed, Ana Pauker had already lost control within the Party. Her only source of authority was the protection of leaders in Moscow, such as Molotov and Manuilsky. In 1952, the influence of the latter was much diminished, and Stalin was preparing to purge them, and perhaps to have them shot. Another source of power for Gheorghiu-Dej was the subordination of the secret services via Soviet agents, they too fellow inmates at Aiud, Doftana and Caransebeș. Emil Bodnăraș, Pantiușa Bodnarenko, Sergey Nikonov et al. are men whom he can trust. They serve Moscow, above all the secret services, but also Gheorghiu-Dej. As the Soviets rely above all else upon the secret services, Gheorghiu-Dej manages to win their trust. Information received from their spies tips the balance in Gheorghiu-Dej's favour. In the conflict within the Kremlin between the Comintern (which, although dissolved, continued to operate, having metamorphosed into the Kominform in 1947) and the secret services, Stalin rules in favour of the latter. He viewed the Comintern people with the greatest of suspicion; they reminded him of Trotsky, Zinoviev, Bukharin, Racovski etc. The 'espionage-itis', rife within the Kremlin, leads Stalin to rely on the reports of Beria. Under the patronage of Moscow, a muffled war unfolds between the two Romanian nuclei of power. They do not represent different policies or visions. Their subordination to the Kremlin is total and unconditional. It would be wrong to suppose that the 'camp inmates', because they had spent the war in Romania, opposed 'Stalin's expansionist tendencies'. In a way, things were exactly the opposite. We can observe that sometimes Pauker and Luca have timid reserves regarding orders from Moscow and try to limit their effect or delay their implementation. The 'Muscovites', having lived for a while in the USSR, were up to date on the negative effects of the collective farms, forced industrialisation and the Terror. Gheorghiu-Dej had won control of the Party because he had proven himself to be more obedient to Stalin than the others. In any case, the accusations that were levelled against him in 1952 include exactly these things. Later, in December 1961, Gheorghiu-Dej will claim, mystifying matters, that he had aligned himself with positions that protected 'Romanian interests', in contrast to Ana Pauker, who, he claimed, pursued the opposite: Russification. A political myth, 'national communism', which will supplant the other myth of 'proletarian internationalism', is placed in circulation. Gheorghiu-Dej was a proponent of Stalinism, as method whereby to maintain a grip on absolute power. This meant an extreme personalisation of the regime and its corollary – the use of repression against any heresy or dissidence, whether real or imaginary. In other words, Dej defended his *right* to judge and punish adversaries. He could do so only by preserving 'ideological purity'. He regarded it as his privilege to hold the power over life and death. Gheorghiu-Dej was not an ideological fanatic, but a pragmatist, an opportunist, a chameleon, of a type frequently encountered among the survivors of the underground. He saw Stalinism exclusively as the praxis of power, as exercised by his mentor, Stalin. Gheorghiu-Dej was a natural imitator. He adapted to any environment, with the aim of conquering and conserving power. The rationale of power was prevalent in him. During the period 1944-1952, both the Pauker and the Dej groups did nothing more than what they were ordered to by the Kremlin. They did so because they were under Red Army occupation, but also because they were prisoners of the Marxist-Leninist-Stalinist ideology. Dej, Pauker, Pătrăşcanu, Bodnăraş, Pîrvulescu, and all the other 'illegals' saw themselves as the standard bearers of a revolution, the missionaries of a utopia that required Romania to be violently subjugated. Had they hesitated or behaved differently, they would have been branded enemies of the Kremlin. The vocabulary of the communist vulgate contained untranslatable terms that led straight to a prison cell, if not the firing squad: 'right-wing deviationism', 'left-wing deviationism', 'liquidationism', 'pacificationism'. Or, put more simply: 'traitor', 'nationalist chauvinist', 'in the pay of the West'. And even more simply: 'agents of the Siguranţa' and 'spy'. All of these were the festering wounds, the perennial obsessions of the underground.

The Kremlin is always the judge in all the episodes in the struggle for supremacy. In the winter of 1945, Pauker and Dej go to Moscow, where they are received by Stalin himself. It was Gheorghiu-Dej's first visit to Moscow. Ana Pauker was familiar with the city. She had been visiting it frequently since 1922. Her relations in the spheres of power mark out another difference between the two. Gheorghiu-Dej is her opposite here – an unknown. Moscow prefers not to settle the dispute. And after this visit, matters within the sphere of power remain unclear. The two have to share. It is an extension of the techniques of divide and rule employed in the inter-war period. The Kremlin maintained rivalries between factions in order to ensure its control. There follows a period of status quo, with shifting fortunes. We always find the presence of Soviet advisers, the embassy, and emissaries from Moscow. They play games; they alleviate and/or aggravate tensions. The formation of the Dr Petre Groza Government, the royal strike,[29] and agrarian reform give rise to endless conflict.

Not even another visit in tandem to Moscow, in September 1945, can resolve the situation. At the close of the PCR national conference of 19-21 October 1945, the members of the CC gather to elect a new head of the Party. The conflict for supremacy is at its height. Vasile Luca proposes that Gheorghiu-Dej should officially hold the position of Secretary General but that Ana Pauker should run the Party *de facto*. It was a compromise formula, a reflection of the situation in the Kremlin, where the supporters of the two rival clans in Bucharest are evenly matched. Nevertheless, Pauker maintains control of the Secretariat. Together with Luca and Teohari Georgescu – a 'permanent faction' as Dej will later say – she frequently forces Gheorghiu-Dej into a minority position. At the end of 1945, Andrey Vyshinsky suggests to Dej that he should depose her. For Vyshinsky, no one had the right to infringe upon the authority of the head of the Party. The same as no one dared to do so in Moscow. If Gheorghiu-Dej was Secretary General, then it was up to him to decide in every matter. What Ana Pauker was doing seemed like heresy to Vyshinsky. It is the first of the episodes in which her head will be demanded. For the time being, Ana Pauker manages to save herself. Stalin summons them both to Moscow, and the status quo is preserved. In these ambiguous circumstances, the intrigues, backstabbing, and denunciations delivered to Soviet emissaries in Bucharest or directly to Moscow follow their course. The situation is mutable. This small band of quislings is completely isolated from the populace and dependent upon the Kremlin. The life of erstwhile clandestinity goes on the same as before, regardless of the change of scene and the higher stakes.

In the summer of 1947, Emil Bodnăraş denounced Gheorghiu-Dej to the Kremlin. Bodnăraş, a man of the Soviet secret service, informed his

---

[29] Between August 1945 and January 1946, King Mihai went 'on strike', refusing to ratify laws passed by the pro-communist Petre Groza Government. – *Translator's note.*

masters that Dej's willingness to increase economic ties with the Anglo-Americans "beyond the previously set 'clearly defined limits' of cooperation ... resulted in a conflict between Dej and Pauker, Luca and Bodnăraș himself, who wanted to assure that Dej did not go farther than necessary in his relations with the Anglo-Americans."[30] Gheorghiu-Dej never finds himself in the situation of having all the others against him at the same time. This would have led to the end of his career. He has the knack of dividing his adversaries and waiting for the right moment to strike. His patience when it came to hatching plots surpassed that of the others, although they too were veteran intriguers from the corridors of the Hotel Lux and the prisons. For Dej, the critical moment comes a year after the denunciation by Bodnăraș. Tito and Dimitrov visited Bucharest in the winter before the crisis. Stalin becomes irate, suspecting a plot against him. Gheorghiu-Dej is accused of 'Titoism' and investigated by Soviet advisers. A trial is prepared, in which he will appear in the dock alongside Pătrășcanu. A note from the General Department of State Security elucidates: "It is rumoured that Mr Gheorghiu-Dej, who has been arrested and who according to some was supposed to have been deported to Kharkov, has now been rehabilitated and is going to take the place of Dr Petre Groza as president of the Council of Ministers. This change is supposed to be going to happen in at most 10 days."[31] Ana Pauker seems to be the beneficiary of this reversal of situation. She suggests to the Soviet Ambassador, Sergey Kavtaradze, to whom she is close, that Gheorghiu-Dej should be replaced. Moscow limits itself to keeping Gheorghiu-Dej on probation, without taking further measures. Gheorghiu-Dej, frightened at what might happen to him, becomes even more prudent, displaying a vociferous Stalinism on all occasions, intended to disadvantage Ana Pauker. To what extent either of them are true believers or hypocrites is hard to determine. After the critical moment of summer 1948, Gheorghiu-Dej, having got rid of Foriș and Pătrășcanu, follows his usual tactic. He makes no direct attack. He has learnt this in prison. He hatches a plot, patiently. He begins by gathering compromising information about the three: Pauker, Luca and Georgescu. The secret service intercepts their telephone calls. Informers are planted in their entourages. This was not at all difficult, because Ana Pauker kept an open house. It was here

---

[30] Robert Levy, *Ana Pauker: The Rise and Fall of a Jewish Communist*, University of California Press, 2001, p. 82.

[31] ANCR, Archive of the CC of the RCP, Fund 95, Dossier 790, p. 42.

that the communist leaders used to meet, toady, or observe. It was here that generals and diplomats used to come. Here, you would find numerous Soviets, agents, diplomats, officers from the garrisons, advisers assigned to the ministries or those in transit through Bucharest. You would frequently meet prominent intellectuals, eager to get in with the new regime. The meetings were discreetly watched by the secret services controlled by Dej loyalists. Preparations to oust Pauker continued for another four years. A number of favourable circumstances, promptly exploited by Gheorghiu-Dej, hastened the denouement: 1) Ana Pauker's cancer, discovered at a medical check in Moscow, in 1949; convalescence and treatment deactivate her politically and she gradually loses her grip on power; 2) Stalin's anti-semitic phobias reach the point of paranoia; she is Jewish; 3) The regime's difficulties demand scapegoats; 4) Purges were periodically demanded by the Comintern, as a means of settling accounts, eliminating rival clans, bringing new lifeblood to the Party, and disciplining activists. The same procedure was employed in the campaigns of verification in 1948-1952. Gheorghiu-Dej's clan held almost complete control over the Party. Nevertheless, Ana Pauker preserved a large share of power: the proof of this is the circumspect strategy adopted by the conspirators. Gradually, Gheorghiu-Dej wins over a number of Ana Pauker's supporters to his side: Iosif Chișinevschi, Miron Constantinescu, and Alexandru Moghioroș, who, out of opportunism, and/or following the indications of the Soviet secret services on which they were dependent, join the conspiracy.

The attack occurs at the beginning of 1952. The target of criticism is firstly Vasile Luca, under the pretext of irregularities at the Ministry of Finance, of which he is in charge. But he is a decoy; the real target is Ana Pauker. The attack in itself seems unremarkable. In spite of lengthy preparations and frequent meetings with Soviet advisers and diplomats, and in spite of a number of visits to Moscow, the true extent of the operation had been kept secret. The attack on Luca takes Pauker and Teohari Georgescu by surprise. They are rash enough to side with him, not suspecting anything. It was a provocation, a typical underground manoeuvre. It is only now that the real assault begins. The strategists and executors are Chișinevschi, Moghioroș, Apostol and Miron Constantinescu, backed up by Pîrvulescu, Bodnăraș and Chivu Stoica. Remaining in the background, Gheorghiu-Dej closely follows the unfolding events. The three targets are isolated, sitting ducks. The plot gathers steam at the end of August 1951, when Gheorghiu-

Dej and Chișinevschi go to the Kremlin and are received by Stalin. There follow five months of meticulous preparations. Lists are drawn up of those loyal to the adversary camp, supporters are recruited, accomplices are briefed, advantages are promised, and the hesitant are threatened. The intrigue entails betrayal, abjuration, denunciation, backstabbing. It is a conspiratorial atmosphere, one they know all too well. The preparations are complete by New Year. At a meeting of the Political Bureau, which promised to be routine, Luca is castigated by Miron Constantinescu. He is seconded by other initiates in the plot. During the 'unmasking', Luca collapses. He is taken home by ambulance. A few days later, he is sacked from the government.

A month later, a second move is made, at a meeting of the Central Committee. The onslaught resembles a settling of accounts. It was the same ritual as in the clandestine period. All the actors knew their roles by heart. There are winners and losers. The losers concede and make a self-denunciation, as stipulated in the catechism of the professional revolutionary. It is exactly what was expected of them, but this does not save them. The game is up. Quite apart from his thirst for power, Gheorghiu-Dej also holds personal grudges. The rivalry between Dej and Luca dated from the 1930s, from Grivitza and Doftana. Luca had 'discovered' the CFR electrician and promoted him in the trades union hierarchy. It was also Luca who had encouraged him to join the Party. Imprudently, Luca used to remind Dej of these humble beginnings. The third move is further meeting of the Political Bureau, on 13 March. The pressure increases on those marked out for sacrifice. The victims are ritually accused of 'right-wing deviationism', of 'liquidationaism', of being 'class enemies', and so on. It is decided that the situation should be dealt with by Party members, based on a letter from the Political Bureau, in which the accusations would be reiterated. In this way, the attack does not remain confined to a handful of members of the leadership: it is broadened to include the whole Party. It is a manoeuvre typical of factional fighting, with which they were all long familiar. They were the survivors of these struggles. The letter was a stigmatisation of Luca and his accomplices. The intended effect: their elimination. But the ceremonial proper has yet to begin. Vasile Luca was not the real target. Provoked, Pauker and Teohari Goergescu put up opposition and lose. The rival clan is determined to eliminate them. In April, Gheorghiu-Dej, together with other plotters, goes to the Kremlin to meet with Stalin, who is impatient to see the execution carried out. Why had Luca remained in the Political Bureau? Gheorghiu-Dej strikes him as undecided, weak. "If I were in your place, I would have shot her in the head a long time ago. … I was convinced that only proletarian blood flowed through your veins, but [I now see that] it's petit bourgeois blood."[32] Prudent, Gheorghiu-Dej tried to assure Stalin that he really did desire the elimination of Ana Pauker. Previously, Stalin had warned Dej that the PCdR was being transformed "from a social and class party to a race party."[33] It was an allusion to the fact that Pauker was Jewish. Dej would go on to 'Romanianise' the Party. Stalin's reaction in April 1952 let him understand that as far as the Kremlin was concerned, the fate of Ana Pauker was sealed. On their return to Bucharest, the plotters proceed to stage the final act of the drama. The denouement takes place a month later. The scene is a plenary of the CC of the PMR. A star-studded cast, a gripping drama. Intransigent characters, hosts of extras, a full auditorium. The ritual unfolds according to the rules of the political sect, which is what the Party had remained, even eight years since emerging from 'illegality' and four years since seizing absolute power. It is a ceremony of stigmatisation, a public execution. The three, Pauker, Luca and Georgescu, are subjected to a concentric attack orchestrated from behind the scenes. They are accused of all the diseases known to the underground. Finally, they are fired from the Political Bureau and the Secretariat. One theme frequently recurs in the incriminations: they have contested of the authority of Gheorghiu-Dej. All the other accusations are secondary, merely part of the ritual. It is a full-blown squaring of accounts. The complexes, frustrations and resentments accumulated over time come to the surface. Fear dominates. The terror of 'not being in line'. If you are out of the Party, you are nothing. The Soviet advisers supervise the plenary session, to make sure all goes according to plan. Ana Pauker and Teohari Georgescu remain ministers and members of the CC of the PMR for a short while. Vasile Luca is arrested in the middle of August. In October 1954 he is tried, along with other 'accomplices' likewise accused of undermining the national economy. Luca is sentenced to death, commuted to life imprisonment. He dies in Aiud in 1963. Pauker and Georgescu do not survive politically. They are deposed from all their functions, and in the middle of February they are arrested

---

[32] Robert Levy, *Ana Pauker: The Rise and Fall of a Jewish Communist*, University of California Press, 2001, p. 203.
[33] *Ibid.*, p. 80.

and interrogated. The death of Stalin supervenes on 5 March 1953. Thanks to the insistent interventions of Molotov and Manuilsky, Ana Pauker is released at the end of April. In May 1954, she is expelled from the PMR. In 1956, she is once more investigated by a Party commission. She refuses to oblige with the declarations demanded. The atmosphere had changed. In February, Khrushchev had presented his report in which he denounced Stalin's personality cult. In those years, there were rumours that she would be rehabilitated and return to the top. But once her protectors, Molotov and Kaganovich, were eliminated, in June 1957, any insistence on the part of Moscow to resolve the situation ceased. In 1958, she receives confirmation of the execution of Marcel Pauker in Moscow 20 years previously. After 1952, Ana Pauker is a non-person, isolated, kept under watch. She dies of cancer on 3 June 1960. She is cremated. The family refuse to intone *The Internationale*, as would have been customary at the funeral of a veteran communist.

Teohari Georgescu is arrested on 18 February and investigated for three and a half years. Naturally, the main accusation against him was that he had been an agent of the Siguranţă. The fact that, as a minister, he had destroyed archive documents connected to his past activity lends weight to the accusation. What was aimed at was to implicate him in a political trial. But also to dishonour him, to de-legitimise him for the years when he had been one of the leaders, while Gheorghiu-Dej was still a lowly activist. He is branded as an accomplice of Vasile Luca and forced to confess imaginary sins, for example, that together with Luca, in the summer of 1940, when they met at the headquarters of the Comintern in Moscow, he had created a factional, anti-Party group, or that he had betrayed Party secrets to the Siguranţă. The inquiry accuses him of complicity with his adjunct, Iosif Şraier, the erstwhile head of the PCdR Legal Bureau in the 1930s. Teohari Georgescu is accused of knowing that Şraier was a Siguranţă informer, and of having covered for him when he was planning to flee to the West. Teohari Georgescu survived Gheorghiu-Dej. In the 1960s, he was rehabilitated and appointed director of the printing press where he had worked in his youth. He died in 1976 (the same year as Emil Bodnăraş) and was buried in the communist pantheon in Liberty Park.

On the fall of the three, those identified as their supporters are also purged. In every institution, there are ceremonies to stigmatise the 'anti-Party group', and the leaders of the PMR are thanked for their foresight and the decision to depose them. *Scînteia* widely reports the official version of events. A press campaign is ordered, conducted by Iosif Chişinevschi and Leonte Răutu. Tens of thousands of official portraits of the three are removed from institutions over night. Books about them or which quote them are banned; most of them are destroyed. The censors forbid any mention of their names in the press. The populace viewed the whole spectacle with indifference. People were hoping for a better life, hoping that the repression and the poverty would abate. None of these things would happen.

***

The fall of the three hastened the conclusion of another murky affair: the Pătrăşcanu case. The death of Stalin led the Romanian communists – after hesitation that related to the power games within the Kremlin – to the decision to liquidate him. It was the manner in which Beria had been tried and executed that inspired the solution settled upon by the Bucharest regime. This was not a trial open to the public and the press. They no longer had Moscow's blessing. The trial unfolded behind closed doors, in a courtroom packed with Securitate officers and Party cadres. Gheorghiu-Dej and Chişinevschi listened to the speeches of the trial in their offices, where they had had speakers installed. They eavesdropped on the magistrates, prosecutors, lawyers and, above all, Pătrăşcanu. The fact that the victim denied any wrongdoing meant the trial was a shambles. Kamenev, Zinoviev, Rykov, Momsky, Radek, Racovski, Bukharin et al., and, in the 1940s, Rajk, Dodja, Slansky and Kostov (who later retracted) recognised that they were enemies of the Party, that they had been traitors working for foreign secret services. An admission of guilt by Pătrăşcanu would have meant that his six-year detention had been justified. It would have also brought what Gheorghiu-Dej wanted: annulment of the historic role Pătrăşcanu had played in 1944. Gheorghiu-Dej and his accomplices did not manage to exploit the propaganda potential of the trial of April 1954. A brief announcement published in *Scînteia* announced the holding of the trial and the execution of the sentence. The reason: a public confession on the part of Pătrăşcanu was lacking. The trial also had another unusual aspect. It was not held during Stalin's lifetime, but a year after his death. The Kremlin no longer mustered this amount of manpower when it wanted to get rid of undesirables. The epoch of show trials had passed. Pătrășcanu could not be released, as it would have been a political problem. If Gheorghiu-Dej and his cronies wished to maintain their supremacy, they had to make him disappear.

The trial was popular among party activists. The scent of blood united them, lent them the cohesion of a clan. Gheorghiu-Dej is acknowledged as the legitimate boss only after the execution of Pătrășcanu. He had proven himself to be the most ruthless of them all. There is a kind of morbid fascination to being in the power of another, of a god who can kill you 'for the good of the cause'. Now that Stalin was gone, there was a risk of things becoming volatile if there was no local dictator to wield absolute authority and take over his attributes. The ambiguities of the deposal of the Ana Pauker group had not made Dej truly master. Corpses and blood were lacking. In 1952, it had all culminated in merely sackings, denunciations and purges. The trial of Vasile Luca would not take place until October 1954, and the death sentence was commuted to life imprisonment. Gheorghiu-Dej needed to kill. Only the death of one of their own would maintain discipline in the ranks. The matter was urgent, because signs of a 'thaw' were coming from Moscow, which might have led to the sacrifice of Gheorghiu-Dej himself. The effect would have been the dismemberment of the clan. Gheorghiu-Dej decided to go all the way and to commit murder. He makes accomplices of the most powerful men in the Political Bureau and the Secretariat. In April 1954, all are in agreement with the death sentence for Pătrășcanu and Koffler. Assassination was part of the Bolshevik catechism. A 'professional revolutionary' had to kill in cold blood, if the 'proletarian revolution' demanded it. The cast of characters implicated in the murder of April 1954 replicate the old prototypes. Wielding ideology as their weapon, the killers behind closed and padded doors are Gheorghiu-Dej, Iosif Chișinevschi, Miron Constantinescu, Alexandru Drăghici, Dumitru Coliu, Emil Bodnăraș, Alexandru Moghioroș and Petre Borilă. As psychological types, they bear a striking resemblance to Virginsky, Verkhovensky, Liputin.[34] They are demons emerging from the underground of clandestinity. They shun the light. Their eyes have grown accustomed to the dark. For them, Pătrășcanu was necessarily an object of resentment, and Gheorghiu-Dej was the prototype of their frustrations.

---

[34] The murderers of former fellow-conspirator Shatov, in Dostoevsky's *The Demons – Translator's note.*

The underground could exist only in abjection. It needs demons as its reason to survive. It sees enemies all around because it feels continually threatened. These apparatchiks, who rule in the shadow of the Red Army barracks, have lived with the same feeling of fear since their clandestine days. Beyond the underground are to be found their historical enemies – the bourgeoisie, the landowners, the elite – and they must be destroyed. But there were, they believed, other, more dangerous enemies, infiltrated within their sect. They had to be discovered and annihilated. There is an endemic fear of betrayal. 'Agents' have to be unmasked. And whoever has been unmasked, whether guilty or not, is necessarily a traitor. Otherwise, it would mean that the Party had made a mistake: something that was impossible. Even if he is not a real traitor, his murder will be a lesson to the others. Otherwise, they too might be tempted to make a pact with the enemy. Once exposed, Pătrăşcanu becomes the Devil incarnate. Thanks to the illumination of the supreme boss, Gheorghiu-Dej, the former comrade is all of a sudden revealed to be the incarnation of the 'class enemy'. It is a fiction centred on betrayal and duplicity. In order to murder the excluded man, he must above all be demonised, dehumanised, isolated from the rest of the world. Only thus – vilified, crushed like an insect, dragged through the mire by the press, arrested, brought to his knees, handed over to the interrogators to be tortured – does he become expendable. Then, he will be forgotten in a basement cell. The underground is a reality that is time-honoured and immutable. It is the paranoia manifest in the struggles for supremacy in any secret society. The underground always operates by means of schisms and 'factional struggles'. Its instinct is to depose and murder any rival. The 'other' is a negative, detestable figure. It is enough for him to exist in order to be hated and for his death to be desired. This derives from the logic of the cell – the Party cell and of the prison cell – the logic of walls and hushed secrets. Pătrăşcanu made a descent into hell; he lost himself in the endless labyrinth of the underground. He was slain, but had circumstances allowed, he too would have slain, in order to conserve his power, to dishonour his adversaries. It was for this that he was schooled, intoxicated with the catechism of the professional revolutionary. Once he had joined his first clandestine cell, while still an adolescent, there was no return. He would go on to triumph or be slain. This was the code. He remained a conspirator, a secret personage, until he was murdered by his own accomplices, with a bullet to the back of his neck. Only at that moment did the conspiracy cease.

Pătrăşcanu had understood the mechanism of the Great Terror since the 1930s. He had closely followed the trials whereby Stalin liquidated the old guard. In Paris in 1946, he had read Arthur Koestler's *Darkness at Noon*. He frequently used to comment upon it. The book, which caused a great stir at the time, tells the story of a Bolshevik leader arrested and forced to confess to imaginary betrayals before being tried and killed on the basis of his confessions. Rubashov, the hero, was inspired by Nikolay Bukharin, Lenin's favourite. Vasile Luca had once accusingly compared Pătrăşcanu to Bukharin. Pătrăşcanu held no illusions as to the denouement. Once enmeshed in the grinding cogs, there was no escape. The mechanism of the investigation is appropriate to the utopia served by all the denizens of the underground. Once the man under arrest has been branded a criminal for political reasons, the investigators set about fabricating evidence of his 'crimes'. Because he has committed no crime, fiction takes the place of reality. Many calmly stepped into the meat grinder confident that 'they had done nothing wrong'. They had not betrayed, they had not been agents of the Siguranţă, they were not spies – therefore they felt safe. They were naïve. The system had other rules. 'Party-minded' fiction dictated the law. Ideology sliced into the living flesh. What was demanded of those under investigation was to confess imaginary crimes, in order to serve a non-existent 'Party cause'.

In the cells of the Securitate, fiction was highly prized. The histories narrated by prisoners under torture or out of fear led to the maximum penalties: life, hard labour, or execution. Some 'confess' to imaginary crimes not only out of fear, but also as a mental exercise and out of discipline. They know the ritual well. They know they cannot be released from under arrest unless they make a confession to the Party. They flagellate themselves, as proof of their limitless devotion. This language has its secrets, and only an initiate can navigate it. During the investigation of the Pătrăşcanu group, we meet Belu Zilber, a long-standing denizen of the underground. He has the most experience to be the agent of death. He is also the most imaginative. He is beaten savagely. "It was preparatory to the operation to extract the soul, a preparation carried out with the meticulousness of a perfect machine. … I had lost the status of human being."[35] Zilber knows there is no escape. His imagination becomes a priceless gift for the Party. He not only offers

---

[35] Belu Zilber, *Actor în procesul Pătrăşcanu. Prima versiune a memoriilor lui Belu Zilber*, Humanitas, 1997, p. 62.

to relate unconfessed deeds, but also to tell the imaginary story of a large-scale plot in which real persons are caught up. The rest is simple. Those under arrest are forced to recognise the fiction as reality. Does the regime not share the same nature? Zilber's imagination is not original: he copies to the last detail the scenarios of the Great Terror in Moscow. He transfers to Bucharest the horrors confessed to by the old guard in the Lyubyanka in the 1930s. Conspiracies involving Anglo-American agents, secret meetings, plots to assassinate beloved leaders, shady financial dealings, sordid affairs, betrayal of the country to Tito, imaginary pogroms, the poisoning of the populace through the water supply, the blowing up of trains, coups d'état, the destruction of harvests through deliberate spread of crop diseases. Of course, the prize most sought-after by the improvising scriptwriter is the denunciation of someone for collaborating with the Siguranţă. This is the most infamous of accusations. Death must be accompanied with dishonour. The confession of having basely betrayed comrades to the enemy was one of the Ten Commandments. No firing squad, no reading of the death sentence. A bullet in the back of the neck, in the dead of night. Exactly the way in which Pătrăşcanu and Koffler are killed. With scorn. It is a ritual. The Siguranţă is the patron of the naïve, the visionary, the disinterested, the stupid and the base who descend into the underground. As this is not enough, other fictive accusations are added: espionage for various secret services. We are in the same area. Had many Comintern agents spied? All of them. How many had been condemned, not for their ideas, but for gathering secret information and passing it on to the Soviets? The communists were traitors to their country, wherever they were to be found. Fictive guilt is added: crimes against the Party, world peace, the proletariat etc. The logic is to liquidate the other. The real motive does not appear in the speech for the prosecution. It is an absurd spectacle, one that is incomprehensible today. It is indicative of the madness that grips certain epochs. This madness is recurrent. Whoever views it as a thing of the past, something gone forever, is deluded.

In Sentence no. 49 of 14 April 1954 of the Supreme Court, Lucreţiu Pătrăşcanu is found guilty of crimes against humanity and the crime of high treason.

> "In fact, from the mass of evidence administered it can be concluded that … the accused established in our country an agency in the service of imperialist circles, acting as the lackeys of the bourgeoisie and the

landowner class, bourgeois nationalists, agents of the Siguranţă and spies, inveterate enemies of the working class and of socialism. Engaging in their treacherous activity under the command of the Anglo-American espionage services, they in effect propped up the fascist/Antonescu regime, and after 23 August 1944 they recruited a group to plot against the state with the aim of overthrowing the democratic regime installed in Romania on 6 March, counting on the support of the Anglo-American imperialists and internal reactionaries ... This treacherous agency with Pătrăşcanu at its head, made up of degenerate elements including Ştefan Foriş, Remus Koffler, Herbert Zilber and their ilk ... supplied the Siguranţă with information regarding the organisation, members, activity of the PCR and other democratic organisations, thereby supporting the repressive activity of exterminating patriotic elements that was savagely carried out by the fascist Antonescu dictatorship and, at the same time, paralysing the struggle against fascism and the war ... They targeted, under orders from the British espionage service, the organisation of the activity of the Romanian Communist Party, aiming to annihilate its members and then transform the Party into a tool to be manipulated in the hands of the imperialists ... These criminals ... in the spring of 1941, surrendered to the Siguranţă a part of the members of the Party's Central Committee, they forbade the organisation of acts of sabotage and groups of partisans. ... Betraying safe houses to the Siguranţă, they planned the organisation of acts of sabotage directed at the Soviet Army. ... With the aim of carrying out provocative actions in the ranks of the communists interned in prison camps, in 1943 Lucreţiu Pătrăşcanu arranged his own internment in the Tîrgu Jiu camp for a few months. ... Lucreţiu Pătrăşcanu, concealing his treacherous and criminal activity, managed to infiltrate himself into the government, within the CC of the Party and then within the Political Bureau of the CC, positioning himself at the same time at the head of a counter-revolutionary group, plotting against the state ... Throughout its activity the criminal group headed by Pătrăşcanu supported, inside Romania, the monarchy, the representatives of the bourgeois parties and the major capitalists, who financed these actions, and supported, outside Romania, American-British imperialism via the espionage services."

What we can read in this document is the rewriting of the underground's history. It is a prolongation of those times into the 1950s. The old stories are still alive, make their presence felt, and must be disposed of. History is rewritten, and the tool of choice, one of deadly force, is the speech for the prosecution. Although they are in power, the illegals remain prisoner to their old obsessions. They hate each other, without exception; they fear each other. The fearful demonisation of Pătrășcanu is merely the most notorious example. The rule is that you must exterminate the other before he you. Any attempt to step outside the boundaries of the clandestine canons is sanctioned. The victim has no right to respect.

"During the speech for the prosecution we heard murmurs from the courtroom many times. But now, there is a general uproar. In response to … the unrelenting voice of Lucrețiu Pătrășcanu, the men and women who pack the court start laughing. I hear them laughing. There are gales of laughter. I hear the deep laughter of the men. I hear the hysterical tittering of the women. The verdict is as good as pronounced. They had packed the court with activists. Communists for pay. They had been given the order to create an atmosphere unfavourable to the accused. They were laughing. Blind, deaf, emptied of any human sentiment, gripped by collective hysteria, slogans, hatred, greed, and fear, the demented were laughing," recalls Lena Constante,[36] one of the later victims. She was in the dock when Pătrășcanu protested against the trial. His final exchange with the judge is revealing. I reproduce the shorthand record.

"*Presiding Judge*: The accused Pătrășcanu has the final word. What do you have to say in your defence? *Pătrășcanu*: I have nothing to say except that I spit upon the accusations brought against me. *Presiding Judge*: Sit down then. The accused Pătrășcanu says that he has nothing to say. *Pătrășcanu*: And that I spit on the accusations brought against me. *Presiding Judge*: These are insults. *Pătrășcanu*: They are not insults. *Presiding Judge*: You are making a spectacle of yourself. *Pătrășcanu*: Yes, let me make a spectacle, life is short but there are people who will take notice of all this beastliness. *Presiding Judge*: You're making a fool of yourself."[37]

---

[36] *Evadarea tăcută*, Florile Dalbe, 1995, p. 117.

[37] *Principiul bumerangului. Documente ale procesului Lucrețiu Pătrășcanu*, Vremea, 1996, p. 746.

Three days later, the execution takes place: a bullet in the back of the neck.

Somewhere, not far away, the man who has ordered the assassination is eavesdropping on what is happening in the courtroom: like the conspirator in a melodrama, lurking behind the arras. On hearing the sentence, which he had been preparing for so long, he is jubilant. The man he hated, who gave him a complex and whom he feared the most, no longer existed. The other, Koffler, had also fallen for reasons that related to murky affairs. His killing supplies Gheorghiu-Dej with an alibi for the assassination of Foriş. The authors of this travesty of justice celebrate the event the next day. The plot had succeeded. A messenger informed them in the morning that the two had been shot. Gheorghiu-Dej sought to assure himself that Pătrăşcanu and Koffler were really dead. He kept asking whether they had been buried. He wanted to know every detail. He wanted to ensure that the episode had come to a close and that he could breathe easily.

***

The underground knows no respite. No sooner does one conflict end than another crisis is brewing. No sooner is one scapegoat dead than another has to be found. The cult constantly demands sacrifices. Since oppressed society demands periodic satisfaction in order not to revolt, other heads must roll. They must pay the toll for the regime's survival. As long as the rulers are not assimilated, they are isolated from society. Because of their illegitimacy, the underground exists until December 1989. Power itself is transformed into an underground. We find its denizens in the labyrinths and bunkers where the erstwhile professional revolutionaries turned masters now dwell. They are surrounded by thick walls, guarded by the political police. Alongside them stands an immense propaganda apparatus with the task of portraying them in a light other than their wretched reality. The denunciations, epidemic purges and factional struggles never stop. The masses must be kept mobilised. Any respite would bring lethal dangers for the regime. The demonstrations for world peace and harvest campaigns do not always have the desired anaesthetic effect. Nor is the ruthless war against kulaks or the unmasking of factory saboteurs sufficient. Other campaigns target speculators, slackers, the remnants of the bourgeois-landowner class, and ideological heretics. Then there are the homages to the heroes of the proletariat, to the fellow travellers, and the dead, who are unable to contradict the mystification. There are also the unending celebrations of fictive achievements. And nevertheless, the procedure has limits. In critical situations, when the pretexts to mobilise society are not strong enough, mass repression is employed, as in 1948-1953 and 1958-1963. And at regular intervals, the underground makes blood sacrifices within its own ranks.

Having emerged from the 'anti-Party Pauker/Luca/Teohari Georgescu group' affair and the Pătrășcanu/Koffler and Luca trials, the governing elite can afford to relax. The authority of Gheorghiu-Dej is seemingly uncontested. External events interrupt this respite. The speech given by Nikita Khrushchev in February 1956 comes as a shock. The exposure of the tyrannical nature of the Stalin regime transforms the 'Greatest Man in Human History', the 'Liberator of Nations', into a ruthless dictator. The Romanian delegates at the congress, Gheorghiu-Dej, Petre Borilă, Iosif Chișinevschi and Miron Constantinescu interpret the consequences of this reversal differently. Does Bucharest have to follow the new line? It was another about-turn, such as the Kremlin had made dozens of times. Periodically, that which had once been true became false. That which had once been the expression of Leninist policy, and as such purely revolutionary, became gross error, treachery and counter-revolution. Each such about-turn brought fresh purges and victims. The executors of the old line paid the cost, usually by losing their positions, often their lives. A veteran of the clandestine life, Gheorghiu-Dej knew full well that he was stalked by the danger of losing power. When the political flow changed course, the Kremlin would impose other figures at the top; it required new, uncompromised lackeys. Dej was the most vulnerable of all the leaders of the Soviet bloc to losing his position. The PMR Congress of December 1955, which had certified his supremacy, was a distant memory. The repercussions are not long in appearing. Two of the members of the delegation that had accompanied him to Moscow attack him at a meeting of the Political Bureau. Iosif Chișinevschi and Miron Constantinescu try to brand him as a 'Romanian Stalin'. If the tactic succeeded, Gheorghiu-Dej's days as head of the PMR would be numbered. The two demand a public debate on the Khrushchev report. They are not the only ones to break ranks. Intellectuals, students and, in particular, writers begin to grow restless, likewise Romania's ethnic Hungarian minority. Within the Party too, there is unrest. Besides the two 'rebels', who had found an excuse to contest the status quo in the Political Bureau, others also displayed centrifugal tendencies. As a warning and a riposte, in July a plenary session of the CC of the PMR eliminated a group in which the prominent figures were Dumitru Petrescu (Vice-Premier, a Comintern agent; he had stood in the dock with Gheorghiu-Dej in the trials of 1933-1934, escaped from prison in 1935, graduated from the V. I. Lenin School for Cadres, was a member of the International Brigades in Spain, as political commissar of the Tudor Vladimirescu Division, and later a general, minister, and member of the CC of the PMR) and Constantin Agiu (a legendary figure of the underground, involved in 1920 in the bomb attack on the Senate, a veteran, mixed up in all the communist clandestine activities, head of Patriotic Defence in the 1940s, one of the Party's secretaries in 1943-1944, also a member of the CC of the PMR). Other figures in the 'counter-revolutionary plot' are Ion Eremia (General, author of a manuscript, *Gulliver in the Land of Lies*, a violent satirical parable against the regime, in which Romania is named Kukunia, the *Land of Lies*, printed in 1992 by the Romanian Cultural Foundation Press), and Victor Dușa, also an illegal, with a prison term in his curriculum vitae. Other 'conspirators' are Mihai Levente, Bucur Șchiopu, likewise illegals.[38] They are investigated in 1955, by a commission led by Constantin Pîrvulescu and Gheorghe Stoica. They are eliminated in the summer of 1956, in the context of the Polish crisis and the effects produced by the Khrushchev report. The 'anti-Party Group' also considered ousting Gheorghiu-Dej by force. A denunciation is forthcoming, and the conspirators are discovered.[39] They are arrested, interrogated, by the Party and Securitate, and accused of having formed an anti-Party, factional group of plotters etc., according to the usual formulas. They are unmasked at a meeting of the Political Bureau, subjected to harsh criticisms and expelled from the Party. The affair is barely touched upon by the press. *Scînteia* publishes only the conclusions of the inquiry. There are no debates, no speech for the prosecution, in contrast to the ceremonies of unmasking at the plenary sessions of 1952.

The disturbances sparked by the death of Stalin, and the Khrushchev report, are far from being laid to rest after this episode. The machinations

---

[38] ANCR, Archive of the CC of the RCP, Fund 1, Dossier 11/1956, Decision of the Plenary CC of the PMR of 16-17 June as regards the anti-Party activity of some Party members.

[39] Author's interview with General Ion Eremia, April 1991.

and the behind the scenes intrigue intensify. The signals from the Kremlin are getting worse. The crisis in Poland indicates what effects the repudiation of the cult of personality could have for the leaders of the satellite countries. 'Opponents' are encouraged. The lesson learned by the 'prisons group' and their allies is that if you 'loosen the screw' and allow free discussion, society, which had otherwise been resigned, will revolt. Another lesson is that dissent at the top leads to a weakening of power and brings with it great risks. 'Factionalism' is yet again decried and viewed as the principal threat. Fears are heightened by what occurs in Budapest in October and November. Bucharest hastens to offer support to Khrushchev. The reasons: the precariousness of the Gheorghiu-Dej group's position and the existence of a significant Hungarian minority in Romania, ready to revolt. Following the arrest of Imre Nagy and his ministers, after the arrival of Red Army tanks in Budapest, the balance of forces changes rapidly. The Soviet bloc is not prepared for reform. Gheorghiu-Dej and his henchmen make a strong comeback; they take control of the situation. They order repression of the students who, in many university centres, had tried to organise protests. Censorship is tightened. Punitive measures are taken in many segments of society. The atmosphere deteriorates. Consolidated, having earned the trust of Khrushchev, to whom he remains vassal, Gherghiu-Dej finds a suitable opportunity to settle accounts with those who had contested him. In the period 28 June-3 July, an extended plenary session of the CC of the PMR raises the issue of Iosif Chişinevschi and Mion Constantinescu, the authors of the attack in March 1956.[40] They are unmasked as enemies of the Party, branded with having attempted to depose Gheorghiu-Dej. Down to the very last detail, it is a spectacle identical with that of 1952. The script is the same, but the cast and the masks are different. The aim was 'to rebuild the unity of the Party'. The great obsession of these veterans of clandestinity – factionalism, the danger of splits – rises to the surface once more. The threat of the conflicts from the inter-war period was still present. All the members of the Political Bureau and the Secretariat in 1958 had lived in the underground. Iosif Chişinevschi and Miron Constantinescu, Gheorghiu-Dej's seconds, lose their positions in the Political Bureau. The ritual is identical. The two submit. The entire cast knows its lines well. On the one hand, there are incriminations, which employ all the old stratagems and

---

[40] Details in Stelian Tănase, *Guvernarea Gheorghiu-Dej, Elite și societate, 1948-1965*, Humanitas, 1998, pp. 127-135.

clichés, on the other hand, there are self-denunciations, a retreat to defensive positions. This time, Chişinevschi and Miron Constantinescu are cast in the roles of those sacrificed for the good of the Party. The same ritualistic words from their 'wooden tongue'[41] are intoned; the same gestures are made. The ceremony is identical and simultaneous with what is happening in Moscow, where, in the very same days, also at a plenary session of the CC, Molotov, Kaganovich and Malenkov are deposed, they too the ringleaders, naturally, of an 'anti-Party group'. The shorthand reports of the two plenary sessions are indistinguishable from each other. The communiqués, proceedings, and results are quasi-identical. It was less observable that in Bucharest what took place was a mirror image. Whereas in Moscow, those fallen into disgrace were accused of not toeing the line of denouncing 'Stalin's personality cult', in Bucharest they were eliminated for the opposite reason. Chişinevschi and Constantinescu had played the Khrushchev hand, and as such, they were promoters of de-Stalinisation. Gheorghiu-Dej was at summit of his powers of machination. His prison schooling, his knack at hatching conspiracies, and his vocation for secrecy and violence were once again demonstrated.

The factional struggles do not fizzle out as soon as the two false rebels are deposed. 1957 marks the beginning of an ebb in the timid reforms launched by the Kremlin. It is a period of 'anti-revisionism', of the left-wing offensive sustained by Mao, of a new crisis with Tito. The conference of Communist and Workers Parties in Moscow in November-December 1957 marks this moment. In May 1958, a communiqué from the Warsaw Pact announces the withdrawal of the Red Army from Romania. It was foreign propaganda and political calculations that led Khrushchev to take this step. He wanted to demonstrate that the puppet regimes of Eastern Europe had popular support. The presence of tanks in Budapest and the threat of force in Warsaw, in 1956, were mere accidents. Romania was, thanks to the 'loyal Gheorghiu-Dej', a safe country. In Bucharest, Moscow's decision provokes new and heightened fears. The Soviet occupation was the regime's guarantor. The ruling group continued to live on a double periphery: one in relation to Romanian society, the other in relation to the Kremlin. It was thus extremely exposed. In order to emerge intact from the new situation, the group around Gheorghiu-Dej, overcome by panic (the decision had come as a surprise and had to be executed within a few weeks),

---

[41] "Limba de lemn" – a term used to denote the obfuscatory, impenetrable language of the communist apparatus and bureaucracy – *Translator's note*.

launches a new wave of terror. It is a reflex of clandestinity and of Stalinism, which saw in repression the solution to all problems. The 'Party cell' led by Gheorghiu-Dej wanted to make sure that all centrifugal tendencies would be annihilated. It wanted to prove to the Kremlin that it was indeed master of the situation and that Moscow had no reasons to change the composition of the Political Bureau. Gheorghiu-Dej's counter attack showed that the tactics of the underground still had an effect. The diversion, in this case, worked. The summer and autumn of 1958 did not lead to disturbances, protests. The populace, still cowed by the Soviet military invasion of Hungary, and anaesthetised by the passivity of the West, did not react. The wave of terror, launched simultaneously with the withdrawal of the Soviet Army, paralysed society. The example of Budapest was not repeated, as the Political Bureau and its clientele had feared.

It is nonetheless a long hot summer for the small world of the underground veterans. A large group of illegals is eliminated at the plenary session of the CC of the PMR. Their crime: they commit the imprudence of presenting a version of the inter-war past other than the official version. The secrets of the underground must be left to lie. Whoever rakes up the past opens a Pandora's box. In addition, the illegals express dissatisfaction with the clan that rules the Party. In totalitarian regimes, history gives or takes away legitimacy – even a history that is fictive. This is why those who hold power are obliged, for reasons of power, to fabricate their own version of the past. To say that things took place otherwise is tantamount to undermining the position of those in power, a grave offence, treated as such. The illegals, as the depositories of their own memories, did not always march to the official version. The idea of collecting documentary materials and testimonies, especially those of the survivors, in order to reconstruct the history of the underground, was nothing short of subversive: it attacked the very foundations of the regime. The PMR leaders found themselves threatened. Their imposture is in danger of being unmasked, being made known beyond the closed circle of a few hundred veterans. The past had been contradicted; the contribution of one or other of the protagonists had been contested. The counter-attack launched by those affected by the revelations was brutal. Constantin Doncea, Ştefan Pavel, Grigore Răceanu, Ovidiu Şandor, Vasile Bîgu, Ofelia Manole (tried in the 1930s along with Grigore Preoteasa), Leonte Tismeneţki, Ştefan Voicu (Aurel Rotemberg, the editor-in-chief of *Class Struggle* magazine, formerly an inmate at the camp at Vapnyarka) et al. are punished. It is a "veritable St Bartholomew's Night à la PMR."[42] The elimination of Constantin Doncea, Gheorghiu-Dej's great rival, came about because he had gathered around him countless veterans dissatisfied with the positions they held. Intellectuals and artists had also gathered around him (Milița Petrașcu, Jacques Costin, Marius Nasta etc.). They "held unprincipled discussions" and criticised those in power from the safety of the patronage offered by Doncea, who seemed untouchable. The group had become dangerous because it had the authority conferred by the former leader from Grivitza and attracted similar attitudes in other circles. Ovidiu Șandor, himself a railway worker, had been the leader of the communist cell at Tîrgu Jiu, appointed by Foriș. His rivalry with Pătrășcanu had given rise to intense factional fighting. Gheorghiu-Dej had reinstated him in the job, before himself taking over the role of head of the Tîrgu Jiu cell and expelling Șandor from the Party. Ștefan Pavel had been a lieutenant of Foriș's adversary, Petre Gheorghe, and was the husband of 'working-class heroine' Elena Pavel. Grigore Răceanu, also a railway worker, had tried to form an independent communist party. Vasile Bîgu was a veteran of the pro-communist inter-war trades union movement. Gheorghiu-Dej organises a settling of accounts within his own ranks. The measures adopted at the plenary session (17 expulsions from the Party) extend to a frenzied witchhunt among the illegals. Other well-known names of the 1930s are also targeted: Tudor Bugnariu, Nicolae Goldberger and Leontie Tismăneanu are purged.

The authority of Gheorghiu-Dej is contested by the very ones who had conferred it upon him in the 1940s, in the prisons: the illegals. His riposte is brutal. He eliminates prominent figures from the underground, in order to reduce the others to silence. Like Stalin in the 1930s, his suspicion of the old guard mounts. He sees here a zone that contests his position. An extremely dangerous situation. If Moscow decided to fire him, it is precisely from the old guard that a replacement would be picked. The history of clandestinity was full of such examples. The memory of the splits, of the internal conflicts, which brought the involvement of the Kremlin, was still vivid. On numerous occasions the ruling group had been sacked and replaced over night. Those chosen as replacements always came from the inside, from the underground. In 1958, the upstarts are expelled from the

---

[42] Pavel Câmpeanu, *Ceaușescu. Anii numărătorii inverse*, Polirom, 2002, p. 266.

Party, they lose their positions, and the purge widens. Those targeted are primarily the illegals. The disputants, veterans of clandestinity, were more dangerous than those who had made a name for themselves in the apparatus after 1944, because they invoked the same sources of authority as Gheorghiu-Dej, Chivu Stoica, Bodnăraş, Apostol, Moghioroş, Borilă et al. They had a common past. It was from among them that Khrushchev could choose another team to rule in Bucharest. At the plenary of June 1958, another episode of factional fighting unfolded. Nor was it to be the last.

The repression extends rapidly and on a large scale outside the Party. The period undergoes a severe 'freeze'. Many segments of society are attacked: former politicians and businessmen, intellectuals, artists, etc. Hundreds of trials are staged, resulting in very heavy sentences. The prisons fill up once more.[43] Compared with the first wave of terror in 1948-1953, the forms of repression diversify. Methods of annihilation and intimidation, not encountered 10 years previously, are now utilised. The 'unmasking' of groups of persons considered dangerous is orchestrated, on the grounds that they had dared to comment critically upon regime policies or poor living conditions. The press orchestrates a campaign of vilification in order to frighten the populace. The so-called unmaskings were frequently practised in the inter-war Party cells, but now they extend beyond the boundaries of the PMR to encompass the whole of society.

In Moscow in the autumn of 1961, Khrushchev resumes the policy of de-Stalinisation at the Twenty Second Congress of the CPSU. The mummified corpse of Stalin is removed from the Lenin Mausoleum. Gheorghiu-Dej and his cronies find themselves in the same situation as in 1956, after the first denunciation of the 'cult of personality'. This time, they do no not wait for a year to pass in order to re-entrench themselves. By the end of the year, they hold a plenary session of the CC of the PMR, in which the new course promoted by the Kremlin is hailed. It lasts for many days. Dozens of speeches are given. There are no purges, no one is expelled or sanctioned. Many political cadavers are present in the auditorium. The dead are invoked, but also the living, the losers and above all the winners of the underground. The plenary session is a recapitulation of the factional struggles within the Party, especially those after the seizure of power. In the version controlled by the 'prisons group', of course. A fictive history is once

---

[43] See the analysis in Stelian Tănase, *Anatomia mistificării*, Humanitas, 2003.

more employed for political ends. According to this version, the effects of Stalinism had been counteracted as early as 1952, with the elimination of the Pauker/Luca/Teohari Georgescu group. Interrupting the proceedings, Gheorghiu-Dej denies that "Pătrășcanu was repressed as the result of some cult of personality or other. It was a battle against the enemy. In fact, he was an agent of the bourgeoisie infiltrated into the leadership of our Party."[44]

The absurdity of this claim is revealed by the fact that in 1952 Stalin was still alive and was in the middle of a campaign of terror. In May 1952, the three losers had been accused of exactly the opposite: grave deviations from the line imposed by Stalin. The cases of Foriș and Pătrășcanu are supposed to have confirmed the 'foresight of Gheorghiu-Dej' who had protected the lives and careers of the communist activists during the repression ordered by Stalin. The fact that no show trial had been held in Bucharest was presented as a merit of Gheorghiu-Dej. The entire plenary is a 'paean of glory' to Gheorghiu-Dej. Instead of being contested, he is the new god of a personality cult. And this exactly when Khrushchev was criticising Stalin for the same practice. Gheorghiu-Dej had been the most zealous Stalinist, and was the first to be targeted for replacement by the Kremlin. The message of the plenary: he was firmly supported by the Party activists; there was no dissidence, no alternative to his leadership. Instead of falling from power, of being overthrown by those who had become reformers over night, Gheorghiu-Dej manages a tour de force and is – by means of a ceremony of consecration – adulated. His supremacy is acknowledged. The denizens of the underground, his political clients, outdo each other in eulogising him and recognising him as their patron. "The plenary ... proved to be a large-scale diversion."[45]

However, this is only one facet of the affair. The other is that these veterans skilled in manipulation take measures to emancipate themselves in relation to the despotic power. The clan did not want to include intruders in its ranks. The Kremlin might demand at any time figures from outside Gheorghiu-Dej's entourage. It would have been the beginning of the end. The Kremlin's privilege of dictating the composition of the governing elite is contested. The Gheorghiu-Dej clan falls back to the trench of nationalist manipulation. The populace harboured strong anti-Russian sentiments and detested the Soviet system imposed upon the country. The price is a

---

[44] ANCR, Archive of the CC of the RCP, Dossier 41/1961, p. 373.
[45] Ghiță Ionescu, *Comunismul în România*, Litera, 1994, p. 370.

prolongation of Stalinist techniques of government upon a partly different ideological base. Control and manipulation in place of terror. A better life in exchange for accepting the regime. Tactically, the governing elite chooses to emancipate itself from Moscow, which has become, under Khrushchev, the main source of instability for them. It was not the regime in itself that was brought into question (the USSR would not have accepted a pluralist system or any reduction in its sphere of influence), but only the fate of the Gheorghiu-Dej clan. For, Gheorghiu-Dej had for many years superimposed his personality upon the regime, as well as that of his acolytes, the members of the Political Bureau. What they were contesting was the Kremlin's privilege to designate who should rule. They wanted to relinquish the subordination imposed by the Comintern since March 1919. Each dictator is master in his own house, 'he does what he wants with his people' without interference 'from outside' i.e. 'from the USSR'. However, the illegals had to answer the following question: who had chosen them to govern Romania? Moscow demanded vassalage, because they were in power solely thanks to the will of the Kremlin, and not that of the Romanian people. Here we find the essence of the 'April declaration' of 1964. The operation to break away from Moscow is conducted in parallel with the utilisation of nationalist discourse, which replaces the previous discourse of proletarian internationalism. The latter discourse had been the source of subordination to the Kremlin and Party discipline, of dedication to the so-called world revolution and communist utopia, to the cult of Lenin and Stalin. The PMR simulates openness towards the West and Romanian society, as a means of political survival. The measures taken are de-Russification of the public sphere, allocation of a larger share of the budget to the everyday needs of the populace, the emptying of the prisons, and relaxation of censorship and travel restrictions. The manipulation is huge. The Gheorghiu-Dej gang presents itself as a victim of the Kremlin. It is yet another exercise in mystification, an about-turn, the same as Stalin used periodically to make in order to consolidate his power. The break with the Soviets made Gheorghiu-Dej popular, for the first time since he had become dictator of Romania. Anti-Russian feelings ran high. By defying Moscow, Gheorghiu-Dej and his clique are obliged to take measures that benefit the populace in order to garner a minimum of support. He does not go as far as reform. Nothing changes in the mechanism of power. None of the illegals sacrificed in the past are rehabilitated. The type of regime imposed by the Kremlin remains the same. It is claimed that the refusal to make fundamental changes comes from the fear of giving Moscow a motive to intervene, as it had done in Berlin and Budapest. People content themselves with as much as they are given: a more breathable air in cultural life, an end to the worst of the terror, meagre improvements in the standard of living. The April Declaration of 1964 was a typical operation of re-entrenchment. The mystification of the real stakes, under the mask of liberalisation, succeeded. The Gheorghiu-Dej clan's decision was not to change anything essential in the exercise of power, while mimicking radical change.

A few months after the April declaration, Gheorghiu-Dej is diagnosed with cancer. The evolution of the illness is rapid. He dies on 17 March 1965. In an archaic political set-up such as that of the PMR leadership, the death of a *capo di tutti capi* is a fracture that brings the very existence of the clan into discussion. An extremely perilous moment. The internal pressure, on the part of the pretenders – they too veterans, sidelined, 'victimised' up to then – but also the pressure from outside, exerted by Moscow, might change the composition and the position of the 'prisons group' and the Allied illegals.

Conservation of the clan was imperative in order to hold on to their positions. In the closed circle of the Political Bureau, the danger of schism was most acute. Rivalries might lead to a split, with unpredictable consequences. The pretenders are Gheorghe Apostol and Nicolae Ceauşescu. Nor should the role played by I. Gh. Maurer be overlooked, who was asked by Gheorghiu-Dej to succeed him. Nor that of Emil Bodnăraş, always ready to pounce, with whom Moscow would long ago have wanted to replace Gheorghiu-Dej. The cast of the drama that was unfolding in an atmosphere of intrigue and sordid backstabbing also included Chivu Stoica, eager to cling to his position and preserve his influence after the death of his protector. Another player is Alexandru Drăghici, the much-feared Minister of the Interior, an occasional ally of Ceauşescu, who is playing his own game, a repeat of the Beria-1953 scenario. There were also other characters, whom the rapid change of context disadvantaged: Al. Moghioroş, Petre Borilă, Dumitru Coliu. Others hoped to make a comeback, primarily Teohari Georgescu, Miron Constantinescu, Constantin Doncea, and Constantin Pîrvulescu. The rapidity with which Ceauşescu is designated by Gheorghiu-Dej's seconds relates to the time factor. The guardians of power take the decision not to enlarge the circle of those who are playing a role in the crisis of succession. Everything is resolved at the level of the Party cell, at the upper echelons. The complex of clandestinity held sway. The group remained hermetically sealed, as demanded by the rules of the underground. Secrecy was maintained. The decision had already been made before the convocation of the CC of the PMR or any congress, to allow time for behind the scenes manoeuvring. The fear of intervention by the Kremlin, which would have imposed its own candidate, precipitated the designation of a successor. Here we find the by now familiar starting point for an operation to manipulate the Party members. Outside the PMR, by means of propaganda and mobilisation, a defensive reaction against the danger of foreign meddling was created. For all that, however, nothing changes in the vassal relations between the ruling group in Bucharest and their patrons in the Kremlin.

***

Ceaușescu was a creature of the underground. Born in 1918, and having joined a communist network in his adolescence, he spent a number of years in prison. In Doftana Prison, he was initiated into the Stalinist creed by veterans such as Gheorghiu-Dej, Emil Bodnăraș, Vasile Luca, and Constantin Pîrvulescu. In Caransebeș Prison, he took an apprenticeship in the ways of conspiracy, intrigue and subversion, alongside Teohari Georgescu and Iosif Chișinevschi. The fact that he was uneducated (he was semi-literate, in fact) meant that he had no formative experience other than what he gained here. He was socialised in prison. He was an exclusive product of the underground, to an even greater extent than his mentors. He was sent to prison at a much younger age than them and had no other horizons prior to this experience. All Ceaușescu knows about politics, about life, is acquired in the prisons through which he passes. After his release, he builds a career in the Party apparatus. An interesting detail: after 23 August 1944, he is assigned the task of rebuilding the UTC. Ceaușescu does so based on the idea of a clandestine organisation, the only type of organisation he knows anything about. Within a few months, the plan is stillborn and this UTC is dissolved. As a man of the apparatus, Ceaușescu continues to live in a closed world after 1944. He existed solely within the sphere of power, isolated from the real, 'profane' world, which he views with contempt and fear. Nor can he even comprehend it. He is the product of an artificial world, but one no less real for that. The dogmatic, Stalinist ideological stamp imprinted on him by the Party cell remains intact until his death, on Christmas Day, 1989.

His designation as Boss of the Party was the result of a plot, which had all the hallmarks of those hatched before and after 1944. It was brought to fruition within the closed circle of the Political Bureau. The loser in this intrigue emerges as Ceauşescu's rival (designated by Gheorghiu-Dej as his successor): Gheorghe Apostol. No sooner has he been ensconced as head of the Party than he demands unconditional fealty from the others. Submission, discipline, and strict hierarchy were part of the lesson of prison. He had observed this as early as his first days as an inmate, when the communist Mafia controlled the closed world of Doftana Prison. After being designated, he demands to be treated as an infallible leader, a quality conferred on him by the mere fact that he had become head of the Party. He takes measures to affirm his supremacy. The methods are those he has picked up from Gheorghiu-Dej. He abolishes the Political Bureau and enlarges the Central Committee, filling it with his own people. He feels hindered by the presence of Gheorghiu-Dej's veterans and deposes them. The first sacrificial victim is his long-standing ally, Drăghici. At a plenary of unmasking, of a type unchanged since the days of the underground, held in April 1968, Drăghici is sacrificed. It is a well-orchestrated ceremony, held in secret, the culminating moment of a plot that begins in 1966, when a 'commission for investigation of abuses' during Gheorhgiu-Dej period is set up. Ceauşescu did not want to unmask those guilty of the terror of 1948-1952 and 1958-1962, but rather to depose Drăghici. Likewise, he was pursuing the demolition of the Gheorghiu-Dej myth. In addition, he accused the members of the Political Bureau – Bodnăraş, Apostol, Stoica, Moghioroş etc. – of having been Gheorghiu-Dej's accomplices in the execution of Foriş, in the rigging of the Pătrăşcanu and Luca trials. It was an intrigue whereby he confiscated all power for himself. He did not act from a desire to re-establish the rule of law or right the wrongs of the past. He invented a powerful means for blackmail and pressure. In April 1968, the plot is ready and the performance can commence. It is a musical score known by heart to all the participants, those at the plenaries of 1952, 1957, 1958, and 1961. It has the same aspect, of a spectacle meticulously prepared behind the scenes. In the auditorium, there was a select audience, who had previously taken part in political executions of the same type. The ritual unfolds exactly as it used to do in prison, when there were few participants, and later, in the 1950s, to packed houses. These were ceremonies of stigmatisation, well described by Orwell. The task is made easier because the victim is among the most hated figures of the regime. Ceaușescu ably makes use of the tide of hatred, vendetta, resentment. He proves as able as his mentor. Drăghici is isolated and subjected to vehement criticism by the vassals of the new master. Taken by surprise, Drăghici defends himself by denying the accusations, without any chances of escape. He is excluded. It was a manipulation of large proportions, which achieved what Ceaușescu had set out to do: to diminish the Gheorghiu-Dej myth, the basis to incriminate Bodnăraș, Apostol, Maurer, Moghioroș et al. When he wanted to get rid of Malenkov, Molotov, Kaganovich, Voroshilov, Bulganin and the rest, Khrushchev accused them of the crimes of their common patron, Stalin. The deposal of Drăghici targeted the positions of the other members of the Political Bureau, and the entire entourage of his predecessor. The rehabilitation of Foriș, Luca, Pătrășcanu, Koffler, Ana Pauker etc. was aimed at inculpating the old guard for these crimes and at exculpating himself. Ceaușescu was just as implicated in repression and terror as the others. However, as he was the one who wielded power, he created for himself an image of a redeemer, of an individual not mixed up in the past dirty work and horrors of the underground whence he originated. It was nothing but an image. The ideological, sectarian settling of accounts, factional struggles, and the successive purges in which he had participated up to then provided him with the necessary technique. At the same time, he made use of the fall of Drăghici to present himself as a different leader. He managed to put the most powerful people of the regime on the defensive. Then he deposed them.

One by one, those who had surrounded Gheorghiu-Dej were purged. Like every denizen of the underground, Ceaușescu made use of plenary meetings and rehabilitations to eliminate the 'comrades in the struggle': Alexandru Bîrlădeanu (in December 1968), followed by Gheorghe Gaston Marin. A year later, Petre Borilă, an old Comintern agent, and Al. Moghioroș, also a man of the Soviet secret services, are deposed. Then there follows the mysterious episode of Chivu Stoica's suicide. He is not the only one to vanish in unelucidated circumstances. Virgil Trofin, close to Ceaușescu since the 1950s, a member of the younger guard, falls into disgrace. He is purged and sent to a farm in the Bărăgan steppe, where he is the victim of a suspicious fatal accident. Vasile Patilineț, former secretary of the CC of the RCP, who had headed the commission of inquiry for the rehabilitation of Foriş, Pătrăşcanu etc., also falls into disgrace, and is subsequently killed in a motor car accident, while Ambassador to Turkey, Gh. Apostol and Ion Gh. Maurer are involved in strange motor car accidents. In 1974, Corneliu Mănescu is deposed as Foreign Minister. In 1974, Ion Gh. Maurer withdraws from the post of Prime Minister, which he has held for 13 years. In November 1976, through two personal letters addressed to Ceauşescu, Emil Bodnăraş[46] also withdraws, for reasons of health.

Two aspects are to be highlighted: the police-state character of his regime, which is an expression of Ceauşescu's prison experiences; and his paranoid obsession with his image in history. The mythmaking extends from falsification of documents and photographs to massive propaganda, its aim the fabrication of a heroic past. Ceauşescu suffered chronic delusions of grandeur. It was a reflex of the periphery, of the clandestinity whence he originated, of the ambiguous status – neither peasant, nor proletarian – which had given rise to his multiple complexes and behavioural deviance. Such an exacerbated personality is frequently to be encountered in political sects and secret societies, in the underground. He saw himself projected against a sweeping historical backdrop, as the avatar of mediaeval Romanian warlords and princes. This huge cinematic screen was the opposite of the Party cell, enclosed by imaginary walls, but also the opposite of the prison cell, of the restricted space in which he had developed. The rats of the underground imagined themselves as omnipotent gods, they dreamed of conquering empires, of glory, of historical immortality. The history of which Ceauşescu saw himself as part had nothing real about it; it was one that was falsified and glorified. The rewriting of history, in which all dictators engage, once more becomes a reflex of the officials who glorify their boss at every opportunity for his imaginary merits, of the historians who dedicate tomes to him by special order, of the propagandists. The personalisation of power reaches unimaginable heights. Another effect is the ever more pronounced police-state character his regime takes. Every individual is a potential enemy of the regime; the presumption of guilt is prevalent. He regards himself as chosen by destiny to fulfil a historical mission. Like Gheorghiu-Dej, he sees society as a carceral universe, as a prison, where there are guards, cells, inmates, sleeping hours fixed by the regime, working hours, meagre

---

[46] *Sfera Politicii*, no. 43/1996, pp. 37-38.

pay, distribution of rations, a canteen. Everything is controlled. There are punishments and rewards for good behaviour. There is a pronounced infantilisation in this world. A wall encloses this space. The life of every person is controlled. Contacts with foreigners are forbidden. The borders are sealed. This world is an inverted utopia. Everything is founded upon mistrust of others, upon universal suspicion. The organs of repression take on unprecedented proportions and acquire new functions. For example, they regularly check all women to see whether they are pregnant. They keep a record of all typewriters. The institution of denunciation expands to a never-before-seen breadth. Huge investments are made to enable the interception of all telephone calls. Institutions and housing blocks are required to have paid informers, who operate around the clock. Often two or three networks intersect, reciprocally checking each other. The dictator trusts no one, starting with his own relatives. Ceaușescu rules a ramified clan, which establishes relations of vassalage with other clans. As the regime degenerates, secret police surveillance extends. The whole of society is exposed.

Like Stalin, Ceaușescu viewed the old guard, the illegals, with the greatest of mistrust. He was no different from them: he himself was a creature of the underground. It was one more reason to harbour resentments against the other survivors. In 1930s, he would have sent them to the Lubyanka. In Bucharest, in the years 1965-1989, he contents himself with purging/ sidelining them. He wants to be the sole repository of the presumptive aura of a non-existent revolution. The illegals remain symbolic presences, wheeled out at ceremonies and public rituals in order to present him to his subjects as their legitimate successor. One such example is the rehabilitation of Gheorghe Cristescu, the first head of the Party, invited to the Tenth Congress in 1969. But as time goes on, such cases become increasingly rare. There is continual tension between the 'senior comrades' and the new generation of apparatchiks imposed by Ceaușescu. When Constantin Pîrvulescu, former head of the PCR, turns up 10 years later, also at a congress, in order to ask the auditorium not to re-elect Ceaușescu, it is an effect of this tension. In any case, the upstart is greeted with a chorus of booing and ushered out of the Congress hall.

The final year of the Ceaușescu dictatorship opens with a document signed by six veterans of pre-war clandestinity: Gheorghe Apostol and Constantin Pîrvulescu, former heads of the Party; Alexandru Bîrlădeanu, a former member of the Political Bureau and erstwhile vice-president of the Government; Corneliu Mănescu, a former foreign minister; Silviu Brucan, the former editor-in-chief of *The Spark* newspaper and previously ambassador to Washington; and Grigore Răceanu, an activist from the underground years. Their letter denounces "the betrayal of revolutionary ideals" and condemns Ceaușescu. "From a political point of view, the December 1989 revolution is not the culmination of an anti-communist assault against the PCR, but rather a conflict which, within that Party, pitted reform-minded illegals against an anti-reformist dictator literally lacking in any support."[47] Ceaușescu is deposed in December of the same year, during a popular uprising. He flees, but is captured, convicted in a sham trial, and executed. Thus ends the political regime of the underground.

Some of its denizens survived to see the collapse of the regime installed in the middle of the 1940s. C. Pîrvulescu, Gh. Apostol, Alexandru Drăghici, I. Gh. Maurer, Gogu Rădulescu, Al. Bîrlădeanu, Corneliu Mănescu, Grigore Răceanu, Simion Bughici, Al. Sencovici, Leonte Răutu, Ana Toma, Manea Mănescu, Constanța Crăciun, Ion Vincze etc. lived on during their own posterity, the fossils of a vanished world. The political regime prepared by a conspiracy and imposed by foreign occupation ended in December 1989. The illegal activists and their disciples ruled the country for decades, but in all that time they never emerged from the underground. They remained hidden in a bunker, far away, cut off from society, plotting continually against it. They never succeeded in emerging on the surface, in gaining legitimacy for so much as a single day in the almost half a century that they ruled Romania. They remained condemned to the eternal condition of creatures of the darkness.

---

[47] Pavel Câmpeanu, *op. cit.*, p. 268.

Romanian and *Russian* acronyms used in the text and notes

ANCR	Central National Archives of Romania
ANR	National Archives of Romania
ARLUS	Romanian Association for the Strengthening of Ties with the Soviet Union
ASRI	Archives of the Romanian Intelligence Service
CFR	Romanian Railways
INST	National Institute for the Study of Totalitarianism
MAI	Ministry of Administration and Home Affairs
MAN (MApN)	Ministry of National Defence
MOPR	International Organisation for Aid to fighters of the Revolution – International Red Aid
MStM	Greater General Staff
PCdR	The Communist Party from Romania – during the period before the communists seized power
PCR	The Romanian Communist Party – during the period the communists were in power
PMR	The Romanian Workers Party – name adopted by the PCR during the Dej period
PNL	The National Liberal Party
PNI	The National Peasant Party
PSD	The Social Democrat Party
SRI	Romanian Intelligence Service, since 1991
SSI	Special Intelligence Service, during the pre-communist period
UTC	Union of Communist Youth
VOKS	All-Union Society for Cultural Relations Abroad

The Author

Stelian Tănase (born 17 February, 1952) has a long and established literary, journalistic and broadcasting career. An authoratative Romanian intellectual, he is a respected historian and maker of documentary films, striving for the uncovering of classified material of fomer totalitarian regimes. He is a well-known face on Romanian television and has been elected to parliamentary posts in his home town of Bucharest. In 1990 he co-founded the magazine *22*, so named to commemorate the day the communist regime was overthrown in Romania – 22 December, 1989.

Regarding his writing, Tănase's fiction and non-fiction is currently widely published and translated. Of his novels, those banned by censors during the 1980s are now available for an international readership. His first novel, published under the Ceauşescu regime in 1982, *The Luxury of Melancholy*, was followed by *Light Fittings*. *At Home the Talk is in a Whisper* is a volume of his communist era diaries, in print. *Maestro, A Melodrama* and *Pavlov's Dogs* followed. *Auntie Varvara's Clients* is the first full translation published in English by the University of Plymouth Press.

Tănase lives in Bucharest where he originally studied philosophy at the University of Bucharest, where he now teaches.

The Translator

Alistair Ian Blyth was born in Sunderland in 1970 and educated at Bede School, Cambridge University (BA), and Durham University (MA). From Romanian he has translated a number of works, including *An Intellectual History of Cannibalism* by Cătălin Avramescu (Princeton University Press), the novel *Little Fingers* by Filip Florian (Houghton-Mifflin Harcourt), the novel *Our Circus Presents ...* by Lucian Dan Teodorovici (Dalkey Archive Press), *Auntie Varvara's Clients: Clandestine Histories* by Stelian Tănase (Spuyten Duyvil), and two books by Constantin Noica; *Six Maladies of the Contemporay Spirit* (University of Plymouth Press) and *The Becoming within Being* (Marquette UP). His most recent translation is Filip and Matei Florian's *The Băiuţ Alley Lads* (University of Plymouth Press). He lives in Bucharest.

Hardback edition first published in the United Kingdom in 2010 by University of Plymouth Press, Scott Building, Drake Circus, Plymouth, Devon, PL4 8AA, United Kingdom.

ISBN 978-1-84102-221-5

A CIP catalogue record of this book is available from the British Library

Translation: Alistair Ian Blyth
Publisher: Paul Honeywill
Publishing Assistants: Victoria Halliday, Charlotte Carey and Alex Hannon
Series Art Director: Sarah Chapman
Consulting Editor: Liz Wells

© Fototeca online a comunismului românesc, Arhivele Naționale ale Românie

Typeset by University of Plymouth in Janson 10/14pt
Printed and bound by R. Booth Limited, Penryn, Cornwall

Visit www.uppress.co.uk/romanian.htm to learn more about this series

Published with the support of the Romanian Cultural Institute

Index